LEGAL RESEARCH AND WRITING

Some Starting Points

FIFTH EDITION

LEGAL RESEARCH AND WRITING

Some Starting Points

FIFTH EDITION

William P. Statsky

WEST

™

THOMSON LEARNING

Africa • Australia • Canada • Denmark • Japan • Mexico • New Zealand • Philippines
Puerto Rico • Singapore • Spain • United Kingdom • United States

NOTICE TO THE READER

Cover Design: Susan Mathews, Stillwater Studio

Cover Photo/: Stock Studios Photography

Library Cover Photo: Courtesy of Albany Law School.

Column and CD Photos: Courtesy of Photodisc.

Delmar Staff

Publisher: Susan Simpfenderfer
Acquisitions Editor: Joan Gill
Developmental Editor: Rhonda Dearborn
Production Manager: Wendy Troeger
Production Editor: Laurie A. Boyce
Marketing Manager: Katherine Hans

Printed in the United States of America
5 6 7 8 9 10 XXX 03 02

For more information, contact Delmar, 3 Columbia Circle, PO Box 15015, Albany, NY 12212-0515; or find us on the World Wide Web at http://www.westlegalstudies.com

International Division List

Asia
Thomson Learning
60 Albert Street, #15-01
Albert Complex
Singapore 189969
Tel: 65 336 6411
Fax: 65 336 7411

Japan:
Thomson Learning
Palaceside Building 5F
1-1-1 Hitotsubashi, Chiyoda-ku
Tokyo 100 0003 Japan
Tel: 813 5218 6544
Fax: 813 5218 6551

Australia/New Zealand:
Nelson/Thomson Learning
102 Dodds Street
South Melbourne, Victoria 3205
Australia
Tel: 61 39 685 4111
Fax: 61 39 685 4199

UK/Europe/Middle East
Thomson Learning
Berkshire House
168-173 High Holborn
London
WC1V 7AA United Kingdom
Tel: 44 171 497 1422
Fax: 44 171 497 1426

Latin America:
Thomson Learning
Seneca, 53
Colonia Polanco
11560 Mexico D.F. Mexico
Tel: 525-281-2906
Fax: 525-281-2656

Canada:
Nelson/Thomson Learning
1120 Birchmount Road
Scarborough, Ontario
Canada M1K 5G4
Tel: 416-752-9100
Fax: 416-752-8102

Library of Congress Cataloging-in-Publication Data
Statsky, William P.
    Legal research and writing : some starting points / William P. Statsky. — 5th ed.
        p.   cm.
    Includes bibliographical references and index.
    ISBN 0-314-12901-4
    1. Legal research—United States. 2.—Legal composition.
I. Title.
KF240.S783   1998
340'.07'2073—dc21

BY THE SAME AUTHOR

Case Analysis and Fundamentals of Legal Writing, 4th edition, St. Paul: West Publishing Company, 1995 (with J. Wernet)

Essentials of Paralegalism, 3d ed. St. Paul: West Publishing Company, 1997

Essentials of Torts. St. Paul: West Publishing Company, 1994

Family Law: The Essentials St. Paul: West Publishing Company, 1997

Family Law, 4th ed. St. Paul: West Publishing Company, 1996

Inmate Involvement in Prison Legal Services: Roles and Training Options for the Inmate as Paralegal, American Bar Association, Commission on Correctional Facilities and Services, 1974

Introduction to Paralegalism: Perspectives, Problems, and Skills, 5th ed. St. Paul: West Publishing Company, 1997

Legal Desk Reference, St. Paul: West Publishing Company, 1990 (with B. Hussey, M. Diamond & R. Nakamura)

The Legal Paraprofessional as Advocate and Assistant: Training Concepts and Materials. New York: Center on Social Welfare Policy and Law, 1971 (with P. Lang)

Legal Thesaurus/Dictionary: A Resource for the Writer and Computer Researcher. St. Paul: West Publishing Company, 1985

Legislative Analysis and Drafting, 2d ed. St. Paul: West Publishing Company, 1984

Paralegal Employment: Facts and Strategies for the 1990s, 2d ed. St. Paul: West Publishing Company, 1993

Paralegal Ethics and Regulation, 2d ed. St. Paul: West Publishing Company, 1993

Torts: Personal Injury Litigation, 3d ed. St. Paul: West Publishing Company, 1995

Rights of the Imprisoned: Cases, Materials, and Directions. Indianapolis: Bobbs-Merrill Company, 1974 (with R. Singer)

What Have Paralegals Done? A Dictionary of Functions. Washington D.C.: National Paralegal Institute, 1973

QUESTIONS/COMMENTS?
Contact the author:
WSTATSKY@DELMAR.COM

Preface

The law library can be a fascinating arena of discovery. Not only is it the place to carry out research assignments, but also it can be a major source for exploring the rationale behind nonresearch tasks in other courses and on the job. Every day literally thousands of judges, legislators, administrators, and private citizens write materials that fill and enliven the shelves and computer screens of a law library. Knowing how to find, assess, and apply this material is an invaluable skill. To achieve it, we will be examining the integrated skills of legal analysis, legal research, and legal writing.

Before covering the specifics of using legal research tools in the text, you are given an overview introduction to our legal system and the ten categories of laws that it produces. Early chapters cover the terminology of legal research through definitions, excerpts, and photographs. This material is then incorporated into scores of practical techniques and checklists that can be used to find answers to research problems.

The process of research is divided into three stages: first, background research in which you obtain a general understanding of the area of law involved in the research problem; second, specific fact research in which you find primary and secondary authority on the specific facts of your problem; and third, validation research in which you assess the current validity of all primary authority you intend to use in your answer to the problem.

Every chapter begins with an outline of the topics covered in that chapter. Where needed, an introductory overview of the chapter follows the outline. Key terms are printed in bold in the text. They are defined in the text and in the comprehensive glossary at the end of the book. To illustrate a research topic, you will often find an excerpt from a relevant library book or computer screen. For many of the major research materials, photographs are also provided. One of the major themes of legal research is the possibility of using a variety of legal research materials to find the same laws. To take advantage of this diversity, you are given many comprehensive checklists covering available options. For example, Exhibit 8.1 in Chapter 8 lists nine different sets of materials where you can obtain background information on areas of the law that are new to you. To provide further assistance in grasping important and sometimes difficult research concepts, additional guidance is available through specially designed techniques such as the CARTWHEEL (to help generate search terms) and RESEARCH LINKS (to show special relationships between two sets of materials). Research problems are included within most chapters as well as at the end of chapter 14.

The legal writing chapters follow a similar pattern in introducing you to every major category of legal writing found in a modern law office, including letters, instruments, pleadings, memoranda of law, and appellate briefs. Also included are writing fundamentals that you should use when preparing any kind of document.

CHANGES IN THE FIFTH EDITION

- The terminology list in chapter 1 has been divided into two lists: an essentials list (Exhibit 1.1) and a comprehensive list (Exhibit 1.2).
- A feature called **RESEARCH LINKS** has been added. These links show the special relationship that exists between two sets of materials.
- A course-long assignment on creating your own state research manual has been added to the end of chapter 1 (Assignment 1.3).
- A new chapter 2 covers kinds of laws and the legal institutions that create them.
- The federal government organization chart that was in the appendix has been moved into chapter 2.

- Chapter 3 contains an overview of the major categories of media in which you can find legal research material: paper, online, CD-ROM, and microform.
- New legal research concepts and services, such as KeyCite, are covered.
- Chapter 3 contains a chart on the twelve possible places where you may be able to read the same court opinion (Exhibit 3.1).
- Extensive coverage is given throughout the book to the legal research options available on the Internet and the World Wide Web. This includes Internet terminology (chapters 1 and 13), the citation of materials found on the Internet (chapter 5), statutory law on the Internet (chapter 11), and case law on the Internet (Appendix D).
- Chapter 4 contains a more in-depth treatment of dictum.
- Chapter 5 presents a chart on when a parallel cite is needed according to the Bluebook (Exhibit 5.2).
- Generic or public-domain citation is covered in chapter 5.
- New assignments have been added in many chapters, particularly in chapter 9 on the nine major search resources.

There are full opinions in Appendix C for some of the case briefing and analysis assignments.

- Chapter 7, on the CARTWHEEL, now includes other index search systems such as TAPP.
- The nine techniques for doing background research on a topic (Exhibit 8.1) now include sample excerpts for the sources mentioned.
- A checklist has been added to chapter 8 on the kinds of information you want to obtain through background research (Exhibit 8.2).
- The shepardizing material in chapter 9 has been revised to reflect major recent changes in this citator.
- Chapter 10 contains a thumbnail format for briefing a case along with the comprehensive format.
- Chapter 10 contains a new section on statutes of construction in many codes, such as the statute on ejusdem generis.
- Chapter 14, on validation research, contains a discussion of why it is relatively easy to fall into the trap of relying on invalid law.
- Chapter 14 also contains a research audit in the form of a checklist so you can determine whether your strategy has been sufficiently comprehensive (Exhibit 14.1).
- Chapter 18, on writing fundamentals, includes additional writing guidelines and assignments.
- The state legal research bibliography of resources has been moved to Appendix A.
- A new appendix contains additional usage guidelines for formal writing (Appendix D).

TEACHING AIDS AND SUPPLEMENTS

- **Student Workbook:** Written by the text author, the Student Workbook includes review questions, research and writing exercises, and related material.
- **Instructor's Manual, with Test Bank:** Written by the text author, the instructor's manual includes Class Ideas, such as lecture ideas and suggestions for using selected Assignments. The instructor's manual also includes detailed competency lists for each chapter.
- **Test Bank:** Contains many test questions. Each chapter contains a variety of questions in true/false, multiple-choice, and essay format.
- **Survival Manual for Paralegal Students,** written by Bradene Moore and Kathleen Reed of the University of Toledo, provides tips for making the most of paralegal courses. ISBN 0-314-221-115.
- **Strategies and Tips for Paralegal Educators,** written by Anita Tebbe and Johnson County Community College, provides teaching strategies specifically designed for paralegal educators. It concentrates on how to teach and is organized in three parts:

the WHO of paralegal education—students and teachers; the WHAT of paralegal education—goals and objectives, and the HOW of paralegal education—methods of instruction, methods of evaluation, and other aspects of teaching. A copy of this pamphlet is available to each adopter of a West text. ISBN 0-314-04971-1.

- **Sample Pages, Third Edition.** This 231-page pamphlet introduces all of West's legal research materials. The accompanying *Instructor's Manual* gives ideas for effectively using the material in the classroom. Classroom quantities are available. Contact your West representative.
- **Citation-At-A-Glance, Revised Edition.** This handy reference card provides a quick, portable reference to the basic rules of citation for the most commonly cited legal sources, including judicial opinions, statutes, and secondary sources, such as legal encyclopedias and legal periodicals. *Citation-At-A-Glance, Revised Edition* uses the rules set forth in *A Uniform System of Citation,* Sixteenth Edition (1996). A free copy of this card is included with every student text. ISBN 0-314-22430-0.
- **How to Shepardize: Your Guide to Complete Legal Research Through Shepard's Citations** is a brief (64-page) pamphlet that helps students understand the research technique of shepardizing citations. The pamphlet is available in classroom quantities (one copy for each student who purchases a new text). Contact your West representative.
- **WESTLAW,** West's online computerized legal research system, offers students "hands-on" experience with a system commonly used in law offices. Qualified adopters can receive ten free hours of WESTLAW. Contact your West representative.
- **West's Paralegal Video Library** includes:
  - The Drama of the Law II: Paralegal Issues video (ISBN 0-314-07088)
  - *I Never Said I Was a Lawer* paralegal ethics video (ISBN 0-314-08049-X)
  - The Making of a Case video (ISBN 0-314-07300-0)
  - Mock Trial Videos—Business Litigation (ISBN 0-314-07343-4)
  - Mock Trial Videos—Trial Techniques: A Products Liability Case (ISBN 0-314-07342-6)
  - Arguments to the United States Supreme Court video (ISBN 0-314-07070-2)

These videos are available to qualified adopters.

ACKNOWLEDGMENTS

Valuable contributions have been made to this edition by the team at West Legal Studies, an imprint of Delmar Publishers.

A word of thanks to the reviewers who made valuable suggestions for improving the text:

Sandra Batemann, Fort Lauderdale College

Beverly Wooddall Broman, Esq., Duffs Business Institute

Michele Dorsey Brooks, Esq., Casco Bay College

Konnie G. Kustron, J.D., Eastern Michigan University

Barbara J. Leff, Roosevelt University

Virginia C. Noonan, Northern Essex Community College

Mary Rogan, Bronx Community College

Roy F. Steele, J.D., Metropolitan College of Legal Studies

Laurel A. Vietzen, Elgin Community College

Credits (page numbers are in boldface type): **33** (bottom) Courtesy of West Group. **37** (top right) Courtesy of West Group. **46** Courtesy of West Group. **61** (top left) *The National Law Journal* is a registered trademark of The New York Law Publishing Company. Copyright 1998, The New York Law Publishing Company. All rights reserved. **61** (middle left) Courtesy of *Marquette Law Review.* **61** (middle right) *Courtesy of Yale Law Journal.* **73** Courtesy of West Group. **96** (top) From *Shepard's Southwestern Reporter Citations.* Reproduced by permission of Shepard's. Further reproduction of any kind is strictly prohibited. **148** Reprinted with permission of

DEDICATION

For Jess and Randy Cairns

Table of Contents—Summary

Table of Contents—Detailed

PART II
LEGAL WRITING 287

Part I

LEGAL RESEARCH

Contents

Chapter 1

PRELIMINARY CONSIDERATIONS

Chapter Outline

SECTION A   INTRODUCTION

This book does not cover every aspect of legal research, nor does it treat every conceivable legal resource that could be used in a law library. Rather, our goal is to examine the major components of legal research with the objective of identifying effective starting points.

A researcher in the law library

A great deal of information is provided in the pages that follow. You should first skim through the chapters quickly to obtain an overview and to see where some concepts are covered in more than one place. Then begin collecting the terminology called for in Assignments 1.1 and 1.2. (See Section E of this chapter.) The best way to avoid becoming overwhelmed is to start feeling comfortable with terminology as soon as possible.

When you walk into a law library, your first impression is likely to be one of awe. You are confronted with row upon row of books, most of which seem unapproachable; they do not invite browsing. To be able to use the law library, your first responsibility as a legal researcher is to break down any psychological barrier that you may have with respect to the books and other resources in it. This is done not only by learning the techniques of research but also by understanding the limitations of the law library.

A major misunderstanding about the law library is that it contains the answer to every legal question. In many instances, legal problems have no definitive answers. The researcher often operates on the basis of "educated guesses" of what the answer is. To be sure, your guess is supported by what you uncover through legal research. The end product, however, is only the researcher's opinion of what the law is, rather than the absolute answer. No one will know for sure what the "right" or final answer is until the matter is litigated in court. If the problem is never litigated, then the "right" answer will be whatever the parties accept among themselves through negotiation or settlement. The researcher will not know what answer carries the day for the client until the negotiation process is over.

Many simple problems, however, can be answered by basic legal research that is relatively easy to perform. Suppose, for example, that someone wants to know the name of the government agency in charge of incorporating a business or the maximum number of weeks one can receive unemployment compensation. Finding the answer is not difficult if the researcher knows what books or other resources to go to and how to use their indexes or other points of access. Many legal research problems, however, are not this simple.

Perhaps the healthiest way to approach the law library is to view it not so much as a source of answers but as a storehouse of ambiguities that are waiting to be identified, clarified, manipulated, and applied to the facts of a client's case. You may have heard the story of a client who walked into a law office and asked to see a one-armed attorney. When asked why he required an attorney meeting such specifications, he replied that he was tired of presenting problems to attorneys and having them constantly tell him that "on the one hand" he should do this but "on the other hand" he should do that; he hungered for an attorney who would give him an answer. This concern is well taken. A client is entitled to an answer, to clear guidance. At the same time (or, on the other hand), part of the attorney's job is to identify alternatives or options and to weigh the benefits and disadvantages of each particular course of action. Good attorneys are so inclined because they understand that our legal system is infested with unknowns and ambiguities. All good legal researchers also have this understanding. They are not frightened by ambiguities; they thrive on them.

There are fourteen chapters in Part I of this book on legal research. Chapters 8 through 14 present checklists and strategies for finding the ten main categories of law that might be needed to resolve a legal issue that has arisen out of the facts of a client's problem. The ten categories of law are:

opinions	charters
statutes	ordinances
constitutions	rules of court
administrative regulations	executive orders
administrative decisions	treaties

For definitions of these categories (plus a special eleventh category—the opinions of the attorney general), see Exhibit 2.2 later in chapter 2.

Before we learn how to find these categories of law, we need to do two things: cover some of the *basics* needed to perform any research task, and study the major *research resources*. These will be our goals in chapters 1 through 7.

Basics

The basics include the following topics:

- Terminology of legal research
- Kinds of legal authority
- Citation of legal authority
- Indexes

Once we have grasped these fundamentals, we turn to the research resources, beginning in chapters 8 and 9.

Research Resources

The major research resources we will use to find the law needed to resolve a legal issue are as follows:

card catalogs	legal periodicals
digests	legal encyclopedias
annotations	treatises
Shepard's	phone and mail
looseleaf services	computers

Our approach in this book, therefore, will be as follows: first, we will cover the basics and the research resources; then, we will use this material to find the ten major categories of law.

SECTION B   IMPORTANCE OF LEGAL RESEARCH

You will eventually forget most of the law that you learn in school. If you do not forget most of it, you should! No one can know all of the law at any given time, even in a specialty. Furthermore, the law is always changing. Nothing is more dangerous than someone with out-of-date "knowledge" of the law. Law cannot be practiced on the basis of the rules learned in school. Those rules may no longer be valid by the time you try to use them in actual cases. Thousands of courts, legislatures, and administrative agencies spend considerable time writing new laws and changing or adapting old ones.

The law library and the techniques of legal research are the indispensable tickets of admission to current law. School teaches you to think. *You teach yourself the law through the skill of legal research.* Every time you walk into a law library, you are your own professor. You must accept nothing less than to become an expert on the topic of your research, no matter how narrow the topic. The purpose of the law library is to enable you to become an expert on the current law of your topic. Do not fall into the trap of thinking that you must be an expert in an area of the law to research it properly. The reverse is true. A major way for you to become an expert in an area is by discovering on your own what the law library can teach you about that area.

Never be reluctant to undertake legal research on a topic simply because you know very little about the topic. Knowing very little can be a beneficial starting point for the researcher! Preconceptions about the law can sometimes lead you away from avenues in the library that you should be traveling.

Becoming an expert through comprehensive legal research does not necessarily mean that you will know everything about a particular topic or issue. Experts are not people who simply know the answers; they also know how to *formulate the questions that remain unanswered even after comprehensive legal research.* An expert is someone who can say:

> This is what the current law says, and these are the questions that the law has not yet resolved.

Of course, you cannot know what is unresolved until you know what is resolved. The law library will help tell you both.

SECTION C   FRUSTRATION AND LEGAL RESEARCH

You are in the position of the king who sadly discovered that there is no royal road to geometry. If he wanted to learn geometry, he had to struggle through it like everyone else. Legal research is a struggle and will remain so for the rest of your career. The struggle will eventually become manageable and even enjoyable and exciting—but there is no way to avoid the struggle no matter how many shortcuts you learn. The amount of material in a law library is simply too massive for legal research to be otherwise, and the material is growing every day with new laws, new formats for law books, new technology, and new publishers offering new services that must be mastered.

Unfortunately, many cannot handle the pressure that the law library sometimes seems to donate in abundance. Too many attorneys, for example, stay away from the library and consequently practice law "from the hip." They act on the basis of instinct and bravado rather than on the basis of the most current law uncovered through comprehensive legal research. Such attorneys need to be sure that they have extensive malpractice insurance!

Legal research will be difficult for you at the beginning, but with experience in the law library, the difficulties will become manageable. The most important advice you can receive is *stick with it*. Spend a lot of time in the library. Be inquisitive. Ask a lot of questions of fellow students, teachers, librarians, attorneys, paralegals, legal secretaries, etc. Be constantly on the alert for tips and techniques. Take strange books from the shelf and try to figure out what they contain, what they try to do, how they are used, and how they duplicate or complement other law books with which you are more familiar. Do not wait to be taught how to use sets of books that are new to you. Strike out on your own.

The coming of computer technology to legal research is of some help, but computers cannot eliminate your need to learn the basics. The struggle does not disappear if you are lucky enough to study or work where computers are available. Intelligent use of computers requires an understanding of the fundamental techniques of legal research. Furthermore, legal research can be expensive. Making cost comparisons between computer research and traditional research presupposes an ability to do both.

At this stage of your career, most of the frustration will center on the question of how to *begin* your legal research of a topic. Once you overcome this frustration, the concern will then become how to *end* your legal research. After locating a great deal of material, you will worry about when to stop. In this book, our major focus will be the techniques of beginning. Techniques of stopping are more troublesome for the conscientious researcher. It is not always easy to determine whether you have found everything that you should find. Although guidelines do exist and will be examined in chapter 14, a great deal of experience with legal research is required before you can make the judgment that you have found everything available on a given topic. Don't be too hard on yourself. The techniques will come with time and practice. You will not learn everything now; you can only begin the learning that must continue throughout your career.

Keep the following "laws" of legal research in mind:

1. *The only books that will be missing from a shelf are those that you need to use immediately.*
2. *A vast amount of information on law books and research techniques exists, most of which you will forget soon after learning.*
3. *Each time you forget something, relearning it will take half the time it previously took.*
4. *When you have relearned something for the fourth time, you own it.*

At times you will walk away from a set of law books that you have used and wonder what you have just done—even if you obtained an answer from the books. At times you will go back to a set of books that you have used in the past and draw a blank on what the books are and how to use them again. These occurrences are natural. You will forget and you will forget again. Stay with it. Be willing to relearn. You cannot master a set of books after using them only a few times. Learning legal research is a little like learning to play a musical instrument: a seat is waiting for you in the orchestra, but you must practice. A royal road does not exist.

SECTION D   FLEXIBILITY IN LEGAL RESEARCH

Researchers have reached an enviable plateau when they understand the following paradox: *You sometimes do not know what you are looking for until you find it.* As researchers pursue avenues and leads, they invariably come upon new avenues and thoughts that never occurred to them initially. An entirely new approach to the problem may be uncovered that radically changes their initial perceptions. They reached this stage not because they consciously sought it out but because they were flexible and open-minded enough to be receptive to new approaches and perceptions.

This phenomenon is by no means peculiar to legal research. Take the situation of the woman in need of transportation. She sets herself to the task of determining the most economical way to buy a good car. In her search, she stumbles upon the practice of leasing cars. After studying this option, she concludes that leasing is the most sensible resolution of her transportation problem. She did not know what she was looking for—a car leasing deal—until she found it. Compare this situation with that of a client who comes into a law office for advice on how to write a will so that a certain amount of money will pass to designated individuals upon death. The attorney asks you to do some legal research in the area of wills. While in the law library studying the law of wills, you see reference to life insurance policies as a *substitute* for wills in passing cash to beneficiaries at death. You bring this to the attention of the attorney, who decides that this option is indeed worth pursuing. You did not know what you were looking for—a will substitute—until you found it.

SECTION E   TERMINOLOGY OF LEGAL RESEARCH: TWO CHECKLISTS

This section contains two lists of research concepts and materials. The first is a list of fifty essential terms that you should understand before you start doing any legal research (see Exhibit 1.1 and Assignment 1.1). The second is a comprehensive list of more than 250 terms that you need to understand by the time you finish studying legal research (see Exhibit 1.2 and Assignment 1.2). All of the concepts and materials in the essentials list are also in the comprehensive list. Assignment 1.1 should be done now. Assignment 1.2 should be completed by the end of the course. You need to learn to use the language of legal research as well as to do legal research. Assignments 1.1 and 1.2 will help you start acquiring this language.

Don't be intimidated by the comprehensive list. You are not expected to grasp everything in it right away. Start collecting definitions now. When you start doing research problems in the library, the terms will have increased meaning for you.

Both lists contain page numbers in parentheses that direct you to pages in the book where the terms are covered. All the terms are also defined in the glossary at the end of the book.

SECTION F   FINDING LAW LIBRARIES

The availability of law libraries depends to a large degree on the area where you live, study, or work. Rural areas, for example, have fewer possibilities than larger cities or capitals.

1.1

Exhibit
The Terminology of Legal
Research: The Essentials

1. act (34)
2. administrative code (35)
3. administrative decision (24)
4. administrative regulation (24)
5. advance sheet (for reporters, for Shepard's, for statutory code) (36)
6. *American Jurisprudence 2d* (Am. Jur. 2d) (37)
7. annotation (38)
8. authority (80)
9. bill (39)
10. *Bluebook: A Uniform System of Citation* (39)
11. brief of a case (39)
12. case (also called opinion) (24)
13. cause of action/defense (211)
14. CARTWHEEL (186)
15. cite/citation (47)
16. cite, parallel (47)
17. code/codify (48)
18. common law (193)
19. constitution (24)
20. *Corpus Juris Secundum* (C.J.S.) (48)
21. cumulative (49)
22. dictum (plural, dicta) (189)
23. digests (for reporters) (50)
24. executive order (24)
25. headnote (57)
26. *Index to Legal Periodicals and Books* (ILP) (58)
27. key number (50)
28. KF call number (142)
29. legal dictionary (60)
30. legal encyclopedia (60)
31. legal periodical (61)
32. legal treatise (62)
33. legislative history (216)
34. LEXIS, LEXIS-NEXIS (247)
35. looseleaf/looseleaf service (63)
36. National Reporter System (43)
37. online (33)
38. ordinance (24)
39. pocket part (122)
40. precedent (189)
41. regional reporter/regional digest (52)
42. reporter: official/unofficial (40)
43. rules of court (also called court rules) (24)
44. section (§) (204)
45. serial publication (388)
46. session law (67)
47. Shepardize (67)
48. statute (24)
49. statutory code: official/unofficial (72)
50. WESTLAW (247)

1.2

Exhibit
The Terminology of
Legal Research: A
Comprehensive Checklist

1. abstract (also called squib) (34)
2. act (34)
3. administrative agency (234)
4. administrative code (35)
5. administrative decision (24)
6. administrative law judge (ALJ) (236)
7. Administrative Procedure Act (APA) (237)
8. administrative regulation (24)
9. advance session law service/legislative service (36)
10. advance sheet (for reporters, for Shepard's, for statutory code) (36)
11. *A.L.R. Blue Book of Supplemental Decisions* (39)
12. *A.L.R. Digest to 3d, 4th, 5th, Federal* (149)
13. *A.L.R. (1st, 2d, 3d, 4th, 5th, Fed.* (37)
14. *ALR Federal Tables* (150)
15. *ALR Index* (149)
16. *A.L.R.2d Digest* (149)
17. *A.L.R.2d Later Case Service* (151)
18. (A.L.R.) *Permanent A.L.R. Digest* (149)
19. American Digest System (37)
20. *American Jurisprudence 2d* (Am. Jur. 2d) (37)
21. analogous/on point (82)
22. annotated (38)
23. annotated bibliography (38)
24. annotated statutory code (38)
25. annotated reporter (38)
26. annotation (38)
27. annotation: superseded/supplemented (151)
28. Annotation History Table (151)
29. appellant (187)
30. appellee (also called respondent) (187)
31. *Atlantic Digest* (38)
32. *Atlantic 2d* (A.2d) (38)
33. authority (80)
34. authority: primary/secondary, mandatory/persuasive (80)
35. authority reference in C.F.R. (237)
36. *Auto-Cite* (38)
37. *Bankruptcy Reporter* (B.R.) (43)
38. bicameral/unicameral legislature (216)
39. bill (39)
40. *Black's Law Dictionary* (39)
41. black letter law (179)
42. *Bluebook: A Uniform System of Citation* (39)
43. *Blue and White Book* (39)
44. Boolean search/natural language search (262)
45. brief, amicus curiae (39)
46. brief, appellate (39)
47. brief of a case (39)
48. bulletin (39)
49. *California Reporter* (Cal. Rptr.) (39)
50. caption (of case, of appellate brief) (103, 310)
51. CARTWHEEL (126)
52. case (also called opinion) (24)
53. casebook (45)
54. case: history of case/treatment of case (158)
55. *Case Names Citator, Shepard's* (96)
56. case note (174)
57. cause of action/defense (211)
58. CD-ROM (45)
59. *Century Digest/Decennial Digest/General Digest* (51)
60. certiorari, writ of (103)
61. charter (24)

1.2

Exhibit
The Terminology of
Legal Research: A
Comprehensive
Checklist—continued

Continued on next page

1.2

Exhibit
The Terminology of
Legal Research: A
Comprehensive
Checklist—continued

122.   *Index Medicus*/MEDLINE (177)
123.   *Index to Legal Periodicals and Books* (ILP) (58)
124.   In re (103)
125.   Insta-Cite (58)
126.   interfiling (33)
127.   Internet (58)
128.   interstate compact (60)
129.   kardex (142)
130.   KeyCite (60)
131.   key facts/issues/holdings (190, 191)
132.   key number (50)
133.   KF call number (142)
134.   Jurisdictional Table of Cited Statutes and Cases (in A.L.R.5th) (150)
135.   law directory (182)
136.   law review/law journal (61)
137.   legal dictionary (60)
138.   legal encyclopedia (60)
139.   legal newsletter (61)
140.   legal newspaper (61)
141.   legal periodical (61)
142.   *Legal Resource Index* (LRI) (176)
143.   legal thesaurus (62)
144.   LegalTrac (62)
145.   legal treatise (62)
146.   legislative history (216)
147.   legislative intent (81)
148.   legislation (63)
149.   LEXIS, LEXIS-NEXIS (247)
150.   lexsee/lexstat (263)
151.   Library of Congress (LC) Classification System (141)
152.   listserv (60)
153.   looseleaf/looseleaf service (63)
154.   *LSA: List of Sections Affected* (239)
155.   Maroon Book (63)
156.   *Martindale-Hubbell Law Directory* (63)
157.   memorandum of law (296)
158.   memorandum opinion (188)
159.   microforms: microfiche/microfilm/ultrafiche (34)
160.   *Military Justice Reporter* (M.J.) (43)
161.   monitor a bill (226)
162.   *National Reporter Blue Book* (39)
163.   National Reporter System (43)
164.   *New York Supplement* (N.Y.S.) (64)
165.   nominative reporter (104)
166.   *North Eastern 2d* (N.E.2d) (64)
167.   *North Western Digest* (64)
168.   *North Western 2d* (N.W.2d) (64)
169.   notes of decisions (205)
170.   nutshell (64)
171.   on all fours (82)
172.   online (33)
173.   opinion: concurring/dissenting/majority (190)
174.   Opinion of the Attorney General (25)
175.   opinion: unpublished/unreported (41)
176.   ordinance (24)
177.   outlines (64)
178.   overrule/reverse/override (159, 218)
179.   *Pacific Digest* (64)
180.   *Pacific 2d* (P.2d) (65)
181.   Parallel Table of Authorities and Rules (in C.F.R.) (237)
182.   Pattern Jury Instructions (65)

Exhibit
The Terminology of
Legal Research: A
Comprehensive
Checklist—continued

183. per curiam opinion (188)
184. Plaintiff-Defendant Table/Defendant-Plaintiff Table (in digests) (146)
185. pocket part (122)
186. Popular Name Table (213)
187. precedent (189)
188. prospective statute (204)
189. public law/private law (63)
190. public law number (Pub. L.) (107)
191. query, computer search (249)
192. record (66)
193. regional reporter/regional digest (52)
194. register (66)
195. remand (189)
196. report, committee (221)
197. reporter: official/unofficial (40)
198. Restatements (66)
199. retroactive statute (204)
200. root expander (!)/universal character (*) (255)
201. rules of court (also called court rules) (24)
202. search engine (for Internet) (265)
203. section (§) (204)
204. serial publication (388)
205. series/edition (66)
206. session law (67)
207. Shepardize (67)
208. slip law/slip opinion (68)
209. *South Eastern Digest* (71)
210. *South Eastern 2d* (S.E.2d) (71)
211. *Southern 2d* (So. 2d) (71)
212. *South Western 2d* (S.W.2d) (72)
213. special edition state reporter/offprint reporter (44)
214. stare decisis (83)
215. star paging (42)
216. statute (24)
217. statute: mandatory/discretionary (209)
218. statutory code: official/unofficial (72)
219. statutory history table (121)
220. superscript number (159)
221. supra/infra (115, 116)
222. Supremacy Clause (83)
223. *Supreme Court Reporter* (S. Ct.) (72)
224. syllabus (in reporters) (188)
225. Table of Courts and Circuits (in A.L.R.) (150)
226. Table of Jurisdictions Represented (in A.L.R.) (150)
227. Table of Key Numbers (in *General Digests*) (147)
228. Table of Laws, Rules, and Regulations (in A.L.R.) (150)
229. Table of Statutes, Rules, and Regulations Cited (in Am. Jur. 2d) (179)
230. TAPP (131)
231. term of art (134)
232. Thomas (59)
233. Total Client-Service Library (73)
234. transcribed (227)
235. treaty (24)
236. uniform state laws (73)
237. *U.S. Code* (U.S.C.) (73)
238. *U.S. Code Annotated* (U.S.C.A.) (73)
239. *U.S. Code Service* (U.S.C.S.) (74)
240. *U.S. Code Service Advance* (72)
241. *U.S. Code Congressional and Administrative News* (U.S.C.C.A.N.) (73)
242. U.S. Court of Appeals (43)

Continued on next page

1.2

Exhibit
The Terminology of
Legal Research: A
Comprehensive
Checklist—continued

243. U.S. District Court (43)
244. *U.S. Law Week (U.S.L.W.)* (74)
245. *U.S. Reports (U.S.)* (74)
246. *U.S. Statutes at Large (Stat.)* (74)
247. *U.S. Supreme Court Bulletin (S. Ct. Bull.)* (42)
248. *U.S. Supreme Court Digest* (LEXIS) (52)
249. *U.S. Supreme Court Digest* (West) (52)
250. *U.S. Supreme Court Reports, Lawyers' Edition (L. Ed.)* (75)
251. validation research (278)
252. *Veterans Appeals Reporter* (43)
253. veto/pocket veto of chief executive (218)
254. WESTLAW (247)
255. *West's Legal Directory* (272)
256. World Wide Web (WWW) (265)
257. *Words and Phrases* (75)

  Assignment 1.1

For each of the words and phrases in Exhibit 1.1, prepare a three-by-five-inch (or a little larger) index card on which you include the following information:

- The word or phrase
- The pages in this text where the word or phrase is discussed (begin with the page number given in parentheses, then add other page numbers as the word or phrase is discussed elsewhere in the text, as well as in the glossary)
- The definition or function of the word or phrase
- Other information about the word or phrase that you obtain as you use the law library
- Comments by your instructor in class about any of the words and phrases

Some words and phrases may call for more than one card. You should strive, however, to keep the information on the cards brief. Place the cards in alphabetical order. The cards will become your own file system on legal research that you can use as a study guide for the course and as a reference tool when you do legal research in the library. Be sure to add cards for new words and phrases that you come across in class and in the library.

See also Assignment 9.2 in chapter 9 for other data that you can add to your cards.

  Assignment 1.2

Do Assignment 1.1 for the list in Exhibit 1.2. Turn in this assignment when you complete your study of legal research.

Twelve different law library possibilities are listed below. Find out which ones exist in your area. You may need permission to use some of them. (This is certainly true of a private law firm's library.) Find out where the nearest **depository library** is located. This is a public or private library that receives free federal government publications to which it must admit the general public. If a private law school or university is a depository library, it must allow you to use the publications it receives free, but you may be denied access to the rest of the library's collection.

Locations of Law Libraries

- Law school library
- General university library (may have a law section)
- Law library of a bar association
- State law library (in the state capital and perhaps in branch offices in counties throughout the state)
- Local public library (may have a small law section)
- Law library of the legislature or city council
- Law library of the city solicitor or corporation counsel
- Law library of the district attorney or local prosecutor
- Law library of the public defender
- Law library of a federal, state, or local administrative agency (particularly in the office of the agency's general counsel)
- Law library of a court
- Law library of a private law firm

You may need some ingenuity to locate these libraries and to gain access to them. Try more than one avenue of entry. Do not become discouraged when the first person you contact tells you that the library is for members or private use only. Some students adopt the strategy of walking into a library—particularly a library supported by public funds—and acting as if they belong. Rather than asking for permission, they wait for someone to stop them or to question their right to be there. Other students take the more conservative course of seeking permission in advance. Yet, even here, some creativity is needed in the way that you ask for permission. The bold question, "Can I use your library?" may be less effective than an approach such as, "Would it be possible for me to use a few of your law books for a short time for some important research that I must do?"

Once you gain access to a law library, you may face another problem. Some library employees resent spending a great deal of time answering students' questions. At a recent conference of the American Association of Law Libraries, an entire session was devoted to the theme of student requests for assistance that "can take a tremendous amount of the law librarian's time and energy." Even if an employee at the desk is willing to give you all the time you need, the supervisor of that employee may be opposed to the attention you are getting. Use your common sense in such situations. Keep your requests to a minimum, particularly if other students are seeking the same kind of help. Before you ask a question, reread the textbook. Many questions can be answered on your own.

There is one other law library that you need to consider: your own. It is not too soon for you to start collecting your own law books, beginning with your course books on law. But never buy a practice book or manual without checking with at least two attorneys or paralegals on the practical value of the book. Ask them how often they consult the book. It is not necessarily wise to purchase a book simply because it treats an area of the law you need to know something about. Also, be prepared for sticker shock when you find out what many of these books cost.

Another option is the **virtual law library** available to many computer users. In the computer age, something is *virtual* if it exists in a computer-generated environment. The primary example of such an environment is the **Internet,** which is a self-governing network of networks to which millions of computer users all over the world have access. Among the many kinds of information available on the Internet are court opinions, statutes, administrative regulations, and other legal materials. In this sense, the Internet serves as a virtual law library for people who have the right equipment and connection. (Many local public libraries offer their patrons free Internet access on the premises of the library.) Because the Internet is largely unregulated, however, you must be somewhat cautious about the accuracy of the information you find on what is called the "information superhighway." Although you cannot yet rely on material obtained through the Internet to the same extent as you can rely on traditional library volumes or on the commercial databases discussed in chapter 13, the scope and sophistication of the Internet continues to grow daily.

SECTION G   **COMPILING YOUR OWN RESEARCH MANUAL ON STATE LAW**

Assignment 1.3 asks you to prepare your own research manual on the law of your state. If you prepare it carefully and keep it up to date, you can use this manual for the remainder of your legal career.

Assignment 1.3

Prepare a research manual on the state law of your state. Although the first draft of this assignment will not be due until the latter part of the course, it is presented here at the beginning of the course so that you can start your preparation. Check the glossary at the end of this book for the meaning of any terms used in this assignment that you do not understand. Also check the index for references to pages in the book where these terms are explained.

Partial or comprehensive guides on the law of your state may already exist, and you may consult them in the preparation of your own manual. (See Appendix A for bibliographies on state law.) In the preparation of your manual, however, you are asked to try to make physical contact with every set of materials or computer resource that you cite. Physical contact simply means that you were able to see one of the volumes or issues on the shelf or that you were able to see a screen that contained a page of the computer resource you refer to in your manual. At the end of the manual, include a list of everything you were not able to make physical contact with for reasons such as its unavailability at the libraries you used.

The focus of the manual will be the law of your state, although the manual will also briefly cover important federal courts such as those that sit in your state.

Throughout the following instructions for this assignment, you are asked to list "every source" or every "other source" where you will be able to find a particular category of law. Sources include: reporters, codes, legal periodicals, legal newsletters, legal newspapers, looseleaf services, special volumes, CD-ROMs, microforms, and online resources such as WESTLAW, LEXIS, and the Internet. When you cite a computer source, be specific in identifying the database or file to which you are referring.

The cover sheet of your manual should say:

"_____ Research Manual"
by _____ _____

Fill in the first blank with the name of your state. Place your own name on the by-line. The next page should contain the Table of Contents, as follows:

TABLE OF CONTENTS
I.   Libraries
II. Primary Authority
   A. Cases
   B. Statutes
   C. Rules of Court
   D. Constitution
   E. Administrative Law
   F. Local Law
   G. Citation Rules
III. Secondary Authority
   A. Legal Encyclopedias
   B. Legal Periodicals
   C. Legal Newspapers
   D. Legal Treatises
IV. Ethics
V.   Miscellaneous

Next to each item on this Table of Contents, place the page number where the discussion of that item begins in your manual.

Assignment 1.3—continued

I. Libraries

Give the name, address, and telephone number of every law library in the area to which you have access. Also state their hours of operation and any restrictions that might exist on using their collections. Indicate which of the libraries are federal depository libraries.

For each library, state what kind of catalog it uses (card, microform, computer), what CD-ROM resources are available, and what computer databases you can use.

II. Primary Authority

A. Cases

1. Give the name, address, telephone number, e-mail address (if any), and Internet address (if any) of:

(a) every state court in your state that publishes opinions
(b) the U.S. District Court(s) that sit in your state
(c) the U.S. Bankruptcy Court(s) that sit in your state
(d) the U.S. Court of Appeals with jurisdiction over your state

2. List every reporter and other source where you will find the opinions of the following courts:

(a) the state court(s) in your state that publish opinions
(b) the U.S. District court(s) that sit in your state
(c) the U.S. Bankruptcy Court(s) that sit in your state
(d) the U.S. Court of Appeals with jurisdiction over your state

3. What set(s) of Shepard's will allow you to shepardize opinions of:

(a) the state court(s) in your state that publish opinions
(b) the U.S. District Court(s) that sit in your state
(c) the U.S. Bankruptcy Court(s) that sit in your state
(d) the U.S. Court of Appeals with jurisdiction over your state

4. What national, regional, topical, or individual state digests cover:

(a) your state courts
(b) the U.S. District Court(s) that sit in your state
(c) the U.S. Bankruptcy Court(s) that sit in your state
(d) the U.S. Court of Appeals with jurisdiction over your state

B. Statutes

1. Give the name, address, telephone number, e-mail address (if any), and Internet address (if any) of:

(a) your state legislature
(b) the chairpersons of the major committees of both houses of the state legislature that propose legislation governing procedures in any trial court of your state

2. List every code, set of session laws, and other source where you will find current statutes of your state legislature.
3. List every legislative service and other source where you will find current bills under consideration by your state legislature.
4. Describe every source you would check to determine the legislative history of a statute of your state.
5. What set of Shepard's will allow you to shepardize your state statutes?

Continued on next page

C. Rules of Court

1. List every code, deskbook, and other source where you will find the rules of court that apply to:

(a) state trial courts in your state
(b) state appellate courts in your state

2. List every code, deskbook, and other source where you will find the rules of court that apply to:

(a) the U.S. District Court(s) that sit in your state
(b) the U.S. Court of Appeals with jurisdiction over your state

3. What set of Shepard's will allow you to shepardize any of the rules of court mentioned in C1 and C2?

D. Constitution

1. List every code and other source where you will find the constitution of your state.
2. What set of Shepard's will allow you to shepardize provisions of your state constitution?

E. Administrative Law

1. List every code and other source where you will find the administrative regulations of any of the administrative agencies of your state.
2. List every looseleaf service and other source where you will find the administrative decisions of any of the administrative agencies of your state.

F. Local Law

1. List every code and other source where you will find the charters of any of the local governments in your state.
2. List every code and other source where you will find the ordinances of any of the local governments in your state.
3. What set of Shepard's will allow you to shepardize charter provisions or ordinances of your state?

G. Citation Rules

List all statutes and rules of court, if any, that require you to use a specific citation format in motions, briefs, or other documents submitted to a state trial or appellate court of your state.

III. Secondary Authority

A. Legal Encyclopedias

List all legal encyclopedias, if any, whose coverage is limited to the law of your state.

B. Legal Periodicals

List every legal periodical published in your state by law schools, bar associations, or private companies that regularly devotes all or some of its space to the law of your state.

C. Legal Newspapers

List every legal newspaper published in your state. Give the name, address, telephone number, e-mail address (if any), and Internet address (if any) of the publisher. State the subscription cost of each.

D. Legal Treatises

List every legal treatise (paperback, hardcover, looseleaf, CD-ROM, or online) that is devoted entirely to the law of your state. Include the name of the publisher of each treatise. (If there are many, limit yourself to any twenty-five current treatises.)

Assignment 1.3—continued

IV. Ethics

1. List every source where you will find the ethical rules that govern attorneys in your state.
2. List every source where you will find opinions applying the ethical rules governing attorneys in your state.

V. Miscellaneous

List any other legal materials on the law of your state that a comprehensive law library would want to have.

———————

At the end of this manual, include a list of every item cited in the manual with which you were not able to make physical contact. Briefly state why (e.g., the libraries you used did not subscribe to the volume, periodical, CD-ROM, or online service you cited).

 CHAPTER SUMMARY

The right attitude about the law library is the first step in mastering the skill of legal research. The researcher must be conscientious, determined, relaxed, and realistic. Legal research does not answer every legal question that can arise. But it can set us in the right direction and help us articulate the ambiguity that often remains even after comprehensive legal research.

Your education will teach you how to think in a legal environment. It cannot reliably teach you what the law is. To find this out, you must know how to use the law library. Furthermore, the law is changing every day. The only dependable way to find out about all of these changes is through legal research.

There is a great deal to learn about legal research. Do not expect to absorb it all in one course. Initially, you may forget almost as much as you learn. When you go through the relearning process, you will start internalizing what is required to be a competent researcher.

Finally, you need to know where to find law libraries that are accessible to you in your community, particularly depository libraries. Once in a library, it is important to be courteous and tactful in using its resources.

 KEY TERMS

depository library   virtual law library   Internet

Chapter 2

CATEGORIES OF LAWS AND RESEARCH MATERIALS

Chapter Outline

SECTION A   **INTRODUCTION**

This is a chapter about classifications and categories. Our first goal will be to define the major categories of law that are created by the different levels and branches of government and that are found in great abundance on the shelves of law libraries and in the databases of computer research programs. Our second goal is to introduce you to the four categories of research materials that serve four sometimes overlapping functions: (1) find these laws so that you can (2) read them, (3) apply them to the facts of a client's problem, and (4) check their current validity before relying on them. In the remainder of the book we will be covering these four categories in greater depth.

SECTION B   **LEVELS AND BRANCHES OF GOVERNMENT**

Our legal system is really three systems consisting of three levels of government. They are the federal government (called the U.S. government), fifty state governments,[1] and a large variety of local governments (called counties, cities, and townships). For an overview of the structure of the federal government, see Exhibit 2.1.

One of the most important characteristics of our legal system is the division of powers between the federal government and the state governments. Only the federal government, for example, has the power to declare war, whereas only a state government has the power to issue a marriage license or a divorce decree. The term **federalism** refers to the division of powers between the federal government and the state governments. Federalism simply means that we live in a society where some powers are exercised by the federal government, others by the state governments, and still others by both the federal and the state governments.

Within the federal, state, and local levels of government, there are three branches: one that makes laws (**legislative branch**), one that carries out laws (**executive branch**), and one that interprets laws and resolves disputes that arise under them (**judicial branch**).

Federal Government

Legislative branch: The Congress

Executive branch: The President and the federal administrative agencies

Judicial branch: The U.S. Supreme Court, the U.S. Courts of Appeal, the U.S. District Courts, and other federal courts

State Government

Legislative branch: The state legislature

Executive branch: The governor and the state administrative agencies

Judicial branch: The state courts

Local Government

Legislative branch: The city council or county commission

Executive branch: The mayor or county commissioner and the local administrative agencies

Judicial branch: The local courts (many local courts, however, are considered part of the state judiciary)

---

1. Plus the District of Columbia, which has a special status but in some respects is treated as a state.

2.1 ....The Federal Government

Exhibit

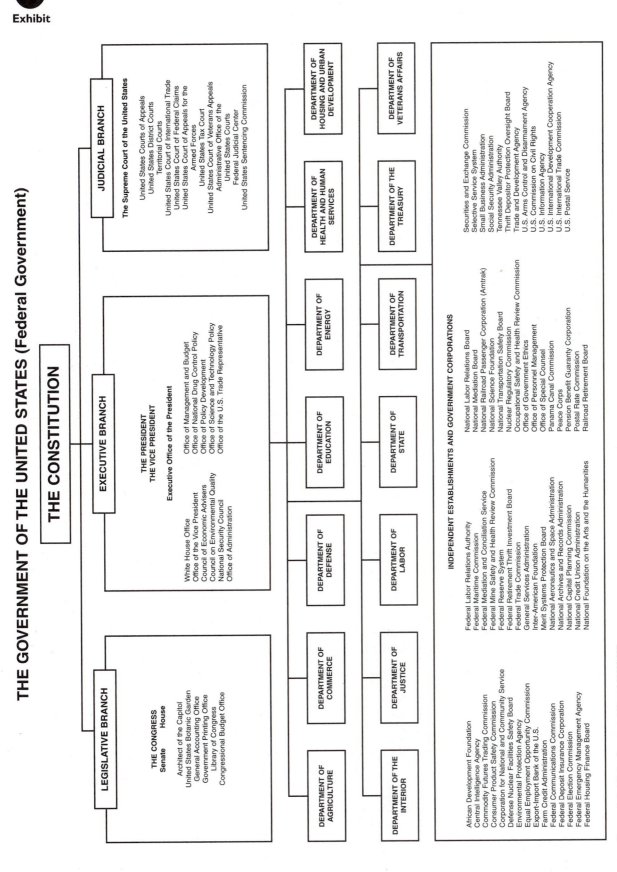

THE GOVERNMENT OF THE UNITED STATES (Federal Government)

THE CONSTITUTION

LEGISLATIVE BRANCH

THE CONGRESS
Senate   House

Architect of the Capitol
United States Botanic Garden
General Accounting Office
Government Printing Office
Library of Congress
Congressional Budget Office

EXECUTIVE BRANCH

THE PRESIDENT
THE VICE PRESIDENT

Executive Office of the President

White House Office
Office of the Vice President
Council of Economic Advisers
Council on Environmental Quality
National Security Council
Office of Administration

Office of Management and Budget
Office of National Drug Control Policy
Office of Policy Development
Office of Science and Technology Policy
Office of the U.S. Trade Representative

JUDICIAL BRANCH

The Supreme Court of the United States

United States Courts of Appeals
United States District Courts
Territorial Courts
United States Court of International Trade
United States Court of Federal Claims
United States Court of Appeals for the Armed Forces
United States Tax Court
United States Court of Veterans Appeals
Administrative Office of the United States Courts
Federal Judicial Center
United States Sentencing Commission

DEPARTMENT OF AGRICULTURE

DEPARTMENT OF COMMERCE

DEPARTMENT OF DEFENSE

DEPARTMENT OF EDUCATION

DEPARTMENT OF ENERGY

DEPARTMENT OF HEALTH AND HUMAN SERVICES

DEPARTMENT OF HOUSING AND URBAN DEVELOPMENT

DEPARTMENT OF THE INTERIOR

DEPARTMENT OF JUSTICE

DEPARTMENT OF LABOR

DEPARTMENT OF STATE

DEPARTMENT OF TRANSPORTATION

DEPARTMENT OF THE TREASURY

DEPARTMENT OF VETERANS AFFAIRS

INDEPENDENT ESTABLISHMENTS AND GOVERNMENT CORPORATIONS

African Development Foundation
Central Intelligence Agency
Commodity Futures Trading Commission
Consumer Product Safety Commission
Corporation for National and Community Service
Defense Nuclear Facilities Safety Board
Environmental Protection Agency
Equal Employment Opportunity Commission
Export-Import Bank of the U.S.
Farm Credit Administration
Federal Communications Commission
Federal Deposit Insurance Corporation
Federal Election Commission
Federal Emergency Management Agency
Federal Housing Finance Board

Federal Labor Relations Authority
Federal Maritime Commission
Federal Mediation and Conciliation Service
Federal Mine Safety and Health Review Commission
Federal Reserve System
Federal Retirement Thrift Investment Board
Federal Trade Commission
General Services Administration
Inter-American Foundation
Merit Systems Protection Board
National Aeronautics and Space Administration
National Archives and Records Administration
National Capital Planning Commission
National Credit Union Administration
National Foundation on the Arts and the Humanities

National Labor Relations Board
National Mediation Board
National Railroad Passenger Corporation (Amtrak)
National Science Foundation
National Transportation Safety Board
Nuclear Regulatory Commission
Occupational Safety and Health Review Commission
Office of Government Ethics
Office of Personnel Management
Office of Special Counsel
Panama Canal Commission
Peace Corps
Pension Benefit Guaranty Corporation
Postal Rate Commission
Railroad Retirement Board

Securities and Exchange Commission
Selective Service System
Small Business Administration
Social Security Administration
Tennessee Valley Authority
Thrift Depositor Protection Oversight Board
Trade and Development Agency
U.S. Arms Control and Disarmament Agency
U.S. Commission on Civil Rights
U.S. Information Agency
U.S. International Development Cooperation Agency
U.S. International Trade Commission
U.S. Postal Service

Source: United States Government Manual 1996/1997.

SECTION C   CATEGORIES OF LAWS

What kinds of laws do these branches of government create? As we saw in chapter 1, the ten major categories of law are:

opinions	charters
statutes	ordinances
constitutions	rules of court
administrative regulations	executive orders
administrative decisions	treaties

To this list we also add opinions of the attorney general, although they technically are not laws. Exhibit 2.2 defines these categories of law and lists who writes or creates them.

2.2 .... Kinds of Laws

Exhibit

Category	Definition	Who Writes This Kind of Law?
(a) **Opinion**	A court's written explanation of how it applied the law to the facts before it to resolve a legal dispute. Also called a **case**.	Courts—usually appellate courts.
(b) **Statute**	A law that declares, commands, or prohibits something. Also called **legislation**. (An **act** is the official document that contains the statute.)	The legislature. Some states also allow a direct vote of the people by referendum.
(c) **Constitution**	The fundamental law that creates the branches of government and identifies basic rights and obligations.	Varies. Often a combination of the legislature and a vote of the people. Another option might be a constitutional convention.
(d) **Administrative Regulation**	A law designed to explain or carry out the statutes and executive orders that govern an administrative agency. Also called an **administrative rule**.	Administrative agency.
(e) **Administrative Decision**	A resolution of a controversy between a party and an administrative agency involving the application of the regulations, statutes, or executive orders that govern the agency. Also called an **administrative ruling**.	Administrative agency.
(f) **Charter**	The fundamental law of a municipality or other local unit of government authorizing it to perform designated governmental functions.	Varies. The state legislature often writes charter provisions for cities in the state.
(g) **Ordinance**	A law that declares, commands, or prohibits something. (Same as a statute, but at the local level.)	The local legislature (e.g., city council, county commission).
(h) **Rules of Court**	The procedural laws that govern the mechanics of litigation (practice and procedure) before a particular court. Also called **court rules**.	Varies. The legislature and/or the highest court in the jurisdiction.
(i) **Executive Order**	A law issued by the chief executive pursuant to specific statutory authority or to the executive's inherent authority to direct the operation of governmental agencies.	President (for U.S. government); governor (for state government); mayor (for local government).
(j) **Treaty**	An international agreement between two or more foreign governments.	The President makes treaties by and with the consent of the U.S. Senate.

2.2 .... Kinds of Laws—continued

Exhibit

Category	Definition	Who Writes This Kind of Law?
(k) **Opinion of the Attorney General**	Formal legal advice given by the chief law officer of the government to another government official or agency. Also called opinions of **legal counsel**. (Technically, this is *not* a category of law, but it is often relied on as a source of law.)	Attorney General.

Assignment 2.1

Find a recent article in your local general newspaper that meets the following criteria: (a) it refers to more than one kind of law listed in Exhibit 2.2, and (b) it refers to more than one level of government. Because the article will have no formal citations to laws, you must do your best to guess what kinds of law and levels of government are involved. Clip out the article. In the margin, next to each reference to a law, place the appropriate abbreviation: FO (if you think the reference is to a federal court opinion); SO (if you think the reference is to a state court opinion); FS (federal statute); SS (state statute); FC (United States Constitution); SC (state constitution); FAR (administrative regulation of a federal agency); SAR (administrative regulation of a state agency). Make up your own abbreviations for any other kind of law listed in Exhibit 2.2. If the article refers to the same law more than once, make a margin note only the first time the law is mentioned.

Another way to classify laws is to distinguish between common law and enacted law. You need to understand the role of the courts with respect to both kinds of laws.

The critically important phrase **common law** has at least four meanings, the last of which will be our primary concern in this book:

- At the broadest level, common law simply means case law—court opinions—as opposed to statutory law. In this sense, all case law develops and is part of the common law.
- Common law also refers to the legal system of England and America. Its counterpart is the **civil law system** of many Western European countries other than England (e.g., France). The origin of civil law includes the jurisprudence of the Roman Empire set forth in the Code of Justinian. (Louisiana is unique in that, unlike the remaining forty-nine common law states, its state law is in large measure based on the civil law—the Code Napoléon.) Although there is overlap between the two systems, common law systems generally place greater reliance on case law, whereas civil law systems tend to place greater emphasis on code or statutory law.
- More narrowly, common law refers to all of the case law *and* statutory law in England and in the American colonies before the American Revolution. The phrase **at common law** often refers to this colonial period.
- The most prevalent definition of common law is judge-made law in the absence of controlling statutory law or other higher law. As we shall see, statutes are superior in authority to the common law. Indeed, statutes are often passed with the express purpose of changing the common law in a particular area. Such statutes are referred to as **statutes in derogation of the common law.** Another meaning of the phrase "at common law," therefore, is judge-made law that exists until changed by statute.

Courts are sometimes confronted with disputes for which there is no applicable law. There may be no constitutional provisions, statutes, or administrative regulations governing the dispute. When this occurs, the court will apply—and if necessary, create—common law to resolve the controversy. Here common law is used in the fourth sense. That is, it is made by judges to compensate for the lack of statutory and other law applicable to the case at hand. In creating the common law, the court relies primarily on the unwritten customs and values of the community from time immemorial. Very often these customs and values are described and enforced in old opinions that are heavily cited by modern courts during the continuing process of developing the common law.

In addition to creating new common law (and interpreting common law created earlier), courts also interpret **enacted law,** the second large category of law we need to consider. Whereas common law is created in the context of disputes that are litigated, enacted law is any law that is *not* created within litigation. Enacted law is written by deliberative bodies such as legislatures, city councils, constitutional conventions, and administrative agencies (acting in their rule-making capacity). The major enacted laws are statutes, ordinances, constitutions, charters, administrative regulations, rules of court, executive orders, and treaties. Courts spend a great deal of time writing opinions that interpret these enacted laws.

To sum up, courts serve the following three roles:

- They interpret enacted laws
- They create common law (when needed to fill the gap caused by the absence of enacted law)
- They interpret common law previously created

SECTION D   CATEGORIES OF RESEARCH MATERIALS

With this understanding of the kinds of laws that exist, we turn now to the four major categories of research materials designed to bring you to these laws so that you can read the laws, apply them to the facts of a client's problem, and determine their current validity. These goals have led publishers to create legal research materials that serve these four functions:

- Materials that contain the full text of the law
- Materials that help you locate the law
- Materials that help you understand and interpret the law
- Materials that help you determine the current validity of the law

The four main columns of Exhibit 2.3 classify research materials by these four functions. As we will see, some materials serve more than one function. Legal periodicals, for example, can help you find laws as well as understand them. Exhibit 2.3 is our point of departure for the remaining chapters in Part I of this book. In these chapters we will be spending a great deal of time defining these categories of materials and learning how to use them.

2.3 .... The Four Functions of Research Materials

Exhibit

Kind of Law	Materials That Contain the Full Text of This Kind of Law	Materials That Can Be Used to Locate This Kind of Law	Materials That Can Be Used to Help Understand This Kind of Law	Materials That Can Be Used to Help Determine the Current Validity of This Kind of Law

(a) Opinions	Reports
	Reporters
	A.L.R., A.L.R.2d,
	  A.L.R.3d,
	  A.L.R.4th,
	  A.L.R.5th,
	  A.L.R. Fed.
		Digests
		Annotations in
		  A.L.R., A.L.R.2d,
		  A.L.R.3d,
		  A.L.R.4th,
		  A.L.R.5th,
		  A.L.R. Fed.
			Legal periodicals
			Legal encyclopedias
			Legal treatises
			Legal newsletters
			Annotations in
			  A.L.R., A.L.R.2d,
			  A.L.R.3d,
				Shepard's
				KeyCite
				Insta-Cite
				Auto-Cite

2.3 ································· The Four Functions of Research Materials—continued

Exhibit

Kind of Law	Materials That Contain the Full Text of This Kind of Law	Materials That Can Be Used to Locate This Kind of Law	Materials That Can Be Used to Help Understand This Kind of Law	Materials That Can Be Used to Help Determine the Current Validity of This Kind of Law
(a) Opinions—continued	Legal newspapers Looseleaf services Slip opinions Advance sheets CD-ROMs WESTLAW LEXIS Internet	Shepard's Legal periodicals Legal encyclopedias Legal treatises Looseleaf services Words and Phrases	A.L.R.4th, A.L.R.5th, A.L.R. Fed. Looseleaf services	
(b) Statutes	Statutory Code Statutes at Large Session Laws Compilations Consolidated Laws Slip Laws Acts & Resolves Laws Legislative Service CD-ROMs WESTLAW LEXIS Internet	Index volumes of statutory code Looseleaf services Footnote references in other materials such as legal periodicals, encyclopedias, and treatises	Legal periodicals Legal encyclopedias Legal treatises Legal newsletters Annotations in A.L.R., A.L.R.2d, A.L.R.3d, A.L.R.4th, A.L.R.5th, A.L.R. Fed. Looseleaf services	Shepard's
(c) Constitutions	Statutory Code Separate volumes containing the constitution CD-ROMs WESTLAW LEXIS Internet	Index volumes of statutory code Looseleaf services Footnote references in other materials	Legal periodicals Legal encyclopedias Legal treatises Legal newsletters Annotations in A.L.R., A.L.R.2d, A.L.R.3d, A.L.R.4th, A.L.R.5th, A.L.R. Fed. Looseleaf services	Shepard's
(d) Administrative Regulations	Administrative Code Separate volumes containing the regulations of certain agencies Register Bulletin Looseleaf services CD-ROMs WESTLAW LEXIS Internet	Index volumes of the administrative code Looseleaf services Footnote references in other materials	Legal periodicals Legal treatises Legal newsletters Annotations in A.L.R., A.L.R.2d, A.L.R.3d, A.L.R.4th, A.L.R.5th, A.L.R. Fed. Looseleaf services	Shepard's (for some agencies) *List of Sections Affected* (LSA) (for federal agencies)
(e) Administrative Decisions	Separate volumes of decisions of some agencies Looseleaf services WESTLAW LEXIS	Looseleaf services Index to (or digest volumes for) the decisions Footnote references in other materials	Legal periodicals Legal treatises Legal newsletters Annotations in A.L.R., A.L.R.2d, A.L.R.3d,	Shepard's (for some agencies)

Continued on next page

Kind of Law	Materials That Contain the Full Text of This Kind of Law	Materials That Can Be Used to Locate This Kind of Law	Materials That Can Be Used to Help Understand This Kind of Law	Materials That Can Be Used to Help Determine the Current Validity of This Kind of Law
(e) Administrative decisions— continued	Internet		A.L.R.4th, A.L.R.5th, A.L.R. Fed. Looseleaf services	
(f) Charters	Separate volumes containing the charter Municipal Code Register Bulletin State session laws Official journal Legal newspaper Internet	Index volumes to the charter or municipal code Footnote references in other materials	Legal periodicals Legal treatises Annotations in A.L.R., A.L.R.2d, A.L.R.3d, A.L.R.4th, A.L.R.5th, A.L.R. Fed.	Shepard's
(g) Ordinances	Municipal Code Official journal Legal newspaper Internet	Index volumes of municipal code Footnote references in other materials	Legal periodicals Legal treatises Annotations in A.L.R., A.L.R.2d, A.L.R.3d, A.L.R.4th, A.L.R.5th, A.L.R. Fed.	Shepard's
(h) Rules of Court	Separate rules volumes Statutory code Practice manuals Deskbooks CD-ROMs WESTLAW LEXIS Internet	Index to separate rules volumes Index to statutory code Index to practice manuals Index to Deskbook Footnote references in other materials	Practice manuals Legal periodicals Legal treatises Legal newsletters Annotations in A.L.R., A.L.R.2d, A.L.R.3d, A.L.R.4th, A.L.R.5th, A.L.R. Fed. Legal encyclopedias Looseleaf services	Shepard's
(i) Executive Orders	Federal Register Code of Federal Regulations Weekly Compilation of Presidential Documents U.S. Code Congressional and Administrative News U.S.C./U.S.C.A./ U.S.C.S. WESTLAW LEXIS Internet	Index volumes to the sets of books listed in the second column Footnote references in other materials	Legal periodicals Legal treatises Legal newsletters Annotations in A.L.R., A.L.R.2d, A.L.R.3d, A.L.R.4th, A.L.R.5th, A.L.R. Fed. Looseleaf services	Shepard's

2.3 .... The Four Functions of Research Materials—continued

Exhibit

Kind of Law	Materials That Contain the Full Text of This Kind of Law	Materials That Can Be Used to Locate This Kind of Law	Materials That Can Be Used to Help Understand This Kind of Law	Materials That Can Be Used to Help Determine the Current Validity of This Kind of Law
(j) Treaties	*Statutes at Large* (up to 1949) *United States Treaties and Other International Agreements* *Department of State Bulletin* *International Legal Materials* WESTLAW LEXIS Internet	Index within the volumes listed in second column *World Treaty Index* *Current Treaty Index* Footnote references in other materials	Legal periodicals Legal treatises Legal newsletters Annotations in A.L.R., A.L.R.2d, A.L.R.3d, A.L.R.4th, A.L.R.5th, A.L.R. Fed. Legal encyclopedias Looseleaf services	Shepard's
(k) Opinions of the Attorney General	Separate volumes containing these opinions WESTLAW LEXIS Internet	Digests Footnote references in other materials		

CHAPTER SUMMARY

Our legal system consists of three levels of government: federal, state, and local. Federalism is the division of powers that exists between the national or federal government and the state governments. Within each level of government, there are three branches of government: executive, legislative, and judicial. The legislative branch makes laws; the executive branch carries out laws; the judicial branch interprets laws and resolves disputes that arise under them.

There are ten main categories of laws: opinions, statutes, constitutions, administrative regulations, administrative decisions, charters, ordinances, rules of court, executive orders, and treaties. (In a special category are opinions of the attorney general.)

The primary meaning of common law is judge-made law in the absence of controlling statutory law or other higher law. Common law grows out of litigation. Enacted law, on the other hand, consists of any law that is not created within litigation, such as constitutions, statutes, administrative regulations, charters, ordinances, rules or court, executive orders, and treaties.

The four major categories of research materials are those that provide the full text of the laws, those that help you locate the laws, those that help you understand the laws, and those that help you determine the laws' current validity.

KEY TERMS

federalism
legislative branch
executive branch
judicial branch
opinion
case
statute
legislation

act
constitution
administrative regulation
administrative rule
administrative decision
administrative ruling
charter
ordinance

rules of court
court rules
executive order
treaty
opinion of the attorney general
legal counsel
common law

civil law system
at common law
statutes in derogation of the common law
enacted law

DEFINING RESEARCH MATERIALS: AN INTRODUCTORY OVERVIEW

Chapter Outline

SECTION A   INTRODUCTION

Chapter 3 contains a great deal of information, almost all of which we will revisit in later chapters. After cautioning you about definitions in Section B and introducing you (in Section C) to the major categories of media you might find in a law library, you then come to the longest section in the chapter—Section D, which defines, in alphabetical order, every major legal research term and every major set of materials (in any media) you will encounter in a law library. Here is how you should approach the chapter:

- Skim through the chapter quickly the first time to get a feel for its contents.
- The most important—and the largest—items in Section D are the entries on Case, Digest, and Shepard's. Read these three entries carefully.
- As you read the chapter, continue collecting the definitions and functions needed to complete Assignments 1.1 and 1.2 on terminology in chapter 1.
- As you read the chapter, do Assignment 3.1 found at the beginning of Section D for every book photographed in the section.

You are not expected to walk away from your first visit to chapter 3 knowing everything in it. More than a few visits will be required. Read, take notes, and do the assignments indicated. Then re-read and take more notes. The foundation of this course is a familiarity with the basic concepts of legal research. Chapter 3 is designed to give you this familiarity before you are required to use the concepts to solve research problems.

SECTION B   ARE THERE STANDARD DEFINITIONS?

Yes, there are standard definitions to most of the words and phrases used in legal research. You need to be cautious, however, because there are a few dramatic exceptions. For example:

- The phrase *Supreme Court* means the highest court in our federal judicial system (the United States Supreme Court) and the highest court in many state judicial systems (e.g., California Supreme Court). In New York State, however, one of the main *trial* courts is called the Supreme Court.
- The word *digest* usually refers to a set of volumes that contain small-paragraph summaries of court opinions. In Minnesota, there is a digest called *Minnesota Digest* that fits this definition—it gives small-paragraph summaries of Minnesota court opinions. There is another digest in Minnesota, however, called *Dunnell Minnesota Digest,* that is a state encyclopedia rather than a traditional digest.

Although standard definitions are generally used, you should be prepared to find variations.

SECTION C   LEGAL RESEARCH MEDIA: PAPER, ONLINE, CD-ROM, MICROFORMS

In Exhibit 2.2 of chapter 2, we identified the kinds of laws that exist (opinions, statutes, administrative regulations, etc.), and who writes them (courts, legislatures, administrative agencies, etc.). Here we examine the various formats for which the legal community spends over $4 billion a year to be able to find and to read these laws. What media are available? Today's legal researcher often has considerable choice. It may be possible, for example, to read a statute of the New York Legislature or to search for opinions of the United States Supreme Court in each of the following media:

Legal Research Media
1. Paper
   a) Pamphlet
   b) Hardcover, fixed pages
   c) Hardcover, looseleaf

2. Online (CALR)
    a) Commercial
    b) Public domain
3. CD-ROM
4. Microform
    a) Microfilm
    b) Microfiche
    c) Ultrafiche

Of course, it can be very expensive for a law firm to purchase all of these media. Few, if any, law libraries in the country are comprehensive enough to provide access to all of them for every category of law. A cost-conscious law firm, therefore, must determine what media will be the most cost-effective. **CALR** (computer-assisted legal research), for example, is sometimes more expensive than using traditional library volumes, yet CALR often allows you to find something in a few minutes that might take a day or two using other media. A law firm may decide that it is more cost-effective to charge a client for computer costs than for the hours needed to use a slower method of research.

Paper

Traditional library books are pamphlets or hardcover volumes made of paper. Very often the pamphlets are considered temporary. They tend to contain recent legal research material that will eventually be printed in more permanent hardcover volumes. When the latter become available, the law library throws away the pamphlets.

Most hardcover volumes contain pages that you cannot remove without ripping the book. A **looseleaf** book, in contrast, is a hardcover with removable pages. It has a ring-binder structure that snaps open and shut for easy insertion and removal of pages. (**Interfiling** means inserting pages anywhere in a text rather than just at the end.) The great benefit of looseleaf materials is that publishers can send subscribers new pages containing updated material along with instructions on what pages to remove because they contain outdated material.

Inserting pages into a looseleaf book

Online (CALR)

Online has several meanings. The broadest definition is using a computer. For example, some software programs have built-in manuals that you can read on your computer screen without being connected to other computers. They are called online manuals. In legal research, the more common meaning of *online* (the one used in this book most of the time) is using a computer that *is* connected to other computers, usually through regular telephone lines hooked up by a modem. This connection allows you to do online computer-assisted legal research (CALR). The two major fee-based (i.e., commercial) online services in the law are WESTLAW and LEXIS. Some online services, however, are in the **public domain,** meaning that they are accessible to anyone at no cost. Most of this material is on the constantly growing Internet, which we introduced in chapter 1 when we discussed the virtual law library.

Examples of CD-ROM products

CD-ROM

CD-ROM ("compact disk with read-only memory") is an optical information-storage system that operates much like a compact disk sold in music stores. Through your computer system, you gain access to the vast amount of information stored on the disk. Up to sixty large volumes of law books can be stored on one disk! Users cannot add any information to the disk; they can only read the information on it through their computer screen or monitor. (Hence the phrase *read only.*) Unlike more traditional computer-assisted research systems, you do not need a modem to use CD-ROM, because you do not use them online.

Microform

Microforms are images or photographs that have been reduced in size. Among the materials stored on microforms are pages from reporters, codes, treatises, periodicals, etc. Vast amounts of material can be stored in this way. An entire volume of a 1,000-page law book can fit on a single plastic card! Special machines (*reader-printers* and *fiche readers*) magnify the material so that it can be read. These machines are sometimes awkward to use. The major value of microforms is the space savings that can result by storing (i.e., archiving) a large quantity of materials that no longer need to take up shelf space. In general, these are older materials that researchers do not use on a regular basis. Several kinds of microforms are available. (a) *Microfilm* stores the material on film reels or cassettes. (b) *Microfiche* stores the material on single sheets of film. (c) *Ultrafiche* is microfiche with a considerably greater storage capacity, providing a reduction factor of 100 or more.

Example of ultrafiche that contains an entire reporter volume

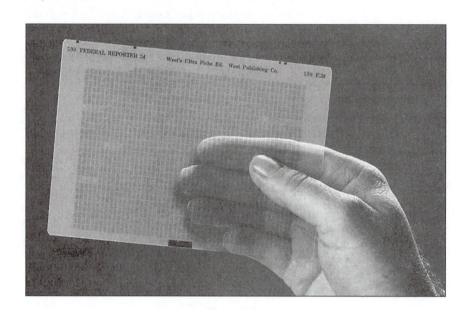

SECTION D　　　FIRST LOOK: A WALKING TOUR

This section provides you with a more detailed first look at some of the major legal research terms and materials in a large law library. In later chapters, we tackle the question of how to use these materials to find what you need. At this stage of the course, our goal is more modest: finding out what exists. Assignment 3.1 asks you to locate as many of the pamphlets and books pictured in this section as you can. Doing the assignment, in effect, asks you to take a walking tour of one or more law libraries in your area.

Assignment 3.1

Section D contains approximately sixty-five photographs of books and pamphlets, not counting the photos of page excerpts. Some of the photos contain more than one volume. In this assignment, you are to go to the most comprehensive law library or libraries near you and find the books and pamphlets depicted in the photographs (or close substitutes). There are several reasons why you may not be able to find the exact book or pamphlet in one of the photos:

- The library may not have purchased or subscribed to the book or pamphlet.
- The library has the book or pamphlet, but not the volume number or issue depicted in the photo. (Some pamphlets, for example, are thrown away when bound volumes come out that include the material in the pamphlets.)

Assignment 3.1—continued

- The library has the book or pamphlet, but the one you want is simply not on the shelf. (It may be in use or have been misshelved.)
- The photograph is not clear enough to allow you to make out the volume number or other identifying information about the book or pamphlet in the photo.

If any of these reasons apply, try to find as close a substitute as possible in the law library. A close substitute might be a different volume number in the same set; a different title in the same category of book; or the same category of book but for a different state. Proceed as follows:

1. Make a list of every book or pamphlet photographed in Section D (not including photos of page excerpts). If more than one book or pamphlet is depicted in a photo, list each separately.
2. Place a checkmark (✓) in front of a book or pamphlet on the list if you found it *exactly* as pictured in the photograph, e.g., the same volume number. Include a one-sentence description of the kind of material found in that book or pamphlet.
3. Place an **(s)**, meaning substitute, in front of a book or pamphlet on the list if you substituted another book or pamphlet for the one in the photo for any of the reasons listed above. State why you had to use a substitute and make clear what your substitute is. Include a one-sentence description of the kind of material found in the book or pamphlet.
4. Place an **(x)** in front of a book or pamphlet on the list if you were not able to find it or a substitute. State why this was so. Still include a one-sentence description of the kind of material found in the book or pamphlet you were seeking.

Abstract An **abstract** is a summary of the important points of a text; it is an overview. Summaries of opinions are sometimes called *abstracts* or *squibs*. One of the major places they are printed is in *digests*, which are volumes of small-paragraph summaries of opinions. *See* Digests (page 49).

Act An **act** is the official document that contains a statute passed by the legislature. A *bill* (which is a proposed statute) becomes an act once the legislature enacts it into law. It can be printed in several formats: as a *slip law* (which consists of a single act), in the *session laws* (which is a collection of every private and public act arranged chronologically), and in a *statutory code* (which is a collection of every public act arranged by subject matter). Session laws are also called Statutes at Large, Acts and Resolves, Laws, etc. *See* Slip Law (page 68); Session Law (page 67); Statutory Code (page 72).

Administrative Code An **administrative code** is a collection of the regulations of one or more administrative agencies. Generally, the regulations of state and local administrative agencies are poorly organized and difficult to find. Not so for the regulations of *federal* administrative agencies, as we will see when we cover the *Code of Federal Regulations*. A distinguishing feature of a code is that the material in it is organized by subject matter rather than chronologically. A subject-matter organization would mean that all or most regulations on the environment, for example, are together in one place in the code. A chronological printing, however, would mean that laws on totally different subject matters could follow each other, depending on the order in which the laws were passed. The following sets of laws often have a subject-matter organization: administrative codes (that print administrative regulations) and statutory codes (that print statutes).

Advance In general, the word *advance* or **advance sheet** refers to a pamphlet that comes out prior to (in advance of) a thicker pamphlet or a bound volume. Very often the material in the advance publication is reprinted in the thicker pamphlet or hardcover volume so that the advance publication can be thrown away. Here are the three main kinds of publications that have this advance feature:

1. Advance sheet for a reporter. A reporter is a publication that contains the full text of court opinions. A reporter advance sheet prints these opinions soon after they are written by the courts. Once several reporter advance sheets are available, the opinions in them are all printed in a hardcover volume so that all the advance sheets can be thrown away.

Advance sheet for a reporter (here the *Supreme Court Reporter*). An advance sheet contains the full text of court opinions that will later be printed in a hardcover reporter volume (here the *Supreme Court Reporter*).

2. Advance sheet for *Shepard's Citations*. A *citator* is a publication (or online service) containing lists of citations that will allow you to assess the current validity of something and also give you leads to other relevant materials. The major citator is *Shepard's Citations*. The advance sheet supplement for Shepard's contains early citator information—the citations—which is later reprinted in larger supplement pamphlets and hardcover volumes. Once the library receives the larger publication, the advance sheet is thrown away.

Advance sheet supplements for Shepard's (here the *Shepard's United States Citations*). The first photo is the advance sheet, the material from which is later reprinted in a thicker supplement pamphlet (middle photo) and finally in a hardcover volume (third photo).

  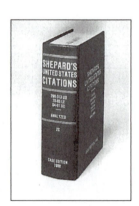

3. Advance sheet for a statutory code. The most current statutes are often first published in a special pamphlet that may be called a **legislative service** or **advance session law service**. Most libraries throw these pamphlets away once they are published in hardcover session law volumes and (if they are public laws) in a bound statutory code.

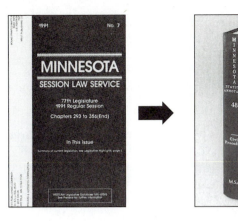

An advance session law service for Minnesota statutes. Many of the statutes in this pamphlet are later printed in the hardcover statutory code for the state, *Minnesota Statutes Annotated.*

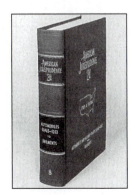

Example of a volume of *American Law Reports, Fifth Series.* All A.L.R. volumes print several opinions plus extensive annotations on selected issues in these opinions.

As we will see later, the advance session law services for federal statutes are *U.S.C.S. Advance* (for the *United States Code Service*) and *United States Code Congressional and Administrative News* (for the *United States Code Annotated*).

A.L.R., A.L.R.2d, A.L.R.3d, A.L.R.4th, A.L.R.5th, A.L.R. Fed.

- A.L.R.: *American Law Reports, First Series*
- A.L.R.2d: *American Law Reports, Second Series*
- A.L.R.3d: *American Law Reports, Third Series*
- A.L.R.4th: *American Law Reports, Fourth Series*
- A.L.R.5th: *American Law Reports, Fifth Series*
- A.L.R. Fed.: *American Law Reports, Federal Series*

These six sets of books contain the complete text of *selected* court opinions along with extensive commentaries, which are, in effect, research papers on issues within the opinions selected. The research papers are called **annotations.** The sets of books are therefore called **annotated reporters,** because they print the full text of opinions plus commentary on them. They are published by Lawyers Co-operative (Lawyers Co-op.), a division of West Group. As we shall see later, annotations are excellent case finders. (Although the abbreviation *A.L.R.* sometimes refers to the First Series only, more commonly it refers to all six sets collectively.) Many annotations have been placed online so that they can now be found and read on a computer screen. The computer systems that provide online access to A.L.R. are WESTLAW and LEXIS.

American Digest System The American Digest System consists of three sets of digests that provide small-paragraph summaries of court opinions written by every federal and every state court that publishes its opinions. The three digests (published by the West Group) are the *General Digest* (containing the most recent summaries), the *Decennial Digests* (containing summaries covering ten-year periods), and the *Century Digest* (containing summaries for cases written prior to 1897). *See* Digests (page 51).

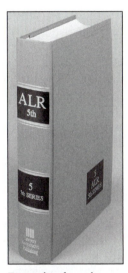

Example of a volume of *American Jurisprudence 2d,* a national legal encyclopedia

American Jurisprudence 2d (Am. Jur. 2d) Am. Jur. 2d is a national **legal encyclopedia** published by Lawyers Co-op., a division of West Group. (Am. Jur. 2d is the second edition of Am. Jur. First.) A legal encyclopedia is a multivolume set of books that summarizes every major legal topic, arranged alphabetically. (Am. Jur. 2d is also available online through WESTLAW and LEXIS.) The other major national legal encyclopedia is *Corpus Juris Secundum* (C.J.S.), also from the West Group.

There are three main uses of national legal encyclopedias such as Am. Jur. 2d and C.J.S.: (1) they are useful as background reading before you begin legal research in a new area of the law; (2) they are good case finders, because of their extensive footnotes to court opinions; and (3) they provide cross-references to other publications of the West Group on whatever topic you are reading about in the encyclopedia. In addition to these two national encyclopedias, several states have state encyclopedias devoted to the law of one state (e.g., Florida and Michigan). *See* Legal Encyclopedia (page 60).

American Law Reports (A.L.R.) *American Law Reports* is an annotated reporter. It prints the full text of selected opinions and extensive annotations based on issues in those opinions. *See* A.L.R., A.L.R.2d, etc. (page 37).

Annotation An *annotation* is a set of notes or commentaries on something. The main volumes containing annotations are the six sets of *American Law Reports:* A.L.R., A.L.R.2d, A.L.R.3d, A.L.R.4th, A.L.R.5th, and A.L.R. Fed. The annotations are research papers that are based on selected court opinions in these volumes. When a supervisor asks you to "find out if there are any annotations," you are being sent to A.L.R., A.L.R.2d, etc.

The verb is **annotated.** If materials are annotated, they contain notes or commentaries. An **annotated statutory code** prints statutes by subject matter and includes research references such as notes of court opinions that have interpreted the statutes (often called **notes of decisions** or *annotations*). The abbreviation for annotated is "Ann." (e.g., Del. Code Ann. for Delaware Code Annotated), or "A." (e.g., U.S.C.A. for United States Code Annotated). An *annotated reporter* such as A.L.R. prints court opinions along with notes or commentaries. An *annotated bibliography* (page 281) contains a list of references along with a brief comment on each reference.

With rare exceptions, annotations are written by private publishers and authors. They are not official documents of courts, legislatures, or agencies.

Atlantic Digest A digest that summarizes state court opinions in the *Atlantic Reporter.* See Research Link A and Exhibit 3.3. *See also* Digests (page 49).

Atlantic Reporter 2d (A.2d) A regional reporter that prints the full text of state court opinions in the Atlantic region of the country. See Exhibit 3.2. *See also* Cases (page 39).

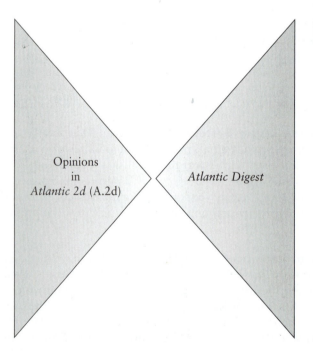

Opinions
in
Atlantic 2d (A.2d)

Atlantic Digest

RESEARCH LINK A

Every opinion in the *Atlantic 2d* reporter written by the state courts in the Atlantic region (Conn., Del., D.C., Me., Md., N.H., N.J., Pa., R.I., and Vt.) is digested (summarized) in *Atlantic Digest.*

Auto-Cite Auto-Cite is an online program of LEXIS that will tell you whether an opinion you are checking is good law. For example, you will be told whether the opinion has been overruled or criticized by another opinion. Auto-Cite also provides parallel cites and other citing material. Auto-Cite is an online citator. *See* Citator (page 47); LEXIS (page 63).

Example of a bill introduced in the House of Representatives of Congress. A bill is a proposed statute.

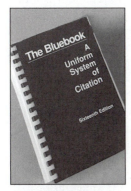

The Bluebook: A Uniform System of Citation, providing guidelines on proper citation form

National Reporter Blue Book, providing parallel cites to court opinions

Ballentine's Law Dictionary *See* Legal Dictionary (page 60).

Bill A **bill** is a proposed statute (one that has not yet been enacted into law). The steps a bill goes through before it becomes a law is known as its **legislative history.**

Black's Law Dictionary A single-volume legal dictionary. *See* Legal Dictionary (page 60).

Blue Book The phrase **blue book** (sometimes spelled *bluebook*) usually refers to one of the following four books or sets of books:

- *The Bluebook: A Uniform System of Citation*
  This is a small blue pamphlet published by the law reviews of several law schools. The pamphlet covers the "rules" of citation form. It is considered by many to be the bible of citation form, although as we will see, not everyone follows it.
- *National Reporter Blue Book*
  This set of books, published by the West Group, enables you to find a *parallel cite* to a court opinion. A parallel cite is simply an additional reference to printed or online sources where you will be able to read the same material word-for-word. A parallel cite to an opinion would be a reference to another reporter that prints the entire text of the opinion. The *National Reporter Blue Book* covers every state. Some states have a *Blue and White Book,* which covers parallel cites for the opinions of one state only.
- *A.L.R. Blue Book of Supplemental Decisions*
  This set of books allows you to update the annotations in A.L.R.1st.
- State directory. Many states have a directory or manual that gives names, addresses, telephone numbers, and e-mail addresses of their state agencies. They may also include information about the functions of each agency. Most of these directories are called *bluebooks.*

Brief The word *brief* means a summary or outline of an argument. In the law, the word is used in four main senses. First, a brief is a document submitted to an appellate court in which a party asks the court to approve, modify, or reverse what a lower court has done. Such briefs are called **appellate briefs.** If a nonparty receives permission to submit an appellate brief, it is called an **amicus curiae** (or friend-of-the-court) **brief.** For example, the American Civil Liberties Union might ask an appellate court (in a case in which the ACLU is not a party) to be allowed to submit an amicus curiae brief that supports the position of a racist organization that is being denied a city permit to march in a parade. (It is possible to locate appellate briefs in some large law libraries and online through LEXIS and WESTLAW. For briefs on the Internet, see <http://www.briefreporter.com>.) Second, a brief is a document submitted to a trial court in support of a particular position, e.g., a brief in support of a motion to dismiss. (In some courts, this kind of brief is called a *memorandum of law* in support of the motion.) Third, a brief is a summary of the main components of a single court opinion, including the key facts, the issues, the holdings, the reasoning, etc. When you *brief a case,* you are providing such a summary. (See Exhibit 10.1 in chapter 10.) Fourth, a *trial brief* is an attorney's personal set of notes on how to conduct a trial.

Bulletin A bulletin is a publication issued on an ongoing or periodic basis (such as the *Internal Revenue Bulletin*).

***California Reporter* (Cal. Rptr.)** A court reporter containing selected California state cases. *See* Cases (page 39).

Cases The word *case* has three meanings. First, a case is a court **opinion,** which is a court's written explanation of how it applied the law to the facts before it to resolve a legal dispute. (See Exhibit 2.2 in chapter 2.) Opinions are printed in volumes called **reporters.**[1] The words *case* and *opinion* are often used interchangeably. For example,

---

1. If the reporter is an official reporter, it is sometimes called **Reports,** e.g., *United States Reports.* The word *reporter* is also sometimes used for volumes containing administrative decisions written by agencies, although the more common usage is for volumes containing opinions written by courts.

Front cover of an appellate brief submitted to the United States Supreme Court. (An appellate brief asks a court of appeals to approve, modify, or reverse what a lower court has done.)

you will hear researchers say that they "read a case" as often as you will hear them say that they "read an opinion." Second, *case* means a pending matter before a court—a matter that is still in litigation. (Every trial and appellate court, for example, has a **docket** that lists the cases on its calendar.) Third, *case* means any client matter in a law office, whether or not litigation is involved. (A large law office, for example, may have hundreds of cases in its active case file and thousands in its closed case files.)

The first meaning of case—an opinion—is our primary concern in this book. Every year over 130,000 opinions are written by more than 3,500 judges sitting in 600 different courts throughout the United States.[2] Our study of this vast array of law will focus on three major themes:

- Where can you read these opinions?
- How do you find them?
- How do you read (i.e., *brief*) and apply them?

On the following pages, we will cover the first theme as we provide an overview of the materials that contain opinions. In chapters 9 and 10 we cover the themes of finding, briefing, and applying opinions. For now, our focus is limited to the question of where you can read them.

For many opinions, there are twelve possible places where you can read them. They are outlined in Exhibit 3.1. The most common is the unofficial reporter. (See the fourth option in Exhibit 3.1.) An **official reporter** is a reporter printed under the authority of the government, often by a government printing office. An **unofficial reporter** is a reporter printed by a commercial publishing company without special authority from the government. As we will see, the West Group is the major publisher of unofficial reporters, particularly through its National Reporter System. Unofficial does not mean unreliable. In fact, West's unofficial reporters are so reliable that many states have discontinued their own official reporters. In such states, most people, including judges, rely almost exclusively on the unofficial reporter.

3.1 .... Twelve Possible Places to Read the Same Court Opinion

Exhibit

Category	Definition	Currency (How soon is the opinion available in this format after the court writes it?)	Frequency of Use (How often do researchers read the opinion in this format?)	Editorial Enhancements (How many features are available in this format in addition to the text of the opinion?)
1. Slip Opinion	A single option printed by the court.	Very current	Seldom	Almost none
2. Advance Sheet	A pamphlet (containing several opinions) printed in advance of a hardcover reporter volume.	Very Current	Very often	Many (e.g., headnotes with key numbers)
3. Reporter (official)	A hardcover volume containing many opinions. An official reporter is one printed under the authority of the government, often by the government itself. Official reporters are sometimes called reports.	Not very current	Not very often	Not many
4. Reporter (unofficial)	A hardcover volume containing many opinions. An unofficial reporter is one printed by a commercial publishing company (e.g., West) without special authority from the government.	Fairly current	Very often	Many (e.g., headnotes with key numbers)

2. Ancil Ramey, *West Publishing Company to Print West Virginia Reports,* 5 W. Va. Law. 7 (Oct. 1991).

3.1 .... Twelve Possible Places to Read the Same Court Opinion—continued

Exhibit

Category	Definition	Currency (How soon is the opinion available in this format after the court writes it?)	Frequency of Use (How often do researchers read the opinion in this format?)	Editorial Enhancements (How many features are available in this format in addition to the text of the opinion?)
5. Looseleaf Service	A hardcover volume with removable pages often containing many opinions.	Very current	Fairly often	Many (e.g., suggestions on practicing law)
6. Legal Newspaper	A newspaper (published daily, weekly, etc.) devoted to legal news; may print text of opinions of local courts.	Very current	Fairly often	Almost none
7. Legal Newsletter	A special-interest publication (printed monthly, bimonthly, etc.) covering a particular area of law; may print text of opinions in that area.	Fairly current	Fairly often	Some
8. Microforms (microfilm, microfiche, ultrafiche)	Images or photographs that have been reduced in size.	Very current	Not often	Many
9. CD-ROM	An optical information-storage system that operates much like a compact disk containing music.	Fairly current	Not very often (although increasing)	Many
10. Online Commercial Database	Online companies sell access to legal materials (e.g., opinions) and law-related materials. The major companies are WESTLAW and LEXIS. (See chapter 13 for an overview of these online services.)	Very current	Fairly often	Many
11. Bulletin Boards	A local dial-in online service for the exchange of messages and information. Some courts have their own bulletin boards that print their opinions.	Very current	Not very often	Almost none
12. Internet	A self-governing special network of networks to which millions of computer users all over the world have access. Among the information available online through the Internet are court opinions. (See Appendix B for the World Wide Web addresses that will allow you to find federal and state court opinions on the Internet.)	Very current	Not very often	Almost none

Courts do not formally publish every opinion they write. An **unpublished opinion** is one that the court does not deem to be important enough for general publication. Because publishers do not print such opinions in their reporters, the opinion is called an **unreported opinion**. It may still be possible, however, to read an unpublished or unreported opinion, particularly in the online commercial databases of WESTLAW and LEXIS. You may be able to read them, but you cannot rely on them to the same extent as reported opinions. Courts place severe limitations on when you can cite and rely on an unpublished opinion.

We turn now to an overview of the major reported opinions, focusing first on federal court opinions and then on state court opinions.

Federal Court Opinions The opinions of the United States Supreme Court are printed in an official reporter, *United States Reports* (abbreviated "U.S."), and in several unofficial reporters: the *Supreme Court Reporter* published by the West Group (abbreviated "S. Ct.") and *United States Supreme Court Reports, Lawyers' Edition,* published by LEXIS Law Publishing Co. (abbreviated "L. Ed.").

The three major reporters containing opinions of the United States Supreme Court

 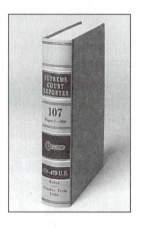 

When an opinion is printed in the *United States Reports,* it will also be printed word-for-word in S. Ct. and in L. Ed., the unofficial reporters—but not necessarily on the same page numbers. Suppose that you are reading an opinion in an unofficial reporter and you want to quote from it. The standard practice is to give the reference or citation to the quote as it appears in the *official* reporter. Suppose, however, that the latter is not available in your library, but one of the unofficial reporters is. How do you quote a page number in an official reporter when all you have available is an unofficial reporter? You use a technique called **star paging.** While you are reading a page in an unofficial reporter, you will find a notation of some kind provided by the printer (an asterisk, a star, or other special notation) plus a page number, often in bold print. The latter is a reference to a page number of the same case in the official reporter. Star paging therefore enables you to determine on what pages the same court language can be found in official and unofficial reporters.[3]

Example of star paging. This excerpt is from page 658 of a reporter. Note the special mark telling you that you will find the same text on page 378 of another reporter.

> **658**
> to determine which crimes have been punished too leniently, and which too severely. § 994(m). Congress has called upon the Commission to exercise its judgment about which ⌐378types of crimes and which types of criminals are to be considered similar for the purposes of sentencing.

Two looseleaf services (page 64) also print the text of all U.S. Supreme Court opinions:

- *United States Law Week* (U.S.L.W.) published by Bureau of National Affairs (BNA)
- *United States Supreme Court Bulletin* (S. Ct. Bull.) published by Commerce Clearing House (CCH)

3. In chapter 5, we discuss vendor-neutral citation systems that use paragraph numbers rather than page numbers in the citation of the opinion. In such systems, star paging is unnecessary because the text you want to quote will always be in the same paragraph number regardless of what reporter you are using. See footnote 3 in chapter 5.

Federal Reporter,
Third Series (F.3d).
Currently contains the
full text of the opin-
ions written by the
United States Courts
of Appeals. (For a
photo of F.2d on ultra-
fiche, see page 34.)

Federal Supplement (F.
Supp.). Currently con-
tains the full text of
the opinions written
by the United States
District Courts.

Example of an official
state reports volume

It is also possible to read U.S. Supreme Court opinions in electronic formats. They are all available online from the main computer services, LEXIS and WESTLAW. Increasingly, the opinions are becoming available on the **Internet,** a special network of networks to which millions of individual computer users have access (see page 58). For a list of Internet addresses where you can read court opinions (federal and state) online, see Appendix B. Finally, West and Lawyer's Co-op publish U.S. Supreme Court opinions on CD-ROM, an optical information-storage system (see page 33).

We now turn to reporters for the *lower* federal courts, primarily the U.S. Courts of Appeals and the U.S. District Courts. (The latter are the main trial courts in the federal judicial system.) Two major reporters contain the full text of opinions from these lower federal courts:

* *Federal Reporter, First Series* (abbreviated "F.")
* *Federal Reporter, Second Series* (abbreviated "F.2d")
* *Federal Reporter, Third Series* (abbreviated "F.3d")
* *Federal Supplement* (abbreviated "F. Supp.")

The first set of reporters (F., F.2d, F.3d) primarily contains opinions written by the U.S. Courts of Appeals. The second set of reporters (F. Supp.) primarily contains opinions written by the U.S. District Courts. Both sets are unofficial reporters published by West.

In addition to F., F.2d, F.3d, and F. Supp., West publishes several specialty or topical reporters that also cover federal courts. For example:

Federal Rules Decisions (F.R.D.)
* Contains opinions of the U.S. District Courts on the Federal Rules of Civil and Criminal Procedure, and also
* Contains articles, speeches, and conference reports on federal procedural issues

Military Justice Reporter (M.J.)
* Contains opinions of the United States Court of Military Appeals and the Courts of Military Review for the Army, Navy-Marine, Air Force, and Coast Guard

Bankruptcy Reporter (B.R.)
* Contains opinions of the United States Bankruptcy Courts and selected bankruptcy opinions of other federal courts

Federal Claims Reporter
* Contains opinions of the United States Court of Federal Claims (formerly called the United States Claims Court)

Veterans Appeals Reporter
* Contains opinions of the United States Court of Veterans Appeals and of federal courts hearing appeals from this court.

In addition to these bound reporters, the opinions of lower federal courts are available online through LEXIS and WESTLAW. Many may also be accessible on the Internet (see Appendix B).

State Court Opinions At one time, all states had official reporters containing the opinions of their highest state courts. As indicated earlier, however, a large number of states have discontinued their official reports. For such states, the unofficial reporters are the main or only source where you can find the opinions of their state courts.

The major publisher of unofficial state reports is the West Group through its *National Reporter System.* There are seven **regional reporters** in the System. (West's other reporters are also part of the National Reporter System.) For a photo of each regional reporter, see page 46. A regional reporter is simply an unofficial reporter that contains state court opinions of several states within one of seven regions of the country. (See Exhibit 3.2.)

If a law office subscribes to a regional reporter covering its own state, the office is also receiving opinions of other states in the same region. These other opinions may be of little practical value to the office. West therefore publishes special state editions for

3.2

Exhibit

Seven Regional Reporters in the National Reporter System

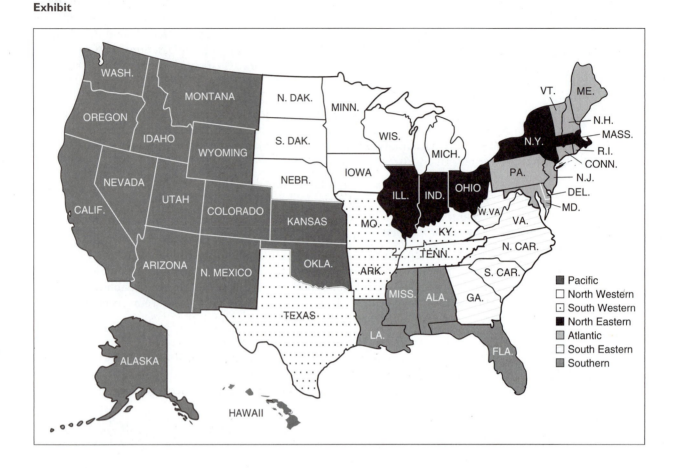

A volume of *Kansas Cases* (a special edition state reporter) containing all the Kansas opinions printed in *Pacific Reporter 2d.*

over half the states. These **special edition state reporters** (sometimes called *offprint reporters*) contain only the opinions of an individual state that are also printed in the regional reporter. For example, the opinions of the highest court in Kansas are printed in the *Pacific Reporter.* A Kansas attorney who does not want to subscribe to the *Pacific Reporter* can subscribe to the special edition Kansas reporter, called *Kansas Cases.* (See Research Link B.)

Finally, West publishes three separate reporters containing state court opinions of New York, California, and Illinois:

- *New York Supplement* (N.Y.S.)
- *California Reporter* (Cal. Rptr.)
- *Illinois Decisions* (Ill. Dec.)

Each contains the opinions of the highest court in the state as well as selected opinions of its lower courts.

Major Characteristics of West Reporters
- The reporters contain the full text of court opinions.
- The opinions are arranged in roughly chronological order according to the date of the decision; they are not arranged by subject matter. A murder case, for example, could follow a tax case.
- The reporters have advance sheets that come out before the hardcover volumes. When the hardcover reporter volume comes out, all the advance sheets are thrown away.
- A Table of Cases appears at the beginning of each reporter volume.
- Many reporters have a statutes table listing the statutes construed (i.e., interpreted) within an individual reporter volume.

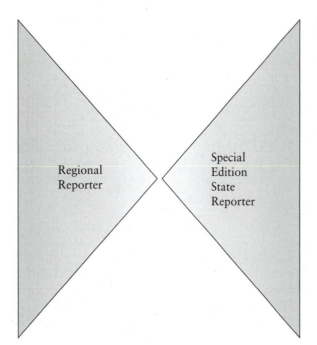

RESEARCH LINK B
The seven regional reporters each contain the opinions of several states. If all of the opinions of one of these states are taken out and also printed in a separate reporter, the latter is called a special edition state reporter.

- There is no traditional index to the opinions in a reporter volume. How then do you find opinions? Later we will see that digests are one of the major ways of locating what is in reporters. A **digest** is a separate set of volumes that contain small-paragraph summaries of opinions. In effect, the digest acts as an index to the opinions in reporter volumes.
- Each opinion is summarized in a series of small paragraphs called **headnotes.** They are written by West editors, not by the court. Headnotes are eventually printed in at least five places: first, just before the opinion begins; second, at the beginning of the advance sheet containing the opinion; third, at the end of the hardcover reporter volume containing the opinion; fourth, in West digests (again, it is this feature of digests that enables them to become indexes to court opinions); fifth, in WESTLAW.

Where else is the full text of state court opinions found?

- Online through LEXIS and WESTLAW
- On CD-ROM
- On **ultrafiche,** which is a single sheet of film containing material that has been reduced by a factor of 100 or more. West publishes an ultrafiche edition of the National Reporter System. *See* Microform (page 34).
- Online on the Internet (see Appendix B for Internet addresses covering specific courts)
- Online on bulletin boards

For a summary of up to twelve places where you may be able to read the same opinion, see Exhibit 3.1.

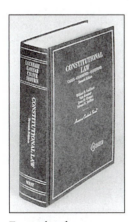

Example of a casebook used in a law school classroom

Casebook A **casebook** is a law school textbook. It consists mainly of a collection of edited court opinions and other materials relating to a particular area of the law, e.g., Lockhart, Kamisar, Choper, and Shiffrin, *Constitutional Law: Cases, Comments, Questions.* Casebooks are not used for legal research; they are classroom texts.

CD-ROM CD-ROM ("compact disk with read-only memory") is an optical information storage system. See the discussion of this medium in Section C of this chapter. For the large number of CD-ROM products available in the law, see *Directory of Law-Related CD-ROMs* by Information Publishing (<http://www.infosourcespub.com>).

The Seven Regional Reporters in the National Reporter System

Atlantic Reporter (A.), *Atlantic Reporter, Second Series* (A.2d). The opinions of the highest state court and some intermediate appellate courts in the following states: Conn., Del., D.C., Me., Md., N.H., N.J., Pa., R.I., Vt.

North Eastern Reporter (N.E.), *North Eastern Reporter, Second Series* (N.E.2d). The opinions of the highest state court and some intermediate appellate courts in the following states: Ill., Ind., Mass., N.Y., Ohio.

North Western Reporter (N.W.), *North Western Reporter, Second Series* (N.W.2d). The opinions of the highest state court and some intermediate appellate courts in the following states: Iowa, Mich., Minn., Neb., N.D., S.D., Wis.

Pacific Reporter (P.), *Pacific Reporter, Second Series* (P.2d). The opinions of the highest state court and some intermediate appellate courts in the following states: Alaska, Ariz., Cal., Colo., Haw., Idaho, Kan., Mont., Nev., N.M., Okla., Or., Utah, Wash., Wyo.

South Eastern Reporter (S.E.), *South Eastern Reporter, Second Series* (S.E.2d). The opinions of the highest state court and some intermediate appellate courts in the following states: Ga., N.C., S.C., Va., W. Va.

Southern Reporter (So.), *Southern Reporter, Second Series* (So. 2d). The opinions of the highest state court and some intermediate appellate courts in the following states: Ala., Fla., La., Miss.

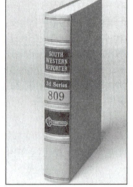

South Western Reporter (S.W.), *South Western Reporter, Second Series* (S.W.2d). The opinions of the highest state court and some intermediate appellate courts in the following states: Ark., Ky., Mo., Tenn., Tex.

Century Digest The *Century Digest* is one of the three digests in the American Digest System published by the West Group. The *Century Digest* contains small-paragraph summaries of court opinions written prior to 1897. The other two digests in the American Digest System are the *Decennial Digests* and the *General Digest*. *See* Digests (page 49) and the photo on page 51.

CIS *CIS* is the abbreviation for the Congressional Information Service. It is one of the major publishers of information that will allow you to trace the legislative history of a federal statute.

Citation A citation (also called a *cite*) is a reference to any material printed on paper or stored in a computer database, e.g., an opinion, statute, legal periodical article, legal treatise, or treaty. The citation is the "address" where you can locate and read the material. Most citations are to printed materials; such citations consist of information such as volume number, page number, and date. As we will see later in chapter 5, there are citation guidelines for citing different kinds of legal materials. One of the major publications containing citation guidelines is *The Bluebook: A Uniform System of Citation,* which we saw earlier. Law school teachers and legal periodical publishers love the *Bluebook.* But many courts do not follow it; they may have their own official citation rules that must be followed.

A **parallel cite** is an additional reference to the *same* material. If, for example, there are two parallel cites to an opinion, you will be able to find the opinion, word-for-word, in two different reporters.

A new development in the arena of citations is the **public domain citation.** This is a citation that is medium-neutral, which means that the references in the citation are not to traditional volume and page numbers of commercial publishers. As we will see later, courts assign paragraph numbering systems that go into the public domain citation.

Citator A **citator** is a book (CD-ROM or online service) that contains lists of citations that can help you assess the current validity of an item and can give you leads to other relevant materials. It is an organized list of citations to legal materials that have referred to (i.e., cited) whatever you are checking. For example, if you are checking the validity of an opinion, the citator will tell you what the courts have said about that opinion and what legal periodical articles have mentioned it. The same is true if you want to check the validity of a statute, constitutional provision, administrative regulation, rule of court, etc. (see Research Link C). The two main reasons to use a citator are to assess the validity of what you are checking and to locate additional laws or other materials on the issues covered in what you are checking. The major citator in legal research is *Shepard's Citations.* You can find Shepard's in a set of printed volumes (pamphlets and hardcover) and online in WESTLAW and LEXIS. The other major online citators are Insta-Cite and KeyCite (found in WESTLAW), and Auto-Cite (found in LEXIS). *See* Shepard's (page 67).

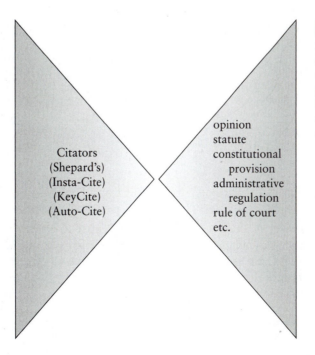

Citators
(Shepard's)
(Insta-Cite)
(KeyCite)
(Auto-Cite)

opinion
statute
constitutional
provision
administrative
regulation
rule of court
etc.

RESEARCH LINK C

A citator will help you determine the current validity of an opinion, statute, constitutional provision, administrative regulation, rule of court, etc. The citator will also lead you to additional relevant laws.

CLE Materials **CLE materials** are continuing-legal-education materials prepared for attorneys after they have completed law school. Many states require attorneys to participate in a designated number of CLE hours per year. Materials for CLE programs often contain checklists, sample forms, and the full text of recent cases, statutes, and administrative regulations that would be of practical value to an attorney working in a particular specialty.

Code A **code** is a collection of laws or rules classified by subject matter regardless of when they were enacted. To **codify** something means to rearrange it by subject matter. *Un*codified material is arranged chronologically by date of enactment; *codified* material is arranged by subject matter or topic regardless of when passed or enacted. When a statute or act is first passed by the legislature, it appears initially as a **slip law** (which is a single act, often printed as a small pamphlet) and then is printed in uncodified books called Session Laws or Statutes at Large. Finally, statutes of general interest are later codified in statutory codes. *See* Legislation (page 64); Statutory Code (page 72). Administrative regulations are also often codified. *See* Administrative Code (page 35).

Sample volumes of the *Code of Federal Regulations* (C.F.R.), which contain many administrative regulations of federal agencies

Code of Federal Regulations (C.F.R.) The C.F.R. is an administrative code in which many of the administrative regulations of federal agencies are organized by subject matter. The C.F.R. is printed by the United States government in a large number of pamphlets that are reissued each year in a different color. It is also possible to read the C.F.R. online on WESTLAW and LEXIS. Before a federal administrative regulation is adopted and printed in the C.F.R., it must be proposed and printed in the daily *Federal Register* (Fed. Reg.) (see Research Link D). *See* Administrative Code (page 35); Federal Register (page 56).

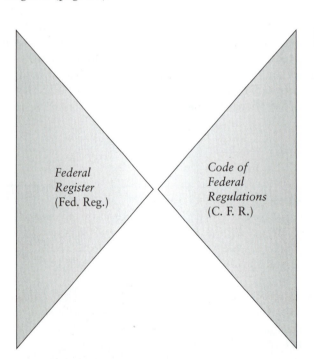

Federal Register (Fed. Reg.)

Code of Federal Regulations (C. F. R.)

RESEARCH LINK D

Before a federal administrative regulation is adopted and printed in the *Code of Federal Regulations* (C.F.R.), it is proposed in the daily *Federal Register* (Fed. Reg.).

Sample volumes of *Corpus Juris Secundum,* a national legal encyclopedia

Congressional Record The *Congressional Record* (Cong. Rec.) is an official collection of the day-to-day happenings of Congress, particularly on the floor of the House and Senate when Congress is in session. It is one source of legislative history (page 225) for federal statutes. It also contains many relatively trivial items that are relevant only to the districts of individual legislators.

Corpus Juris Secundum (C.J.S.) *Corpus Juris Secundum* is a national encyclopedia published by the West Group. (It is the second edition of *Corpus Juris*.) A *legal encyclopedia*

is a multivolume set of books that summarizes every major legal topic, arranged alphabetically. (Parts of C.J.S. are also available online through WESTLAW.) The other major national legal encyclopedia is Am. Jur. 2d, also from the West Group. There are three main uses of national legal encyclopedias such as C.J.S. and Am. Jur. 2d: (1) they are useful as background reading before you begin legal research in a new area of the law; (2) they are good case finders, because of their extensive footnotes to court opinions; and (3) they provide cross-references to other publications of the West Group on whatever topic you are reading in the encyclopedia. In addition to these two national encyclopedias, several states have state encyclopedias devoted to the law of one state (e.g., Florida and Michigan). *See* Legal Encyclopedia (page 60).

Cumulative Cumulative means that which repeats earlier material and consolidates it with new material in one place. A cumulative supplement, for example, is a pamphlet or volume that repeats, updates, and consolidates all earlier pamphlets or volumes. Because of the repetition, the earlier pamphlets or volumes can be thrown away. Similarly, pocket parts (containing supplemental material at the end of a book) are often cumulative. When the most recent pocket part comes out, the old one can be thrown away. Here is an example of a cumulative pocket part in a statutory code:

> **UNITED STATES CODE ANNOTATED**
>
> Title 28
> Judiciary and Judicial Procedure
> §§ 171 to 1250
>
> Cumulative Annual Pocket Part
>
> *For Use in 1996*
>
> Replacing prior pocket part in back of volume

Current Law Index *Current Law Index* (CLI) is the most comprehensive general index to legal periodical literature available. (The other major one is the *Index to Legal Periodicals and Books*.) The CLI comes out in three versions: a paper version (consisting of pamphlets and hardcover volumes), a CD-ROM version (called *LegalTrac*), and an online version (called *Legal Resource Index*). The online version is available on WESTLAW and LEXIS. *See* Legal Periodical (page 61).

Decennial Digest The *Decennial Digest* is one of the three digests in the American Digest System published by the West Group that contains small-paragraph summaries of court opinions written by every federal and state court that publishes its opinions. Each *Decennial Digest* covers a ten-year period. (Recent decennials are published in two five-year parts.) The other two digests in the American Digest System are the *Century Digest* and the *General Digest*. *See* Digests (page 49) and the photo on page 51.

Deskbook A deskbook is a single-volume collection of the rules of procedure for one or more courts, usually in the same judicial system. These rules of procedure are called court rules or rules of court. See the photo of several deskbooks on page 66.

Digests Our goals in this section are to define *digest,* to identify the major digests, and to explain the relationship between digests and reporters. Later in this book we will cover the techniques of using digests in research (page 143).

Digests are volumes containing small-paragraph summaries of court opinions organized by subject matter. (These summaries are sometimes called **abstracts** or **squibs.**)
The primary purpose of digests is to summarize—to digest—case law. For this reason,
digests serve as excellent case finders. The major publisher of digests is West. Its **key
number system** is the organizational principle used to classify the millions of small-
paragraph summaries in the digests. Here is how this principle works. West divides all
of law into 450 general topics such as Arson, Infants, Marriage, Negligence, and
Obscenity. Each of these general topics is further classified into subtopics, and each
subtopic is then assigned a number. The phrase *key number* refers to two things: the
general topic and the number of the subtopic. Examine the following examples of
subtopics under the general topic of Negligence:

Examples of key
numbers

> # NEGLIGENCE
>
> ☞ 22. Dangerous instrumentalities
>   and operations
>
> ☞ 28. Care required in general
>
> ☞ 32(2.9). Deliverymen and haulers

The second key number in this example is referred to as "Negligence 28." (It is *not*
referred to as "28 Care required in general.") The key number must include the general topic. You usually do not have to state what the subtopic is; giving the general
topic and the number is enough. If a supervisor asks you to check Negligence 28 in a
West digest, you simply go to the N volume of the digest where you will check number 28 under Negligence.

Once you find a key number (consisting of a general topic and a number) that is
relevant to your research problem, you will find summaries of court opinions under
that key number. For example, the following excerpt from a digest contains opinions
that are summarized (or digested) under key number Obscenity 1, and key number
Obscenity 2:

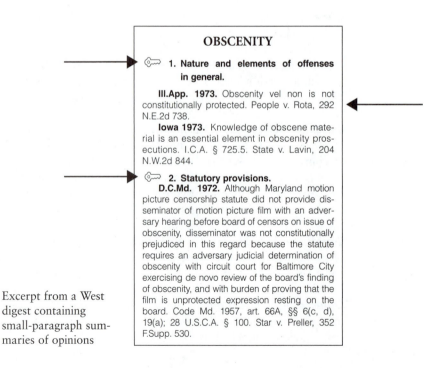

Excerpt from a West
digest containing
small-paragraph sum-
maries of opinions

> ## OBSCENITY
>
> ☞ 1. Nature and elements of offenses
>   in general.
>
>   **Ill.App. 1973.** Obscenity vel non is not
> constitutionally protected. People v. Rota, 292
> N.E.2d 738.
>   **Iowa 1973.** Knowledge of obscene mate-
> rial is an essential element in obscenity pros-
> ecutions. I.C.A. § 725.5. State v. Lavin, 204
> N.W.2d 844.
>
> ☞ 2. Statutory provisions.
>   **D.C.Md. 1972.** Although Maryland motion
> picture censorship statute did not provide dis-
> seminator of motion picture film with an adver-
> sary hearing before board of censors on issue of
> obscenity, disseminator was not constitutionally
> prejudiced in this regard because the statute
> requires an adversary judicial determination of
> obscenity with circuit court for Baltimore City
> exercising de novo review of the board's finding
> of obscenity, and with burden of proving that the
> film is unprotected expression resting on the
> board. Code Md. 1957, art. 66A, §§ 6(c, d),
> 19(a); 28 U.S.C.A. § 100. Star v. Preller, 352
> F.Supp. 530.

Beneath each summary paragraph is a citation to the case being summarized. For example, see the citation for *People v. Rota* in the first paragraph listed.

Where do these summary paragraphs come from? They come from the *headnotes* of court opinions in West reporters. (For an example of three headnotes at the beginning of an opinion, see Exhibit 9.6 in chapter 9.) As we saw earlier, a headnote is a summary of a portion of the opinion that is printed before the opinion begins.

We now turn to an overview of the following four kinds of West digests:

- A national digest covering most state and federal courts
- Federal digests covering only federal courts
- Regional digests covering the courts found in the regional reporters
- Digests of individual states

National Digest   West publishes one national digest: the American Digest System. This massive set (containing over 100 volumes) gives you small-paragraph summaries of the court opinions of most appellate state and federal courts and some lower state and federal courts. The American Digest System has three main units:

- *Century Digest,* covering summaries of opinions written prior to 1897.
- *Decennial Digests,* covering summaries of opinions written during ten-year periods starting in 1897. The more recent Decennials are printed in two five-year parts. Part 1 of the Tenth Decennial, for example, covers the period from 1986 to 1991. Part 2 covers 1991 to 1996. (Prior to the Ninth Decennial, all of the Decennial Digests were issued in one part only—covering the entire ten years.)
- *General Digests,* covering summaries of opinions written since the last Decennial was published. The *General Digest* volumes are kept on the shelf only until they are eventually consolidated (cumulated) into the next *Decennial Digest.* When the latter arrives, all of the *General Digest* volumes are thrown away.

Here are examples of volumes from each of the three units of the American Digest System:

Federal Practice Digest 4th. Digests federal court opinions.

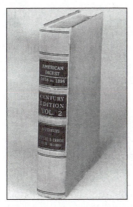

Example of a *Century Digest* volume

Example of a *Decennial Digest* volume

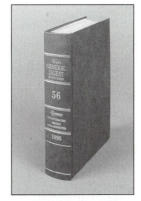

Example of a *General Digest* volume

Federal Digests Covering Only Federal Courts   West publishes five large digests that cover the three main federal courts: the U.S. Supreme Court, the U.S. Courts of Appeals, and the U.S. District Courts. The five digests are:

- *Federal Digest*
- *Modern Federal Practice Digest*
- *Federal Practice Digest 2d*
- *Federal Practice Digest 3d*
- *Federal Practice Digest 4th*

The last digest listed—*Federal Practice Digest 4th*—is the most important because it covers the most recent period; it digests federal cases from 1975 to the present. The other four cover earlier time periods and are therefore used less frequently.

Finally, West publishes a number of special digests that cover specific federal courts or specific topics of federal law:

- *West's Bankruptcy Digest*
- *West's Education Law Digest*
- *West's Federal Claims Court Digest*
- *West's Military Justice Digest*
- *West's Social Security Digest*
- *U.S. Court of Appeals Digest for the Fifth Circuit*
- *U.S. Court of Appeals Digest for the Eleventh Circuit*
- *United States Supreme Court Digest* (West)

The *United States Supreme Court Digest* (West) covers opinions of the United States Supreme Court only. A competing digest is the *United States Supreme Court Digest, Lawyers Edition* published by LEXIS. Because it is not a West digest, it does not use the key number system to classify the small-paragraph summaries in it. It has its own headnote system.

United States Supreme
Court Digest. Published
by West.

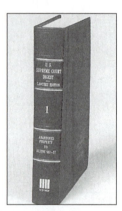

United States Supreme
Court Digest, L. Ed.
Published by LEXIS.

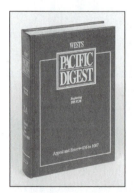

Pacific Digest, one of
the regional digests.
Digests opinions in the
Pacific Reporter.

Regional Digests   A regional digest contains small-paragraph summaries of those court opinions that are printed in its corresponding regional reporter. The opinions in the *Pacific Reporter,* for example, are digested in the *Pacific Digest.* As we shall see in Exhibit 3.3, only four of the seven regional reporters have corresponding regional digests. Those digests are *Atlantic Digest, North Western Digest, Pacific Digest,* and *South Eastern Digest* (see Research Link E). Regional digests for the other three regions either do not exist or have been discontinued.

Digests of Individual States   An individual state digest contains small-paragraph summaries of the opinions of the state courts within that state, as well as the opinions of the federal courts that are relevant to that state. Almost every state has its own digest. (The main exceptions are Delaware, Nevada, and Utah.) See the bottom of page 53 for a photo of several state digests.

To summarize, examine Exhibit 3.3 where you will find a list of reporters, the names of the courts whose full opinions are currently printed in those reporters, and the names of the digests that give small-paragraph summaries of those opinions.

Digests in CD-ROM and Online   All of the digests we have been discussing are printed in hardcover volumes. West also provides two alternatives. First, some of its digests are available on CD-ROM. Second, all of the digests are available online through WESTLAW. Earlier we looked at key numbers Negligence 28, Obscenity 1,

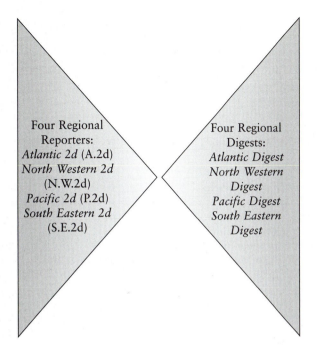

Four Regional
Reporters:
Atlantic 2d (A.2d)
North Western 2d
(N.W.2d)
Pacific 2d (P.2d)
South Eastern 2d
(S.E.2d)

Four Regional
Digests:
Atlantic Digest
North Western
Digest
Pacific Digest
South Eastern
Digest

RESEARCH LINK E

The opinions in four of the
regional reporters (A.2d,
N.W.2d, P.2d, and S.E.2d) are
summarized (digested) in their
corresponding regional
digests.

and Obscenity 2 as they would appear in a digest volume. One of the ways to find them on WESTLAW is to use a special WESTLAW "k" number assigned to each of the 450 general topics in the West digest system. For example, Negligence is number 272 and Obscenity is number 281. Here is how you would find Negligence 28, Obscenity 1, and Obscenity 2 in WESTLAW:

272k28

281k1

281k2

If you are using hardcover digest volumes and want to look at the potentially thousands of cases summarized under Negligence 28, you would go to the N volume of the digest and find number 28 under Negligence. If, however, you are online on WEST-LAW, you would simply type 272k28 at the keyboard after selecting the database you

Examples of
state digests

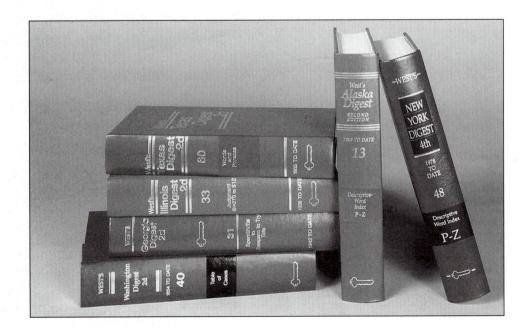

3.3

Exhibit
Reporters and Digests:
A Checklist

Name of Reporter	The Courts Whose Opinions Are Currently Printed in Full in This Reporter	The Digests that Contain Small-Paragraph Summaries of the Opinions in This Reporter
United States Reports (U.S.) *Supreme Court Reporter* (S.Ct.) *United States Supreme Court Reports, Lawyers' Edition* (L.Ed.) *United States Law Week* (U.S.L.W.) *United States Supreme Court Bulletin* (CCH) (S. Ct. Bull.)	United States Supreme Court	American Digest System *United States Supreme Court Digest* (West) *United States Supreme Court Digest, L. Ed.* *Federal Digest* *Modern Federal Practice Digest* *Federal Practice Digest, 2d* *Federal Practice Digest, 3d* *Federal Practice Digest, 4th* Individual state digests (for Supreme Court cases relevant to that state)
Federal Reporter 2d (F.2d) *Federal Reporter 3d* (F.3d)	United States Courts of Appeals	American Digest System *Federal Digest* *Modern Federal Practice Digest* *Federal Practice Digest, 2d* *Federal Practice Digest, 3d* *Federal Practice Digest, 4th* Individual state digests (for federal cases relevant to that state)
Federal Supplement (F. Supp.)	United States District Courts	American Digest System *Federal Digest* *Modern Federal Practice Digest* *Federal Practice Digest, 2d* *Federal Practice Digest, 3d* *Federal Practice Digest, 4th* Individual state digests (for federal cases relevant to that state)
Atlantic Reporter 2d (A.2d)	The highest state court and some intermediate appellate courts in Conn., Del., D.C., Me., Md., N.H., N.J., Pa., R.I., Vt.	American Digest System *Atlantic Digest* Individual state digests for Conn., D.C., Me., Md., N.H., N.J., Pa., R.I., Vt.
North Eastern Reporter 2d (N.E.2d)	The highest state court and some intermediate appellate courts in Ill., Ind., Mass., N.Y., Ohio	American Digest System Individual state digests for Ill., Ind., Mass., N.Y., Ohio (There is *no* North Eastern Digest)
North Western Reporter 2d (N.W.2d)	The highest state court and some intermediate appellate courts in Iowa, Mich., Minn., Neb., N.D., S.D., Wis.	American Digest System *North Western Digest* Individual state digests for Iowa, Mich., Minn., Neb., N.D., S.D., Wis.

Exhibit
Reporters and Digests:
A Checklist—continued

Name of Reporter	The Courts Whose Opinions Are Currently Printed in Full in This Reporter	The Digests that Contain Small-Paragraph Summaries of the Opinions in This Reporter
Pacific Reporter 2d (P.2d)	The highest state court and some intermediate appellate courts in Alaska, Ariz., Cal., Colo., Haw., Idaho, Kan., Mont., Nev., N.M., Okla., Or., Utah., Wash., Wyo.	American Digest System *Pacific Digest* Individual state digests for Alaska, Ariz., Cal., Colo., Haw., Idaho, Kan., Mont., N.M., Okla., Or., Wash., Wyo.
South Eastern Reporter 2d (S.E.2d)	The highest state court and some intermediate appellate courts in Ga., N.C., S.C., Va., W.Va.	American Digest System *South Eastern Digest* Individual state digests for Ga., N.C., S.C., Va., W. Va.
Southern Reporter 2d (So. 2d)	The highest state court and some intermediate appellate courts in Ala., Fla., La., Miss.	American Digest System Individual state digests for Ala., Fla., La., Miss. (There is *no* Southern Digest)
South Western Reporter 2d (S.W.2d)	The highest state court and some intermediate appellate courts in Ark., Ky., Mo., Tenn., Tex.	American Digest System Individual state digests for Ark., Ky., Mo., Tenn., Tex. (There is *no* South Western Digest)

want. This would lead you to the potentially thousands of cases summarized under 272k28. See Research Link F. Later we will cover both kinds of searches in greater depth.

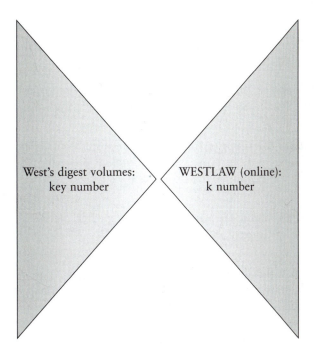

West's digest volumes: key number

WESTLAW (online): k number

RESEARCH LINK F

Every key number in a bound West digest volume (which allows you to find cases summarized under a particular topic) has a corresponding k number in WESTLAW (which allows you to find the same cases summarized under that k number online).

Federal Cases *Federal Cases* is the name of the West reporter that contains very early opinions of the federal courts (up to 1880) before F., F.2d, F.3d, and F. Supp. came into existence.

Federal Practice Digest 2d; Federal Practice Digest 3d; Federal Practice Digest 4th See Exhibit 3.3.

Federal Register (Fed. Reg.) The *Federal Register* is a daily publication of the federal government that prints proposed regulations of the federal administrative agencies; executive orders and other executive documents; and news from federal agencies, such as announcements inviting applications for federal grants. (The *Federal Register* is published by the United States government.) Many of the proposed regulations that are adopted by the federal agencies are later printed in the *Code of Federal Regulations* (C.F.R.). See Research Link D (page 48).

Examples of the *Federal Register* and the *Code of Federal Regulations*. The C.F.R. prints regulations in force that were first proposed in the Fed. Reg.

Federal Reporter 2d; Federal Reporter 3d A West reporter currently containing opinions of the United States Courts of Appeals. See photo on page 43.

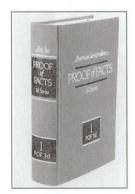

Federal Rules Decisions (F.R.D.) A West reporter containing opinions of United States District Courts on issues of civil and criminal procedure, plus articles, speeches, and conference reports on federal procedural issues. *See* Cases (page 39).

Federal Supplement (F. Supp.) A West reporter containing opinions of the United States District Courts. See photo on page 43.

Example of a formbook

Formbook A formbook is a legal treatise in the form of a manual. A **legal treatise** is a book written by a private individual (or by a public official writing as a private citizen) that provides an overview, summary, or commentary on a legal topic. Manuals often contain summaries of the law, checklists, sample forms, etc. A formbook (also called a *practice manual* or *handbook*) is a single-volume or multivolume how-to-do-it text.

General Digest The *General Digest* is one of three digests within the American Digest System published by West. The other two are the *Century Digest* and the *Decennial Digests*. All three digests contain small-paragraph summaries of court opinions by every federal and state court that publishes its opinions. The *General Digest* covers opinions written since the date of the last *Decennial Digest*. Eventually, every *General Digest* volume will be thrown away and the material in them will be consolidated into the next *Decennial Digest* (see Research Link G). See the photo of these three digests on page 51.

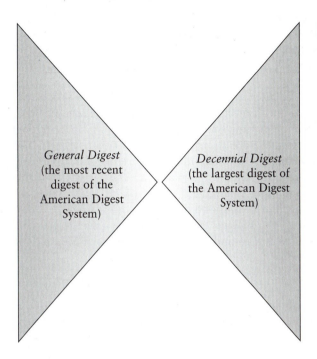

General Digest
(the most recent digest of the American Digest System)

Decennial Digest
(the largest digest of the American Digest System)

RESEARCH LINK G

The *General Digest* is a multi-volume digest that summarizes (digests) opinions of every state and federal court. All *General Digest* volumes will eventually be thrown away. The material in them will be printed in the next *Decennial Digest* covering a ten-year period, in two five-year parts.

Headnote A *headnote* is a small-paragraph summary of a portion of an opinion, printed just before the opinion begins. Most headnotes are written by a private publisher such as West. (A few courts, however, ask one of their clerks or other employees to write them.) In West reporters, each headnote has two numbers. First is a consecutive number. In an opinion with four headnotes, for example, the headnotes will be numbered 1, 2, 3, and 4. (Later, we will see that these consecutive numbers are important when shepardizing opinions.) Second, each headnote is assigned a key number, which consists of a general topic and a number. These headnotes with key numbers are also printed in digests. Here is an example of the third headnote from an opinion that has the key number "Libel and Slander 28":

The third headnote from an opinion in a West reporter

> **3. Libel and Slander** 🔑 **28**
>
> One may not escape liability for defamation by showing that he was merely repeating defamatory language used by another person, and he may not escape liability by falsely attributing to others the ideas to which he gives expression.

For another example, see the headnotes at the beginning of the opinion in Exhibit 9.6 in chapter 9. Again, all headnotes from opinions in reporters are also printed in West digests that cover those reporters. See Exhibit 3.3 for a checklist of what digests cover what reporters. For a list of other places where headnotes are printed, see page 45.

Examples of horn-
books

Hornbook A **hornbook** is another kind of *legal treatise*. (*See* Formbook, page 56.) Hornbooks summarize the law but tend to be less practical than formbooks. Hornbooks are more popular with law students than with practitioners.

Index to Legal Periodicals and Books (ILP) *Index to Legal Periodicals and Books* (ILP) is one of the two major general indexes to legal periodical literature. (The other is the *Current Law Index*.) The ILP is available in three versions: paper (consisting of pamphlets and hardcover volumes), CD-ROM, and online. *See* Legal Periodical (page 61).

Insta-Cite Insta-Cite is an online program of WESTLAW that will tell you whether an opinion you are checking is good law. For example, you will be told whether the opinion has been overruled or criticized by another opinion. Insta-Cite is a citator. *See* Citator (p. 47).

Internet The Internet is a special network of networks to which millions of individual computer users all over the world have access. It is not run or controlled by any single government or organization. A *network* is a group of computers connected by telephone lines, fiber optic cables, satellites, or other systems. The members of the network can communicate with each other to share information that is placed on the network.[4] Vast quantities of data are available on the networks of the Internet, including legal information. Examples include court opinions, statutes, administrative regulations, treaties, court addresses, and directories of attorneys. (See the discussion at the end of chapter 1 on the Internet as a virtual law library.) Here, for example, is the online "site" where you can find New Jersey statutes, bills, names of state legislators, the current legislative calendar, etc.:

```
http://www.njleg.state.nj.us
```

At the federal level, a number of major Internet sites provide laws and information from and about Congress, federal courts, and federal administrative agencies. For example:

```
http://thomas.loc.gov
http://www.fedworld.gov
```

(We will cover such sites in greater detail later in chapter 13 and in Appendix B.) There is no charge for most of this information once you have paid for the computer equipment and start-up connections that are needed. Because the Internet is essentially unregulated, however, data found there do not have the kind of assurance of accuracy as would the same data printed in bound volumes and in the more traditional research computer databases such as LEXIS and WESTLAW. This may change, however, as the Internet continues to grow.

One of the best ways to find information on the Internet is through the **World Wide Web.** The Web allows you to gain access to other data through **hypertext,** which is a method of displaying and *linking* together information that is located in different places on the Internet. For example, if you are in a document that contains the court opinions of your state, you may be able to "click" the phrase *state statutes* to switch to another document or site that contains the information on the statutes of your state.

Here, for example, is a recent announcement on a resource that is available on the Internet, the Legal Explorer. Note the extensive amount of material available by hypertext linking:

> We invite you to take a look at our "recently updated Legal Explorer web site (URL: http://www.ll.georgetown.edu). The Georgetown University Legal Explorer contains links to many sources of law and law-related information. Some of these links are accessed by clicking on buttons for the following areas: Federal, State and Territorial, and Foreign and International. State and

---

4. A different concept is an *intranet,* which connects computers within a particular company or other organization so that they can share information. A law office with branch offices, for example, might have an intranet for sharing briefs, memos, or other data. If the organization allows selected individuals (e.g., clients) to have access to some of this information, the system becomes an *extranet.* The Internet, in contrast, is dramatically different in that it allows unrelated computer users all over the world to share "virtually" unlimited information.

Thomas
http://thomas.loc.gov

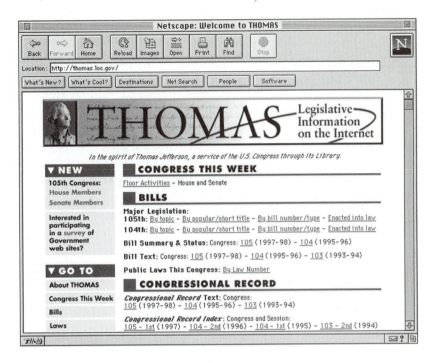

Fedworld
http://www.fedworld.gov

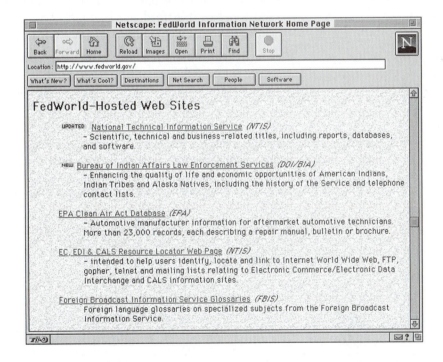

Territorial coverage is provided through a clickable map of the United States whose links lead to separate pages for each of the states and territories. These pages cover the law and government of each state or territory. Additional links are provided to sites relating to state and local government. The links for Federal and Foreign and International coverage are not quite as comprehensive yet, but new links are being added on a daily basis. The Library also maintains databases of the opinions of the U.S. Court of Appeals for the District of Columbia Circuit and the U.S. Court of Appeals for the Federal Circuit. The opinions of both are downloaded nightly and are reformatted for viewing and for downloading in WP5.1, Word 2 and ASCII formats. The opinions of all of the U.S. Courts of Appeals are available both from a clickable map and from the Federal Judicial page on the Legal Explorer. The Legal Explorer continually grows and evolves. [W]e invite you to visit it."

Another major legal research benefit of the Internet is the **listserv,** which is a program that manages computer mailing lists (e-mail lists) automatically. When you join a listserve that relates to the law, you may be able to ask research questions that are read by potentially thousands of other members of the list. For example, the following legal and factual research questions were recently sent ("posted"):

I need a copy of the Air Force Instruction, which has replaced AF Regulation 126-7 (dated 28 August 1987). If you have it and can fax it to me, I would appreciate it. My fax number is . . . .

We have a case that involves a '92 Chev Cavalier in which during impact with a tree, the door-mounted seat belt failed, allowing the passenger to be thrown from the vehicle. Would anyone in cyberspace have dealt with a case involving GM and door-mounted seat belts? Or have web sites that I might check involving such? Any help would be appreciated.

We are in need of the current cost of living figures for clerical workers in Boston, MA, Hartford and Stamford, CT. Does anyone know how to get this information? I would appreciate any leads.

Anyone on the list can read these questions and the answers given in response. After answers are posted, you will often find another message sent by the grateful person who posted the original question, exclaiming, "Thanks for saving my life!"

Interstate Compact An **interstate compact** is an agreement between two or more states governing a problem of mutual concern, such as the resolution of a boundary dispute. The compact is passed by the legislature of each state and is therefore part of the statutes of the states involved. Congress must give its approval. Hence, the compact also becomes part of the statutes of Congress.

KeyCite KeyCite is an online citator (available on WESTLAW) that claims to be more comprehensive and current than the paper and online versions of Shepard's. *See* Citator (page 47).

Black's Law Dictionary

Legal Dictionary A **legal dictionary** contains definitions of words and phrases used in the law. Examples include *Black's Law Dictionary* (West), *Ballentine's Law Dictionary* (Lawyers Co-op), and *West's Legal Thesaurus/Dictionary* (West). The major multivolume legal dictionary is *Words and Phrases* from West. The definitions in this set consist of thousands of excerpts from court opinions that have treated the word or phrase. Hence, this massive dictionary can also serve as an excellent case finder. See photo of this set on page 75.

Legal Encyclopedia A *legal encyclopedia* is a multivolume set of books that summarizes every major legal topic. It is valuable (a) as background reading for a research topic that is new to you, and (b) as a case finder (due to its extensive footnotes). The two national encyclopedias are *American Jurisprudence 2d* (Am. Jur. 2d) and *Corpus Juris Secundum* (C.J.S.), both published by West. (For photos of these two encyclopedias, see pages 37 and 48.) A number of states have their own encyclopedias covering the law of that state, e.g. *Florida Jurisprudence* and *Michigan Law and Practice*.

Legal Newsletter Many private companies and public-interest groups publish **legal newsletters** that provide practical guidelines and current developments in very specific areas of the law. Examples: *Corporate Counsellor, Daily Tax Report, AIDS Policy & Law, Matrimonial Strategist.* Printed weekly, biweekly, or monthly, they are often quite expensive even though they tend to be relatively brief.

Example of a national legal newspaper

Legal Newspaper There are two kinds of **legal newspapers:** local and national. Local legal newspapers are usually published weekly or every business day. They print court dockets (calendars), the full text of selected opinions of local courts, information on new rules of court, job announcements, etc. Most large cities have their own legal newspaper. Examples: *New York Law Journal, Daily Washington Law Reporter, San Francisco Daily Journal.* There are several national legal newspapers such as the weekly *National Law Journal.* They cover more than one state on topics such as law firm mergers and dissolutions, salary surveys, careers of prominent attorneys, trends in federal areas of the law, etc.

Legal Periodical In the broadest sense, a **legal periodical** is a pamphlet on a legal topic that is usually sold by subscription and issued at regular intervals—other than a pamphlet that simply updates or supplements another publication. All periodicals are first printed as pamphlets (often called *issues*) and are then placed in hardcover volumes if the law library considers them sufficiently important. This broad definition of legal periodical would include legal newspapers and legal newsletters. More commonly, however, the phrase refers to three categories of periodicals:

- *Academic* legal periodicals (often called **law reviews** or **law journals**) are published by law schools, and hence are scholarly in nature. Law students are selected to do some of the writing and all of the editing for most academic legal periodicals. (It is a mark of considerable distinction for a student to be "on law review.") Most academic legal periodicals are general in scope, covering a wide variety of legal topics. Others are special-interest legal periodicals that concentrate on specific subject areas such as women's rights or environmental law.

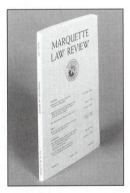 

Examples of academic legal periodicals

- *Commercial* legal periodicals are published by private companies. They tend to be more practice-oriented, specialized, and expensive than the academic legal periodicals.
- *Bar association* legal periodicals are published by national, state, or local bar associations. Their focus is on practical articles and features of interest to the membership.

There are two major general indexes to legal periodical literature:

- *Current Law Index* (CLI)
- *Index to Legal Periodicals and Books* (ILP)

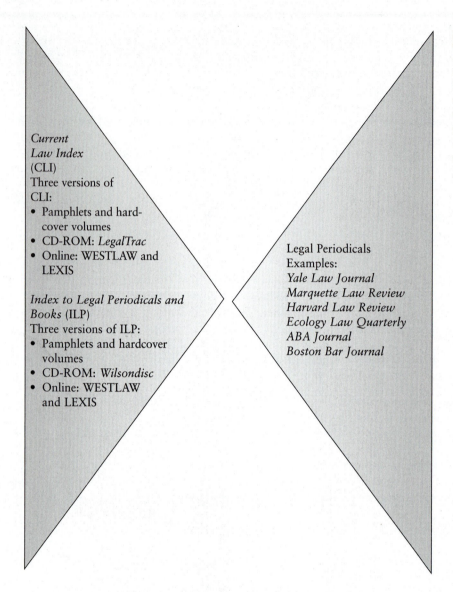

RESEARCH LINK H
A great deal of literature exists in the three kinds of legal periodicals (academic, commercial, and bar association). The two major indexes to this literature are the *Current Law Index* (CLI) and the *Index to Legal Periodicals and Books* (ILP).

Current Law Index (CLI)
Three versions of CLI:
• Pamphlets and hardcover volumes
• CD-ROM: *LegalTrac*
• Online: WESTLAW and LEXIS

Index to Legal Periodicals and Books (ILP)
Three versions of ILP:
• Pamphlets and hardcover volumes
• CD-ROM: *Wilsondisc*
• Online: WESTLAW and LEXIS

Legal Periodicals Examples:
Yale Law Journal
Marquette Law Review
Harvard Law Review
Ecology Law Quarterly
ABA Journal
Boston Bar Journal

These indexes are available in different formats:

• Paper (pamphlets and hardcover volumes)
• CD-ROM (*LegalTrac* is the CD-ROM version of CLI; *Wilsondisc* is a CD-ROM program that contains ILP)
• Online (primarily through WESTLAW and LEXIS).

See Research Link H. In addition to these general indexes, there are special indexes to legal periodical literature on topics such as tax law.

Legal Thesaurus A legal thesaurus provides word alternatives for words used in legal writing. The thesaurus may also be helpful when you need word alternatives to form queries for computer-assisted legal research (page 251). Two examples: Burton's *Legal Thesaurus,* 2d ed. (Macmillan 1992), and Statsky's *Legal Thesaurus/Dictionary: A Resource for the Writer and Legal Researcher* (West 1985).

LegalTrac *LegalTrac* is a major general index to legal periodical literature. It is the CD-ROM version of the *Current Law Index,* the most comprehensive general index to legal periodical literature available. (See page 174.)

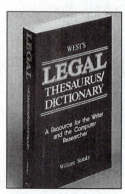

Example of a legal thesaurus

Legal Treatise A *legal treatise* (not to be confused with treaty) is any book written by a private individual (or by a public official writing as a private citizen) that provides an overview, summary, or commentary on a legal topic. The treatise will usually attempt to give an extensive treatment of that topic. Hornbooks, handbooks, and formbooks are also treatises. Some treatises are designed primarily as study aids for students. (*See* Nutshell, page 64.) Treatises are printed in several formats, such as single volume, multivolume, and looseleaf.

Legislation **Legislation** is the process of making statutory law by the legislature. The word *legislation* also refers to the statutes themselves.

There are two main categories of statutes:

- **Public laws** (also called *public statutes*): statutes that apply to the general public or to a segment of the public and have permanence and general interest. Example: a statute defining a crime. Such statutes are published as slip laws, as session laws, and as codified laws.
- **Private laws** (also called *private statutes*): statutes that apply to specifically named individuals or groups and have little or no permanence or general interest. Example: a statute naming a bridge after a deceased senator. These statutes are published as slip laws and as session laws; they are not codified.

LEXIS LEXIS is a legal research computer system owned by the Reed Elsevier company. (See page 247.) LEXIS also refers to the LEXIS Publishing Company.

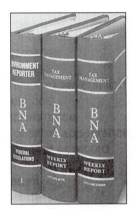

Looseleaf Service A **looseleaf** text or **service** is a ring-binder hardcover volume or set of volumes containing pages that can easily be inserted or taken out. As new material is written covering the subject matter of the looseleaf text, it is placed in the binder, often replacing the pages that the new material has changed or otherwise supplemented. This kind of updating can sometimes occur as often as once a week, so looseleaf services frequently contain the most current material available in print.

Some looseleaf services are legal treatises, others are reporters, and others are combination treatise-reporters. There are few areas of the law that are *not* covered by one or more looseleaf services. Examples of such services include *Environmental Reporter, Tax Management, Employment Practices Guide, Standard Federal Tax Reports, United States Law Week, Criminal Law Reporter, Family Law Reporter, Media Law Reporter, Sexual Law Reporter, Labor Relations Reporter.*

Examples of a loose-
leaf service

Although some looseleaf services do little more than print the most current opinions in their specialty, most have a variety of features:

- The full text plus summaries of court opinions in the area of the specialty
- The full text plus summaries of administrative regulations and decisions in the area of the specialty (some of which may not be easily available elsewhere)
- The full text plus summaries of the major statutory provisions in the area of the specialty
- Suggestions on how to practice in the specialty

The major publishers of looseleaf services are Commerce Clearing House (CCH), Bureau of National Affairs (BNA); Clark Boardman Callaghan; Warren, Gorham & Lamont; and Matthew Bender.

Maroon Book The **maroon book** is the citation guide formally called *The University of Chicago Manual of Legal Citation.* It is the major competitor of the more widely used citation guide, *The Bluebook: A Uniform System of Citation. See* Bluebook (page 39).

Martindale-Hubbell Law Directory The *Martindale-Hubbell Law Directory,* published by Reed Elsevier, is a multivolume set of books that serves three major functions by providing:

- An alphabetical listing of attorneys and law firms by state and city—this is the **law directory,** which is the main component of the set; for some firms, the listing includes paralegals and other nonattorney personnel
- Short summaries of the law of all fifty states (in its separate Digest volume)
- Short summaries of the law of many foreign countries (in its separate Digest volume)

*Martindale-Hubbell
Law Directory*

The *Martindale-Hubbell Law Directory* is also available on the Internet at the following site:

http://www.martindale.com

Microfiche *See* Microform (page 34).

NEXIS An online service affiliated with LEXIS. (The combined service is often referred to as LEXIS-NEXIS).) NEXIS gives you access to many newspapers; medical, scientific, social science, humanities, and financial journals and reports; public records; wire services; etc. from all over the world. (See page 247.)

New York Supplement **(N.Y.S.)** A reporter containing New York cases. *See* Cases (page 44).

North Eastern Reporter **2d (N.E.2d)** A regional reporter that prints the full text of state court opinions in the North East region of the country. See Exhibit 3.2. *See also* Cases (page 46).

North Western Digest A digest that summarizes state court opinions printed in the *North Western Reporter. See* Research Link I and Exhibit 3.3. *See also* Digests (page 52).

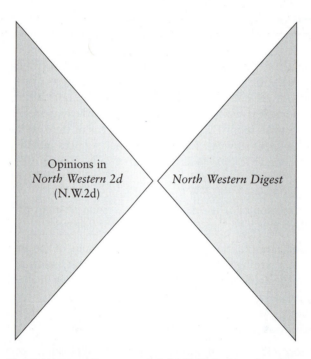

Opinions in
North Western 2d
(N.W.2d)

North Western Digest

RESEARCH LINK I

Every opinion in the *North Western 2d* reporter written by the state courts in the North Western region (Iowa, Mich., Minn., Neb., N.D., S.D., and Wis.) is digested (summarized) in *North Western Digest.*

North Western Reporter **2d (N.W.2d)** A regional reporter that prints the full text of state court opinions in the North West region of the country. See Exhibit 3.2. *See also* Cases (page 46).

Examples of nutshells

Nutshell A nutshell is a legal treatise written in pamphlet form. It summarizes a topic that is often covered in a law school course. Nutshells, therefore, are primarily used as study aids by law students. They are published by West.

Outlines An outline, also called a *study outline,* is a pamphlet that summarizes and outlines a legal subject. Like the nutshell, the topic of an outline often parallels the subject matter of a law school course (e.g., contracts, torts). Some of the most popular outlines are published by Gilberts and Emmanuels. West also publishes outlines in its Black Letter Series.

Pacific Digest A digest that summarizes state court opinions printed in the *Pacific Reporter. See* Research Link J and Exhibit 3.3. *See also* Digests (page 52).

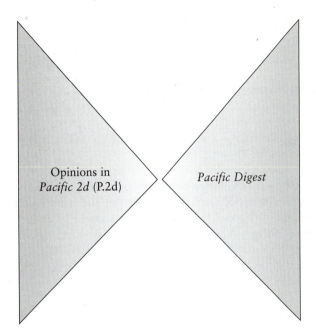

Opinions in
Pacific 2d (P.2d)

Pacific Digest

RESEARCH LINK J
Every opinion in the *Pacific 2d* reporter written by the state courts in the Pacific region (Alaska, Ariz., Cal., Colo., Haw., Idaho, Kan., Mont., Nev., N.M., Okla., Or., Utah, Wash., and Wyo.) is digested (summarized) in *Pacific Digest*.

Pacific Reporter 2d (P.2d) A regional reporter that prints the full text of state court opinions in the Western region of the country. See Exhibit 3.2. *See also* page 46.

Pattern Jury Instructions Toward the end of a jury trial, the judge must give the jury *instructions* (also called the *charge*) on the law that will govern its deliberations. In some states and judicial systems, there are suggested instructions that can be adapted to the specifics of a particular trial. The instructions are called Model Jury Instructions or more commonly, **Pattern Jury Instructions.** They are often printed in hardcover volumes and are widely used.

Pocket Part A **pocket part** is a small pamphlet inserted into a special pocket built into the inside cover of a bound volume (usually the back cover). The pocket part is published after the bound volume is published. The purpose of a pocket part is to update the material in the bound volume. Pocket parts are critically important in legal research. You may be reading something in the bound volume without being aware that it is no longer valid. One of the ways to check its validity is to check the pocket part for that volume. (For a list of law books that often have pocket parts, see Exhibit 6.1 in Chapter 6.)

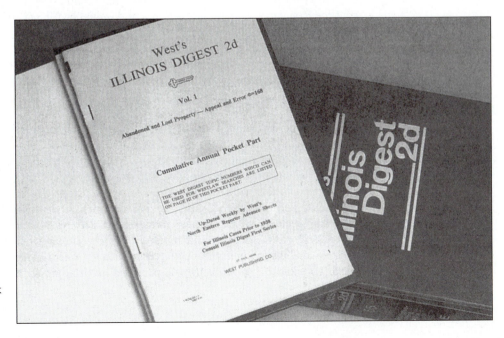

Example of a law book
with a pocket part

Record When referring to a trial, the **record** is the official collection of what happened during the trial. It includes a word-for-word transcript of what was said, the pleadings, and all the exhibits. *See also* Congressional Record (page 48).

Regional Digest A digest that summarizes cases in a regional reporter. See Exhibit 3.3 and Digests (page 52). See also Research Links A, I, J, and L.

Register A **register** is a set of books that contain administrative regulations, e.g., the *Federal Register.*

Reporter A set of volumes containing the complete text of court opinions. An *official reporter* is a reporter published under the authority of the government, often by the government itself. (Official reporters are sometimes called Reports, e.g., *United States Reports.*) An *unofficial reporter* is a reporter printed by a private or commercial publisher without specific authority from the government. (There are also some sets of books called reporters that contain the complete text of administrative decisions.) *See* Cases (page 39). See also Exhibits 3.2 and 3.3 for lists of reporters.

Restatements Restatements are scholarly publications of the **American Law Institute** (ALI) that attempt to formulate (that is, restate) the existing law of a given area. Occasionally, the Restatements also state what the ALI thinks the law *ought* to be.
    Examples of Restatements:

Restatement of Agency   *Restatement of Property*
Restatement of Conflicts of Law *Restatement of Restitution*
Restatement of Contracts   *Restatement of Security*
Restatement of Foreign   *Restatement of Torts*
    Relations Law   *Restatement of Trusts*
Restatement of Judgments

Example of a
Restatement

Because the Restatements are written by a private organization (ALI) rather than by an official government entity, they are not laws. However, because of their scholarly content, they have great prestige in the courts. Judges frequently rely on them in their opinions. One of the reasons this is so is the elaborate procedure the ALI follows before issuing one of its Restatements. First, a renowned scholar in the field prepares an initial draft of the Restatement. This draft is reviewed by a committee of Advisors consisting of other scholars and specialists in the field. A special Council of the ALI then reviews and revises the draft. This leads to a *tentative draft* that is considered by the ALI at one of its annual meetings. After further editing and revision, the final version is approved by the ALI. You can read the Restatements in bound volumes and online in WESTLAW and LEXIS.

Rules of Court Rules of court, also called **court rules,** are the laws of procedure that govern the conduct of litigation before a particular state or federal court. They are often found in the statutory code and in separate volumes or pamphlets, sometimes called *deskbooks* (see page 49).

Examples of rules of
court volumes

Series A new **edition** is a revision of an earlier version of a book or set of books. A new **series,** in contrast, refers to a new numbering order for new volumes within the *same* set of books. Reporters, for example, come in series. *Federal Reporter, First Series* (F.) has 300 volumes. After volume 300 was printed, the publisher decided to start a new series of the same set of books—*Federal Reporter, Second Series* (F.2d). The first volume of F.2d is volume 1. F.2d has 999 volumes. After volume 999 was printed, the publisher decided to start a new series of the same set of books—*Federal Reporter, Third Series* (F.3d). After a large number of F.3d volumes are printed, we will undoubtedly see an F.4th, which will begin again with volume 1. There is no consistent number of volumes that a publisher will print before deciding to start a new series for a set of books.

Session Law **Session laws** are uncodified statutes enacted during a particular session (often lasting two years) of the legislature. (Individual session laws are printed as *slip laws.*) Session laws are printed chronologically rather than by subject matter. Other names for this kind of law include Statutes at Large (e.g., *United States Statutes at Large*), Acts and Resolves, Laws, etc. The generic name *session laws* is often used to refer to all of them. Session laws contain both *public statutes*—also called *public laws* (which are statutes that apply to the general public or to a segment of the public and have permanence and general interest), and *private statutes*—also called *private laws* (which are statutes that apply to specifically named individuals or groups and have little or no permanence or general interest). Public statutes or laws are later *codified,* which means they are placed in statutory codes and arranged by subject matter. See Research Link K. *See also* Act (page 34); Code (page 48); Statutory Code (page 72).

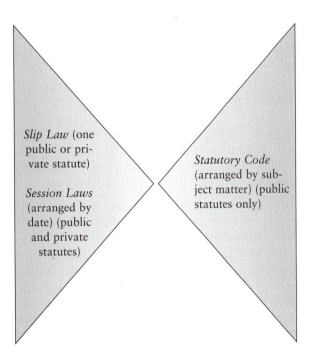

Slip Law (one public or private statute)

Session Laws (arranged by date) (public and private statutes)

Statutory Code (arranged by subject matter) (public statutes only)

RESEARCH LINK K

After public and private statutes are first printed as *slip laws,* they are printed in volumes of *session laws* where they are arranged chronologically (by date of enactment). The public statutes are then arranged by subject matter and printed in a *statutory code.*

Excerpt from a page in a Shepard's volume

Shepard's Our goal here is to provide a brief overview of Shepard's and shephardizing by identifying the major sets of Shepard's volumes that exist. Later in this book, we will learn how to use Shepard's—how to **shepardize**. (See page 153.)

Shepard's Citation's is a citator (page 47), which is a list of citations that can help you assess the current validity of an item and can lead you to other relevant materials. To *shepardize* an item means to use any of the three versions of *Shepard's Citations* (paper, CD-ROM, or online) to obtain validation and other data on whatever you are shephardizing. If, for example, you are shephardizing a case, you may be given the parallel cite of the case (another reporter where you will find the same case), the history of the case (such as citations to all the appeals within the same litigation as the case you are shephardizing), the treatment of the case (such as citations to other cases that have followed or criticized the case you are shephardizing), legal periodical literature on the case, etc. If you are shephardizing a statute, you may be given the session law citation of the statute, amendments or repeals of the statute, cases that have interpreted the statute, legal periodical on the statute, etc.

There are two main benefits of citators such as *Shepard's Citations*. First, they can help you determine the current validity of cases, statutes, or whatever you are shephardizing. Second, they can lead you to additional relevant laws, for reasons we will explore in chapter 9. See Research Link C (page 47).

What can you shepardize? Here is a partial list:

- Court opinions
- Statutes
- Constitutions
- Some administrative regulations
- Some administrative decisions
- Ordinances
- Charters

- Rules of court
- Some executive orders
- Some treaties
- Patents, trademarks, copyrights
- Restatements
- Some legal periodical literature

As we will see later, it is important to distinguish between **cited material** and **citing material** within Shepard's. Students sometimes confuse the two categories. The cited material is always what you are checking or sheparding. Everything on the above partial list is cited material. It simply means that which is mentioned—cited—by something else. What do we call the materials that *do* the citing? Answer: cit*ing* materials. Here are some examples:

- Assume you are sheparding *Smith v. Smith,* 100 N.E.2d 458 (Mass. 1980). You find out through Shepard's that this case was once mentioned by the case of *Jones v. Jones,* 105 N.E.2d 62 (Mass. 1982). What was cited? The *Smith* case. Therefore it is the cited material. Who did the citing? The *Jones* case. Therefore it is the citing material.
- Assume you are sheparding section 100 of the state statutory code. You find out through Shepard's that this statute was once mentioned by the case of *Kiley v. New York,* 296 N.E.2d 222 (N.Y. 1982). What was cited? Section 100. Therefore it is the cited material. Who did the citing? The *Kiley* case. Therefore it is the citing material.

As you can see from the first example, an opinion can be the cited material—what you are sheparding—and another opinion can be the citing material for what you are sheparding. See page 156.

On pages 69–71, there is an overview of some of the major items that can be sheparded, with the appropriate set of *Shepard's Citations* that you would use to do so.

Slip Law A slip law is a single act passed by the legislature. It is printed separately, often in a small pamphlet. It is the first official publication of the act. All slip laws are later printed chronologically in volumes that may be called Session Laws, Acts, Statutes at Large, etc. Finally, if the slip law is a public law or statute, it is also printed in a **statutory code,** where the arrangement is by subject matter.

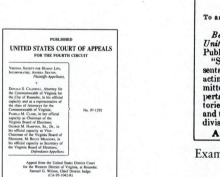

Example of a slip opinion

> **Public Law 87-17**
> **87th Congress, H. R. 4363**
> **April 7, 1961**
>
> **AN ACT**   75 STAT. 41.
>
> To amend Public Law 86–272 relating to State taxation of interstate commerce.
>
> *Be it enacted by the Senate and House of Representatives of the United States of America in Congress assembled,* That section 201 of Public Law 86–272 (73 Stat. 556) is amended to read as follows: Interstate commerce.
> "Sec. 201. The Committee on the Judiciary of the House of Representatives and the Committee on Finance of the United States Senate, acting separately or jointly, or both, or any duly authorized subcommittees thereof, shall make full and complete studies of all matters pertaining to the taxation of interstate commerce by the States, territories, and possessions of the United States, the District of Columbia, and the Commonwealth of Puerto Rico, or any political or taxing subdivision of the foregoing."   Taxation studies. 15 USC 381 note.
> **Approved April 7, 1961.**

Example of a slip law

Slip Opinion When a court first announces a decision, it is usually published in what is called a **slip opinion** or slip decision. It contains a single case in pamphlet form. The slip opinions are later printed in advance sheets for reporters, which in turn become hardcover reporters.

An Overview of Major Items That Can Be Shepardized

Assume that you want to shepardize an opinion of the United States Supreme Court:

Here is the set of Shepard's you use to shepardize an opinion of the United States Supreme Court:

Supreme
Court
Reporter

*Shepard's
United
States
Citations*

Assume that you want to shepardize opinions found in *Federal Reporter, 2d:*

Here is the set of Shepard's you use to shepardize an F.2d opinion:

*Federal
Reporter
2d* (F.2d)

*Shepard's
Federal
Citations*

Assume that you want to shepardize opinions found in *Federal Supplement:*

Here is the set of Shepard's you use to shepardize an F. Supp. opinion:

*Federal
Supplement*
(F. Supp.)

*Shepard's
Federal
Citations*

Continued on next page

Assume that you want to shepardize a federal statute of Congress: a statute found in U.S.C.A. *(United States Code Annotated)* or in U.S.C.S. *(United States Code Service)* or in U.S.C. *(United States Code)*:

Here is the set of Shepard's you use to shepardize a federal statute:

United States Code Annotated (U.S.C.A.)

Shepard's Federal Statute Citations

Assume that you want to shepardize a regulation of a federal agency found in C.F.R.:

Here is the set of Shepard's that will enable you to shepardize a regulation in C.F.R.:

Code of Federal Regulations (C.F.R.)

Shepard's Code of Federal Regulations Citations

Assume that you want to shepardize opinions found within the following regional reporters:

> *Atlantic Reporter 2d*
> *Pacific Reporter 2d*
> *South Western Reporter 2d*
> *South Eastern Reporter 2d*
> *North Eastern Reporter 2d*

At the right are the sets of Shepard's that you use to shepardize the opinions in these regional reporters.

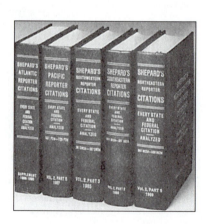

Assume that you want to shepardize the following:
   A Rhode Island court opinion
   A Rhode Island statute
   A Rhode Island constitutional
      provision
   A New Hampshire court opinion
   A New Hampshire statute
   A New Hampshire constitutional
      provision

Here are the sets of Shepard's that you would use:

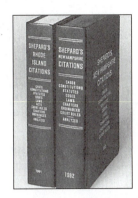

Note: Every state has its own set of Shepard's similar to *Shepard's Rhode Island Citations* and *Shepard's New Hampshire Citations* above.

South Eastern Digest A digest that summarizes state court opinions printed in the *South Eastern Reporter.* See Research Link L and Exhibit 3.3. *See also* Digests (at page 52).

South Eastern Reporter 2d (S.E.2d) A regional reporter that prints the full text of state court opinions in the southeastern region of the country. See Exhibit 3.2. *See also* Cases (page 46).

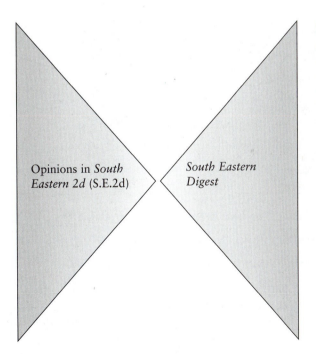

Opinions in *South Eastern 2d* (S.E.2d)

South Eastern Digest

RESEARCH LINK L

Every opinion in the *South Eastern 2d* reporter written by the state courts in the southeastern region (Ga., N.C., S.C., Va., and W. Va.) is digested (summarized) in *South Eastern Digest.*

Southern Reporter 2d (So. 2d) A regional reporter that prints the full text of state court opinions in several southern states. See Exhibit 3.2. *See also* Cases (page 46).

South Western Reporter 2d (S.W.2d) A regional reporter that prints the full text of state court opinions in the southwest region of the country. See Exhibit 3.2. *See also* Cases (page 46).

Statutes at Large An uncodified printing of statutes. Statutes at Large (Stat.) are session laws. *See* Act (page 34); Session Law (page 67); United States Statutes at Large (page 74).

Statutory Code Statutes are first published as *slip laws,* then in *session law* volumes, and finally, if they are of general public interest, in a *statutory code.* A statutory code is a collection of statutes of the legislature organized by subject matter. For example, the statutes on murder are together, the statutes on probate are together, etc. An **official statutory code** is one printed under the authority of the government, often by the government itself. An **unofficial statutory code** is one printed by a commercial publishing company without special authority from the government. Statutory codes are often annotated (particularly unofficial codes), meaning that notes or commentaries accompany the full text of the statutes. The notes might include summaries of cases (often called *notes of decisions*) that have interpreted the statute and information on the legislative history of the statute, such as the dates of earlier amendments. Statutes are published in printed volumes and online through WESTLAW and LEXIS. *See* Act (page 34); Legislation (page 63).

The three major *federal* statutory codes are:

Example of a state statutory code

U.S.C.—*United States Code* (published by the U.S. Government Printing Office) (official)
U.S.C.A.—*United States Code Annotated* (published by West) (unofficial)
U.S.C.S.—*United States Code Service* (published by LEXIS) (unofficial)

The three major federal statutory codes: U.S.C., U.S.C.A., U.S.C.S.

Updating The *United States Code* is updated by:

- bound supplement volumes

The *United States Code Annotated* is updated by:

- pocket parts
- pamphlet supplements
- *United States Code Congressional and Administrative News* (U.S.C.C.A.N.)

The *United States Code Service* is updated by:

- pocket parts
- *U.S.C.S. Advance*

Supreme Court Reporter (S. Ct.) An unofficial reporter that prints every opinion of the United States Supreme Court. It is published by West. Before the final volumes are printed, it comes out in pamphlet advance sheets and in hardcover *Interim Edition* volumes. *See* Cases (page 40) and the photos on pages 36, 42, and 69.

Total Client-Service Library The **Total Client-Service Library** is the system by which Lawyers Co-op refers you to many of the books and other materials Lawyers Co-op (and its parent, the West Group) publishes. For example, Lawyers Co-op publishes American Law Reports (A.L.R.1st, A.L.R.2d, etc.). If you are reading an annotation on felony murder in one of the A.L.R. volumes, you will find a Total Client-Service Library reference section to other Lawyers Co-op and West Group publications (e.g., Am. Jur. 2d) on the same or similar felony murder issues.

Ultrafiche *See* Microform (page 34).

Uniform State Laws **Uniform state laws** are statutes that cover areas of law where uniformity across state lines is deemed appropriate. Examples are the Uniform Reciprocal Enforcement of Support Act and the Uniform Arbitration Act. One of the major organizations that writes and proposes uniform state laws is the National Conference of Commissioners on Uniform State Laws (NCCUSL). The proposals are submitted to every state legislature, which is free to adopt, modify, or reject them. To find out whether an individual state has adopted one of the proposed uniform state laws, you would check the index of the statutory code of that state. All of the uniform state laws are printed in at set of books called *Uniform Laws Annotated* (U.L.A.), published by West. The U.L.A. is also available online on WESTLAW. Drafts of uniform state laws can be found on the Internet at

<http://www.law.upenn.edu/library/ulc/ulc.htm>

Another major national organization that writes and proposes laws is the American Law Institute (ALI), which also publishes the Restatements that we examined earlier. Some of the ALI proposals are called "model acts," such as the Model Penal Code. Again, legislatures are free to adopt, modify, or reject what is proposed. Occasionally, the NCCUSL and the ALI will work together to jointly propose a law. A major example is the important Uniform Commercial Code (UCC).

United States Code (U.S.C.) The official code published by the United States government containing federal statutes. *See* Statutory Code (page 72).

United States Code Annotated (U.S.C.A.) An unofficial code published by West containing federal statutes. *See* Statutory Code (page 72).

United States Code Congressional and Administrative News (U.S.C.C.A.N.)
U.S.C.C.A.N., published by West, will enable you to:

- Obtain the complete text of public laws or statutes of Congress before they are published in U.S.C./U.S.C.A./U.S.C.S.
- Obtain the complete text of some congressional committee reports (important for legislative history)
- Translate a Statute at Large cite into a U.S.C./U.S.C.A./U.S.C.S. cite (through Table 2)
- Obtain leads to the legislative history of federal statutes (primarily through Table 4)

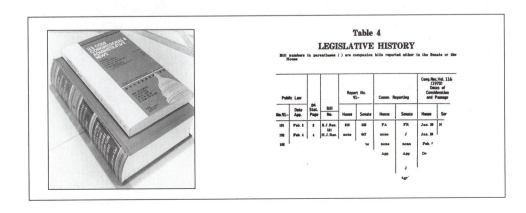

- Obtain the complete text of some federal agency regulations (duplicating what is found in the *Federal Register*—Fed. Reg. and in the *Code of Federal Regulations*—C.F.R.)
- Obtain the complete text of executive orders and other executive documents
- Obtain the complete text of all current United States Statutes at Large (see below)

United States Code Service (U.S.C.S.) An unofficial code published by LEXIS Law Publishing Co. containing federal statutes. *See* Statutory Code (page 72).

United States Law Week (U.S.L.W.) U.S.L.W. is a looseleaf service published by the Bureau of National Affairs (BNA) that prints the full text of every United States Supreme Court case on a weekly basis. It also prints other data on cases in the Supreme Court and summarizes important cases from other courts.

United States Reports (U.S.) An official reporter that prints every opinion of the United States Supreme Court. *See* Cases (page 39) and the photo on page 42. The advance sheets for *United States Reports* are called **preliminary prints.**

United States Statutes at Large (Stat.) The *United States Statutes at Large* (Stat.) contains the full text of every public law or statute and every private law or statute of Congress. (A private law or private statute applies to specifically named individuals or to groups and has little or no permanence or general interest, unlike a public law or public statute.) The statutes within Stat. are printed chronologically. See Research Link M. All current statutes at large are now also printed in *U.S. Code Congressional and Administrative News* as well as in separate Stat. volumes. (The public laws of general interest are later codified and printed in each of the three sets of codified federal statutes: U.S.C., U.S.C.A., U.S.C.S.) *See* Statutory Code (page 72).

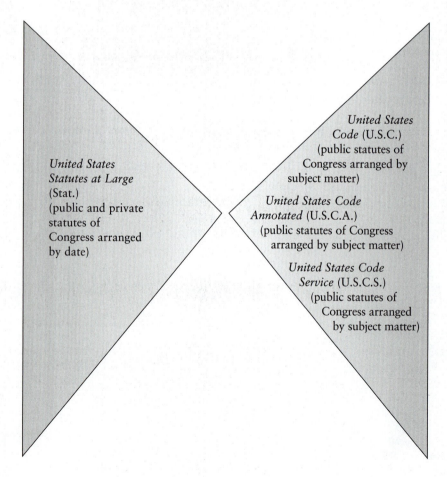

United States Statutes at Large (Stat.) (public and private statutes of Congress arranged by date)

United States Code (U.S.C.) (public statutes of Congress arranged by subject matter)

United States Code Annotated (U.S.C.A.) (public statutes of Congress arranged by subject matter)

United States Code Service (U.S.C.S.) (public statutes of Congress arranged by subject matter)

RESEARCH LINK M

All public and private statutes of Congress are printed chronologically as session laws in *United States Statutes at Large* (Stat.). If they are public statutes, they are also codified and printed by subject matter in the three codes containing federal statutes: U.S.C. (official), U.S.C.A. (unofficial), and U.S.C.S. (unofficial).

Words and Phrases, a multivolume legal dictionary

United States Supreme Court Reports, Lawyers' Edition (L. Ed.) An unofficial reporter that prints every opinion of the United States Supreme Court. It is published by LEXIS Law Publishing Co. *See* Cases (page 39) and the photo on page 42.

WESTLAW WESTLAW is a legal research computer system owned by the West Group. (See page 247.)

Words and Phrases A multivolume legal dictionary. Most of the definitions in this dictionary are quotations from court opinions. *See* Legal Dictionary (page 60).

SECTION E   OUTLINE

For a summary of many of the glossary entries we have been examining, see Exhibit 3.4.

3.4

Exhibit

Major Legal Reference Materials: An Outline

BOOKS OF LAW	Federal Statutes	*U.S. Statutes at Large* *U.S. Code* *U.S. Code Annotated* *U.S. Code Service*
	State Statutes	Session laws State statutory codes
	Federal Court Opinions	
	U.S. Supreme Court	*U.S. Reports* *Lawyers' Edition* *Supreme Court Reporter* *U.S. Law Week* *U.S. Supreme Court Bulletin* (CCH)
	U.S. Courts of Appeals	*Federal Reporter 3d*
	U.S. District Courts	*Federal Supplement* *Federal Rules Decisions*
	State Court Opinions	
	Regional Reporters of the National Reporter System . . .	*Atlantic Reporter 2d* *North Eastern Reporter 2d* *North Western Reporter 2d* *Pacific Reporter 2d* *South Eastern Reporter 2d* *Southern Reporter 2d* *South Western Reporter 2d*
	Others	Official state reporters Special edition state reporters (offprint reporters)
	Federal & State Constitutions	Within statutory code
	Federal Administrative Regulations	*Federal Register* *Code of Federal Regulations*

Continued on next page

3.4

Major Legal Reference
Materials: An Outline—
continued

BOOKS OF LAW (Cont.)

State Administrative
Regulations . . . .
- State register
- State administrative code

Charters & Ordinances . . . .
- Municipal code

BOOKS OF SEARCH AND/OR INTERPRETATION

Digests . . . .
- American Digest System
  - *Century Digest*
  - *Decennial Digests*
  - *General Digests*
- U.S. Supreme Court digests
- Regional digests
- Individual state digests
- *Federal Digest*
- *Modern Federal Practice Digest*
- *Federal Practice Digest 2d*
- *Federal Practice Digest 3d*
- *Federal Practice Digest 4th*
- *Bankruptcy Digest*
- *Military Justice Digest*
- *Federal Claims Court Digest*
- *Education Law Digest*
- *Social Security Digest*

Legal Encyclopedias . . . .
- *American Jurisprudence 2d*
- *Corpus Juris Secundum*

Legal Periodicals . . . .
- *Index to Legal Periodicals and Books*
- *Current Law Index*
- *LegalTrac*
- *Wilsondisc*

Annotations . . . .
- *American Law Reports*
- *American Law Reports 2d*
- *American Law Reports 3d*
- *American Law Reports 4th*
- *American Law Reports 5th*
- *American Law Reports Fed.*

Others . . . .
- Looseleaf services
- Legal treatises
- Legal newsletters
- Legal newspapers

COMPUTER RESEARCH SYSTEMS . . . .
- WESTLAW
- LEXIS

CITATORS . . . .
- Shepard's
- KeyCite (WESTLAW)
- Insta-Cite (WESTLAW)
- Auto-Cite (LEXIS)

PARALLEL CITATION TABLES . . . .
- *National Reporter Blue Book*
- *Blue and White Book*

3.4

Exhibit

Major Legal Reference
Materials: An Outline—
continued

LEGAL DICTIONARIES	*Black's Law Dictionary* *Ballentine's Law Dictionary* West's *Legal Thesaurus/Dictionary* *Words and Phrases*
CITATION GUIDELINES	*Bluebook: A Uniform System of Citation* *Chicago Manual of Legal Citation* (Maroon Book)

C HAPTER SUMMARY

Although standard definitions of legal research terms exist, there are some fairly dramatic exceptions. Hence you need to determine whether any of the terms have special definitions in your area.

The four major categories of legal research media are paper (pamphlet, hardcover—fixed pages, hardcover—looseleaf), online (commercial, public domain), CD-ROM, and microform (microfilm, microfiche, ultrafiche).

Most of this chapter introduced you to the major legal research terms in use. We also provided an introductory look at all of the major sets of books and other kinds of materials found in a law library. Our focus was on identifying what exists. In later chapters, we will reinforce the material in this chapter as we focus on the more demanding question of how to find what exists. Step one is a catalog of what is available, which was the theme of chapter 3.

K EY TERMS

CALR	opinion	deskbook	maroon book
looseleaf	reporter	abstracts	law directory
interfiling	reports	squibs	nutshell
online	docket	key number system	outline
public domain	official reporter	regional digest	Pattern Jury Instructions
CD-ROM	unofficial reporter	formbook	pocket part
microform	unpublished opinion	legal treatise	record
abstract	unreported opinion	hornbook	register
act	star paging	Insta-Cite	Restatements
administrative code	Internet	World Wide Web	American Law Institute
advance sheet	regional reporters	hypertext	rules of court
legislative service	special edition state reporters	listserve	court rules
advance session law service	digest	interstate compact	edition
annotations	headnotes	KeyCite	series
annotated reporters	ultrafiche	legal dictionary	session laws
legal encyclopedia	casebook	legal newsletters	shepardize
annotated	citation	legal newspapers	cited material
annotated statutory code	parallel cite	legal periodical	citing material
notes of decisions	public domain citation	law reviews	statutory code
Auto-Cite	citator	law journals	slip opinion
bill	CLE materials	legal thesaurus	official statutory code
legislative history	code	legislation	unofficial statutory code
blue book	codify	public laws	Total Client-Service Library
appellate briefs	slip law	private laws	uniform state laws
amicus curiae brief	cumulative	looseleaf service	preliminary prints

Chapter 4

AUTHORITY IN RESEARCH AND WRITING

► *Chapter Outline*

SECTION A   **INTRODUCTION**

The purpose of legal research is to help a client solve a legal dispute, prevent such a dispute from arising, or prevent the dispute from getting worse. All three are accomplished by analyzing the facts of the client's case and by applying any existing *mandatory primary authority* to these facts. Our goal in this chapter is to identify what we mean by this kind of authority and to explore what must be done if such authority cannot be found. First, some definitions.

Authority is any source that a court can rely on in reaching its decision.

Primary and Secondary Authority

Primary authority is any *law* that the court can rely on in reaching its decision. Examples include statutes, administrative regulations, constitutional provisions, executive orders, charters, ordinances, treaties, and other court opinions (see Exhibit 2.2 in chapter 2).

Secondary authority is any *nonlaw* that the court can rely on in reaching its decision. Examples include legal and nonlegal periodical literature, legal and nonlegal encyclopedias, legal and nonlegal dictionaries, legal and nonlegal treatises. (See Exhibit 4.1 later in this chapter.)

As we study primary and secondary authority, keep in mind that it makes no difference whether this authority is in a printed pamphlet or book; on a CD-ROM; online through WESTLAW, LEXIS, or the Internet; or on microform. Most primary and secondary authority can be found in a variety of media. (See Section C in Chapter 3 on the kinds of media available.) In chapter 4, we want to identify the variety of authority that a court might consider, regardless of the kind of media in which this authority could be read.

Mandatory Authority and Persuasive Authority

Mandatory authority is whatever the court *must* rely on in reaching its decision. Only primary authority—such as another court opinion, a statute, or a constitutional provision—can be mandatory authority. A court is never required to rely on secondary authority, such as a legal periodical article or legal encyclopedia. Secondary authority cannot be mandatory authority.

Persuasive authority is whatever the court relies on when it is not required to do so. There are two main kinds of persuasive authority: (a) a prior court opinion that the court is not required to follow but does so because it finds the opinion persuasive, and (b) any secondary authority that the court is not required to follow but does so because it finds the secondary authority persuasive.

Nonauthority

Nonauthority is (a) any primary or secondary authority that is not on point because it is not relevant and does not cover the facts of the client's problem, (b) any invalid primary authority, such as an unconstitutional statute, or (c) any book that is solely a finding aid, such as *Shepard's Citations* or digests.

SECTION B   **MANDATORY AUTHORITY**

Courts *must* follow mandatory authority. There are two broad categories of mandatory authority: (a) **enacted law** such as a statute, a constitutional provision, an ordinance, or an administrative regulation,[1] and (b) other court opinions. Each category will be considered separately.

---

1. *Enacted law* is law that is not produced through litigation. The most common enacted laws are the statutes of legislatures.

Enacted Law as Mandatory Authority

Any enacted law is mandatory authority and must be followed if the following three tests are met:

- The enacted law is being applied in a geographic area over which the authors of the law have power or jurisdiction (e.g., a Florida statute being applied to an event that occurred in the state of Florida).
- It was the intention of the authors of the enacted law (e.g., the legislature that wrote the statute) to cover the facts that are currently before the court.
- The application of this enacted law to these facts does not violate some other law that is superior in authority (e.g., the statute does not violate the constitution).

If an enacted law such as a state statute meets these three tests, it is mandatory authority in every state court in the state.

For example, assume that § 14 of the Florida statutory code provides, "It shall be a felony to break and enter a dwelling for the purpose of stealing property therein." Smith is charged with violating § 14 after being arrested for breaking down the door of a Miami apartment and taking jewelry from within. Is § 14 mandatory authority in a Florida criminal court where Jones is being prosecuted? Yes. The author of § 14 is the Florida legislature. The alleged crime occurred in Miami, a geographical area over which the Florida legislature clearly has power or jurisdiction. The first test is met. There is little doubt that an apartment is a "dwelling." Hence the legislature intended § 14 to cover stealing from an apartment. The second test is met. There is no indication that § 14 violates the state constitution or any other higher authority. Assuming there is no such violation, the third test is met. Therefore, § 14 is mandatory authority in the criminal trial of *Florida v. Smith*.

Suppose, however, that Smith is arrested for breaking into a *car* and stealing valuables from the glove compartment. Is § 14 mandatory authority in this case? We need to know whether a car is a "dwelling" for purposes of § 14. (In part, it might depend on whether the owner of the car ever slept in it.) To answer this question, we need to ask whether the Florida legislature intended to include motor vehicles within the meaning of "dwelling" in § 14. This is a question of **legislative intent**. If the statute was not intended to cover these facts, it is not applicable; it cannot be mandatory authority. In this instance it would be nonauthority.

Furthermore, even if the enacted law *was* intended to cover the facts before the court, it is not mandatory authority if it violates some higher law. The authors of an administrative regulation, for example, may intend to cover a particular individual's activities, but if this regulation is inconsistent with the statute that the regulation is supposed to be carrying out, the regulation is not mandatory authority; it is invalid. Similarly, a statute may clearly cover a given set of facts but be invalid because the statute is unconstitutional. For example, a statute that prohibits marriage between the races is clearly intended to prevent interracial marriage, but the statute is not mandatory authority because it is in violation of the constitution.

State enacted law (e.g., a state statute, a state administrative regulation) is usually mandatory only in the state that enacted that law. Suppose, however, that a state court is considering a *federal* enacted law.

Federal enacted law (e.g., the United States Constitution, a federal statute, a federal administrative regulation) can sometimes be mandatory authority in *state* courts. The United States Constitution is the highest authority in the country. If a provision of this Constitution applies, it controls over any state law to the contrary. Federal statutes and the regulations of federal administrative agencies are also superior in authority to state laws in those areas entrusted to the federal government by the United States Constitution, such as interstate commerce, patents, bankruptcy, or foreign affairs. Federal statutes and regulations in these areas are mandatory authority in state courts.

Court Opinions as Mandatory Authority

When is a court *required* to follow an opinion, so that the opinion is mandatory authority? Two conditions must be met:

- The opinion is on point, that is, it must be analogous.
- The opinion was written by a higher court that is superior to the court currently considering the applicability of the opinion.

In general, something is **on point** when it is relevant because it covers the facts of your research problem, and something is **analogous** when it is similar, although there may be differences. More specifically, a court opinion is on point and analogous when:

- there is a sufficient similarity between the **key facts** of the opinion and the facts of the client's case, *and*
- there is a sufficient similarity between the rule of law (e.g., statute, common law principle) that was interpreted and applied in the opinion and the rule of law that must be interpreted and applied in the client's case.

A *key fact* is a fact that was essential or very important to the conclusion or holding of the court's opinion. The easiest case is when the opinion is **on all fours** with the facts of the client's case. This means that the key facts of the opinion are exactly the same or almost exactly the same as the facts of the client's case. In chapter 10, we will examine in greater detail the process of applying an opinion by comparing it to a client's case.

If the opinion is not on point or analogous because there is not sufficient similarity between the opinion and the client's case, the opinion cannot be mandatory authority; it is nonauthority.

The second condition for the existence of mandatory authority requires us to examine the relationship between the court that wrote the opinion and the court that is currently considering that opinion. We will briefly cover six variations:

1. The highest court in the judicial system is considering an opinion written by a lower court in the same judicial system.
2. A lower court is considering an opinion written by the highest court in the same judicial system.
3. A court is considering an opinion written in the past by the same court.
4. A court in one state is considering an opinion written by a court from another state.
5. A state court is considering an opinion written by a federal court.
6. A federal court is considering an opinion written by a state court.

In each of these six situations, a court is attempting to determine whether the ruling (called a *holding*) in a prior opinion is binding in the litigation currently before the court. Assume that each opinion *is* analogous: the facts currently before the court are sufficiently similar to the key facts in the opinion under consideration, and the rules of law are also the same or sufficiently similar.

1. *The highest court is considering an opinion written by a lower court in the same judicial system.*

    A higher court is never required to follow an opinion written by a lower court in the same judicial system, whether or not the opinion is analogous. The California Supreme Court, for example, does not have to follow the holding in an opinion written by a California Superior Court, one of the lower courts in the California judicial system. Similarly, the United States Supreme Court does not have to follow the holding in an opinion written by a United States District Court, the trial court in the federal judicial system. If the opinion is analogous, it can only be persuasive authority; the higher court can follow the holding if it chooses to do so.

2. *A lower court is considering an opinion written by the highest court in the same judicial system.*

    An opinion written by the highest court in a judicial system *is* mandatory on every lower court in the same judicial system—if that opinion is analogous. An analogous opinion by the Supreme Court of Montana, for example, must be followed by every lower state court in Montana.

3. *A court is considering an opinion written in the past by the same court.*

    Does a court have to follow its *own* prior opinions? If, for example, the Florida Supreme Court wrote an opinion in 1970, is the holding in that opinion mandatory authority for the Florida Supreme Court in 1999 if the opinion is analogous? No. A court is always free to **overrule** and in effect invalidate its own prior opinions. This, however, rarely happens. A court is reluctant to change holdings in prior opinions unless there are good reasons to do so. This reluctance is known as **stare decisis.** Stated more positively: If a precedent exists, a court will follow it in a later similar case unless there are good reasons for the court to change the precedent. A **precedent** is simply a prior decision that can be used as a standard in a later similar case. To maintain fairness and stability, stare decisis means that courts should decide similar cases in the same way unless there is good reason to do otherwise.

The Florida example just used involved the highest state court considering an earlier opinion written by the same court. Suppose the opinion had been written by an intermediate or middle appeals court. Sometime later, this same court is asked to follow its own prior opinion because it is analogous to the case currently before the court. Does it have to? No. Any court can later overrule itself and reach a holding that differs from the holding it reached in the earlier opinion as long as no opinion written by a higher court is contrary to the result the court now wants to reach.

4. *A state court is considering an opinion written by a state court in another state.*

A state court generally does not have to follow an opinion written by a state court in another state, no matter how similar or analogous the opinion is. An Idaho court, for example, does not have to follow an opinion written by a Texas court.

There are two main exceptions to the principle that an opinion of one state is not mandatory authority in another state. The first involves conflicts of law and the second, full faith and credit:

- **Conflicts of law.** Suppose that an accident occurs in New York, but the negligence suit based on this accident is brought in a state court in Ohio where the defendant lives. Assume that the Ohio court has **subject-matter jurisdiction** over the dispute (meaning that the court has the power to hear this kind of dispute) and **personal jurisdiction** over the parties (meaning that the court has the power to render a decision that would bind these particular parties). What negligence law does the Ohio court apply? Ohio negligence law or New York negligence law? The negligence law of the two states may differ in significant respects. This is a conflicts-of-law problem, which arises whenever there is an inconsistency between the laws of two different, co-equal legal systems such as two states. Under the principles of the conflicts of law, a court of one state may be required to apply the law of another state. For example, the law to be applied may be the law of the state where the injury occurred or the law of the state that is at the center of the dispute. If this state is New York, then the Ohio court will apply New York negligence law. Analogous opinions of New York courts on the law of negligence will be mandatory authority in the Ohio court.

- **Full faith and credit.** The United States Constitution provides that "Full Faith and Credit shall be given in each State to the public Acts, Records, and judicial Proceedings of every other State" (art. IV, § 1). Suppose that Richards sues Davis for breach of contract in Delaware. Davis wins. Richards cannot go to another state and bring a breach-of-contract suit against Davis arising out of the same facts. If the Delaware court had proper jurisdiction (subject matter and personal) when it rendered its judgment, the Delaware opinion must be given full faith and credit in every other state. The case cannot be relitigated. The Delaware opinion is mandatory authority in every other state.

5 and 6. *A state court is considering an opinion written by a federal court and vice versa.*

The general rule is that state courts have the final say on what the state law is, and federal courts have the final say on what the federal law is. State courts do *not* have to follow opinions written by federal courts *unless* the issue before the state court involves a federal question—one arising out of the United States Constitution or out of a statute of Congress. (The clause in the United States Constitution that says federal law controls over state or local law whenever a federal question is raised is the **Supremacy Clause.**)

Federal courts do not have to follow state court opinions except to the extent that the federal court needs to know what the state law is on a given topic, and the state court opinions provide this information. When does a federal court need to know what the state law is on a given topic? Mainly in *diversity of citizenship* cases. Also, the case before the federal court must raise a state question rather than a federal question arising under the United States Constitution or statute of Congress. In a proper diversity case,[2] a federal court will apply state law to resolve the controversy. In such cases, state court opinions will be mandatory authority in the federal court.

SECTION C   PERSUASIVE AUTHORITY

We turn next to persuasive authority, which is any law or nonlaw that a court decides to follow because of its persuasiveness rather than because of a mandate or duty to follow it. The most common categories of persuasive authority we need to consider are (1) other court opinions and (2) secondary authority.

Court Opinions as Persuasive Authority

Review the two conditions mentioned earlier on when an opinion is mandatory authority: The opinion must be analogous, or on point, *and* it must have been written by a court that is superior to the court currently considering that opinion. If both these tests are not met, either the opinion is nonauthority, or it might be *persuasive authority*.

Suppose that you are reading an opinion that is analogous, or on point, but is not mandatory because of one of the following:

*   It was written by an inferior court and is now being considered by a court within the same judicial system that is superior to the court that wrote the opinion; or
*   It was written by a court from a judicial system that is different from the judicial system where the court considering that opinion sits. (Assume that there are no conflict-of-interest or full-faith-and-credit issues.)

If either of these two situations exists, the court, as we have seen, does *not* have to follow the opinion; it is not mandatory authority. If, however, the opinion is analogous or on point, the court would be free to adopt it as persuasive authority.

A number of factors go into a court's determination of whether a prior opinion is persuasive enough to adopt. A judge is usually interested in knowing how many other courts have adopted the result (the holding) of this opinion. Is there a "majority rule" or school of thought that has developed around that result? Has the opinion been frequently cited with approval? (To find out, check **citators** such as Shepard's and KeyCite.) How well reasoned is the opinion? These considerations will help a judge decide whether to adopt an opinion as persuasive. Finally, it is human nature for judges to gravitate toward opinions that are most in tune with their personal philosophies and biases—although preferences on this basis are never acknowledged.

Finally, we need to consider **dictum** as persuasive authority. Dictum is a statement made by a court that was not necessary to resolve the narrow question or issue before the court. Assume that a tenant (Mr. Kiley) sued his landlord (ABC Properties, Inc.) for failing to repair the main elevator in the building. The landlord claimed the tenant should repair it. The court rendered its decision in the opinion of *Kiley v. ABC Properties, Inc.,* ruling in favor of the tenant. In the *Kiley* opinion, the court says, "Landlords have an obligation to maintain elevators as well as all common passageways in the rented premises." The court's statement about the elevator is its **holding**; its statement about common passageways, however, is dictum. (A holding is a court's specific answer to a specific question or issue that arises out of specific facts before the court.)

---

2. The amount in controversy must exceed $50,000 and the parties must be citizens of different states. 28 U.S.C.A. § 1332(a) (1993).

The narrow issue before the court was whether the landlord must repair the *elevator*. The court's answer to this issue is its holding. Everything else is dictum. There was no need for the court to tell us about the landlord's legal obligation concerning *passageways*. The law governing passageways should be resolved in a future case when the dispute before the court involves parties fighting over who must maintain passageways. To be sure, it was convenient for the court in the *Kiley* opinion to add its view about passageways; they seem to be similar in function to elevators. But in our legal system, we prefer that courts stick to the disputes arising from the facts before them. Occasionally they don't, leading to dictum.

Now assume that, years later, another landlord-tenant case comes before the court. Jackson (the tenant) is being sued by Weber (the landlord) over repair of the passageway in the building where Jackson lives. Is *Kiley v. ABC Properties, Inc.* mandatory authority? No. Jackson is very happy about the language in *Kiley* that says landlords must maintain passageways. But the *Kiley* opinion is not mandatory authority on the issue of a landlord's responsibility to maintain passageways, because this issue was never before the *Kiley* court. The language about passageways in *Kiley* was dictum. Does this mean that the court in the Jackson/Weber case must ignore the dictum in *Kiley* on passageways? No. The court can decide to adopt the *Kiley* statement on passageways because it finds the statement persuasive. It is not required to follow the *Kiley* statement, but may decide to do so as persuasive authority.

Secondary Authority as Persuasive Authority

Secondary authority such as a legal treatise or a legal periodical article is not the law itself. It is not written by the legislature, a court, an agency, a city council, etc. Secondary authority can never be mandatory authority; it can only be persuasive. The chart in Exhibit 4.1 provides an overview of the major kinds of secondary authority that a court could decide to rely on in reaching its conclusion.

4.1

Exhibit
Categories of Secondary
Authority

Kind	Contents	Examples
1a. Legal Encyclopedias	Summaries of the law, organized by topic	*Corpus Juris Secundum* *American Jurisprudence 2d*
1b. Nonlegal Encyclopedias	Summaries of many topics on science, the arts, history, etc.	*Encyclopedia Britannica*
2a. Legal Dictionaries	Definitions of legal terms taken almost exclusively from court opinions	*Words and Phrases*
2b. Legal Dictionaries	Definitions of legal terms that come from a variety of sources	*Black's Law Dictionary* *Ballentine's Law Dictionary* West's *Legal Thesaurus/ Dictionary*
2c. Nonlegal Dictionaries	Definitions of all words in general use	*Webster's Dictionary*
3a. Legal Periodicals (academic)	Pamphlets (often later bound) containing articles on a variety of legal topics	*Harvard Law Review* *Utah Law Review* *Yale Journal of Law and Feminism*

Continued on next page

4.1

Exhibit
Categories of Secondary
Authority—continued

Kind	Contents	Examples
3b. Legal Periodicals (commercial)	Pamphlets (often later bound) containing articles on a variety of legal topics	*Case and Comment* *Practical Lawyer*
3c. Legal Periodicals (bar association)	Pamphlets (often later bound) containing articles on a variety of legal topics	*American Bar Association Journal* *California Lawyer* *Colorado Lawyer*
3d. Nonlegal Periodicals	Pamphlets (often later bound) containing articles on a variety of mainly nonlegal topics	*Newsweek* *Foreign Affairs*
4a. Legal Treatises	Summaries of and commentaries on areas of the law	*McCormick on Evidence* Johnstone and Hopson, *Lawyers and Their Work*
4b. Nonlegal Treatises	Summaries of and commentaries on a variety of mainly nonlegal topics	Samuelson, *Economics*
5. Formbooks, Manuals, Practice Books	Same as legal treatises with a greater emphasis on the "how-to-do-it" practical dimensions of the law	Dellheim, *Massachusetts Practice* Moore's *Federal Practice* Am. Jur. *Pleading and Practice Forms Annotated*
6. Looseleaf Services	Collections of materials in ring binders covering current law in designated areas	*State Tax Guide* (CCH) *Labor Relations Reporter* (BNA)
7a. Legal Newspapers	Daily or weekly information relevant to a law practice	*Daily Washington Law Reporter* *National Law Journal*
7b. Nonlegal Newspapers	General-circulation newspapers	*New York Times* *Detroit Free Press*
8. Legal Newsletters	Weekly, biweekly, or monthly practical information on a specific area of the law	*Washington Tax Review* *AIDS Policy & Law*

Almost all secondary authorities quote from the law itself; they quote primary authority. For example, here is an excerpt from page 321 of the third edition of a 1990 legal treatise called *Administrative Law and Process in a Nutshell* by Ernest Gellhorn and Ronald M. Levin. Note that this excerpt quotes from § 553 (b)(3)(B) of the Administrative Procedure Act (APA), which is within title 5 of the United States Code Annotated (U.S.C.A.):

> The final exemption to the APA's notice-and-comment procedures applies when "notice and public procedure . . . are impracticable, unnecessary, or contrary to the public interest." 5 U.S.C.A. § 553 (b)(3)(B). In practice this exception applies primarily when delay in the issuance of the rule would frustrate

the rule's purpose . . . . Ernest Gellhorn & Ronald M. Levin, *Administrative Law and Process in a Nutshell* 321 (3d ed. 1990).

If you want to quote § 553 (b)(3)(B) in your memorandum or other writing, do not do it solely by quoting a secondary authority such as this legal treatise. Go directly to the current United States Code (using U.S.C., U.S.C.A., or U.S.C.S.) and quote from § 553 (b)(3)(B) itself. Do not rely solely on the Gellhorn/Levin quotation of § 553 (b)(3)(B). You may *also* want to cite the Gellhorn/Levin observation that includes the quote from § 553 (b)(3)(B), but not as a substitute for a direct quote. As a general rule, *you should never use someone else's quotation of the law.* Quote *directly* from the primary authority. Use the secondary authority to bolster your arguments on the interpretation of the primary authority. This is one of the main functions of secondary authority: to help you persuade a court to adopt a certain interpretation of primary authority. You are on very dangerous ground when you use secondary authority as a substitute for primary authority.

Secondary authority frequently paraphrases or summarizes primary authority, e.g., a legal treatise or encyclopedia summarizes the law on a particular topic. (For an example, see the excerpt from the legal encyclopedia *Corpus Juris Secundum* in Exhibit 9.8 in chapter 9). You will be very tempted to use such summaries in your own writing. Generally, secondary authority is clearly written and quotable. It provides summaries of the law that often seem to fit very nicely into what you are trying to say. There are serious dangers, however, in relying on quotes containing these summaries. Although there are circumstances in which the summaries can be used (with appropriate citation to avoid the charge of **plagiarism**), you need to be aware of the five major dangers of doing so:

* The excerpts are secondary authority, and the goal of your writing is to use primary authority to support your arguments.
* The excerpts may contain summaries of several court opinions; these opinions should be individually analyzed before you use any of them in your writing. As indicated earlier, you need to go to the source, whether it be a statute, an opinion, or any other primary authority.
* The excerpts may be based on opinions from different states, and your legal writing must focus on the law of the state in which the client is litigating the case.
* The excerpts may contain summaries of opinions written by federal courts, and your case may be in a state court where there are no federal issues.
* The excerpts may contain summaries of opinions on state issues written by state courts, and your case may be in a federal court where there are no state issues.

In short, too much reliance on such excerpts from secondary authority amounts to laziness in legal research and analysis. It is sometimes difficult to find and apply primary authority. If someone else at least appears to have done all the work for you in secondary authority, why not use it? The answers to this question are the five dangers just mentioned.

Even if you never use secondary authority in your writing, it may still be of value to you. For example, the footnotes in a legal treatise, encyclopedia, or periodical might give you leads to the primary authority that you need to find and analyze. Furthermore, if you are doing research in an area of the law that is new to you, some background reading in a legal treatise, encyclopedia, or periodical often provides an excellent introduction to the area, as we will see in Exhibit 8.1 in chapter 8. Armed with some basic definitions and a general understanding, you will be better equipped to launch your research and analysis into the specific issues before you.

Suppose you want to use an excerpt from a secondary authority in your legal writing. You may, for example, want to quote from a treatise to bolster your argument on the interpretation of a statute or other primary authority. As such, you are asking the court to accept the secondary authority as persuasive authority. What steps are necessary to do so properly? What is the proper foundation for the use of secondary authority in legal writing? Exhibit 4.2 presents this foundation.

4.2 ································ The Foundation for Using a Quote from a Legal Treatise or Any Other Secondary Authority in Your
Legal Writing as Possible Persuasive Authority

Exhibit

1. The quote from the legal treatise (or other secondary authority) is not a substitute for a direct quote from the
court opinion, statute, or other primary authority. When you need to tell the reader what the primary authority
says, you do not do so solely through secondary authority.
2. The quote from the legal treatise (or other secondary authority) that you want to use does not contradict case
law, statutory law, or any other primary authority that exists in the jurisdiction where the client is in litigation.
Stated more simply, there must be no contrary mandatory authority.
3. If the quote from the legal treatise (or other secondary authority) *does* contradict case law, statutory law, or any
other primary authority, you cannot use the quote unless you satisfy yourself:
  • that the court (before which the client is in litigation) has the power to change the law that contradicts what
    the legal treatise (or other secondary authority) says and, in effect, to adopt a new interpretation of the law
    in the jurisdiction; and
  • that there is a reasonable likelihood that a court with such power is inclined to change the law.

Most well-written and comprehensively researched legal memoranda and appellate
briefs make relatively few references to secondary authority. Experienced advocates
know that judges are suspicious of secondary authority. It is true that some secondary
authorities are highly respected, such as *Prosser on Torts* or any of the Restatements
of the American Law Institute. Yet even these must be used with caution. The preoc-
cupation of a court is with primary authority. Before you use secondary authority in
your writing, you must be sure that (a) the secondary authority is not used as a substitute for the primary authority; (b) the secondary authority is not unduly repetitive
of the primary authority; (c) the secondary authority will be helpful to the court in
adopting an interpretation of primary authority, particularly when there is not a great
deal of primary authority on point; (d) you discuss the secondary authority after you
have presented the primary authority; and (e) the foundation for the use of secondary
authority (see Exhibit 4.2) can be demonstrated if needed.

Suppose you find a quote in a legal treatise that not only does not contradict any
law within the jurisdiction where the client is in litigation, but also concisely states the
law that does exist. In this instance, the treatise quote is, in effect, an accurate summary
of the law. Although you are on much safer ground in using such a quote, you should
provide some indication in your legal writing that such a parallel exists between the law
and the treatise quote. At the very least, you should state in your writing that the quote
from the secondary authority is consistent with the law of the jurisdiction and be prepared to back up this statement if it is later challenged or questioned by anyone.

Finally, you may find statements in secondary authority that neither contradict nor
summarize the law of your jurisdiction. The issue being discussed in the secondary
authority may simply have never arisen in your jurisdiction. Such issues are called
issues of **first impression.** (A case raising such issues is called a *case of first impression.*)
Again, you are on relatively safe ground in using such discussions in your legal writing. In
fact, the use of secondary authority is usually most effective when it treats issues that have
not yet been resolved in your jurisdiction. Courts are often quite receptive to adopting secondary authority as persuasive authority when novel questions or issues are involved.

  Assignment 4.1

Are the following statements true or false? Explain why you think any of the statements are false.

(a) All primary authority is mandatory authority, because primary authority consists of statutes,
constitutional provisions, or other laws.
(b) Secondary authority can be mandatory authority.
(c) An invalid state statute can be persuasive authority if a court decides to follow the statute
even though it does not have to.

Assignment 4.1—continued

(d) A federal administrative regulation can be mandatory authority in a state court.

(e) An opinion of the United States District Court can be mandatory authority for the United States Supreme Court.

(f) Because dictum is a comment by the court that was not necessary to resolve the issues before the court, dictum is nonauthority.

(g) An opinion in one state cannot be mandatory authority in the court of another state.

(h) A federal court can overrule an opinion of a state court.

(i) If your library does not have a copy of the statute you need to cite, you can cite the language of the statute that is printed in a scholarly analysis of the statute in a legal periodical article.

(j) A dissenting opinion can be persuasive authority.

Assignment 4.2

Mary Franklin is pregnant. The father, Bob Vinson, disappears before the baby is born. Mary agrees to let a Missouri couple adopt the baby. Bob was never notified of the adoption. When he finds out, he seeks to have the adoption nullified so that he can have full custody of the child.

Assume that each of the following authorities is relevant to the issue of whether Bob Vinson can invalidate the adoption, and that you want to cite all of them in your memorandum of law. In what order would you cite them if you wanted to cite the most controlling first? Place them in ascending order of importance, starting with the most important.

(a) An administrative regulation of a Missouri agency

(b) A statute of the Missouri legislature

(c) A statute of Congress

(d) A *Harvard Law Review* article on parental consent to adoption

(e) An opinion of the highest state court in Missouri interpreting a statute of the Missouri legislature

(f) A provision of the Missouri Constitution

(g) A legal treatise written by a Missouri judge on adoption

(h) An opinion of the highest state court in New York

(i) A provision of the United States Constitution

 CHAPTER SUMMARY

Authority is any source a court could rely on in reaching its conclusion. The authority can be primary, secondary, mandatory, or persuasive. It is primary if it is a law; it is secondary if it is a nonlaw; it is mandatory if the court must follow it; it is persuasive if the court follows it even if not required to do so. Only primary authority can be mandatory authority. Primary authority and secondary authority can be persuasive authority.

Enacted law is mandatory authority if it is being applied in the appropriate geographic area, if its authors intended it to apply to the facts in question, and if applying it does not violate a higher law. A court opinion is mandatory authority if it is on point or analogous, and if it was written by a higher court in the same judicial system. In several instances, however, a court may be required to follow an opinion written by a different judicial system. Examples include cases involving conflicts of law, full faith and credit, the Supremacy Clause, and diversity of jurisdiction.

A court opinion can be persuasive authority if other courts have adopted the holding in the opinion, if it is well reasoned, etc.

Dictum in an opinion cannot be mandatory authority, but it can be persuasive authority if a court wishes to adopt the dictum.

Great caution is needed when using secondary authority in legal writing. For example, quoting secondary authority must never be a substitute for quoting primary authority directly. Also, secondary authority often summarizes the law of more than one state, but you must concentrate on analyzing the specific law of the state where the case is in litigation.

Use secondary authority for leads to primary authority. As needed, use secondary authority to help persuade a tribunal to adopt an interpretation of primary authority that you are advocating. When you do the latter, be sure that there is no mandatory authority that contradicts this interpretation. This is part of the foundation that must be laid before trying to use secondary authority as persuasive authority.

KEY TERMS

authority	legislative intent	precedent	dictum
primary authority	on point	conflicts of law	holding
secondary authority	analogous	subject-matter jurisdiction	plagiarism
mandatory authority	key facts	personal jurisdiction	first impression
persuasive authority	on all fours	full faith and credit	
nonauthority	overrule	Supremacy Clause	
enacted law	stare decisis	citator	

Chapter *5*

CITATION FORM

► *Chapter Outline*

SECTION A   **INTRODUCTION**

A **citation** (or **cite** for short) is a reference to any written material. Here are two examples of citations, first of a federal statute and then of a state opinion:

28 U.S.C.A. § 44(c)
Smith v. Jones, 76 N.Y.2d 533, 563 N.E.2d 11 (1931)

Cites such as these give you the "address" where you can go in a traditional library or online to locate and read whatever is cited.

Are there any consistent rules on citation form? If you pick up different law books and examine the citations of similar material within them, you will notice great variety in citation form. You will find that people abbreviate things differently, do not include the information in the same order in the cite, use parentheses differently, use punctuation within the cite differently, include different amounts of information in the same kind of cite, etc. There does not appear to be any consistency. Yet, in spite of this diversity and confusion, you are often scolded by supervisors for failing to use "proper citation form." What, you may well ask, is "proper"?

Start by checking the rules of court or statutes governing the court that will have jurisdiction over the problem you are researching. They may or may not contain *official citation rules* on the format you must use when submitting documents to a particular court.[1] If such rules exist, they must obviously be followed no matter what any other citation guidebook may say. These are, in effect, citation *laws*.

Suppose, however, that there are no official citation laws in your state or that such laws do not cover the citation question that you have. In such circumstances, *ask your supervisor what citation form you should use.* You will probably be told, "Use the **Bluebook.**" This is a reference to *The Bluebook: A Uniform System of Citation,* which we looked at earlier (see photo on page 39). It is a small blue pamphlet (although in earlier editions, white covers were used). The Bluebook is published by a group of law students on the law reviews of their law schools.

Caution is needed in using the Bluebook. It is a highly technical and sometimes difficult-to-use publication because it packs so much information into a relatively small space. Primary users of the Bluebook are law schools that typeset their law reviews by using professional printers. What about those of us who use regular typewriters or word processors and do not typeset what we produce? Although the Bluebook does cover many of our citation needs, keep in mind that we are not the main audience of the Bluebook. Also, be aware that many courts do *not* follow the Bluebook even if there are no court rules on citation form for their courts. Judges often simply use their own "system" of citation without necessarily being consistent.

Why, then, is the Bluebook so important? Two reasons: First, it is the most comprehensive citation system in existence, and second, most attorneys had the Bluebook drilled into them during their first year of law school. Today more and more law firms are instructing all of their attorneys, paralegals, and secretaries to follow it, unless official citation rules exist.

We turn now to the fundamentals of citation form based on the rules in the Bluebook. Here are the categories that we will learn to cite:

Opinions
Constitutions and charters
Federal statutes
State statutes
Administrative regulations and decisions
Documents of legislative history
Secondary authority
Internet sources

---

1. States that have their own citation systems include California, Florida, Louisiana, Maine, Michigan, New Jersey, New York, Ohio, Pennsylvania, Tennessee, and Texas. For an extensive list, see A. Darby Dickerson, *An Un-Uniform System of Citation: Surviving with the New Bluebook,* 26 Stetson Law Review 53, 167 (1996).

> **GENERAL CITATION GUIDELINES**
>
> 1. Find out if there are citation laws in the rules of court or in statutes.
> 2. Ask your supervisor if he or she has any special instructions on citation form.
> 3. Consult the Bluebook.
> 4. Consult the specific citation guidelines presented below, which are based on the Bluebook.
> 5. Remember that the functional purpose of a citation is to enable readers to use a library to locate whatever you are citing. You must give enough information in the cite to fulfill this purpose. Courtesy to the reader in providing this help is as important as compliance with the niceties of citation form.
> 6. Often a private publisher of a book will tell you how to cite the book. ("Cite this book as . . . .") Ignore this instruction! Instead, follow guidelines 1–5 above.
> 7. When in doubt about whether to include something in a citation after carefully following guidelines 1–5 above, resolve the doubt by including it in the cite.

Our focus will be on providing complete or full citations for each of these authorities. Later we will also learn how to provide a **short form citation,** which is an abbreviated citation of an authority that you provide after you have already given a full citation of that authority.

SECTION B CITING OPINIONS

First let's look at the components of a typical citation of an opinion. See Exhibit 5.1. Not all opinions are cited in the same way, however. The citation format that you use depends on the kind of court that wrote the opinion. Before examining the guidelines that explain these differences, here is an overview:

Example A: Format of a citation to an opinion of the highest federal court (the United States Supreme Court):

> *Taglianetti v. United States,* 394 U.S. 316 (1969)

Example B: Format of a citation to an opinion of a federal middle appeals court (the United States Court of Appeals for the Second Circuit):

> *Sterling Nat'l Bank & Trust Co. v. Fidelity Mortgage Investors,* 510 F.2d 870 (2d Cir. 1975)

Example C: Format of a citation to an opinion of a federal trial court (the United States District Court for the Western District of Wisconsin):

> *Stone v. Schmidt,* 398 F. Supp. 768 (W.D. Wis. 1975)

Example D: Format of a citation to an opinion of the highest state court (New Jersey Supreme Court):

> *Petlin Associates, Inc. v. Township of Dover,* 64 N.J. 327, 316 A.2d 1 (1974)

Example E: Format of a citation to an opinion of a lower state court (Connecticut Superior Court, Appellate Session):

> *Huckabee v. Stevens,* 32 Conn. Supp. 511, 338 A.2d 512 (Super. Ct. 1975)

Example F: Format of a public domain citation

> *Jenkins v. Patterson,* 1997 Wis. Ct. App. 45, ¶ 157, 612 N.W.2d 1043

Example G: Format of a citation to an administrative decision (National Labor Relations Board):

> *Standard Dry Wall Products, Inc.,* 91 N.L.R.B. 544 (1950)

Example H: Format of a citation to an opinion of the Attorney General:

> 40 Op. Att'y Gen. 423 (1945)

Guidelines for Citing Opinions

1.   The names of the parties in a case should be *italicized* (if your printer has this capacity) or <u>underlined</u> (i.e., underscored). If you are able to use italics, an example would be as follows:

    Steck v. Farrell, 479 F.2d 1129 (7th Cir. 1990)

If you cannot italicize the names of the parties, underline (underscore) them:

    <u>Steck v. Farrell</u>, 479 F.2d 1129 (7th Cir. 1990)

2.   You will note that some of the citations in the above boxed examples have **parallel cites** (see Examples D, E, and F) and some do not. Before examining the rules of providing parallel cites and the techniques of finding such cites, some basics need to be covered.

The same opinion can be printed in more than one place. (See Exhibit 3.1 in chapter 3 for twelve possibilities in traditional reporters, CD-ROM, and online services.) A parallel cite is an additional reference to the same material; it is a second "address" for

Exhibit
Components of a Typical Citation of an Opinion

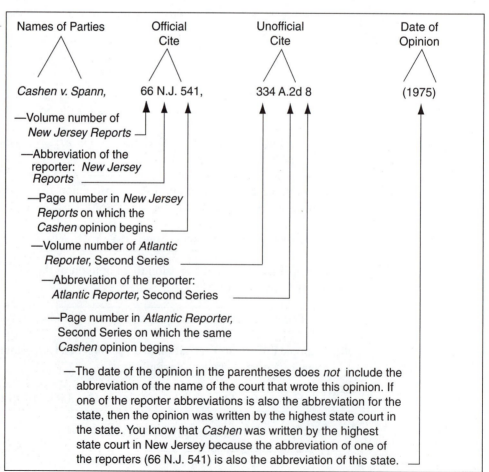

whatever is being cited. If there is a parallel cite to an opinion, you will be able to find that opinion (word-for-word) in at least two different reporters. Note that in Example D, the *Petlin* opinion can be found in *New Jersey Reports* (abbreviated "N.J.") and in *Atlantic Reporter 2d* ("A.2d"). Similarly, both the *Huckabee* opinion in Example E and the *Jenkins* opinion in Example F have a parallel cite. The other opinions cited in Examples A, B, C, G, and H do not have parallel cites.

3. Do not confuse parallel cite with the **same case on appeal.** Examine the citations of the following two opinions:

Jarrett v. Jarrett, 64 Ill. App. 3d 932, 382 N.E.2d 12 (1978)
Jarrett v. Jarrett, 78 Ill. 2d 337, 400 N.E.2d 421 (1979)

- Note that each opinion has its own parallel cite. the first *Jarrett* opinion begins on page 932 of volume 64 of *Illinois Appellate Court Reports,* Third Series (Ill. App. 3d) *and* also on page 12 of volume 382 of *North Eastern Reporter,* Second Series (N.E.2d). The second *Jarrett* opinion begins on page 337 of volume 78 of *Illinois Reports,* Second Series (Ill. 2d) *and* also on page 421 of volume 400 of *North Eastern Reporter,* Second Series (N.E.2d).

- The 1979 *Jarrett* opinion is the *same case on appeal* as the 1978 *Jarrett* opinion. In fact, the 1979 opinion reversed the 1978 opinion. "Same case on appeal" means that the opinions are part of the same litigation. The first *Jarrett* opinion is *not* a parallel cite of the second *Jarrett* opinion. Although part of the same litigation, the 1978 opinion and the 1979 opinion are totally separate opinions, each of which has its own parallel cite.

- Assume that you wanted to cite the 1978 opinion. As we will see later, you need to tell the reader about anything significant that has happened to an opinion on appeal, such as a reversal. Here is how you would do this for the *Jarrett* opinions:

Jarrett v. Jarrett, 64 Ill. App. 3d 932, 382 N.E.2d 12 (1978), *rev'd,* 78 Ill. 2d 337, 400 N.E.2d 421 (1979)

4. There are six main techniques of finding a parallel cite. See Research Link N.

- Check the top of the caption. Go to the reporter that contains the opinion. At the beginning of the opinion, there is a **caption** giving the names of the parties, the name of the court that wrote the opinion, the date of the decision, and other information about the litigation that led to the opinion. See if there is a parallel cite at the top of the caption. This technique does not always work, but it is worth a try. It works primarily when you check the captions of the opinions printed in the seven regional reporters we examined in Exhibit 3.2 of Chapter 3. Here is an example from the *North Western Reporter,* one of the seven regional reporters:

Finding a parallel cite by checking the top of the caption. If you go to 504 N.W.2d 728 and check the top of the caption of *Asher v. Exxon Co., U.S.A.,* you will find that its parallel cite is 200 Mich. App. 635.

728 Mich.   504 NORTH WESTERN REPORTER, 2d SERIES

200 Mich.App. 635
Farmer ASHER and Lucy Marie Asher,
his wife, Plaintiffs-Appellants,

v.

EXXON COMPANY, U.S.A., a Division
of Exxon Corporation, a Foreign
Corporation, Defendant-Appellee,

Court of Appeals of Michigan.
Submitted March 10, 1993, at Detroit.
Decided July 19, 1993, at 9:25 a.m.

- **Shepardize** the case in the standard sets of *Shepard's Citations,* such as *Shepard's Southwestern Reporter Citations* (see photo on page 70). To *shepardize* a case means to obtain the validation and other data on that case provided by any of the three versions of *Shepard's Citations* (paper, CD-ROM, or online). Among the data provided for a court opinion are available parallel cites. The first cite in *Shepard's* found in parentheses is the parallel cite. If you find no cite in parentheses, it means (a) that no parallel cite exists, (b) that the reporter containing the parallel cite has not been printed yet, or (c) that the parallel cite was given in one of the earlier volumes of Shepard's and was not repeated in the volume you are examining.

Using *Shepard's Citations* to find a parallel cite. If you shepardized the *E.I. DuPont* case (that begins on page —756—), you are told that its parallel cite is volume 280, page 477 of *Arkansas Reports* (280Ark477).

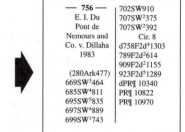

- Use the *Shepard's Case Names Citator.* Shepard's also has a separate set of citators called Case Name Citators. Their sole function is to give you parallel cites. Court opinions are listed alphabetically by party names along with the parallel cites.

Using *Shepard's Case Names Citator* to find a parallel cite. The parallel cites for *Wilson v. Peters* are 343 Ill App 354 and 99 NE2d 150.

Wil-Win	ILLINOIS CASE NAMES CITATOR
Wilson v. Parker 132 Ill App 2d 5, 269 NE2d 523 (1971)	Wilson v. Reeves Red-E-Mix Concrete Products 29 Ill App 3d 448. 330 NE2d 521 (1975)
Wilson v. Peters 343 Ill App 354, 99 NE2d 150 (1951)	Wilson & Tavridges Inc. v. Industrial Commission 32 Ill 2d 355, 204 NE2d 446 (1965)
Wilson, Ranson v. 335 Ill App 7, 80 NE2d 381 (1948)	Wilson Enterprises Inc., Thakkar v. 120 Ill App 3d 878, 76 Ill Dec 331, 458 NE2d 985 (1983)

- Go to the *National Reporter Blue Book,* a set of books published by West. (See photo on page 39.) The *National Reporter Blue Book* will also tell you which official reporters have been discontinued. If your state has a *Blue and White Book,* you can also use it to try to find a parallel cite.
- Check the Table of Cases in a digest. Go to every digest that gives small-paragraph summaries of court opinions for the court that wrote the opinion, e.g., the American Digest System. Go to the Table of Cases in these digests. See if there is a parallel cite for your case. In the following excerpt from a digest Table of Cases, you find two cites for *Ames v. State Bar*—106 Cal. Rptr. 489 and 506 P.2d 625:

 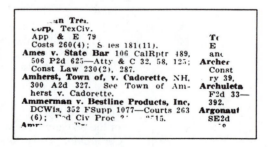

Finding a parallel cite by checking the Table of Cases in digests

- Use WESTLAW and LEXIS. When you call up your case on either of the two main online research systems, WESTLAW and LEXIS, you are always given existing parallel cites.

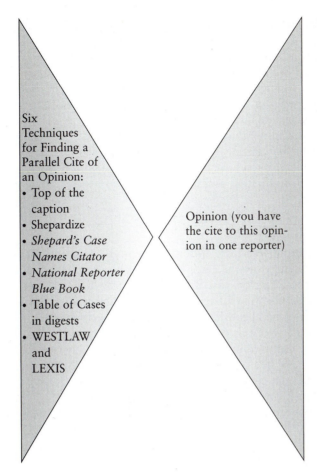

Six Techniques for Finding a Parallel Cite of an Opinion:
• Top of the caption
• Shepardize
• *Shepard's Case Names Citator*
• *National Reporter Blue Book*
• Table of Cases in digests
• WESTLAW and LEXIS

Opinion (you have the cite to this opinion in one reporter)

RESEARCH LINK N
You have the citation to one reporter where you can read an opinion. You now want a parallel cite so that you can read the same opinion—word-for-word—in another reporter. There are six techniques you can use to try to find a parallel cite. For example, assume you know the cite of the *Smith* case in *New York Reports,* but you don't know its cite in the *North Eastern Reporter.* Use the six techniques to try to find the N.E.2d parallel cite.

5.   When do you provide a parallel cite? When you are citing an opinion in your memorandum or other writing, when are you required to give a parallel cite? For many opinions there is:

- an official cite to an **official reporter** (an official reporter is a reporter printed under the authority of the government, often by the government itself), and
- an unofficial cite to an **unofficial reporter** (an unofficial reporter is a reporter printed by a commercial printing company without special authority from the government)

When must you provide both the official cite and the unofficial cite of an opinion? The answer for *federal* court opinions is fairly simple: never.

- When you want to cite an opinion of the United States Supreme Court, cite only the official reporter: *United States Reports* (U.S.). Do not cite the two major unofficial reporters, *Supreme Court Reporter* (S. Ct.) and *Lawyer's Edition* (L. Ed. 2d). See Example A at the beginning of this chapter.
- When you want to cite a current opinion of a United States Court of Appeals, cite only the *Federal Reporter 3d* (F.3d). See Example B at the beginning of this chapter.
- When you want to cite a current opinion of a United States District court, cite only the *Federal Supplement* (F. Supp.). See Example C at the beginning of this chapter.

Next we cover the need for parallel cites when you are citing *state* court opinions. Assume that you are in the law library doing legal research. You find a state court opinion that you want to consider using in a document needed for the client's case. Do you provide the parallel cite for this opinion? Unfortunately, this simple question does not have a simple answer. According to the Bluebook, the answer depends on three factors: (a) whether a parallel cite exists, (b) the kind of writing you are preparing, and (c) who publishes the unofficial reporter that would be used for the unofficial cite.

(a) The Existence of a Parallel Cite Of course, you can't give a parallel cite if none exists! Several reasons may account for the absence of a parallel cite. First, it may not exist because the official reporter has been discontinued.[2] Second, the official reporter may not have been published yet. (Official reporters are sometimes printed as much as a year after the printing of the unofficial reporter. See Exhibit 3.1 in chapter 3.) If the official reporter has been discontinued or has not been printed yet, all you have is the unofficial cite in a regional reporter. If so, here are the guidelines to follow:

Suppose, for example, that you want to cite the case of *Nace v. Nace* decided by the Supreme Court of Arizona. Assume that because the case is so recent, the official cite is not available. All you have is the unofficial cite in the *Pacific Reporter 2d* (P.2d). Here is how you would cite this case:

Nace v. Nace, 790 P.2d 48 (Ariz. 1998)

Note the abbreviation *Ariz.* just before the date in the parentheses. This is an abbreviation of the court that wrote the case. When the abbreviation is the abbreviation of the state itself, you know that the case was written by the highest state court in the state. If you did not provide this abbreviation, someone looking at the cite would not know what court wrote it. The general rule is to provide an abbreviation of the court that wrote the case unless the identity of this court is unambiguously clear by looking at the abbreviation of any of the reporters in the cite. The reporter in this cite is *Pacific Reporter 2d* (P.2d). Looking at the cite of this reporter certainly does not tell you what court wrote *Nace.* (Many states are covered in P.2d. See Exhibit 3.2 and Research Link J in chapter 3.) Hence, you must abbreviate the court in the parentheses before the date.

Suppose, however, that the official cite of the *Nace* case *was* available and you needed to provide it. Assume that the case began on page 411 of volume 162 of *Arizona Reports* (abbreviated Ariz.), the official state reporter. Here is how you would cite the case:

Nace v. Nace, 162 Ariz. 411, 790 P.2d 48 (1998)

Note that there is no need to include the abbreviation of the court that wrote the case in the parentheses before the date. As we have seen, if the abbreviation of a reporter is the abbreviation of a state, you can assume that the case was written by the highest state court in that state. Hence, there is no need to abbreviate the court in the parentheses with the date. You can tell by looking at the abbreviation of the official reporter (162 Ariz. 411) that the highest state court in Arizona wrote the case, because *Ariz.* is the abbreviation of the state.

(b) The Kind of Writing You Are Preparing What are you preparing? A memo? An appellate brief? Who is the audience? Your supervisor? A court? Answers to such questions will provide us with the next important guideline on when to provide a parallel cite.

In a document to be submitted to a state court (such as an appellate brief), all citations to cases decided by courts *of that state* must include a citation to the official state reporter (if available) in addition to the unofficial regional reporter. Only these cases require a parallel cite. Consequently, the following case citations *never* require a parallel cite:

- A state court citation that you want to use in a document that will be submitted to a court in a different state
- A state court citation that you want to use in a document that will not be submitted to any court

2. You can find out if an official reporter has been discontinued by consulting the *National Reporter Blue Book* or the *Blue and White Book.* See page 39.

In these two instances, the cite to the unofficial regional reporter is sufficient. For a summary of these rules, see Exhibit 5.2.

Let's look at some additional examples. Assume that during your research, you come across the *Lausier* case whose full cite is as follows:

Lausier v. Pescinski, 67 Wis. 2d 4, 226 N.W.2d 180 (1975)

This case was written by the highest state court in Wisconsin. You can tell this because *Wis.* is the abbreviation of the state. Under the above guidelines, if you are preparing an appellate brief to be submitted to a state court in New York or in Hawaii, here is how you cite *Lausier* in your brief:

Lausier v. Pescinski, 226 N.W.2d 180 (Wis. 1975)

If, however, you are preparing an appellate brief to be submitted to a state court in Wisconsin, here is how you cite it in your brief:

Lausier v. Pescinski, 67 Wis. 2d 4, 226 N.W.2d 180 (1975)

If the document you are preparing is not going to be submitted to any court, here is how you would cite this opinion in your document:

Lausier v. Pescinski, 226 N.W.2d 180 (Wis. 1975)

Again, the only time you provide a parallel cite is when the document you are preparing is to be submitted to a state court, and the opinion you are citing was decided by a state court in the same state.

 5.2 .... When Do You Need to Provide a Parallel Cite?

Exhibit

For Opinions Printed in These Reporters:	Is a Parallel Cite Needed When Citing One of These Opinions?	Comments
• *United States Reports* (U.S.)	No	The two main parallel cites are to the *Supreme Court Reporter* (S. Ct.) and to *Lawyer's Edition* (L. Ed. 2d). If the official cite to *United States Reports* (U.S.) is available, do not give the parallel cites in S. Ct. and L. Ed. 2d.
• *Federal Reporter 3d* (F.3d)	No	Opinions in F.3d have no widely used parallel cites.
• *Federal Supplement* (F. Supp.)	No	Opinions in F. Supp. have no widely used parallel cites.
Seven regional reporters: • *Atlantic* (A.2d) • *North Eastern* (N.E.2d) • *North Western* (N.W.2d) • *Pacific* (P.2d) • *South Eastern* (S.E.2d) • *Southern* (So. 2d) • *South Western* (S.W.2d) See Exhibit 3.2 in chapter 3.	Yes, cite the regional (unofficial) reporter *and* the official reporter when you will be using the cite in a document that will be submitted to a court in the same state as the state that wrote the opinion you want to cite. For example, use a parallel cite of a N.Y. case that will be used in a document to be filed in a N.Y. court.	But no parallel cite of a state court opinion is needed if you are using the cite in a document that will *not* be submitted to a court in the same state that wrote the opinion. The regional reporter cite is sufficient. You do not have to use the official cite. For example, do *not* give the parallel cite of a N.Y. case that will be used in a document to be filed in an Ohio court.

One final example involves a middle appeals state court opinion. Assume that you want to cite *Bowser v. Lee Hospital,* a 1990 opinion decided by the Superior Court of Pennsylvania. Here is how you would cite this opinion if you were citing it in an appellate brief or other document to be submitted to a Pennsylvania state court:

Bowser v. Lee Hosp., 399 Pa. Super. 332, 582 A.2d 369 (1990)

You need to give the parallel cite because you are using the cite in a document to be submitted to a state court that is the same state as the state where the opinion was written. Here, however, is how you would cite the opinion if you were citing it in an appellate brief or other document to be submitted to a New York state court, to a Florida state court, or to any court other than a Pennsylvania state court:

Bowser v. Lee Hosp., 582 A.2d 369 (Pa. Super. Ct. 1990)

No parallel cite is needed. The regional reporter citation is sufficient because the cite is not being used in a document to be filed in a state court that is the same state as the state where the opinion was written. The key concerns are: In what state are you in litigation? and What state wrote the opinion you want to cite?

| STATE OF OPINION | $\neq$ | STATE OF COURT WHERE YOU ARE LITIGATING | $\rightarrow$ | NO PARALLEL CITE NEEDED |
| STATE OF OPINION | $=$ | STATE OF COURT WHERE YOU ARE LITIGATING | $\rightarrow$ | PARALLEL CITE NEEDED |

Note that the *Bowser* citation with the parallel cite does not abbreviate the name of the court in the parentheses at the end of the cite. It simply says (1990). There is no need to abbreviate the name of the court because we can tell by looking at one of the reporters (399 Pa. Super. 332) that the case was written by a Pennsylvania Superior Court. (Pa. is the abbreviation of Pennsylvania and Super. is the abbreviation of Superior Court.) Again, the rule is that you do not need to abbreviate the court at the end of a citation if the identity of the court is unambiguously clear by looking at the abbreviation of any of the reporters in the cite.

(c) Where the Unofficial Cite Is Published Our examples thus far have assumed that the unofficial cite was one of the seven regional reporters (*Atlantic, North Eastern, North Western, Pacific, South Eastern, Southern,* and *South Western.* See Exhibit 3.2 in chapter 3). Suppose, however, that the opinion is published in a different unofficial source, e.g., a looseleaf service, an annotated reporter such as A.L.R.5th, a CD-ROM, an Internet address, or a database in WESTLAW or LEXIS. Do you ever cite one of these unofficial sources? No—unless the cite to the regional reporter does not exist. The only unofficial cite to use is the regional reporter except when it is unavailable.

It must be pointed out that *not* everyone agrees with the above Bluebook guidelines on when to provide a parallel cite to a state court opinion. The better rule is as follows: If parallel cites to an official state reporter and to an unofficial regional reporter exist, *always* provide both as a courtesy to the reader. If the cite to the regional reporter does not exist, cite other unofficial sources such as a looseleaf service. If, however, your supervisor insists that you follow the Bluebook, use the above guidelines.

6.   Looseleaf services often provide the most current legal material available. Some services send out opinions within a week of their issuance by the court. As indicated above, however, do *not* include the citation to the looseleaf service *unless* the citation to the regional reporter is not available at the time.

7.   Court opinions are found in traditional library volumes (reporters) and on computerized legal research services. Some opinions, however, are found only online in these services. An example is *Bucknum v. Bucknum,* which was decided on February

Assignment 5.1

Here are two citations to the same case:

(a) *Velletri v. Lussier,* 88 R.I. 352, 148 A.2d 360 (1959)
(b) *Velletri v. Lussier,* 148 A.2d 360 (R.I. 1959)

Assume that you wanted to cite the *Velletri* case in the following documents. According to the Bluebook, which citation would you use and why?

(1) A memorandum submitted to a Rhode Island Superior Court in support of a motion to dismiss.
(2) A law review article.
(3) An appellate brief to be submitted to the United States Supreme Court.
(4) An interoffice memorandum prepared by a paralegal for the paralegal's supervisor who is preparing an appellate brief that will be submitted to the Rhode Island Supreme Court.

19, 1991, by the Minnesota Court of Appeals. Its docket number is No. C6-90-1798. This opinion is found on WESTLAW and on LEXIS but not in a traditional library reporter volume. Here is how the case is cited in WESTLAW and LEXIS, respectively:

Bucknum v. Bucknum, 1991 WL 17881 (Minn. App.)
Bucknum v. Bucknum, 1991 Minn. App. LEXIS 145

The number 17881 is an internal WESTLAW number, and 145 is an internal LEXIS number.

The Bluebook does *not* follow these citation formats. The Bluebook has its own format for citing cases found in WESTLAW and LEXIS:

Bucknum v. Bucknum, No. C6–90–1798, 1991 WL 17881 (Minn. App. Feb. 19, 1991)
Bucknum v. Bucknum, No. C6–90–1798, 1991 Minn. App. LEXIS 145 (Feb. 19, 1991)

Note that in these Bluebook cites, the docket number and the WESTLAW/LEXIS cite are given, along with the full date of the decision in parentheses at the end.

When do you cite a case in WESTLAW or LEXIS? Only when the case is not available in traditional library volumes such as reporters.

8. There is some disagreement as to whether parallel cites are needed for opinions of the U.S. Supreme Court. The Bluebook says you should never provide a parallel cite for such opinions if you have the official cite (U.S.), even if the parallel cites in S. Ct. and L. Ed. are also available. (See Example A at the beginning of the chapter.) The better view, however, is to give all three cites when they are available.

9. When parallel cites are used, always place the official cite first before the unofficial cite. (See Examples D and E.)

10. There is never a parallel cite for *Federal Reporter 2d* cases (F.2d) (see Example B) or for *Federal Reporter 3d* cases (F.3d). See Exhibit 5.2. Abbreviate the circuit in parentheses at the end of the cite before the year. 2d Cir. means the case was decided by the U.S. Court of Appeals for the Second Circuit. D.C. Cir. would mean the case was decided by the U.S. Court of Appeals for the District of Columbia Circuit. Fed. Cir. would mean the case was decided by the United States Court of Appeals for the Federal Circuit. The caption of the opinion will tell you which circuit court wrote the opinion.

11. There is never a parallel cite for *Federal Supplement* cases (F. Supp.). (See Example C and Exhibit 5.2.) Abbreviate the U.S. District Court in parentheses at the end of the cite before the year. W.D. Wis. means the opinion was written by the United States District Court, Western District, sitting in Wisconsin. The caption of the opinion will tell you which U.S. District Court wrote the opinion.

12. In Example D, the parentheses at the end of the cite to the *Petlin* case contain the date of the decision, but nothing more. As stated earlier, there is no need to indicate the name of the court in the parentheses if the identity of the court is unambiguously clear from the abbreviation of a reporter in the cite. In Example D, the *Petlin* case was written by the highest court (the Supreme Court) in the state of New Jersey. You know this by examining the abbreviation of the official reporter in the cite (64 N.J. 327). When the abbreviation of the reporter (here, N.J.) is the abbreviation of the state, you can assume that the case was written by the highest court in that state. Suppose, however, that you did not have this official reporter cite. If all you had was the unofficial Atlantic 2d cite (316 A.2d 1), you would cite the case as follows:

Petlin Associates, Inc. v. Township of Dover, 316 A.2d 1 (N.J. 1974)

By looking at the abbreviation of the reporter (A.2d), you cannot tell which court wrote this opinion. Therefore, you must abbreviate the name of the court in the parentheses before the date. Using the abbreviation of the state alone (N.J.) tells you that it was the highest state court in the state.

13. In Example E, "Super. Ct." appears before the date in the parentheses. This is the abbreviation of the Connecticut Superior Court, which wrote the opinion. This abbreviation is necessary because the identity of the court is not unambiguously clear from the abbreviation of any of the reporters in the cite. The abbreviations "Conn. Supp." and "A.2d" do not clearly tell you that the case was written by a Connecticut Superior Court. Note, however, that it is not necessary to tell the reader in the parentheses that this court is in Connecticut because it is clear from the abbreviation of the reporter (32 Conn. Supp. 511) that it is a Connecticut case.

14. Include only the last name of parties who are people. For example, if the parties are listed as "Frank Taylor v. Mary Smith" in the caption, your cite should list them as *Taylor v. Smith*.

15. When a party is a business or organization, you need to determine whether to abbreviate part of the party's name. There are eight words that are almost always abbreviated: and (&), Association (Ass'n), Brothers (Bros.), Company (Co.), Corporation (Corp.), Incorporated (Inc.), Limited (Ltd.), and Number (No.). The abbreviation of other words in a party's name depends on whether the citation is a stand-alone citation or is part of a sentence. Here is an example of a stand-alone citation:

Erie R.R. Bldg. Preservation Ass'n v. Smith Co., 100 F.3d 23 (5th Cir. 1998)

Here is an example of the same citation that is part of a sentence:

In *Erie Railroad Building Preservation Ass'n v. Smith Co.,* 100 F.3d 23 (5th Cir. 1998), the court discussed the reversion doctrine.

Note that the words "Association" and "Company" are abbreviated in both examples. They are among the eight that are almost always abbreviated. The abbreviation of "Railroad" and "Building," however, differs in the examples. The Bluebook gives a list of words that you must abbreviate in stand-alone citations, but not when you use them in a citation that is part of a sentence (which the Bluebook refers to as a citation "in a textual sentence"). The list includes words such as Authority (Auth.), Board (Bd.), Building (Bldg.), Committee (Comm.), Department (Dep't), Education (Educ.), Government (Gov't), Railroad (R.R.), and University (Univ.). The general rule is: abbreviate these words only in stand-alone citations. A major exception exists for the first word of a party's name. Such words are rarely abbreviated even in stand-alone citations. For example, compare the two ways "Board" is treated in the following stand-alone citation:

Davis Bd. of Inquiry v. Board of Governors Ass'n, 672 F.2d 23 (9th Cir. 1980)

16. When the United States is a party, do not use the abbreviation "U.S." Spell it out. See Example A.

17. Assume that Maine is a party. Your cite should say "State" (rather than "State of Maine" or "Maine") *if and only if* the opinion was written by a Maine state court. Suppose, however, that Maine is a party in an opinion written by an Ohio court. In such a case, use "Maine" (not "State of Maine" or "State") in your cite as the name of this party. This same guideline applies for the words "Commonwealth" and "People." These words are used alone in a cite only if the court that wrote the opinion you are citing is in the same state referred to by the words "Commonwealth" and "People." Example: You are citing an opinion of the California Supreme Court, whose caption describes the parties as follows:

People of California v. Gabriel S. Farrell

Your cite of this opinion would be *People v. Farrell.*

18. When an opinion consolidates more than one litigation, it is referred to as a **consolidated litigation.** A supreme court, for example, may use one opinion to resolve similar issues raised in several different lower court cases. The caption of such an opinion will probably list all the parties from these different lower court cases. For example, the caption might say: *A v. B; C v. D; E v. F.* When you cite this opinion, include only the *first* set of parties listed in the caption—here, *A v. B.* If the caption says *et al.* (meaning "and others") after the name of a party, do not include the phrase *et al.* in your cite.

19. Often the court will tell you the **litigation status** of the parties, such as plaintiff, defendant, appellant, or appellee. Do not include this information in your cite.

20. Titles of individual parties (such as administrator or secretary) should be omitted from your cite. One exception is the Commissioner of Internal Revenue. Cite this party simply as "Commissioner"—for example, *Jackson v. Commissioner.*

21. When the caption of an opinion contains the phrase *In re* (meaning "in the matter of"), include this phrase in your cite—for example, *In re Jones.*

22. Include the year of the decision at the end of the cite in parentheses. If more than one date is given in the caption of the opinion, use the year from the date the opinion was decided.

23. Do not include the **docket number** of the case in the cite unless the case is not printed in a traditional reporter (see guideline 7), or unless the case is still pending. (The docket number is the number assigned to a case by the court.)

24. Once an opinion is written, two things can occur. First, it might be appealed one or more times, leading to more opinions that are part of the same litigation (all referred to as the *same case on appeal*). What happens to an opinion on appeal is known as its **subsequent history** or the **history of the case.** Second, other opinions that are not part of the same litigation might agree with it and therefore follow it, or criticize it and therefore refuse to adopt its conclusions. How other opinions react to a particular opinion in any of these ways is known as the **treatment of the case** in the courts. When you give the citation of an opinion, you need not include any information about treatment of this kind. But, as indicated earlier, your citation *does* have to alert the reader to important subsequent history events. Here is an example:

Herbert v. Lando, 568 F.2d 974 (2d Cir. 1977), *rev'd,* 444 U.S. 111 (1979)

It would obviously be important to let the reader know that the *Herbert* case was reversed *(rev'd)* on appeal. In addition, you would want to let the reader know whether the case was affirmed *(aff'd)* on appeal, and whether an appellate court accepted certiorari *(cert. granted),* or denied certiorari *(cert. denied).* (Certiorari refers to the **writ of certiorari.** This is an order by an appellate court requiring a lower court to certify the record of a lower court proceeding and to send the record "up" to the appellate court, which has decided to accept the appeal.) For older cases, a reader would usually not be interested in knowing whether an appellate court accepted or denied certiorari. Hence this information is included in your cite only if the case you are citing is less than two years old. If, however, you feel it is important for the reader to have this kind of information on the subsequent history of older cases, include it in the citation.

25.   The reporter volumes that contain current opinions are conveniently arranged by volume number. All the volumes of the same set have the same name, e.g., *Atlantic Reporter 2d*. At one time, however, life was not this simple. Volumes of opinions were identified by the name of the individual person who had responsibility for compiling the opinions written by the judges. These individuals were called reporters. "7 Cush. 430," for example, refers to an opinion found on page 430 of volume 7 of Massachusetts cases when Mr. Cushing was the official reporter. When he ended his employment, Mr. Gray took over, and the cite of an opinion in the volume immediately after "7 Cush." was "1 Gray." By simply looking at the cover of the volume, you *cannot* tell what court's opinions are inside unless you happen to be familiar with the names of these individuals and the courts for which they worked. These volumes are called **nominative reporters** because they are identified by the name of the individual person who compiled the opinions for the court.

26.   Assume that all you know are the names of the parties and the name of the court that wrote the opinion. How do you obtain the full cite so that you can find and read the opinion?

- Go to every digest that covers that reporter. See Exhibit 3.3 in chapter 3 for a list of what digests cover what reporters. Check the table of cases in the digests.
- Call the court clerk for the court that wrote the opinion. If it is a recent case, the clerk may be able to send you a copy. Occasionally, the clerk will give you the cite of the case. (It will help if you can tell the clerk the docket number of the case.)
- Go to the reporter volumes that cover the court that wrote the opinion. Because you do not have a volume number, you cannot go directly to the volume that has the opinion. If you can *approximate* the date of the case, however, you can check the table of cases in each reporter volume that probably covers that year. You may have to check the table of cases in ten to fifteen volumes before achieving success. The opinions are printed in the reporters in roughly chronological order.
- Use *Shepard's Case Names Citator* referred to (and excerpted) on page 96.
- If you have access to WESTLAW or LEXIS, simply enter the name of the case in the appropriate database or file. Suppose, for example, you were looking for the full cite of the *Miranda* opinion. You could type the word *Miranda* as one of your search terms. This should lead you to numerous references to every case in which Miranda was one of the parties. These references will usually include all of the parallel cites for the opinions.

27.   When you are quoting specific language in an opinion or in a legal periodical article, you need to give two page numbers: first, the page number on which the opinion or legal periodical article begins; and second, the page number on which the quote is found. This is known as a **pinpoint cite,** which is a reference to a specific page in a document in addition to the page on which the document begins. The page on which the quote is found is the "pinpointed" number. For opinions, this number goes immediately after the page number on which the opinion begins, separated by a comma. Assume that you want to quote from an opinion that has a parallel cite. Hence your quote will be found in the opinion printed in both reporters, but on different page numbers. A pinpoint cite of this opinion would state the page number in each reporter where the opinion begins *plus* the page number in each reporter on which your quote is found. In the following example, the *Bridgeton* opinion begins on page 17 of *Maryland Reports* (Md.) and on page 376 of the *Atlantic Reporter 2d* (A.2d). The quote from the *Bridgeton case,* however, is found on page 20 and on page 379 of these reporters:

> "Even though laches may not apply, one must use reasonable promptness when availing himself of judicial protection." *Bridgeton Educ. Ass'n v. Board of Educ.,* 147 Md. 17, 20, 334 A.2d 376, 379 (1975).

28.   The vast majority of citations to cases contain volume and page numbers, e.g., *Smith v. Smith,* 300 N.E.2d 202 (N.Y. 1996). In this example, the volume number is to a particular reporter—volume 303 of the *North Eastern Reporter,* Second Series. The case begins on page 202. Critics have argued that we need to get ready for the paperless law library when all or most legal materials, particularly primary authority, will be available online through computers. (See discussion of *virtual law library* at the end of chapter 1.) When this time comes, we should be able to cite cases and other documents without referring to volume and page numbers. Indeed, proposals have been advanced for what is called a **generic citation** system—one that gives references to documents without using traditional volume and page numbers.

The system has different names. It is referred to as **electronic citation** because the references are to online documents. It is also called a **public domain citation** system when it refers you to free materials that are not dependent on the volumes of commercial companies such as West, the publisher of the widely used National Reporter System (see Exhibit 3.2 in chapter 3). Something is *in the public domain* when it is free and open to anyone who wants it. The format of traditional case citations is dependent on volume and page numbers. A generic or public domain citation system is referred to as "medium neutral," "format neutral" or "vendor neutral" (the vendor being the seller/publisher of reporter volumes).

The essence of a generic citation system is sequential opinion and paragraph numbering. When a court writes an opinion, it will assign a sequential number to it (perhaps similar to a docket number) and then a sequential number to every paragraph: ¶ 1, ¶ 2, ¶ 3, ¶ 4, etc. If, for example, you wanted to quote a sentence that appeared in the eighty-ninth paragraph of *Davis v. Cardiff,* the citation might be:

> *Davis v. Cardiff,* 1996 Wis. Ct. App. 234, ¶ 89

This would refer you to the 89th paragraph in *Davis v. Cardiff,* which was the 234th opinion issued in 1996 by the Wisconsin Court of Appeals. If researchers wanted to check this citation, they would go online. For example, they might go to the site on the Internet that contains opinions of Wisconsin state courts, find opinion no. 234, and quickly "click" to ¶ 89 of the opinion.[3]

A few states have already adopted generic citation systems like this. Such systems, however, do not replace the traditional volume/page citation system. At least not yet. Comprehensive law libraries will continue to add traditional reporter volumes to their shelves. But an alternative is slowly emerging. In the meantime, if a state has adopted an official public domain citation system, use it, but also include a traditional reporter cite where available. For example:

> *Stevens v. State,* 1996 S.D. 1, ¶ 217, 402 N.W.2d 327

See also Example F at the beginning of this chapter. For a report on the Internet that gives the details of the generic systems adopted by specific courts, see <http://www.aallnet.org/committee/citation>.

SECTION C   CITING CONSTITUTIONS AND CHARTERS

Constitutions and charters are cited to (a) the abbreviated name of the constitution or charter, (b) the article, and (c) the section.

> U.S. Const. art. I, § 9
> N.M. Const. art. IV, § 7

---

3. Of course, if page numbers are no longer needed, we will no longer need star paging. As we saw in chapter 3 (page 42), **star paging** is a notation (such as an asterisk or star) next to text within a page in an unofficial reporter that indicates where the same text can be found in the official reporter. If every opinion has the same paragraph numbering system, there will be no need to tell a reader where material can be found within parallel cites. Under a generic citation system, a reference to ¶ 13 of an opinion, for example, will lead you to the same material in every official reporter and in every unofficial reporter that prints the opinion.

When citing constitutions and charters currently in force, do not give the date of enactment.

SECTION D   CITING FEDERAL STATUTES

1.   All federal statutes of Congress are collected in chronological order of passage as session laws in the *United States Statutes at Large* (abbreviated "Stat."). **Session laws** are statutes of the legislature that are organized chronologically by date of enactment rather than by subject matter. If the statute is of general public interest, it is also printed in *each* of three codes in which the statutes *are* organized by subject matter:

- United States Code (U.S.C.)
- United States Code Annotated (U.S.C.A.)—West Publishing Co.
- United States Code Service (U.S.C.S.)—LEXIS

The preferred citation format is to U.S.C., which is the official code.

42 U.S.C. § 3412(a)(1970)

or

Narcotic Rehabilitation Act of 1966, 42 U.S.C. § 3412(a)(1970)

Although it is not necessary to give the **popular name** of the statute (as in the second version of the above example), citing the popular name when known is often helpful.

2.   A new edition of the U.S.C. comes out every six years. The date you use in citing a statute in U.S.C. is the date of the edition you are using unless your statute is found in one of the annual Supplements to the U.S.C., which come out in between editions. If your statute is in a Supplement, you cite the volume and year of this Supplement. Suppose your statute is found in the sixth Supplement published in 1983. Your cite would be as follows:

29 U.S.C. § 169 (Supp. VI 1983)

The date you use in citing a statute in U.S.C. is not the year the statute was enacted or passed by the legislature. Nor is it the year the statute became effective. The date you use is the date of the edition of the code or of the Supplement year.

3.   Although citation to U.S.C. is preferred, it is not uncommon to find citations to the other codes: U.S.C.A. and U.S.C.S. (There is never a need, however, to cite more than one of the three codes.) The format is as follows:

29 U.S.C.A. § 169 (West 1983)

29 U.S.C.S. § 169 (LEXIS 1982)

In parentheses before the date, include the name of the publisher. Use the year that appears on the title page of the volume, or its latest copyright year, in this order of preference. If your statute is in one of the annual pocket parts of either of these two codes, include "Supp." and give the year of the pocket part—for example: (West Supp. 1998).

4.   There is one instance in which you *must* cite to the *United States Statutes at Large* (Stat.) rather than to U.S.C. The rule is as follows: Cite to the statute in Statutes at Large if (a) there is a difference in the language of the statute between Stat. and U.S.C. and (b) the statute in U.S.C. is in a title that has not been enacted into positive law by Congress.

It is highly unlikely that you will find a difference in language between Stat. and U.S.C. Yet the conscientious researcher must check this out before relying on any statutory language.

All the statutes in U.S.C. fall within one of fifty titles—for example, title 11 on Bankruptcy, title 39 on the Postal Service. If Congress goes through all the statutes in a particular title and formally declares that all of them are valid and accurate, then that title has been enacted into positive law. You can rely exclusively on the language of such statutes even if the language is different from the statute as it originally appeared in Statutes at Large. At the beginning of the first volume of U.S.C., you will be told which titles of the U.S.C. have been enacted into positive law.

   5.   A Statute at Large cite, when needed, should include:

- the name of the statute if one exists; if one does not exist, include "Act of" and give the full date of enactment—month, day, and year
- the **Public Law** (Pub. L.) number of the statute or its chapter number
- the section of the statute you are citing
- the volume number of the Statutes at Large used
- the abbreviation "Stat."
- the page number on which your statute is found in the Stat. volume
- in parentheses, the year the statute was enacted or passed by the legislature. Do not include the year, however, if you used the "Act of" option referred to in the first bullet.

   Narcotic Addict Rehabilitation Act, Pub. L. No. 80–793, § 9, 80 Stat. 1444 (1966)

Note again that the year in parentheses at the end of the cite is the year the statute was passed. Guideline 2 above said that you do not use the date of enactment when citing a statute in U.S.C. The rule is different when giving a Stat. cite.

   This example referred you to section number 9 of this Public Law (Pub. L.). The statute might also have several title numbers. If so, § 9 would be found within one of these titles. Assume, for example, that § 9 is in title III of the Public Law. It is important to remember that these section and title numbers are found in the original *session law* edition of the statute. When this statute is later printed in U.S.C. (assuming it is a public law of general interest), it will *not* go into § 9 of the third title. The U.S.C. has its own title and section number scheme. (For example, title III, § 9 of the above statute might be found in title 45, § 1075(b) of the U.S.C.) This can be very frustrating for the researcher new to the law. If you are reading a statute in its original session or Public Law form, you will not be able to find this statute under the same title and section number in U.S.C. You must translate the Public Law or Stat. cite into a U.S.C. cite. Phrased another way, you must translate the session law cite into a code cite. Later, we will see that this is done by using one of two tables: Table III in a special Tables volume of U.S.C./U.S.C.A./U.S.C.S., or Table 2 in *U.S. Code Congressional and Administrative News* (U.S.C.C.A.N.). See Research Link O.

   Rarely will you need to cite a session law when its codified cite is available. The latter is usually all that is needed. If, however, you need to cite a session law that has

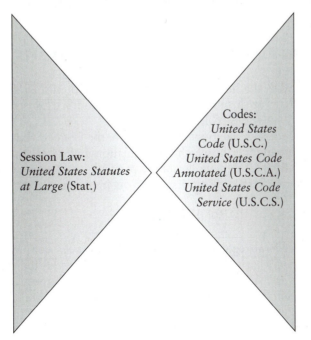

Session Law:
United States Statutes at Large (Stat.)

Codes:
United States Code (U.S.C.)
United States Code Annotated (U.S.C.A.)
United States Code Service (U.S.C.S.)

RESEARCH LINK O

If you have a federal statute with a Stat. (session law) cite and you want to read this statute in one of the three federal codes, you must find the code cite of your Stat. (session law) cite by checking:

- Table III in the tables volume of U.S.C./U.S.C.A./U.S.C.S., or
- Table 2 in U.S.C.C.A.N.

already been codified, let the reader know where it will found in the code, i.e., give both the session law *and* the codified cite.

Health Insurance Portability Act of 1996, Pub. L. No. 104-191, § 102, 110 Stat. 1936 (codified at 42 U.S.C.A. § 300gg (West Supp. 1997))

6. Of course, if the statute is a private law that is deemed to be of no general public interest, it will not be printed in the U.S.C. or the U.S.C.A. or the U.S.C.S. It will be found only in Statutes at Large (Stat.).

7. The Internal Revenue Code (I.R.C.) is within the United States Code (U.S.C.). Hence, to cite a tax statute, use the guidelines presented earlier on citing U.S.C./U.S.C.A./U.S.C.S.

26 U.S.C. § 1278 (1976)

There is, however, another option that is considered acceptable:

I.R.C. § 1278 (1976)

8. There is a special format for citing Federal Rules of Civil Procedure, Federal Rules of Criminal Procedure, Federal Rules of Appellate Procedure, and the Federal Rules of Evidence.

Fed. R. Civ. P. 15
Fed. R. Crim. P. 23
Fed. R. App. P. 3
Fed. R. Evid. 310

SECTION E   CITING STATE STATUTES

1. Like federal statutes, the statutes of the various states are compiled in two kinds of collections: state *codes* (arranged by subject matter) and *session laws* (arranged in chronological order of enactment).

2. Citations to state codes vary from state to state. Exhibit 5.3 shows examples of standard Bluebook citation formats. Use these as guides unless local rules of court dictate otherwise. The year at the end of the cite should be the year that appears on the spine of the volume, or the year that appears on the title page, or the latest copyright year—in this order of preference.

SECTION F   CITING ADMINISTRATIVE REGULATIONS AND DECISIONS

1. Federal administrative regulations are published in the *Federal Register* (Fed. Reg.). Many of these regulations are later codified by subject matter in the *Code of Federal Regulations* (C.F.R.).

2. Federal regulations that appear in the *Code of Federal Regulations* are cited to (a) the title number in which the regulation appears, (b) the abbreviated name of the code—C.F.R., (c) the number of the particular section to which you are referring, and (d) the date of the code edition that you are using.

29 C.F.R. § 102.60(a) (1975)

3. Federal regulations that have not yet been codified into the *Code of Federal Regulations* are cited to the *Federal Register* using (a) the volume in which the regulation appears, (b) the abbreviation "Fed. Reg.", (c) the page on which the regulation appears, and (d) the year of the *Federal Register* you are using.

27 Fed. Reg. 2092 (1962)

5.3

Exhibit
State Statutory Code
Citations

These examples of state statutory code citations comply with the Bluebook (local rules may require a different format).

Alabama:	Ala. Code § 37-10-3 (1977)
Alaska:	Alaska Stat. § 22.10.110 (Michie 1962)
Arizona:	Ariz. Rev. Stat. § 44-1621 (1956)
	Ariz. Rev. Stat. Ann. § 44-1621 (West 1956)
Arkansas:	Ark. Code Ann. § 20-316 (Michie 1968)
California:	Cal. Prob. Code § 585 (West 1956)
	Cal. Prob. Code § 585 (Deering 1956)
Colorado:	Colo. Rev. Stat. § 32-7-131 (1971)
	Colo. Rev. Stat. Ann. § 32-7-131 (West 1971)
Connecticut:	Conn. Gen. Stat. § 34-29 (1989)
	Conn. Gen. Stat. Ann. § 53a-135 (West 1972)
Delaware:	Del. Code Ann. tit. 18, § 2926 (1974)
District of Columbia:	D.C. Code Ann. § 16-2307 (1981)
Florida:	Fla. Stat. ch. 2.314 (1986)
	Fla. Stat. Ann. ch. 6.341 (Harrison 1985)
	Fla. Stat. Ann. § 1078 (West 1976)
Georgia:	Ga. Code Ann. § 110-118 (1973)
	Ga. Code Ann. § 22-1414 (Harrison 1977)
Hawaii:	Haw. Rev. Stat. § 431:19-107 (1988)
	Haw. Rev. Stat. Ann. § 431:19-107 (Michie 1988)
Idaho:	Idaho Code § 18-3615 (1987)
Illinois:	5 Ill. Comp. Stat. 100/5-80 (West 1993)
	5 Ill. Comp. Stat. Ann. 100/5-80 (West 1993)
Indiana:	Ind. Code § 9-8-1-13 (1976)
	Ind. Code Ann. § 9-8-1-13 (Michie 1983)
	Ind. Code Ann. § 9-8-1-13 (West 1979)
Iowa:	Iowa Code § 455.92 (1958)
	Iowa Code Ann. § 98.14 (West 1984)
Kansas:	Kan. Stat. Ann. § 38-1506 (1986)
	Kan. Corp. Code Ann. § 17-6303 (West 1995)
Kentucky:	Ky. Rev. Stat. Ann. § 208.060 (Banks-Baldwin 1988)
	Ky. Rev. Stat. Ann. § 44.072 (Michie 1986)
Louisiana:	La. Rev. Stat. Ann. § 15:452 (West 1981)
	La. Code Civ. Proc. Ann. art. 3132 (West 1961)
Maine:	Me. Rev. Stat. Ann. tit. 36, § 1760 (West 1964)
Maryland:	Md. Code Ann., Fam. Law § 7-106 (1984)
	Md. Ann. Code art. 78, § 70 (1957)
Massachusetts:	Mass. Gen. L. ch. 106, § 2-318 (1984)
	Mass. Gen. Laws Ann. ch. 156, § 37 (West 1970)
	Mass. Ann. Laws ch. 123, § 15 (Law. Co-op. 1988)
Michigan:	Mich. Comp. Laws § 550.1402 (1980)
	Mich. Comp. Laws Ann. § 211.27 (West 1986)
	Mich. Stat. Ann. § 28.1070 (Law. Co-op. 1987)
Minnesota:	Minn. Stat. § 336.1-101 (1988)
	Minn. Stat. Ann. § 104.08 (West 1987)
Mississippi:	Miss. Code Ann. § 19-13-57 (1972)
Missouri:	Mo. Rev. Stat. § 545.010 (1986)
	Mo. Ann. Stat. § 334.540 (West 1989)
Montana:	Mont. Code Ann. § 37-5-313 (1989)
	Mont. Rev. Code Ann. § 37-5-313 (Smith 1990)
Nebraska:	Neb. Rev. Stat. § 44-406 (1983)
	Neb. Rev. Stat. Ann. § 44-406 (Michie 1995)
Nevada:	Nev. Rev. Stat. § 463.150 (1987)
	Nev. Rev. Stat. Ann. § 679B.180 (Michie 1986)
New Hampshire:	N.H. Rev. Stat. Ann. § 318:25 (1984)
New Jersey:	N.J. Rev. Stat. § 40:62-127 (1961)
	N.J. Stat. Ann. § 14A:5-20 (West 1969)
New Mexico:	N.M. Stat. Ann. § 31-6-2 (Michie 1978)

Continued on next page

5.3

Exhibit
State Statutory Code
Citations—continued

New York:	N.Y. Penal Law § 155.05 (McKinney 1988)
	N.Y. Town Law § 265 (Consol. 1978)
North Carolina:	N.C. Gen. Stat. § 15A-1321 (1988)
North Dakota:	N.D. Cent. Code § 23-12-11 (1989)
Ohio:	Ohio Rev. Code Ann. § 2935.03 (Anderson 1987)
	Ohio Rev. Code Ann. § 2305.131 (Banks-Baldwin 1996)
Oklahoma:	Okla. Stat. tit. 42, § 130 (1979)
	Okla Stat. Ann. tit. 21, § 491 (West 1983)
Oregon:	Or. Rev. Stat. § 450.870 (1987)
Pennsylvania:	1 Pa. Cons. Stat. § 1991 (1972)
	18 Pa. Cons. Stat. Ann. § 3301 (West 1983)
	Pa. Stat. Ann. tit. 24, § 7-708 (West 1990)
Puerto Rico:	P.R. Laws Ann. tit. 7, § 299 (1985)
Rhode Island:	R.I. Gen. Laws § 34-1-2 (1956)
South Carolina:	S.C. Code Ann. § 16-23-10 (Law. Co-op. 1976)
South Dakota:	S.D. Codified Laws § 15-6-54(c) (Michie 1984)
Tennessee:	Tenn. Code Ann. § 33-1-204 (1984)
Texas:	Tex. Penal Code Ann. § 19.06 (West 1989)
	Tex. Rev. Civ. Stat. Ann. art. 5336 (West 1962)
Utah:	Utah Code Ann. § 41-3-8 (1953)
Vermont:	Vt. Stat. Ann. tit. 19, § 708 (1987)
Virginia:	Va. Code Ann. § 18.2-265.3 (Michie 1950)
Washington:	Wash. Rev. Code § 7.48A.010 (1987)
	Wash. Rev. Code Ann. § 11.17.110 (West 1967)
West Virginia:	W. Va. Code § 23-1-17 (1985)
Wisconsin:	Wis. Stat. § 52.28 (1967)
	Wis. Stat. Ann. § 341.55 (West 1971)
Wyoming:	Wyo. Stat. § 26-18-113 (1977)

4. Federal regulations are often divided into several parts in the *Federal Register*. If you are not citing the entire regulation, give the page in the *Federal Register* where the regulation begins *and* the page that contains the part to which you are referring.

27 Fed. Reg. 2092, 2094 (1962)

Often the *Federal Register* will tell you where in the *Code of Federal Regulations* a particular regulation will also be found. If so, tell the reader by giving both the Fed. Reg. cite and the codified cite.

58 Fed. Reg. 7185 (1996) (to be codified at 14 C.F.R. § 39.13)

5. On citing administrative decisions, see Example G at the beginning of this chapter.

SECTION G   CITING THE DOCUMENTS OF LEGISLATIVE HISTORY

1. **Legislative history** consists of all the events that occur in the legislature before a bill is enacted into law (page 216). The main documents of legislative history are bills, reports and hearings of congressional committees, transcripts of floor debates, etc.

2. Bills are cited by reference to (a) the number assigned to the bill by the House of Representatives or Senate, (b) the number of the Congress during which the bill was introduced, and the year of the bill.

H.R. 3055, 94th Cong. (1976)
S. 1422, 101st Cong. (1989)

3.   Reports of congressional committees are cited by reference to (a) the abbreviation of the House (H.) or Senate (S.) where the report was written, (b) the number of the Congress and the number of the report connected by a hyphen, (c) the page number of the report to which you are referring, and (d) the year in which the report was published. If the report is also printed in the set of books called *United States Code Congressional and Administrative News* (U.S.C.C.A.N.), include the volume number of U.S.C.C.A.N. (which will be a year), the page number in U.S.C.C.A.N. where the report begins, and the specific page number of the report to which you are referring.

H.R. Rep. No. 92-238, at 4 (1979)
S. Rep. No. 92-415, at 6 (1971), *reprinted in* 1971 U.S.C.C.A.N. 647, 682

4.   Hearings held by congressional committees are cited by reference to (a) the title of the hearing, (b) the number of the Congress during which the hearing was held, (c) the number of the page in the published transcript to which you are referring, and (d) the year in which the hearing was held.

Hearings on S. 631 Before the Subcomm. on Labor of the Senate Comm. on Labor and Public Welfare, 92d Cong. 315 (1971)

5.   The *Congressional Record* is issued on a daily basis and later collected into bound volumes. The *bound* volumes are cited by referring to (a) the number of the volume in which the item appears, (b) the abbreviation Cong. Rec., (c) the number of the page on which the item appears, and (d) the year. The *daily* volumes are cited in the same manner except that (a) the page number should be preceded by the letter "H" or "S" to indicate whether the item appeared in the House pages or the Senate pages of the volume, (b) the date should include the exact day, month, and year, and (c) the phrase "daily ed." should go before the date.

Bound volumes:
103 Cong. Rec. 2889 (1975)
Daily volumes:
122 Cong. Rec. S2395 (daily ed. Feb. 26, 1976)
132 Cong. Rec. H1385 (daily ed. Mar. 13, 1990)

SECTION H   CITING SECONDARY AUTHORITY

1.   Legal *treatises* are cited to (a) the number of the volume being referred to (if part of a set), (b) the full name of the author, (c) the full title of the book as it appears on the title page, (d) the number of the section or page to which you are referring, (e) the edition of the book, if other than the first, and (f) the date of publication. The title of the book should be italicized or underscored. The name of the publisher is almost never given.

6 Melvin M. Belli, *Modern Trials* § 289 (1963)
George Osborne, *Handbook on the Law of Mortgages* 370 (2d ed. 1970)

2.   Legal periodical *articles* are cited by reference to (a) the full name of the author, (b) the title of the article, (c) the number of the volume in which the article appears, (d) the abbreviated name of the legal periodical, (e) the number of the page on which the article begins, and (f) the year of publication. The title of the article should be italicized or underscored.

Robert Catz & Susan Robinson, *Due Process and Creditor's Remedies,* 28 Rutgers L. Rev. 541 (1975)
William P. Statsky, *The Education of Legal Paraprofessionals: Myths, Realities, and Opportunities,* 24 Vand. L. Rev. 1083 (1971)

If you are referring to material on a specific page in an article, you need to add a pinpoint cite that will give the page number containing that material. The page number you are pinpointing goes immediately after the page number on which the article begins. Suppose, for example, that you were quoting from page 550 of the above Rutgers Law Review article. The cite would be:

> Robert Catz & Susan Robinson, *Due Process and Creditor's Remedies,* 28 Rutgers L. Rev. 541, 550 (1975)

3. Legal periodical *notes* and *comments* written by law students are cited in the same manner as articles (see guideline 2) except that the word *Note, Comment,* or *Special Project* is placed after the author's name just before the title.

4. Legal *encyclopedias* are cited by reference to (a) the number of the volume, (b) the abbreviated name of the encyclopedia, (c) the subject heading to which you are referring—in italics or underscored, (d) the number of the section to which you are referring, and (e) the date of publication of the volume you are citing.

> 83 C.J.S. *Subscriptions* § 3 (1953)
> 77 Am. Jur. 2d *Vendor and Purchaser* § 73 (1975)

5. *Restatements of the Law* published by the American Law Institute are cited by reference to (a) the title of the Restatement, (b) the edition being referred to (if other than the first edition), (c) the number of the section being referred to, and (d) the date of publication.

> *Restatement (Second) of Agency* § 37 (1957)

6. Annotations in A.L.R., A.L.R.2d, A.L.R.3d, A.L.R.4th, A.L.R.5th, and A.L.R. Fed. are cited by (a) the full name of the author, if available, (b) the word, "Annotation," (c) the title of the annotation—in italics or underscored, (d) the volume number, (e) the abbreviation of the A.L.R. unit, (f) the page number where the annotation begins, and (g) the date of the volume.

> James J. Watson, Annotation, *Attorney's Fees: Cost of Services Provided by Paralegals or the Like as Compensable Element in Award in State Court,* 73 A.L.R.4th 938 (1989)

SECTION I   CITING INTERNET SOURCES

The **Internet** is a self-governing network of networks to which millions of computer users all over the world have access. The Bluebook discourages citation of material on the Internet unless the material is unavailable elsewhere in more traditional formats. Given the rapidly changing nature of the Internet, what you cite today may be unavailable tomorrow. When you do want to cite something on the Internet, provide (a) the name of the author, if given; (b) the title or top-level heading of the material you are citing; (c) the date of publication or the last modification date, or (if neither is available) the date you visited the site; and (d) the Uniform Resource Locator (URL) placed in angled brackets (< >). The URL is the electronic address of material on the Internet.

> National Federation of Paralegal Associations, *Informal Ethics and Disciplinary Opinion No. 96-2* (visited July 19, 1997) <http://www.paralegals.org/ Development/ethics96-2.html>

For an outstanding citation guide on the Internet, see Peter W. Martin, *Introduction to Basic Legal Citation* (visited May 6, 1998) <http://www.law.cornell.edu/citation/ citation.table.html>.

Assignment 5.2

Each of the following citations has one or more things wrong with it. Describe the errors and gaps in format. For example, a parallel cite is missing or something is abbreviated incorrectly. You do not have to go to the library to check any of these cites. Simply use the guidelines presented above.

(a) *Smith v. Jones,* 135 Mass. 37, 67 N.E. 2d 316, 320 (1954). First assume that you are citing this case in a motion submitted to a state trial court in Massachusetts. Then assume that you are citing it in a memorandum submitted to the United States District Court sitting in Boston.

(b) *Paul Matthews v. Edward Foley, Inc.,* 779 F. 2d 729 (W.D.N.Y., 1979). First assume that you are citing this case in a motion submitted to the United States District Court sitting in Manhattan. Then assume that you are citing it in an appellate brief submitted to the highest state court in New York.

(c) *Jackson v. Jackson,* 219 F.Supp. 1276, 37 N.E. 2d 84 (1980). First assume that you are citing this case in a motion submitted to a state trial court in California. Then assume that you are citing it in a law review article.

(d) *Davis v. Thompson, et al,* 336 P. 2d 691, 210 N.M. 432 (1976). First assume that you are citing this case in a motion submitted to a state appellate court in Florida. Then assume that you are citing it in an appellate brief submitted to the New Mexico Supreme Court.

(e) *Washington Tire Company v. Jones,* 36 N.J.Super. 222, 351 A. 2d 541 (1976). First assume that you are citing this case in a news story for a paralegal newsletter published by a New Jersey paralegal association. Then assume that you are citing it in a memorandum submitted to the New Jersey Supreme Court.

(f) *State of New Hampshire v. Atkinson,* 117 N.H. 830, 228 A. 2d 222 (N.H.Super., 1978). First assume that you are citing this case in an appellate brief submitted to the New Hampshire Supreme Court. Then assume that you are citing it in an appellate brief submitted to the Ohio Supreme Court.

(g) *Richardson v. U.S.,* 229 U.S. 220 (1975).

(h) American Law Institute, *Restatement of Torts* (2d ed 1976).

(i) U.S.Const. Art. III (1797).

(j) Smith, F., Products Liability (3rd ed. 1985).

(k) 42 USC 288 (1970).

(l) 17 U.S.C.A. 519 (1970).

(m) 40 Fed. Reg. § 277 (1976).

Assignment 5.3

(a) For your state, check the state code and rules of court of the highest state court in the state to find out whether any special citation rules must be followed in documents submitted to the courts. If so, redo Assignment 5.2 by stating which, if any, of the citations in (a) to (m) would have to be changed to conform to these special citation rules, and how.

(b) Find any court opinion written by the highest state court in your state. Locate this opinion by using the regional reporter for your state. (See Exhibits 3.2 and 3.3.) Pick an opinion that is at least ten pages long.

   (i)   Write down every citation in this opinion (up to a maximum of twenty-five).

   (ii) State whether these citations conform to the Bluebook citation rules outlined in chapter 5. Point out any differences.

   (iii) State whether these citations conform to the special citation rules, if any, you identified in answering question (a) above. Point out any differences.

SECTION J   ALTERNATE CITATION AUTHORITY?

For years, many have criticized *The Bluebook: A Uniform System of Citation*. People find its citation rules too arbitrary and the book itself difficult to use. In 1989, a major challenger to the Bluebook appeared: *The University of Chicago Manual of Legal Citation,* also known as the **Maroon Book** because of the color of its cover. Whereas the Bluebook tries to include citation rules for almost every situation, the Maroon Book adopts a substantially different point of view. Because "it is neither possible nor desirable to write a particular rule for every sort of citation problem that might arise," the citation rules in the Maroon Book "leave a fair amount of discretion to practitioners, authors, and editors." To a devotee of the Bluebook, such discretion is very distasteful. It is too early to tell what impact the Maroon Book will have on the world of citation. Because the Bluebook is so firmly entrenched, it is unlikely that a competitor will replace it any time soon.

SECTION K   CITE CHECKING

When an assignment involves **cite checking,** you are given a document written by someone else and asked to check the citations provided by the author of the document. The assignment is quite common in law firms, particularly when the document to be checked is an appellate brief. Students on law review in law school also do extensive cite checking on the work of fellow students and outside authors.

Although our focus in this section will be cite checking documents written by others, the guidelines discussed here are in large measure equally applicable to your own writing. (Subjecting what you have written to your own criticism and review is what is known as **self-editing.**)

Guidelines for Cite Checking

The first step is to obtain clear instructions from your supervisor on the scope of the assignment. Should you do a "light check" or a comprehensive one? Should you focus solely on citation form, or should you determine the accuracy of all quotes used by the writer of the document? On citation form, what rules should you use? The Bluebook?

The following guidelines assume that you have been asked to undertake a comprehensive check.

    1.   Make sure that you have a *copy* of the document on which you can make comments. Avoid using the original.

    2.   If the pages of the document already have pencil or pen markings made by others (or by the author who made last-minute insertions), use a pencil or pen that is a different color from all other markings on the pages. In this way it will be clear to any reader which corrections, notations, or other comments are your own. If you find that you do not have enough room to write in the margins of the pages, use separate sheets of paper. You can increase the size of the margins by photocopying the document on a machine that will reduce the size of what is copied.

    3.   If the document will be submitted to a court, be sure that you are using the official citation rules, if any, that must be followed for all citations in documents submitted to that court. If official citation rules do not exist, find out what rules or guidelines on citation format the supervisor wants you to use. The Bluebook?

    4.   Before you begin, try to find a model. By going through the old case files of the office, you may be able to locate a prior document, such as an old appellate brief, that you can use as a general guide. Ask your supervisor to direct you to such a document. Although it may not cover all the difficulties you will encounter in your own document, you will at least have a general guide approved by your supervisor.

    5.   Check the citation form of *every* cite in the document written by the author of that document. This includes any cites in the body of the text, the footnotes, the appendix material, and the introductory pages of the document, such as the Table of Authorities (page 311) at the beginning of a brief. (A **table of authorities** is a list of the primary and secondary authority the writer is using in an appellate brief or other document. The table will usually indicate on what page(s) in the document each authority is discussed or mentioned.)

6. For longer documents, you need to develop your own system for ensuring the completeness of your checking. For example, you might want to circle every cite that you have checked and found to be accurate, and place a small box around (or a question mark next to) every cite that is giving you difficulties. You will want to spend more time with the latter, seeking help from colleagues and your supervisor.

7. When you find errors in the form of the citation, make the corrections in the margin of the pages where they are found.

8. For some errors, you will not be able to make the corrections without obtaining additional information, such as a missing date or a missing parallel cite. If you can obtain this data by going to the relevant library books (or available online resources), do so. Otherwise make a notation in the margin of what is missing or what still needs correction.

9. Consistency in citation format is extremely important. On page 2 of the document, for example, the author may use one citation format, but on page 10, he or she may use a completely different format for the same kind of legal material. You need to point out this inconsistency and make the consistency corrections that are called for.

10. Often your document will quote from opinions, statutes, or other legal materials. Check the accuracy of these quotations. Go to the material being quoted, find the quote, and check it against the document line by line, word by word, and punctuation mark by punctuation mark. Be scrupulous about the accuracy of quotations.

11. Shepardize anything that can be shepardized, such as opinions and statutes. Here are some examples of what you need to determine through shepardizing:

- Whether any of the cited opinions have been overruled or reversed
- Whether any of the cited statutes have been repealed or amended by the legislature, or have been invalidated by a court

12. Check the accuracy of all **supra** references.

The word *supra* means "above" or "earlier." It refers to something already mentioned (and cited) in the document you are cite checking. For example, assume that footnote 8 on page 23 of the document contains the following cite:

[8]Robert G. Danna, *Family Law* 119 (1992).

The particular reference is to page 119 of Danna's book. Now assume that ten pages later—in footnote 17—the document again refers to Danna's book, this time to page 35. A full citation to this page would be as follows:

[17]Robert G. Danna, *Family Law* 35 (1992).

But a full citation is not needed. You can use a *short form citation*. This is an abbreviated citation of an authority that you use after you have already given a full citation of that authority earlier in the document. For the short form citation of a legal treatise such as the Danna *Family Law* book, use the author's last name followed by the *supra* reference:

[17]Danna, *supra* note 8 at 35.

This means that the full cite of Danna's book was already given earlier *(supra)* in the document in footnote 8. There is no need to repeat the full cite. The cite checker must simply go to footnote 8 and make sure that the full cite of the book is provided there.

Finally, assume that Danna's book was cited in full in the body of the text of the document rather than in a footnote. A later footnote reference to the same book would be as follows:

[17]Danna, *supra,* at 35.

The accuracy of this reference is checked in the same way: make sure that the full cite of Danna's book is in fact provided earlier in the body of the document.

Infra means "below" or "later" and refers to something that will come later in the document. In the same manner as you checked the *supra* references, you must determine whether the *infra* references are accurate.

13.   Check the accuracy of all of short form case citations.

Assume that the document you are cite checking gives the following reference early in the document:

Sierra Club v. Sigler, 695 F.2d 957, 980 (5th Cir. 1983).

The cite is to page 980 of the *Sierra Club* case, which begins on page 957 of the *Federal Reporter,* Second Series. Now assume that the author wants to refer to page 962 of the same case later in the document. Generally, there is no need to repeat the entire citation. The following short form may be used:

Sierra Club, 695 F.2d at 962.

To check the accuracy of this cite, you must go back in the document to make sure that *Sierra Club* has already been cited in full.

Do not, however, use *supra* when you are citing court opinions. *Supra* can be used for many items, such as legal treatises and legal periodicals. With rare exceptions, however, do not use it in citations to court opinions. When you wish to avoid repeating the full citation of an opinion, use the short form case citation just discussed.

14.   All **id.** references should also be checked. *Id.* means the same as something previously mentioned. Use *id.* when you are citing an authority that is also the *immediately preceding* authority cited in a footnote. (*Id.* is more specific than *supra;* the latter means above or earlier. *Id.,* however, means *immediately* above.) Assume, for example, that footnote 21 in the appellate brief you are cite checking says:

²¹*Kohler v. Tugwell,* 292 F. Supp. 978 (E.D. La. 1968).

And footnote 22 says:

²²*Id.* at 985.

The *Id.* reference means that here in footnote 22 you are referring to the immediately preceding authority—the *Kohler* opinion in footnote 21.

Be careful about *id.* references. A writer cannot use *id.* if more than one authority is cited in the preceding footnote. Suppose, for example, that footnote 21 cited *Kohler* and another opinion:

²¹*Smith v. Harris,* 260 F.2d 601 (2d Cir. 1956); *Kohler v. Tugwell,* 292 F. Supp. 978 (E.D. La. 1968).

If footnote 22 wanted to cite *Tugwell,* you could not use *id.* because there is more than one authority in footnote 21. Footnote 22 should use the short form citation as follows:

²²*Tugwell,* 292 F. Supp. at 985.

Cite-Checking Software

Computer companies have developed two kinds of cite-checking software. First, there is *format* software that tells you whether a particular citation conforms to *The Bluebook: A Uniform System of Citation.* The developers placed the entire Bluebook into the program so that it can recognize discrepancies between the rules of the Bluebook and citations that are typed into the computer. In addition to pointing out citation errors, the program will refer you to specific rules in the Bluebook that have been violated. Two examples of such software are The Electronic Bluebook and CiteRite. The second kind of cite-checking software provides *validation* data on citations. You will be told, for example, whether a particular court opinion has been overruled and whether a particular statute has been repealed. Two examples of such software are WESTcheck, used in conjunction with WESTLAW, and CheckCite, used in conjunction with LEXIS. Unlike the format cite-checking software, the validation programs are online and hence are used through a modem.

Assignment 5.4

In Appendix C you will find the opinion of *Brown v. Hammond* by Judge Waldman. Assume that the opinion in Appendix C is only the first draft of the opinion. After writing it, Judge Waldman hands it to you and asks you to cite check it. Make sure all the citations are in Bluebook form according to the guidelines presented in this chapter. Check the accuracy of every quote. Check other references as well. If, for example, the text cites an opinion and summarizes what is in the opinion, check whether the summary is accurate. If you cannot check some of the cites, point out why (e.g., the library you are using does not have whatever you need to check a particular cite).

CHAPTER SUMMARY

A citation or a cite is an "address" where an opinion, a statute, a treatise, or other authority can be found in a library. Unfortunately, people are often inconsistent in the way they cite material. For some courts there are official citation rules that must be followed in all documents submitted to those courts. When this is not so, the bible of proper citation form is the The Bluebook: A Uniform System of Citation. Supervisors often—but by no means always—instruct all of their employees to follow the Bluebook.

Because there is a great variety of primary and secondary authority that can be cited, there are a great many rules on what constitutes proper citation form. Our focus in this chapter is on the essentials.

When citing cases, four of the essential concerns are parallel cites, names of the court, abbreviations, and spaces. Here are some of the major citation questions that you must ask yourself: [1] When do you include available parallel cites? (For example, do you include the cite to the regional reporter?) [2] When do you include the name of the court in the parentheses before the date? (For example, do you include the name of the court for cases in F.3d?) [3] What should and should not be abbreviated in the cite? (For example, do you abbreviate "United States" when the federal government is a party? Is "Wisconsin" abbreviated "Wis." or "WS"?) [4] Where should you include spaces in the cite? (For example, is the Federal Supplement abbreviated "F.Supp." or "F. Supp."?)

The future of traditional case citations is in doubt. Some courts are moving toward a generic citation system. Because this system will number every paragraph, it can be vendor-neutral.

When citing statutes, four of the essential concerns are code, date, abbreviations, and spaces. Here are some of the major citation questions that you must ask yourself: [1] Which code do you cite? (For example, when do you cite the statute in U.S.C. as opposed to U.S.C.A. or U.S.C.S.?) [2] What date do you use? (For example, do you provide the date the statute was passed by the legislature or the date of the edition of the code you are using?) [3] What should and should not be abbreviated in the cite? (For example, is "Public Law" abbreviated "PL" or "Pub. L."?) [4] Where should you include spaces in the cite? (For example, when you want to cite section 23, do you say "§ 23" or "§23"?)

Cite checking a document can involve four tasks: First, identify and correct inaccuracies in citation form according to official citation rules, the Bluebook, or other citation system required by a supervisor. Second, shepardize (or use another citator) to be sure that cited cases have not been overruled or cited statutes have not been repealed. Third, check the accuracy of every quotation against the original source, word for word, punctuation mark by punctuation mark. Fourth, check the accuracy of every authority cited more than once in the document through supra, infra, and id. references, and check all short form citations.

KEY TERMS

citation	consolidated litigation	pinpoint cite	Maroon Book
cite	et al.	generic citation	cite checking
Bluebook	litigation status	electronic citation	self-editing
short form citation	*In re*	public domain citation	table of authorities
parallel cites	docket number	star paging	supra
same case on appeal	subsequent history	session laws	infra
caption (of opinion)	history of the case	popular name	id.
shepardize	treatment of the case	Public Law	
official reporter	writ of certiorari	legislative history	
unofficial reporter	nominative reporters	Internet	

COMPONENTS OF MANY LAW BOOKS

➤ *Chapter Outline*

SECTION A   INTRODUCTION

Before we begin our examination of the structure of law books, review Section B in chapter 3 on the variety of legal research media in existence: paper volumes, online services, CD-ROM, and microform. Here in chapter 6, our primary focus is on the structure of paper products on the shelves of law libraries: pamphlets, hardcover books, and looseleaf texts.

SECTION B   COMPONENTS

Many law books are similar in structure. To be sure, some books, such as *Shepard's Citations,* are unique. In the main, however, the texts follow a pattern. The following components are contained in many.

Outside Cover

On the outside cover, you will find the title of the book, the author(s) or editor(s), the name of the publisher (usually at the bottom), the edition of the book (if more than one edition has been printed), and the volume number (if the book is part of a set or series of books). After glancing at the outside cover, you should ask yourself the following questions:

- Is it a book *containing* law (written primarily by a court, a legislature, or an administrative agency), or is it a book *about* the law (written by a scholar who is commenting on the law)? Is the book a combination of both? (See the four categories of legal materials by function in Exhibit 2.3 in chapter 2.)
- Is this book the most current available? Look at the books on the shelf in the area where you found the book that you are examining. Is there a replacement volume for your book? Is there a later edition of the book? Check your book in the card or computer catalog to see if other editions are mentioned.

Publisher's Page

The first few pages of the book often include a **publisher's page** containing information about the publisher. The page may list other law books published by the same company.

Title Page

The **title page** repeats most of the information contained on the outside cover: title, author, editor, publisher. It also contains the date of publication.

Copyright Page

The **copyright page** (often immediately after the title page) has a copyright mark © plus a date or several dates. The most recent date listed indicates the timeliness of the material in the volume. Given the great flux in the law, it is very important to determine how old the text is. If the book has a pocket part (see below), it has been updated to the date on the pocket part.

COPYRIGHT © 1979, 1983, 1989, 1994 WEST PUBLISHING CO.

COPYRIGHT © 1998

By

WEST PUBLISHING CO.

The dates on this copyright page indicate that the material in the book is current up to 1998, the latest copyright date. Caution, however, is needed in reaching this conclusion. Publishers like to have their books appear to be as current as possible. A book with a 1998 copyright date may in fact have been published *at the beginning* of 1998 or *at the very end* of 1997! A 1998 date does not necessarily mean that you are current up to December of that year. We will return to this concern later when we discuss pocket parts.

Foreword or Preface

Within the **foreword** or **preface**, you may find some basic information about the book, particularly material on how the book was prepared and guidance on how to use it.

Summary Table of Contents

On one or two pages, you may find the main topics treated in the book.

Detailed Table of Contents

When provided, the detailed **table of contents** can be very extensive. The major headings of the summary table of contents are repeated, and detailed subheadings and sub-subheadings are listed. Use this table as an additional index to the book.

Table of Cases

The **table of cases** lists, alphabetically, every case that is printed or referred to in the text, with page(s) or section(s) where the case is found or discussed. This table is sometimes printed at the end of the book.

Table of Statutes

The **table of statutes** gives the page numbers where every statute is interpreted or referred to in the text. This table is sometimes printed at the end of the book.

List of Abbreviations

The abbreviation list, if provided, is critical. A reader who is unfamiliar with law books should check this list immediately. It may be the only place in the book that spells out the abbreviations used in the body of the text. In *Shepard's Citations*, for example, abbreviations are found in the first few pages of the bound volumes and in most of its pamphlets.

Example of abbreviations
used by Shepard's

History of Case		
a	(affirmed)	Same case affirmed on appeal.
cc	(connected case)	Different case from case cited but arising out of same subject matter or intimately connected therewith.
D	(dismissed)	Appeal from same case dismissed.
m	(modified)	Same case modified on appeal.
r	(reversed)	Same case reversed on appeal.
s	(same case)	Same case as case cited.
S	(superseded)	Substitution for former opinion.
v	(vacated)	Same case vacated.
US cert den		Certiorari denied by U. S. Supreme Court.
US cert dis		Certiorari dismissed by U. S. Supreme Court.
US reh den		Rehearing denied by U. S. Supreme Court.
US reh dis		Rehearing dismissed by U. S. Supreme Court.
Treatment of Case		
c	(criticised)	Soundness of decision or reasoning in cited case criticised for reasons given.
d	(distinguished)	Case at bar different either in law or fact from case cited for reasons given.
e	(explained)	Statement of import of decisions in cited case. Not merely a restatement of the facts.
f	(followed)	Cited as controlling
h	(harmonized)	Apparent inconsistency explained and shown not to exist.
j	(dissenting opinion)	Citation in dissenting opinion.
L	(limited)	Refusal to extend decision of cited case beyond precise issues involved.
o	(overruled)	Ruling in cited case expressly overruled.
p	(parallel)	Citing case substantially alike or on all fours with cited case in its law or facts.
q	(questioned)	Soundness of decision or reasoning in cited case questioned.

Statutory History Table

Some texts, particularly statutory codes, may include a **statutory history table** that lists every statute cited in the book and indicates whether it has been repealed or whether it has a new section number and title. The legislature may have changed the entire name of the statutory chapter (from Prison Law to Correction Law, for instance) and renumbered all the sections. Without this table, the researcher can become lost. In the example below, note that former Prison Law sections 10–20 are now found in Correction Law sections 600–610. You may find a citation to a Prison Law section in a book that was published before the state changed to Correction Law sections. When you go to look up the Prison Law section, you will find nothing unless you have a way to translate the section into a Correction Law section. The statutory history table will be one way to do it.

TABLE OF PRISON LAW SECTIONS

Showing the distribution of those sections of the former Prison Law in effect prior to the general amendment by L.1929, c. 243, which are contained wholly or in part in the Correction Law, or which have been omitted or repealed.

Prison Law Section	Correction Law Section
1	1
10–20	600–610
21	Repealed
22 L.1919, c. 12	611
22 L.1920, c. 933	612
23–32	613–622
40–50	40–50

Example of a statutory history table

Body of the Text

The fundamental characteristic of the body of many legal texts is that it is arranged according to units such as parts, subparts, divisions, subdivisions, chapters, subchapters, sections, subsections, etc. Often each unit covers a similar subject matter and is numbered or lettered in sequence. You should thumb through the entire book to obtain a feel for the numbering and classification system used by the author or editor.

Footnotes

Footnotes are very important in law books; researchers place great emphasis on them. They often give extensive citations to cases and other cross-references, and hence can be an excellent lead to additional law.

Pocket Parts and Other Updating Features

A unique and indispensable feature of many law books is the **pocket part.** It is a small booklet addition to the text, usually placed at the very end of the text in a specially devised pocket built into the inside of the rear cover. (See photo on page 65.) The pocket part is published after the book is printed and is designed to bring the book up-to-date with the latest developments in the field covered by the book. Of course, a pocket part can also grow out of date. Normally, it is replaced once a year. On the front cover of the pocket-part booklet, there is a date telling you what period is covered. The title page (see above) may say that the last edition of the book was published in 1990, but the front page of the pocket part may say "for use during 1998–1999." Again, however, use caution in interpreting these dates. The publisher may have prepared this pocket part at the end of 1997 or at the beginning of 1998. You cannot assume that the material in the pocket part is current up to December of 1999.

Normally, the organization of the pocket part exactly parallels the organization of the main text. For example, to find out if there has been anything new in the area covered by chapter 7, part 2, section 714 of the main text, you go to chapter 7, part 2, section 714 of the pocket part. If you find nothing there, then nothing new has happened. If changes or additions have occurred, they will be found there. The changes may appear in different formats. <u>All new text might appear underlined.</u> ~~All old text might appear with a strikeout line through it.~~ Or, you may be able to assume that any text that appears in the pocket part is new text.

Pocket parts are **cumulative** in that, whenever a pocket part is replaced by another pocket part, everything in the early pocket part is consolidated into the most recent one. The earlier pocket part is thrown away. *Cumulative* means that the most recent volume or issue contains all the material in the prior volumes or issues and consolidates this older material with new material.

Not all law books have pocket parts. For an overview, see Exhibit 6.1.

How is new material added to law books without pocket parts—the ones listed in the second column of Exhibit 6.1? Shepard's is kept current by advance sheets (p. 36) and supplemental pamphlets; the American Digest System by adding *General Digest* volumes, which are thrown away when the next *Decennial Digest* is published; looseleaf services by inserting pages with new material into the binders and removing pages with outdated material (a process called **interfiling**). For the other items in the second column of Exhibit 6.1—West reporters, session laws, etc.—new material is added simply by adding new volumes or issues.

Some sets of books use a variety of methods to bring them up to date: pocket parts, supplement pamphlets, supplement volumes, reissued volumes, revised volumes, etc.

Appendix

The text may include one or more **appendixes** at the end. Normally, they include tables, charts, or the entire text of statutes or regulations, portions of which are discussed in the body of the book.

Glossary

The book may include a **glossary**, which is a dictionary that defines a selected number of words used in the body of the book.

Bibliography

A brief or extended **bibliography** of the field covered by the book may be included at the end of each chapter or at the end of the book.

6.1

Exhibit
Pocket Parts

Law Books That Always or Often Have Pocket Parts:	Law Books That Never Have Pocket Parts:
• State statutory codes (e.g., *Georgia Code Annotated*)	• Shepard's (e.g., *Shepard's Federal Citations*)
• Unofficial federal codes (e.g., *U.S.C.A.* and *U.S.C.S.*)	• American Digest System (*Century Digest, Decennial Digests,* and *General Digests*)
• Annotated reporters (e.g., *A.L.R.5th*)	• Looseleaf services (e.g., *United States Law Week*)
• Legal encyclopedias (e.g., *C.J.S.* and *Am. Jur. 2d*)	• West Reporters (e.g., regional reporters, S. Ct., F.3d, F. Supp.)
• State digests (e.g., *Illinois Digest 2d*)	• Session laws (e.g., *United States Statutes at Large*)
• Regional digests (e.g., *Pacific Digest*)	• Legal periodicals (e.g., *Boston College Law Review*)
• Federal digests (e.g., *Federal Practice Digest 4th*)	• Legal newspapers (e.g., *San Francisco Daily Journal*)
• Legal treatises written for practitioners (e.g., C.Z. Nothstein, *Toxic Torts*)	• Legal newsletters (e.g., *The Guardian*)

Index

The **index** is a critical part of the book. Unfortunately, some books either have no index or do a sloppy job of indexing. The index is arranged alphabetically and should refer the reader to the page number(s) or to the section number(s) where topics are treated in the body of the text. The index is found at the end of the book. If there are many volumes in the set, you may find more than one index. For example, there may be a **general index** for the entire set and a series of smaller indexes covering individual volumes.

 Assignment 6.1

Compare the features that are similar and dissimilar among the following four law books. Be specific in your comparison. For example, don't just say which books have an index. After you point this out, indicate the differences among the indexes in the books that have them. Be sure to identify each volume that you use.

(a) A recent bound volume of the regional reporter that contains state court opinions of your state (see Exhibit 3.2 in chapter 3).

(b) Any bound volume of the state digest that covers state court opinions of your state (see Exhibit 3.3 in chapter 3).

(c) Any recent bound volume of *Shepard's Citations* that covers state court opinions of your state.

(d) Any bound volume of the statutory code of your state (see Exhibit 5.3 in chapter 5).

K EY TERMS

publisher's page	table of contents	cumulative	index
title page	table of cases	interfiling	general index
copyright page	table of statutes	appendix	
foreword	statutory history table	glossary	
preface	pocket part	bibliography	

Chapter 7

THE CARTWHEEL AND OTHER INDEX SEARCH SYSTEMS

Chapter Outline

SECTION A   INTRODUCTION

In chapter 8 we will identify some of the law books you can use to begin your legal research. Before we get to this chapter, however, we need to cover a more urgent skill that you will need before picking up any law book or approaching any legal materials. That skill is identification of search terms through the technique we have called the CARTWHEEL. Professor Roy Steele, a veteran teacher of legal research, made the following observations about new students:

> I think it is important for students to understand that they cannot just walk into a library and start pulling books off the shelf. That is the quickest way to become frustrated. Legal research requires thoughtful planning. A student must determine which resources will be checked. It is not enough that a student knows [that] a certain resource has an index or table of contents. The student must know what he/she is looking for. This requires the student to develop a list of search terms. Some people would call the development of this list *brainstorming*. However, brainstorming is somewhat hit or miss; it lacks structure and organization. The CARTWHEEL is one of the most effective ways of systematically developing a list of search terms. [It is] a method of analyzing a legal problem and developing a list of descriptive words, which can be used to search indexes.

SECTION B   THE CARTWHEEL

The major sets of law books that contain indexes are digests, statutory codes, administrative codes, legal encyclopedias, and legal treatises. Some sets of law books have more than one index. Many statutory codes and legal encyclopedias, for example, have a general index at the end of the set as well as individual indexes that cover specific volumes or units of the set. In addition, some sets of books consist entirely of index material. The major examples are the *Index to Legal Periodicals and Books* (ILP) and the *Current Law Index* (CLI), both of which are multivolume sets of books that index the hundreds of legal periodicals in existence.

Most people think that using an index is a relatively easy task—until they start trying to use indexes of law books! These indexes are often poorly written because they are not comprehensive. To be comprehensive, an index might have to be as long as the text it is indexing. Hence, publishers are reluctant to include such indexes.

Because of this reality, one of the most important skills in legal research is the creative use of indexes in law books. When you master this skill, 70 percent of the research battle is won. The **CARTWHEEL** is a word-association technique designed to assist you in acquiring the skill. (See Exhibit 7.1.)

The objective of the CARTWHEEL can be simply stated: to develop the habit of phrasing every word involved in the client's problem *fifteen to twenty different ways!* When you go to the index (or to the table of contents[1]) of a law book, you naturally begin looking up the words and phrases that you think should lead you to the relevant material in the book. If you do not find anything relevant to your problem, two conclusions are possible:

- There is nothing relevant in the law book.
- You looked up the wrong words in the index and table of contents.

Although the first conclusion is sometimes accurate, nine times out of ten the second conclusion is the reason you failed to find material that is relevant to the client's problem. The solution is to be able to phrase a word in as many different ways and in as many different contexts as possible. Hence, the CARTWHEEL.

---

1. See chapter 6 on the distinction between a summary table of contents and a detailed table of contents.

7.1 ....   The CARTWHEEL: Using the Index of Law Books

Exhibit

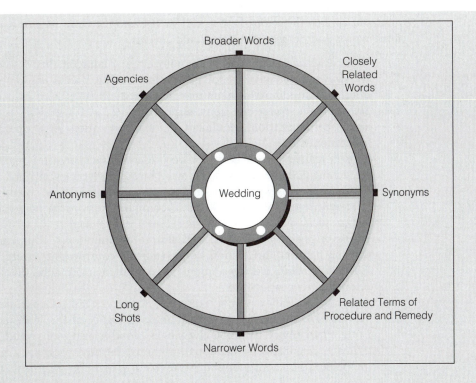

1. Identify all the *major words* from the facts of the client's problem, e.g., wedding (most of these facts can be obtained from the intake memorandum written following the initial interview with the client). Place each word or small set of words in the center of the CARTWHEEL.
2. In the index, look up all of these words.
3. Identify the *broader categories* of the major words.
4. In the index, look up all of these broader categories.
5. Identify the *narrower* categories of the major words.
6. In the index, look up all of these narrower categories.
7. Identify all *synonyms* of the major words.
8. In the index, look up all of these synonyms.
9. Identify all of the *antonyms* of the major words.
10. In the index, look up all of these antonyms.
11. Identify all words that are *closely related* to the major words.
12. In the index, look up all of these closely related words.
13. Identify all terms of *procedure* and *remedy* related to the major words.
14. In the index, look up all of these procedural and remedial terms.
15. Identify all *agencies,* if any, that might have some connection to the major words.
16. In the index, look up all of these agencies.
17. Identify all *long shots.*
18. In the index, look up all of these long shots.

Note: The above categories are not mutually exclusive.

Suppose the client's problem involved, among other things, a wedding. The first step would be to look up the word *wedding* in the index of any law book you are examining. Assume that you are not successful with this word, either because the word is not in the index or because the page or section references do not lead you to relevant material in the body of the book. The next step is to think of as many different phrasings and contexts of the word *wedding* as possible. This is where the eighteen steps of the CART-WHEEL can be useful. Use the CARTWHEEL to compile a comprehensive list of search words, which you then take to the index of statutory codes, digests, encyclopedias, treatises, or any other law book that contains an index.

If you applied the steps of the CARTWHEEL to the word *wedding*, here are some of the words and phrases that you would check:

1. *Broader words:* celebration, ceremony, rite, ritual, formality, festivity, etc.
2. *Narrower words:* civil wedding, church wedding, golden wedding, proxy wedding, sham wedding, shotgun marriage, etc.
3. *Synonyms:* marriage ceremony, nuptial, etc.
4. *Antonyms:* alienation, annulment, divorce, separation, legal separation, judicial separation, etc.
5. *Closely related words:* license, blood test, contract, minister, matrimony, marital, conjugal, domestic, husband, wife, bride, anniversary, custom, children, premarital, spouse, relationship, family, home, consummation, cohabitation, sexual relations, betrothal, wedlock, oath, community property, name change, domicile, residence, etc.
6A. *Terms of procedure:* action, suit, statute of limitations, complaint, discovery, defense, petition, jurisdiction, court, superior court, county court, etc.
6B. *Terms of remedy:* damages, injunction, specific performance, divorce, partition, rescission, revocation, etc.
7. *Agencies:* Bureau of Vital Statistics, County Clerk, Department of Social Services, License Bureau, Secretary of State, Justice of the Peace, etc.
8. *Long shots:* dowry, common law, single, blood relationship, fraud, religion, illegitimate, remarriage, antenuptial, alimony, bigamy, pregnancy, gifts, chastity, impotence, incest, virginity, support, custody, consent, paternity, etc.

If the CARTWHEEL can generate this many words and phrases from a starting point of just one word *(wedding)*, potentially thousands more can be generated when you subject all of the important words from the client's case to the CARTWHEEL. Do you check them all in the index volume of every code, digest, encyclopedia, practice manual, and treatise? No. You can't spend your entire legal career in the law library working on one case! Common sense will tell you when you are on the right track and when you are needlessly duplicating your efforts. You may get lucky and find what you are after in a few minutes. For most important tasks in any line of work (or play), however, being comprehensive is usually time-consuming.

As indicated in Exhibit 7.1, the categories may overlap; they are not mutually exclusive. There are two reasons for checking antonyms: they might cover your topic, or they might give you a cross-reference to your topic. It is not significant whether you place a word in one category or another so long as the word comes to your mind as you comb through all available indexes. The CARTWHEEL is, in effect, a word-association game that should become second nature to you with practice. Perhaps some of the word selections seem a bit far-fetched. You will not know for sure, however, whether a word is fruitful until you try it. Be imaginative and take some risks.

Assignment 7.1

CARTWHEEL the following words or phrases:
(a) Paralegal
(b) Woman
(c) Rat bite
(d) Rear-end collision
(e) Monopoly

Indexes and tables of contents are often organized into headings, subheadings, sub-subheadings and perhaps even sub-sub-subheadings. Examine the following excerpt from an index. Note that "Burden of proof" is a sub-subheading of "Accidents" and a subheading of "Unavoidable accident or casualty." The latter is a subheading of "Accidents," which is the main heading of the index entry. If you were looking for law on burden of proof, you might be out of luck unless you first thought of looking up "accidents" and "unavoidable accident."

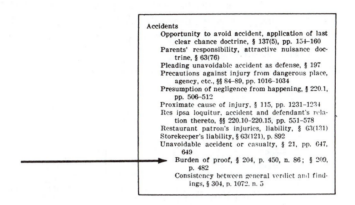

Accidents
Opportunity to avoid accident, application of last clear chance doctrine, § 137(5), pp. 154–160
Parents' responsibility, attractive nuisance doctrine, § 63(76)
Pleading unavoidable accident as defense, § 197
Precautions against injury from dangerous place, agency, etc., §§ 84–89, pp. 1016–1034
Presumption of negligence from happening, § 220.1, pp. 506–512
Proximate cause of injury, § 115, pp. 1231–1234
Res ipsa loquitur, accident and defendant's relation thereto, §§ 220.10–220.15, pp. 551–578
Restaurant patron's injuries, liability, § 63(131)
Storekeeper's liability, § 63(121), p. 892
Unavoidable accident or casualty, § 21, pp. 647, 649
   Burden of proof, § 204, p. 450, n. 86; § 209, p. 482
Consistency between general verdict and findings, § 304, p. 1072, n. 5

Excerpt from an index

Suppose that you identify the following words to check in an index:

minor	sale
explosion	warranty
car	damage

The index may have no separate heading for "minor," but "minor" may be a subheading under "sale." If so, you would not find "minor" unless you first thought of checking "sale." Under each of the above six words, you should be alert to the possibility that the other five words may be subheadings for that word. Hence the process of pursuing these six words in an index would be as follows: (The word in bold letters is checked first and then the five words *under it* are checked to see if any of them are subheadings.)

Car	**Damage**	**Explosion**	**Minor**	**Sale**	**Warranty**
damage	car	car	car	car	car
explosion	explosion	damage	damage	damage	damage
minor	minor	minor	explosion	explosion	explosion
sale	sale	sale	sale	minor	minor
warranty	warranty	warranty	warranty	warranty	sale

Assignment 7.2

One way to gain an appreciation for the use of indexes is to write one of your own. When you write an index for this assignment, be sure to use headings, subheadings, sub-subheadings, etc. in each index.

(a) Write a comprehensive index of your present job or the last job that you had.
(b) Pick one area of the law that you have covered in class or read about. Write your own comprehensive index on what you have learned.
(c) Write a comprehensive index of the following statute:

§ 132. Amount of force. The use of force against another for the purpose of effecting the arrest or recapture of the other, or of maintaining custody of him, is not privileged if the means employed are in excess of those which are reasonably believed to be necessary.

Assignment 7.3

Examine the index from the legal encyclopedia *Corpus Juris Secundum* (C.J.S.) in Exhibit 7.2. It is an excerpt from the heading of "Evidence." "Death" is the subheading of "Evidence." What sub-subheadings or sub-sub-subheadings of "Evidence" would you check to try to find material on the following topics?

(a) Introducing a death certificate into evidence
(b) The weight that a court will give to the personal conclusions of a witness
(c) Introducing the last words of a decedent into evidence
(d) A statement by the person who died disclaiming ownership of land around which he or she had placed a fence

Exhibit

Excerpt from Encyclopedia
Index (C.J.S.)

EVIDENCE

Dealers,
    Securities, judicial notice, § 29, p. 890
    Value,
        Household goods, opinion evidence, § 546(121), p. 479, n. 95
        Property, § 546(115), p. 430
            Opinion evidence, § 546(122), p. 483
Death,
    Autopsy, generally, ante
    Best evidence rule, § 803, p. 136
    Book entries,
        Entrant, proof of handwriting, § 693, p. 942
        Supplemental testimony respecting entries by clerks and third persons, § 693, p. 939
        Supporting entries by deceased persons by oath of personal representative, § 684, p. 910
    Clerk or employee making book entries, § 692
    Copy of record, certification by state registrar, § 664, p. 865, n. 69
    Declaration against interest, death of declarant, § 218, p. 604
    Declarations, § 227, p. 624
        Death of declarant as essential to admission, § 230
    Dying declarations, generally, post
    Experiments, object or purpose, § 588(1)
    Former evidence, death of witness, § 392
    General reputation, § 1048
    Hearsay, § 227, p. 624
        Death certificates, § 194, pp. 561, 562; § 766, p. 66
        Death of declarant, § 205
        Impossibility of obtaining other evidence, § 204
    Letters, § 703, p. 976
    Maps and diagrams of scenes of occurrence, § 730(1), p. 1045
    Memorandum, § 696, p. 955
    Mortality tables, generally, post
    Newspaper announcement, § 227, p. 625
    Opinion evidence,
        Animals, § 546(68)
        Cause and effect, § 546(11), p. 129
        Effect on human body, § 546(97), p. 374
        Fixing time, § 546(91), n. 16
    Owners, admissions, § 327
        Personal property, § 334
    Parol or extrinsic evidence, rule excluding, action to recover for, § 861, p. 230
    Photographs, personal appearance or identity, § 710
    Presumptions, ancient original public records, official making, § 746, p. 37
    Prima facie evidence, record of, § 644
    Private documents, recitals, § 677
    Public records and documents, registers of, § 623
    Reputation, § 227, p. 626
    Res gestae, statements, § 410, p. 991
    Rumor, § 227, p. 625
    Self-serving declarations, effect of death of declarant, § 216, p. 591
    Services, value, opinion evidence in death action, § 546(124), p. 489, n. 96
    Statements, weight of evidence, § 266
    Value of service rendered by claimant, opinion evidence, § 546(125), p. 493, n. 41

Death—Continued
    Witness, unsworn statements, circumstances tending to disparage testimony, § 268
    Wrongful death,
        Admissions, husband and wife, § 363
        Admissions of decedent, privity, § 322, n. 96.5
        Declarations against interest, § 218, p. 607
        Loss of life, value, opinion evidence, § 546 (121), p. 473, n. 54
        Municipal claim, evidence of registry, § 680, n. 21
        Value of decedent's services, opinion evidence, § 546(124), p. 489, n. 96
Death certificates,
    Certified copies, § 651, p. 851
        Officer as making, § 664, p. 865, n. 69
        Prima facie evidence, § 773
    Church register, competency, § 727
    Conclusiveness, § 766, p. 64
    Expert testimony, supporting opinion, § 570
    Foreign countries, authenticated copies, § 675, p. 885
    Hearsay, § 194, pp. 561, 562; § 766, p. 66
    Kinship, § 696, p. 949, n. 2
    Official document, § 638, pp. 823, 824
    Prima facie case or evidence, post
Debate, judicial notice, United States congress, § 43, p. 995
Debs, judicial notice, § 67, p. 56, n. 17
Debtor and creditor, admissions, § 336
Debts. Indebtedness, generally, post
Decay,
    Judicial notice, vegetable matter, § 88
    Opinion evidence, buildings, § 546(73), p. 290
Decedents' estates,
    Judicial admissions, claim statements, § 310
    Judicial records, inferences from, § 765
    Official documents, reports and inventories of representatives, § 638, p. 818
    Value, opinion evidence, § 546(121), p. 478
Deceit. Fraud, generally, post
Decisions, judicial notice, sister states, § 18, p. 861
Declaration against interest, §§ 217–224, pp. 600–615
    Absence of declared from jurisdiction, § 218, p. 604
    Account, § 224
    Admissions, distinguished, § 217, p. 603
    Adverse character, § 222
    Affirmative proof as being best evidence obtainable, § 218, p. 604
    Apparent interest, § 219, p. 608
    Assured, § 219, p. 611
    Best evidence obtainable, necessity of, § 218, p. 604
    Boundaries, § 219, p. 611
    Coexisting, self-serving interest, § 221
    Contract, § 224
    Criminal prosecution, statement subjecting declarant to, § 219, p. 608
    Death action, § 218, p. 607
    Death of declarant, § 218, p. 605
    Dedication to public use, § 219, p. 611
    Deeds, § 224
    Disparagement of title § 219, p. 611
    Distinctions, § 217, p. 603
    Enrollment of vessel, § 224

SECTION C   OTHER INDEX SEARCH SYSTEMS

The CARTWHEEL is not the only technique for using indexes (and tables of contents) effectively. Here are some others.

Descriptive Words

West Publishing Company (the West Group) suggests a five-part **descriptive word** framework for generating search terms: Parties, Places or Things, Basis of Action or Issue, Defenses, and Relief Sought. By trying to identify terms that fall into these categories, you will be generating numerous words to check in the indexes (and tables of contents) of law books you are examining.

Parties Identify persons of a particular class, occupation, or relation involved in the problem you are researching (e.g., commercial landlords, children born out of wedlock, physicians, sheriffs, aliens, collectors). Include any person who is directly or indirectly necessary to a proper resolution of the legal problem.

Places or Things Identify all significant objects—those places and things perceptible to the senses that are involved in the problem being researched (e.g., automobiles, sidewalks, derricks, garages, office buildings). An object is significant if it is relevant to the **cause of action** or dispute that has arisen. (A cause of action is a set of facts that give a party a right to judicial relief; it is a legally acceptable reason for suing.)

Basis of Action or Issue Identify the alleged wrong suffered or infraction (e.g., negligence, loss of goods, assault, failure to pay overtime, sex discrimination).

Defenses Identify those reasons in law or fact why there arguably should be no recovery (e.g., assumption of the risk, failure of consideration, act of God, infancy).

Relief Sought Identify the legal remedy being sought (e.g., damages, injunction, annulment).

Example At a professional wrestling match the referee was thrown from the ring in such a way that he struck and injured the plaintiff, who was a front-row spectator. The following descriptive words for this problem should be checked:

Parties—spectator, patron, arena owner, wrestler, referee, promoter
Places and things—wrestling match, amusement place, theater, show
Basis of action or issue—negligence, personal injury to spectator, liability
Defense—assumption of risk
Relief sought—damages

TAPP

Lawyers Co-operative Publishing Company (now owned by International Thomson, which also owns West) suggests generating search terms by thinking of **TAPP** categories: Things, Acts, Persons, or Places involved in the problem you are searching.

Things—automobile, pool, knife, blood, etc.
Acts—swimming, driving, rescuing, accounting, etc.
Persons—mother, pedestrian, driver, etc.
Places—state freeway, residence, etc.

Assignment 7.4

This assignment asks you to identify as many index (and table of contents) entries as you can that may cover designated topics. Use the CARTWHEEL, descriptive words, and TAPP systems. Go to the indexes (and tables of contents) in the sets of books indicated. Make a notation of *every* index (and table of contents) entry that appears to cover the topic. Try to find multiple entries in the indexes (and tables of contents) for the topic you are searching. In class, the teacher will call

Continued on next page

Assignment 7.4—continued

on you to indicate what entries you found that appeared to be successful so that others in the class can compare their entries with yours.

(a) Rape. Books to use: your state statutory code.
(b) Race discrimination. Books to use: the state digest that covers your state courts.
(c) Suicide. Books to use: *American Jurisprudence 2d.*
(d) Divorce. Books to use: *Corpus Juris Secundum.*
(e) Homosexuality. Books to use: *Index to Annotations.*

HAPTER SUMMARY

Indexes and tables of contents in law books are often difficult to use because they are not comprehensive. One consequence of this is that you may be failing to find relevant material in law books simply because you looked up the wrong words in the index and table of contents. The CARTWHEEL is a technique that may be of assistance in overcoming this small (or large) disaster.

The technique assumes that the words you first checked in the index or table lead nowhere, and that you must now think of other words to check that might be more productive. The following categories of the CARTWHEEL will help you identify them: broader words, narrower words, synonyms, antonyms, closely related words, terms of procedure and remedy, agency-related words, and long shorts.

One of the unique features of indexes and tables of contents is that headings are often divided into subheadings, sub-subheadings, and sub-sub-subheadings. What you want may be one of these "sub" entries, but unless you have thought of the headings of which they are "subs," you may miss relevant material. Again, the CARTWHEEL should help you overcome this.

Two other techniques for generating search terms for use with the indexes and tables of contents of law books are the descriptive word method and TAPP.

**EY TERMS**

CARTWHEEL   descriptive words   cause of action   TAPP

Chapter 8

THE FIRST LEVEL OF LEGAL RESEARCH: BACKGROUND

Chapter Outline

SECTION A   INTRODUCTION

There are three interrelated levels of researching a problem:

Background Research. Provides you with a general understanding of the area of law involved in your research problem.

Specific Fact Research. Provides you with primary and secondary authority that covers the specific facts of your research problem.

Validation Research. Provides you with information on the current validity of all the primary authority you intend to use in your research memorandum on the problem.

At times all three levels of research go on simultaneously. If you are new to legal research, however, it is recommended that you approach your research problem in the three stages just listed. Our concern in this chapter is the first level: background research. The other two levels are covered in chapters 9 through 14.

Let us assume you are researching a topic that is totally new to you. Where do you begin? What law books do you take off the shelves or what computer databases or files do you start checking? More specifically:

- Should you start looking for federal law or state law?
- Should you begin looking for statutes or for court opinions?
- Should you check constitutional law?
- Should you check procedural law?
- Should you check administrative law?
- Should you check ordinances or other local laws?

By definition, you don't know the answers to such questions—we are assuming that you have never researched a problem like the one now before you. Of course, you will want to ask your supervisor for direction on where to begin. Also, you should try to seek out a colleague who may have some time to provide you with initial guidance. But suppose that such assistance is fairly minimal or is simply not available. Where do you begin?

SECTION B   RESOURCES FOR BACKGROUND RESEARCH

Start with some of the nine techniques for doing background research outlined in Exhibit 8.1. Spend an hour or two (depending on the complexity of the problem) doing some reading in law books that will provide you with an overview and a general understanding of the area(s) of law involved in your research problem. You will then be in a better position to be able to identify the major **terms of art** you need to understand and the major questions or issues you need to address. (A legal term of art is a word or phrase that has a special or technical meaning in the law.) Of course, while doing this background research, you will probably also come up with leads that will be helpful in the second and third levels of research.

Let's look at an example. Suppose you were researching a case involving child emancipation. You begin by doing some background research in the categories listed in Exhibit 8.1. Here are examples of information you might find in these categories:

Background Research Notes on Problem
Involving Child Emancipation

1. Legal Dictionary

   "'Emancipation' means the relinquishment of parental control and it terminates the parental obligation of support." 14 *Words and Phrases* 168 (Supp. 1997). [Barks v. Barks, Mo. App., 686 S.W.2d 50, 51.]

2. Legal Encyclopedia

   "The significance of the term 'emancipation' is not exact. Emancipation, as employed in the law of parent and child, means the freeing of the child for all

8.1 ································· Techniques for Doing Background Research on a Topic

Exhibit

---

1. Legal Dictionaries

Have access to a **legal dictionary** throughout your research. For example:

> *Black's Law Dictionary*
> *Ballentine's Law Dictionary*
> *Oran's Law Dictionary*
> West's *Legal Thesaurus/Dictionary*
> *Words and Phrases*

Look up the meaning of all important terms that you come across in your research. These dictionaries are starting points only. Eventually you want to find primary authority that defines these terms.

---

2. Legal Encyclopedias

Find general discussions of your topic in the major national **legal encyclopedias:**

> *American Jurisprudence 2d*
> *Corpus Juris Secundum*

Also check encyclopedias, if any, that cover only your state. Use the CARTWHEEL to help you use their indexes.

---

3. Legal Treatises

Find discussions of your topic in **legal treatises.** Go to your card or computer catalog in the library. Use the CARTWHEEL to help you locate treatises such as hornbooks, nutshells, formbooks, practice manuals, scholarly studies, etc. Many of these books will have *KF call numbers*. If there are open stacks in the library, go to the KF section to browse through the selections on the shelf. You may find some treatises that you missed in the catalog. Use the CARTWHEEL to help you use the indexes of these books.

---

4. Annotations

Find discussions of your topic in the **annotations** of A.L.R., A.L.R.2d, A.L.R.3d, A.L.R.4th, A.L.R.5th, and A.L.R. Fed. Use the CARTWHEEL to help you find these discussions through indexes such as the *Index to Annotations.*

---

5. Legal Periodical Literature

Find discussions of your topic in **legal periodical** literature. The main indexes to such literature are:

> *Index to Legal Periodicals and Books* (ILP)
> *Current Law Index* (CLI)
> LegalTrac (the CD-ROM version of CLI)

Use the CARTWHEEL to help you use these indexes to locate legal periodical literature on your topic.

---

6. Agency Reports/Brochures

If your research involves an administrative agency, call or write the agency. Find out what **agency reports,** brochures, or newsletters are available to the public. Such literature often provides useful background information.

---

7. Committee Reports

Many research projects involve one or more statutes. Before statutes are passed, committees of the legislature often write reports that comment on and summarize the legislation. (See Exhibit 11.5 in chapter 11.) In addition to being good sources of legislative history on the statute, the reports are excellent background reading. If practical, contact both houses of the legislature to find out which committees acted on the statute. If the statute is fairly recent, they may be able to send you copies of the **committee reports** or tell you where to obtain them. If you live near the library of the legislature, you may be able to find committee reports there. The committee reports of many recent federal statutes are printed in *U.S. Code Congressional and Administrative News* (U.S.C.C.A.N.).

---

8. Reports/Studies of Special Interest Groups

There are **special interest groups** for almost every area of the law, e.g., unions, bar associations, environmental associations, tax associations, insurance and other business associations. They often have position papers and studies that they might be willing to send you. Although one-sided, such literature should not be ignored.

---

9. *Martindale-Hubbell Law Digest*

The *Digest* volume of *Martindale-Hubbell Law Directory* provides concise summaries of the law of the fifty states and many foreign countries. (For a photo, see page 63.)

the period of minority from the care, custody, control, and service of the parents; the relinquishment of parental control, conferring on the child the right to his or her own earnings and terminating the parent's legal obligation to support the child." 67A Corpus Juris Secundum, *Parent & Child* § 5 (1978).

3. Legal Treatise

"[S]upport orders may be terminated before majority if the child becomes emancipated by events other than attaining majority, such as contracting a marriage or leaving home becoming self-supporting." 2 Homer H. Clark, Jr., *The Law of Domestic Relations in the United States* 358 (1987).

4. Annotation

"The courts . . . held or recognized that a decree ordering payment of child support until a child attains his or her majority, or the happening of some other specified contingency, such as emancipation or graduation from high school or college, evidences an intent on the part of the parties to the divorce or the court entering the order, or justifies the conclusion that the child support obligation is not terminated by the earlier death of the obligated parent." Susan L. Thomas, Annotation, *Death of Obligor Parent as Affecting Decree for Support for Child,* 14 American Law Reports 5th 557, 607 (1994).

5. Legal Periodical Literature

"The attributes of parental status in our society strengthen parents' natural incentives to care for their own offspring. Parents stand in a long-run relationship with their children: they are obliged to raise and support them until emancipation. This arrangement encourages parents to love their children, if for no other reason than that it is unpleasant to be legally encumbered with massive and continuing responsibilities for a person whom one dislikes." Stephen G. Gilles, *On Educating Children: A Parentalist Manifesto,* 63 University of Chicago Law Review 937, 954 (1996).

6. Agency Report/Brochure

"Recommendation: Duration of Support. States shall have and use laws that mandate a continuing support obligation by one or both parents until a child reaches the age of 18, graduates from or is no longer enrolled in secondary school or its equivalent, or is otherwise emancipated by a court of competent jurisdiction." U.S. Commission on Interstate Child Support, *Supporting Our Children: A Blueprint for Reform* 45 (1992).

7. Committee Report

"The Committee has stressed the importance of preserving the integrity of the family relationship by requiring, in general, the written consent of a parent or guardian before a suit is filed for a child under eighteen years of age. Such written consent is necessary for legal representation of a youngster, other than a married or legally emancipated child, except where consent is provided by a court of competent jurisdiction . . . ." House of Representatives Report 93-247, at 26 (1973).

8. Report/Study of Special Interest Group

"She also discussed the pain caused by seeing her family and relatives dispersed . . . [and] anguishes about securing her children's emancipation." Afro-American Law and Policy Report, *African Americans and Property Ownership: Creating Our Own Meanings, Redefining Our Relationships,* 1 African-Am. L.J. Policy Report, 79, 88 (Fall 1994).

9. *Martindale-Hubbell Law Digest*

"Unless otherwise emancipated, child support terminates at age 19, unless parties otherwise agree, child is mentally or physically disabled, or child is still in high school or its equivalent." *Martindale-Hubbell Law Digest* CO-35 (Colorado) (1997).

All this background research will be in **secondary authority**—legal dictionaries, legal encyclopedias, legal treatises, legal periodical literature, etc. Use these materials for the limited purposes of (1) background reading and (2) providing leads to **primary authority**—particularly through footnotes. You will not have time to use all of the nine techniques of background research presented in Exhibit 8.1. Usually, one or two of the techniques is sufficient for the limited purpose of providing an overview and getting you started.

Exhibit 8.2 illustrates the kind of information you should be able to derive from background research.

8.2 ································ Checklist of Information to Be Obtained Through Background Research

Exhibit

MAJOR AREAS OF LAW THAT MAY BE INVOLVED IN THE RESEARCH PROBLEM
(circle those that preliminarily seem applicable)

antitrust	criminal law	international	sports
bankruptcy	employment	labor relations	taxation
children	environment	landlord-tenant	torts
civil procedure	estate and probate	military	trademarks
civil rights	ethics	municipalities	transportation
commercial	evidence	partnership	women
communications	family	patents	other _____
constitutional law	fraud	public benefits	_____
consumer	gifts	real estate	_____
contracts	health	sales	
copyright	immigration	sea	
corporations	insurance	securities	

JURISDICTIONS THAT MAY NEED TO BE CHECKED
(circle those that preliminarily seem applicable)

Federal	State	Local	International

PRIMARY AUTHORITY THAT MAY NEED TO BE CHECKED
(circle those that preliminarily seem applicable; see Exhibit 2.2 in chapter 2)

opinions	administrative decisions	executive orders
statutes	charters	treaties
constitutions	ordinances	
administrative regulations	rules of court	

MAJOR CAUSES OF ACTION AND DEFENSES THAT NEED TO BE EXPLORED

MAJOR TERMS OF ART THAT APPEAR TO BE CRITICAL AND THAT NEED TO BE DEFINED

CITATIONS TO MAJOR STATUTES THAT MIGHT BE APPLICABLE

Continued on next page

8.2 ························· Checklist of Information to Be Obtained Through Background Research—continued

Exhibit

CITATIONS TO MAJOR ADMINISTRATIVE REGULATIONS THAT MIGHT BE APPLICABLE

CITATIONS TO MAJOR COURT OPINIONS THAT MIGHT BE APPLICABLE

Can you ever use (e.g., quote from) secondary authority in your writing? Review page 87 in chapter 4 on the five major dangers of relying on secondary authority. In particular, see Exhibit 4.2 on the foundation for using secondary authority in legal writing as possible persuasive authority.

 Assignment 8.1

Fill out the checklist in Exhibit 8.2 for the following research questions. Assume that the individuals involved in each of these questions live in your state.

(a) Can a woman agree to bear the child of another woman using in vitro fertilization?
(b) Can a doctor assist a patient to commit suicide?
(c) Can someone sell pornography on the Internet?
(d) Can a church be forced to pay taxes on profits from its bingo games?

 C HAPTER SUMMARY

There are three levels of legal research: background research in which you start identifying the basic vocabulary and the major principles of an area of the law that is relatively new to you; specific fact research in which you look for primary and secondary authority on the facts of a specific client's case; and validation research in which you check the current validity of whatever authority you initially felt was relevant to the problem you are researching. Occasionally, aspects of all three levels of research will be going on simultaneously.

The nine major sources of background research are: legal dictionaries, legal encyclopedias, legal treatises, annotations, legal periodical literature, agency reports and brochures, committee reports, reports and studies of special interest groups, and the *Martindale-Hubbell Law Digest.*

Caution is needed in using secondary authority. It should never be a substitute for primary authority, which is the major focus of your research.

 K EY TERMS

background research	legal dictionary	legal periodical	*Martindale-Hubbell Law Digest*
specific fact research	legal encyclopedia	agency reports	secondary authority
validation research	legal treatises	committee reports	primary authority
terms of art	annotations	special interest groups	

Chapter 9

CHECKLISTS FOR USING NINE MAJOR SEARCH RESOURCES

Chapter Outline

SECTION A   INTRODUCTION

We have said that the main objective of legal research is to locate mandatory primary authority. **Mandatory primary authority** is any law (opinion, statute, constitutional provision, etc.) that a court must follow to help it resolve the legal dispute before the court (see the beginning of chapter 4). There are three levels of government—federal, state, and local. Exhibit 9.1 presents an overview of their primary authority.

9.1

Exhibit
Kinds of Primary Authority

FEDERAL LEVEL OF GOVERNMENT	STATE LEVEL OF GOVERNMENT	LOCAL LEVEL OF GOVERNMENT (CITY, COUNTY, ETC.)
U.S. Constitution	State constitution	Charter
Statutes of Congress	State statutes	Local ordinances
Federal court opinions	State court opinions	Local court opinions
Federal administrative regulations	State administrative regulations	Local administrative regulations
Federal administrative decisions	State administrative decisions	Local administrative decisions
Federal rules of court	State rules of court	Local rules of court
Executive orders of the president	Executive orders of the governor	Executive orders of the mayor
Treaties		

How do you find the categories of primary authority outlined in Exhibit 9.1? The main way is to use the following **search resources** or tools:

- catalogs
- digests
- annotations
- Shepard's
- looseleaf services
- legal periodical literature
- legal encyclopedias
- legal treatises
- phone and mail

A tenth resource, computers, will be covered separately in chapter 13.

Before we begin our examination of these search resources, we need to make a number of important observations about them:

- You were first introduced to many of them during the "tour" that we took in chapter 3.
- Four of the search resources (looseleaf services, legal periodicals, legal encyclopedias, and legal treatises) are secondary authorities, which were defined and outlined in Exhibit 4.1 of chapter 4.
- Four of the search resources (annotations, legal periodicals, legal encyclopedias, and legal treatises) were listed in Exhibit 8.1 of chapter 8 as valuable ways to conduct background research.
- Three of the search resources (catalogs, digests, and Shepard's) are pure finding aids; they are not secondary authorities in themselves and hence are never cited as authority.
- Some of the search resources, particularly Shepard's, are also helpful in doing the third level of research—validation research, which we will cover in chapter 14.

In later chapters, we will be referring to the search resources extensively as we cover ways to find the primary authorities listed in Exhibit 9.1. Because the search resources are needed for finding more than one category of primary authority, the techniques for using the search resources are presented together here in chapter 9.

In short, the search resources are extraordinarily important. Indeed, they can be considered the foundation of legal research itself.

TOPICS FOR ASSIGNMENTS 9.1 AND 9.3–9.11

The following topics will be used for most of the assignments in chapter 9. You will be referred back to these topics throughout our study of the search resources covered in this chapter. In each assignment, you are to assume that your legal research problem involves the topic indicated in (a) to (o) below. Use the CARTWHEEL to help you locate material in whatever search resources the assignment is asking you to check.

For these assignments, your instructor may require you to do all of the topics (a to o) or selected ones.

TOPICS

(a) A local government uses its zoning laws to try to close a bar that features topless dancers.

(b) A daughter challenges the validity of a deceased parent's will that leaves everything to the parent's pet cat.

(c) A newspaper falsely prints that an individual had been convicted of child molestation.

(d) A client is angry at his attorney for revealing to the police that the client fantasized about killing the President of the United States.

(e) A civil suit against a homeowner is brought by a burglar for injuries received when the burglar fell because of a defective floor in the house being burglarized.

(f) A high school teacher is disciplined for using a Scientology workbook in class.

(g) A husband is arrested after his wife accuses him of raping her.

(h) A father wants to revoke the adoption of a child he did not know existed at the time of the adoption; the mother told him the baby died in childbirth.

(i) A man sues to prevent an abortion from being performed on the woman he impregnated; the woman is a mentally retarded, unmarried adult living with her parents, who are arranging the abortion.

(j) A lesbian sues the Girl Scouts organization that turned down her application to be a volunteer because of her sexual orientation.

(k) A parent seeks to invalidate the marriage of his thirteen-year-old daughter who married her first cousin, also thirteen years old.

(l) A paralegal is charged with insider trading after buying stock in a company that is a client in the law firm where the paralegal works.

(m) A patient wants to prevent his doctor from telling an insurance company about the patient's AIDS status.

(n) A person wants to cancel a contract to buy a house because the seller failed to disclose that there had recently been a murder in the house.

(o) A patient is scheduled for surgery where her right arm is to be amputated; by mistake the surgeon amputates the left arm.

SECTION B   CATALOG

A well-organized catalog is one of the researcher's best friends. Many librarians, however, say that it is one of the most underutilized resources in the library. If the library has not switched over to a completely computerized catalog, you need to learn some of the basics of the manual card catalog. Most law libraries use the **Library of Congress (LC) classification system.** Under this system, many law books have **KF call numbers.** Here is an example of a card from a card catalog:

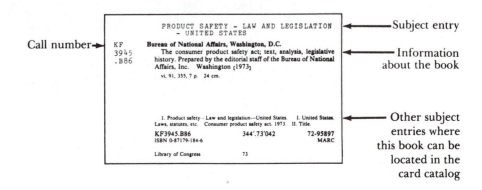

Most law libraries have **open stacks,** meaning that users are free to browse through all or some of the shelves. Take advantage of this opportunity when it exists. Go to the KF section to do some browsing. Here are some examples of topics (with their beginning KF call numbers) that you might want to explore to find out what your library has available on the shelves[1]:

Civil Procedure Law: KF 8810   Marital Relations: KF 501
Constitutional Law: KF 4501   Paralegals: KF 320L
Corporate Law: KF 1384   Real Property Law: KF 560
Criminal Law: KF 9201   Tort Law: KF 1246
Ethics: KF 300   Trials: KF 8910
Lawyers: KF 297   Wills and Trusts: KF 728

Checklist #1   Checklist for Using the Catalog

1. Find out what kind of catalog your library uses. A card (paper) catalog? Microfiche? Computer? Locate the description of how to use the catalog. (The how-to material for computerized catalogs may be online or available through a HELP key on the keyboard.) If the library still uses the card catalog, there may be more than one available. For example, one set of cards may alphabetize all books by author name, while another may be separately alphabetized by book title.

2. Select several entries from the catalog at random. Pick ones that appear to contain different kinds of information. Try to figure out why they are different. If you can't, ask a staff member of the library to briefly explain the differences.

3. Be sure you understand the information in the catalog that tells you where the books are located in the library. Some books may be on reserve, in special rooms, or in other buildings.

4. Select several KF entries at random, particularly on books housed in different locations within the same building. Try to find these books. Ask for help if you cannot locate them.

5. Now try the reverse process. Select at random three different kinds of books from the library shelves (not the same books you looked at in #4 above). Take these books to the catalog and try to find the entries for them. Your goal is to become as proficient in the

structure and use of the catalog as possible. Steps #2–5 are designed to help you achieve this goal *before* you experience the pressure of actual research.

6. Ask a staff member what kinds of research material, if any, are *not* cataloged, such as microfilm, ultrafiche, appellate briefs, or old exams.

7. Ask a staff member what special lists of law books, if any, are in the library, such as a list of legal periodicals or a list of reserve books. These lists may be in notebooks on special tables or in folding "pages" attached to the wall.

8. Ask whether the library can obtain books for you at other libraries through **interlibrary loan.**

9. Ask a staff member to explain the difference between the library's catalog and **Kardex.** (The latter is the place where many libraries keep records of current serial publications that come into the library every day.) If the library does not use a Kardex, ask what it uses instead.

10. When using any catalog, the CARTWHEEL will help you think of words and phrases to check.

11. Never antagonize the employees of a law library! You are going to need all the help you can get! Do not abuse their availability. Do not ask any questions until you first try to find the answer on your own.

 Assignment 9.1

Use the catalog of a law library to find the call number (e.g., a KF number) of one law book that might be helpful in researching each of the topics for the Chapter 9 Assignments (printed at the beginning of the chapter at the end of Section A). Most of the law books you will select will be legal treatises or looseleaf services, but you are not limited to these categories of books. You can use any law book so long as you locate it through the catalog. Pick one per topic. Give the citation of each book and place a check mark next to the citation to indicate that you were able

---

1. If your library does not use the Library of Congress classification, it might use the **Dewey Decimal System.** For legal material under this system, see the books beginning with number 340.

Assignment 9.1—continued

to locate the book on the shelves of the library. (If you can't locate the book, pick a different one from the catalog.) If the title of the book you select does not indicate that the book probably covers the topic, give the heading of a chapter, section, or page in the book showing that the topic is probably covered in the book. At the top of your answer sheet, give the name and address of the law library you used.

Assignment 9.2

Assignment 1.2 in chapter 1 asked you to organize a system of three-by-five-inch index cards for each of the legal research terms listed in Exhibit 1.2. For each card with the name of a law book on it, find out where the book or set of books is located in a law library near you. Obtain this information from the catalog or other library list, and enter it on the index cards.

SECTION C   DIGESTS

We have already examined the major **digests** and the names of reporters whose opinions are summarized (in small paragraphs) in the digests. You should review this material now. See Exhibit 3.3 on page 54. See also Research Links A, E, I, J, and L in chapter 3 on the relationship between regional reporters and regional digests.

Our focus here is on the digests of West.[2] The thousands of opinions summarized in these digests are organized by the **key number system.** Every important issue examined in an opinion is summarized in a small paragraph (called a **headnote**) and assigned a topic and number (called a key number) by West editors. As we will see, these paragraphs are printed in several places, such as in the digests of West. Paragraphs with the same key number are printed together in the digests. This enables a researcher to find numerous opinions on the same point of law. For example, West assigns Searches & Seizures ⚷ 7(10) to the topic of searches and seizures made without warrants. You can to go any West digest, take down the "S" volume, find Searches & Seizures, and turn to number 7(10) to try to find a potentially large number of different opinions that covered this issue.

The beauty of the West digests is that once you know how to use one of the digests, you know how to use them all. To demonstrate this, we begin by following the journey of a court opinion from the time it arrives at West. (See Exhibit 9.2.)

9.2

Exhibit
Journey of a Court
Opinion

JOURNEY OF A STATE COURT OPINION, e.g., CALIFORNIA

1. The California Supreme Court sends a copy of its opinion to West Publishing Company in Minnesota.
2. West editors write brief paragraph *headnotes* for the opinion. Each headnote is a summary of a portion of the opinion.

JOURNEY OF A FEDERAL COURT OPINION, e.g., A U.S. COURT OF APPEALS

1. The U.S. Court of Appeals sends a copy of its opinion to West Publishing Company in Minnesota.
2. West editors write brief paragraph *headnotes* for the opinion. Each headnote is a summary of a portion of the opinion.

Continued on next page

---

2. There are other kinds of digests, such as those that cover annotations in A.L.R., A.L.R.2d, etc. (which we will examine later), but the main digest system in legal research is that published by West.

9.2

Exhibit
Journey of a Court
Opinion—continued

JOURNEY OF A STATE COURT OPINION, e.g., CALIFORNIA

3. The headnotes are printed at the beginning of the full text of the opinion in the reporter—here, the *Pacific Reporter 2d* (P.2d). The editors assign each of these headnotes a key number, which consists of a topic and a number, e.g., Criminal Law ☞ 1064(5).

4. In addition to being printed at the beginning of the opinion in P.2d, the headnotes will also be printed at the beginning of the advance sheet for P.2d that contains the opinion and in the back of the bound P.2d volume that contains the opinion.

5. This headnote is also printed in the appropriate digests of West. The above example will go in the "C" volume of these digests where "Criminal Law" is covered. The headnote will be placed under key number 1064(5) of Criminal Law, along with summaries of other opinions on the same or similar areas of law. In what digests will such headnotes from a recent California opinion be printed? The list follows:

- All headnotes of P.2d cases go into the American Digest System. First, the headnote goes into a *General Digest* volume. After a ten-year period (in two five-year intervals), all the *General Digests* are thrown away, with the material in them printed in the next *Decennial Digest*.
- All headnotes of P.2d cases are also printed in its regional digest—the *Pacific Digest*.
- All headnotes of California cases in P.2d are also printed in the individual state digest—the *California Digest*.

6. Hence, the headnote from the opinion of the California Supreme Court will be printed:

- at the beginning of the opinion in P.2d.
- at the beginning of the P.2d advance sheet containing the opinion.
- at the end of the bound P.2d volume containing the opinion.
- in the American Digest System (first in the *General Digest* and then in the *Decennial Digest*).
- in the regional digest—*Pacific Digest*.
- in the individual state digest—*California Digest*.

In all the above digests, the headnote will be printed in the "C" volume for

JOURNEY OF A FEDERAL COURT OPINION, e.g., A U.S. COURT OF APPEALS

3. The headnotes are printed at the beginning of the full text of the opinion in the reporter—here, the *Federal Reporter 3d* (F.3d). The editors assign each of these headnotes a key number, which consists of a topic and a number, e.g., Appeal and Error ☞ 1216.

4. In addition to being printed at the beginning of the opinion in F.3d, the headnotes will also be printed at the beginning of the advance sheet for F.3d that contains the opinion and in the back of the bound F.3d volume that contains the opinion.

5. This headnote is also printed in the appropriate digests of West. The above example will go in the "A" volume of these digests where "Appeal and Error" is covered. The headnote will be placed under key number 1216 of Appeal and Error, along with summaries of other opinions on the same or similar areas of law. In what digests will such headnotes from a recent F.3d opinion be printed? The list follows:

- All headnotes of F.3d cases go into the American Digest System. First, the headnote goes into a *General Digest* volume. After a ten-year period (in two five-year intervals), all the *General Digests* are thrown away, with the material in them printed in the next *Decennial Digest*.
- All headnotes of F.3d cases are also printed in the most current federal digest—the *Federal Practice Digest 4th*.
- If our F.3d case dealt with a particular state, the headnotes of the F.3d case will also be printed in the individual state digest of that state.

6. Hence, the headnote from the opinion of the U.S. Court of Appeals will be printed:

- at the beginning of the opinion in F.3d.
- at the beginning of the F.3d advance sheet containing the opinion.
- at the end of the bound F.3d volume containing the opinion.
- in the American Digest System (first in the *General Digest* and then in the *Decennial Digest*).
- in the *Federal Practice Digest 4th*.
- in a state digest if the F.3d case dealt with a particular state.

In all the above digests, the headnote will be printed in the "A" volume for Appeal

9.2

Exhibit
Journey of a Court
Opinion—continued

JOURNEY OF A STATE COURT OPINION, e.g., CALIFORNIA

Criminal Law under number 1064(5), along with headnotes from other opinions on the same or similar area of the law.

7. Finally, West publishes all of these opinions and headnotes on WESTLAW, its computer research system. (See Research Link F in chapter 3 on the need to translate a digest key number into a WEST-LAW k number so that you can find cases digested online under the same topics.)

JOURNEY OF A FEDERAL COURT OPINION, e.g., A U.S. COURT OF APPEALS

and Error under number 1216, along with headnotes from other opinions on the same or similar area of the law.

7. Finally, West publishes all of these opinions and headnotes on WESTLAW, its computer research system. (See Research Link F in chapter 3 on the need to translate a digest key number into a WEST-LAW k number so that you can find cases digested online under the same topics.)

Keep the following points in mind about Exhibit 9.2:

- The state court opinions printed in West's reporters from the other forty-nine states go through the process or journey outlined in the *first* column of Exhibit 9.2 for California. Of course, different states have their own reporters and digests (see Exhibit 3.3), but the process is the same.
- All U.S. District Court opinions printed in *Federal Supplement* (F. Supp.) go through the process or journey outlined in the *second* column of Exhibit 9.2.
- All U.S. Supreme Court opinions printed in *Supreme Court Reporter* (S. Ct.) go through the process or journey outlined in the *second* column of Exhibit 9.2. (For additional digests that summarize all U.S. Supreme Court opinions, see Exhibit 3.3.)

Assume that you are doing research on the right of a citizen to speak in a public park. You find that West's digests cover this subject under the following key number:

Constitutional Law 🔑 211

West publishes about sixty digests—state, federal, and national. (See Exhibit 3.3 in chapter 3.) You can go to the "C" volume of *any* of these sixty digests, turn to "Constitutional Law" and look for number "211" under it. Do you want only Idaho case law? If so, go to Constitutional Law 🔑 211 in the *Idaho Digest*. Do you want only case law from the states in the western United States? If so, go to Constitutional Law 🔑 211 in the *Pacific Digest*. Do you want only current federal case law? If so, go to Constitutional Law 🔑 211 in the *Federal Practice Digest 4th*. Do you want only U.S. Supreme Court cases? If so, go to Constitutional Law 🔑 211 in the *U.S. Supreme Court Digest* (West).

Do you want the case law of *every* court in the country? If so, trace Constitutional Law 🔑 211 through the three units of the American Digest System:

- Go to Constitutional Law 🔑 211 in every *General Digest* volume.
- Go to Constitutional Law 🔑 211 in every *Decennial Digest*.
- Go to the equivalent number for Constitutional Law 🔑 211 in the *Century Digest*.

To **trace a key number** through the American Digest System means to find out what case law, if any, is summarized under its topic and number in every unit of the American Digest System. (For the *Century Digest*, you will need an equivalent number, because there are no key numbers in the *Century Digest*. See step 8 in checklist #2.)

One final point: The headnotes and digests we are discussing are written by a private publishing company—West. You never quote headnotes or digests in your legal writing. They *cannot* be authority—primary or secondary. They are mere leads to case law.

Checklist #2   Checklist for Using the Digests of West

1. Locate the right digests for your research problem. This is determined by identifying the kind of case law you want to find. State? Federal? Both? Review pages 49–55 on the American Digest System, the four regional digests, the five major federal digests, the two digests for U.S. Supreme Court cases (only one of which is a West digest), the individual state digests, etc. You must know what kind of case law is summarized in each of these digests. See the chart in Exhibit 3.3 in chapter 3.

2. Find key numbers that cover your research problem. There are thousands of topics and subtopics in West's digests. How do you find the ones relevant to your research problem? There are eight techniques:

   - Descriptive Word Index (DWI). Every digest has a **DWI.** Use the CARTWHEEL to help you locate key topics in the DWI.
   - Table of Contents. There are 450 main topics (e.g., Constitutional Law, Criminal Law), which are covered throughout the volumes of the digest you are using. At the beginning of each main topic, you will find a table of contents. If you can find one of these main topics in the general area of your research, you then use its table of contents to locate specific key numbers. These tables of contents have different names: *"Scope Note,"* "Analysis," or "Subjects Included." Use the CARTWHEEL to help you locate key numbers in them.
   - Headnote in West Reporter. Suppose that you already have an opinion on point. You are reading its full text in a West reporter. Go to the most relevant headnotes at the beginning of this opinion. (For example, see the husband-and-wife and negligence headnotes at the beginning of the *Self* opinion in Exhibit 9.6 later in this chapter and the search and seizure headnotes at the beginning of the *Bruni* opinion on page 186 of chapter 10.) Each headnote has a key number. Use this key number to go to any of the digests to try to find more case law under that number.
   - Table of Cases in the Digests. Suppose again that you already have an opinion on point. You are reading its full text in a reporter. Go to the table of cases in the American Digest System or in any other digest that covers the reporter your opinion is in. Look up the name of the opinion in this table of cases. (If you can't find it, check this table in the pocket part of the volume you are using. Not all digest volumes, however, have pocket parts.) If you find your opinion in the table, you will be told what key numbers that opinion is digested under in the digest. Go to those key numbers in the

body of the digest to find that opinion summarized, along with other opinions under the same key numbers. (Note: the table of cases in some West digests is called *Plaintiff-Defendant Table* or *Defendant-Plaintiff Table,* depending on which party's name comes first. The Defendant-Plaintiff Table is useful if you happen to know only the name of the defendant or if you want many opinions where the same party was sued, e.g., General Motors. Defendant-Plaintiff Tables usually refer you back to the Plaintiff-Defendant Table, where the key numbers are listed.)

   - Library References in a West Statutory Code. After West prints the full text of statutes in the statutory codes it publishes, it also provides research references, such as Historical Note, Cross References, Library References, and Notes of Decisions. The Library References give you key numbers on topics covered in the statutes. For an example, see Exhibit 11.1 in chapter 11 containing an excerpt from a statutory code (§ 146). After the text of the statute, there are Library References to two key numbers: Prisons 13, and Reformatories 7. Hence, a West statutory code has given you a lead to a key number, which you can take to any of the West digests to find case law.
   - Library References in West's *Corpus Juris Secundum* (C.J.S.). As we have seen, C.J.S. is a legal encyclopedia that summarizes almost every area of the law. In addition, it often provides "Library References" to key numbers on the topics summarized in the encyclopedia. Hence, a West encyclopedia has given you a lead to a key number, which you can take to any of the West digests to find case law.
   - Key Number References That Are Part of Annotations in *Recent* Volumes of A.L.R.5th and A.L.R. Fed. (There are no key number references in earlier volumes of A.L.R.5th and A.L.R. Fed. Nor are there any in A.L.R.1st, A.L.R.2d, A.L.R.3d, and A.L.R.4th.)
   - WESTLAW. As we will see in chapter 13, one of the searches you can make on WESTLAW is a digest field search, which will give you almost instant access to the millions of headnotes printed in West digests. (See Research Link F in chapter 3 on the need to translate a digest key number into a WESTLAW k number.)

3. Assume that while using the Descriptive Word Index (DWI) in any of the digests, you come across a key number that appears to be relevant to your research problem. But when you go to check that number in

Checklist #2   Checklist for Using the Digests of West—continued

the body of the digest, you find no case law. The DWI has, in effect, led you to nonexistent case law! The editors are telling you that there are no cases digested under this key number *at this time*. Go to the table of contents for the main topic you are in (see step #2 above). Check the "Analysis" or "Scope Note" there to see if you can find a more productive key number. Or, go to a different digest to see if you will have more luck with your original key number.

4. The West editors occasionally add new topics and numbers to the key number system. Hence, you may find topics and numbers in later digest volumes that are not in earlier digest volumes.

5. The first key number under most topics and subtopics is often labeled "In General." This is obviously a broad category. Many researchers make the mistake of overlooking it in their quest for more specific topic headings. Go after more specific key numbers, but do not neglect this general one.

6. The West digests obviously duplicate each other in some respects. The American Digest System, for example, contains everything that is in all the other digests. A regional digest will duplicate everything found in the individual state digests covered in that region. (See the chart in Exhibit 3.3 in chapter 3.) It is wise, nevertheless, to check more than one digest. Some digests may be more up-to-date than others in your library. You may miss something in one digest that you will catch in another.

7. Be sure you know all the units of the most comprehensive digest—the American Digest System: *Century Digest, Decennial Digests, General Digest.* These units are distinguished solely by the period of time covered by each unit. Know what these periods of time are: *Century Digest* (1658–1896), *Decennial Digests* (ten-year periods, although since the Ninth Decennial they come in two five-year parts), *General Digest* (the period since the last *Decennial Digest* was printed).

8. At the time the *Century Digest* was printed, West had not invented the key number system. Hence, topics are listed in the *Century Digest* by *section* numbers rather than by key numbers. Assume that you started your research in the *Century Digest*. You located a relevant section number and you now want to trace this number through the *Decennial Digests* and the *General Digest*. To do this, you need a corresponding *key* number. There is a parallel table in volume 21 of the First Decennial that will tell you the corresponding key number for any section number in the *Century Digest*. Suppose, however, that you started your research in the *Decennial Digests* or the *General Digest*. You have a key number and now want to find its corresponding section number in the *Century Digest*. In the First and Second Decennial, there is a "see" reference under the key number that will tell you the corresponding section number in the *Century Digest*.

9. Tricks of the trade are also needed in using the *General Digest,* which covers the most recent period since the last *Decennial Digest* was printed. When the current ten-year period is over, all the *General Digest* volumes will be thrown away. The material in them will be consolidated or cumulated into the next *Decennial Digest* (which is issued in two five-year parts beginning with the Ninth Decennial). When you go to use the *General Digest,* there may be twenty to thirty bound volumes on the shelf. To be thorough in tracing a key number in the *General Digest,* you must check *all* these bound volumes. There is, however, one shortcut. Look for the *Table of Key Numbers* within every tenth volume of the *General Digest*. This table tells you which *General Digest* volumes contain anything under the key number you are searching. You do not have to check the other *General Digest* volumes.

Assignment 9.3

Go to any West digest that covers cases of your state courts. (See Exhibit 3.3 in chapter 3.) Find any two key numbers that might be helpful in researching each of the topics for the chapter 9 assignments (printed at the beginning of the chapter at the end of Section A). Pick two per topic. Under both key numbers, find a case written by a state court in your state or by a federal court that sits in your state. If you cannot find a case written by such a court in either of the key numbers, select a different key number until you are able to find one. Give the key number, the citation of the case, and a statement of why you think the case might cover the problem. Also specify which digest you used.

SECTION D   ANNOTATIONS

An **annotation** is a set of notes or commentary on something. It is, in effect, a research paper. The most extensive annotations are those of the Lawyers Co-operative Publishing Company (a division of West Group) in the following six sets of books:

A.L.R.1st	A.L.R.4th
American Law Reports, First	*American Law Reports, Fourth*
A.L.R.2d	A.L.R.5th
American Law Reports, Second	*American Law Reports, Fifth*
A.L.R.3d	A.L.R. Fed.
American Law Reports, Third	*American Law Reports, Federal*

All six sets are reporters in that they print opinions in full. They are **annotated reporters** in that notes or commentaries are provided with each opinion in the form of an annotation. Unlike the regional reporters of West, the A.L.R. reporters contain only a small number of opinions. The editors select opinions raising novel or interesting issues, which then become the basis of an annotation. The following is an example of the beginning of an annotation found on page 1015, volume 91 of A.L.R.3d:

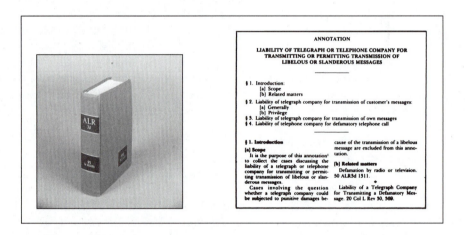

One of the joys of legal research is to find an annotation on point. A wealth of information is contained in annotations, such as a comprehensive, state-by-state survey of law on an issue. A single annotation often contains hundreds of citations to court opinions. Picture yourself having the capacity to hire your own team of researchers to go out and spend weeks finding just about all the case law that exists on a particular point of law. Though none of us is likely to have this luxury, we do have a close equivalent in the form of annotations in the six sets of American Law Reports. They are a gold mine of research references. There are hundreds of volumes in these six sets, so the chances are very good that you will find an annotation that is *on point,* i.e., that covers the facts of your research problem.

Most of the references in the annotations are to case law. Their primary service, therefore, is to act as a case finder. Because of this, the annotation system of Lawyers Co-op is the major competitor of the other massive case finders—the digests of West. The competition has led to a rich source of material at our disposal. (The competition is expected to continue even though both West and Lawyers Co-op are now part of West Group.)

The annotations cover both federal and state law. A.L.R.1st, A.L.R.2d, and most of A.L.R.3d cover both state and federal law. The later volumes of A.L.R.3d and all of A.L.R.4th and 5th cover mainly state law. A.L.R. Fed. covers only federal law. The annotations in these six sets do not follow any particular order. There may be an annotation on zoning, for example, followed by an annotation on defective wheels on baby carriages. The annotations in A.L.R.1st and A.L.R.2d are older than the annotations in the other sets, but this is not significant because all of the annotations can be updated.

We turn now to the two major concerns of the researcher:

- How do you find an annotation on point?
- How do you update an annotation that you have found?

As you will see, it is much easier to find and update annotations in A.L.R.3d, A.L.R.4th, A.L.R.5th, and A.L.R. Fed. than in the earlier A.L.R.1st and A.L.R.2d. This is not a major concern, however; the latter two sets are used fairly infrequently today because of the age of the annotations in them, even though these annotations can be updated to current law.

Finding an Annotation on Point

The major ways of finding annotations on point are outlined in Exhibit 9.3. These methods are most useful when you are at the very beginning of your search and have no leads. As you can see in Exhibit 9.3, the six sets of A.L.R. do not have the same index system: the multivolume *ALR Index* covers all of the sets (except for A.L.R.1st), a Quick Index volume covers all of the sets (except for A.L.R.2d), a LEXIS search will

Exhibit
Finding Annotations When
You Have No Leads

INDEX SYSTEMS FOR A.L.R.1st	INDEX SYSTEMS FOR A.L.R.2d	INDEX SYSTEMS FOR A.L.R.3d, A.L.R.4th, A.L.R.5th	INDEX SYSTEMS FOR A.L.R. FED.
• *ALR First Series Quick Index* • *Permanent ALR Digest*	• *ALR Index* • LEXIS • *ALR2d Digest*	• *ALR Index* • *ALR Quick Index 3d, 4th, 5th* • LEXIS • WESTLAW • *ALR Digest to 3d, 4th, 5th, Federal*	• *ALR Index* • *ALR Federal Quick Index* • LEXIS • WESTLAW • *ALR Digest to 3d, 4th, 5th, Federal*

lead you to annotations in all the sets (except for A.L.R.1st), and a WESTLAW search will lead you to annotations in all sets (except for A.L.R.1st and A.L.R.2d). Finally, all six sets have digests that provide summaries of the annotations in them. Although more awkward to use, these digests can serve as indexes to the annotations in all the sets.

Exhibit 9.4 tells you what to do if you are further along in your research and already have an opinion (state or federal), a statute (state or federal), or a regulation (federal) that is on point, or potentially on point. Use the methods listed in the second column of Exhibit 9.4 to try to find any annotations that discuss or mention that opinion, statute, or regulation.

Exhibit
Finding Annotations When
You Already Have a Lead

IF YOU ALREADY HAVE A CITATION TO:	USE THE FOLLOWING METHODS OF FINDING ANNOTATIONS THAT MENTION THAT CITATION:
A State Court Opinion	• Shepardize the opinion. • Check KeyCite (on WESTLAW). • Check Auto-Cite (on LEXIS).
A Federal Court Opinion	• Shepardize the opinion. • Check KeyCite (on WESTLAW). • Check Auto-Cite (on LEXIS). • Check the separate volume called *ALR Federal Tables*.
A State Statute	• Shepardize the statute.
A Federal Statute	• Shepardize the statute. • Check the "Table of Laws, Rules, and Regulations" in the last volume of *ALR Index*. • Check the separate volume called *ALR Federal Tables*.
A Federal Regulation	• Shepardize the regulation. • Check the "Table of Laws, Rules, and Regulations" in the last volume of *ALR Index*. • Check the separate volume called *ALR Federal Tables*.

In the next section, we will see that annotations are one of the "citing materials" in Shepard's. This simply means that the annotations have discussed or mentioned whatever you are shepardizing. Hence, if you shepardize the items in the first column of Exhibit 9.4, you will be led to all annotations, if any, that have mentioned that item. If you have access to KeyCite (available on WESTLAW) or to Auto-Cite (available on LEXIS), these computer services will tell you what annotations have mentioned your federal or state court opinion. *ALR Federal Tables* will do the same for federal opinions, statutes, and regulations. Finally, use the "Table of Laws, Rules, and Regulations" to find annotations on a federal statute (in U.S.C., U.S.C.A., or U.S.C.S.) or on a federal administrative regulation (in C.F.R.). This excellent table is located in the last volume of the *ALR Index*.

As indicated earlier, some of the annotations in the six sets are very long and comprehensive. How do you find the law of a *particular* state or court within an annotation without having to read the entire annotation? At the beginning of annotations in A.L.R.3d and A.L.R.4th, you will find a "Table of Jurisdictions Represented," which will direct you to specific sections of the annotation that cover the law of your state. At the beginning of annotations in A.L.R. Fed., there is a "Table of Courts and Circuits," which will direct you to sections of the annotation dealing with certain federal courts. In addition to these tables, there will usually be other indexes or tables of contents at the beginning of the annotations.

TABLE OF JURISDICTIONS REPRESENTED
Consult POCKET PART in this volume for later cases

US: §§ 2[b], 3, 4[a], 5[b], 6[a], 7[a], 10[b]	**Miss:** §§ 4[a]
Ala: §§ 2[b], 4[a], 6[a], 7[a], 8, 10[b]	**Mo:** §§ 4[a], 6[a], 10[b]
Cal: §§ 4[a, b], 7[a, b], 10[b], 11	**NH:** §§ 3, 4[b]
Fla: §§ 5[a]	**NC:** §§ 7[a]
Ga: §§ 3, 4[b], 5[b], 6[b], 10[a]	**Ohio:** §§ 4[a, b], 6[a], 7[a, b], 10[b]
Ill: §§ 4[b], 5[a, b], 6[a, b], 10[a]	**Or:** §§ 4[a], 10[b]
Ind: §§ 4[a], 5[b], 6[a], 7[a, b], 8, 9, 10[b]	**Pa:** §§ 4[a], 7[a], 10[b]
Iowa: §§ 7[a], 8	**Tenn:** §§ 4[a], 5[b], 6[a]
Ky: §§ 3, 4[a], 5[b]	**Tex:** §§ 4[a], 7[a], 10[b]
La: §§ 5[b], 7[a, b]	**Vt:** §§ 9
Me: §§ 5[b], 7[a], 10[b]	**Wash:** §§ 6[a], 7[a], 8
Md: §§ 4[b]	**Wis:** §§ 7[a], 8, 10[b], 11
Mich: §§ 4[a], 10[b]	

TABLE OF COURTS AND CIRCUITS
Consult POCKET PART in this volume for later cases and statutory changes

Sup Ct: §§ 2[a], 3[a], 5, b, 14	**Sixth Cir:** §§ 5[b], 6[b], 10[a, b], 12[a], 13[a], 15[b]
First Cir: §§ 5[b], 6[b], 15[b], 16[a], 18[a]	**Seventh Cir:** §§ 2[a, b], 4[b], 5[b], 10[b], 15[b]
Second Cir: §§ 2[b], 3[a, b], 5[a], 12[a], 16[a], 18[a]	**Eighth Cir:** §§ 3[a], 4[a, b], 5[a, b], 6[a], 12[a], 13[a], 15[b], 16[a], 17, 19
Third Cir: §§ 3[a], 5[a], 7, 11[b], 12[b], 13[a], 15[b]	**Ninth Cir:** §§ 2[a, b], 3[a], 4[a], 5, a, 6[b], 7, 8, 10[a], 11[a, b], 12[a, b], 13[a, b], 15[a, b], 16[b], 17, 18[a, b]
Fourth Cir: §§ 2[b], 3[a], 4[b], 5[a, b], 8, 9, 10[b], 12[a, b], 13[b], 14, 15[a, b], 16[a], 17, 18[a]	**Tenth Cir:** §§ 2[b], 3[a], 5[a, b], 6[a, b], 9, 11[a, b], 12[a], 14, 17, 18[b]
Fifth Cir: §§ 3[a], 5[a, b], 8, 10[a], 11[a, b], 13[a], 15[a], 16[b], 18[b]	**Dist Col Cir:** §§ 3[b], 5[b], 6[b], 10[a, b]
	Ct Cl: § 16[a]

The table at the beginning of annotations in A.L.R.5th is called "Jurisdictional Table of Cited Statutes and Cases." The state-by-state breakdown in the table includes full citations to the statutes and cases discussed in the annotation.

Jurisdictional Table of Cited Statutes and Cases

ALABAMA

A R Civ P, Rule 60(a). See §§ 4[a], 14[a]
Alabama R Civ P, Rule 60(a). See § 5[b]

Antepenko v Antepenko (1991, Ala Civ App) 584 So 2d 836—§ 4[a]
Cornelius v Green (1988, Ala) 521 So 2d 942—§ 5[b]
Merchant v Merchant (1992, Ala Civ App) 599 So 2d 1198— § 14[a]

ARIZONA

16 A R S R Civ P, Rule 60(a). See § 10[b]

Harold Laz Advertising Co. v Dumes (1965) 2 Ariz App 236, 407 P2d 777—§ 10[b]

CALIFORNIA

Cal Code Civ Proc § 473. See §§ 6[a, b], 7[b], 10[a]
Cal Code Civ Proc § 579. See § 10[a]

Bastajian v Brown (1941) 19 Cal 2d 209, 120 P2d 9—§ 10[a]
Benway v Benway (1945) 69 Cal App 2d 574, 159 P2d 682—§ 4[a]

Updating an Annotation

Suppose that you have found an annotation on point. It has led you to very useful law. This annotation, however, may be ten, twenty, thirty, or more years old. How do you update this annotation to find the most current law on the points covered in the annotation? Of course, any opinion or statute found within the annotation can be shepardized as a technique of finding more law. But our focus here is the updating systems within A.L.R. itself. Exhibit 9.5 outlines these systems.

9.5

Exhibit
How to Update an
Annotation

UPDATING AN ANNOTATION IN A.L.R.1st	**UPDATING AN ANNOTATION IN A.L.R.2d**	**UPDATING AN ANNOTATION IN A.L.R.3d, A.L.R.4th, A.L.R.5th, AND A.L.R. Fed.**
• *A.L.R. Blue Book of Supplemental Decisions*	• *A.L.R.2d Later Case Service*	• Pocket part of volume containing the annotation
• "Annotation History Table" in the last volume of *ALR Index*	• "Annotation History Table" in the last volume of *ALR Index*	• "Annotation History Table" in the last volume of *ALR Index*
	• 1-800-225-7488	• 1-800-225-7488

Note: Any opinion or statute you find in an annotation can also be updated by shepardizing that opinion or statute.

If the annotation you want updated is in A.L.R.1st, start with the *A.L.R. Blue Book of Supplemental Decisions.* (Check each volume of this *Blue Book,* because the volumes are noncumulative.) If the annotation you want updated is in A.L.R.2d, start with the *A.L.R.2d Later Case Service.* (Check the volume that covers your annotation, plus the pocket part of this volume of the *Later Case Service.*) If the annotation you want updated is in A.L.R.3d, or in A.L.R.4th, or in A.L.R.5th, or in A.L.R. Fed., you check the pocket part of the volume containing the annotation.

There are no pocket parts to the volumes of A.L.R.1st and A.L.R.2d. Hence you must use the *Blue Book* and *Later Case Service* in order to perform needed updating. Thankfully, the volumes of A.L.R.3d, A.L.R.4th, A.L.R.5th, and A.L.R. Fed. *do* have pocket parts that can be used to update annotations in them. The existence of these pocket parts makes it much easier to update annotations in A.L.R.3d, A.L.R.4th, A.L.R.5th, and A.L.R. Fed. than to update annotations in A.L.R.1st or A.L.R.2d.

A toll-free number is available for obtaining additional updating information on the annotations in A.L.R.2d, A.L.R.3d, A.L.R.4th, A.L.R.5th, and A.L.R. Fed. Any member of the public can use this number; you do not have to be a subscriber. Currently, the number is 1-800-225-7488. It is called the *Latest Case Service Hotline.*

One final updating feature must be covered: the "Annotation History Table." Note that Exhibit 9.5 lists this table as a further method of updating annotations in all six sets of A.L.R. The law in some annotations may become so outdated that it is replaced by another annotation. The outdated annotation is called a **superseded annotation,** which should no longer be read. If, however, an annotation is substantially updated but not totally replaced by another annotation, the older annotation is called a **supplemented annotation,** which can be read along with the newer annotation. There are two ways to find out which annotations have been superseded or supplemented. Check the "Annotation History Table" found in the last volume of the *ALR Index.* Another way to find out is to check the standard method for updating annotations in A.L.R.1st (the *Blue Book*), in A.L.R.2d *(Later Case Service),* in A.L.R.3d (pocket parts), in A.L.R.4th (pocket parts), in A.L.R.5th (pocket parts), and in A.L.R. Fed. (pocket parts).

Note on Another Annotated Reporter of Lawyers Co-op Lawyers Co-op publishes *United States Supreme Court Reports, Lawyers' Edition* (abbreviated L. Ed.). This is also an annotated reporter in that it prints the full text of opinions (those of the U.S. Supreme Court) with annotations on issues within some of these opinions. (See photo of this reporter on page 42.)

Checklist #3   Checklist for Finding and Updating Annotations in A.L.R.1st, A.L.R.2d, A.L.R.3d, A.L.R.4th, A.L.R.5th, and A.L.R. Fed.

1. Your goal is to use the six sets to find annotations on your research problem. The annotations are extensive research papers on numerous points of law.

2. The most current annotations available are in A.L.R.3d, in A.L.R.4th, in A.L.R.5th, and in A.L.R. Fed. Start with these sets. Then try to find annotations in A.L.R.2d and in A.L.R.1st. Use the CARTWHEEL to help you locate annotations in the following index resources:

(a) To find annotations in A.L.R.3d, in A.L.R.4th, and in A.L.R.5th:
- Use *ALR Index*
- Use *ALR Quick Index 3d, 4th, 5th*
- Use LEXIS or WESTLAW
- Use *ALR Digest to 3d, 4th, 5th, Federal*

(b) To find annotations in A.L.R. Fed.:
- Use *ALR Index*
- Use *ALR Federal Quick Index*
- Use LEXIS or WESTLAW
- Use *ALR Digest to 3d, 4th, 5th, Federal*

(c) To find annotations in A.L.R.2d:
- Use *ALR Index*
- Use LEXIS
- Use *ALR2d Digest*

(d) To find annotations in A.L.R.1st:
- Use *ALR First Series Quick Index*
- Use *Permanent ALR Digest*

3. If you have already found a particular law (see list below) and you want to know if there is an annotation that mentions that law, check the following resources:

(a) If you already have a state court opinion:
- Shepardize the opinion
- Check KeyCite (on WESTLAW)
- Check Auto-Cite (on LEXIS)

(b) If you already have a federal court opinion:
- Shepardize the opinion
- Check KeyCite (on WESTLAW)
- Check Auto-Cite (on LEXIS)
- Check *ALR Federal Tables*

(c) If you already have a state statute:
- Shepardize the statute
- Check KeyCite (on WESTLAW)
- Check Auto-Cite (on LEXIS)
- Check *ALR Federal Tables*

(d) If you already have a federal statute:
- Shepardize the statute

- Check the "Table of Laws, Rules, and Regulations" in the last volume of *ALR Index*
- Check *ALR Federal Tables*

(e) If you already have a federal administrative regulation:
- Shepardize the regulation
- Check the "Table of Laws, Rules, and Regulations" in the last volume of *ALR Index*
- Check *ALR Federal Tables*

4. Use the tables or other indexes at the beginning of the annotation to help you locate specific sections of the annotation. Section 1[a] of the annotation will give you the *scope* covered in the annotation. (Before you spend much time with the annotation, however, check the "Annotation History Table" to determine if it has been superseded or supplemented by another annotation. See step 6 below.)

5. Section 1[b] of the annotation will give you citations to related annotations and materials you may want to check. In § 1[b] you might find a reference to annotations that are more relevant than (or as relevant as) the annotation you are about to examine.

6. Update all annotations that are on point.

(a) To update an annotation in A.L.R.1st:
- Check the *A.L.R. Blue Book of Supplemental Decisions*
- Check the "Annotation History Table" in the last volume of *ALR Index*

(b) To update an annotation in A.L.R.2d:
- Check the *A.L.R.2d Later Case Service*
- Check the "Annotation History Table" in the last volume of *ALR Index*
- Call 1-800-225-7488

(c) To update an annotation in A.L.R.3d, in A.L.R.4th, in A.L.R.5th, or in A.L.R. Fed.:
- Check the pocket part
- Check the "Annotation History Table" in the last volume of *ALR Index*
- Call 1-800-225-7488

7. Within the six sets of annotations, Lawyers Co-op will give you lists of its other publications (e.g., Am. Jur. 2d) that cover the same or similar topics in its annotations. As we saw earlier, the main vehicle used to provide these leads is the list called Total Client-Service Library References. (See page 73.)

Assignment 9.4

Find one annotation that might be helpful in researching each of the topics for the chapter 9 assignments (printed at the beginning of the chapter at the end of Section A). Locate one per topic. In each annotation, find a case written by a state court of your state or by a federal court that sits in your state. If you cannot find a case written by such a court, select a different annotation that does contain one. Give the citation of the annotation and of the case that it cites.

SECTION E   SHEPARD'S

There have been four great research inventions in the law:

- The key number system of the West digests
- The annotations in A.L.R.1st, A.L.R.2d, A.L.R.3d, A.L.R.4th, A.L.R.5th, and A.L.R. Fed
- CALR (computer-assisted legal research), particularly WESTLAW and LEXIS
- Shepard's

The first three are extensively used as case finders. Although Shepard's is not primarily designed to be a case finder, it can serve this function, along with other functions, as we shall now see.

Shepardize

> "[D]iligent research, which includes Shepardizing cases, is a professional responsibility."
>
> —*Cimino v. Yale University,* 638 F. Supp. 952, 959 (D. Conn. 1986).

The verb **shepardize** means to use the volumes (or CD-ROM or online version) of *Shepard's Citations* to obtain validation and other data on the primary authority you are checking. (You can also shepardize some secondary authorities, such as legal periodical articles, although this is not as common as shepardizing primary authority.) When you shepardize opinions, statutes, and other primary authorities, Shepard's will help you answer questions such as the following:

- Is this opinion that I just found still good law? Is it still valid? Have other courts followed it or rejected it?
- How can I find other opinions like it?
- Is this statute that I found still good law? Is it still valid? Has it been changed by the legislature? How have the courts interpreted it?

Before we examine how Shepard's provides you with this kind of information, review the following material:

- page 67 on the kinds of Shepard's volumes that exist
- page 96 on the use of Shepard's as one of the six techniques of finding a parallel cite
- page 36 on the meaning of an advance sheet for Shepard's

Shepard's is a **citator,** which is a book (CD-ROM or online service) that contains lists of citations that can help you assess the current validity of an item and can give you leads to other relevant materials. We will examine Shepard's as a citator through the following topics:

    (a)   The units of a set of Shepard's
    (b)   Determining whether you have a complete set of Shepard's
    (c)   The distinction between cited material and citing material
    (d)   Abbreviations in Shepard's
    (e)   Shepardizing a case (court opinion)
    (f)   Shepardizing a statute
    (g)   Shepardizing a regulation

We will limit ourselves to shepardizing cases, statutes, and regulations. Knowing how to shepardize these items, however, will go a long way toward equipping you to shepardize other primary authorities as well, such as constitutions, administrative decisions, charters, and rules of court.

(a) The Units of a Set of Shepard's

By "set of Shepard's" we mean the group of volumes of Shepard's that cover whatever you are trying to shepardize. Every set of Shepard's includes two main units: (a) *hardcover* or bound red volumes and (b) white, gold, blue, gray, yellow, or red *pamphlet* supplements. The hardcover volumes and the pamphlet supplements are sometimes broken into parts, e.g., Part 1, Part 2. The white pamphlet is the advance sheet that is later thrown away and **cumulated** (or consolidated) into a larger pamphlet. Eventually, all the pamphlets are thrown away and cumulated into hardcover or bound red volumes. The pamphlet supplements contain the most current shepardizing material.

Example of a set of
Shepard's

(b) Determining Whether You Have a Complete Set of Shepard's

Shepard's Citations comes in three formats: paper (pamphlets and hardcover or bound volumes), CD-ROM, and online (through WESTLAW and LEXIS). The CD-ROM and online versions are the easiest to use. In most instances, you simply enter what you want to shepardize once in order to call up all available citing materials on the computer screen. Paper Shepard's, which most researchers must use, are not as easy.

As we saw earlier, Shepard's comes in sets, e.g., the set for Illinois, the set for federal statutes. For some sets, there may be ten hardcover or bound volumes and three or four pamphlet supplements. Before you start shepardizing, you must determine whether you have a complete set in front of you on the shelf. To determine whether your set is complete, go through the following steps:

1. Pick up the most recently dated pamphlet supplement—usually the advance sheet—that the library has received for that set of Shepard's (see photo of pamphlet supplements on page 36). The date is at the top of the supplement. Be careful, however; the pamphlet supplement you find on the shelf may *not* be the most recent; someone else may be using it or it may have been misshelved. To determine the most recent Shepard's supplement received by the library, check the library's computer catalog. Type in the name of the set of Shepard's. Among the information provided, the computer should tell you the most recent supplement received by the library. If the library does not have a computer catalog, ask a librarian how you can determine what is the most recent.
2. Once you are satisfied that you have the most recent unit, find the following statement on the front cover: WHAT YOUR LIBRARY SHOULD CONTAIN. This will

tell you what is a complete set of Shepard's for the set you are using. Go down the list and make sure everything you are told should be on the shelf is indeed there. (The last entry on the list should be the pamphlet supplement that contains the list you are reading.)

Assume, for example, that today's date is January 1998. You want to shepardize a Wisconsin state case and a Wisconsin state statute. You go to *Shepard's Wisconsin Citations*. On the front cover of a January 1998 advance sheet for this set of Shepard's, you find the following:

WHAT YOUR LIBRARY SHOULD CONTAIN

1995 Bound Volumes 1 and 2, Cases*
1995 Bound Volume 3, Statutes*
1995 Bound Volume 4, Case Names*
Supplemented with:
—*April, 1997 Annual Cumulative Supplement Vol. 90 No. 4*
—*January, 1998 Advance Sheet Vol. 91 No. 1*

DESTROY ALL OTHER ISSUES

To be complete, therefore, the following units of *Shepard's Wisconsin Citations* should be on the shelf:

- a 1995 bound volume (vol. 1) of *Shepard's Wisconsin Citations* covering cases; and
- a 1995 bound volume (vol. 2) of *Shepard's Wisconsin Citations* covering cases; and
- a 1995 bound volume (vol. 3) of *Shepard's Wisconsin Citations* covering statutes; and
- a 1995 bound volume (vol. 4) of *Shepard's Wisconsin Citations* covering case names; and
- an April, 1997 Annual Cumulative Supplement pamphlet (vol. 90, no. 4) of *Shepard's Wisconsin Citations* covering cases, statutes, and case names; and
- a January, 1998 Advance Sheet pamphlet (vol. 91, no. 1) of *Shepard's Wisconsin Citations* covering cases, statutes, and case names.

The last item on the list is always the pamphlet that contains the list you are reading. Hence, the above list is found on the January, 1998 Advance Sheet (vol. 91, no. 1) of *Shepard's Wisconsin Citations*.

Occasionally, the list can become quite involved. For example, you may find two lists on the pamphlet. One list tells you what should be on the shelf before a certain bound Shepard's volume is received by the library, and a second list tells you what should be on the shelf after that bound volume is received by the library. Yet the same process is followed. Carefully go through the list (or lists) one unit at a time, checking to see if what the list says should be on the shelf is there.[3]

Why do you need to take the time to be sure that the set of Shepard's you want to use is complete? Because the failure to do so might result in your missing vital information about what you are shepardizing. Assume you are in the library reading the case of *Smith v. Smith* decided in 1990. At the time you are reading this case, you are not aware that it was overruled in 1995. The reporter containing the opinion does not give you this information, because the overruling occurred after the reporter volume was printed. Before you rely on a case, you know that you must shepardize it. You go to the right set of Shepard's and check the *Smith* case in every

---

3. It is also possible to shepardize *after* the date of the most recent supplement received by the library. For a fee, a researcher can find out what has happened since the last supplement. This is done on the phone, by fax, or online.

bound volume and pamphlet supplement on the shelf. None of them, however, tells you that there are problems with the case. Unfortunately, the pamphlet that says *Smith* was overruled is not on the shelf. Someone else may be using it in another room of the library. Careless researchers would not even know that the pamphlet was missing. Careful researchers, however, make it their business to know what should be on the shelf. They do this by checking the "What Your Library Should Contain" list. When you do this, as a conscientious researcher, you realize that you can't complete your sheparizing of *Smith* until you find the missing pamphlet. You go from table to table in the library looking for it. If this doesn't work, you ask a librarian for help in locating it.

(c) The Distinction between "Cited Material" and "Citing Material"

- **Cited material** is whatever you are sheparizing, such as a case, statute, or regulation.
- **Citing material** is whatever mentions, treats, or discusses the cited material, such as another case, a legal periodical article, an annotation in A.L.R., etc.

Suppose you are sheparizing the case found in 75 F.2d 107 (a case that begins on page 107 of volume 75 of *Federal Reporter 2d*). While reading through the columns of Shepard's, you find the following cite: f56 S.E.2d 46. The *cited* material is 75 F.2d 107. The *citing* material is 56 S.E.2d 46, which followed (f) or agreed with the decision in 75 F.2d 107.

Suppose you are sheparizing a statute: 22 U.S.C. § 55.8 (section 55.8 of title 22 of the United States Code). While reading through the columns of Shepard's, you find the following cite: 309 U.S. 45. The *cited* material is 22 U.S.C. § 55.8. The *citing* material is 309 U.S. 45, which interpreted, treated, or mentioned 22 U.S.C. § 55.8.

Shepard's always indicates the cited material by the black bold print along the top of every page of Shepard's and by the black bold print numbers that are the volume or section numbers of the cited material. In the following excerpt, the cited material is 404 P.2d 460. The citing material follows the number –460–:

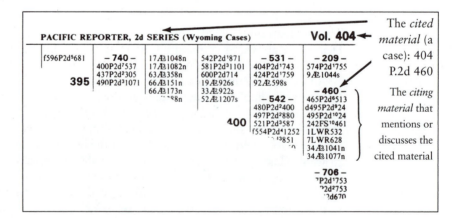

In the following excerpt, the cited material is a statute: § 37–31, which is in Article (Art.) 2 of the Wyoming Statutes. The citing material is indicated beneath **§ 37–31.**

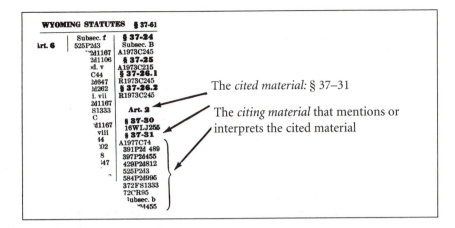

In recent sets of Shepard's the volume number or title number of the cited material is placed in a small box. In the following example, the citing material is 131 *Arizona Reports* 93. The cited material is the Ninth Circuit case, 106F3d⁵1475.

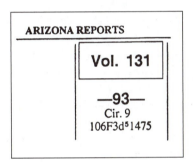

As we will see later (in Exhibit 9.7), another change in recent sets of Shepard's is the addition of the actual name of the parties in the cited case.

(d) Abbreviation in Shepard's

Shepard's packs a tremendous amount of information (the cites) into every one of its pages. Each page contains up to eight columns of cites for the cited and the citing materials. For the sake of economy, Shepard's uses many abbreviations that are peculiar to Shepard's. For example:

FS → means *Federal Supplement*

A³ → means *American Law Reports 3d*

* → (asterisk) means that the year that follows the citing case is the year of the cited statute or regulation; it is not the year of the citing case

Δ → (delta symbol) means that the year that follows the citing case is the year of the citing case; it is not the year of the cited statute or regulation

Most researchers do not know the meaning of every abbreviation and signal used by Shepard's. *But you must know where to find their meaning.* There are two places to go:

- The abbreviations tables at the beginning of most units of Shepard's (for an example, see page 121).
- The preface or explanation pages found at the beginning of most units of Shepard's.

Many researchers neglect the latter. Buried within the preface or explanation pages may be an interpretation of an abbreviation or symbol that is not covered in the abbreviation tables.

(e) Shepardizing a Case (Court Opinion)

Almost every reporter has a corresponding set of Shepard's that will enable you to shepardize cases in that reporter (page 69). For example, if the case you want to shepardize is 40 N.Y.2d 100, you go to the set of Shepard's that covers cases in New York—*Shepard's New York Citations*. If the case you want to shepardize is 402 F.2d 1064, you go to the Shepard's that covers F.2d cases—*Shepard's Federal Citations*.

Of course, many cases have parallel cites—the case is found word-for-word in more than one reporter. You can shepardize most cases with parallel cites through either reporter. Assume you want to shepardize the following case:

> *Welch v. Swasey,* 193 Mass. 364, 79 N.E. 745 (1907)

This case is found in two reporters: *Massachusetts Reports* and *North Eastern Reporter.* Hence, you can shepardize the case and obtain similar citing material from two different sets of Shepard's: *Shepard's Massachusetts Citations* and *Shepard's Northeastern Citations.* A thorough researcher will shepardize his or her case by using *both* sets of Shepard's.

To shepardize a *case* means to obtain the following six kinds of information about the cited case (the case you are shepardizing):

1. The **parallel cite** of the case. The first entry in parentheses is the parallel cite. (See page 96 for the reasons why you may find no parallel cite here.)
2. The **history of the case.** Here you will find all cases that are part of the same litigation, e.g., appeals, reversals.
3. The **treatment of the case.** Here you will find all citing cases that have analyzed or mentioned the cited case—for example, followed it, distinguished it, criticized it, or just mentioned it.
4. Citing legal periodical literature (law review article, case note, etc.) that has analyzed or mentioned the cited case.
5. Citing annotations in A.L.R.1st, A.L.R.2d, A.L.R.3d, A.L.R.4th, A.L.R.5th, or A.L.R. Fed. that have analyzed or mentioned the cited case.
6. Citing opinions of the attorney general that have analyzed or mentioned the cited case.

A *parallel cite* (item 1 above) is an additional reference where you will be able to read the same material word-for-word. There are two main reasons you may need a parallel cite. First, the rules of citation may require you to include a parallel cite (see chapter 5). Second, the cite to a case you have may be to a reporter your library does not subscribe to; a parallel cite may lead you to a reporter your library does have.

The *history of the case* (item 2) gives you every decision that was part of the same litigation as the case you are shepardizing. For example, you will be given abbreviations that tell you whether the case went up on appeal where it was affirmed (a), dismissed (D), modified (m), reversed (r), etc. Citations to each of these decisions are provided. If one of the decisions is so recent that its traditional citation is not yet available, Shepard's will give you the **docket number** of the decision. (A *docket number* is the consecutive number assigned to a case by the court when it is filed by the party bringing the litigation.) The most obvious reason you need the history of a case is that you do not want to cite a case that is no longer valid. Even if this has not yet happened to the case, knowing that it has been appealed should alert you that the case might be drastically changed on appeal.

The *treatment of the case* (item 3) tells you how other cases in unrelated litigation have responded to (treated) the case you are shepardizing. For example, you will be given abbreviations that tell you whether the case has been criticized (c), questioned (q), explained (e), followed (f), overruled[4] (o), etc. by other cases—the *citing cases*. You need to know how a case has been treated in order to assess how much weight it can be given. A case that has been ignored or criticized is obviously of less weight than one that other cases have cited with approval (followed—f).

As you can see, both the history and the treatment of a case help you perform the third level of legal research, validation research, which we introduced in chapter 8 and will examine again in chapter 14.

The great value of Shepard's as a case finder comes through items 3 to 5. If a citing case (item 3) analyzes or mentions the cited case (which you are shepardizing), the two cases probably deal with similar facts and law. All citing cases, therefore, are potential leads to more case law on point. Similarly, a citing legal periodical article (item 4) or a citing A.L.R. annotation (item 5) will probably discuss a variety of cases in addition to the cited case. Hence again, you are led to more case law through Shepard's.

One final point before we examine an extended excerpt from a Shepard's page. Recall that cases in reporters are broken down into headnotes at the beginning of the case (see page 57). These headnotes, written by private publishers such as West, are small-paragraph summaries of portions of the case printed just before the text of the case begins.[5]

A case can involve many issues, only a few of which may be relevant to your research problem. Is it possible to narrow your shepardizing to those parts of the case that are most relevant to your research problem? Yes. It is possible to shepardize a portion of a case through its headnote numbers. In effect, you are shepardizing the headnote! Let's examine how this is done:

- Every headnote of the cited case has a consecutive number: 1, 2, 3, 4, etc.

  Assume, for example, that you are shepardizing the *Jackson* case—the cited case—and that there are ten headnotes to this case. But as you read *Jackson,* it is clear that you are interested in only the fifth headnote. The other nine summarize parts of the case that are not relevant to your research problem.

- When the editors of Shepard's come across a *citing* case that deals with only one of the headnotes of the *cited* case, they include the number of this headnote as part of the reference to the *citing* case in the columns of Shepard's. The number is printed as a small raised, or elevated, number—called a **superscript** number—within the reference to the citing case. For example, the number 3 in the following cite is printed as a superscript number: 23N.Y.^3487 (1965). You've seen superscript numbers before. Footnote numbers, for example, are almost always in superscript on a page.[6]

  When you shepardize the *Jackson* case in our example, you find that many citing cases have analyzed or mentioned *Jackson*. It might take hours for you to read them all. Here are three that you find:

  $$102\text{N.Y.}^334$$
  $$111\text{N.Y.}^5109$$
  $$116\text{N.Y.}21$$

  Two of these citing cases have superscript numbers. The second one is of particular interest to you because it dealt with the fifth headnote of the *Jackson* case. Though you don't ignore the other two, you concentrate on 111 N.Y. 109.

---

4. A case is **reversed** when it is invalidated by a court in a later case involving the same litigation. A case is **overruled** when it is invalidated by a court in a later case involving different litigation.
5. Most reporters, such as those published by West, call these summaries *headnotes*. A few, however, call them *syllabi* (plural of **syllabus**). West has a different meaning for *syllabus*. In West reporters, a syllabus is a one-paragraph summary of the entire case, which is printed just below the caption and just before the headnotes.
6. In the language of printing, a number printed slightly *below* the line is a **subscript** character. In the following example, the number 7 is superscript and the number 8 is subscript: court^7, court_8.

You leave Shepard's and go read this case in a reporter (on CD-ROM or online). Be careful. It is easy to become confused. The superscript number refers to the headnote number of the *cited* case, not of the *citing* case, even though this number is printed within the reference of the citing case. The number 5 in the citing case, 111 N.Y. 109, refers to the fifth headnote of the *Jackson* case, It is not the fifth headnote of 111 N.Y. 109.

Let's look at another example. Assume that you are shepardizing *Welch v. Swasey,* 193 Mass. 364. In the columns of Shepard's you find the following:

f196Mas^{8}476

The *citing* is 196 Mass. 476. This case follows (agrees with) the *cited* case of *Welch v. Swasey,* 193 Mass. 364. Note the raised number 8—the superscript figure. This 8 refers to the eighth headnote of the *cited* case, *Welch v. Swasey.* The *citing* case dealt with that portion of *Welch* that was summarized in the eighth headnote of the *Welch* case. Again, do not make the mistake of thinking that the small raised number refers to a headnote in the citing case. It refers to a headnote number of the *cited* case.

A final example. Assume that you are researching the problem of whether a person can sue his or her spouse for negligence: Are spouses immune from tort actions against each other? In your research you come across the promising case of *Self v. Self,* which starts on page 65 of volume 376 of *Pacific Reporter 2d* (376 P.2d 65). The beginning of this case is excerpted in Exhibit 9.6.

9.6

Exhibit
Excerpt from a Case
(Self v. Self) in *Pacific Reporter 2d*

SELF v. SELF   Cal. **65**
Cite as 376 P.2d 65

26 Cal.Rptr. 97
Catherine SELF, Plaintiff and Appellant,
v.
Adrian SELF, Defendant and Respondent.
L.A. 26878.

Supreme Court of California,
In Bank.
Nov. 9, 1962.

Action against husband by wife, whose arm allegedly was broken in course of unlawful assault by husband. The Superior Court, Los Angeles County, John F. McCarthy, J., granted the husband's motion for summary judgment and the wife appealed. The Supreme Court, Peters, J., held that wife could recover if husband broke her arm in course of unlawful assault.

Reversed.

Opinion, 20 Cal.Rptr. 781, vacated.

1. Husband and Wife 205(2)
Rule of interspousal immunity for intentional torts is abandoned; one spouse may sue the other in tort where tort is intentional.

2. Husband and Wife 205(2)
Wife could recover from husband if he broke her arm in course of unlawful assault; disapproving Peters v. Peters, 156 Cal. 32, 103 P. 219, 23 L.R.A.,N.S., 699; Watson v. Watson, 39 Cal.2d 305, 246 P.2d 19. West's Ann.Civ.Code, § 163.5.

3. Negligence 14
Generally, in absence of statute or some other compelling reason of public policy, where there is negligence proximately causing injury, there should be liability.

Robert H. Lund and John R. Brunner, Long Beach, for plaintiff and appellant.

Wolver & Wolver and Eugene L. Wolver, Los Angeles, amici curiae, on behalf of plaintiff and appellant.

Baird, Mooney & Baird, C. Duane Mooney and Woodrow W. Baird, Long Beach, for defendant and respondent.

9.6

Exhibit
Excerpt from a Case
(Self v. Self) in *Pacific
Reporter 2d*—continued

PETERS, Justice.

[1, 2]   The sole problem involved in this case is whether California should continue to follow the rule of interspousal immunity for intentional torts first announced in this state in 1909 in the case of Peters v. Peters, 156 Cal. 32, 103 P. 219, 23 L.R.A., N.S., 699. Because the reasons upon which the Peters case was predicated no longer exist, and because of certain legislative changes made in recent years, we are of the opinion that the rule of the Peters case should be abandoned. In other words, it is our belief that the rule should be that one spouse may sue the other in tort, at least where that tort is an intentional one. . . .

Note the following characteristics of the case in Exhibit 9.6:

- The case has three headnotes.
- The headnotes are numbered consecutively: 1, 2, 3.
- The headnotes also have key numbers consisting of a topic and a number [Husband and Wife 205(2) for the first two headnotes, and Negligence 14 for the third].
- The headnotes summarize portions of the opinion that begins after the name of the judge who wrote the opinion (Justice Peters). The consecutive numbers of the headnotes correspond to the bracketed numbers in the opinion. For example, the first two headnotes summarize that portion of the opinion that begins with the bracketed numbers [1, 2] just below the justice's name. The third headnote summarizes the portion of the opinion that begins with the bracketed number [3] (not shown in Exhibit 9.6).

As indicated, you find this case promising in your research. You want to use this case in the memorandum of law that you will be submitting to your supervisor. (A **memorandum of law** is a written explanation of what the law is and how it might apply to a fact situation.) But you are not ready to use this case—you haven't shepardized it yet. You must never rely on a case until you find out its history and treatment, as explained earlier. Shepard's will tell you.

To shepardize a case in the *Pacific Reporter 2d,* you use *Shepard's Pacific Reporter Citations,* as we saw in the chart on page 70 in chapter 3. Exhibit 9.7 shows a sample page from *Shepard's Pacific Reporter Citations* that will enable you to start shepardizing the *Self v. Self* case. Let's examine this sample page closely.

Note the following characteristics of the Shepard's page in Exhibit 9.7:

- There are six columns on this page.
- The names of the cases to be shepardized—the *cited cases*—are all given in full. Toward the bottom of the fifth column is the full name of the case you are shepardizing, *Self v. Self*. This is a recent feature of Shepard's. Earlier editions of Shepard's did not give the actual names of the parties of the cited case. You were simply given the numbers of its citation. Now you are given both. The first cited case shepardized on this page is the *Cocanougher* case in the first column; the last cited case is *Self*.
- Another recent feature is the date of the cited case printed just below its name. *Self* was decided in 1962.
- The volume number of the cited cases is placed in a box. See the top of the second column. All the cited cases following this box are in volume 376 of the *Pacific Reporter 2d*. All the cited cases before this box are in volume 375 of the *Pacific Reporter 2d*.

9.7

.... Sample page from *Shepard's Pacific Reporter Citations*

Exhibit

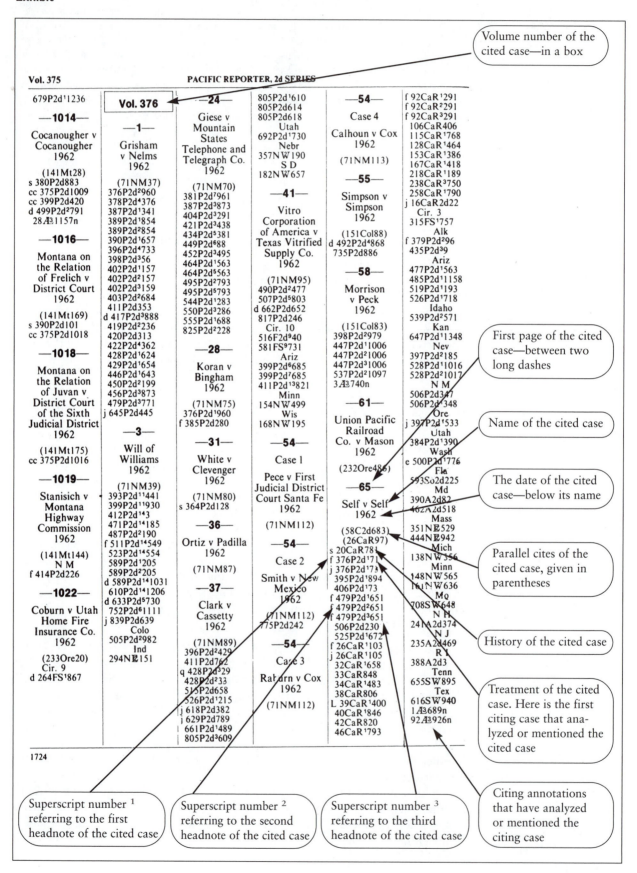

Volume number of the cited case—in a box

Vol. 375

PACIFIC REPORTER, 2d SERIES

679P2d¹1236	**Vol. 376**	**—24—**	805P2d¹610	**—54—**	f 92CaR¹291

First page of the cited case—between two long dashes

Name of the cited case

The date of the cited case—below its name

Parallel cites of the cited case, given in parentheses

History of the cited case

Treatment of the cited case. Here is the first citing case that analyzed or mentioned the cited case

Citing annotations that have analyzed or mentioned the citing case

Superscript number ¹ referring to the first headnote of the cited case

Superscript number ² referring to the second headnote of the cited case

Superscript number ³ referring to the third headnote of the cited case

- The first page number of the cited cases is centered in the column between two long dashes. The first page of the *Cocanougher* case is 1014. The first page of the *Self* case is 65. (Look back at the actual text of the *Self* case in Exhibit 9.6. You can confirm that this case begins on page 65 of volume 376 of the *Pacific Reporter 2d*. See the top right corner of Exhibit 9.6.)
- Parallel cites are given in parentheses beneath the name and year of the case. There are two parallel cites to *Self v. Self*: (58C2d683) and (26CaR97). You are not expected to know what C2d, CaR, or any other abbreviation means. Check the abbreviations table and preface material in any Shepard's unit (other than the advance sheet) for the meaning of abbreviations. There we are told that C2d means *California Supreme Court Reports, Second Series* and that CaR means *California Reporter*. Hence the *Self* case can be found in three places: 376 P.2d 65, 58 C2d 683, and 26 CaR 97. (Note that the top of the caption in Exhibit 9.6 gives us the *California Reporter* parallel cite, but not the C2d parallel cite. The C2d cite was not available at the time the *Pacific Reporter 2d* volume in Exhibit 9.6 was printed.)
- There are a number of abbreviations that lead you to the *history of the cited case*. Small "s", for example, means same case at a different stage of the litigation. The *Self* case includes the following notation: s 20CaR781. If you went to volume 20 of the *California Reporter* and turned to page 781, you would find that something occurred (we are not told what) in the *Self* litigation. For example, the court might have denied a particular motion or rendered an opinion against one of the parties. To find out, you need to go to 20 CaR 781. There are other history notations on the sample page in Exhibit 9.7. Find the "cc" reference for the *Cocanougher* case. This means connected case. The reference may be to a case involving the same parties, but in a different action.
- Most of the other references in Exhibit 9.7 give you the *treatment of the cited case*. This is done by providing numerous citing cases that have analyzed or mentioned the cited case. The first citing case for *Self* is: f 376P2d[1]71. This tells you that the cited case *(Self)* was followed (f) by the citing case found at 376 P.2d 71. Page 71 refers to the page number where the citing case makes specific reference to the cited case, *Self*. What does this citing case say about *Self*? We are not told other than that it followed (f) *Self*. To find out, you need to go to page 71 of volume 376 of the *Pacific Reporter 2d*. (In a moment we will discuss the superscript number 1 before the page number: [1]71.)
- Examine the other notations in front of citing cases: "e" means the citing case explained the cited case; "L" means the citing case limited or restricted the application of the cited case; "j" means the cited case was analyzed or mentioned in a dissenting opinion of the citing case. Again, all these abbreviations are explained for you at the beginning of the Shepard's volume or pamphlet.
- The overwhelming number of citations for the *Self* case constitute the *treatment of the case* in which citing cases have analyzed or mentioned the cited case, *Self*. Note that these citing cases are broken down by court. The citing cases begin with the courts of the same state as the cited case—California for the *Self* case. Then you get federal citing cases, if any, and the state citing cases, if any. There are many state citing cases for *Self* in the sixth column, beginning with Alaska state cases (Alk) and ending with Texas state cases (Tex).
- Citing annotations also analyze or mention the cited case. The references to these annotations, if any, are printed after the citing cases. There are two citing annotations for *Self*, the first in volume 1 and the second in volume 92 of *American Law Reports, Third Series*.
- Finally, note the numerous superscript numbers within the citing cases: [1], [2], [3], [4], [5], [6], etc. Although these numbers are found within the cites of citing cases, they refer to headnote numbers of the cit*ed* case. They tell you that the citing case dealt with the points of law that are summarized in that particular headnote number of the cited case. Of the many citing cases for *Self*, let's look at the following three in the fifth column:

376P2d^{1}71
479P2d^{2}651
479P2d^{3}651

These three citing cases analyzed or mentioned the cited case, *Self.* In particular, the first citing case dealt with the portion of *Self* that was summarized in the first headnote of *Self.* The next citing case dealt with the portion of *Self* that was summarized in the second headnote of *Self.* The last citing case dealt with the portion of *Self* that was summarized in the third headnote of *Self.*

- Look back at the *Self* excerpt in Exhibit 9.6. Note again that there are three consecutively numbered headnotes: 1, 2, 3. These numbers correspond to the superscript numbers ^{1}, ^{2}, ^{3} in the citing cases for *Self* in the Shepard's excerpt in Exhibit 9.7. Assume that when you read the *Self* case, you were particularly interested in the court's discussion of negligence, because your research problem has negligence issues in it. Read the third headnote in Exhibit 9.6. It specifically refers to negligence. Hence, when you shepardize *Self,* you want to give particular attention to any citing case that has a superscript number ^{3}. There are four of them in the fifth and sixth columns of the Shepard's excerpt in Exhibit 9.7: 479P2d^{3}651, 92CaR^{3}291, 238CaR^{3}750, and 435P2d^{3}9. You may want to read all the citing cases, but these four will get your immediate attention because they are potentially more relevant to your research.
- Of course, when you shepardize a case, you need to check the cited case *(Self)* in every unit of Shepard's. See the earlier discussion on determining whether you have a complete set of Shepard's. In the other units of Shepard's you will use to shepardize *Self,* you may find other citing cases containing the superscript ^{3}.
- Note that some of the citing cases have no superscript numbers. This makes it a little more difficult to assess how they treated the cited case. Like all citing references, however (including those with superscript numbers), you must read the actual text of a citing case (in reporters, on CD-ROM, or online) to determine in what manner it analyzed or mentioned the cited case. Shepard's is only the first step in finding out.
- When shepardizing a case, you may find citing legal periodical literature that has analyzed or mentioned the cited case. The excerpt from Shepard's in Exhibit 9.7, however, has no citing legal periodical literature for *Self.* (Nor do any of the other cited cases in the excerpt have any citing legal periodical literature.)
- When shepardizing a case, you may find citing opinions of the attorney general that have analyzed or mentioned the cited case. The excerpt from Shepard's in Exhibit 9.7, however, has no citing opinions of the attorney general for *Self.* (Nor do any of the other cited cases in the excerpt have any citing opinions of the attorney general.)

Checklist #4a   Checklist for Shepardizing a Case

1. You have a case you want to shepardize. In what reporter is this case found? Go to the set of Shepard's in the library that covers this reporter. (See page 69.)

2. If the case you want to shepardize has a *parallel cite* that you already have, find out if the library has a set of Shepard's for the other reporter volumes in which the case is also printed. You may be able to shepardize the case through two sets of Shepard's. If so, shepardize the case twice. You may be able to find information about the cited case in one set of Shepard's that is not available in the set of Shepard's used to shepardize it through its parallel cite.

3. Know whether you have a complete set of Shepard's in front of you by reading the "What Your Library Should Contain" list on the most recent pamphlet of that set.

4. The general rule is that you must check the cite of the case you are shepardizing (the cited case) in *every* unit of a set of Shepard's. With experience you will learn, however, that it is possible to bypass some of the units of the set. There may be information on the front cover of one of the Shepard's volumes, for example, that will tell you that the date or volume number of the reporter containing your cited case is not covered in that Shepard's volume. You can bypass it and move on to other units of the set.

Checklist #4a   Checklist for Shepardizing a Case—continued

5. In checking all the units of Shepard's, it is recommended that you work *backward* by examining the most recent Shepard's pamphlets first so that you start with the latest *history* of the case and the latest citing materials in the *treatment* of the case.

6. Suppose that in one of the units of a set of Shepard's, you find nothing listed for the cited case. This could mean one of three things:

   (a) You are in the wrong set of Shepard's.

   (b) You are in the right set of Shepard's, but the Shepard's unit you are examining does not cover the particular volume of the reporter that contains your cited case. (See guideline 4 above.)

   (c) You are in the right set of Shepard's. The silence in Shepard's about your cited case means that since the time of the printing of the last unit of Shepard's for that set, nothing has happened to the case—there is nothing for Shepard's to tell you.

7. Know the six kinds of information that you can try to obtain when shepardizing a case: parallel cites, history of the cited case, the treatment of the cited case (found in the citing cases), citing legal periodical literature, citing annotations, and citing opinions of the attorney general.

8. The *history* of the case tells you what has happened in different stages of the litigation involved in the cited case. If a decision in the litigation is very recent, Shepard's might give you its docket number rather than its citation. More information on docket numbers is found at the end of the unit of Shepard's you are using.

9. The page number listed for every citing case is the page on which the ci*ted* case is mentioned. It is not the page on which the ci*ting* case begins.

10. Use the abbreviations tables and the preface pages at the beginning of most units of Shepard's—and use them often.

11. A small "n" to the right of the page number of citing material (e.g., 23ALR198n) means the cited case is mentioned within an annotation. A small "s" to the right of the page number of citing material (e.g., 23ALR198s) means the cited case is mentioned in a supplement to (or pocket part of) the annotation.

12. You can also shepardize a case online through either WESTLAW or LEXIS. For a photograph of a WESTLAW screen containing Shepard's, see Exhibit 13.4 in chapter 13.

13. For more information about Shepard's:
    • 800-899-6000
    • http://www.shepards.com

 Assignment 9.5

Pick any case that you found while doing any one of the parts of Assignments 9.3 or 9.4. Do questions (a)–(g) below on this case.

(a) What set of *Shepard's Citations* would you use to shepardize this case?

(b) Is this set of *Shepard's Citations* on the shelf complete? List everything that should be on the shelf. Place a check mark next to each unit that is on the shelf and an "x" next to each unit that is missing.

(c) List the parallel cites, if any, for this case provided by Shepard's.

(d) State the history of this case according to Shepard's. Give the meaning of abbreviations of all symbols that Shepard's uses to indicate this history. If there is no history of the case provided by Shepard's, redo this assignment until you find a case that does have such a history.

(e) In the treatment of the cited case, find a citing case written by a state court in your state. Give the meaning of abbreviations of all symbols, if any, that Shepard's uses to indicate this treatment. If there is no citing case written by a state court of your state, redo this assignment until you find a cited case that does have such a citing case. Give the citation of the citing case.

(f) Go to the reporter that prints the full text of the citing case you found in (e). Find the citing case in it and quote the sentence from the case that refers to the cited case.

(g) Question (a) asked you to identify a set of Shepard's that you would use to shepardize the case you selected, and question (c) asked you if the case had a parallel cite.

   (i) If there is a parallel cite, is there another set of Shepard's that would allow you to shepardize your case? If so, what is the name of this set of Shepard's?

   (ii) Go to this other set of Shepard's. Is it complete? Redo question (b) for this set.

   (iii) Can you find the same information in this set that you found when answering questions (c), (d), and (e) for the other set?

(f) Shepardizing a Statute

You shepardize a *statute* to try to find the following seven kinds of information:

1. A parallel cite of the statute (found in parentheses immediately after the section number of the statute). The parallel cite (if given) is to the *session law* edition of the statute.
2. The history of the statute in the legislature, such as amendments, added sections, repealed sections, renumbered sections, etc.
3. Citing cases that have analyzed or mentioned the statute, declared it unconstitutional, etc.
4. Citing administrative decisions, such as agency decisions that have analyzed or mentioned the statute.
5. Citing legal periodical literature, such as law review articles that have analyzed or mentioned the statute.
6. Citing annotations in A.L.R.1st, A.L.R.2d, A.L.R.3d, A.L.R.4th, A.L.R.5th, and A.L.R. Fed. that have analyzed or mentioned the statute.
7. Citing opinions of the attorney general that have analyzed or mentioned the statute.

To learn how to shepardize a statute, you must first learn the distinction between a statute's session law cite and its codified cite. First let's review some basics.

A **statute** is a law passed by the legislature declaring, commanding, or prohibiting something. The official document that contains the statute is called an **act.** There are two main kinds of statutes:

- **public laws,** which are statutes that apply to the general public or to a segment of the public and have permanence and general interest (example: a statute changing welfare eligibility)
- **private laws,** which are statutes that apply to specifically named individuals or groups and have little or no permanence or general interest (example: a statute that names a Wyoming post office building after a recently deceased senator)

Statutes can be found in three major formats printed in the following order:

- **slip law:** A single statute (public or private law) that is printed separately, often in a small pamphlet. (For a picture of an act, see page 68.)
- **session law:** A single statute (public or private law) that is printed in chronological order along with every other statute passed during a particular session of the legislature, usually lasting one or two years. (If, for example, the legislature passes a bankruptcy statute and a murder statute on the same day, they will be printed in the session laws one after the other.) Other names for session laws include *Acts, Laws,* and most commonly, **Statutes at Large.** (The major set of federal session laws is called *United States Statutes at Large* (abbreviated Stat.) (see page 74). The citation to a session law is called its **session law cite.**
- **code:** A collection of statutes (public laws only) that are printed by subject matter regardless of when the legislature passed them. When we say a statute has been **codified,** we mean that it has been printed in a code where the rules or laws in it are printed by subject matter rather than chronologically. (For example, all of the bankruptcy statutes are printed together, and all of the murder statutes are printed together elsewhere in the code.) The citation to a statute in a code is called its **codified cite.**

Every private law will have only a session law cite, because it will not be printed in a code. Every public law, however, will have both a session law cite *and* a codified cite. Here are examples of session law and codified law cites of a state statute (Ohio) and of a federal statute, both of which are public laws:

Session Law Cite of a Statute	Codified Cite of the Same Statute
1975 Ohio Laws, C. 508 ⟵————⟶	Ohio Rev. Code Ann. § 45 (1978)
87 Stat. 297 (1965) ⟵————⟶	34 U.S.C. § 18(c) (1970)

Notice the totally different numbering system in the codified and session law cites—yet they are the same statutes. Section 45 of the Ohio Revised Code Annotated is found word-for-word in Chapter (C.) 508 of the 1975 session laws of Ohio. And section 18(c) of title 34 of the United States Code is found word-for-word in volume 87 of *Statutes at Large* (Stat.) on page 297. Notice also the different years for the same statute. The year in the session law cite is the year the legislature passed the statute. The year in the codified cite, however, is usually the year of the edition of the code.

Assume that you want to shepardize a statute. (The cited material will be a cited statute.) The question becomes: When do you shepardize a statute through its session law cite and when do you shepardize through its codified cite?

There are two instances when you *must* shepardize the statute through its session law cite:

• If the statute will never be codified because it is a private law and therefore of no general public interest
• If the statute has not yet been codified because it is so recent (codification will come later).

If the statute *has* been codified, you must shepardize it through its latest codified cite. But suppose you know only the session law cite of the statute. How do you find its codified cite? Go to the current code that should contain your statute. Look for special tables at the beginning or end of the code. For federal statutes in the United States Code, for example, there is a *Tables volume* in which you will find Table III. (See Research Link O in Chapter 5.) Table III will enable you to translate a session law cite into a codified law cite (page 213). (A Tables volume also exists for U.S.C.A. and for U.S.C.S.)

Shepard's has its own abbreviation system for session laws. Suppose that you are sheparidizing Kan. Stat. Ann. § 123 (1973)—a codified cite. Section 123 is the *cited statute*—what you are shepardizing. In the Shepard's columns for Kansas statutes, you might find:

> §123
>
> (1970C6)
> A1972C23
> Rp1975C45

The *parallel cite* in parentheses is 1970C6, which means Chapter 6 of the 1970 Session Laws of the state of Kansas. The mention of a year in Shepard's for statutes usually refers to the session laws for that year. (You find the meaning of "C" by checking the abbreviations tables at the beginning of the Shepard's volume.)

Immediately beneath the parentheses in the above example for section 123 (the cited statute), you find two other references to session laws:

A1972C23	This means that in Chapter 23 of the 1972 Session Laws of Kansas, there was an amendment to section 123 (which is what "A" means according to Shepard's abbreviations tables).	Rp1975C45	This means that in Chapter 45 of the 1975 Session Laws of Kansas, section 123 was repealed in part (which is what "Rp" means according to Shepard's abbreviations tables).

You will note that Shepard's does *not* tell you what the amendment was, nor what was repealed in part. How do you find this out? Two ways. First, you go to the actual session laws, if your library has them. Second, you go to the cited statute (§ 123) in the codified collection of the statutes (here the *Kansas Statutes Annotated*). At the bottom of the statute in the code, there may be historical or legislative history notes that will summarize amendments, repeals, etc. For an example of this kind of information on a

New York statute, see Exhibit 11.1 in Chapter 11. (Be sure to check these notes for the cited statute in the pocket part of the code volume you are using.)

Other citing material given in Shepard's for a statute is less complicated. For example, there are cites to citing cases, citing legal periodical articles, etc., that follow a pattern very similar to the citing material for cases you are shepardizing (see checklist #4a on shepardizing a case).

Assume that you want to shepardize a federal statute in the *United States Code* (U.S.C.). The set of Shepard's you would use is *Shepard's Federal Statute Citations* (see page 70 for a photo of a volume from this set). There are two major kinds of citing cases that analyze or mention a federal cited statute. Both kinds give you a year in front of the citing case, but the year can have two very different meanings:

- When there is an asterisk (*) in front of the year, Shepard's is telling you that the court that wrote the citing case specified the year of the U.S.C. in which the cited statute is found. The year in front of the asterisk is the year *of the U.S.C.* that contains the cited statute, not the year of the citing case. In an asterisk cite, you are not told the year of the citing case.
- When there is a delta symbol (Δ) in front of the year, Shepard's is telling you that the court that wrote the citing case did *not* specify the year of the U.S.C. in which the cited statute is found. The year in front of the delta symbol is the year *of the citing case,* not the year of the U.S.C. In a delta cite, you are not told the year of the U.S.C. that contains the cited statute.

Assume, for example, that the federal statute you were shepardizing—the cited statute—is section 2506 in title 22 of the *United States Code* (22 U.S.C. § 2506). Here is an excerpt from one of the units of *Shepard's Federal Statute Citations* that you would use to shepardize this statute:

Excerpt from *Shepard's Federal Statute Citations* (used to shepardize 22 U.S.C. § 2506)

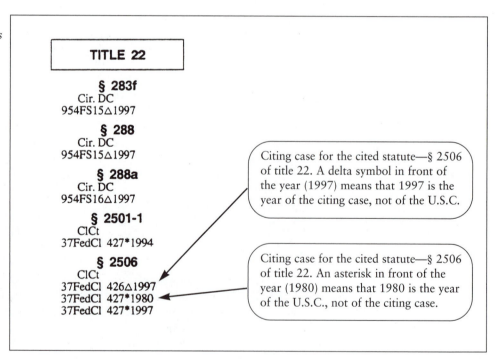

The first citing case is 37FedCl 426. The abbreviations tables at the beginning of Shepard's tell you that FedCl means the Federal Claims Court. On page 426 of volume 37 of this reporter, you will find that the court analyzed or mentioned the cited statute, 22 U.S.C. § 2506. Note the year 1997 in front of the delta symbol. This means that the court that wrote the citing case did not specify the year of 22 U.S.C. § 2506. Hence 1997 is the year of the citing case, 37FedCl 426; it is not the year of 22 U.S.C. § 2506.

The next citing case is 37FedCl 427. Again the abbreviations tables tell you that this is a Federal Claims Court case. On page 427 of volume 37 of this reporter, you will find that the court analyzed or mentioned the cited statute, 22 U.S.C. § 2506. Note the year 1980 in front of the asterisk. This means that the court that wrote the citing case *did* specify the year of 22 U.S.C. § 2506. Hence 1980 is the year of 22 U.S.C. § 2506; it is not the year of the citing case, 37FedCl 427.

Checklist #4b   Checklist for Shepardizing a Statute

1. Go to the set of Shepard's that will enable you to shepardize your statute. For federal statutes, it is *Shepard's Federal Statute Citations.* For state statutes, go to the set of Shepard's for your state. This set of Shepard's may cover both state cases and state statutes in the same units or in different case and statute editions of the set.

2. If the statute has been codified, shepardize it through its latest codified cite. If all you have is the session law cite of the statute, translate it into a codified cite by using the tables in the current code. For federal statutes, go to Table III of the Tables volume of U.S.C./U.S.C.A./U.S.C.S. and Table 2 in *United States Code Congressional and Administrative News* (U.S.C.C.A.N.).

3. If the statute has not been codified, you can shepardize it through its session law cite.

4. Know whether you have a complete set of Shepard's in front of you by reading the "What Your Library Should Contain" list on the most recent pamphlet of that set.

5. Check your cite in *every* unit of Shepard's. It is recommended that you work backward by examining the most recent Shepard's pamphlets first so that you obtain the latest history and citing material first.

6. At the top of a Shepard's page, and in its columns, look for your statute by the name of the code, year, article, chapter, title, or section. Repeat this for every unit of Shepard's.

7. Know the seven kinds of information you can try to obtain by shepardizing a statute: parallel cite (not always given), history of the statute in the legislature, citing cases, citing administrative decisions, citing legal periodical literature, citing annotations, citing opinions of the attorney general.

8. The history of the statute in the legislature will give you the citing material in session law form, e.g., A1980C45. This refers to an amendment (A) printed in the 1980 Laws of the legislature, Chapter (C) 45. Another example: A34St.654. This refers to an amendment (A) printed in volume 34, page 654, of the *Statutes at Large.* If you want to locate these session laws, find out if your library keeps the session laws. Also, check the historical note after the statute in the statutory code (page 205).

9. The notation **et seq** means "and following" *(et sequens).* The citing material may be analyzing more than one statutory section.

10. Find the meaning of abbreviations used by Shepard's in its tables and preface material at the beginning of most of the units of the set of Shepard's.

11. If your state code has gone through revisions or renumberings, read the early pages in the statutory code and in the Shepard's volumes to try to obtain an explanation of what has happened. This information may be of considerable help to you in interpreting the data provided in the Shepard's units for your state code.

12. You can also shepardize a federal statute (and many state statutes) online through either WESTLAW or LEXIS.

13. For more information about Shepard's:
    • 800-899-6000
    • http://www.shepards.com

Assignment 9.6

(a) Go to your state statutory code. Pick any statute in this code that might be helpful in researching any *one* of the topics for the chapter 9 assignments (printed at the beginning of the chapter at the end of Section A). Which topic did you select, (a) to (o)? Give the citation of the statute. Give a brief quote from this statute indicating that it might be relevant to the topic you selected.

(b) What set of *Shepard's Citations* would you use to shepardize this statute?

(c) Is this set of *Shepard's Citations* on the shelf complete? List everything that should be on the shelf. Place a check mark next to each unit that is on the shelf and an "x" next to each unit that is missing.

Continued on next page

Assignment 9.6—continued

(d) According to Shepard's, have there been any amendments, or has the legislature taken any other action on this statute? If so, give the meaning of abbreviations of all symbols that Shepard's uses to indicate this action. (Be sure to check every unit of Shepard's for this set.)

(e) Find a citing case written by a state court in your state. Give the meaning of abbreviations of all symbols, if any, that Shepard's uses to indicate how this citing case treated the cited statute. If there is no citing case written by a state court of your state, redo this assignment until you find a cited statute that *does* have such a citing case. Give the citation of the citing case.

(f) Go to the reporter that prints the full text of the citing case you found in (e). Find the cited statute in it and quote the sentence from the case that refers to the cited statute.

(g) Sheperdizing a Regulation

You cannot sheperdize administrative regulations of state agencies. No sets of Shepard's cover state regulations. You can, however, sheperdize federal regulations in the *Code of Federal Regulations* (C.F.R.). This is done through *Shepard's Code of Federal Regulations Citations.* (See photo on page 70.) It will also allow you to sheperdize presidential proclamations, executive orders, and reorganization plans.

To sheperdize a C.F.R. regulation means to obtain the following three kinds of information about the *cited regulation* (the regulation you are sheperdizing):

1. The history of the regulation in the courts—for example, citing cases that have invalidated or otherwise discussed the cited regulation.
2. Citing legal periodical literature that has analyzed or mentioned the cited regulation.
3. Citing annotations in A.L.R.1st, A.L.R.2d, A.L.R.3d, A.L.R.4th, A.L.R.5th, and A.L.R. Fed. that have analyzed or mentioned the cited regulation.

The C.F.R. comes out in a new edition every year. All the changes that have occurred during the year are incorporated in the new yearly edition. (Each year is printed in a different color.) Two kinds of changes can be made:

- Those changes made *by the agency* itself, e.g., amendments, repeals, renumbering—this is the history of the regulation in the agency.
- Those changes forced on the agency *by the courts*, e.g., declaring a section of the regulation invalid—this is part of the history of the regulation in the courts.

Unfortunately, Shepard's will give you only the history of the regulation in the courts (plus references to the regulation in legal periodical literature and in annotations). The columns of Shepard's will *not* give you the history of the regulation in the agency. (As we will see later on page 239, to obtain the latter, you must check elsewhere, e.g., the "CFR Parts Affected" tables in the *Federal Register.*) The main value of the Shepard's for C.F.R. is that it will lead you to what the courts have said about the regulation (plus the periodical and annotation references).

When sheperdizing through the *Shepard's C.F.R. Citations,* the cited material, of course, is the federal regulation—which we refer to as the cited regulation. Shepard's provides two categories of *citing* material:

- Citing cases, periodicals, and annotations that refer to the cited regulation *by year,* that is, by C.F.R. edition.
- Citing cases, periodicals, and annotations that refer to the cited regulation *without* specifying the year or edition of the regulation in the C.F.R.

To indicate the first kind of citing material, Shepard's gives you a small elevated asterisk just before a given year. If, for example, the cited regulation you were sheperdizing is 12 C.F.R. § 218.111(j) (1965), you might find the following:

§ 218.111(j)
420F2d90*1965

The citing material is a citing case—420 F.2d 90. The small asterisk means that this case specifically identified the year of the cited regulation—1965. This year is *not* the year of the citing case. It is the year of the cited regulation. We are not given the year of the citing case.

Now let us examine the second kind of citing material mentioned above. There may be citing material that mentions the regulation but does *not* tell us the specific year or edition of that regulation. Shepard's uses a delta symbol (Δ) in such situations. If, for example, the cited regulation you were shepardizing is 12 C.F.R. § 9.18(a)(3) (1962), you might find the following:

$$\text{§9.18(a)(3)}$$
$$274\text{FS}628^{\Delta}1967$$

The citing material is a citing case—274 F. Supp. 628. The delta symbol means that the citing case did not refer to the year or edition of section 9.18(a)(3). When this occurs, the year next to the delta symbol is the year of the citing case and *not* the year of the cited regulation. The citing case of 274 F. Supp. 628 was decided in 1967.

Checklist #4c   Checklist for Shepardizing a Federal Regulation

1. Go to *Shepard's Code of Federal Regulations Citations*. (For a photo, see page 70.)
2. Know whether you have a complete set of Shepard's in front of you by reading the "What Your Library Should Contain" list on the most recent pamphlet in that set.
3. Shepardize your regulation through every unit of this set of Shepard's.
4. Know the three kinds of information you can obtain when shepardizing a federal regulation: history of the regulation in the courts, citing legal periodical literature, and citing annotations.
5. An asterisk or a delta symbol will appear next to the year of all citing material: the citing cases, the citing periodical literature, and the citing annotations.
   (a) The asterisk means that the citing material referred to the specific year of the cited regulation. Hence the year is the year of the cited regulation, not of the citing material.
   (b) The delta symbol means that the citing material did not refer to the specific year of the cited regulation. Hence the year is the year of the citing material, not of the cited regulation.
6. The set of Shepard's for C.F.R. does not directly tell you what amendments, revisions, or other changes

were made *by the agencies* to the regulations. You are told only what *the courts* have said about the regulations. (To find out what the agencies have done to the regulations, you must check sources such as the "CFR Parts Affected" tables in the *Federal Register.*)

7. Check the meaning of abbreviations in the tables and preface at the beginning of most of the Shepard's units.
8. All regulations in C.F.R. are based on statutes of Congress. (A statute that is the basis or authority for the actions of a person or agency is called an **enabling statute**.) As we will see later, you can find out what statutes in U.S.C. are the authority for particular regulations in C.F.R. by checking the "authority" reference under many of the regulations in C.F.R. Once you know the statute that is the basis for the regulation, you might want to shepardize that enabling statute for more law in the area. (See checklist 4b on shepardizing a statute.)
9. You can also shepardize a federal regulation online through either WESTLAW or LEXIS.
10. For more information about Shepard's:
    • 800-899-6000
    • http://www.shepards.com

Note on KeyCite: An Online Competitor to Shepard's

A competitor to Shepard's has emerged. The West Group now has **KeyCite**, a new *online* citator that you use on WESTLAW. For an example of a KeyCite screen, see Exhibit 13.5 in chapter 13.) Shepard's is available in paper format (hardcover volumes and pamphlets), on CD-ROM, and online through WESTLAW and LEXIS. Now WESTLAW has added KeyCite, its own online citator system. (KeyCite is *not* available in hardcover or pamphlet format.) KeyCite claims to be better than Shepard's in a number of respects.

For example, KeyCite will provide more citing legal periodical literature than Shepard's. Also, it will give citing cases that are **unreported cases;** Shepard's does not cite such cases. (An unreported case—also called an *unpublished case*—is a full opinion written by a court that refuses to allow it to be printed in standard reporters; unreported cases therefore cannot be relied upon in the same manner as reported opinions.[7])

SECTION F   LOOSELEAF SERVICES

Inserting pages into a looseleaf service

A **looseleaf** is a hardcover book with easily removable pages, which usually uses a three-ring binder structure. The primary advantage of this structure is the ease of inserting updating material. Because looseleafs can be frequently updated (e.g., weekly), they often contain the most current material available on a subject—almost as current as what is available online. Normally the buyer of a looseleaf pays for the initial volume(s) plus a subscription that consists of new pages that periodically come in the mail. New pages might simply be added to the end of the volume, or they might be **interfiled.** Interfiling means inserting pages anywhere within an existing text, not just at the end. The pages come with instructions telling the filer which pages to remove from the volume(s) and which to insert as replacements or additions. (This task, sometimes performed by paralegals, is called **looseleaf filing.**)

Several different kinds of legal materials are published as looseleafs:

- Legal treatises. Some looseleafs are standard legal treatises that provide a comprehensive overview of a legal topic, perhaps along with some checklists and forms. An example is *Larson's Workmen's Compensation Law.*
- Reporters. Reporters are volumes containing court opinions. Although most reporters have a permanent binding with nonremovable pages, a few are looseleafs. An example is *United States Law Week,* which contains every opinion of the United States Supreme Court (see page 74).
- Services. A **looseleaf service** is a multipurpose collection of materials on a particular area of law. They might be called guides, reporters, indexes, coordinators, libraries, etc. Examples include *Congressional Index, Employment Practices Guide,* and *AIDS Law and Litigation Reporter.*

For a comprehensive list of what is available, see *Legal Looseleafs in Print,* published by Infosources Publishing. (Its Internet address is <http://www.infosourcespub.com>.)

Our primary focus in this section is the third category—the looseleaf service. There is no prescribed definition of a looseleaf service. A publisher might use this phrase for any of its looseleaf books. More commonly, however, the phrase refers to volumes containing a wide variety of legal materials. For example:

- Recent court opinions or summaries of opinions
- Relevant legislation—usually explained in some detail
- Administrative regulations and decisions, or summaries of them (some of this material may not be readily available elsewhere)
- References to relevant studies and reports
- Practice tips

In short, looseleaf services can be extremely valuable. The major publishers of them are Commerce Clearing House (CCH), Bureau of National Affairs (BNA), Clark Boardman Callaghan (CBC), Warren, Gorham & Lamont, and Matthew Bender. They cover numerous areas of the law, e.g., criminal law, taxes, corporate law, and unions. You should assume that one or more looseleaf services exist on the general topic of your research problem until you prove otherwise to yourself.

---

7. Unreported opinions are useful to know about because they can give a researcher an indication of what a court's thinking might be on the areas covered in the opinion. Both WESTLAW and LEXIS give the text of unreported cases, but until KeyCite, you could not obtain citator references to them as citing cases.

Unfortunately looseleaf services are sometimes awkward to use. Occasionally library users misfile pages that they take out for photocopying. There is no standard structure for a looseleaf. You might find the following, for example:

- One volume or multivolume
- Organization by page number, organization by section number, organization by paragraph number, or a combination of these
- Different colored pages to indicate more recent material
- New pages inserted by interfiling, by addition to the end of one of the volumes, or a combination of both methods
- Indexes at the end, in the middle, or at the beginning of the volumes
- Bound volumes that accompany the three-ring volumes
- Transfer binders that contain current material

You should approach the structure of each looseleaf service as a small puzzle sitting on the shelf waiting to be put together.

Checklist #5   Checklist for Finding and Using the Looseleaf Services

1. Divide your research problem into its major topics, such as family law, tax law, antitrust law, etc. Assume that one or more looseleaf services exist for these topics until you demonstrate otherwise to yourself.

2. Find out where the looseleaf services are located in your library. Are they all together? Are they located in certain subject areas? Does the library have a separate list of them?

3. Check the library's card or online catalog. Look for subject headings on your topics to see if looseleaf services are mentioned. Check the names of the major publishers of looseleaf services, e.g., Bureau of National Affairs and Matthew Bender. (See checklist #1 on using the catalog.)

4. Ask library staff members if they know of looseleaf services on the major topics of your research.

5. Call other law libraries in your area. Ask the staff members there if they know of looseleaf services on the major topics of your research. See if they can identify looseleaf services that you have not yet found.

6. Speak to experts in the area of the law, e.g., professors. (See checklist #9.) Ask them about looseleaf services.

7. Once you have a looseleaf service in front of you, you must figure out how to use it:

    (a) Read any preface or explanatory material in the front of the volumes of the looseleaf service.

    (b) Ask library staff members to give you some help.

    (c) Ask attorneys or paralegals who are experts in the area if they can give you a brief demonstration of its use.

    (d) Ask a fellow student who is familiar with the service.

    (e) Read any pamphlets or promotional literature by the publishers on using their looseleaf services.

    For each looseleaf service, you need to know the following:
    - What it contains and what it does not contain
    - How it is indexed
    - How it is supplemented
    - What its special features are
    - How many volumes or units it has and the interrelationship among them

    You obtain this information through techniques (a) to (e) above.

8. In your research memo, you rarely cite a looseleaf service unless the material you found there does not exist elsewhere. Use the looseleaf service mainly as background research (see Exhibit 8.1 in chapter 8) and as a search tool for leads to find primary authority, such as cases, statutes, and regulations.

Assignment 9.7

Find one looseleaf that might be helpful in researching each of the topics for the chapter 9 assignments (printed at the beginning of the chapter at the end of Section A). Locate one per topic. In each looseleaf, find a case written by a state court in your state or by a federal court that sits in your state. If you cannot find a case written by such a court, use a different looseleaf until you find one. Give the citation of the looseleaf and of the case.

SECTION G   LEGAL PERIODICAL LITERATURE

Legal periodical literature consists of the following:

- Lead articles and comments written by individuals who have extensively researched a topic
- **Case notes** that summarize and comment on important court opinions
- Book reviews

There are three major publishers of periodicals: academic institutions, including almost all of the nation's law schools (where the students running the periodicals have the prestige of being "on law review"); commercial companies; and bar associations. Legal periodicals are either general, covering a wide variety of legal topics, e.g., *Harvard Law Review*, or specialized, e.g., *Family Law Journal*. (See Exhibit 4.1 in chapter 4 for additional examples of legal periodicals and other secondary authorities.) The large number of legal periodicals that exist provide researchers with a rich source of material.

How can you locate legal periodical literature on point? What index systems will allow you to gain access to the hundreds of legal periodicals and the tens of thousands of articles, comments, case notes, book reviews, and other material in them? Two major general index systems exist:

- *Index to Legal Periodicals and Books* (ILP) published by H.W. Wilson Co.
- *Current Law Index* (CLI) published by Information Access Corporation

Of the two, the CLI is more comprehensive because it indexes more legal periodicals. Both are available in three different versions: a paper version (consisting of pamphlets and hardcover volumes), a CD-ROM version, and an online version. Few law libraries subscribe to all the legal periodicals indexed in the ILP and the CLI. Hence you may be obtaining leads to periodicals that your library does not have. If so, check other libraries in the area.

In addition to ILP and CLI, which are general indexes, there are special indexes to legal periodical literature on topics such as tax law.

Examples of the paper versions of the *Index to Legal Periodicals and Books* (ILP) and the *Current Law Index* (CLI). Both are also available online and on CD-ROM.

Index to Legal Periodicals and Books (ILP)

- The ILP first comes out in pamphlets that are later consolidated (i.e., cumulated) into bound volumes.
- You must check each ILP pamphlet and each ILP bound volume for whatever years you want.
- The ILP regularly adds new periodicals that are indexed.
- Every ILP pamphlet and bound volume has four indexes:
  (1)   A Subject and Author Index
  (2)   A Table of Cases commented on
  (3)   A Table of Statutes commented on (added recently)
  (4)   A Book Review Index
- Abbreviation tables appear at the beginning of every pamphlet and bound volume.
- The Subject and Author Index in the ILP is easy to use. You simply go to the topic on which you are seeking periodical literature, e.g. abortion, smoking. If you have the name of an author and want to know if he or she has written anything on the topic of your research, you simply check that author's last name in this index.[8]
- Toward the end of every ILP pamphlet and hardcover volume is a Table of Cases. Suppose that elsewhere in your research you come across an important case, and you now want to know if that case was ever commented on (i.e., noted) in the legal periodicals. Go to the ILP pamphlet or hardcover volume that covers the year of the case and check the Table of Cases. (See Research Link P on page 176.)
- The Table of Statutes serves the same function for statutes. This table will tell you where you can find periodical literature commenting on certain statutes. (See Research Link Q on page 177.)
- At the end of every pamphlet and hardcover ILP volume is a Book Review Index. If you are looking for a review of a law book you have come across elsewhere in your research, go to the ILP pamphlet or hardcover volume that covers the year of publication of the book for which you are seeking reviews.
- The ILP is also available:
  (1)   On WILSONLINE, the publisher's online research system
  (2)   On WILSONDISC, a CD-ROM system
  (3)   On WESTLAW
  (4)   On LEXIS

Current Law Index (CLI)

The CLI indexes substantially more periodicals than the ILP. In fact, one of the reasons the CLI was created was the unwillingness of the publisher of the ILP (H.W. Wilson Co.) to expand the number and kind of periodicals it indexed.

- The CLI first comes out in pamphlets that are later consolidated (i.e., cumulated) into hardcover volumes.
- You must check each CLI pamphlet and each annual CLI issue for the years you want.
- There are four indexes within each CLI unit:
  —A Subject Index
  —An Author-Title Index
  —A Table of Cases
  —A Table of Statutes
- Abbreviation tables appear at the beginning of every CLI unit.
- The Subject Index gives full citations to periodicals under a topic (e.g., child welfare, zoning) and under an author's name.

---

8. Prior to 1983, the entries under an author's name had to be cross-referenced to the "subject" portions of the index. Today, there are full bibliographic entries under both topics and author names.

- Book reviews are included under the Author-Title Index along with cites to periodical literature by the authors.
- The Table of Cases is valuable if you already know the name of a case located elsewhere in your research. To find out if that case was commented on, check the Table of Cases in the CLI unit that covers the year of the case. (See Research Link P.)

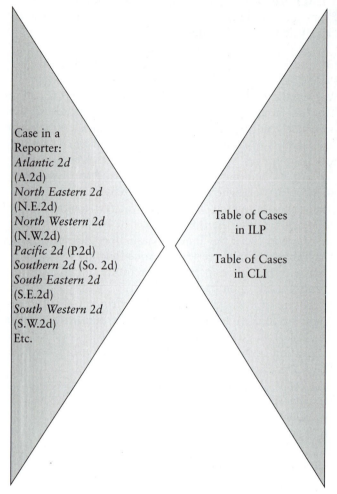

RESEARCH LINK P

If you have found a case in a reporter that is important to your research, find out if that case has been commented on in a case note in legal periodical literature. To find out, check the tables of cases in ILP and CLI.

Case in a
Reporter:
Atlantic 2d
(A.2d)
North Eastern 2d
(N.E.2d)
North Western 2d
(N.W.2d)
Pacific 2d (P.2d)
Southern 2d (So. 2d)
South Eastern 2d
(S.E.2d)
South Western 2d
(S.W.2d)
Etc.

Table of Cases
in ILP

Table of Cases
in CLI

- The Table of Statutes is equally valuable. If you already have the name of a statute from your other research (such as Atomic Energy Act; California Fair Employment Practices Act), look for the name of that statute in the Table of Statutes for the CLI unit that covers the approximate time the statute was passed. (See Research Link Q.)
- The CLI began in 1980; it does not index periodicals prior to this date. The ILP must be used for the period before 1980.

Legal Resource Index (LRI) The Legal Resource Index (LRI) is the online version[9] of the *Current Law Index*. The LRI is available on WESTLAW and LEXIS.

LegalTrac LegalTrac is the CD-ROM version of the *Current Law Index*.

Other Index Systems

A number of other periodical index systems exist:

- Index to Federal Tax Articles
- Index to Foreign Legal Periodicals
- Index to Canadian Legal Periodical Literature

---

9. The LRI is also available on a special microfilm reader. However, due to the popularity of the CD-ROM version of the CLI *(LegalTrac)*, many libraries do not have this microfilm version.

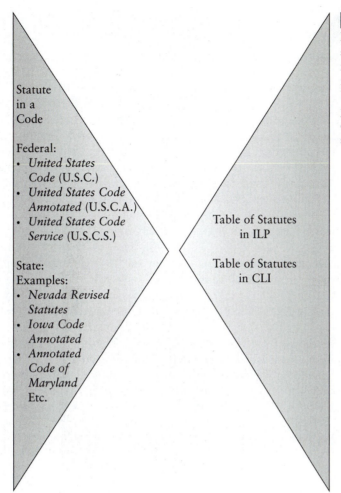

Statute
in a
Code

Federal:
- *United States Code* (U.S.C.)
- *United States Code Annotated* (U.S.C.A.)
- *United States Code Service* (U.S.C.S.)

State:
Examples:
- *Nevada Revised Statutes*
- *Iowa Code Annotated*
- *Annotated Code of Maryland*
Etc.

Table of Statutes in ILP

Table of Statutes in CLI

RESEARCH LINK Q

If you have found a federal or state statute in a code that is important to your research, find out if that statute has been commented on in a legal periodical literature. To find out, check the tables of statutes in ILP and CLI.

- Jones-Chipman Index to Legal Periodical Literature (covering periodical literature up to 1937 only)
- Index Medicus (covers medical periodicals—usually available only in medical libraries)
- MEDLINE (a computer search system for medical periodicals—available mainly in medical libraries). Free access to MEDLINE is possible through the "Internet Grateful Med" page of the United States National Library of Medicine (<http://igm.nlm.nih.gov>).

Legal Periodicals on the Internet

There is a great deal of legal periodical literature on the Internet. You can find lists (directories) of legal periodicals, as well as legal newsletters and magazines, some written solely online *(cyberjournals)*. There are also extensive indexes to this literature that allow you to do key word searches to find literature on a vast number of legal topics. Here are some of the Internet addresses to check, many of which have links to each other and to other legal resources on the Internet:

- http://www.lawreview.org
- http://www.regent.edu/lawlib/bookmark/bk-e-jnl.html
- http://www.hg.org/journals.html
- http://www.usc.edu/dept/law-lib/legal/journals.html
- http://www.findlaw.com/03journals/index.html
- http://lawlib.wuacc.edu/washlaw/lawjournal/lawjournal.html
- http://www.andersonpublishing.com/lawschool/directory/directory.html

Checklist #6   Checklist for Finding Legal Periodical Literature

1. Use legal periodical literature mainly for background research and for leads to primary authority, particularly through the extensive footnotes in this literature. (See Exhibit 8.1 in chapter 8.)

2. There are two major general index systems: *Index to Legal Periodicals and Books* (ILP) and *Current Law Index* (CLI). They are issued in pamphlets and hardcover volumes. (There are also CD-ROM versions and online versions, which are considerably easier to use. One of the most popular is LegalTrac, the CD-ROM version of CLI.)

3. The CARTWHEEL will help you locate material in ILP and CLI.

4. Both ILP and CLI also contain separate indexes. You should become familiar with all these internal index features.

5. Start with the subject headings index within ILP and CLI.

6. Identify the name and date of every important case that you have found in your research thus far. Go to the Table of Cases in ILP and in CLI to find out if any periodical literature has commented on that case. (Go to the ILP and CLI units that would cover the year the case was decided. To be safe, also check their units for two years after the date of the case.) See Research Link P.

7. If you are researching a statute, find out if any periodical literature has commented on the statute. (See Research Link Q.) This is done in two ways:
   (a) Check the Table of Statutes in ILP and CLI.
   (b) Break your statute down into its major topics. Check these topics in the Subject Indexes of ILP and CLI to see if any periodical literature on these topics discusses your statute.

8. If you have the name of an author who is known for writing on a particular topic, you can also check for literature written by that author under his or her name in ILP and CLI.

9. Ask library staff members if the library has any other indexes to legal periodical literature, particularly in specialty areas of the law.

10. It is possible to shepardize some legal periodical literature. If you want to know whether the periodical article, note, or comment was ever mentioned in a court opinion, go to *Shepard's Law Review Citations*.

11. It is possible to search for legal periodical literature online in WESTLAW, LEXIS, and WILSONLINE.

12. There are many sites on the Internet that allow you to obtain lists of legal periodicals and to find specific information within these periodicals.

Assignment 9.8

Find one legal periodical article that might be helpful in researching each of the topics for the chapter 9 assignments (printed at the beginning of the chapter at the end of Section A). Choose one per topic. In each article, find a case written by a state court in your state or by a federal court that sits in your state. If you cannot find a case written by such a court, choose a different legal periodical article until you find one. Give the citation of the article. Quote the sentence (or footnote) from the article that mentions this case.

SECTION H

LEGAL ENCYCLOPEDIAS

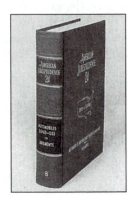

The major multivolume **legal encyclopedias** are *Corpus Juris Secundum* (C.J.S.), a dark blue set, and *American Jurisprudence 2d* (Am. Jur. 2d), a green set. Both are published by the West Group. In many law libraries, they are the most frequently used volumes on the shelf because they are easy to use and are comprehensive. If you know how to use a general encyclopedia, you know how to use a legal encyclopedia. The volumes contain hundreds of alphabetically arranged topics on almost every area of the law. For each topic, you are given explanations of the basic principles of law and extensive footnote references supporting these principles. The vast majority of the references are to cases, although for certain topics, such as federal taxation, there are references to statutes as well. Legal encyclopedias have two main values. They are excellent as background research in a new area of the law. (See Exhibit 8.1 in chapter 8.) They are also valuable as leads to primary authority, particularly case law. In addition to the national legal encyclopedias, some states have state-specific encyclopedias devoted to the law of one state, e.g., *Florida Jurisprudence*.

For a sample page from C.J.S., see Exhibit 9.8. Every section begins with a summary of that section in black bold print. The phrase **black letter law** has come to mean any summary or overview that contains basic principles of law.

9.8

Exhibit
Excerpt from a Page in
Corpus Juris Secundum

§§ 22–23 BURGLARY

c. Use of Instrument, Explosives, or Torch

In order to constitute burglary, entry need not be made by any part of accused's body, but entry may be made by an instrument, where the instrument is inserted for the purpose of committing a felony.

In order to constitute a burglary, it is not necessary that entry be made by any part of the body; it may be by an instrument,[5] as in a case where a hook or other instrument is put in with intent to take out goods, or a pistol or a gun with intent to kill.[6] It is necessary, however, that the instrument shall be put within the structure, and that it shall be inserted for the immediate purpose of committing the

felony or aiding in its commission, and not merely for the purpose of making an opening to admit the hand or body, or, in other words, for the sole purpose of breaking.

A statute making it an offense to break and enter a building with intent to commit a crime, and defining "enter" as including insertion into the building of any instrument held in defendant's hand and intended to be used to detach or remove property, does not require that the offender intend the detachment or removal of property to occur at the moment of insertion only, and the intended detachment or removal relates to a later time as well. . . .

5. Cal.—People v. Walters, 57 Cal.Rptr. 484, 249 C.A.2d 547. Del.—Bailey v. State, 231 A.2d 469.
Me.—State v. Liberty, 280 A.2d 805.
N.J.—**Corpus Juris Secundum quoted in** State v. O'Leary, 107 A.2d 13, 16, 31 N.J.Super 411.
N.M.—State v. Tixier, 551 P.2d 987, 89 N.M. 297.
Or.—Terminal News Stands v. General Cas. Co., 278 P.2d 158, 203 Or. 54.

Tenn.—State v. Crow, 517 S.W.2d 753.
Tex.—Tanner v. State, Cr., 473 S.W.2d 936.
Wyo.—Mirich v. State, 593 P.2d 590.
6. N.J.—**Corpus Juris Secundum quoted in** State v. O'Leary, 107 A.2d 13, 16, 31 N.J.Super. 411.
Pa.—Commonwealth v. Stefanczyk, 77 Pa.Super. 27.
Tex.—Stroud v. State, 60 S.W.2d 439, 124 Tex.Cr. 56.

At the end of both C.J.S. and Am. Jur. 2d is a huge *general index*. There are also extensive topic indexes within individual volumes.

Checklist #7   Checklist for Using Legal Encyclopedias

1. Use the two national legal encyclopedias (Am. Jur. 2d and C.J.S.) for the following purposes:
   (a) As background research for areas of the law that are new to you.
   (b) For leads in their extensive footnotes to primary authority, such as cases and statutes.
2. Both legal encyclopedias have multivolume general indexes at the end of their sets. Use the CARTWHEEL to help you locate material in them. In addition to these general indexes, Am. Jur. 2d and C.J.S. have separate indexes in many of the individual volumes.
3. Neither Am. Jur. 2d nor C.J.S. includes a table of cases.
4. C.J.S. does not have a table of statutes. Am. Jur. 2d, however, has a separate volume called *Table of Statutes, Rules, and Regulations Cited.* Check this

table if you have found a relevant statute, regulation, or rule of court from your other research that you want to find discussed in Am. Jur. 2d.
5. Am. Jur.2d and C.J.S. are published by the West Group. Within these legal encyclopedias, the publisher provides library references to other research books that it publishes, e.g., annotations in A.L.R.1st, A.L.R.2d, A.L.R.3d, A.L.R.4th, A.L.R.5th, and A.L.R. Fed.
6. Find out if your library has a *local* encyclopedia that is limited to the law of your state. States with such encyclopedias include California, Florida, Kentucky, Illinois, Maryland, Michigan, Minnesota, New York, Ohio, Pennsylvania, and Texas.
7. Am. Jur. 2d is available online through LEXIS and WESTLAW.

Assignment 9.9

(a) Find one section in C.J.S. that might be helpful in researching each of the topics for the chapter 9 assignments (printed at the beginning of the chapter at the end of Section A). Find one per topic. Within this section, find a case cited in the footnotes written by a state court in your state or by a federal court that sits in your state. If you cannot find a case written by such a court, choose a different section of C.J.S. until you find one. Give the citation of the C.J.S. section you used. Quote the sentence (or footnote) from the section that mentions this case.

(b) Find one section in Am. Jur. 2d that might be helpful in researching each of the topics for the chapter 9 assignments (printed at the beginning of the chapter at the end of Section A). Find one per topic. Within this section, find a case cited in the footnotes written by a state court in your state or by a federal court that sits in your state. If you cannot find a case written by such a court, choose a different section of Am. Jur. 2d until you find one. Give the citation of the Am. Jur. 2d section you used. Quote the sentence (or footnote) from the section that mentions this case.

SECTION I   LEGAL TREATISES

A **legal treatise** is any book written by private individuals (or by public officials writing in a private capacity) on a topic of law. Some treatises are scholarly; others are more practice oriented. The latter are often called *hornbooks, handbooks, formbooks,* and *practice manuals.* Treatises give overview summaries of the law, plus references to primary authority. There are single-volume treatises such as *Prosser on Torts,* as well as multivolume treatises such as *Moore's Federal Practice, Collier on Bankruptcy,* etc.

Checklist #8   Checklist for Finding and Using Legal Treatises

1. Always look for legal treatises on the topics of your research problem. Assume, until you prove otherwise to yourself, that three or four such treatises exist and are relevant to your problem.

2. Treatises are useful for background research and for leads to primary authority. See Exhibit 8.1 in chapter 8.

3. Many treatises are updated by pocket parts, supplemental volumes, and page inserts if the treatise is printed as a looseleaf.

4. Start your search for treatises in the card or computer catalog (see checklist #1 on using the catalog).

5. Check with experts in the area of law in which you are interested, e.g., teachers, for recommendations on treatises you should examine. See checklist #9.

6. If your library has open stacks, find the treatise section. For example, go to the section of the stacks containing books with KF call numbers. (For a list of KF numbers by subject area, see page 142.) Locate the section of the stacks containing treatises on your topic. Browse through the shelves to try to find additional treatises. Some treatises that you need, however, may be on reserve rather than in the open stacks.

7. Once you have found a treatise, check that author's name in the *Index to Legal Periodicals and Books* (ILP) or the *Current Law Index* (CLI) to try to find periodical literature on the same topic by this author. You can also use these indexes to see if there are any book reviews on the treatises. (See checklist #6 on finding legal periodical literature.)

8. Libraries do not always purchase subsequent editions of treatises. The library's catalog will probably not tell you of such editions. One way to find out if there is a later edition of a treatise you have found on the shelf is to check *Law Books & Serials in Print* or *Books in Print.*

Assignment 9.10

Find one legal treatise that might be helpful in researching each of the topics for the chapter 9 assignments (printed at the beginning of the chapter at the end of Section A). Find one per topic. The legal treatise you select must be different from any of the legal treatises you used in

Assignment 9.10—continued

Assignments 9.1 and 9.7. In each legal treatise, find a citation to a case written by a state court in your state or by a federal court that sits in your state. If you cannot find a case written by such a court, choose a different legal treatise until you find one. Give the citation of the legal treatise and of the case. Quote the sentence (or footnote) from the legal treatise that mentions this case.

SECTION J   PHONE AND MAIL—CONTACT THE EXPERTS

In law offices throughout the country, many attorneys and paralegals use the telephone as a research tool. They call colleagues and experts for leads. As students, you also can use this resource. With caution—and, if needed, with the approval of instructors or supervisors—you should consider contacting experts on the topics of your research. If you can get through to them and if you adopt a sufficiently humble attitude, they may give you leads to important laws and may even discuss the facts of your research problem. Many experts are quite willing to help you free of charge, as long as you are respectful and do not give the impression that you want more than a few moments of their time. You do not ask to come over to spend an afternoon!

Making contact through the mail is less likely to obtain a response unless you use e-mail rather than traditional "snail" mail. It takes very little effort—and no cost—for a prospective expert to respond to a brief question e-mailed from you.

 Assignment 9.11

Give the names, addresses, and telephone numbers of two experts you would try to contact because they might be helpful in researching each of the topics for the chapter 9 assignments (printed at the beginning of the chapter at the end of Section A). Give two per topic. State why you think they might be helpful and where you obtained their names, addresses, and phone numbers.

Checklist #9   Checklist for Doing Phone and Mail Research

1. Your goal is to contact someone who is an expert in the area of your research problem. You want to try to talk with him or her briefly on the phone. (As an alternative, try to e-mail your question to the expert. Some of the sources listed below that give names and addresses of experts may also give their e-mail addresses.)

2. Do not try to contact an expert until you have first done a substantial amount of research on your own. For instance, you should have already checked the major cases, statutes, regulations, legal treatises, legal periodical literature, annotations, etc., that are readily available in the library.

3. Prepare the questions you want to ask the expert. Make them short and to the point. For example, "Do you know of any recent case law on the liability of a municipality for . . .?" ."Could you give me any leads

to literature on the doctrine of promissory estoppel as it applies to . . .?" "Do you know of any good Internet sites I could check on . . . ?" "Do you know anyone I could contact who has done empirical research on the new EPA regulations?" "Do you know of anyone currently litigating § 307?" Do *not* recite all the facts of the research problem to the expert and say, "What should I do?" If the expert wants more facts from you, let him or her ask you for them. You must create the impression that you want no more than a few moments of the expert's time. If the experts want to give your request more attention, they will let you know.

4. Introduce yourself as a student doing research on a problem. State how you got the expert's name (see the next guideline) and then state how grateful you would be if you could ask him or her a "quick question."

Continued on next page

Checklist #9   Checklist for Doing Phone and Mail Research—continued

5. Your introductory comments should state how you came across the expert's name and learned of his or her expertise. For example, say "I read your law review article on . . . ." "I saw your name as an attorney of record in the case of . . . ." "Mr./Ms. _____ told me you were an expert in this area and recommended that I contact you."

6. Where do you find these experts? A number of possibilities exist:

   (a) *Special interest groups and associations*

   Contact attorneys within groups and associations such as unions, environmental groups, and business associations. Ask your librarian for lists of such groups and associations, for example, the *Encyclopedia of Associations.*

   (b) *Government agencies*

   Contact the law departments of the government agencies that would be involved in the area of your research.

   (c) *Specialty libraries*

   Ask your librarian for lists of libraries, such as the *Directory of Special Libraries and Information Centers.*

   (d) *Law professors*

   Ask a librarian if the library has the *AALS Law Teacher's Directory,* which lists teachers by name and specialty across the country.

   (e) *Attorneys of Record*

   If you have found a recent court opinion on point, the names of the attorneys for the case are printed at the beginning of the opinion (see page 187). Try to obtain the phone number and address of the attorneys from *West's Legal Directory* (available on WESTLAW) or from the *Martindale-Hubbell Law Directory.* These attorneys may be willing to send you a copy of appellate briefs on the case. Also ask them about any ongoing litigation in the courts.

   Often you are permitted to go to the court clerk's office and examine pleadings, appellate briefs, etc., on pending cases. All of these documents will give the names and addresses of the attorneys of record who prepared them. Finally, don't forget to check the closed case files of your own office for prior research that has already been done in the same area as your problem.

   (f) *Authors of legal periodical literature and of legal treatises*

   Try to contact the author of a treatise or law review article that is relevant to your research. (See checklists ##6 and 8 on legal periodicals and legal treatises.) The author's business address can often be found in sources such as the *AALS Law Teacher's Directory, West's Legal Directory, Martindale-Hubbell,* etc. On locating individuals on the Internet, see chapter 13.

C HAPTER SUMMARY

The nine major search resources will often lead you to more than one of the following categories of primary authority: opinions, statutes, constitutions, administrative law, local law, rules of court, and international law. Hence, before covering the techniques of finding this primary authority, we needed to cover the nine major search resources.

To determine what primary and secondary authority a library has, check its card or online catalog. In effect, this is the index to the library itself. Although a catalog is usually comprehensive, you need to determine whether the library has any special lists of materials that may not be in the catalog. Kardex is a separate tool used by some libraries. In it the staff records the latest issues, pamphlets, volumes, or supplements the library has received on its subscription or serial publications.

The digests of West consist of hundreds of volumes that contain millions of small-paragraph summaries of court opinions. (These summaries were originally published as headnotes at the beginning of court opinions.) The summaries are organized in the digests by the key number system. Opinions on similar points of law are assigned a topic and number, called the key number. Once you find a key number that covers the area of your research, you are led to case summaries in that area. Ways to find a key num-

ber include the DWI, the table of contents for digest topics, leads from headnotes in court opinions, etc.

The annotations in A.L.R.1st, A.L.R.2d, A.L.R.3d, A.L.R.4th, A.L.R.5th, and A.L.R. Fed. are another major case finder. To find an annotation within one of the six sets, use the various index systems that are provided. For the more recent annotations, the most important index to use is the *ALR Index.* Because annotations are one of the citing materials in Shepard's, shepardizing is another way to find annotations. The most efficient way to update an annotation is to check the pocket part of the volume that contains the annotations—if such pocket parts exist. (The only sets that do *not* have pocket parts are A.L.R.1st and A.L.R.2d; annotations in these sets have their own updating features.)

As a citator, Shepard's enables you to assess the current validity of what you are shepardizing, called the cited material. This can be a cited case, a cited statute, a cited federal regulation, etc. The citing material in Shepard's also gives you leads to additional law. After you find the right set of Shepard's, be sure that the set is complete. When shepardizing a case, you are trying to find parallel cites, the history and treatment of the cited case, citing legal periodical literature, citing annotations, and citing opinions of the attorney general. (It is also possible to shepardize a headnote in a cited case.) When shepardizing a statute, you are trying to find a parallel cite, the history of the statute in the legislature, the treatment of the statute in the courts, citing administrative decisions, citing legal periodical literature, citing annotations, and citing opinions of the attorney general. (Before you can shepardize a statute, you may need to translate a session law cite into a codified cite.) In recent sets of Shepard's covering federal statutes, the citing material may have a date. It will be the date of the cited statute (if an asterisk is present) or it will be the date of citing material (if a delta symbol is present). When shepardizing a federal regulation, you are trying to find the history of the regulation in the courts, citing legal periodical literature, and citing annotations. When you shepardize a federal regulation, the citing material will always have a date. It will be the date of the cited regulation (if an asterisk is present), or it will be the date of the citing material (if a delta symbol is present).

Looseleaf services can be invaluable in research. It is relatively easy for the library to keep them current by inserting pages with new material and by removing pages with outdated material (interfiling). The services can provide leads to and explanations of primary authority.

Legal periodical literature consists of lead articles and comments, case notes, and book reviews. There are two major index systems to this literature: ILP and CLI. Within these systems, there are separate indexes that allow you to search specific subjects, specific authors, and book reviews. Both ILP and CLI have a table of cases and a table of statutes that allow you to find periodical literature on specific cases and statutes. Legal periodical literature can provide leads to, and explanations of, primary authority. It is also useful for background research.

Corpus Juris Secundum and *American Jurisprudence 2d* are national legal encyclopedias that summarize almost every area of the law. They are comprehensive and easy to use. In addition, they are effective for background research and for case finding because of the extensive footnotes within them.

Scholarly or practical legal treatises are available on most areas of the law. Another important search resource are experts who might be available to you by phone or mail.

KEY TERMS

mandatory primary authority	annotated reporters	superscript	enabling statute
search resources	superseded annotation	subscript	KeyCite
Library of Congress (LC) Classification System	supplemented annotation	memorandum of law	unreported cases
	shepardize	statute	looseleaf
KF call number	citator	act	interfiled
open stacks	cumulated	public laws	looseleaf filing
Dewey Decimal System	cited material	private laws	looseleaf service
interlibrary loan	citing material	slip law	legal periodical
Kardex	parallel cite	session law	case notes
digests	history of the case	Statutes at Large	LegalTrac
key number system	treatment of the case	session law cite	legal encyclopedias
headnote	docket number	code	black letter law
trace a key number	reversed	codified	legal treatise
DWI	overruled	codified cite	
annotation	syllabus	et seq.	

Chapter 10

CASE LAW

Chapter Outline

SECTION A   BRIEFING COURT OPINIONS

The word *brief* has several meanings.

First, to **brief** a court opinion is to summarize its ten essential components (e.g., key facts, issues, reasoning, disposition). Such a brief is your own summary of the opinion for later use. Second, a **trial brief** is an attorney's set of notes on how he or she will conduct the trial. The notes (often placed in a **trial notebook**) will be on the opening statement, witnesses, exhibits, direct and cross-examination, closing argument, etc. This trial brief is sometimes called a trial manual or trial book. (Trial brief has other meanings as well. In some states, for example, when an attorney submits a written argument in support of a motion during a trial, the writing is called a trial brief.) Third, the **appellate brief** is the formal written argument to a court of appeals on why a lower court's decision should be affirmed, modified, or reversed. The focus of the appellate brief is on the claimed errors made "below." An appellate brief is submitted to the appellate court and to the other side.

Here our concern is the first meaning of the word *brief*—a summarization of the ten essential components of a court opinion. (See Exhibit 10.1) These ten components will give you a comprehensive brief of the opinion. After we cover the comprehensive brief, we will also look at a shorter version, the thumbnail brief. It should be pointed out, however, that not all attorneys use the same format for briefing opinions. Indeed, the same attorney may use more than one format. Nevertheless, the guidelines in this chapter for preparing comprehensive and thumbnail briefs should prepare you to adapt to any format.

The briefs we will be examining are not legal documents submitted to a court or other institution. Your supervisors may not even ask to see them. Their primary value is to help you understand an opinion of a court. Opinions cannot be read like novels or the morning newspaper. Understanding them requires discipline and a method of analysis. Briefing is that method. Before we examine the comprehensive and thumbnail brief, we will study an opinion as it might appear in a library reporter volume.

The circled numbers are explained after the opinion.

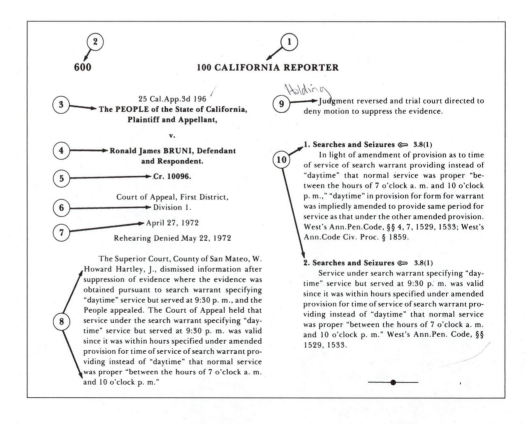

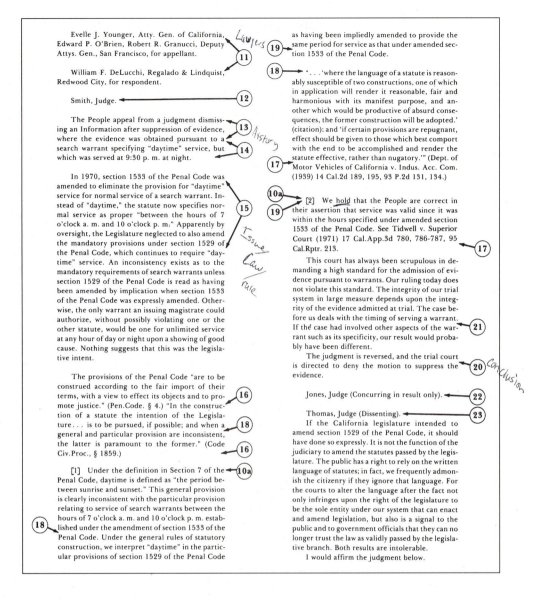

1. The *California Reporter* is an unofficial reporter of state opinions in California. The "100" indicates the volume number of the reporter.

2. The *Bruni* case begins on page 600. The **citation** of this case is *People v. Bruni*, 25 Cal. App. 3d 196, 100 Cal. Rptr. 600 (1972). The official cite is given at the top of the first column above the word PEOPLE.

3. When the *People* or the state brings an action, it is often a criminal case. *People v. Bruni* is an appellate court decision. Trial court decisions are appealed to the appellate court. The **appellant** is the party bringing the appeal because of dissatisfaction with the ruling or decision of the lower court. The state of California brought the case as the plaintiff and prosecutor in the lower court (Superior Court, County of San Mateo) and is now the appellant in the higher court (Court of Appeal, First District, Division 1).

4. Bruni was the defendant in the lower court because he was being sued or, in this case, charged with a crime. The appeal is taken against him by the People (appellant), because the lower court ruling was favorable to Bruni, to the dissatisfaction of the People. The party against whom a case is brought on appeal is called the **respondent.** Another word for respondent is **appellee.**

5. "Cr. 10096" refers to the **docket,** or calendar number of the case assigned by the court. "Cr." stands for *criminal.* (Docket numbers are not used in the citation of **reported** cases. *Reported* here means printed in a traditional reporter. See number 7 below.)

6. Make careful note of the name of the court writing the opinion. As soon as possible, you must learn the hierarchy of state courts in your state. In many

states, there are three levels of courts: trial level, middle appeals level, and supreme level. (Most cases are appealed from the trial court to the middle appeals level, and then to the supreme level.) Here, we know from the title of the court (Court of Appeal) that it is an appellate court. It is not the supreme court, because in California the highest court is the California Supreme Court.

The name of the court is significant because of legal authority. If the court is the highest or supreme court of the state, then the case would be applicable throughout the state. A middle appeals court case, in contrast, applies only in the area of the state over which that court has jurisdiction. When you see that the case was written by a trial or middle appeals court, you are immediately put on notice that you must check to determine whether the case was ever appealed subsequent to the date of the case. One of the main systems for checking is called **shepardizing** (see Checklist 4a in chapter 9).

⑦ When a reported case is being cited, only the year (here, 1972) is used, not the month or day (April 27). (If the case has not yet been reported, the month, day, and year are used—along with the docket number.) Sometimes, the text of the reported opinion will also give you the date of the hearing or rehearing as well as the date of the decision. The year of the decision is still the critical one for citation purposes.

⑧ Here the editors provide the reader with a summary of what the case says. The court did not write this summary; the editors did. Therefore, it is not an official statement of the law. It is merely an aid to the reader, who can quickly read this summary to determine whether the case covers relevant areas of law. This summary paragraph is often called the **syllabus.**

⑨ Here continues the unofficial summary, providing the reader with what procedurally must happen as a result of the April 27 case.

⑩ These are editor's **headnotes,** which are small-paragraph summaries of portions of the case. When the editors first read the case, they decide how many major topics or issues are covered in the case. Each of these topics is summarized in a headnote, all of which are then given consecutive numbers, here 1 and 2. These numbers correspond with the bracketed numbers [1] and [2] in the case itself. (See ⑩ₐ) If, for example, you wanted to read the portion of the case that was summarized in the second headnote of the case, you would go to the text of the case that begins with the bracketed [2].

The headnotes also have a **key number,** which consists of a topic and a number, here "Searches and Seizures ⊙⊶ 3.8(1)." Each headnote will also be printed in the **digests** of West Publishing Company. *Digests* are volumes that contain nothing but the headnotes of court opinions. You can find out what other courts have said about the same or similar points by going to the digest volumes, looking up the key number of a headnote (e.g., Searches and Seizures ⊙⊶ 3.8(1)), and reading summary paragraphs from many court cases such as our case, *People v. Bruni.*

Caution is needed in reading the syllabus and headnotes of opinions. As indicated earlier, they are not written by the court and therefore should never be relied on or quoted. They are merely preliminary guides to what is in an opinion. To understand the opinion, you must carefully study the language of the opinion itself through the process called *briefing.*

⑪ Here are the attorneys who represented the appellant and respondent on appeal. Note that the attorney general's office represented the People. The attorney general or the district attorney's office represents the state in criminal cases.

⑫ The opinion begins with the name of the judge who wrote the opinion, Judge Smith. In this spot you will sometimes find the words **Per Curiam Opinion.** A per curiam opinion is a court opinion that does not name the individual judge who wrote the opinion for the court, and is usually a short opinion. Most per curiam opinions raise issues the court has decided frequently. It may also be called a *memorandum opinion.*

⑬ In reading or briefing a case, make note of the history of the litigation to date. The lower court rendered a judgment dismissing the information (similar to an indictment) against Bruni after certain evidence was suppressed and declared inadmissible. (This is the prior proceeding.) The People have now appealed the judgment. (This is the present proceeding.)

If the words *information* or *suppression* are new to you, look them up in a legal dictionary before proceeding. Do this for every new word.

⑭ It is critical to state the facts of the case accurately. Here the facts are relatively simple: A search warrant that said "daytime" service was served at

9:30 P.M., and evidence was taken pursuant to this search warrant. Defendant objected to the admission of this evidence at trial. In most cases, the facts are not this simple. The facts may be given at the beginning of the case, or they may be scattered throughout the case. If you confront the latter situation, you must carefully read the entire case to piece the facts together. Ultimately, your goal is to identify the **key facts** of the opinion. A key fact is simply one that was essential or very important to the result or holding of the court.

(15) The next critical stage of reading a case is to state the **issue** (or issues) that the court was deciding in the case. When phrasing an issue, you should make specific reference to the language of the rule in controversy (e.g., a statute) along with important facts that raise this controversy. The issue in *Bruni* is as follows: When § 1533 was amended to allow service up to 10:00 P.M., did the legislature impliedly also amend § 1529, which continues to require "daytime" service, so that evidence obtained pursuant to a warrant served at 9:30 P.M. can be admitted into evidence?

(16) The court refers to other statutes to support the conclusion it will reach. Note the interrelationship of the statutory sections. One statute is interpreted by interpreting other statutes. Section 4 of the Penal Code ("Pen. Code") says that the sections of the Penal Code are to be interpreted ("construed") rationally in order to carry out their purpose or objective and to promote justice. Section 1859 of the Code of Civil Procedure ("Code Civ. Proc.") says that when a general and a particular section are inconsistent, the latter is preferred.

The interrelationship of the statutes in this case is as follows:

- Section 1529 of the Penal Code says "daytime."
- Section 7 of the Penal Code defines daytime as sunrise to sunset.
- Section 1533 of the Penal Code, as amended, says between 7:00 A.M. and 10:00 P.M.
- Section 4 of the Penal Code and § 1859 of the Code of Civil Procedure provide principles of interpreting statutes that are inconsistent.

(17) In the same manner, a court will refer to other cases to support its ruling. In this way, the court argues that the other cases are **precedents** for the case before the court. (A *precedent* is a prior decision that can be used as a standard in a later similar case.) The court in *People v. Bruni* is saying that *Dept. of Motor Vehicles of California v. Indus. Acc. Com.* and *Tidwell v. Superior Court* are precedents for its own ruling. Precedent is important because of the principle of **stare decisis,** which means that courts should decide similar cases in the same way unless there is good reason to do otherwise.

(18) Here is the **reasoning** of the court to support its ruling: If there is a general statute (such as § 1529) and a specific statute (such as § 1533) that are inconsistent, the latter is paramount and is preferred. Hence the legislature probably intended to amend the more general statute—§ 1529—when it amended § 1533.

(19) The result, or **holding,** of the court must then be identified. A *holding* is a court's specific answer to a specific issue that arises out of specific facts before the court.) The holding is that § 1529 was impliedly amended to authorize service up to 10:00 P.M. The holding is also called the court's *ruling.*

(20) The procedural consequences of the court's resolution of the issue are then usually stated, as here, toward the very end of the case. The judgment of the lower court is reversed. The lower court cannot continue to suppress (i.e., declare inadmissible) the evidence seized at the 9:30 P.M. search. This is the **disposition** of the case.

An appeals court could take a number of positions with respect to a lower court's decision. It could affirm it; modify it (reverse it only in part); **remand** the case (send it back to the lower court) with instructions on retrying the case or taking other corrective action, etc.

(21) In theory, a judge must be very precise in defining the issue before the court—and in resolving only that issue. The judge should not say more than *must* be said to decide the case. This theory, however, is sometimes not observed. Judges will go off on tangents, giving long dissertations or speeches through their opinions. As indicated, this can make your job more difficult; you must wade through all the words to identify (1) the key facts, (2) the precise issues, (3) the precise holding, and (4) the precise reasoning.

The worst tangent that a judge can stray into is called **dictum.** Dictum is a judge's or court's view of what the law is, or might be, on facts that are *not* before the court. Judge Smith indicated that the result of the case might be different if the warrant were not specific, e.g., if it did not name the individual to be searched or what the investigator was looking for. This was not the situation in the *Bruni* case; therefore, Judge Smith's commentary or speculation is dictum.

㉒ On any court there may be several judges. They do not always agree on what should be done in a case. The majority controls. In *Bruni,* Judge Smith wrote the **majority opinion,** which is the opinion agreed upon by at least half of the judges plus one. A **concurring opinion** is one that votes for the result reached by the majority but for different reasons. In *Bruni,* Judge Jones concurred but specified that he accepted only the result of Judge Smith's opinion. Normally, judges in such situations will write an opinion indicating their own point of view. Judge Jones chose not to write an opinion. He simply let it be known that he did not necessarily agree with everything Judge Smith said; all he agreed with was the conclusion that the warrant was validly served. To reach this result, Judge Jones might have used different reasoning, relied on different cases as precedent, etc.

㉓ A **dissenting opinion** disagrees with part or with all of the result of the majority opinion. Dissenting opinions are sometimes heated. Of course, the dissenter's opinion is not controlling. It is often valuable to read, however, in order to determine what the dissenter thinks that the majority decided.

We turn now to the ten components found in a **comprehensive brief** of a court opinion (Exhibit 10.1) followed by a ten-part brief of *Bruni* that conforms to the guidelines of briefing presented in Exhibit 10.1.

 10.1 ························· Comprehensive Brief of a Court Opinion

Exhibit

I.   CITATION
Where can the case be found? Provide a full *citation* to the case you are briefing, e.g., the volume of the reporter, the abbreviation of the reporter, the page on which the case begins, the date of decision.

II. PARTIES
Who are the *parties*? Identify the lead parties, their relationship to each other, their litigation status when the case began (e.g., defendant), and their litigation status now (e.g., appellant).

III. OBJECTIVES OF PARTIES
When the litigation began, what were the parties seeking? State the ultimate objectives of the parties in terms of the end result they want from the litigation. At this point, do not focus on tactical or procedural objectives.

IV. THEORIES OF THE LITIGATION
What legal theories are the parties using? At the trial level of a civil case, state the cause of action and the main defense. (A **cause of action** is a set of facts that give a party a right to judicial relief; it is a legally acceptable reason for suing.) In a criminal case, state what the prosecution was for and the response of the defendant. If the case is now on appeal, briefly state the main theory of each party. Where relevant, always refer to specific rules.

V.   HISTORY OF THE LITIGATION
What happened below—what are the prior proceeding(s)? For each *prior proceeding,* briefly state the nature of the proceeding, the party initiating it, the name of the court or agency involved, and the result of the proceeding. For the *present proceeding,* briefly state the nature of the proceeding, who initiated it, and the name of the court or agency involved.

VI. FACTS
What are the facts of the case? Specifically, state the facts that were very important or *key* to the holding(s) reached by this court.

VII. ISSUE(S)
What are the questions of law now before the court? Provide a comprehensive statement of each *issue* by making specific reference to the language of the rule in controversy (e.g., a statute) along with important facts that raise this controversy.

VIII.   HOLDING(S)
What are this court's answers to the issues? If you have stated each issue comprehensively, its holding will be a simple YES or NO response.
   IX.   REASONING
Why did the court answer the issues the way it did? State the reasons for each holding.
    X.   DISPOSITION
What order did this court enter as a result of its holding(s)? State the procedural consequences of the court's resolution of the issue(s).

Comprehensive Brief of *People v. Bruni*

CITATION:	*People v. Bruni*, 25 Cal. App. 3d 196, 100 Cal. Rptr. 600 (1972).
PARTIES:	People of California/prosecution/plaintiff below/appellant here v. Bruni/accused/defendant below/respondent here
OBJECTIVES OF PARTIES:	The People want to convict and punish Bruni for criminal conduct. Bruni wants to avoid conviction and punishment.
THEORIES of the LITIGATION:	1. TRIAL: The People sought to prosecute Bruni for the alleged commission of a crime. (The opinion does not tell us which crime. The legal theory that justifies the bringing of the prosecution is the alleged commission of a crime.) Because Bruni is resisting the prosecution, we can assume that the basis and theory of his case is simply that he did not commit the crime. At the trial this was probably his main defense. 2. APPEAL: Bruni says that the state violated § 1529 when the search warrant was served at 9:30 P.M. The People say § 1529 was impliedly amended by § 1533, which allows service up to 10:00 P.M.
HISTORY of LITIGATION Prior Proceeding:	1. TRIAL: A criminal prosecution was brought by the People (the state) in the Superior Court (San Mateo). RESULT: Judgment for Bruni dismissing the information after the court granted a motion to suppress the evidence obtained from the search warrant.
Present Proceeding:	2. APPEAL: The People now appeal the dismissal of the information to the Court of Appeals (First District).
FACTS:	A search warrant that said "daytime" service was served at 9:30 P.M. Evidence was obtained during this search, which the People unsuccessfully attempted to introduce during the trial.
ISSUE:	When § 1533 was amended to allow service up to 10:00 P.M., did the legislature impliedly also amend § 1529 which continues to require "daytime" service, so that evidence obtained pursuant to a warrant served at 9:30 P.M. can be admitted into evidence?
HOLDING:	YES.
REASONING:	If there is a general statute (such as § 1529) and a specific statute (such as § 1533) that are inconsistent, the latter is paramount and is preferred. Hence the legislature probably intended to amend the more general statute—§ 1529—when it amended § 1533.
DISPOSITION:	The trial court's judgment dismissing the information is reversed. When the trial resumes, the court must deny the motion to suppress the evidence based on the time of the service.

At the end of your brief, you should consider adding some notes that cover the following topics:

- What has happened to the case since it was decided? Has it been overruled? Has it been expanded or restricted by later cases? You can find the history and treatment of a case by shepardizing it. See checklist #4a in chapter 9.
- Summary of concurring opinions, if any.
- Summary of dissenting opinions, if any.
- Interesting dictum in the majority opinion, if any.
- Your own feelings about the opinion. Was it correctly decided? Why or why not?

Thumbnail Brief

A **thumbnail brief** is, in effect, a brief of a brief! It is a shorthand version of the comprehensive brief. A thumbnail brief includes abbreviated versions of six of the components (i.e., citation, facts, issues, holding, reasoning, and disposition) and leaves out four of the components (i.e., parties, objectives, theories, and history of the litigation). By definition, you must know how to do a comprehensive brief before you can do a shorthand one. Many students fall into the trap of doing *only* shorthand briefs. It takes considerable time to write a comprehensive brief. It is highly recommended, however, that early in your career you develop the habit and skill of preparing briefs comprehensively. Without this foundation, your shorthand briefs will be visibly superficial. Shorthand briefs are valuable time savers when communicating with colleagues, but they are not substitutes for comprehensive briefs.

Thumbnail Brief of *People v. Bruni*

CITATION:	*People v. Bruni*, 25 Cal. App. 3d 196, 100 Cal. Rptr. 600 (1972)
FACTS:	A "daytime" search warrant served at 9:30 P.M. produces evidence that the People unsuccessfully attempt to introduce during the trial.
ISSUE:	Did § 1533 (which allows service up to 10:00 P.M.) impliedly amend § 1529 (which requires "daytime" service) so that evidence obtained from a 9:30 P.M. warrant is admissible?
HOLDING:	Yes
REASONING:	A specific statute (§ 1533) is preferred over an inconsistent general one (§ 1529).
DISPOSITION:	Dismissal of information is reversed; motion to suppress the 9:30 P.M. evidence must be denied.

 Assignment 10.1

Prepare a comprehensive and a thumbnail brief of each of the following three opinions printed in Appendix C:

(a) *United States v. Kovel*

(b) *Quinn v. Lum* (You do not need to give the citation of this opinion. It is an actual opinion, but was not reported in a traditional reporter.)

(c) *Brown v. Hammond*

SECTION B   APPLYING COURT OPINIONS

Our next concern is: How do you apply an opinion to the facts of a research problem? Before we examine this question, we need to take a closer look at the kind of law found within an opinion. The function of a court's opinion is to apply one or more rules of law to the facts involved in the legal dispute before the court. What kind of rules of law does a court interpret and apply? There are two broad categories:

> Enacted law
> Common law

Enacted law is any law that is not created within litigation. Here is a list of the major categories of enacted laws and their definitions (see also Exhibit 2.2 in chapter 2):

* *Constitution:* The fundamental law that creates the branches of government and identifies basic rights and liberties. The legislature often writes the constitution, sometimes with a vote of the people. (Another possibility is a constitutional convention.)
* *Statute:* A law that declares, commands, or prohibits something. The legislature writes statutes. (The people sometimes can also do so by referendum.)
* *Administrative regulation:* A law designed to explain or carry out the statutes and executive orders that govern an administrative agency. The agency writes its own administrative regulations.
* *Ordinance:* A law that declares, commands, or prohibits something. It is written by the local legislature such as the city council.
* *Rules of court:* The procedural laws that govern the mechanics of litigation before a court. They are written by the legislature and/or by the highest court of the jurisdiction.

Although rules of court are enacted laws, they are not created within litigation. When a high court creates (or participates in the creation of) rules of court, there are no parties before it in litigation. Rules of court are created to govern all procedural steps in every case that will come before a court (e.g., the rules of evidence that will govern every civil trial, the rules of procedure that will govern wills and estate cases in probate court).

There is another category of law that the courts apply. This kind of law *does* grow out of litigation. It is called **common law.** This is judge-made law created by the courts to resolve a dispute within a particular litigation in the absence of controlling enacted law such as a statute or constitutional provision that governs the dispute. When a court has a dispute before it in litigation, it seeks to resolve the dispute by applying enacted law to the dispute. If no controlling enacted law exists, the court has the power to create new law—called common law—to resolve the dispute. For example, most of the law of negligence was initially created as common law by the courts because the legislatures had not created (enacted) any statutes in this area of the law. If, however, such statutes did exist, the courts would have to apply them. Because statutes are superior in authority to common law, new statutes can always change the common law. Statutes that bring about this change are called **statutes in derogation of the common law.**

To sum up, courts resolve legal disputes by applying two different kinds of rules of law to the facts before them: enacted law and common law.

Assume that you are in the law library researching the facts of a client's problem or the facts presented to you by your instructor for a school assignment. You find an opinion that looks promising, but you need to analyze it carefully before concluding that it applies to the facts you are researching. The opinion reached a certain result, called a *holding.* The conclusion of your legal analysis will be your assessment of whether this holding applies to the facts of your research problem. How do you make this assessment? You go through two separate comparisons:

* **Rule comparison.** First, you compare the *rule of law* (enacted law or common law) that was interpreted and applied in the opinion with the rule of law (enacted law or common law) that you have uncovered elsewhere in your research as potentially applicable to the facts of your research problem.
* **Fact comparison.** Second, you compare the *key facts* of the opinion (i.e., those that were essential or very important to its holding) with the facts of your research problem.

Rule Comparison

Suppose your client is charged with a violation of § 23(b) of the state code on the payment of certain taxes. One of your first steps is to go to the law library and find § 23(b). You want to know whether § 23(b) applies to your client. After a preliminary analysis of this statute on your own, you search for court opinions that interpreted and applied § 23(b). You would not try to find opinions that interpreted housing or pollution statutes. You focus on opinions that cover the *same* rule of law involved in the case of the client—here, § 23(b). This is also true of the common law. If the client has a negligence case, for example, you search for opinions that interpret the law of negligence.

Rule comparison in the analysis of opinions, therefore, is fairly simple. The general principle is: you compare the rule involved in your client's case (or school assignment) with the rule interpreted and applied in the opinion, and you proceed only if the rule is exactly the same. Although there are some exceptions, this principle will be sufficient to guide you most of the time.

Fact Comparison

Here is the heart of the analysis. Before the holding of an opinion can apply, you must demonstrate that the key facts of the opinion are substantially the same as the facts in the client's case (or school assignment). If the facts are exactly the same or almost exactly the same, the opinion is said to be **on all fours** with your facts. If so, then you will have little difficulty convincing someone that the holding of the opinion applies to your facts. It is rare, however, that you will find an opinion on all fours. Consequently, careful analysis of *factual similarities and differences* must be made. In general, if the facts are substantially similar, the ruling applies; if they are substantially different, it does not.

You must determine what the *key facts* are in the opinion, because these facts alone are the basis of the comparison. As indicated earlier, a key fact is a fact that was essential or very important to the holding of the court. In a divorce opinion, for example, it will probably not be key that a plaintiff was thirty-three years old. The court would have reached the same result if the plaintiff were thirty-two or thirty-four. Age may have been irrelevant or of very minor importance to the holding. What *may* have been key is that the plaintiff beat his wife, because without this fact the court may not have reached the conclusion that the ground of cruelty existed. You carefully comb the opinion to read what the judge said about the various facts. Did the court emphasize certain facts? Repeat them? Label them as crucial or important? These are the kinds of questions you must ask yourself to determine which facts in the opinion were key.

Let us assume that you have been able to identify the key facts of opinion. Your next concern is *comparing* these facts and the facts of your own problem. For example:

Facts of Your Research Problem

Client sees an ad in the paper announcing a sale at a local store. He goes to the back of the store and falls into a pit. There was a little sign that said *danger* near the pit. The client wants to sue the store owner, J. Jackson, for negligence in failing to use reasonable care in preventing his injury. The law office assigns you to research the case. You find the case of *Smith v. Apex Co.* and want to argue that it applies.

The Opinion: *Smith v. Apex Co.*

This case involved a man (Mr. Smith) who is looking for an address. He is walking down the street. He decides to walk into an office building to ask someone for directions. While coming down the corridor, he slips and falls on a wet floor. There was a small sign in the corridor that said *wet floor*, which Smith saw. Smith sued the owner of the building (Apex Co.) for negligence. The court held that the owner was negligent for failure to exercise reasonable care for the safety of users of the building. The cite of the opinion is *Smith v. Apex Co.*, 223 Mass. 578, 78 N.E.2d 422 (1980).

First, identify all factual similarities:

- The client was in a public place (a store). Smith was also in a public place (an office building).
- Both situations involved some kind of warning (the *danger* sign and the *wet floor* sign).
- The warning in both situations was not conspicuous (the *danger* sign was "little"; the *wet floor* sign was "small").

Next, identify all factual differences:

- The client was in a store, whereas Smith was in an office building.
- The client's case involved a hole or pit, whereas *Smith v. Apex Co.* involved a slippery surface.
- The client was there about a possible purchase, whereas Smith was looking for directions and therefore not trying to transact any business in the office building.

Next, identify any factual gaps:

- Smith saw the *wet floor* sign, but we do not know whether the client saw the *danger* sign.

Ninety percent of your legal analysis is complete if you have been able to make the above identifications. Many students do a sloppy job at this level. They do not carefully pick apart the facts to identify similarities, differences, and gaps.

Once you have done this properly, you make your final arguments about the opinion:

- If you want the holding in the opinion to apply, you emphasize the similarities between your facts and the key facts in the opinion. If any of your facts differs from a fact in the opinion, you try to point out that this is not significant because the latter was not a key fact in the opinion.
- If you do not want the holding in the opinion to apply, you emphasize the differences between your facts and the key facts in the opinion. If any of your facts is similar to a fact in the opinion, you try to point out that this is not significant because there is still a dissimilarity with at least one of the key facts in the opinion.

Factual Gaps   *Factual gaps* sometimes pose a problem. If the factual gap is in the facts of your client's case, you simply go back to the client and ask him or her about the fact. In the above case, for example, the paralegal asks the client whether he saw the "danger" sign. Suppose, however, that the factual gap is in the opinion itself. Assume that your client was running when he fell into the pit, but that the opinion does not tell you whether Smith was running, walking, etc. You obviously cannot go to Smith or to the judge who wrote the opinion and ask. You must make a guess of what the judge would have done in the opinion if Smith had been running at the time he slipped on the corridor floor. You may decide that it would have changed the result or that this additional fact would have made no difference to the ruling reached.

Application in Memorandum of Law

We turn now to an overview of how *Smith v. Apex Co.* would be applied to the client's case in a **memorandum of law.** The latter is simply a written analysis of a legal problem. In chapter 16 we will discuss the components of a memorandum of law in greater detail. For now, we concentrate on only three components: legal issue, facts, and analysis.

The client's case and the *Smith* opinion involve exactly the same rule—the law of negligence. Assume that the part of this rule that is in contention (the *element in contention*) between the client and the store owner, J. Jackson, is the requirement that "reasonable care" be used.

> *Issue:* Did the store use "reasonable care" for the safety of users of the store when the only warning of a pit in the store was a small *danger* sign near the pit?

Facts: The client saw an ad in the newspaper announcing a sale. He went to the back of the store and fell into a pit. There was a small sign that said *danger* near the pit.

Analysis: An opinion on point is *Smith v. Apex Co.,* 233 Mass. 578, 78 N.E.2d 422 (1980). In this opinion, the holding of the court was that the owner of an office building was liable for negligence when Smith slipped on a wet corridor floor in the building. There was a small *wet floor* sign in the corridor. This opinion is substantially similar to our own client's case. Both were in public buildings where owners can expect people to be present. In both situations, the warning was insufficient. The *wet floor* sign in the opinion was "small." The *danger* sign in our situation was "little." Because of all these important similarities, it can be argued that the holding in *Smith v. Apex Co.* applies.

It is true that in the opinion the judge pointed out that Smith saw the sign. Our facts do not state whether the client saw the *danger* sign in the store. This should not make any difference, however, as the judge in the opinion would probably have reached the same result if Smith had not seen the *wet floor* sign. In fact, the case would probably have been stronger for Smith if he did *not* see the sign. The building was dangerous in spite of the fact that users of the building such as Smith could see the sign. Obviously, the danger would be considered even greater if such users could not see the sign. We should find out from our client whether he saw the *danger* sign, but I do not think that it will make any difference in the applicability of the holding in *Smith v. Apex Co.*

The store owner will try to argue that the opinion does not apply. The argument might be that a pit is not as dangerous as a wet floor, because a pit is more conspicuous than a wet floor and hence not as hazardous. A user is more likely to notice a hole in the floor than to know whether a floor is slippery enough to fall on. Our client could respond by pointing out that the pit was in the back of the store where it may not have been very noticeable. Furthermore, the wet floor in the opinion was apparently conspicuous (Smith saw the *wet floor* sign), yet in the opinion the judge still found the defendant liable.

Assignment 10.2

In the following situations, point out any factual similarities, differences, and gaps between the client facts and the facts of the opinion.

(a) *Client Facts:* Jim is driving his car 30 MPH on a dirt road at night. He suddenly sneezes and jerks the steering wheel slightly, causing the car to move to the right and run into Bill's fence. Bill sues Jim for negligence.
Opinion: A pedestrian brings a negligence action against Mary. Mary is driving her motorcycle on a clear day. A page of a newspaper unexpectedly flies into Mary's face. Because she cannot see where she is going, she runs into a pedestrian crossing the street. The court finds for Mary, ruling that she did not act unreasonably in causing the accident.

(b) *Client Facts:* Helen is the mother of David, age four. The state is trying to take David away from Helen on the ground that Helen has neglected David. Helen lives alone with David. She works part-time and leaves David with a neighbor. Helen's job occasionally requires her to travel. Once she was away for a month. During this period, David was sometimes left alone, because the neighbor had to spend several days at the hospital. When David was discovered alone, the state began proceedings to remove David on the ground of neglect.
Opinion: The state charged Bob Thompson with the neglect of his twins, aged ten. The state wishes to place the twins in a foster home. Bob is partially blind. One day he accidentally tripped and fell on one of the twins, causing severe injuries to the child. Bob lives alone with the twins but refuses to hire anyone to help him run the home. The court ruled that Bob did not neglect his children.

Assignment 10.3

(a) Before Helen became a paralegal for the firm of Harris & Derkson, she was a chemist for a large corporation. Harris & Derkson is a patent law firm where Helen's technical expertise in chemistry is invaluable. Helen's next-door neighbor is an inventor. On a number of occasions, he discussed the chemical makeup of his inventions with Helen. The neighbor is being charged by the government with stealing official secrets in order to prepare one of these inventions. Harris & Derkson represents the neighbor on this case. Helen also works directly on the case for the firm. In a prosecution of the neighbor, Helen is called as a witness and is asked to reveal the substance of all her conversations with the neighbor concerning the invention in question. Does Helen have to answer? Apply *United States v. Kovel* to this question. Do not do any legal research. Limit yourself to the application of this one opinion based on the guidelines of this section. For the text of *Kovel*, see Appendix C.

(b) Salem is a factory town of 500 inhabitants in Hawaii. The factory employs 95 percent of the workers in the town. The town has only two private attorneys: Ann Grote and Timothy Farrell. Forty of the employees have decided to sue the factory over a wage dispute. Ann Grote represents all these employees. She works alone except for her only employee, Bob Davis, a paralegal. In this litigation, the factory is represented by Timothy Farrell who has no employees—no secretaries and no paralegals. Grote and Farrell are young attorneys who have just begun their practices. Their only clients are the forty employees and the factory, respectively. The litigation has become quite complicated. Several months before the case is scheduled to go to trial, Farrell offers Davis a job as a paralegal at double the salary he is earning with Grote. Davis accepts the offer. Grote goes to court seeking a preliminary injunction against Davis and Farrell, which would bar them from entering this employment relationship. Apply *Quinn v. Lum* and *Cronin, Fried, Sekiya & Kekina* to the facts of the case of *Grote v. Davis and Farrell*. Do not do any legal research. Limit yourself to the application of this one opinion based on the guidelines of this section. For the text of *Quinn*, see Appendix C.

(c) Anthony Bay is a paralegal who works for Iverson, Kelley, & Winters in Philadelphia. He is an at-will employee. His supervising attorney is Grace Swenson. One day Bay notices that Swenson deposited a client settlement check in the general law firm account. Bay calls the bar association disciplinary committee and charges Swenson with commingling funds unethically. (The ethical obligation of an attorney is to keep client funds and general law firm funds in separate accounts. Commingling these funds in one account is unethical.) Bay is fired for disloyalty. In the meantime, the bar investigates the charge of commingling and finds that the charge is accurate. Swenson is eventually disciplined. Can Bay sue Swenson and Iverson, Kelley, & Winters for wrongful dismissal? Apply *Brown v. Hammond* to answer this question. Do not do any legal research. Limit yourself to the application of this one opinion based on the guidelines of this section. For the text of *Brown*, see Appendix C.

SECTION C

> "There is a high that comes with finding that case on all fours—the one that makes your brief smoke—there's nothing like that sense of triumph."
>
> —James Clay, Paralegal Huffman, Arrington, Kihle, Goberino & Dunn

FINDING COURT OPINIONS

In sections A and B, we covered the structure of a court opinion, the briefing of an opinion, and the application of an opinion to a set of facts. Here our focus is on *finding* these opinions in the library—finding case law.

In searching for case law, you will probably find yourself in one or more of the following situations:

- You already have one case **on point** (or close to being on point) and you want to find additional ones. (Something is on point when it is relevant because it covers the facts of your research problem.)
- You are looking for cases interpreting a statute, constitution, charter, ordinance, rule of court, or administrative regulation that you already have.
- You are starting from square one. You want to find case law when you do *not* have a case, statute, or other law to begin with. You may be looking for cases containing common law or for cases interpreting statutes that you have not found yet.

The following search techniques are not necessarily listed in the order in which they should be tried. Your goal is to know how to use all of them. In practice, you can vary the order.

First, a reminder about doing the first level of legal research: background research. You should review the checklist for background research presented in Exhibit 8.1 in chapter 8. While doing this research, you will probably come across laws that will be of help to you on the specific facts of your problem (which is the second level of research). If so, you may already have some case law and now want to find more.

TECHNIQUES FOR FINDING CASE LAW WHEN YOU ALREADY HAVE ONE CASE ON POINT

1. *Shepardize the case that you have.* (See Checklist #4a on shepardizing cases, in chapter 9.) In the columns of Shepard's, look for cases that have mentioned your case. Such cases will probably cover similar topics. (You can also shepardize a case online through LEXIS and WESTLAW.)

2. *Shepardize cases cited by the case you have.* Almost every court opinion discusses or at least refers to other opinions. Is this true of the case you already have? If so, shepardize every case your case cites that might be relevant to your research. (See Checklist #4a on shepardizing cases in chapter 9.)

3. If you have access to WESTLAW, *do a KeyCite check* on the case you have. As a citator, KeyCite is more comprehensive than Shepard's in giving you access to cases that have cited the case that you have.

4. *Use the West digests.* There are two ways to do this:

   (a) Go to the Table of Cases in all the digests covering the court that wrote the case you already have, such as the Table of Cases in the American Digest System. The Table of Cases will tell you what key numbers your case is digested under in the main volumes of the digest. Find your case digested under those key numbers. Once you have done so, you will probably be able to find other case law under the same key numbers.

   (b) Go to the West reporter that contains the full text of the case you already have. At the beginning of this case in the reporter, find the headnotes and their key numbers. Take the key numbers that are relevant to your problem into any of West's digests to find more case law.

(See Checklist #2 on using digests, in chapter 9.)

5. *Find an annotation.* First identify the main topics or issues in the case you already have. Look up these topics in the *ALR Index* and in the other index systems for finding annotations in A.L.R.1st, A.L.R.2d, A.L.R.3d, A.L.R.4th, A.L.R.5th, and A.L.R. Fed. (For a description of these annotation index systems, see Exhibit 9.3 in chapter 9 and Checklist #3 in chapter 9.) Another way to try to find annotations is by shepardizing the case you have. Annotations are among the citing materials of Shepard's. (See Checklist #4a on shepardizing cases, in chapter 9.) Once you find an annotation, you will be given extensive citations to more case law. (See Checklist #3 on finding annotations, in chapter 9.)

6. *Find a discussion of your case in the legal periodicals.* Go to the Table of Cases in the *Index to Legal Periodicals and Books* (ILP) and the *Current Law Index* (CLI). There you will be told if your case was analyzed (noted) in the periodicals. If so, the discussion may give you additional case law on the same topic. (See Checklist #6 on finding legal periodical literature, in chapter 9. See also Research Link P in chapter 9.)

7. *Go to Words and Phrases.* Identify the major words or phrases that are dealt with in the case you have. Check the definitions of those words and phrases in the multivolume legal dictionary called *Words and Phrases.* (See photo on page 75.) By so doing you will be led to other cases defining the same words or phrases.

Assignment 10.4

Go to the regional reporter that covers your state. (See Exhibit 3.2 in chapter 3.) Pick any opinion in this reporter that meets the following criteria: it was decided by the highest state court of your state, it is at least twenty years old, and it has at least five headnotes in it. Assume that this case is relevant to your research problem. What is the citation of this case? Find *additional* cases by using the "Techniques for Finding Case Law When You Already Have One Case on Point." Try to find one additional case through each technique. Describe each of the techniques you used. Explain how you used it and give the cite to the additional case it led you to. If you were not able to use any of the techniques, explain why (e.g., your library did not have the materials you needed for the technique).

Now let us assume that you already have a statute and you want case law interpreting that statute. The techniques for doing so (many of which are the same when seeking case law interpreting constitutions, regulations, etc.) are as follows:

TECHNIQUES FOR FINDING CASE LAW INTERPRETING A STATUTE

1. *Shepardize the statute that you have.* (See Checklist #4b on shepardizing statutes in chapter 9.) In the columns of Shepard's, look for cases that have mentioned your statute. (You can also shepardize a statute online through LEXIS and WESTLAW.)

2. *Examine the Notes of Decisions for your statute in the statutory code.* At the end of your statute in the statutory code, there are paragraph summaries of cases (often called **Notes of Decisions**) that have interpreted your statute. (See Exhibit 11.1 in chapter 11.) Look for these summaries in the bound volume of the code, in the pocket part of this volume, and in any supplemental pamphlets at the end of the code. (For federal statutes, the codes to check are U.S.C.A. and U.S.C.S. The U.S.C. will *not* have such case summaries.)

3. *Find an annotation on your statute.* There are several ways to find out if there is an annotation in A.L.R.1st, A.L.R.2d, etc. that mentions your statute. First, shepardize that statute. Such annotations are among the citing materials of Shepard's. Second, check the *Table of Laws, Rules, and Regulations* in the last volume of the *ALR Index.* See Exhibit 9.4 in chapter 9. Such annotations will probably lead you to more case law on the statute. (If the statute you have is a federal statute, you can also find annotations on that statute through a separate volume called *ALR Federal Tables.*)

4. *Find legal periodical literature on your statute.* Law review articles on statutes, for example, often cite cases that interpret the statutes. There are three ways to find such articles:
   (a) Shepardize the statute. (See technique 1 above.) Citing material for a statute often includes citing legal periodical literature.
   (b) Check the Table of Statutes in the *Index to Legal Periodicals and Books* (ILP) and in the *Current Law Index* (CLI). See Research Link Q in chapter 9.
   (c) Go to the Subject Indexes in ILP and CLI and check the topics of your statute.
   (See Checklist #6 on legal periodicals in chapter 9.)

5. *Go to looseleaf services on your statute.* Find out if there is a looseleaf service on the subject matter of your statute. Such services often give extensive cites to cases on the statute. (See checklist #5 on looseleaf services, in chapter 9.)

6. *Go to legal treatises on your statute.* Most major statutes have treatises on them that contain extensive cites to cases on the statute. (See checklist #8 on legal treatises, in chapter 9.)

7. *Shepardize any cases you found through techniques 1–6 above.* You may be led to additional case law on the statute. (You can shepardize in pamplets and hardcover volumes, on CD-ROM, or online through WESTLAW and LEXIS. If you have access to WESTLAW, KeyCite is another citator you can use.)

 Assignment 10.5

Go to the state statutory code for your state. Pick any statute in this code that meets the following criteria: it is printed in the bound volume rather than in a pocket part or supplement and there are at least ten court opinions interpreting this statute summarized beneath the statute (Notes of Decisions). Assume that this statute is relevant to your research problem. What is the citation of this statute? Find cases interpreting this statute using the "Techniques for Finding Case Law Interpreting a Statute." Try to find one case through each technique. Describe each of the techniques you used. Explain how you used it and give the cite to the case it led you to. If you were not able to use any of the techniques, explain why (e.g., your library did not have the materials you needed for the technique).

Finally, we assume that you are starting from scratch. You are looking for case law and you do not have a starting case or statute with which to begin. You may be looking for common law or for cases interpreting statutes that you have not found yet.

TECHNIQUES FOR FINDING CASE LAW
WHEN YOU DO NOT HAVE A CASE OR STATUTE TO BEGIN WITH

1. *West digests.* In the Descriptive Word Indexes (DWI) of the West digests, try to find key numbers on the topics of your research. (See checklist #2 on using the West digests, in chapter 9.)

2. *Annotations.* Try to locate annotations on the topics of your research through the index systems for A.L.R.1st, A.L.R.2d, A.L.R.3d, A.L.R.4th, A.L.R.5th, and A.L.R. Fed. (See Exhibit 9.3 and checklist #3 on finding annotations, in chapter 9.)

3. *Legal treatises.* Try to find treatises on the topics of your research in the card or online catalog. (See checklist #8 on finding treatises, in chapter 9.)

4. *Looseleaf services.* Find out if there are looseleaf services on the topics of your research. (See checklist #5 on finding looseleaf services, in chapter 9.)

5. *Legal periodical literature.* Try to find legal periodical literature on the topics of your research in the Subject Indexes of ILP and CLI. (See checklist #6 on finding legal periodical literature, in chapter 9.)

6. *Legal encyclopedias.* Go to the indexes for Am. Jur. 2d and C.J.S. Try to find discussions in these legal encyclopedias on the topics of your research. (See checklist #7 on using legal encyclopedias, in chapter 9.)

7. *Computers* (see page 245 in chapter 13).

8. *Phone and mail research.* Find an expert. (See checklist #9 on doing phone and mail research, in chapter 9.)

9. *Words and Phrases.* Identify all the major words or phrases from the facts of your research problem. Look up these words or phrases in the multivolume legal dictionary, *Words and Phrases,* which gives definitions from court opinions.

10. *Shepardizing.* If techniques 1–9 lead you to any case law, shepardize what you have found in order to look for more cases. (See checklist #4a on shepardizing a case, in chapter 9.)

Assignment 10.6

Go to today's general-circulation newspaper. Select any topic in any of the stories in the newspaper that interests you. Select one that you think is related to the law in some way. Assume that you want to do legal research on this topic, starting with case law. What topic did you select? Find cases on this topic by using the "Techniques for Finding Case Law When You Do Not Have a Case or Statute to Begin With." Try to find one case through each technique. Describe each of the techniques you used. Explain how you used it and give the cite of the case it led you to. If you were not able to use any of the techniques, explain why (e.g., your library did not have the materials you needed for the technique). If the topic you selected has never been involved in court cases, select another topic from the newspaper after describing the steps you took with the techniques that were unsuccessful.

Where can you read the opinions found through the techniques discussed in this chapter? As we saw in chapter 3, you can read opinions in traditional reporter volumes (or other paper media), on CD-ROM, on microforms, and online. See Exhibit 3.1 in chapter 3 on "Twelve Possible Places to Read the Same Court Opinion." For a comprehensive list of court opinions on the Internet, see also Appendix B, "Case Law on the Internet."

 CHAPTER SUMMARY

To brief an opinion comprehensively means to identify its ten essential components: citation, parties, objectives of parties, theories of litigation, history of the litigation, facts, issues(s), holding(s), reasoning, and disposition. Dictum is something said by the court that was not necessary to resolve the issues before the court. It goes beyond the facts of the case. By definition, therefore, dictum is nonessential. The opinion may consist of several opinions: a majority opinion (which controls), one or more concurring opinions (which vote for the result reached by the majority, but for different reasons), and one or more dissenting opinions (which disagree with all or part of the result reached by the majority). When reading an opinion in a West reporter, you will find a syllabus (summarizing the entire opinion) and headnotes (summarizing portions of the opinion). These features enable you to make a quick determination of whether anything in the opinion is relevant to your research.

There are two main steps in applying an opinion to a set of facts from a client's case: compare rules and compare facts. First, you compare the rule (which will either be an enacted law or a common law) that was interpreted in the opinion with the rule you are considering in the client's case. With limited exceptions, the opinion cannot apply unless these two rules are the same. Second, you identify factual similarities, factual differences, and factual gaps between all the facts in the opinion and all the facts in

the client's case. Then you compare the key facts in the opinion with the facts of the client's case. The opinion will apply if these facts are the same or are substantially similar.

If you already have a court opinion and are looking for more, shepardize the opinion you have, do a KeyCite check on it, shepardize the relevant opinions cited in the opinion you have, use the West digests, find an annotation, find legal periodical literature, and check *Words and Phrases*. If you are looking for cases interpreting a statute, shepardize the statute, use the Notes of Decisions after the statute in the code, and check for annotations, legal periodical literature, looseleaf services, and legal treatises. If you are starting from point zero, check West digests, annotations, legal treatises, looseleaf services, legal periodical literature, legal encyclopedias, computer services, phone and mail research, and *Words and Phrases*.

◖K◗EY TERMS

brief	syllabus	disposition	statutes in derogation of the
trial brief	headnotes	remand	common law
trial notebook	key number	dictum	rule comparison
appellate brief	digests	majority opinion	fact comparison
citation	per curiam opinion	concurring opinion	on all fours
appellant	key facts	dissenting opinion	memorandum of law
respondent	issue	comprehensive brief	on point
appellee	precedents	cause of action	Notes of Decisions
docket	stare decisis	thumbnail brief	
reported	reasoning	enacted law	
shepardizing	holding	common law	

STATUTORY LAW

Chapter Outline

SECTION A   INTRODUCTION

Statutes are laws written by legislatures that declare, command, or prohibit something. Statutes are among the most important primary authorities you will research. The vast majority of court opinions interpret and apply one or more statutes or administrative regulations based on those statutes. Indeed, one of the reasons there are so many opinions is that people constantly disagree over the meaning of statutes.

In the hierarchy of laws, constitutional law is the highest form of primary authority. (For the definition of the categories of law, see Exhibit 2.2 in chapter 2.) Next in the hierarchy are statutes. As long as a statute does not violate the constitution, the statute controls. Courts cannot change a statute, but they can declare it unconstitutional. As we saw in chapter 10, courts create common law, yet legislatures can change the common law by enacting statutes in derogation of the common law. In short, statutes play a central role in our legal system.[1]

SECTION B   READING STATUTES

In Exhibit 11.1, there is an excerpt from a New York statutory code. It is an **annotated statutory code,** which simply means that the statutes are organized by subject matter (rather than chronologically), and that a variety of research references are provided along with the text of the statutes. (On the definitions of *code, session law,* and *slip law,* see page 166 in chapter 9.) Here is an explanation of the circled numbers in Exhibit 11.1:

(1) This is the **section** number of the statute. The symbol "§" before "146" means section.

(2) This is a heading summarizing the main topic of the statute. Section 146 covers who can visit state prisons in New York. This summarization was written by the private publishing company, not by the New York state legislature.

(3) Here is the body of the statute written by the legislature.

(4) At the end of a statutory section, you will often find a reference to **session laws,** which are statutes enacted during a particular session of the legislature and printed in chronological order rather than by subject matter. The references to session laws will use abbreviations such as L. (laws), P.L. (Public Law), Stat. (Statutes at Large), etc. Here you are told that in the Laws (L) of 1962, chapter (c) 37, § 3, this statute was amended. The Laws referred to are the session laws. See the Historical Note (6) below for a further treatment of this amendment.

(5) The amendment to § 146 was effective (*eff.*) on February 20, 1962. The amendment may have been passed by the legislature on an earlier date, but the date on which it became the law of New York was February 20, 1962. It is important to know the effective date of a statute. Attorneys sometimes take cases that involve facts that occurred prior to the effective date of an otherwise applicable statute. Unless the statute is **retroactive** (i.e., one that applies to facts arising before as well as after its date of enactment), you must locate the earlier version of the statute, often available only as session laws. Although no longer in effect, the earlier version may be the statute that governs the client's case.[2]

(6) The **Historical Note** provides the reader with some of the legislative history of § 146. First, the reader is again told that § 146 was amended in 1962. Note that early in the body of the statute, there is a reference to the title "commissioner of general services." The 1962 amendment simply changed the title from "superintendent of standards and purchase" to "commissioner of general services."

(7) Also, part of the Historical Note is the *Derivation* section. This tells the reader that the topic of § 146 of the Corrections Law was once contained in § 160 of the Prison Law, which dates back to 1847. In 1929 there was another amendment. The Historical Note was written by the private publisher, not by the New York state legislature.

---

1. For a discussion of when federal law controls over state law, see section B in chapter 4.
2. Most statutes are **prospective** in that they apply only to facts arising after their date of enactment.

Exhibit
Excerpt from a Statutory
Code (New York State)

§ 146.   Persons authorized to visit prisons

The following persons shall be authorized to visit at pleasure all state prisons: The governor and lieutenant-governor, commissioner of general services, secretary of state, comptroller and attorney-general, members of the commission of correction, members of the legislature, judges of the court of appeals, supreme court and county judges, district attorneys and every minister of the gospel having charge of a congregation in the town wherein any such prison is situated. No other person not otherwise authorized by law shall be permitted to enter a state prison except under such regulations as the commissioner of correction shall prescribe. The provisions of this section shall not apply to such portion of a prison in which prisoners under sentence of death are confined.

As amended L.1962, c. 37, § 3, eff. Feb. 20, 1962.

Historical Note

L.1962, c. 37, § 3, eff. Feb. 20, 1962, substituted "commissioner of general services" for "superintendent of standards and purchase".

Derivation. Prior to the general amendment of this chapter by L.1929, c. 243, the subject matter of this section was contained in former Prison Law, § 160; originally derived from R.S., pt. 4, c. 3, tit. 3, § 159, as amended L.1847, c. 460.

Cross References

Promoting prison contraband, see Penal Law, §§ 205.20, 205.25.

Library References

Prisons ⟜13.
Reformatories ⟜7.

C.J.S. Prisons §§ 18, 19.
C.J.S. Reformatories §§ 10, 11.

Notes of Decisions

I. Attorneys

Warden of maximum security prison was justified in requiring that interviews of prisoners by attorney be conducted in presence of guard in room, in view of fact that attorney, who sought to interview 34 inmates in a day and a half, had shown no retainer agreements and had not stated purpose of consultations. Kahn v. La Vallee, 1961, 12 A.D.2d 832, 209 N.Y.S.2d 591.

Supreme court did not have jurisdiction of petition by prisoner to compel prison warden to provide facilities in prison which would not interfere with alleged violation of rights of prisoner to confer in private with his attorney. Mummiani v. La Vallee, 1959, 21 Misc.2d 437, 199 N.Y.S.2d 263, affirmed 12 A.D.2d 832, 209 N.Y.S.2d 591.

Right of prisoners to confer with counsel after conviction is not absolute but is subject to such regulations as commissioner of correction may prescribe, and prisoners were not entitled to confer with their attorney privately within sight, but outside of hearing of a prison guard, when warden insisted on having a guard present in order to insure against any impropriety or infraction of prison rules and regulations during interview. Id.

⑧ The *Cross References* refer the reader to other statutes that cover topics related to § 146.

⑨ The *Library References* refer the reader to other texts that address the topic of the statute. On the left-hand side, there are two key numbers (Prisons 13 and Reformatories 7) that can be used to find more case law in the digests of West Publishing Company. In the right column, the library reference is to specific sections of C.J.S. *(Corpus Juris Secundum)*, a West legal encyclopedia.

⑩ The most important research resource in an annotated code is the **Notes of Decisions**. It includes a series of paragraphs that briefly summarize every court decision that has interpreted or applied § 146. Of course, the decisions cover cases decided before the code volume containing § 146 was published. For later decisions, the reader must look to the *pocket part* of this code volume, and to any supplemental pamphlets that have been added to the code.

The first decision that you are given is *Kahn v. La Vallee*. Next is *Mummiani v. La Vallee*. At the end of the final paragraph, you will find **Id.**, which means that the paragraph refers to the case cited in the immediately preceding paragraph, the *Mummiani* case. (In addition to using the Notes of Decisions, another way to find later decisions is to shepardize § 146. See checklist #4b on shepardizing a statute, in chapter 9.)

Assignment 11.1

Compare Exhibit 11.1 with the three codes mentioned in parts (a), (b), and (c) of this assignment. In each code, select any statute that has Notes of Decisions beneath it. (In some codes this feature may have other names, e.g., "Interpretative Notes and Decisions.") Photocopy the statute you have selected along with its features. (Try to keep the photocopying to no more than two pages.) Describe the features of the page in a manner similar to Exhibit 11.1. Place numbered circles by specific features, which you will explain on separate sheets of paper. Point out what is similar to the features of the New York statute in Exhibit 11.1. Also, note and try to explain features that are not in Exhibit 11.1.

(a) Your state code (see Exhibit 5.3 in chapter 5.) (If your state is New York, pick the code of any other state where you might want to become employed someday.)

(b) *United States Code Annotated* (U.S.C.A.).

(c) *United States Code Service* (U.S.C.S.). The statute you pick for part (c) should be the same statute you picked for part (b).

With this perspective of what a statute in an annotated code looks like, we turn to some general guidelines on understanding statutes:

1. *The organization of a statutory code is often highly fragmented because it contains a large number of units and subunits.* A statutory code can contain anywhere from 5 to 150 volumes. If you are unfamiliar with a code, you should examine the first few pages of the first volume. There you will usually find the subject matter arrangement of all the volumes, e.g., "agency," "corrections," "corporations."

   An individual subject in a code may be further broken down into titles, parts, articles, or chapters, which are then broken down into sections and subsections. Here is an example of a possible categorization for the state of "X":

   > X State Code Annotated
   > Title 1. Corporate Law
   > Chapter 1. Forming a Corporation
   > Section 1. Choosing a Corporate Name
   > Subsection 1(a). Where to File the Name Application
   > Subsection 1(b). Displaying the Name Certificate
   > Subsection 1(c). Changing the Corporate Name
   > Section 2 . . . .
   > Chapter 2 . . . .
   > Etc.

   Of course, each state may adopt its own classification terminology. What is called a chapter in one state may be called a title in another.

   You also need to be sensitive to the internal context of a particular statutory section. A section is often a sub-sub-subunit of larger units.

   > **Example:** Examine § 1183 in Exhibit 11.2.
   > Note that § 1183 is within Part II, which is within Subchapter II, which is within Chapter 12, which is within Title 8.

   In view of this structure, you should not simply pick up a statutory code volume and read a section in isolation. That section is part of several units. The meaning of specific statutory language in a section sometimes depends on what unit it is in. Often you will see introductory phrases in a section such as,

- For purposes of this Title, . . .
- As used in this Chapter, . . .
- For purposes of this Subchapter, . . .
- For purposes of this Part, . . .
- As used in this article, . . .

This kind of language should alert you to the need to view the section in context. The legislature is telling you that the law contained in the section you are reading may be limited to the unit of which that section is a part.

As indicated earlier, a legislature may completely revise its labeling system (page 122). What was once "Prison Law," for example, may now fall under the topic heading of "Correction Law." What was once section 73(b) of "Corporations Law" may now be section 13(f) of "Business and Professions Law." If such a reordering

11.2

Exhibit
Sections, Parts, Subchapters, Chapters, and Titles in a Statutory Code

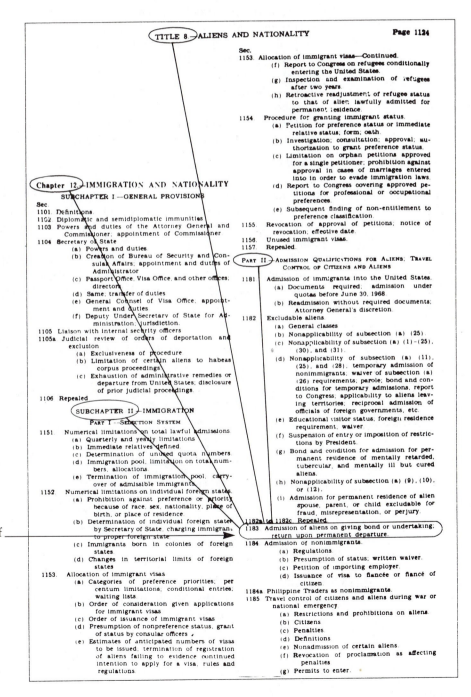

§ 1183 is within Part II of Subchapter II of Chapter 12 of Title 8

has occurred, you should be able to find out about it either in a transfer or conversion table at the beginning of one of the code volumes or in the Historical Note at the bottom of the section. One of the advantages of CARTWHEELING (see Exhibit 7.1 in chapter 7) is that you are less likely to miss such statutes in the index of the code; the CARTWHEEL forces you to think of synonyms and broader/narrower categories of every word you are checking in an index.

2. *Statutes on administrative agencies often follow a common sequence.* A large number of statutes in a code cover administrative agencies. In fact, statutes are carried out mainly by administrative agencies. The agency may be a grant-making or service agency (such as the Social Security Administration) or a regulatory agency (such as the Federal Power Commission or the State Utilities Commission).[3] Statutes that cover administrative agencies are sometimes organized in the following sequence:

   - The agency is created and named.
   - The major words and phrases used in this cluster of statutes are defined.
   - The administrators of the agency are given titles and powers.
   - The budgetary process of the agency is specified.
   - The method by which the public first comes into contact with the agency is established, such as applying for the benefits or services of the agency.
   - The way in which the agency must act when a citizen complains about the agency's actions is established.
   - How the agency must go about terminating a citizen from its services is established.
   - The way in which a citizen can appeal to a court, if not satisfied with the way the agency handled his or her complaint, is established.

3. *All statutes must be based on some provision in the constitution that gives the legislature the power to pass the statute.* Legislatures have no power to legislate without constitutional authorization. The authorization may be the general constitutional provision vesting all legislative powers in the legislature; more often, it will be a specific constitutional provision such as the authority to raise revenue for designated purposes.

4. *Check to see if a statutory unit has a definition section.* At the beginning of a cluster of statutes, look for a definition section. If it exists, the section will define a number of words used in the remaining sections of the unit. Here is an example of such a definition section:

§ 31. **Definitions.**—As used in this article, unless the context shall require otherwise, the following terms shall have the meanings ascribed to them by this section:

1. "State" shall mean and include any state, territory or possession of the United States and the District of Columbia.

2. "Court" shall mean the family court of the state of New York; when the context requires, it shall mean and include a court of another state defined in and upon which appropriate jurisdiction has been conferred by a substantially similar reciprocal law.

3. "Child" includes a step child, foster child, child born out of wedlock or legally adopted child and means a child under twenty-one years of age, and a son or daughter twenty years of age or older who is unable to maintain himself or herself and is or is likely to become a public charge.

4. "Dependent" shall mean and include any person who is entitled to support pursuant to this article.

5. *Find the statutes of construction.* Many codes have statutes that give you guidelines on how to interpret the statutes in the code. (**Construction** simply means interpretation; the verb is **construe.**) For example, there may be a statute of construction

---

3. As we will see in chapter 12, agencies are also classified as executive department agencies, independent regulatory agencies, and quasi-independent regulatory agencies.

on how to interpret a statute that contains a list of specific items followed by a general item. The rule of construction is that the general item should be construed (interpreted) as being of the same kind (*ejusdem generis*) as the specific items. Suppose § 100 of a statute prohibits "hunting, fishing, horse racing, and other public events." What does "other public events" mean? The statute of construction says you are to interpret a general item as being of the same kind as the specific items in the list. This would lead to the conclusion that "other public events" in § 100 means other *outdoor sporting* events, not any public event or even any sporting event. Why? Because all of the specific items in the list are outdoor sporting events. Hence, under this interpretation, § 100 would prohibit ocean swimming races, but not necessarily indoor swimming races. Statutes of construction such as these can be very helpful in understanding statutes.

Assignment 11.2

Each of the following problems consists of a statute and a set of facts. Determine whether *ejusdem generis* is helpful in deciding whether the statute applies to the facts.

(a) *Statute.* § 88. An injunction can be obtained against any person who falsely claims to be the inventor of a product by circular, advertisement, or otherwise.

Facts: George writes a letter to Sam falsely stating that he (George) invented the portable radio.

(b) *Statute:* § 608.7. Evidence of abandonment shall include exposure of the child in a street, field, or other place with the intent to leave the child there indefinitely.

Facts: Roger took his infant child to the church rectory. When no one was looking, he left the child in a corner of the hallway and ran out.

---

6. *Statutes should be briefed.* A "brief" of a statute consists of answers to the following questions:
   (a) What is the citation of the statute? (On citing statutes, see Exhibit 5.3 in chapter 5.)
   (b) What are the *elements* of the statute? (See discussion of elements below.)
   (c) To whom is the statute addressed? Who is the audience? (Everyone? The director of an administrative agency? Citizens who want to apply for a permit? Etc.)
   (d) What condition(s) make the statute operative? (Many statutes have "when" or "if" clauses that specify condition(s) for the applicability of the statute.)
   (e) Is the statute mandatory or discretionary? A **mandatory statute** requires that something happen or be done ("must", "shall"). A **discretionary statute** permits something to occur, but does not impose it ("may", "can").
   (f) What is the internal statutory context of the statute? To what other statutes, if any, does your statute refer?
   (g) What is the effective date of the statute?
   (h) Has the statute been amended in the past? (Check the Historical Notes that follow the statute. Briefly summarize major relevant changes.)
   (i) Has the statute been declared valid or invalid by the courts? (Check Notes of Decisions following the statute and shepardize the statute.)
   (j) Do administrative regulations exist that interpret and carry out the statute? (On finding regulations based on statutes, see Research Link R in chapter 12. Give citations to any such regulations.)
7. *Statutory language tends to be unclear.* Seldom, if ever, is it absolutely clear what a statute means or how it applies to a given set of facts. For this reason, statutory language regularly requires close scrutiny and interpretation.
8. *Statutes are to be read line by line, pronoun by pronoun, punctuation mark by punctuation mark.* Statutes cannot be speed read. They should be read with the

same care that you would use if you were translating a foreign language to English. Sentences sometimes appear endless. Occasionally so many qualifications and exceptions are built into a statute that it appears incomprehensible. Don't despair. The key is perseverance and a willingness to tackle the statute slowly, piece by piece—through its elements.

9. *Break each statute into its elements.* Statutes, like all rules, have consequences. There are statutes that impose punishments, require payments, establish norms of behavior, make declarations of policy, institute procedures, etc. How do you determine when a statute applies so that its consequences must be followed? The answer is: When *all* of the **elements** of that statute apply. An element is a component or portion of a rule that is a precondition of the applicability of the entire rule. If you can show that *all* of the elements of a rule apply to a fact situation, then the rule itself—and its consequence—applies to the fact situation. The failure of any *one* of the elements to apply means that the entire rule cannot apply.

Let us examine some examples involving statutory rules:

> **§ 971.22. Change of place of trial.** The defendant may move for a change of the place of trial on the ground that an impartial trial cannot be had in the county. The motion shall be made at the time of arraignment.

Step one is to break the rule into its elements. The effect or consequence of the rule is to change the place of the trial. Ask yourself what must happen before this consequence will follow. What conditions or preconditions must exist before the result will occur? The answer will provide you with the elements of the rule:

1. Defendant
2. May move for a change of the place of trial
3. On the ground that an impartial trial cannot be had in the county
4. The motion must be made at the time of the arraignment

Hence, there are four elements to § 971.22. All four must exist before the place of the trial will be moved.

Suppose you are analyzing the following statute:

> **§ 25-403.** A pharmacist must not sell prescription drugs to a minor.

As with almost all rules, this one is not already broken down into elements. You must identify the elements on your own. Ask yourself what conditions must exist before § 25-403 applies. Your answer will consist of its elements:

1. Pharmacist
2. Must not sell
3. Prescription drugs
4. To a minor

No violation exists unless all four elements of the statute are established. If, for example, a pharmacist sells simple aspirin (a nonprescription drug) to a minor, he or she has not violated the statute. The third element cannot be established. Hence, there was no violation, because one of the elements (preconditions) cannot be met.

How long should an element be? This question has no absolute answer. The two main criteria to keep in mind are these: (1) each element must be a precondition to the consequence of the entire rule, and (2) you should be able to discuss each element separately with relative ease.

For a number of reasons, rules such as statutes and regulations can be difficult to break into elements. For example, the rule may be long or may contain:

• Lists
• Alternatives
• Exceptions or provisos

Nevertheless, the same process is used. You must take the time to dissect the rule into its component elements. Examine the following rule as we try to identify its elements.

§ 5. While representing a client in connection with contemplated or pending litigation, a lawyer shall not advance or guarantee financial assistance to his client, except that a lawyer may advance or guarantee court costs, expenses of investigation, expenses of medical examination, and costs of obtaining and presenting evidence provided the client remains ultimately liable for such expenses.

Elements of § 5:

1. A lawyer
2. Representing a client in connection with contemplated litigation or in connection with pending litigation
3. Shall not advance financial assistance to his client or guarantee financial assistance to his client, except that the following is proper:
   a. lawyer advances or guarantees court costs, or
   b. lawyer advances or guarantees expenses of investigation, or
   c. lawyer advances or guarantees expenses of medical examination, or
   d. lawyer advances or guarantees costs of obtaining and presenting evidence

   as long as the client remains ultimately liable for all expenses ("a"–"d").

When an element is stated in the alternative, list all the alternatives within the same element. Alternatives related to one element should be kept within the phrasing of that element. The same is true of exception or proviso clauses. State them within the relevant element, as they are intimately related to the applicability of that element.

In the above example, the most complicated element is the third—(3). It contains lists, alternatives, an exception, and a proviso. But they all relate to the same point—the propriety of financial assistance. None of the subdivisions of the third element should be stated as a separate element. Sometimes you must do some unraveling of a rule to identify its elements. This certainly had to be done with the third element of § 5. Do not be afraid to pick the rule apart in order to cluster its thoughts around unified themes that should stand alone as elements. Diagram the rule for yourself as you examine it.

If more than one rule is involved in a statute, regulation, constitutional provision, charter, ordinance, etc., treat one rule at a time. Each rule should have its own elements, and, when appropriate, each element should be subdivided into its separate components, as in the third element of § 5.

Once you have broken the rule down into its elements, you have the structure of the analysis in front of you. Each element becomes a separate section of your analysis. You discuss one element at a time, concentrating on those that pose the greatest difficulties.

Element identification has many benefits in the law, as demonstrated in Exhibit 11.3.

To a very large extent, as you can see in Exhibit 11.3, legal analysis proceeds by *element analysis.* A major characteristic of sloppy legal analysis is that it does not clearly take the reader (or listener) through the important elements of rules that must be analyzed.

11.3 .... The Benefits of Element Identification

Exhibit

- *Identifying Issues.* Once you identify the elements of a rule, the next step is to find the elements that are most likely to be in contention. These elements become the basis of legal issues (as we shall see in section B of chapter 16, on the memorandum of law).
- *Drafting a Complaint.* When drafting a legal complaint, you often organize your factual allegations around the elements of each important rule in the controversy. (The most important rule is called the **cause of action,** which is a set of facts that give a party a right to judicial relief; it is a legally acceptable reason for suing someone. Negligence is an example.)

Continued on next page

11.3 ························· The Benefits of Element Identification—continued

Exhibit

- *Drafting an Answer.* When drafting an answer to a complaint, you often state your defenses by alleging facts that support the elements of each defense. (Many **defenses,** such as the statute of limitation, are nothing more than rules designed to defeat the claims of another.)
- *Organizing an Interview of a Client.* One of the goals of interviewing a client is to obtain information on facts relevant to each of the elements of the potential causes of action and defenses in the case. Element analysis, therefore, helps you organize the interview and give it direction.
- *Organizing an Investigation.* One of the goals of investigation is to obtain information on facts relevant to each of the elements of the potential causes of action and defenses in the case. Element analysis, therefore, helps you organize the investigation and give it direction.
- *Conducting a Deposition.* During a deposition, many of the questions are designed to determine what facts the other side may be able to prove that support the elements of the potential causes of action and defenses in the case.
- *Organizing a Memorandum of Law.* One of the purposes of a memorandum of law is to tell the reader what rules might apply to the case, what elements of these rules might be in contention, and what strategy should be undertaken as a result of this analysis.
- *Organizing an Examination Answer.* Many essay examinations in school are organized around the key elements of the rules that should be analyzed.
- *Charging a Jury.* When a judge charges (that is, instructs) a jury, he or she will go over each of the elements of the causes of action and defenses in the case in order to tell the jury what standard to use to determine whether facts in support of those elements have been sufficiently proven during the trial.

Assignment 11.3

Break the following statutes into their elements:

(a) § 200. Parties to a child custody dispute shall attempt mediation before filing for a custody order from the court.

(b) § 75(b). A lawyer shall not enter into a business transaction with a client if they have differing interests therein and if the client expects the lawyer to exercise his professional judgment therein for the protection of the client.

(c) § 38. A person or agency suing or being sued in an official public capacity is not required to execute a bond as a condition for relief under this section unless required by the court in its discretion.

(d) § 1.2. A lawyer may not permit his legal assistant to represent a client in litigation or other adversary proceedings or to perform otherwise prohibited functions unless authorized by statute, court rule or decision, administrative rule or regulation or customary practice.

(e) § 179(a)(7). If at any time it is determined that application of best available control technology by 1988 will not assure protection of public water supplies, agricultural and industrial uses, and the protection and propagation of fish, shellfish and wildlife, and allow recreational activities in and on the water, additional effluent limitations must be established to assure attainment or maintenance of water quality. In setting such limitations, EPA must consider the relationship of the economic and social costs of their achievement, including any economic or social dislocation in the affected community or communities, the social and economic benefits to be obtained, and determine whether or not such effluent limitations can be implemented with available technology or other alternative control strategies.

SECTION C   FINDING STATUTES

TECHNIQUES FOR FINDING STATUTES

1. Go to the statutory code in which you are interested. Some states have more than one statutory code. (See Exhibit 5.3 in chapter 5.) For federal statutes, there are the *United States Code* (U.S.C.), the *United States Code Annotated* (U.S.C.A.), and the *United States Code Service* (U.S.C.S.). Know how to use all available statutory codes that cover the same set of statutes. Although they contain the same statutes, the index and research features may differ.

2. Read the explanation or preface pages at the beginning of the first volume of the statutory code. Also read the comparable pages at the beginning of the Shepard's volumes that will enable you to shepardize statutes in that code. These pages can be very helpful in explaining the structure of the code, particularly if there have been new editions, revisions, or renumberings.

3. Most statutory codes have general indexes at the end of the set as well as individual indexes for separate volumes. Use the CARTWHEEL to help you use these indexes. Also check any tables of contents that exist. Some statutes have popular names, such as the Civil Rights Act of 1964. If you know the popular name of a statute, you can find it in the statutory code through a **Popular Name Table** that often exists within the code itself.

4. While reading one statute in the code, you may be given a cross-reference to another statute within the same code. Check out these cross-references.

5. Update any statute that you find in the statutory code by checking the pocket part of the volume you are using; supplement pamphlets at the end of the code; bound supplement volumes; session law pamphlets; advance legislative services; online resources such a WESTLAW, LEXIS, and the Internet; etc.

6. Looseleaf services. Find out if there is a looseleaf service on the topic of your research. Such services will give extensive references to applicable statutes. (See checklist #5 on finding and using looseleaf services, in chapter 9.)

7. Legal treatises. Find out if there are legal treatises on the topics of your research. Such treatises will often give extensive references to applicable statutes. (See checklist #8 on finding and using legal treatises, in chapter 9.)

8. Legal periodical literature. Consult the *Index to Legal Periodicals and Books* (ILP) and the *Current Law Index* (CLI). Use these indexes to locate periodical literature on the topics of your research. This literature will often give extensive references to applicable statutes. (See

checklist #6 on finding legal periodical literature, in chapter 9.) If you already have the citation to a statute and want to know if there is any legal periodical literature discussing it, check the "Table of Statutes" in the *ILP* and the *CLI*.

9. Annotations. Use the available index systems for A.L.R.1st, A.L.R.2d, A.L.R.3d, A.L.R.4th, A.L.R.5th, and A.L.R. Fed. to help you locate annotations. Annotations will sometimes refer you to statutes—particularly in A.L.R. Fed. for federal statutes. (See Exhibit 9.3 and checklist #3 on finding and updating annotations, in chapter 9.)

10. Legal encyclopedias. Occasionally, legal encyclopedias such as Am. Jur. 2d and C.J.S. will summarize important statutes in the text and refer you to important statutes in the footnotes. (See checklist #7 for using legal encyclopedias, in chapter 9.)

11. Computers. State and federal statutes are available online through WESTLAW and LEXIS. Many are also available on the Internet. See Exhibit 11.4 for some of the most commonly used Internet sites for statutes. Finally, most statutes are available on CD-ROM. (See chapter 13 on computer research.)

12. Phone and mail research. Try to find an expert. (See checklist #9 on doing phone and mail research, chapter 9.)

13. Occasionally, in your research you will come across a statute that is cited in its session law form (page 166). To find this statute in the statutory code, you must translate the session law cite into the codified cite. This is done by trying to find transfer or conversion tables in the statutory code. For federal statutes, a session law or Statute at Large cite is translated into a U.S.C./U.S.C.A./U.S.C.S. cite by:

(a) Checking Table III in the Tables volume of U.S.C./U.S.C.A./U.S.C.S.

(b) Checking Table 2 in *U.S. Code Congressional and Administrative News* (U.S.C.C.A.N.)

See Research Link O in chapter 5. Some session laws, however, are never printed in the statutory code. Hence there is no codified cite for such statutes. You must go directly to the session laws in the library—if the library has them. (For federal statutes, the session laws are in *United States Statutes at Large*, page 166.) It is also possible to shepardize session laws that are not codified, page 167.

11.4

Exhibit
Statutes and Legislative
Information from the
Internet

The following Internet sites will lead you (directly or through links) to information about the legislature (e.g., names and addresses of individual legislators, steps on how a bill becomes a law). Many of the sites also allow you to enter search queries (questions) in order (a) to find the status of current bills pending in the legislature (important for monitoring legislation) or (b) to find statutes already enacted and part of the code. Not all of the sites, however, have the complete code online. For additional leads to the law of your state, check the general home page for your state; there you will often find links to a variety of state laws. Here is the address of the home page of most states (insert your state's abbreviation in place of the **xx**): **http://www.state.xx.us**

UNITED STATES (Federal):   http://www.senate.gov
                            http://www.house.gov
                            http://thomas.loc.gov
ALABAMA: http://alaweb.asc.edu/legis.html
ALASKA: http://www.legis.state.ak.us
ARIZONA: http://www.azleg.state.az.us
ARKANSAS: http://www.uark.edu:80/depts/govninfo/public_html
CALIFORNIA: http//www.leginfo.ca.gov
COLORADO: http://www.state.co.us/gov_dir/stateleg.html
CONNECTICUT: http://www.cslnet.ctstateu.edu/statutes/index.htm
DELAWARE: http://www.state.de.us/research/assembly.htm
DISTRICT OF COLUMBIA: http://ci.washington.dc.us
FLORIDA: http://www.leg.state.fl.us
GEORGIA: http://state.ga.us/legis
HAWAII: http://www.hawaii.gov/lrb/lib.html
IDAHO: http://www.state.id.us/search.html
ILLINOIS: http://www.state.il.us/legis
INDIANA: http://www.ai.org/legislative
IOWA: http://www.legis.state.ia.us
KANSAS: http://www.ink.org/public/legislative
KENTUCKY: http://www.lrc.state.ky.us/home.htm
LOUISIANA: http://www.legis.state.la.us
MAINE: http://www.state.me.us/legis
MARYLAND: http://mlis.state.md.us
MASSACHUSETTS: http://www.state.ma.us/legis/legis.htm
MICHIGAN: http://www.umich.edu/~icle/leg-sums/legist.htm
MINNESOTA: http://www.leg.state.mn.us
MISSISSIPPI: http://www.ls.state.ms.us
MISSOURI: http://www.moga.state.mo.us
MONTANA: http://www.mt.gov/leg/branch/branch.htm
NEBRASKA: http://unicam1.lcs.state.ne.us
NEVADA: http://www.leg.state.nv.us
NEW HAMPSHIRE: http://www.state.nh.us/gencourt/gencourt.htm
NEW JERSEY: http://www.njleg.state.nj.us
NEW MEXICO: http://www.nm.org/legislature
NEW YORK: http://unix2.nysed.gov/ils/legislature/legis.html
NORTH CAROLINA: http://www.legislature.state.nc.us
NORTH DAKOTA: http://www.state.nd.us/lr
OHIO: http://www.state.oh.us/ohio/index.htm
OKLAHOMA: http://www.onenet.net/oklegal
OREGON: http://www.leg.state.or.us
PENNSYLVANIA: http://moose.erie.net/~italo/bills.html
RHODE ISLAND: http://www.rilin.state.ri.us/gen_assembly/genmenu.html
SOUTH CAROLINA: http://www.lpitr.state.sc.us
SOUTH DAKOTA: http://www.state.sd.us/state/legis/legis.htm
TENNESSEE: http://www.legislature.state.tn.us/Legislative/Legislative.htm
TEXAS: http://www.capitol.state.tx.us
UTAH: http://www.le.state.ut.us
VERMONT: http://www.leg.state.vt.us
VIRGINIA: http://www.state.va.us/home/governmt.html
WASHINGTON STATE: http://leginfo.leg.wa.gov

11.4

Exhibit
Statutes and Legislative
Information from the
Internet—continued

WEST VIRGINIA:	http://www.wvlc.wvnet.edu/legisinfo/legishp.html
WISCONSIN:	http://www.legis.state.wi.us
WYOMING:	http://legisweb.state.wy.us

ALL LEGISLATURES:	http://law.house.gov/17.htm
	http://lawlib.wuacc.edu/washlaw/uslaw/statelaw.html
	http://www.hg.org
	http://www.law.cornell.edu
	http://www.lawguru.com/search/lawsearch.html
	http://www.legalonline.com/statute2.htm
	http://www.multistate.com
	http://www.piperinfo.com/state/states.html

Once you have found a statute that is relevant to your research problem, you need to do further research on the statute before you rely on it.

TECHNIQUES FOR FURTHER RESEARCH ON STATUTES YOU HAVE FOUND

1. Make sure the statute is still valid:
   - Check your statute in the pocket part of the volume where you found the statute.
   - Check your statute in supplement pamphlets and in hardcover supplements that go with the code.
   - Shepardize the statute. (See checklist #4b on shepardizing statutes, in chapter 9.)
2. Check all cross-references within the statute. If the statute refers to other statutes in the code, check them for their relevance to your research.
3. Find cases interpreting the statute:
   - Check *notes of decisions* following the statute.
   - Shepardize the statute. Among the citing materials are cases that have analyzed or mentioned the statute. (See technique #1 above).
4. Find administrative regulations based on the statute. Many statutes are carried out by administrative regulations. The statute is considered the *authority* for such regulations. It is the **enabling statute,** which is a statute that is the basis or authority for what an agency does. To find the enabling statute for a federal regulation, check what is called the "Authority" reference beneath the regulation in the *Code of Federal Regulations,* or at the beginning of the cluster of reg-

ulations you are examining in the C.F.R. See Research Link R in chapter 12.
5. Find annotations on the statute.
   - If you shepardize the statute, the citing materials include annotations in A.L.R.1st, A.L.R.2d, etc.
   - Check the table called "Table of Laws, Rules, and Regulations" found in the last volume of *ALR Index.* See checklist #3 in chapter 9.
   - For federal statutes, also check the separate volume called *ALR Federal Tables.*
6. Find legal periodical comments or other periodical literature on the statute. Check the Table of Statutes in the ILP and CLI. (See checklist #6 in chapter 9 and Research Link Q in chapter 9).
7. Find out if there are any looseleaf services that cover the statute. (See checklist #5 in chapter 9.)
8. Find out if there are any legal treatises that cover the statute. (See checklist #8 in chapter 9.)
9. Find a discussion of your statute in *American Jurisprudence 2d.* See the separate volume called *Table of Statutes, Rules, and Regulations* that is part of Am. Jur. 2d. (See checklist #7 in chapter 9.)
10. Conduct the legislative history of the statute. See section D of this chapter.

SECTION D   LEGISLATIVE HISTORY

We have four themes to explore here:

- The legislative process
- Why one might search for legislative history: advocacy objectives
- Controversy over the use of legislative history
- Finding legislative history

The Legislative Process

The legislative process consists of the steps that a bill must go through before it becomes a statute. (A **bill** is simply a proposed statute.) Exhibit 11.5 outlines these steps for the federal legislature—Congress. The chart in Exhibit 11.5 assumes that the same idea for a bill is introduced simultaneously in both chambers of Congress, the House of Representatives and the Senate. It is, of course, also possible for a bill to be introduced in one chamber, go through all the steps for passage in that chamber, and *then* be introduced in the other chamber. The conference committee step outlined in the chart occurs only when both chambers have enacted their own version of the bill.

Congress is **bicameral**, meaning that it consists of two chambers, the House of Representatives and the Senate. In some state legislatures, the chambers have different names, such as the Assembly and the House of Delegates. Legislatures with only one chamber are called **unicameral**. Only one state legislature is unicameral (Nebraska). Local legislatures, however, such as city councils, are often unicameral.

The process of enactment can involve six major stages:

- Proposal
- Initial committee consideration
- Floor debate
- Conference committee consideration
- Floor debate
- Response of the chief executive

The **legislative history** of a statute is what occurs at each of these stages.

Proposal The idea for a statute can come from many sources. The chief executive of the government (for example, the president or governor) may initiate the process by sending the legislature a message stating the reasons for a proposed law. Frequently, an administrative agency has made a study of a problem, which is the impetus for the proposal. The agency will usually be the entity with responsibility for administering the proposal if it is enacted into law.

The bar association might prepare a report to the legislature calling for the new legislation. The legislature or chief executive may have established a special commission to study the need for changes in the law and to propose changes as appropriate. The commission might consist of members of the legislature and outside experts. Some states have ongoing law revision commissions that frequently make proposals for legislation. In many areas a council of governments made up of neighboring governments studies problems and proposes legislative changes. The National Conference of Commissioners on Uniform State Laws is an organization with members from each state. The conference makes proposals to the state legislatures for the enactment of **uniform state laws** when it deems uniformity to be desirable.

Finally, the idea for the legislation may be generated within the legislature itself. One or both houses may have established an investigating committee to examine a particular problem and propose needed legislation. Individual legislators can also propose bills. Can private citizens propose a bill? Usually not. They must convince an individual legislator to introduce or sponsor their idea for a bill.

Initial Committee Consideration When a member of the legislature introduces a bill, he or she usually accompanies it with a statement on why the bill should be enacted. As bills are introduced, they are assigned a consecutive number (S 250 is the 250th bill introduced in the Senate during the current session; HR 1753 is the 1753rd bill introduced in the House of Representatives during the current session).

Once the bill is introduced, it follows a similar procedure in each chamber. The bill is sent to the committee with responsibility over the subject matter of the bill— for example, a bill to change the criminal law might go to the Judiciary Committee. The initial draft of the bill might be considered by this committee and by one of its

11.5 .... The Legislative History of a Federal Statute—How a Bill Becomes a Law

Exhibit

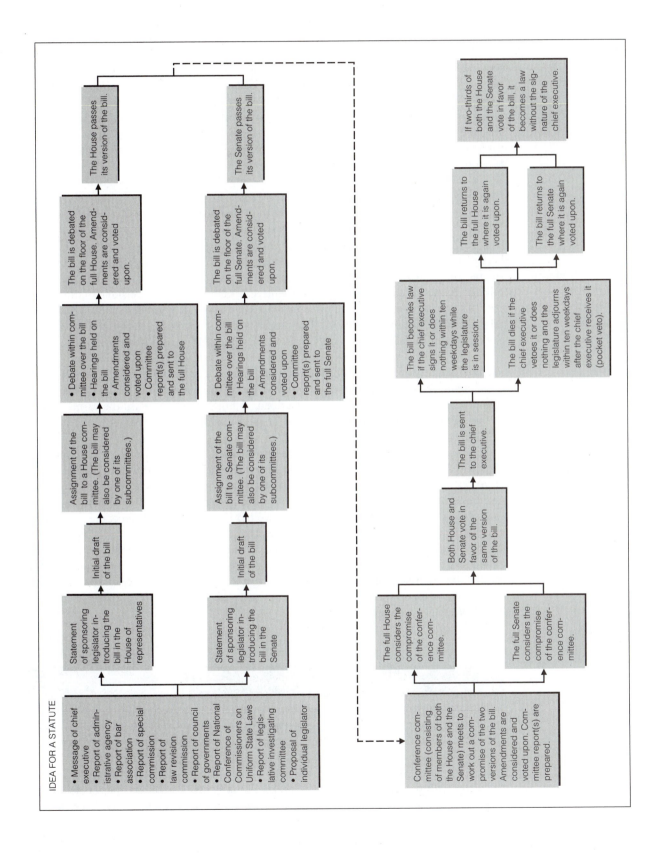

subcommittees. Hearings are held. Citizens and public officials give testimony for or against the bill. In some legislatures this testimony is transcribed so that a word-for-word record is available. Legislators often propose amendments to the bill, which are voted on by the committee. The committee then issues a report summarizing why the bill is needed and what its major provisions are. If there is disagreement within the committee, a minority report is often prepared.

Floor Debate The bill with its accompanying report(s) goes to the floor of the chamber of which the committee is a part. (This occurs after a special committee or a legislative leader establishes the ground rules under which the bill will be debated and voted upon on the floor.) The bill is debated by the full chamber. During the debate, which will usually be recorded or transcribed, members ask questions about the meaning of certain provisions in the bill: what is covered and what is not. Amendments are often made from the floor and voted upon.

Conference Committee Consideration Because both chambers act independently of each other in considering the bill, it is rare that they both produce exactly the same bill. Inevitably, the amendment process leads to different versions of the proposed law. To resolve these differences, a *conference committee* is established, consisting of key members of both chambers, such as the chairpersons of the committees that initially considered the bill or the members who first introduced or sponsored the bill. A compromise is attempted in the conference committee. Amendments are considered and a final report of the conference committee is issued. Dissenting members of the committee might prepare a minority report. The majority report summarizes the major terms of the compromise and explains why it should be enacted by each chamber.

Floor Debate The conference committee compromise then goes back to the floor of each chamber where more debate, explanations, and amendments are considered. Again, everything is recorded or transcribed. If both chambers pass the same version of the bill, usually by a majority vote, it goes to the chief executive.

Response of Chief Executive There are three main ways for the bill to become law after it reaches the chief executive. First, he or she can sign it. Second, the chief executive can do nothing. If the legislature stays in session for at least ten weekdays after he or she receives it, the bill automatically becomes law—without requiring a signature. Third, if the chief executive rejects or **vetoes** the bill, it can still become law if both chambers of the legislature **override** the veto by a two-thirds vote.

There are two main ways for the chief executive to reject a bill. First, he or she can explicitly veto the bill and send it back to the legislature, often with a statement of the reasons for the rejection. Second, he or she can do nothing. If the legislature adjourns within ten weekdays after the chief executive receives it, the bill automatically dies. This is known as a **pocket veto.**

Assignment 11.4

(a) Redraw Exhibit 11.5 so that your chart includes the steps needed for a bill to become a statute in your state legislature. (Among the sources you should try to check is the legislature's Internet site(s). Your state's site may have information on how a bill becomes a law in your state legislature. See Exhibit 11.4.)

(b) Give the name, address, phone number, and fax number of the chief legislator of both chambers of your legislature, e.g., Speaker of the House, President of the Senate. (If your state legislature is unicameral [Nebraska], answer these questions for the one chamber that exists.)

(c) What is the full name of the legislative committee in each chamber (e.g., Judiciary Committee) with primary authority to consider laws that directly affect your state courts,

Assignment 11.4—continued

such as procedural laws that govern the conduct of litigation? Give the name, political party, phone number, and fax number of the current chairperson of each of these committees.

(d) What is the name of the *local* legislature in your city or county? Give the name, address, phone number, and fax number of the chief legislator of this body. (If you have both a city and a county legislature, answer this question for both.)

Why Search for Legislative History: Advocacy Objectives

To understand why researchers try to find the legislative history of a statute, let's look at an example:

> In 1975 the state legislature enacts the Liquor Control Act. Section 33 of this Act provides that "Liquor shall not be sold on Sunday or on any day on which a local, state, or federal election is being held." The Fairfax Country Club claims that § 33 does not apply to the sale of liquor on Sunday or on election day *by membership clubs;* it applies only to bars that provide service to any customers that come in off the street. The question, therefore, is whether the legislature intended to include membership clubs within the restrictions of § 33. The state liquor board says that it did. The Fairfax Country Club argues that it did not.

How can the legislative history of § 33 help resolve this controversy? An advocate has two objectives when researching the legislative history of a statute:

- To determine whether the specific facts currently in controversy were ever discussed by the legislature when it was considering the proposed statute, and
- To identify the broad or narrow purpose that prompted the legislature to enact the statute and to assess whether this purpose sheds any light on the specific facts currently in controversy

For example, when the legislature was considering § 33, was there any mention of country or membership clubs in the governor's message, in committee reports, in floor debates, etc.? If so, what was said about them? What was said about the purpose of § 33? Why was it enacted? What evil or mischief was it designed to combat? Was the legislature opposed to liquor on moral grounds? Did it want to reduce rowdyism that comes from the overuse of liquor? Did it want to encourage citizens to go to church on Sunday and to vote on election day? Were complaints made to the legislature about the use of liquor by certain groups in the community? If so, what groups? Answers to such questions might be helpful in formulating arguments on the meaning and scope of § 33. The advocate for the Fairfax Country Club will try to demonstrate that the legislature had a narrow objective when it enacted § 33: to prevent neighborhood rowdyism at establishments that serve only liquor. The legislature, therefore, was not trying to regulate the more moderate kind of drinking that normally takes place at membership clubs where food and liquor are often served together. The opponent, in contrast, will argue that the legislature had a broader purpose in enacting § 33: to decrease the consumption of liquor by all citizens on certain days. The legislature, therefore, did not intend to exclude drinking at a membership club.

Controversy Over the Use of Legislative History

Several interrelated reasons account for the controversy surrounding the use of legislative history as an aid in the interpretation of a statute:

- Availability and cost
- Reliability
- Manipulation
- Overuse

Availability and Cost   As you can see from Exhibit 11.5, a statute can have a great deal of legislative history. Given the vast numbers of statutes in existence, the task of collecting and researching their legislative histories can be enormous. Justice Jackson suggested that this impracticality raises a basic question of fairness:

> Laws are intended for all of our people to live by; and the people go to law offices to learn what their rights under those laws are. [Controversies exist which affect] every little merchant in many States. Aside from a few offices in the larger cities, the materials of legislative history are not available to the lawyer who can afford neither the cost of acquisition, the cost of housing, or the cost of repeatedly examining the whole congressional history. Moreover, if he could, he would not know any way of anticipating what would impress enough members of the Court to be controlling. *Schwegmann Bros. v. Calvert Distillers Corp.*, 341 U.S. 384, 396, 71 S. Ct. 745, 751, 95 L. Ed. 1035 (1951), concurring opinion.

In spite of the increased availability in recent years of the documents of legislative history (particularly online through LEXIS, WESTLAW, and to a more limited extent, the Internet), the documents are still generally inaccessible, particularly for state statutes. It is much easier to undertake such research for federal statutes than for state statutes. Yet even for the former, the cost of the research can be substantial. An advocate may have to examine thousands of pages in a variety of books. Few clients can afford this kind of service. Later we will explore some of the main resources for researching the legislative history of a statute. Knowing about these books and techniques, however, does not diminish the point made by Justice Jackson. A comprehensive examination of the documents of legislative history can be an expensive and time-consuming task. The records that are needed may not be equally available to everyone.

Reliability   Assume that in a particular case there are no problems of availability and cost—you are able to collect and study the entire legislative history of a statute. At this point, another problem arises. How reliable is the history that you are examining? Information from legislative history is reliable to the extent you can establish that:

- The information was considered by the legislature, and
- The information accurately reflects what the legislature ultimately did.

Suppose that Senator Smith sends a letter to a constituent explaining the meaning of a bill and why she is supporting it. In a broad sense, this letter is part of the legislative history of the statute that came from the bill, but the letter is totally unreliable. There is no rational way of determining whether the legislature *as a whole* considered the letter and acted in accordance with its contents. The strong likelihood is that neither occurred. Would it make any difference if this letter was also printed in the official record or journal of the legislature while the bill was being considered? Probably not. A great deal is printed during the course of a legislature's consideration of a bill. Every legislature prides itself on being an open forum in which a wide variety of viewpoints on proposed legislation is solicited. Also, many viewpoints are received in the form of letters, reports, studies, testimony, etc. Much of it is useful, but a good deal of it is considered junk. According to some commentators, research into legislative history consists in large measure of rummaging through "the ashcans of the legislative process." C. Curtis, *It's Your Law* 52 (1954).

Suppose, however, that this same legislator is speaking to another legislator on the floor of the Senate during a debate on the bill:

> Senator SMITH: The purpose of this bill is to phase the government out of the business of operating a railroad. It establishes an Interim Management Council, which will run the affairs of the railroad until such time as private capital can take over complete management.

> Senator THOMAS: Senator, am I correct in understanding that the bill currently before the Senate applies only to those railroad facilities in which the government acquired an interest prior to 1974?

> Senator SMITH: The senator is indeed correct.

Here we have an exchange between two legislators during a floor debate on the bill. Presumably there are other legislators listening to this debate, so we are on safer ground in concluding that the legislature considered what they had to say. It would be helpful to know who Senator Smith is. Is she the sponsor of the bill or the chairperson of the committee that initially considered it? If so, her comments are likely to be given more weight. Courts are more inclined to conclude that the legislature considered what Senator Smith had to say and, if the bill was enacted, that her comments accurately reflect what the legislature intended. The views of legislators who did not have such a key role in steering the bill through the legislature are usually given less weight. Such views are considered less reliable in deciphering the meaning of the statute.

Yet it must be remembered that this piece of legislative history focuses only on the views of individual legislators. We can *never* be certain that these views accurately record what hundreds of legislators tried to do in passing the bill. This is so even if the individual legislator in question actually wrote the bill. According to an English commentator, Lord Halsbury:

> [I]n construing a statute I believe the worst person to construe it is the person who is responsible for its drafting. He is very much disposed to confuse what he intended to do with the effect of the language which in fact has been employed. At the time he drafted the statute, at all events, he may have been under the impression that he had given full effect to what was intended, but he may be mistaken . . . . *Hilder v. Dexter,* [1902] A.C. 474, 477.

Though there is some merit to this skepticism that English courts have toward the use of legislative history, *American* courts have not gone this far. As indicated, our courts do give weight to the statements of legislators who had an important role in passing the bill.

Perhaps the most reliable documents of legislative history are the committee reports that are written after the committee holds hearings on the bill and debates amendments to it. These reports often have two main components. First, they state the purpose of the bill in terms of what it is trying to accomplish. They will often include discussions of prior law on the subject of the bill (including court opinions). Such discussion is usually provided as background on why the bill is needed. Second, the reports contain a section-by-section summary of the bill. It is sometimes claimed that many legislators do *not* read the technical language of the bill itself. Instead, they rely on the more readable summaries of the bill contained in the committee reports.[4]

Some committees also print transcripts of the testimony of witnesses who appear before the committee on the bill. However, given the diversity of this testimony and the early stage at which it is provided in the legislative process, it is less reliable as an indication of what the legislature intended when it passed the bill.

What about specific commission studies, messages of the chief executive, and reports of councils of government and of commissioners on uniform laws? To what extent can their proposals for legislation be relied upon to determine the legislative intent of the bills that are enacted? These proposals, of course, are also made early in the process, and a great deal may happen between the time of proposal and the date of enactment. The reliability of these initiating documents may depend on whether the language of the bill that was enacted is the same as the language of the bill that was proposed by the commission, chief executive, council, etc. If the language is the same or very similar, then the accompanying study, message, or report of these groups is generally accorded some weight in determining legislative intent.

In summary, therefore, the following are considered the most reliable components of legislative history in the interpretation of statutes:

- Committee reports
- Statements of legislators who sponsored the bill or who chaired committees that favorably considered it
- Studies, reports, and messages of bodies that initially proposed the bill

---

4. Also valuable is the **committee print,** which is a miscellaneous compilation of information prepared by committee staff members on a bill consisting of statistics, studies, reports, comparative analyses of related bills, etc.

Although the use of any legislative history still remains controversial, the above components are most frequently relied upon.

Manipulation Perhaps the most cynical explanation for the reluctance of some courts to use legislative history is the tendency of legislators and legislative staff members to "plant" statements and commentary in the legislative history for the sole reason of influencing later interpretation of the statute:

> But the intentions of some member of the subcommittee staff, buried in a report . . . are not the statute and do not necessarily represent the intentions of Congress. We all know the propensity of people who cannot persuade Congress to include a provision in the statute to insert comments favorable to their position in the legislative history in the hopes of persuading a court later on that what they say is what Congress had in mind. Application of Commonwealth Edison Co. for a Permit for Dresden Unit 3, No. 70–21, Illinois Pollution Control Board, 3/3/71, reported in 5 CCH Atom.En.Rep.Par. 16,613 at 22638. See Murphy A., *Old Maxims Never Die: The "Plain-Meaning Rule" and Statutory Interpretation in the "Modern" Federal Courts,* 75 Colum. L. Rev. 1299, 1312–3, n. 100 (1975).

Under this view, statements and commentary in the legislative history are no more reliable than what someone says on the telephone when he or she knows that there is a wiretap on the phone! Assume that a legislator wants to enact a law that prevents an agency from regulating a particular practice. For various political reasons, the legislator cannot collect enough votes from colleagues to support this provision. Hence the language that is to be voted upon by the legislature is intentionally left vague or general. The legislator then instructs a committee staff member to state in the committee report that the bill is intended to accomplish the specific objective that the legislator had in mind initially. Also, this legislator might conveniently arrange for another legislator to ask a question on the floor during debate on the meaning of the vague or general language in the bill. A response is then made for the record, which is in accord with what the legislator was not able to insert in the bill itself. Such manipulative maneuvers are common enough to cast doubt on the reliability of legislative history in the interpretation of statutes.

Overuse Apart from problems of availability, reliability, and manipulation, critics charge that legislative history is being overused by advocates and by courts. They are too quick to resort to the "ashcans" of the legislative process and tend to overinterpret what they find. Suppose, for example, that while a bill for a statute is being debated in the legislature, an amendment is considered and *rejected* by the legislature. What conclusions should be drawn on the basis of this rejection? That the legislation did not intend to include the provisions of the amendment in the statute that was enacted? Or that the amendment was superfluous because the legislature thought that the provisions of the amendment were already included in the original bill? Given such questions, you cannot assume that legislative history will automatically yield clarity in the search for meaning.

Another complaint of the critics is that the users of legislative history fail to understand that the documents of this history do not constitute law:

> It is not to be supposed that, in signing a bill the President endorses the whole Congressional Record, *Schwegmann Bros. v. Calvert Distillers Corp.,* 341 U.S. 384, 396, 71 S. Ct. 745, 751, 95 L. Ed. 1035 (1951) (Justice Jackson concurring).

The goal of these critics is to limit the use of legislative history to those circumstances in which the language of the statute is ambiguous. If this is not done, there is a danger that legislative history will be used to alter the intent of the legislature as clearly expressed in the language of the statute. In short, the concern is that the legislative history will be substituted for the statute itself. The entire process is turned on its head, as reflected in the standard joke that a court will examine the language of a statute only if the legislative history of the statute is ambiguous! J. Cory, *The Use of Legislative History in the Interpretation of Statutes,* 32 Can. Bar Rev. 624, 636 (1954).

The problem, however, is that advocates frequently disagree over whether the language of a statute is ambiguous. Law offices spend vast amounts of time and resources trying to demonstrate that statutes are ambiguous. Generally, they have been very successful. It is not surprising, therefore, that the use of legislative history is increasing as courts struggle to interpret and apply statutes to concrete facts before them. The criticism of legislative history has had almost no effect on this increase. As indicated earlier, an advocate who does not appear with an argument based on legislative history is usually considered unprepared.

Assignment 11.5

Mary Franklin is a registered practitioner before the U.S. Patent Office. She is a nonattorney who has been registered by and authorized to practice before the Patent Office. She has an office in the state where she meets her clients, renders opinions on patentability, and prepares legal instruments such as applications for letters patent. The state bar association claims that she is illegally practicing law and is seeking an injunction to stop her unless she becomes a member of the bar. In 15 U.S.C. § 31 Congress has provided that the commissioner of patents:

> may prescribe regulations governing the conduct of agents, attorneys, or other persons representing applicants or other parties before the Patent Office.

The commissioner has established procedures for the registration of lawyers and nonattorneys to practice before it. The state bar association, however, claims that these procedures are invalid insofar as they authorize practice by nonattorneys, because Congress did not intend such authorization in § 31. Mary (and the Patent Office) disagree with this interpretation of § 31.

(a) What is Mary's argument based on the language of § 31? What is the bar's argument? Is this language ambiguous? Is there a need to resort to the legislative history of § 31?

(b) When § 31 was first introduced in Congress, it read that the commissioner "may prescribe regulations governing the recognition and conduct of agents, attorneys, or other persons representing applicants or other parties before the Patent Office." This language, however, was amended. The version passed by Congress contained the language quoted above (see indented text). What arguments can be made on the interpretation of § 31 based on this data of legislative history?

(c) On the floor of the Senate during debate on this provision, the following exchange occurred between Senator Davis and Senator Kline:

Senator DAVIS: I would like to ask the distinguished Senator if this bill would allow the Commissioner of Patents to set a maximum limit on the amount of fees that a lawyer can charge clients for services rendered in connection with a case before the Patent Office?

Senator KLINE: We examined that question carefully in committee, Senator, and it was our view that any conduct of representatives can be regulated by the Commissioner including the question of fees. I should point out, however, that we did not find much problem with the way in which the bar associations currently handle the question of excessive fees.

What arguments can be made on the interpretation of § 31 based on this data of legislative history?

(d) In the report of the Senate committee that recommended the adoption of this law, the following comment is made: "This provision is not intended to authorize persons not members of the bar to practice law." What arguments can be made on the interpretation of § 31 based on this data of legislative history?

Finding Legislative History

In tracing legislative history, you are looking for documents such as bills, hearing transcripts, proposed amendments, and committee reports. As indicated, it is often very difficult to trace the legislative history of *state* statutes. The documents are sometimes poorly preserved, if at all.

TECHNIQUES FOR TRACING THE LEGISLATIVE HISTORY OF STATE STATUTES

1. Examine the historical data beneath the statute in the statutory code (see Exhibit 11.1). Amendments are usually listed there.

2. For an overview of codification information about your state, check the introductory pages in the first volume of the statutory code, or the beginning of the volume where your statute is found, or the beginning of the Shepard's volume that enables you to shepardize the statutes of that state.

3. Ask your librarian if there is a book (sometimes called a **legislative service**) that covers your state legislature. If one exists, it will give the bill numbers of statutes, proposed amendments, names of committees that considered the statute, etc. If such a text does not exist for your state, ask the librarian how someone finds the legislative history of a current state statute in your state.

4. Check the Internet site of the state legislature. (See Exhibit 11.4.) It may have links to sources of legislative history, such as an archives link or a legislative research link. Some sites have an e-mail address to which you can send specific questions. If your state has such an address, send an e-mail asking for a lead to the legislative history of the statute you are researching.

5. Contact the committees of both houses of the state legislature that considered the bill. The office of your local state representative or state senator might be able to help you identify these committees. If your statute is not too old, staff members on these com-

mittees may be able to give you leads to the legislative history of the statute. Ask if any committee reports (or committee prints) were written. Ask about amendments, etc.

6. Ask your librarian (or a local politician) if there is a law revision commission for your state. If so, ask a legislative reference librarian there for leads.

7. Is there a state law library in your area? If so, contact it for leads.

8. Check the law library and drafting office of the state legislature for leads.

9. Cases interpreting the statute sometimes give the legislative history of the statute, or portions of it. To find cases interpreting a statute, check the Notes of Decisions after the statute in the statutory code (see Exhibit 11.1) and shepardize the statute (see checklist #4b on shepardizing a statute, in chapter 9).

10. You may also find leads to the legislative history of a statute in legal periodical literature on the statute (see checklist #6 in chapter 9), in annotations on the statute (see checklist #3 in chapter 9), in treatises on the statute (see checklist #8 in chapter 9), and in looseleaf services on the statute (see checklist #5 in chapter 9). Phone and mail research might also provide some leads (see checklist #9 in chapter 9).

11. For an overview of state legislative history sources, check *State Legislative Sourcebook* by Lynn Hellebust or *Guide to State Legislative and Administrative Materials* by M. L. Fisher.

 ### Assignment 11.6

After Congress enacted major welfare reform in 1996, every state passed welfare reform legislation to conform to the changes in federal welfare law. Assume that you want to trace the legislative history of this state legislation for your state. (If there is a great deal of this legislation, select any major state legislation on welfare reform in your state.) What specific steps would you take to find the legislative history of this state welfare legislation? Your answer should include the following sources:

- Complete titles of books and other paper materials you would consult
- Relevant CD-ROMs, microforms, and online databases

Give a brief quote from each source to indicate that it covers this state welfare legislation. (If you cannot quote from it, state why—e.g., your library does not subscribe to it.) In addition, list the names, addresses, and phone numbers of:

- legislative bodies,
- administrative agencies, and
- other organizations (public or private)

that you would check for leads to the legislative history of the state welfare legislation. Your answer to this assignment should constitute a mini-reference manual for compiling the legislative history of your state's statutes.

It is easier to trace the legislative history of a *federal* statute, because the documents are generally more available.

TECHNIQUES FOR TRACING THE LEGISLATIVE HISTORY OF A FEDERAL STATUTE

1. Examine the historical data at the end of the statute in the *United States Code* (U.S.C.), in the *United States Code Annotated* (U.S.C.A.), and in the *United States Code Service* (U.S.C.S.).

2. You will also find the **PL** (Public Law) **number** of the statute at the end of the statute printed in U.S.C./ U.S.C.A./U.S.C.S. This PL number will be important for tracing legislative history. (Note that each amendment to a statute will have its own PL number.)

3. Step one in tracing the legislative history of a federal statute is to find out if the history has already been collected ("compiled") by someone else. There may be a list available telling you which area libraries have collected specific legislative histories.
   - Ask your librarian.
   - Check *Sources of Compiled Legislative Histories* by Nancy Johnson. This book will tell you where to locate already collected (compiled) legislative histories. Performing a similar service is *Federal Legislative Histories* by Bernard Reams.
   - Contact the Library of Congress in Washington, D.C., if convenient. It collects legislative histories.
   - If the statute deals with a particular federal agency, check with the library, law department, or legislative liaison office of that agency in Washington, D.C., or in one of its state or regional offices throughout the country. The agency may have compiled the legislative history and may give you access to it.
   - Contact special interest groups or associations that are directly affected by the statute. (See *Encyclopedia of Associations* by Gale.) They may have compiled the legislative history.
   - One question you can ask through phone and mail research is whether the expert knows if anyone has compiled the legislative history of the statute. See checklist #9 in chapter 9.

4. The *Congressional Record* gives you the transcript of the conversations between legislators on the floor while the bill is being debated. These conversations (though sometimes later altered—"amended"—by participating legislators) may cover the meaning of particular clauses in a bill. The conversations are often used by advocates when citing legislative history. The *Congressional Record* is published by Congress in daily pamphlets and later in permanent hardbound volumes (see page 111 of chapter 5 on citation). Recent issues are also available online through LEXIS, WESTLAW, and LEGI-SLATE.

5. The following materials are also useful in tracing the legislative history of federal statutes:
   - *United States Code Congressional and Administrative News* (contains committee reports of important bills; see its Table 4, which is a status table providing leads to legislative history). U.S.C.C.A.N. is a good place to begin your search for federal legislative history.
   - *Monthly Catalog of U.S. Government Publications* (acts as an index to tell you which committee hearings have been published).
   - *Congressional Index* from Commerce Clearing House (contains digest of bills, status tables, voting records, current news, etc.).
   - The paper, CD-ROM, microform, and online products of CIS (Congressional Information Service) that contain reprints of legislative history documents, abstracts, indexes, and other finding tools. The CIS materials include:
     —*CIS/Annual Index to Publications of the United States Congress (CIS/Index)*
     —*CIS/Annual Legislative Histories of U.S. Public Laws (CIS/Legislative Histories)*
     —*CIS/Annual Abstracts of Congressional Publications*
     —*Congressional Masterfile*
   - *United States Serial Set* (committee reports, legislative studies, and other legislative documents)
   - *Congressional Quarterly Weekly Report* (contains a legislative history table and a status table on current major bills)
   - *Congressional Monitor* (contains a summary of daily events in Congress, lists of printed committee reports and other legislative documents)

6. Contact both committees of Congress that considered the legislation. They may be able to send you:
   - committee reports (summaries of the bill and a statement of the reasons for and against its enactment)
   - committee prints (a miscellaneous compilation of information prepared by committee staff members on a bill consisting of statistics, studies, reports, comparative analysis of related bills, etc.)
   - hearing transcripts (a word-for-word account of the testimony given by a witness), etc.
   - copies of the bill and amendments to it

   If you have any difficulty, ask staff members in the office of your United States Senator and Representative for help in obtaining what you need from the relevant committees.

Continued on next page

TECHNIQUES FOR TRACING THE LEGISLATIVE HISTORY OF A FEDERAL STATUTE—continued

7. Cases interpreting the statute sometimes give the legislative history of the statute. To find cases interpreting the statute, check the Notes of Decisions after the statute in the U.S.C.A. and in the U.S.C.S. Also, shepardize the statute (see checklist #4b on shepardizing a statute, in chapter 9).

8. Find out if there is an annotation on the statute. See the "Table of Laws, Rules, and Regulations" in the last volume of *ALR Index*. For federal statutes, also check the volume called *ALR Federal Tables*. (See Exhibit 9.4 and checklist #3 on finding and updating annotations, in chapter 9.)

9. You may also find leads to the legislative history of a statute in legal periodical literature (see checklist #6 in chapter 9), in legal treatises on the statute (see check-list #8 in chapter 9), in looseleaf services on the statute (see checklist #5 in chapter 9), and through phone and mail research (see checklist #9 in chapter 9).

10. To try to find a discussion of your statute in Am. Jur. 2d, a legal encyclopedia, check a separate volume called *Table of Statutes, Rules, and Regulations Cited*.

11. Examine your statute in its session law form in *United States Statutes at Large* for possible leads (page 166).

12. Check the Internet (e.g., http://thomas.loc.gov) for information on particular statutes as well as on the process of enacting laws in Congress. (See beginning of Exhibit 11.4.)

13. Check legislative histories online through WESTLAW and LEXIS.

 Assignment 11.7

In 1996 Congress enacted major federal welfare legislation.

(a) Give the popular name of this legislation, its public law number, its session law cite, and at least one codified cite of this legislation.

(b) List specific paper, CD-ROM, microform, and online sources you would check if you were researching the legislative history of this federal legislation. Give a brief quote from each source to indicate that it covers this legislation. If you cannot quote from it, state why (e.g., your library does not subscribe to it).

In addition, list the names, addresses, and phone numbers of:

- legislative bodies,
- administrative agencies, and
- other organizations (public or private)

that you would check for leads to the legislative history of the federal welfare legislation.

SECTION E   MONITORING PROPOSED LEGISLATION

Occasionally, you will be asked to **monitor a bill** currently before the legislature that has relevance to the caseload of the law office where you work. If you work for a corporation, you may be asked to monitor bills that affect the business of the company. Large corporations often hire **lobbyists** whose sole function is to monitor and try to influence the content of proposed legislation. To monitor a bill means to determine its current status in the legislature and to keep track of all the forces that are trying to enact, defeat, or modify the bill.

TECHNIQUES FOR MONITORING PROPOSED LEGISLATION

1. Begin with the legislature. Find out what committee in each chamber of the legislature (often called the Senate and House) is considering the proposed legislation. Also determine whether more than two committees are considering the entire bill or portions of it.

2. Ask committee staff members to send you copies of the bill in its originally proposed form and in its amended forms.

3. Determine whether the committees considering the proposed legislation have written any reports on it and, if so, whether copies are available.

4. Determine whether any hearings have been scheduled by the committees on the bill. If so, try to attend. For hearings already conducted, see if they have been **transcribed** (a word-for-word recording).

5. Find out the names of people in the legislature who are working on the bill: legislators "pushing" the bill, legislators opposed to it, staff members of the individual legislators working on the bill, and staff members of the committees working on the bill. Ask for copies of any position papers or statements.

6. The local bar association may have taken a position on the bill. Call the association. Find out what committee of the bar is involved with the subject matter of the bill. This committee may have written a report on the bar's position on the bill. If so, try to obtain a copy.

7. Is an administrative agency of the government involved with the bill? Identify the agency with jurisdiction over the subject matter of the bill. Find out who in the agency is working on the bill and whether any written reports of the agency are available. Determine whether the agency has a legislative liaison office.

8. Who else is lobbying for or against the bill? What organizations are interested in it? Find out if they have taken any written positions.

9. What precipitated consideration of the bill by the legislature? Was there a court opinion that prompted the legislative action? If so, you should know what the opinion said.

10. Are any other legislatures in the country contemplating similar legislation? Some of the ways of finding out include the following:
    (a) Look for legal periodical literature on the subject matter of the bill (see checklist #6 in chapter 9).
    (b) Check looseleaf services, if any, covering the subject matter of the bill (see checklist #5 in chapter 9)—these services often cover proposed legislation in the various legislatures.
    (c) Check legal treatises on the subject matter of the bill (see checklist #8 in chapter 9).
    (d) Organizations such as bar associations, public interest groups, business associations, etc. often assign staff members to perform state-by-state research on what the legislatures are doing. Such organizations may be willing to share this research with you.
    (e) Find out if there is a council of governments in your area. It may have done the same research mentioned in (d) above.
    (f) Contact an expert for leads to what other legislatures are doing (see checklist #9 in chapter 9).

11. Check the Internet site for your state legislature (see Exhibit 11.4). It will often give you links to information on the status of current bills in the legislature. Some of the sites also provide direct e-mail links to individual legislators from whom you can seek information about pending bills.

12. Check online bill-tracking services on WESTLAW (e.g. US-BILLTRK) and LEXIS (e.g., BLTRCK). Also check LEGI-SLATE of the Washington Post Company, ELSS (Electronic Legislative Search System) of Commerce Clearing House, WASHINGTON ALERT of the Congressional Quarterly, GPO Access, online versions of *CIS/Index*, etc.

Assignment 11.8

Check your local general-circulation newspaper for today and for several days prior to today. Find a story about any bill that is currently before your state legislature. Assume that you work for a law firm or company that wants you to monitor this bill. Your first task is to write a report about its current status. In your report, cover the topics listed in (a) to (d) below. If you cannot cover these topics (particularly those in (c)) for the bill you select, because the bill is so recent or so insignificant, select another bill.

(a) Describe the bill. What does it cover? What is its bill number or citation?
(b) Who is sponsoring the bill? Why? Who is opposing the bill? Why?

Continued on next page

Assignment 11.8—continued

(c) What has happened thus far in the legislature? What committee(s) have considered it or will consider it? Have hearings been held? Has the bill been amended? If so, how? What is available in writing (e.g., text of the bill, text of amendments, committee reports, hearing testimony)? Where can this material be found?

(d) What is the next proceeding? When will it occur? What are the chances that this bill will be enacted into law?

CHAPTER SUMMARY

Statutes in annotated codes contain research references after the full text of the statues. The references often include historical information that is relevant to the legislative history of the statute, cross-references to related statutes in the code, library references to other books and materials of the publisher of the code, and most importantly, Notes of Decisions that summarize court opinions interpreting or applying the statute.

Statutory codes are highly fragmented or stratified into titles, parts, articles, chapters, sections, subsections, etc. All statutes must be based on a provision in the constitution. Definitions sections are often helpful in understanding a unit or cluster of statutes on the same subject. Statutes of construction can help you interpret (construe) ambiguity in a statute. Statutes should be briefed by stating the citation; by identifying the audience; by incorporating important cross-references; by identifying stated conditions, inclusions and exclusions; by stating whether the statute is discretionary or mandatory; and by breaking it into elements. Statutes, like all rules, should be broken down into their elements. An element is a component or portion of a rule which is a precondition of the applicability of the entire rule. This kind of element analysis is important for many tasks such as identifying issues, drafting complaints and answers, organizing an interview, etc.

To find statutes, go to the appropriate statutory code and study its features. Other ways to find statutes are to look for leads in looseleaf services, legal treatises, legal periodical literature, annotations, legal encyclopedias, computer research systems, the Internet, phone and mail research, etc. Once you have found a relevant statute, make sure it is still valid. Check cross-references within the statute; find cases interpreting the statute; find administrative regulations based on the statute; find annotations, legal periodical literature, looseleafs, Am. Jur. 2d discussions, and legal treatises on the statute. Conduct a search of its legislative history.

The federal legislature (Congress) and most state legislatures are bicameral, i.e., they consist of two houses. For a bill to become a statute, the bill must go through approximately six stages. First, the bill is proposed and then introduced into one of the houses of the legislature. It may be introduced into the other house simultaneously or at a later date. Second, there is an initial consideration of the bill by a committee of each house. Third, all of the members of one of the houses debate and vote on the bill, and then all of the members of the other house debate and vote on the bill. Fourth, there is a consideration of the bill by a conference committee made up of members of both houses. The role of this committee is to try to reconcile any differences in the two versions of the bill passed by each house. Fifth, the bill goes back to the full membership of each house for a vote on what the conference committee produced. Sixth, the chief executive signs or vetoes the bill. If he or she vetoes the bill, it can still become a statute if two-thirds of each house vote to override the chief executive. The legislative history of a statute consists of what happens during these six stages. As an aid in interpreting statutory language, it is useful to try to find its legislative history to determine if the legislature ever discussed the specific facts now in controversy, and to determine the broad or narrow purpose of the legislature in enacting the statute.

The use of legislative history has been controversial for several reasons. The documents of legislative history are not equally available to everyone. Furthermore, these documents are often unreliable as a guide to understanding legislative intent, and can be unduly manipulated by advocates pushing a certain interpretation of this intent. Although American courts tend to emphasize the importance of the documents of legislative history, they can be overused.

To trace the legislative history of a statute, check the historical data in the statutory code; find out if anyone has already collected the legislative history; ask the appropriate committees of the legislature to send you copies of committee reports; look for cases that might provide some of the legislative history; look for leads in periodical literature, treatises, looseleaf services, check computer research services and the Internet; etc.

When monitoring proposed legislation, identify all the legislative committees considering the legislation. Ask that you be sent copies of the bill, amendments, transcribed hearings, position papers, and statements of individuals pushing and opposing the legislation. Also try to obtain copies of reports of bar associations, administrative agencies, and organizations lobbying for or against the legislation. Know what precipitated consideration of the legislation. Finally, check if other legislatures in the country are considering similar legislation.

KEY TERMS

annotated statutory code	construction	Popular Name Table	override
section (§)	construe	enabling statute	pocket veto
session laws	*ejusdem generis*	bill	committee print
retroactive	mandatory statute	bicameral	legislative service
prospective	discretionary statute	unicameral	PL number
Historical Note	elements	legislative history	monitor a bill
Notes of Decisions	cause of action	uniform state laws	lobbyists
id.	defenses	vetoes	transcribed

Chapter 12

OTHER PRIMARY AUTHORITY

Chapter Outline

SECTION A   **CONSTITUTIONAL LAW**

Reading Constitutional Law

The **constitution** sets out the fundamental ground rules for the conduct of the government in the geographical area over which the government has authority or jurisdiction. The constitution defines the branches of the government, establishes basic rights and obligations of citizens, and covers matters that the framers considered important enough (such as limitations on the power to tax) to be included in the constitution. (See Exhibit 2.2 in chapter 2.) The United States Constitution does this for the federal government, and the state constitution does it for the state government.

The supreme law of the land is the United States Constitution. If there is a conflict between the United States Constitution and a state constitution or any other state law, the United States Constitution controls. This principle is established in the **Supremacy Clause** of the United States Constitution, which says "the laws of the United States . . . shall be the supreme Law of the Land" (art. VI, cl. 2). This does not mean, however, that the United States Constitution controls every aspect of our lives. The state constitution is the final authority on some matters that are considered local (e.g., establishing the grounds for divorce). The United States Constitution, in contrast, is the final authority on national matters (e.g., bankruptcy, currency, foreign policy).

In some areas, the powers are shared (e.g., welfare law). The division of powers between the federal and state governments is called **federalism.** This simply means that in our society, some powers are exercised by the federal government, some by the state governments, and others by both the federal and state governments. Even when state governments are exercising exclusively local powers, however, they must conform to federal constitutional principles in the United States Constitution. For example, a state would be violating the Equal Protection Clause of the United States Constitution if it passed a law that said husbands, but not wives, could use a certain ground for divorce. The federal government cannot start passing divorce laws, but it can insist that the divorce laws passed by the states conform to the United States Constitution.

In reading the constitution, keep the following guidelines in mind:

1. *Thumb through the headings of all the sections or articles of the constitution, or glance through the table of contents.* How is the document organized? What subjects did the framers want covered by the constitution? A quick scanning of the section headings or table of contents is a good way to obtain an overview of the structure of the text.
2. *The critical sections or articles are those that establish and define the powers of the legislative, judicial, and executive branches of government in the geographic area covered by the Constitution.* Who passes, interprets, and executes the law? For the United States Constitution, "all legislative Powers granted herein shall be vested in a Congress" (art. I, § 1); "the judicial Power of the United States, shall be vested in one supreme Court, and in such inferior Courts as the Congress may from time to time ordain and establish" (art. III, § 1); and "the executive Power shall be vested in a President of the United States of America" (art. II, § 1). The exact scope of these powers, as enunciated elsewhere in the Constitution, has been and continues to be an arena of constant controversy and litigation.
3. *The amendments to the constitution change or add to the body of the text.* The main vehicle for changing the constitution is the amendment process, which itself is defined in the constitution. Some constitutions, for example, can be amended by a vote of the people in a general election. A condition for most amendments is that they must be approved by one or more sessions of the legislature. Constitutional amendments usually appear at the end of the document.
4. *Constitutions are written in very broad terms.* There are, of course, exceptions to this, particularly with respect to the constitutions of local governments, which can contain very specific provisions. In the main, however, a common characteristic of constitutions is their broad language. How would you interpret the following section?

Congress shall make no laws respecting an establishment of religion, or prohibiting the free exercise thereof; or abridging the freedom of speech, or of the press; or of the right of the people to assemble, and to petition the Government for a redress of grievances.

How many words in this provision do you *not* understand? What is an "establishment"? If the school board requires a "moment of silence" at the beginning of each day, is the school board establishing a religion? What does "abridging" mean? If a government official leaks secret documents to the press, and the government tries to sue the press to prevent publication of the documents, has the "freedom" of the press been abridged? If the people have a right to "assemble," could the government pass a law prohibiting all gatherings of three or more people at any place within one thousand yards of the White House gates? The questions arising from the interpretation of constitutional law are endless; tens of thousands of court opinions exist on questions such as these. The broader the language, the more ambiguous it is, and therefore the greater the need for interpretation.

5. *One of the central questions for the interpreter of constitutional law is: what meaning did the authors intend?* Common sense dictates that when language is ambiguous, the ambiguity may be resolved in part by attempting to determine what the author of the language intended by it. What was the author's meaning? In what context was the author writing? Does the context shed any light on what was meant? This kind of analysis is fundamental to legal reasoning, whether the document is a constitution, a statute, a regulation, or a case. It is particularly difficult to do, however, for a constitution written over a hundred years ago.

Finding the *original intent* of the authors of the constitution, however, is not the only method used to interpret particular provisions of the constitution. Another approach is to view the constitution as a "living" document that must be interpreted in light of the needs of modern society. The danger in this view is that too much can be read into the constitution based on the personal philosophies of individual judges. The charge is that these individuals rewrite the constitution under the guise of interpreting it to fit modern society. This debate, of course, adds to the controversy and the volume of constitutional law.

Finding Constitutional Law

TECHNIQUES FOR FINDING CONSTITUTIONAL LAW

1. Start with the text of the constitution itself. It is usually found at the beginning of the statutory code of the jurisdiction. (The federal Constitution is in U.S.C./U.S.C.A./U.S.C.S.)
2. Use the CARTWHEEL to help you use the general index of the statutory code and the separate index for the constitution itself. (See Exhibit 7.1 in chapter 7.) Also check the table of contents material for the constitution in the statutory code.
3. Following the text of individual constitutional provisions there are often *Notes of Decisions* containing summaries of cases interpreting the constitution. Some of these notes can run hundreds of pages. Check any available index or table of contents covering these notes.
4. Shepardize the constitutional provision. The set of Shepard's to use is the same set you use for shepardizing a statute. (See checklist #4b on shepardizing a statute, in chapter 9.)
5. Annotations. Find annotations in A.L.R.1st, A.L.R.2d, etc. on the constitutional provisions in which you are interested. (See Exhibits 9.2 and 9.3 and checklist #3 on finding and updating annotations, in chapter 9.)
6. Digests. Go to the *United States Supreme Court Digest* (West) (page 52). Also use the various West digests that cover other jurisdictions. (The American Digest System, of course, covers all jurisdictions.) Use the Descriptive Word Index (DWI) of a digest to locate relevant key numbers. (See checklist #2 on using West digests, in chapter 9.) (For cases on the U.S. Constitution, you can also go to the LEXIS digest—the *United States Supreme Court Digest, Lawyers Ed.*, page 52.)

Continued on next page

TECHNIQUES FOR FINDING CONSTITUTIONAL LAW—continued

7. Legal treatises. Find legal treatises on the entire constitution or on the specific portions of the constitution in which you are interested. Numerous such treatises exist. (See checklist #8 on finding legal treatises, in chapter 9.)

8. Legal periodical literature. Go to the two indexes to legal periodical literature: ILP and CLI. Use them to help you locate what you need among the vast periodical literature on the constitution. (See checklist #6 on finding legal periodical literature, in chapter 9)

9. Looseleaf services. Find out if there are looseleaf services on the area of the constitution in which you are interested. (See checklist #5 on looseleaf services, in chapter 9.)

10. Phone and mail research. Contact an expert. (See checklist #9 on phone and mail research, in chapter 9.)

11. *Words and Phrases.* Identify specific words or phrases within the constitutional provision you are examining. Find court definitions of these words or phrases in the multivolume legal dictionary, *Words and Phrases.*

12. Legal encyclopedias. Find discussions of constitutional law in Am. Jur. 2d and in C.J.S. (See checklist #7 on legal encyclopedias, in chapter 9.)

13. Shepardize every case you found that interprets the constitution. (See checklist #4a on shepardizing a case, in chapter 9.)

14. LEXIS and WESTLAW contain the full text of the United States Constitution and every state constitution. They also can lead you to extensive case law interpreting these constitutions and legal periodical literature analyzing them. See chapter 13.

15. Check the Internet site for the state statutes of your state. See Exhibit 11.4 in chapter 11. Some of these cites will also lead you to the constitution of your state.

 Assignment 12.1

(a) Go to your state constitution. Find any provision in it that grants powers to your governor. Select one of the powers. Quote a sentence from the provision and give its citation.

(b) Go to the set of Shepard's that will allow you to shepardize this constitutional provision. Pick any citing case. Go to the reporter that contains this citing case. Quote the sentence from the case that cites this provision. Give the citation of your quote. (If there are no citing cases, redo part (a) of this assignment until you find a constitutional provision that does have a citing case.)

(c) Go back to the set of books you used in part (a). Are there notes of decisions in this set? If so, find the case you used for part (b). Photocopy this page and circle the case in these notes.

(d) Go to your main state digest. In this digest, find the case you used for part (b). Under what key number(s) was this case digested? On what page(s) of the digest volume (or its supplement) did you find this case digested?

(e) Go to the American Digest System. Find the case you used for part (b). Under what key number(s) was this case digested? In what units of the American Digest System and on what page(s) did you find this case digested?

SECTION B   ADMINISTRATIVE LAW

Kinds and Functions of Administrative Agencies

An **administrative agency** is a unit of government whose primary mission is to carry out—or administer—the statutes of the legislature and the executive orders of the chief of the executive branch of government. At the federal level, the chief is the president; at the state level, it is the governor; and at most local levels, it is the mayor. As we will see in a moment, many agencies also have rulemaking and dispute-resolution responsibilities.

Administrative agencies can have a wide variety of names. Here are some examples:

- Fire Department
- Board of Licenses and Occupations
- Civil Service Commission
- Agency for International Development
- Department of Defense
- Office of Management and Budget
- Legal Services Corporation
- Bureau of Taxation
- Internal Revenue Service
- Division of Child Support and Enforcement
- Social Security Administration
- Worker's Compensation Administration

Certain types of agencies exist at all three levels of government. For example, there is a separate tax collection agency in each of the federal, state, and local governments. Other agencies, however, are unique to one of the levels. For example, only the federal government has a Department of Defense (DOD) and a Central Intelligence Agency (CIA). Nothing comparable exists at the state and local levels of government. The latter have police departments and the highway patrol, but their role is significantly different from the DOD and CIA.

For a list of some of the most important federal agencies, see Exhibit 2.1 in chapter 2. There are three main kinds of administrative agencies:

- Executive department agencies
- Independent regulatory agencies
- Quasi-independent regulatory agencies

Executive department agencies exist within the executive branch of the government, often at the cabinet level. Examples include the Department of Agriculture and the Department of Labor. These agencies are answerable to the chief executive, who usually has the power to dismiss those in charge of them.

Independent regulatory agencies exist outside the executive department and, therefore, outside the day-to-day control of the chief executive. Examples include the Securities and Exchange Commission and the Public Utilities Commission. Their function is usually to regulate an aspect of society—often a particular industry such as securities and public utilities. To insulate these agencies from politics, those in charge usually cannot be removed at the whim of the chief executive.

A **quasi-independent regulatory agency** is a hybrid agency, often with characteristics of the two kinds just described. It has more independence than an executive department agency, yet it might exist within the executive department.

Most administrative agencies have three functions: execution, rulemaking, and dispute resolution:

- *Execution.* The primary function of the agency is to carry out (i.e., execute) the statutes and executive orders governing the agency, and the administrative regulations created by the agency itself. This is the agency's executive function.
- *Rulemaking.* The agency often has the authority to write rules and regulations. (See definition of administrative regulation below.) In so doing, the agency is "making law" like a legislature. Indeed, such laws are often referred to as **quasi-legislation.**
- *Dispute Resolution.* The agency has the authority to interpret the statutes and regulations that govern it. Furthermore, it often has the authority to resolve disputes that arise over the application of such laws. It will hold administrative hearings and issue decisions. (See definition of administrative decision below.) In this sense the agency is acting like a court when the latter resolves (i.e., adjudicates) disputes. The dispute-resolution power of the agency is therefore called a **quasi-judicial power.** The phrase **quasi-adjudication** refers to the process by which agencies act like courts in interpreting laws and resolving disputes. An agency exercises its quasi-judicial power at several

levels. At the first level is a *hearing*, which is similar to a trial in a court of original jurisdiction. The presiding agency official—known variously as **hearing examiner, trial examiner,** or **administrative law judge** (ALJ)—will, like the judge in a trial court, take testimony of witnesses and other evidence, determine the facts of the case, and apply the law to those facts in order to render a decision. In many agencies, the findings of fact and the decision of the hearing officer constitute only a recommendation to the director, commissioner, secretary, or other high official who will make the decision at this level. Like the courts, many agencies then provide a second, "appellate" level where a body such as a board or commission reviews the decision of the hearing examiner (or other official) to correct errors. After the parties to the dispute have used all these avenues of redress within the agency, they have **exhausted administrative remedies** and may then appeal the final administrative decision to a court.

Here is an example of an agency using all three powers:

Securities and Exchange Commission (SEC)

- *Execution.* The SEC accepts filings of registration statements containing financial data on issuers of securities. This is done to carry out the statutes of Congress requiring such registration.
- *Rulemaking.* The SEC writes regulations that provide greater detail on what the registration statements must contain.
- *Dispute Resolution.* The SEC holds a hearing to decide whether a corporation has violated the registration requirements laid out in the statutes and administrative regulations. The end product of the hearing is often an administrative decision.

 Assignment 12.2

Give the name, address, phone number, fax number, and function (stated briefly) of:

(a) Three federal agencies with offices in your state.
(b) Five state agencies in your state.
(c) Five city or county agencies with offices in your city or county.

Finding Administrative Law

An **administrative regulation** is a rule or law of an administrative agency that explains or carries out the statutes and executive orders that govern the agency. (See Exhibit 2.2 in chapter 2.)

Many agencies write regulations, but few have coherent systems of organizing and distributing the regulations. A major exception is the federal agencies, whose regulations are first published in the *Federal Register;* many are then codified in the *Code of Federal Regulations.* A large number of states also follow this pattern of a separate register and code for the regulations of state administrative agencies. The state register and code, however, are not as sophisticated as the *Federal Register* and the *Code of Federal Regulations.*

Normally, an agency does not have the power to write regulations unless it has specific statutory authority to do so. An examination of the statute giving the agency this authority can be helpful in understanding the regulations themselves. In theory, the statutes of the legislature establish the purpose of the agency and define its overall policies, but leave to the agency (through its regulations) the task of filling in the specifics of administration. Regulations, therefore, tend to be very detailed.

The other major kind of administrative law is the **administrative decision.** This is a resolution of a controversy between a party and an administrative agency involving the application of the regulations, statutes, or executive orders that govern the agency. (It is also called an *administrative ruling.* See Exhibit 2.2 in chapter 2.) Not many agencies publish their decisions in any systematic order; some agencies do not publish them at all. Regulatory agencies, such as the Federal Communications Commission and state environmental agencies, often do a better job at publishing their decisions than other agencies.

The federal government and most states have an **Administrative Procedure Act** (APA). This is a statute that governs the steps that an agency must take to write a regulation or issue an administrative decision. Examples of these steps include publishing a notice of a proposed regulation, allowing affected parties to participate in a hearing that leads to an administrative decision, etc. Part of legal research in administrative law should address the question of whether the agency properly complied with the Administrative Procedure Act on such steps.

When looking for an administrative regulation, you must simultaneously be looking for the **enabling statute** that is the authority for the regulation. (An enabling statute is a statute that authorizes the agency to write regulations to perform other specific tasks.) With very few exceptions, agencies do not have their own independent power. In large measure, the very reason for the existence of the agency is to carry out the statutes of the legislature that created the agency and gave it specific responsibilities. Consequently, two questions always confront the researcher:

- Is there an administrative regulation on point?
- If so, does the regulation go beyond what its enabling statute authorizes the agency to do? In other words, is the administrative regulation within the scope of the enabling statute?

To answer the second question, of course, you need to find the enabling statute. Often the lead you need to find this statute will be within the administrative code that contains the regulation.

Assume that you have found a federal administrative regulation in the *Code of Federal Regulations* (C.F.R.) that is on point. You now want to check the authority for that regulation in the enabling statute, which for federal statutes would be within the *United States Code* (U.S.C.) or the *United States Code Annotated* (U.S.C.A.) or the *United States Code Service* (U.S.C.S.). To find the statute, you would check the "Authority" reference within the C.F.R. itself. Beneath the regulation you are reading (or at the beginning of the cluster of regulations of which your regulation is a part), find an "Authority" reference that will tell you what federal statutes are the authority for the regulation. See Research Link R.

Suppose you have not yet found any administrative regulations, but you have found a statute that is on point. You want to determine whether there are any administrative regulations based on that statute. To find out, check the "Parallel Table of Authorities and Rules" in the pamphlet called *CFR Index and Finding Aids* that is part of the C.F.R. set. See Research Link S.

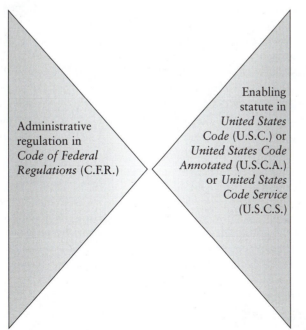

Administrative regulation in *Code of Federal Regulations* (C.F.R.)

Enabling statute in *United States Code* (U.S.C.) or *United States Code Annotated* (U.S.C.A.) or *United States Code Service* (U.S.C.S.)

RESEARCH LINK R

If you have found an administrative regulation, and you now want to find the enabling statute that is the authority for that regulation, check the "Authority" reference beneath the regulation in C.F.R. (or at the beginning of the cluster of regulations of which your regulation is a part). There you will be given the cite in U.S.C. (U.S.C.A or U.S.C.S.) to the federal statute that is the authority for the regulation.

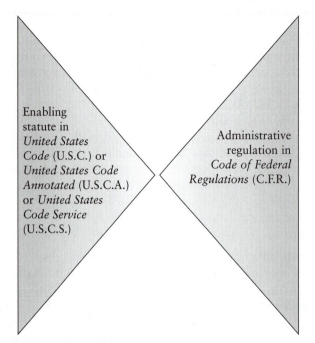

Enabling statute in *United States Code* (U.S.C.) or *United States Code Annotated* (U.S.C.A.) or *United States Code Service* (U.S.C.S.)

Administrative regulation in *Code of Federal Regulations* (C.F.R.)

RESEARCH LINK S

If you have found a federal statute in U.S.C. (or U.S.C.A. or U.S.C.S.) and you now want to know whether there are any administrative regulations in C.F.R. that are based on that statute, you would check the "Parallel Table of Authorities and Rules" in the pamphlet called *CFR Index and Finding Aids* that is part of the C.F.R. set. This pamphlet will tell you if your statute is an enabling statute for any administrative regulations.

TECHNIQUES FOR FINDING ADMINISTRATIVE LAW

1. Start with your law library. Ask where you can find the kind of administrative law you are seeking, e.g., federal administrative regulations, state administrative regulations. Also check the catalog. (See checklist #1 in chapter 9.)

2. Consider calling, or if practical, visiting the agency itself. There may be a regional or district office near you. Contact the library, the law department, or the public information section in the agency. Ask for a list of the agency's publications, such as regulations, decisions, annual reports. Also ask where these materials are located. Find out if you can come to the agency and use the materials. Ask about brochures describing the agency's functions, which can be sent to you.

3. Whenever an agency official is reluctant to let you have access to any publications of the agency, you may have to do separate research to find out whether you are entitled to access—under the federal Freedom of Information Act and its state equivalent, for example.

4. Many federal administrative regulations are printed in the *Code of Federal Regulations* (C.F.R.), which are usually printed first in their proposed form in the *Federal Register* before they are enacted by the agency. The C.F.R. comes out in a new edition—and a new color—every year. See Research Link D in chapter 3. There are six main ways to locate regulations in the C.F.R.:

    (a) The *C.F.R. Index and Finding Aids* volume. This is a single-volume pamphlet that is reissued every year.

    (b) The *Index to the Code of Federal Regulations* published by Congressional Information Service (CIS).

    (c) Looseleaf services. As indicated earlier, there are numerous looseleaf services covering many federal agencies and some state agencies. These services usually give extensive references to administrative regulations and decisions. (See checklist #5 in chapter 9)

    (d) The *Federal Register*. Use the indexes to the *Federal Register* to find proposed regulations that could lead you to regulations in the *Code of Federal Regulations* itself. The main index to the entire *Federal Register* is the *CIS Index to the Federal Register*. There is also an annual index to the *Federal Register*.

    (e) LEXIS and WESTLAW. These commercial online services act as online indexes to federal regulations.

    (f) The Internet.

    • To find the *Code of Federal Regulations,* go to: <http://www.access.gpo.gov/nara/cfr>

    • To find the *Federal Register,* go to: <http://www.access.gpo.gov/su_docs/aces/aces140.html>

    • Many federal agencies have their own sites. For example, to find the Securities and Exchange Commission, go to: <http://www.sec.gov>

    • If you don't know the Internet site of the agency in which you are interested, check FedWorld (page 59), a massive online locator service for access to information disseminated by the federal government. To use this service, go to: <http://www.fedworld.gov>

5. Once you have found a federal regulation on point in the C.F.R., do the following:

    (a) Shepardize the regulation. (See checklist #4c on shepardizing a regulation, in chapter 9.)

    (b) Find the enabling statute that is the authority

TECHNIQUES FOR FINDING ADMINISTRATIVE LAW—continued

for that regulation. Read this statute in U.S.C./ U.S.C.A./U.S.C.S. Make sure the regulation does not contradict, go beyond the scope of, or otherwise violate the statute that the regulation is supposed to implement:

- If you have a regulation and want to find out what statute is the authority for that regulation, look for the "Authority" reference beneath the regulation in the C.F.R. (or at the beginning of the cluster of regulations in C.F.R. of which your regulation is a part). See Research Link R.
- If you have a statute and want to find out if there are any regulations implementing that statute, check the "Parallel Table of Authorities and Rules" in a volume called *CFR Index and Finding Aids* that accompanies the C.F.R. (and is also published separately by LEXIS as part of U.S.C.S.). See Research Link S.

(c) Once you have found a regulation in the C.F.R., you must find out if the regulation has been affected in any way (changed, revoked, added to, renumbered) by subsequent material printed in the *Federal Register.* This is done by checking your C.F.R. cite in:

- The monthly pamphlet called *LSA: List of Sections Affected.*
- The "CFR Parts Affected" table in the daily *Federal Register* from the date of the latest *LSA* pamphlet to the current date. (The "Reader Aids" section of the *Federal Register* has this table in a cumulative list.)

The *LSA* pamphlet and the "CFR Parts Affected" table will tell you what pages of the *Federal Register* contain material that affects your regulation in the C.F.R. (You need to do this only until the next annual edition of the C.F.R. comes out,

because anything affecting the regulation during the preceding year will be incorporated in the next edition of C.F.R.)

(d) Find out if there is an annotation on your regulation. Shepardize the regulation. Annotations in A.L.R.1st, A.L.R.2d, etc. are among the citing materials of Shepard's. Also, check the "Table of Laws, Rules, and Regulations" in the last volume of the *ALR Index.* See also the separate volume called *ALR Federal Tables* for annotations on federal regulations in the C.F.R. (See Exhibit 9.4 in chapter 9.)

6. Many states have an administrative code and an administrative register comparable to the federal C.F.R. and the *Federal Register.* The exact titles of the state codes and registers are found in the "Tables" section toward the end of *The Bluebook: A Uniform System of Citation* (see page 39 for a photo of the Bluebook).

7. LEXIS and WESTLAW contain regulations and other administrative laws of every state.

8. The Internet is also a source for state administrative law. Check the Internet site for the state statutes of your state. (See Exhibit 11.4 in chapter 11.) Some of these sites will also lead you to the regulations and other administrative laws of your state. See also <http://www.nass.org/acr/acrdir.htm> (the administrative codes and registers site of the National Association of Secretaries of State).

9. Federal administrative decisions are printed in separate reporter volumes for each agency. Some federal administrative decisions can be shepardized. See, for example, *Shepard's United States Administrative Citations* and *Shepard's Labor Law Citations.* State administrative decisions are often much more difficult to locate. Looseleaf services that cover a particular federal or state agency are a good source for finding administrative decisions. (See checklist #5 in chapter 9.)

 Assignment 12.3

(a) What is the title of the administrative code of your state? Does your state have a register? If so, what is its title?

(b) Find and cite any state administrative regulation that covers when workers in your state are entitled to worker's compensation for injuries on the job.

 Assignment 12.4

(a) Select any regulation in the *Code of Federal Regulations.* Use the tables in the recent issues of the *Federal Register* to find out how that regulation has been affected within the last year. Give the citation of the regulation. State how it has been affected and give the citation to the page(s) in the *Federal Register* that tells you how it was affected. (If the

Continued on next page

Assignment 12.4—continued

tables in the *Federal Register* tell you that the regulation you selected has not been affected, pick a different regulation.)

(b) Find any five regulations in the *Code of Federal Regulations,* written by five different agencies, that mention attorneys. Quote one sentence from each regulation and give its citation.

(c) Give the cite for the enabling statute for each of the regulations you picked in part (b).

(d) Find any federal statute on taking a home office deduction on your federal income tax return. What is the citation of this statute? Find one regulation that carries out this statute. What is the citation of this regulation? How did you find it? List another way you could have used to find it.

SECTION C   LOCAL LAW

The local level of government consists of thousands of counties, cities, and towns throughout the country. They pass laws that deal with a wide variety of subjects, e.g., zoning, transportation, housing, sanitation. Among the most common kinds of local laws are **charters** (the fundamental law of a municipality or other local unit of government authorizing it to perform designated governmental functions) and **ordinances** (laws passed by the local legislature that declare, command, or prohibit something). See Exhibit 2.2 in chapter 2.

Contact your city, county, or other form of government. Call city hall, the local council, the board of supervisors, the county commissioner's office, etc. Ask what kinds of laws it passes, where those laws can be found, how they are updated, etc. If the clerk you speak to does not know, ask a public information officer or anyone in the law department. You may be able to go to a government office to examine these local laws.

Many local general public libraries have municipal codes and other local laws. Also ask any law librarians in your area where this material can be found.

Many charters are also printed in the state's statutory code. (See "Techniques for Finding Statutes" on page 213 in chapter 11.) Finally, more and more local law is now available on the Internet. For example, to find a large number of municipal codes, go to <http://www.spl.lib.wa.us/collec/lawcoll/municode.html> and <http://www.municode.com>.

Here are some other leads to local law:

- Legal periodical literature exists on local issues such as zoning, municipal bonds, etc. (see checklist #6 on legal periodical literature, in chapter 9).
- The Shepard's volumes for a particular state will enable you to shepardize local charters and ordinances.
- Digests can be used to find case law in charters and ordinances (see checklist #2 on digests, in chapter 9).
- Annotations on *local law* in A.L.R.1st, A.L.R.2d, A.L.R.4th, and A.L.R.5th (see checklist #3 on annotations, in chapter 9).
- Legal treatises on local law (see checklist #8 on legal treatises, in chapter 9).
- Am. Jur. 2d and C.J.S. have discussions on local law (see checklist #7 on legal encyclopedias, in chapter 9).
- Looseleaf services cover aspects of local law (see checklist #5 on looseleaf services, in chapter 9).
- Local legal newspapers often cover charter provisions, new ordinances, etc.
- Phone and mail research; contact an expert (see checklist #9 on phone and mail research, in chapter 9).
- *Ordinance Law Annotations* (published by Shepard's) summarizes court opinions that have interpreted ordinances.

Assignment 12.5

What are the different categories of local laws published where you live? Who enacts them? Where can each be found?

SECTION D   RULES OF COURT

You must always check the **rules of court** (also called *court rules* and *rules of procedure*) governing practice and procedure before a *particular* court. These rules govern the mechanics of litigation. They will tell you how to file a request for an extension of time, the number of days a defendant has to answer a complaint, the format of a complaint or appellate brief, etc.

TECHNIQUES FOR FINDING RULES OF COURT

Rules of Court for State Courts:

- Check your state statutory code for the text of the rules.
- Ask your librarian if there is a rules service company that publishes an updated edition of state rules of court.
- Find out if the court itself publishes its own rules.
- LEXIS and WESTLAW contain the rules of court for many state courts.
- To find rules of court for state courts on the Internet, check the following sites:
  http://www.ljx.com/courthouse/staterules.html
  http://www.llrx.com/columns/litigat.htm
- Shepardize rules of court in the same set of Shepard's you use to shepardize a statute (see checklist #4b, in chapter 9).
- For case law on the rules of court, check the digests for your state (see checklist #2 on digests, in chapter 9).
- Check local practice books, formbooks, or other legal treatises (see checklist #8 on legal treatises, in chapter 9).
- Check with an expert (see checklist #9 on phone and mail research, in chapter 9).

Rules of Court for Federal Courts:

- Check the U.S.C./U.S.C.A./U.S.C.S., such as title 18 (Appendix) and title 28 (Appendix).
- To find rules of court governing specific federal courts, check *Federal Local Court Rules,* a looseleaf published by Lawyers' Co-op.

- LEXIS and WESTLAW contain rules of court of federal courts. Many rules are also available on CD-ROM.
- To find rules of court for federal courts on the Internet, check the following cites:
  http://www.llrx.com/columns/litigat.htm
  http://www.uscourts.gov/links/html
- Shepardize federal rules of court in *Federal Statute Citations* (page 70).
- For case law on rules of court, check the digests, such as *Federal Practice Digest* 4th (see checklist #2 on digests, in chapter 9).
- Check the *Federal Rules Service,* a Lawyers' Co-op publication that contains cases interpreting the Federal Rules of Civil Procedure.
- Check special treatises on the federal rules such as:
  Moore's Federal Practice
  Wright and Miller, *Federal Practice and Procedure*
- Find annotations on the federal rules of court. Check the "Table of Laws, Rules, and Regulations" in the last volume of the *ALR Index* and the separate volume, *ALR Federal Tables* (see checklist #3, in chapter 9).
- Check legal periodical literature on the federal rules of court (see checklist #6 on legal periodical literature, in chapter 9).
- Check Am. Jur. 2d and C.J.S. on the federal rules of court (see checklist #7 on legal encyclopedias, in chapter 9).
- Check with an expert (see checklist #9 on phone and mail research, in chapter 9).

Assignment 12.6

Locate the rules of court governing the three courts listed below. For each court, find and quote from any rule that imposes a time limitation on one or more of the parties for litigation within that court (e.g., the time within which a party must file a particular motion or respond to

Continued on next page

Assignment 12.6—continued

a discovery request). Also give the name, address, and fax number of each of the three courts you select:

(a) any state trial court of your state
(b) any United States District Court sitting in your state
(c) any United States Bankruptcy Court sitting in your state

SECTION E   INTERNATIONAL LAW

International law consists of the law that exists between nations. The primary kind of international law is the **treaty,** which is a formal agreement between two or more foreign governments. The president negotiates treaties with other nations, but the Senate must approve the treaty by at least a two-thirds vote. An **executive agreement,** in contrast, is a formal agreement between two or more foreign governments that does not require a vote of approval by the Senate. The line between what can be covered in an executive agreement rather than a treaty is not clear and has always been the subject of considerable debate between the president and Congress.

The first step in researching international law is to read one or more legal periodical articles or sections of a legal treatise that cover the area of your research. Before you start reading the text of treaties, executive agreements, and case law interpreting them, you need a listing of the cast of participants and an overview of technical terms involved. Secondary sources such as legal periodicals and legal treatises will provide this. See Exhibit 8.1 in chapter 8.

TECHNIQUES FOR FINDING INTERNATIONAL LAW

1. In general, check:
   - *United States Treaties and Other International Acts*
   - *Treaties and Other International Acts Series* (T.I.A.S.)
   - *United States Treaties and Other International Agreements* (U.S.T.)
   - WESTLAW's database, USTREATIES
   - LEXIS's ITRADE, INLAW, etc., libraries
   - The yearly U.S. Statutes at Large (page 74), which contain U.S. treaties (up to 1950)
   - Blaustein and Flanz, *Constitutions of the Countries of the World*
   - *CCH Tax Treaties*
   - *Treaties in Force*
   - *Department of State Bulletin*
   - *United Nations Treaty Series*
   - Catalog of U.S. publications
   - *International Legal Materials*
   - Szladits, *Bibliography on Foreign and Comparative Law: Books and Articles in English*

   For other texts summarizing and commenting on treaties and international law generally, see checklist #8 on legal treatises, in chapter 9.

2. Legal periodical literature. There is extensive periodical literature on international law, both in general legal periodicals and in specialty periodicals devoted

   to international law exclusively. (See checklist #6, in chapter 9)

3. Looseleaf services, such as *CCH Tax Treaties,* mentioned above. (See checklist #5 on looseleaf services, in chapter 9.)

4. American case law on international law. Check the digests. (See checklist #2 on digests, in chapter 9.)

5. Case law of foreign countries. Statutory law of other countries. Go to the international law section of a large law library.

6. Annotations on international law. (See checklist #3 on annotations, in chapter 9.)

7. Legal encyclopedias. For material on international law in Am. Jur. 2d and in C.J.S., see checklist #7, in chapter 9.

8. *Martindale-Hubbell Law Dictionary*—Digest volume. Contains brief summaries of the law of many countries (page 63).

9. Phone and mail research. (See checklist #9 on contacting experts, in chapter 9.)

10. See *Restatement (Second) of Foreign Relations Law of the United States.*

11. Shepardize all treaties. Go to *Shepard's Federal Statute Citations* (page 70).

CHAPTER SUMMARY

Constitutions cover fundamental topics such as the creation of the branches of government and the identification of their powers. The federal government has a constitution. Each state also has its own constitution. The division of powers between the federal government and the state governments, as reflected in their constitutions, is called federalism. The methods of amending the constitution are stated in the constitution itself. The document contains very broad terms that are in constant need of interpretation. Two of the main approaches to interpreting the constitution are to ask what the original intent of the authors was, and to ask how it can be interpreted in the light of the needs of modern society. Techniques for finding constitutional law include checking Notes of Decisions, annotations, digests, legal treatises, legal periodical literature, looseleaf services, Words and Phrases, legal encyclopedias, LEXIS, WESTLAW, the Internet, etc. Provisions in the constitution can be shepardized to find more law.

There are three kinds of administrative agencies: executive department agencies, independent regulatory agencies, and quasi-independent regulatory agencies. Agencies serve three main functions: to carry out statutes and executive orders, to write rules and regulations, and to interpret the laws that govern the agency and to resolve disputes that arise under them. When agencies execute, create, and interpret law, they must comply with the Administrative Procedure Act. When looking for administrative law, contact the agency itself for a list of its publications. For federal regulations, check the Federal Register and the Code of Federal Regulations. Once you have a regulation, shepardize it, find the statutory authority (the enabling statute) for it, determine if the agency has done anything to affect the regulation since it was enacted, and determine whether there are annotations covering the regulation.

To find charters, ordinances, and other local laws, contact the local unit of government to determine what it publishes. Check legal periodical literature, Shepard's, digests, annotations, legal treatises, legal encyclopedias, looseleaf services, local legal newspapers, phone and mail research, the Internet, etc.

To find rules of court of state courts, check the statutory code, the publications of rules service companies, the court itself, Shepard's, digests, legal treatises, etc. To find rules of court of federal courts, check similar sources at the federal level, and also annotations, periodical literature, legal encyclopedias, online resources, etc.

Treaties are formal agreements between two or more foreign governments that require two-thirds approval by the Senate. Executive agreements do not require Senate approval. There are standard materials that contain treaties and other documents of international law, e.g., International Legal Materials. Leads to international law can be found through legal periodical literature, looseleaf services, digests, annotations, legal encyclopedias, Shepard's, Martindale-Hubbell, etc.

KEY TERMS

constitution
Supremacy Clause
federalism
administrative agency
executive department agencies
independent regulatory
   agencies

quasi-independent regulatory
   agency
quasi-legislation
quasi-judicial power
quasi-adjudication
hearing examiner
trial examiner

administrative law judge
exhausted administrative
   remedies
administrative regulation
administrative decision
Administrative Procedure Act
enabling statute

charters
ordinances
rules of court
treaty
executive agreement

COMPUTER RESEARCH

Chapter Outline

SECTION A   SURVIVAL STRATEGIES

Electronic research is becoming more and more critical in the practice of law. Although most research today is still conducted through the traditional paper products of pamphlets, hardcover volumes, and periodicals, the alternative of **CALR** (computer-assisted legal research) is becoming increasingly common. CALR is conducted (a) **online** (being connected to a host computer system or information service, usually through normal telephone lines) or (b) on **CD-ROM** (compact disc read-only memory, an information storage system that uses optical technology or laser beams to store and allow you to read information without needing a telephone or other connection to another system or service; see page 33).

Using a CALR program for the first time can create anxiety. The experience is somewhat like learning to drive a car for the first time. Having a grounding in the basics and knowing where to get help can be a great benefit. The computer survival techniques presented in Exhibit 13.1 apply to any computer program that you are learning for the first time, including CALR.

13.1 .... Computer Survival Strategies

Exhibit

Stage I: Identify Your "Help" Resources

- Line up in-house support. Find out who in the office already knows how to use the program. Ask them if they would be willing to answer your questions about it. If possible, they should be people other than—or in addition to—your supervisor.
- Ask if the program you will be using has an 800 number that you can use for assistance. Free phone service may be available for a period of time after the office purchases the program or equipment. If not, find out if the office has purchased a service agreement that allows unlimited calls during the period of the agreement.
- Ask if the program has an **online tutorial** that explains the basics. If so, ask someone to start the tutorial for you.
- Ask if the program has a **HELP key** that can be used while you are running the program. If so, ask how to use it.
- Find the manual for the program (called the **documentation**). Turn to the index, if one exists. Select some familiar terms in the index, such as underlining and capitalization. Turn to the pages for such items and try to follow the instructions provided for them. In short, start with "easy" tasks.
- Find out if the supermarket-style bookstores in your area sell "how-to" books on the program you will be using in the office. Scores of such books exist for many of the most popular word processing, spreadsheet, and database programs. Buy one of these books and study it on your own.
- Start a computer notebook in which you write definitions of new terms, steps to follow for certain tasks, steps you took just before you seemed to make a mis-

take, questions that you want to ask someone later, etc.
- Expect to learn a new vocabulary. (*Boot*, for example, has nothing to do with what goes on your foot.)

Stage II: Learn the Big Seven Tasks

Learn the seven essential tasks that apply to most programs:
- How to turn on the computer, call up or **load** the program, and start using it
- How to create a new document or file with the program
- How to save a document or file
- How to retrieve a document or file that was created and saved earlier
- How to make a copy of the document or file
- How to turn on the printer and print a document or file
- How to exit from the program and turn the computer off without losing data

Stage III: Take the Initiative

- Find out if your local paralegal association is offering a seminar on computer use. Attend it. If none is planned, call the president of the association and suggest that one be offered.
- Read the local bar association journals to find out what computer seminars are offered by the bar or by **CLE** (continuing legal education) groups. Attend some that are relevant to your job.
- Photocopy a chapter from the computer manual (documentation) at the office. Take the chapter home and read it over the weekend.
- Ask librarians in your area how you can find magazine reviews of the program that you use. Read these reviews.

13.1 ································· Computer Survival Strategies—continued

Exhibit

- Find out if there is a **users group** in your area that meets every month to discuss the program, such as a WordPerfect Users Group. Attend the meetings of this group.
- Find out if there is a **listserv** on the Internet where you can read comments, questions, and answers (called *postings*) about the program from people who use it all over the world. Spend a few minutes each day at work or at home reading these postings. Once

you are comfortable with the listserv, ask your own questions about the program and watch for answers from across town, another city, or another continent.
- Organize a "specialty section" of your paralegal association that consists of paralegals who use the program. Members of this section would meet periodically to learn from each other and to discuss common problems with the program.

SECTION B   WESTLAW AND LEXIS

The major CALR systems are **WESTLAW** and **LEXIS.**

WESTLAW® by the West Group

WESTLAW contains a great deal of material. Here are some examples: federal court opinions; state court opinions; *United States Code;* state statutes; the *Code of Federal Regulations;* administrative decisions; legal treatises published by West, Commerce Clearing House, Bureau of National Affairs, and other publishers; legal periodical literature; a *West's Legal Directory* containing the addresses of attorneys throughout the United States; annotations in A.L.R.3d, A.L.R.4th, A.L.R.5th, and A.L.R. Fed.; *American Jurisprudence 2d,* a national legal encyclopedia; nonlegal data from Dow Jones and DIALOG. (DIALOG provides access to information on business, energy, biotechnology, engineering, electronics, medicine, the social sciences and humanities, current news, etc.) You can check the current validity of cases and statutes by using Insta-Cite, QuickCite, Shepard's Preview, and Shepard's online—without leaving the computer. The newest online citator of WESTLAW is KeyCite, which allows you to check the validity of cases. There are also special databases in many areas, such as international law, professional responsibility (ethics), taxation, securities, medicine, etc. Other special databases that can be of unique value to litigators contain the names and addresses of experts in the fields of science, engineering, economics, etc. There are also bankruptcy records, information on deeds and other data recorded in counties throughout the country, abstracts of tax records, etc. Each day more material is added to WESTLAW.

LEXIS® by Reed Elsevier

LEXIS is also a massive source of online data. Examples include federal and state court opinions; federal and state statutes; *Code of Federal Regulations;* administrative decisions; legal treatises; *Martindale-Hubbell Law Directory;* annotations in A.L.R.2d, A.L.R.3d, A.L.R.4th, A.L.R.5th, A.L.R. Fed., and in *Lawyers' Edition 2d;* legal periodical literature; special libraries on taxation, labor law, insurance, and international law; public records such as deed transfers; treatises published by Commerce Clearing House and the Bureau of National Affairs; *American Jurisprudence 2d,* a national legal encyclopedia; nonlegal databases through NEXIS covering medicine, patents, current news, etc.; validation data through Shepard's and Auto-Cite, etc. (Auto-Cite is an online citator that provides parallel citations, the history of litigation involved in an opinion, references to other opinions that affect the validity of the opinion you are checking, etc.) As with WESTLAW, materials are added to LEXIS regularly.

Terminal using
WESTLAW

Terminal using LEXIS

statutory &
case law

Using WESTLAW and LEXIS

Both WESTLAW and LEXIS provide vastly more information than the text of cases, statutes, regulations, and treaties. Examples:

- Information on the status of pending suits in federal, state, and local courts
- Records of judgments in bankruptcy courts, other federal courts, state courts, county courts, and other local courts
- Statistics on jury awards for specific kinds of injuries
- Mechanic's lien filings
- Identification of major property holdings of particular persons and businesses (e.g., real estate, stock, business equipment)
- UCC (Uniform Commercial Code) filings
- Chain-of-title data
- Addresses of persons and businesses
- Financial information on particular companies (e.g., sales information, stock market prices on designated days)
- Personnel information on particular companies (e.g., names of officers and directors)
- Information on proposed mergers and acquisitions
- Medical research (e.g., reports on whether carpal tunnel syndrome is hereditary)
- News stories on particular topics or persons in newspapers and other media throughout the world
- Date of birth and date of death of particular individuals
- Social science and humanities information (e.g., articles on fetal tissue transplants, family background of felons in a particular state, linguistics, political science)

Let's take a closer look at some of the legal materials that are available via CALR. Assume that you are working on a case involving a client who developed cancer after smoking for many years. You want to know if the client can bring a product liability claim against the tobacco company. One of the first things you need to decide is whether you want to search for cases, statutes, regulations, secondary sources, etc. Assume that you want to find court cases written by any state court in your state. You then need to go to the database in WESTLAW[1] or LEXIS that contains such cases. Once there, the next step is to formulate a question—called a **search query**—for the computer. The query would ask the computer to find cases involving product liability and cigarettes.

There are two ways to formulate queries in WESTLAW and LEXIS. You can use either **Boolean**[2] language or natural (associative) language. Boolean searches are more traditional and more commonly used, so we will examine them first.

Here is an example of a query that could be used in WESTLAW for our tobacco case:

```
cigar! tobacco smok! /p product strict! /5 liab!
```

Later we will examine the meaning of such queries and how to write them. For now, we simply want to give you an overview of what is available.

The screen in Exhibit 13.2 shows a recent case *(Forster v. R.J. Reynolds Tobacco Co.)* that would be retrieved by WESTLAW if you used the above query. It assumed that you asked WESTLAW for Minnesota cases (found in its database, MN-CS). After looking at a large number of such cases, you might want to ask the computer to give you a list of citations of every case that fits your query. The screen in Exhibit 13.3 presents such a list. (It includes the *Forster* case as well as others that fit the query.) If you have a printer connected to your computer, you can ask for a printout of the data on any of these screens.

---

1. The assistance of Laura C. Mickelson is gratefully acknowledged for the material on WESTLAW.
2. A Boolean search is one that allows words to be specifically included or excluded through logical operators such as AND, OR, and NOT.

Exhibit

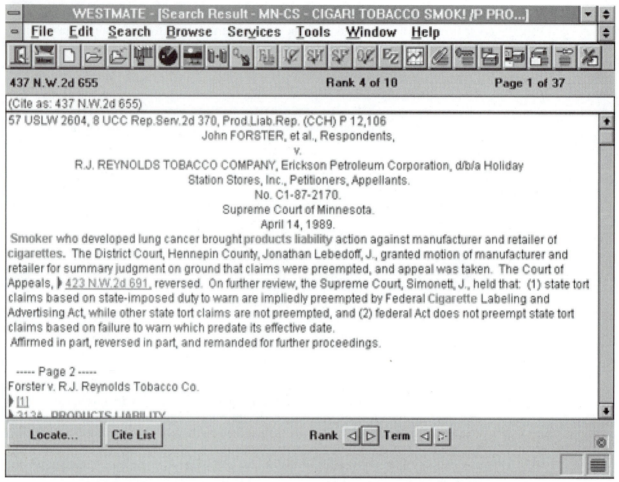

Case retrieved by WESTLAW, with search words highlighted. Note that at the top of the screen you find the database (MN-CS) and the query used.

Almost every citation to a case that you obtain through CALR can be taken to a traditional law library where you can read the case in a reporter volume. Of course, you can also read the case on the computer screen, or you can read a printout of the case, but it is usually cheaper to read material in a library volume than to read it online. The computer is excellent for searching, but not necessarily for extensive reading.

The *Forster* case was decided in 1989. Suppose that you wanted to know what has happened to the case since 1989. Has it been overruled? Has it been cited by other courts? WESTLAW has five different updating or validation services that can give you further information about cases like *Forster.* They are Insta-Cite, Shepard's PreView, Shepard's Citations (see Exhibit 13.4), and QuickCite, which allows you to update Shepard's PreView and Shepard's Citations. The most recent updating or validation service on WESTLAW is **KeyCite,** which is more comprehensive than Shepard's (see Exhibit 13.5).

In litigation, there is often a need to find experts who may be able to provide consultation and possibly deposition or trial testimony.[3] One of the specialized searches that can be performed by computer is a search for such experts. Exhibit 13.6 presents an example of the results of this kind of search from the Forensic Services Directory (FSD) database in WESTLAW.

LEXIS works in a similar way, with many of the same features. Suppose, for example, that you wanted cases in which a juror concealed his or her bias. You would

---

3. See Runde, *Computer Assisted Legal Research,* 10 Facts and Findings 13 (NALA, July/August 1983).

13.3

Exhibit

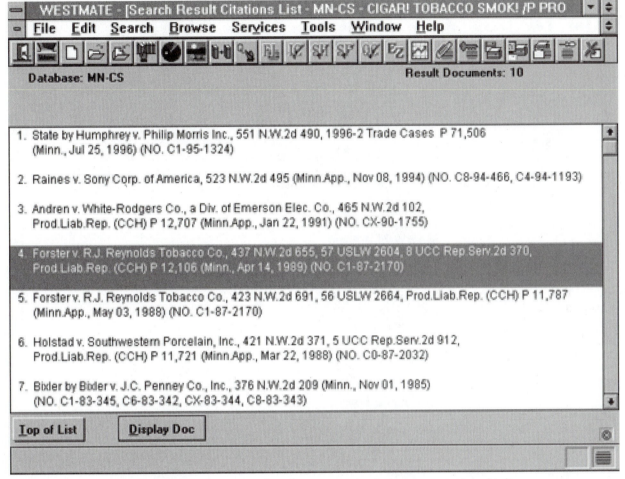

List of cases retrieved by WESTLAW. The case we have been examining is document no. 4 on this list.

instruct LEXIS to find cases in which the word *bias* appears in proximity to the words *juror* and *conceal* or *concealed*. See Exhibit 13.7.

Once you have examined a number of these cases, you can ask the service to display a list of citations of all the cases discovered when LEXIS fulfilled your search request. See Exhibit 13.8.

SECTION C   FORMULATING A SEARCH QUERY

We turn now to one of the critical skills in using WESTLAW and LEXIS: formulating a research question or *query*. Our examination of this skill will explore the following topics:

(a) Universal character (*) and root expander (!) for WESTLAW and LEXIS
(b) WESTLAW queries:

- The OR connector
- The AND connector (&)
- The sentence connector (/s)
- The paragraph connector (/p)
- The BUT NOT connector (%)
- The numerical connector (/n)
- Phrase searching (" ")

13.4

Exhibit

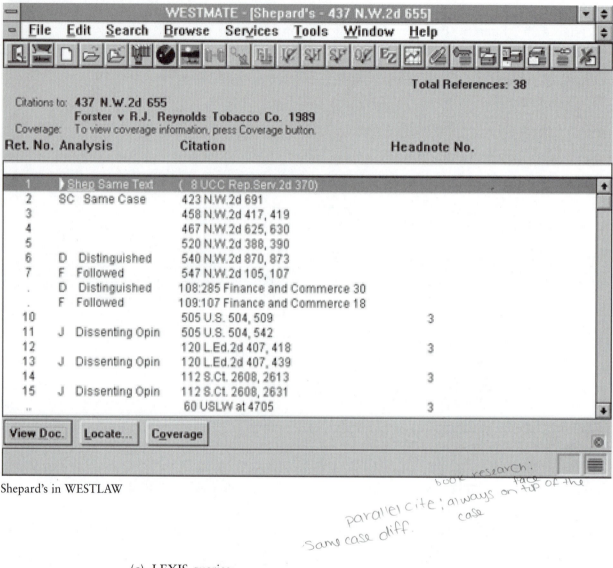

Shepard's in WESTLAW

[handwritten notes:] book research: parallel cite; always on top of the face of the case / same case diff.

    (c) LEXIS queries:

- The OR connector
- The AND connector
- The sentence connector (/s)
- The paragraph connector (/p)
- The numerical connector (w/n)
- The AND NOT connector
- Phrase searching

    (d) Field searches:

- Title search
- Synopsis search
- Topic search
- Digest search
- Judge search

    (e) WIN and Freestyle

    (f) Find and read

13.5

Exhibit

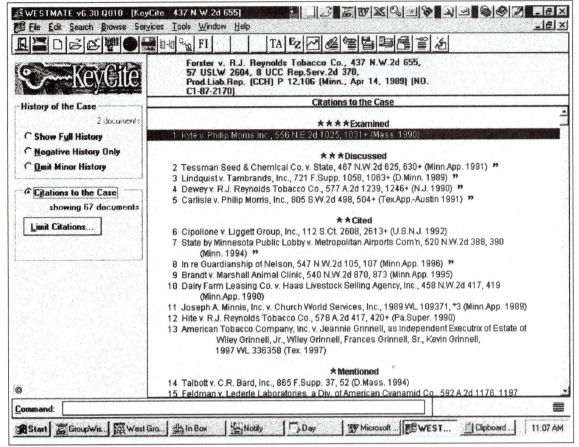

KeyCite on WESTLAW. Note the number of stars next to the categories of citing cases. Four stars indicate that a citing case examined the *Forster* case with some thoroughness. Two or three stars indicate a less thorough treatment of the *Forster* case by the citing cases. One star indicates that the *Forster* case was mentioned but was not discussed by the citing cases.

(a) Universal Character (*) and Root Expander (!) for WESTLAW and LEXIS

An important technique in the formulation of queries in either WESTLAW or LEXIS is the proper use of the asterisk (*) as a **universal character,** and the exclamation mark (!) as a **root expander.** The discussion below of these and other query-formulation techniques will cover searches for cases, although the techniques are generally applicable when searching any kind of document available in the databases and files of WESTLAW and LEXIS.

The Universal Character (*) Suppose that you asked the computer to find cases that contained the following word anywhere in the case:

```
marijuana
```

This search will not find a case that spelled the word *marihuana*. If, however, you changed your query to:

```
mari*uana
```

13.6

Exhibit

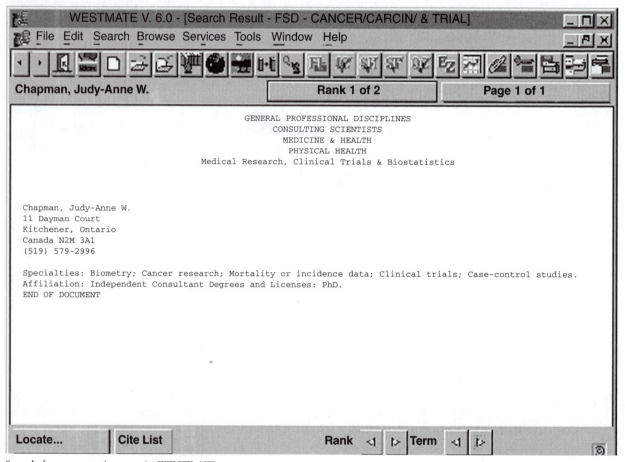

Search for expert witnesses in WESTLAW

you would pick up cases under both spellings. The asterisk stands for any character or letter. Hence the above search would also pick up cases that contain the words *maribuana*, *marituana*, or *marizuana*—if such words exist in any of the cases in the database or file you are searching. Because the asterisk stands for any character, it is called the universal character. It is most commonly used when searching for cases that contain a proper name you are having trouble spelling. If, for example, you were looking for cases decided by a judge whose name is spelled *Falen* or *Falon*, you can enter the query as:

fal*n

You are not limited to one universal character per word. For example, the following search:

int**state

will give you cases containing the word *interstate* and cases containing the word *intrastate*. Similarly, the query:

s****holder

will give you cases containing the word *stockholder*, cases containing the word *stakeholder*, and cases containing the word *shareholder*.

13.7

Exhibit

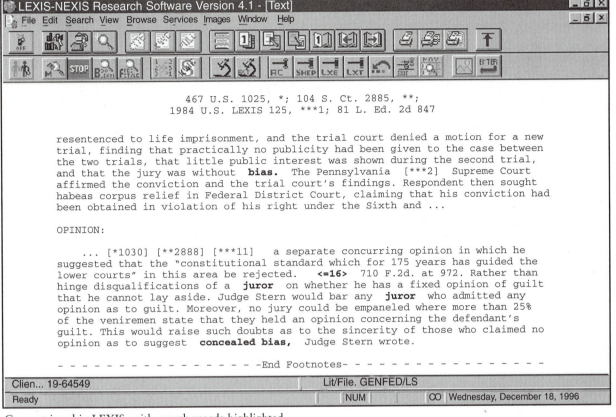

Case retrieved in LEXIS, with search words highlighted

Root Expander (!) Next we consider the exclamation mark (!) as a root expander. When this mark is added to the root of a word, it acts as a substitute for one or more characters or letters. If your query is:

litig!

you will find cases containing one or more of the following words: litig, litigable, litigate, litigated, litigating, litigation, litigator, litigious, litigiousness. The root expander is quite powerful and can be overused. The query:

tax!

will lead you to cases containing any one or more of the following words: tax, taxability, taxable, taxation, taxational, taxes, taxi, tax-deductible, tax-exempt, tax-free, taxicab, taxidermy, taxidermist, taxied, taximeter, taximetrics, taxing, taxis, taxiway, taxol, taxon, taxonomist, taxonomy, taxpayer, taxy, taxying. This will undoubtedly lead to cases that are beyond the scope of your research problem.

Plurals It is not necessary to use universal characters or the root expander to obtain the plural of a word. The query:

guest

will give you cases containing the word *guest* and cases containing the word *guests*. The query *memorandum* will give you cases containing the word *memoranda* and

Exhibit

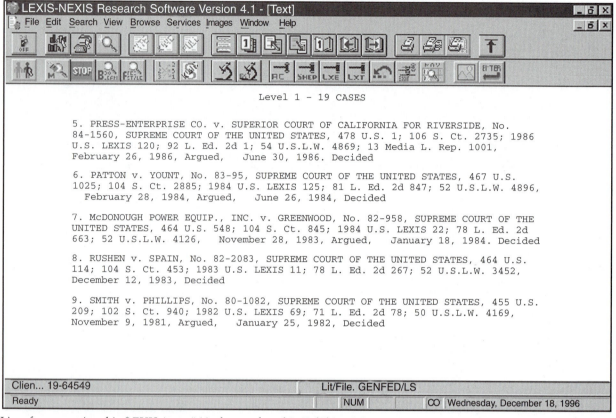

List of cases retrieved in LEXIS (case #6 is the one found in Exhibit 13.7)

those containing the word *memorandums.* The same is true for other irregular plurals. The query *child* will give you cases containing the word *child* as well as those containing the word *children.* Entering the singular form of a word will automatically also search the plural form of that word.

Next we will focus on special guidelines for formulating WESTLAW queries and LEXIS queries.

(b) WESTLAW Queries

When formulating a query in WESTLAW (or in LEXIS, as we will see in a moment), **connectors** can be used to show the relationship between the words in the query. Connectors link query words together to give the query more direction. Some of the main connectors in WESTLAW are:

- The OR connector
- The AND connector (&)
- The sentence connector (/s)
- The paragraph connector (/p)
- The BUT NOT connector (%)
- The numerical connector (/n)

After explaining how to use each of these connectors, we will examine how to search for phrases on WESTLAW through the use of quotation marks (" ") in queries.

The OR Connector   The simplest connector in WESTLAW is OR, which can be expressed by typing the word *or* between two words, or by leaving a blank space between the words. This connector instructs WESTLAW to treat the two words as alternatives and to find cases that contain either or both words. Hence, the query:

```
doctor or physician
```

or the query:

```
doctor physician
```

will find the following cases:

- A case that contains both the word *doctor* and the word *physician*[4]
- A case that contains the word *doctor,* but not the word *physician*
- A case that contains the word *physician,* but not the word *doctor*

Similarly, the query:

```
attorney or lawyer or counsel
```

or the query:

```
attorney lawyer counsel
```

will find the following cases:

- A case that contains all three words: *attorney* and *lawyer* and *counsel*
- A case that contains the word *attorney* but not the words *lawyer* or *counsel*
- A case that contains the words *attorney* and *lawyer* but not the word *counsel*
- A case that contains the words *attorney* and *counsel* but not the word *lawyer*
- A case that contains the word *lawyer* but not the words *attorney* or *counsel*
- A case that contains the words *lawyer* and *attorney* but not the word *counsel*
- A case that contains the words *lawyer* and *counsel* but not the word *attorney*
- A case that contains the word *counsel* but not the words *attorney* or *lawyer*
- A case that contains the words *counsel* and *lawyer* but not the word *attorney*
- A case that contains the words *counsel* and *attorney* but not the word *lawyer*

The AND Connector (&) When you use the & connector in your WESTLAW query, you are asking WESTLAW to find cases that contain every word joined by &. The query:

```
paralegal & fee
```

will find cases in which the word *paralegal* and the word *fee* are found anywhere in the case, no matter how close or far apart they appear in the case. The query will not find cases containing only one of these words.[5]

The Sentence Connector (/s) The sentence connector (/s) requires the search words to appear in the same sentence in the case.[6] The query:

```
paralegal /s termin!
```

will find cases in which the word *paralegal* is found in the same sentence as the word *terminable* or *terminal* or *terminate* or *terminating* or *termination* or *terminator* or *terminology* or *terminus.* Here are examples of two sentences from two different cases that this query would retrieve:

---

4. In all of these examples, remember that the service will retrieve cases containing these words and their plurals, such as physician, physicians; doctor, doctors.

5. It is also possible to write this query as *paralegal and fee* (rather than use the ampersand—&), but this is not recommended.

6. The sentence connector (/s) and the paragraph connector (/p) are referred to as the *grammatical connectors.*

```
Case #1:
"The paralegal did not receive notice of the allegation
until the letter of termination arrived the next day."
```

```
Case #2:
"The patient's terminal condition was negligently diag-
nosed in a report obtained by the paralegal of the oppos-
ing counsel."7
```

The Paragraph Connector (/p) The paragraph connector (/p) requires the search words to appear in the same paragraph in the case. The query:

```
                       paralegal /p certif!
```

will find cases in which the word *paralegal* is found in the same paragraph as the word *certifiable* or *certificate* or *certified* or *certification* or *certifier* or *certify* or *certifying*.

The BUT NOT Connector (%) The BUT NOT connector (%) excludes everything that follows the percentage mark, %. The query:

```
                        paralegal % fee
```

or

```
                      paralegal but not fee
```

will find every case in which the word *paralegal* appears, except for those cases in which the word *fee* plus the word *paralegal* appear. Perhaps you are looking for every case that mentions the word *paralegal* other than those involving paralegal fees or attorney fees.

The Numerical Connector (/n) The numerical connector (/n)[8] requires search words to appear within a specified number[9] of words of each other in the case. The query:

```
                     paralegal /5 license*
```

will retrieve any case in which the word *paralegal* appears within five words of the word *license,* or within five words of the word *licensed.* Here is an example of a line from a case that this query would retrieve:

```
    ". . . the paralegal had no license from the state."
```

A case with the following line, however, would *not* be retrieved by this query because there are more than five words between the search words of the query:

```
   ". . . paralegals as well as notaries and process servers
                      are not licensed."
```

Phrase Searching (" ") Thus far, our examples of queries have involved searches for individual words in cases. Suppose, however, that you wanted to search for phrases such as drug addict, habeas corpus, or legal assistant. If your query was:

```
                        legal assistant
```

7. Note that in case #2, the order in which the search terms appear in the sentence is not the order of the words in the query itself. If you want to limit the search to cases that contain the search words in the sentence in the order presented in the query, you would phrase the query as follows: paralegal +s termin!
8. The numerical connector can also be expressed as w/n. For example: paralegal w/5 fee.
9. Up to 255.

WESTLAW would interpret the space between these two words to mean OR. Hence, it will retrieve

- Any case in which both the word *legal* and the word *assistant* appear
- Any case in which the word *legal* appears but the word *assistant* does not appear
- Any case in which the word *assistant* appears but the word *legal* does not appear

This could lead to thousands of cases, the vast majority of which would have nothing to do with legal assistants.[10] To avoid this problem, we need a way to tell WESTLAW not to interpret the space between the search words to mean OR. This is done by placing quotation marks around any phrase (or group of words) that you want WESTLAW to search as a unit. Hence our query should read:

```
"legal assistant"
```

Later we will see that LEXIS does *not* require quotation marks when conducting a phrase search, because LEXIS does not interpret every space as an OR.

(c) LEXIS Queries

When using LEXIS, connectors are also used in formulating a query. Although there are many similarities between the connectors in WESTLAW and in LEXIS, there are also differences. Some of the main connectors in LEXIS are:

- The OR connector
- The AND connector
- The sentence connector (/s)
- The paragraph connector (/p)
- The numerical connector (w/n)
- The AND NOT connector

After examining these connectors, we need to compare how to search for phrases in LEXIS and in WESTLAW.

The OR Connector The OR connector tells LEXIS to treat the two words joined by OR as alternatives. The query:

```
merger or acquisition
```

will find the following cases:

- A case that contains both the word *merger* and the word *acquisition*
- A case that contains the word *merger* but not the word *acquisition*
- A case that contains the word *acquisition* but not the word *merger*

Hence the OR connector in LEXIS is similar to the OR connector in WESTLAW, except that LEXIS does *not* interpret a space between two words as an OR.

The AND Connector When you use the AND connector in your LEXIS query, you are asking LEXIS to find cases that contain every word joined by AND, no matter how close or far apart they appear in the case. The query:

```
paralegal and fee
```

will find cases in which the word *paralegal* and the word *fee* appear. The query will not find cases containing only one of these words. (In WESTLAW, the preferred way to achieve this result is by using the & connector.)

---

10. WESTLAW will probably flash a message on the screen warning you that your search query may retrieve a large number of cases and suggesting that you rephrase your query to make it narrower.

The Sentence Connector (/s) The sentence connector (/s) requires the search words to appear in the same sentence in the case. The query:

```
boston /s strangler
```

will find cases in which the word *boston* is found in the same sentence as the word *strangler.*

The Paragraph Connector (/p) The paragraph connector (/p) requires the search words to appear in the same paragraph in the case. The query:

```
murder /p drug
```

will find cases in which the word *murder* is found in the same paragraph as the word *drug.*

The Numerical Connector (w/n) The numerical connector (w/n) or (/n) of LEXIS requires search words to appear within a designated number of words of each other in the case. The query:

```
paralegal w/5 license
```

will retrieve any case in which the word *paralegal* appears within five words of the word *license.*[11]

The AND NOT Connector The AND NOT connector in a LEXIS query excludes everything that follows *and not.* The query:

```
paralegal and not fee
```

will find every case in which the word *paralegal* appears, except for those cases in which the word *fee* plus the word *paralegal* appear.[12]

Phrase Searching Recall that phrase searching in WESTLAW required the use of quotation marks around any phrase, because WESTLAW interprets spaces between words to mean OR. This is *not* so in LEXIS, because LEXIS does not equate spaces with ORs. Hence to search for a phrase in LEXIS, you do not have to use quotation marks around the phrase. Simply state the phrase. The query:

```
legal assistant
```

will not lead you to any cases in which the word *legal* appeared but not the word *assistant,* and vice versa.

Assignment 13.1

Below you will find five separate queries. If they were used in either WESTLAW or LEXIS, what words in the documents would they find?

(a) para!
(b) assign!
(c) crim!
(d) legis!
(e) e****e

---

11. The number (n) of words that can be used as the numerical connector in LEXIS is any number up to 255. But LEXIS does not count words such as *the, be,* and *to.* LEXIS considers them "noise words." The numerical connector in WESTLAW also goes up to 255. See footnote 9. But WESTLAW counts every word. In the LEXIS numerical query, if you want the words in the case to appear in the order in which the words are listed in the query, use the pre/n connector. For example: paralegal pre/5 license. See also footnote 7.
12. Another way to phrase this query is: paralegal but not fee. The latter phrasing would make this LEXIS connector the same as the connector in WESTLAW that serves this function.

Assignment 13.2

On page 249, the following query was given as an example of a WESTLAW query:

```
cigar! tobacco smok! /p product strict! /5 liab!
```

Explain this query. State what the symbols mean. What is the query designed to find? Assume that you are using the query to find cases in one of the databases of WESTLAW.

Assignment 13.3

You are looking for cases in which a paralegal is charged with the unauthorized practice of law.

(a) Write a query for WESTLAW.
(b) Write a query for LEXIS.

Assignment 13.4

You are looking for cases in which a law firm illegally failed to pay overtime compensation to its paralegals.

(a) Write a query for WESTLAW.
(b) Write a query for LEXIS.

Assignment 13.5

You would like to know what the courts in your state have said about paralegals.

(a) Write several queries for WESTLAW.
(b) Write several queries for LEXIS.

(d) Field Searches

In addition to full text searches, both WESTLAW and LEXIS allow you to conduct searches that are limited to information found in certain parts of cases or other documents. On LEXIS, these parts are called **segments.** The segments of cases are: name, court, writtenby, dissentby, counsel, number, etc. On WESTLAW, these parts are called **fields.** The fields of cases are: title, synopsis, topic, digest, judge, etc. Here is a fuller explanation and some examples of field searches on WESTLAW.

Field Searches on WESTLAW
Title (abbreviated *ti*) The title field contains only the names of the parties to a case. Use this field to retrieve a case if you know the case name. The computer will quickly retrieve your case and display it so you can either read it online or print it to read at a later time. Suppose, for example, that the title of the case you wanted to read was *Pennzoil v. Texaco.*

Once you select the database you want, a title field search for this case would be as follows:

```
ti(pennzoil & texaco)
```

Synopsis (abbreviated *sy*) The synopsis field contains a summary of the case prepared by the editorial staff of WESTLAW. This summary includes the facts presented by the case, the holding of the lower court, the issues on appeal, and the resolution of those issues. The names of majority, concurring, and dissenting judges are also included in the synopsis field. Because general legal concepts are used to describe the issues before the court, this is a good field in which to run a conceptual search. A conceptual search is helpful for finding cases that fall into a legal category or classification, such as domicile, adverse possession, or product liability. The digest field (to be considered below) also allows you to conduct a search via concepts. Hence it is often worthwhile to combine the synopsis and digest fields in a single search. For example:

```
sy,di("product liability")
```

Topic (abbreviated *to*) Each small-paragraph summary in the West digests (page 53) is assigned a topic classification, such as criminal law, bankruptcy, and divorce. West has tens of thousands of cases summarized under these topics. If you already know a topic classification, you can conduct a WESTLAW search that is limited to this topic field. For example:

```
to(criminal)
to(bankruptcy)
to(divorce)
to("product liability")
```

Digest (abbreviated *di*) In addition to a topic classification, every small-paragraph case summary

in a West digest contains the name or title of the case, the name of the court that decided it, the citation of the case, and the rest of the summary itself, known as a headnote (page 57). All of this information (topic, title, court, citation, headnote) is contained within what is called the digest field of WESTLAW. Here is an example of a search in this field:

```
di(paralegal)
```

This search will find every case that has the word *paralegal* anywhere in a small-paragraph case summary of a West digest. To make sure that your search finds cases mentioning legal assistants as well as those mentioning paralegals, the search would be:

```
di(paralegal "legal assistant")
```

As indicated above, it is often wise to combine searches in the digest and synopsis fields.

Judge (abbreviated *ju*) If you wanted to find cases written by a particular judge, e.g., Justice William Brennan, you could conduct a search in the judge field:

```
ju(brennan)
```

When run in the database containing opinions of the United States Supreme Court (sct), this search will give you every majority opinion written by Justice Brennan.

(e) WIN and Freestyle

Thus far we have been covering Boolean searches in which you broaden or narrow your search query by using connectors such as AND, OR, and NOT. There is now a simpler method. WESTLAW and LEXIS use different terms to describe this alternative:

WESTLAW: **WIN** (WESTLAW Is Natural), a "natural language" method of writing a search query.

LEXIS: **Freestyle**, a "plain English" method of writing a search query.

Under both methods, you simply write out a question using everyday language. For example, instead of writing:

```
cigar! tobacco smok! /p product strict! /5 liab!
```

you would write:

```
Can strict product liability be imposed for harm caused by
smoking cigarettes?
```

Both WESTLAW and LEXIS have a built-in thesaurus that will allow you to select synonyms and closely related words if the ones you used are not productive.

This kind of search is not a substitute for a Boolean search. Natural or plain English searches work best when you are searching general issues at the beginning of your research. Eventually, you may need to refine your search by switching to a search that uses Boolean language.[13]

(f) Find and Read

Suppose that you already have the citation of a case or other document, and you simply want to read it. But you are not in a traditional law library that has the bound volumes you need. If you have access to WESTLAW or LEXIS, there is a relatively easy way to retrieve what you want. On WESTLAW, use the *find* command (abbreviated *fi*). On LEXIS, use the *lexstat* command (abbreviated *lxt*) when you are looking for a statute and the *lexsee* command (abbreviated *lxe*) when you are looking for cases or any other documents available through this route.

Here are four examples that use the *find* command of WESTLAW to retrieve documents in the *Supreme Court Reporter* (sct), the *United States Code Annotated* (usca), the *Code of Federal Regulations* (cfr), and the *Federal Register* (fr). All of these examples assume that you already know the volume, page, and section numbers indicated. You simply want to find these documents and read them on your computer screen.

```
fi 97 sct 451
fi 18 usca 1968
fi 9 cfr 11.24
fi 52 fr 22391
```

The first example below uses the *lexstat* command of LEXIS to locate a statute in *United States Code Service* (uscs), and the next three examples use the *lexsee* command to locate material in *Columbia Law Review* (colum l rev), *American Law Reports, Federal* (alrfed), and an IRS Revenue Ruling (rev rul). Again, all of these examples assume that you already know the volume, page, and section numbers indicated.

```
lxt 11 uscs 101
lxe 87 colum l rev 1137
lxe 44 alrfed 148
lxe rev rul 88-2
```

SECTION D   INTERNET

The **Internet** is one of the most exciting developments in the history of computers. Approximately 40 million people around the world can and do use this enormously flexible communication medium. That figure is expected to grow to 200 million Internet users by the year 1999.[14] The Internet is a massive collection of networks—a network of networks. A **network** is two or more computers (and other devices) that are connected by telephone lines, fiber optic cables, satellites, or other systems in order to share messages, other data, software, and hardware. It isn't difficult to envision how the Internet works because "it parallels, to some extent, how our worldwide, and even national telephone system works. When you place a call to someone in the United States outside your local phone company's service area, you dial a single number (with an area code), and the phone rings at the other end. You do not need to know that you're really using the systems of several phone companies, all of whom have agreed with one another how they're going to bill for connections so that they can all go through unimpeded by differences in each system. The Internet works in much the same way. All of the individuals running the various networks that are connected to it have agreed with one another on a common set of specifications, or **protocols,** in order for information to flow from one network to another."[15] A protocol is a set of standards that allows computers to communicate with each other.

---

13. Brent Roper, *Using Computers in the Law 2d* 302 (1996).
14. *American Civil Liberties Union v. Reno*, 929 F. Supp. 824 (E.D. Pa. 1996).
15. Will Sadler, *Introduction to the Internet*, 65 Bar Examiner 45, 46 (May 1995).

The Internet was developed in the 1960s by the U.S. Department of Defense to link a handful of computers in the event of a nuclear attack. The idea was to design a system that would allow communication over a number of different routes between linked computers. Thus, a message sent from a computer in Washington, D.C., to a computer in Palo Alto, California, might first be sent to a computer in Philadelphia, and then be forwarded to a computer in Pittsburgh, and then to Chicago, Denver, and Salt Lake City, before finally reaching Palo Alto. If the message could not travel along that path (because of military attack, simple technical malfunction, or other reason), the message would automatically (without human intervention or even knowledge) be rerouted, perhaps, from Washington, D.C., to Richmond, and then to Atlanta, New Orleans, Dallas, Albuquerque, Los Angeles, and finally to Palo Alto. This type of transmission and rerouting would likely occur in a matter of seconds.[16]

When the government no longer needed this link, it, in effect, turned the system over to the public. Hence no single entity—academic, corporate, governmental, or nonprofit—administers the Internet. It exists and functions because hundreds of thousands of separate operators of computers and computer networks independently decided to use common data transfer protocols to exchange communications and information with other computers (which in turn exchange communications and information with still other computers). There is no centralized storage location, control point, or communications channel for the Internet, and it would not be technically feasible for a single entity to control all of the information conveyed on the Internet.[17]

Some have called the Internet the most important new communication medium in decades. "The Internet attracts educational institutions doing research, commercial organizations advertising their products electronically, sports networks, artists, musicians, financial analysts, television networks, lawyers, and . . . governments." Small wonder that many use the metaphor "information superhighway" to describe the Internet.[18]

Why are attorneys interested in the Internet? First of all, many of their clients are on the Internet. Very few large businesses today do not have an Internet address where consumers can find out about their products and organizational structure. Second, the Internet is an additional way for attorneys to communicate with each other. Third, the Internet provides a great deal of legal, financial, and other information for relatively little cost. Much of this data is also available for a fee from the major commercial online services such as WESTLAW and LEXIS. Neither of these giants, however, is likely to go out of business soon because of competition from the Internet. WESTLAW and LEXIS spend a great deal of editorial time and resources compiling and ensuring the accuracy of the data they make available. No such control mechanisms exist for the even larger quantity of data found on the Internet. Internet reliability is increasing, but it has not reached the stage where it is ready to satisfy the legal community's need for online information to the exclusion of the traditional providers.

To use the Internet, you need a computer, a modem, a regular telephone line, and an Internet account through an access or service provider.[19] Examples of commercial or fee-based providers are America Online, CompuServe, Microsoft Network, and Prodigy. If you are part of a university, you may be able to gain access to the Internet through the university's direct connection.

In addition to using the national commercial online services, individuals can also access the Internet using some (but not all) of the thousands of local dial-in computer services, often called **bulletin board systems** or "BBSs." Individuals, nonprofit organizations, advocacy groups, and businesses can offer their own dial-in computer "bulletin board" service where friends, members, subscribers, or customers can exchange ideas and information. BBSs range from single computers with only one telephone line into the computer (allowing only one user at a time), to single computers with many telephone lines into the computer (allowing multiple simultaneous users), to multiple

16. *American Civil Liberties Union v. Reno,* 929 F. Supp. at 832.
17. *Id.* at 832.
18. Sadler, *Introduction to the Internet,* 65 Bar Examiner at 45.
19. Roper, *Using Computers in the Law 2d,* 313.

linked computers each servicing multiple dial-in telephone lines (allowing multiple simultaneous users). Some (but not all) of these BBSs offer direct or indirect links to the Internet. Some BBSs charge users a nominal fee for access, whereas many others are free to individual users.[20]

The **World Wide Web** is a tool that allows you to navigate locations on the Internet that are often linked by **hypertext.** Hypertext is a method of displaying and linking information located in different places in the same document or in different documents. On a page on the World Wide Web, you will see words or pictures that are highlighted, perhaps by being in a different color. When you click on the words or picture, you are sent to another location on the Internet. Suppose, for example, you are on the World Wide Web site of the National Federation of Paralegal Associations (NFPA). One of the pages on this site is the "Legal Resources" page. See Exhibit 13.9. Note the fifteen resources available on this page. By clicking any of these fifteen options, you will be sent to over 1,000 other Web sites on the Internet that will help you do factual and legal research. Do you want information on federal statutes? Click the option called "Federal Laws, Codes, Statutes" at the top of the second column. Do you want information about the Federal Trade Commission? Click the option called "Federal Agencies and Departments" at the top of the first column. A great many other Internet sites operate in the same way to lead you to a vast quantity of legal materials. Some sites are **search engines** that operate as indexes and points of entry to any topic on the Internet.

13.9

Exhibit
Information Options on the World Wide Web Site of the NFPA

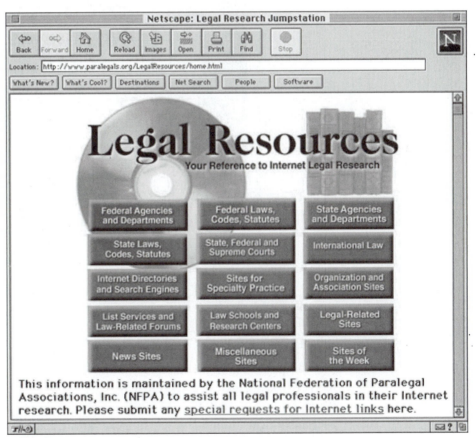

http://www.paralegals.org
Web site of the National Federation of Paralegal Associations (NFPA)

---

20. *American Civil Liberties Union v. Reno,* 929 F. Supp. at 833–34.

Legal Research on the Internet

Here are some Internet addresses that are relevant to legal research.

- State and federal statutes on the Internet:

  See Internet addresses in Exhibit 11.4 in chapter 11.

- State and federal cases on the Internet:

  See Internet addresses in Appendix B.

- ABANet:

  http://www.abanet.org

  This is the site of the American Bar Association that contains information on its sections and divisions (including the Legal Assistant Division), news releases, and a calendar of events. Some of the publications of the ABA and a list of Internet discussion groups hosted by the ABA are also included.

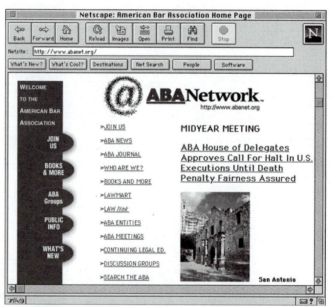

ABANet

- Chicago-Kent guide to Legal Resources:

  http://www.kentlaw.edu/legal_resources

  This site provides instructions on finding legal materials on the Internet. In addition, you are given lists covering computer law, family law, environmental law, human rights, health law, federal government, state government, etc.

- Counsel Connect Web:

  http://www.counsel.com

  This online service has links to other legal resources on the Internet. There are also online seminars on legal topics conducted for subscribers.

Chicago-Kent College of Law
Illinois Institute of Technology

| Welcome | News | Admissions | Academics | Departments |
| Overview | Faculty | Students | Legal Resources | Search |

Legal Resources

**Downtown Campus
Information Center Resources**

IIT's Downtown Campus <u>Information Center</u> contains
three libraries:
     Chicago-Kent Law Library
     Library of International Relations
     Stuart Business Library

Pollution Prevention Resources
A database containing a searchable, annotated bibliography of
over 500 documents relating to pollution prevention provided by
Chicago-Kent, the Chicago Legal Clinic, and Gardner, Carton &
Douglas.

IC³

An **online document collection** providing full-text access
to documents of both U.S. and foreign governments and
international organizations. The documents complement and
provide research resources for the institutes and programs of
IIT's law and business schools. Links to papers and
presentation transcripts from institute conferences and
programs are included.

**Online Resources from the
Center for Law and Computers**

Chicago-Kent's <u>Center for Law and Computers</u> maintains a variety of <u>online legal resources</u>:

Chicago-Kent Guide to Legal Resources

- Federal Court Locator:

    http://www.law.vill.edu/Fed-Ct/fedcourt.html

    This site provides information on the U.S. Supreme Court, the U.S. Courts of
    Appeals, and the federal agencies that work with these courts, e.g., the U.S.
    Department of Justice and the U.S. Sentencing Commission.

- Federal Web Locator:

    http://www.law.vill.edu/Fed.Agency/fedwebloc.html

    This is an index of all the Internet sites covering the federal government.

- FindLaw:

    http://www.findlaw.com

    This site is a comprehensive legal research site called a "one-stop shopping center."
    It was voted one of the "Best of the Web" sites in the category of overall research
    by the legal newsletter *legal.online*. The index of FindLaw contains numerous links
    to legal resources on the Internet. Its LawCrawler feature allows you to search for
    key terms in the contents of other Internet sites as well as within FindLaw itself.

LegalMinds   Laws   LegalNews   LawCrawler
Community   Cases & Codes   Today's News   Web Search

US Supreme Court Cases
1893+ Free!

Free Legal EMail!
you@**JusticeMail**.com!

FindLaw Guide   [options]

LawCrawler - LegalMinds - Law Reviews - Real Time SEC EDGAR Filings - Bookstore - Microsoft v. DOJ
Stock Quotes - Message Boards - Chat - Online CLE - Career Center - Legal Jobs - Legal News

Legal Subject Index
Constitutional, Intellectual Property Labor...

Law Schools
Law Reviews, Outlines, Student Resources...

Professional Development
Career Development, CLE, Employment...

Legal Organizations
National Bars, State Bars, Local Bars ...

Law Firms & Lawyers
Lawyers WWW sites, NLJ 250...

Consultants & Experts

Directories
Government, Yellow Pages, Phone, Maps...

Laws: Cases & Codes
Supreme Court Opinions, Constitution, State Laws...

U.S. Federal Government Resources

State Law Resources
California, New York, Texas...

Foreign & International Resources
Country Pages, Int'l Law, Int'l Trade...

News & Reference
Legal News, Library Information...

Legal Practice Materials
Forms, Publishers, Software & Technology...

LegalMinds - Community
Message Boards, Mailing List Archives, Chat...

FindLaw

- GPO Access:

    http://www.acess.gpo.gov/su_docs

  This site provides comprehensive coverage of information on the executive branch of the federal government, including the full text of the *Code of Federal Regulation,* the *Federal Register,* GAO reports, and Comptroller General Decisions. Data on Congress are also included.

- LawCrawler:

    http://www.lawcrawler.com

  A search tool ("engine") devoted to legal topics. See also FindLaw above.

- Law Group Network, Lawyers Legal Research:

    http://www.llr.com

  This site has an extensive database of court opinions, including all opinions of the U.S. Supreme Court since 1900, all opinions of the U.S. Courts of Appeals since 1992, and all recent opinions of the highest appellate court in every state. It also has numerous links to other kinds of laws, law firms, financial services, e-mail addresses, etc.

CSDNet

Code of Federal
Regulations

Congress

Federal Budget

Federal Register

GILS

MOCAT

Sales Products

Statistical
Abstract of the
United States

FDLP
Administrator

Welcome to the Superintendent of Documents Home Page and

GPO Access

A Service of the U.S. Government Printing Office

What Is GPO Access?   Search Databases
New/Noteworthy Products from GPO   Find Government Information
Browse Federal Bulletin Board Files   Find Products for Sale by GPO
            Government Information at a Library Near You

Questions or comments regarding this service? Contact the *GPO Access* **User Support Team** by Internet e-mail at *gpoaccess@gpo.gov* ; by telephone at **1-202-512-1530** or **toll free at 1-888-293-6498** ; by fax at **1-202-512-1262** .

March 26, 1998

GPO Access

- Law Journal Extra, Practice Areas:

    http://www.ljextra.com/Practice.pointer.html

  This site provides links to statutes, opinions, and related materials for specific areas in which attorneys practice.

- Law Journal Extra, State Courts:

    http://www.ljextra.com/courthouse/states.html

  This site contains state law resources, including the state court rules of selected states and materials from the National Conference of Commissioners on Uniform State Laws.

- Law Journal Extra, U.S. Supreme Court:

    http://www.ljextra.com/courthouse/supindex.html

  This site provides links to federal laws including opinions of the U.S. Supreme Court, federal statutes governing federal procedure, and news involving the U.S. Supreme Court.

- Legal Information Institute of Cornell Law School:

  http://www.law.cornell.edu

  Here you obtain access to federal and state court opinions, the current U.S. Code, e-mail addresses, etc.

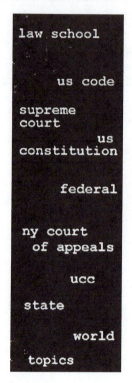

Welcome to the Legal Information Institute

a research activity of the <u>*Cornell Law School*</u>

This web site holds the Internet publications of the Legal Information Institute, a part of the <u>Cornell Law School</u>.

The server offers the LII's collection of <u>recent</u> and <u>historic</u> Supreme Court decisions, its hypertext versions of the full <u>U.S. Code</u>, <u>U.S. Constitution</u>, Federal <u>Rules of Evidence</u> and <u>Civil Procedure</u>, <u>recent opinions of the New York Court of Appeals</u> and commentary on them from the <u>liibulletin-ny</u>, the <u>American Legal Ethics Library</u>, and other important legal materials -- <u>federal</u>, <u>state</u>, <u>foreign and international</u>. It holds the LII's <u>e-mail address directory of faculty and staff at</u> <u>U.S. law schools</u> as well as contact information on <u>other people and organizations</u> in the field of law. It is host to the <u>*Cornell Law Review,*</u> and offers information about <u>Cornell Law School</u> and <u>the Cornell Law Library.</u>

Internet activity is only one of the LII's activities, which include consulting, software development, and electronic publication on disk and CD-ROM. All electronic products of the LII can be <u>ordered and purchased</u> directly from this site.

- <u>Site tour</u>
- <u>Items of Special Current Interest</u>
- <u>Main Menus (Legal Topics, Sources, Organizations, People)</u>
- <u>About This Site and the LII</u>
- <u>Additional WWW Sources (Law and Other)</u>

law school

us code

supreme court

us constitution

federal

ny court of appeals

ucc

state

world

topics

Legal Information Institute

- LEXIS Counsel Connect's LAWlinks:

  http://www.counsel.com

  This site provides links to federal and state laws, classified ads from legal newspapers, stock quotations, law library materials (including the Library of Congress), etc.

- Moye, Giles, O'Keefe, Vermeire & Gorrell, Denver:

  http://www.mgovg.com

  This site was voted one of the "Best of the Web" sites in the category of medium-sized law firms by the legal newsletter *legal.online.* It contains the full text of a number of legal treatises on banking and commercial law. The site also has a "Funny Stuff" feature covering humorous transcripts and "war stories."

- P-LAW Legal Resource Locator:

    http://www.dorsai.org/p-law

    This locator provides links to federal and state research sites, statistical data, and specialized research on a variety of topics.

- Tax Prophet:

    http://www.taxprophet.com

    This site contains links to numerous other tax resources on the Internet as well as columns, newsletters, and articles on tax planning and law. The site is arranged to be a useful teaching tool for attorneys and the general public. It includes a forms-based questionnaire you can use to help distinguish between an employee and an independent contractor for tax purposes. A law firm that uses independent paralegals might find this feature helpful.

- U.S. House of Representatives, Internet Law Library:

    http://law.house.gov

    This site contains the full text of the U.S.C. *(United States Code)* and the C.F.R. *(Code of Federal Regulations).* Historical documents are included such as the Constitution, Declaration of Independence, *Federalist Papers,* etc. You can also gain access to the federal budget, *Congressional Record,* hearings of congressional committees, House and Senate committee reports, presidential documents, etc. In addition, there are links to state laws, treaties, and the catalogs of law school libraries.

---

http://law.house.gov/   U.S. House of Representatives Internet Law Library   Monday, July 27, 1998

Internet Law Library

The U.S. House of Representatives Internet Law Library Welcome!

 Search the U.S. Code

 U.S. Code Classification Tables

 Codification legislation

- ☐ About the House Internet Law Library
- ☐ U.S. Federal laws (arranged by original published source)
- ☐ U.S. Federal laws (arranged by agency)
- ☐ U.S. state and territorial laws
- ☐ Laws of other nations
- ☐ Treaties and international law
- ☐ Laws of all jurisdictions (arranged by subject)
- ☐ Law school law library catalogues and services
- ☐ Attorney and legal profession directories
- ☐ Law book reviews and publishers

◆

 FRAMES version of the Law Library

 Fast-loading GRAPHIC-FREE version of our homepage

Internet Law Library (U.S. House of Representatives)

- Villanova Center for Information Law and Policy:

  http://www.law.vill.edu

  This site has links to the Federal Web Locator on the federal government, Federal Court Locator on the federal courts, and State Court Locator on state courts.

- West's Legal Directory:

  http://www.wld.com

  This site allows you to locate attorneys in particular cities and towns across the country. *West's Legal Directory* covers more attorneys than the *Martindale-Hubbell Law Directory.*

---

http://www.wld.com/   West Legal Directory   Friday, August 7, 1998

HELP   CONTACT US   SITE MAP

▶ The Informed Client
Find an Attorney, Info about the Law, Secure Communication...

▶ Attorney Resources
Find an Attorney, Secure Communication, Services from West...

Legal Lines
Monica Lewinsky's Illicit Fixation: Scandal Tests The Limits Of Copyright Law, Cowan Liebowitz & Latman PC

Same-Sex Ruling: Bold but Strict, Campion, Rodolff, Van Riper & Procopio LLP

Who Is a Witness?, The Crow Law Firm

Subcontractor's Employee Can't Sue Builder, Campion, Rodolff, Van Riper & Procopio LLP

What's New
West Legal Directory Takes the Law to the People in Los Angeles

West Legal Directory Named Most Incredibly Useful Web Site by *Yahoo! Internet Life* Magazine

WEST GROUP   Help | Contact Us | Site Map | Home
© 1998 West Group | West Group Home

West's Legal Directory

- WWW Virtual Library Law:

  http://www.law.indiana.edu/law/v-lib/lawindex.html

  This site provides a connection to a great deal of legal material on various sites. You are led to law firms, law schools, federal government information, state government information, international law, etc.

World Wide Web Virtual Library: Law: Main Index

Sponsored by
The Indiana University School of Law Library and
The World Wide Web Virtual Library

Table of contents

- **About this website**
- **Search this website**
- **Browse the links**
  - **Legal Information by Organization Type**
  - **Legal Information by Topic**
  - **Search Tools and Other Comprehensive Sites**

- **Add a link to this list**
- View **New Submissions** to this list.

Search for documents containing the following:

Top of Page

Legal Information by Organization Type

Virtual Law Library

Other Useful Sites

- Alta Vista (general search engine):

   http://www.altavista.digital.com

- Internal Revenue Service:

   http://www.irs.ustreas.gov/prod

- Internet Sleuth (Law):

   http://www.isleuth.com/lega.html

- Lawyers Weekly:

   http://www.lweekly.com

- Legal List:

   http://www.lcp.com/The-Legal-List/TLL-home.html

- Martindale-Hubbell:

   http://www.martindale.com

- Securities & Exchange Commission:

   http://www.sec.gov/index.html

- Thomas (federal legislative information):

    http://thomas.loc.gov
    See page 59 in chapter 3.

- U.S. Federal Courts Finder:

    http://www.law.emory.edu/FEDCTS

- WashLaw Web (an indexer of legal sites):

    http://www.lawlib.wuacc.edu

- West's Legal News:

    http://www.westlaw.com/wlntop/front.htm

- West Group:

    http://www.westgroup.com

- Yahoo (general search engine):

    http://www.yahoo.com

 Assignment 13.6

Using the Internet, find:

(a) your street address or that of your parents

(b) the Internet address of any independent paralegal who has a **home page** on the Internet (a home page is the page on the Internet, usually the opening page, that introduces a computer user to the site of an organization or individual)

(c) one Internet site dealing with a subject that will be covered in each course in your curriculum (one different Internet address per course).

(d) the Internet address of a government agency that answers the question of whether a tomato is a vegetable or a fruit.

Explain how you obtained each answer.

HAPTER SUMMARY

The major CALR (computer assisted legal research) systems are: WESTLAW and LEXIS. Use standard survival techniques such as finding out if any of the products has an 800 number that you can use, and taking advantage of online tutorials and HELP keys.

One of the most important skills in this area is the ability to formulate a question, or query, for the computer to answer. Most queries ask the computer to find data within a designated database. In formulating a query using Boolean language, you need to know how to use the universal character (*) and the root expander (!). You also need to know when to use connectors (such as the OR connector, the AND connector, and the numerical connector) to specify the relationship among the search words in the query in order to give the search more direction. You

also need to know how to search for phrases, how to conduct field and segment searches, and how to perform simple "find" searches when you already have the citation to something you want to read.

Recently, a more natural way to phrase queries by using plain English has been developed. WESTLAW calls its method WIN (WESTLAW Is Natural); LEXIS calls its method Freestyle.

The Internet has been a major development in the computer revolution. Internet users have access to a vast network of resources at a reasonable cost. The power of hypertext has made the World Wide Web the dominant vehicle for navigating the resources of the Internet.

KEY TERMS

CALR	users group	root expander	protocols
online	listserv	connectors	bulletin board systems
CD-ROM	WESTLAW	segments	World Wide Web
online tutorial	LEXIS	fields	hypertext
HELP key	search query	WIN	search engines
documentation	Boolean	Freestyle	home page
load	KeyCite	Internet	
CLE	universal character	network	

Chapter 14

VALIDATION—THE THIRD LEVEL OF RESEARCH: ENDING YOUR RESEARCH

► *Chapter Outline*

SECTION A   INTRODUCTION

In chapter 8, we introduced the three levels of legal research:

- Background research
- Specific fact research
- Validation research

Exhibit 8.1 examined the steps for conducting *background research* on an area of law that is new to you. Chapter 9 examined the techniques of *specific fact research* through a series of extensive checklists. If you have done a comprehensive job on the first two stages of research, you may also have completed most of the third stage—**validation research**. At the validation stage, you ensure that everything you want to use from your research is still good law. This means making sure that the law is current and has not been affected by any later laws that you have not yet found.

SECTION B   WHY THERE IS A HIGH RISK THAT YOU WILL RELY ON INVALID LAW

The importance of validation research cannot be overestimated. It is easy to understand why you do not want to rely on a case that has been overruled, or on a statute that has been amended, repealed, or declared unconstitutional. Surprisingly, however, it is relatively easy to fall into such potentially disastrous traps. This is because some invalid laws are never removed from the shelves. This means that while you are reading such laws, you are given no indication that they are invalid and therefore are tempted—very tempted—to rely on them.

For example, a reporter volume may contain several hundred court opinions. Some of their holdings may have been overruled or declared unconstitutional years after the reporter volume was published. Yet no one goes back to this volume to insert corrections or warnings. An invalid case will be printed right next to a valid case. You must perform validation research before you rely on any law. For cases, you must use citator services such as Shepard's and KeyCite.

The same danger exists with statutes. A code volume may contain several thousand statutory sections and subsections. Some of them may have been amended, repealed, or declared unconstitutional years after the code volume was published. Yet no one goes back to this volume to insert corrections or warnings. Eventually, however, statutory code volumes (unlike reporter volumes) *are* updated so that the code volumes containing invalid statutes are replaced by volumes containing valid statutes. But for some codes, this replacement may take more than ten years! Consequently, when you are reading a statute, there may be invalid statutes printed right next to valid statutes without any indication of which were rendered invalid by subsequent action of the legislature or courts. To find out which statutes fall into this category, you must perform validation research. For statutes, you check available pocket parts, supplementation volumes or pamphlets, and paper or online citator services such as Shepard's.

In short, appearances are deceptive. Don't fall into the inviting trap of relying on invalid law simply because the law looks valid. Perform validation research on everything you want to use.

SECTION C   PERSPECTIVE OF THE OTHER SIDE

A good way to approach validation research is to take the perspective of the other side. Suppose that you have helped do some of the research for an appellate brief. It has been filed in court and served on the attorney for the other side. Your brief is handed over to a researcher in the law office of your opponent. That person will do the following:

- Read the full text of all *primary authority* (see Exhibit 2.2 in chapter 2) on which you rely to see if you have interpreted the statutes, cases, regulations, etc., properly; to see whether you have taken quotations out of the context, etc.

- *Shepardize* the statutes, cases, regulations, etc., that you cite to find out whether the law is still valid.
- Read the *secondary authority* (see Exhibit 4.1 and Exhibit 4.2 in chapter 4) that you cite to see whether you have interpreted the legal treatise, legal periodical article, etc., properly; to see whether you have taken quotations out of context, etc.
- Look for other applicable primary authority that you failed to mention.
- Look for other applicable secondary authority that you failed to mention.

Proper validation research means that you will be able to predict what this imaginary researcher will find when he or she checks your research through these steps. In short, at the validation stage of your research you must ask yourself:

- Have I found everything I should have found?
- Is everything I found good law?
- Have I properly interpreted what I found?

The answer to the first two questions should be *no* if:

- You did an incomplete job of CARTWHEELING the indexes of all the sets of books mentioned in the checklists and techniques in this book (see Exhibit 7.1 in chapter 7).
- You failed to shepardize cases, statutes, constitutional provisions, rules of court, ordinances, treaties, etc., as called for in these checklists and techniques (see checklists #4a, 4b, and 4c in chapter 9).
- You failed to take other standard validation steps, such as updating regulations in C.F.R. through the *LSA* pamphlet and the proper tables in the *Federal Register*.

Someone "who tries to respond to a motion or brief without conducting fresh research is courting sanctions or a malpractice suit."

—United States Court of Appeals for the Seventh Circuit, *Continental Illinois Securities Litigation v. Continental Illinois Corp.*, 962 F.2d 566, 570 (7th Cir. 1995)

SECTION D   RESEARCH AUDIT

The checklist in Exhibit 14.1 is designed to help you achieve the comprehensiveness that is essential to all aspects of legal research, especially validation research. *Fill out a separate research audit for each issue you research.* Start by summarizing the issue in the box at the top of the form. The checklist should act as a self-audit to make sure that you have covered all bases. It consists of a series of reminders. They are needed because you have so many resources to check in a comprehensive law library. Note that part IV reminds you to keep a "Research Log." You not only want to be comprehensive, you also want to be able to tell others (and remind yourself) what steps you took along the way.

 14.1 ·································· Research Audit

Exhibit

ISSUE # _____ (briefly state issue researched)

I. What I Have Checked: Legal Materials

A. *Primary Authority*

☐ federal cases	☐ international law	☐ ordinances
☐ federal statutes	☐ state cases	☐ charter
☐ federal constitution	☐ state statutes	☐ local rules of court
☐ federal rules of court	☐ state constitution	☐ local administrative regulations
☐ federal administrative regulations	☐ state rules of court	☐ local administrative decisions
☐ federal administrative decisions	☐ state administrative regulations	
	☐ state administrative decisions	*Continued on next page*

14.1 .... Research Audit—continued

Exhibit

B. *Secondary Authority*

☐ legal periodicals   ☐ legal treatises   ☐ looseleaf services
☐ ALR annotations   ☐ legal encyclopedias   ☐ legal newsletters
☐ *Words & Phrases*
(legal dictionary)

II. What I Have Checked: Nonlegal Materials *only in civil cases*
As relevant to the research problem, I have checked nonlegal literature in the areas of:

☐ medicine   ☐ psychology   ☐ psychiatry   ☐ economics
☐ statistics   ☐ accounting   ☐ sociology   ☐ other
☐ biology   ☐ chemistry   ☐ business management

III. What I Intend to Rely on in My Research Memo
For every primary authority I intend to use, I have:

☐ used paper citators to determine whether it is still valid (e.g., Shepard's)
☐ used CD-ROM or online citators to determine whether it is still valid (e.g., Shepard's, Auto-Cite, KeyCite)
☐ checked other standard updating features (e.g., pocket part, supplement pamphlets, history tables)

IV. Research Log
For each paper, CD-ROM, or online resource, I have made the following brief notations in my research notebook or log:

☐ the name of the resource
☐ the major words/phrases I have checked in the resource
☐ which library I used for this resource (if more than one)

V. People Consulted for Guidance/Leads Before Completion
People with whom I have shared my research strategy to determine whether they think I have omitted something:

☐ supervisor
☐ other attorney(s) in office
☐ law librarian
☐ law clerk
☐ experienced paralegal
☐ other experts (see checklist #9 in chapter 9)
☐ other _____

SECTION E   TIME TO STOP?

At the outset of your research, the difficulty you face is often phrased as: "Where do I begin?" As you resolve this difficulty, another one emerges: "When do I stop?" Once the research starts flowing, you are sometimes faced with a mountain of material, and yet you do not feel comfortable saying to yourself that you have found everything there is to be found. Exhibit 14.2 presents some guidelines on handling this concern. With experience, you will begin to acquire a clearer sense of when it is time to stop, but it is rare for you to know this with any certainty. You will always have the suspicion that if you pushed on just a little longer, you would find something new and more on point than what you have come up with to date. Also, there is no way around the reality that comprehensive research requires a substantial amount of time. It takes time to dig. It takes more time to dig comprehensively.

14.2 ....

Exhibit
Guidelines for Determining
When to End Your Legal
Research

1. *Instructions from your supervisor.* You must, of course, live within time guidelines imposed by your supervisor. You cannot spend the rest of your career in the law library working on one problem! If your supervisor has not set specific time guidelines for the research project, ask him or her to do so as soon as you determine that the project is going to take a significant amount of time. This may be an opportunity for the supervisor to narrow the focus of the project or to redirect your energies entirely. It may also be

14.2

Exhibit
Guidelines for Determining
When to End Your Legal
Research—continued

an opportunity for the supervisor to let you know that you misunderstood the question to be researched!

2. *Repetition.* If you find that all the different avenues you are taking in the law library appear to be leading to the same primary and secondary authority, it may be time to stop. This repetition may be a good indication that you have already found what there is to find. Many legal materials are designed to be finding aids to the same kind of law, as we saw in chapter 9 on the nine major search resources. Digests and ALR annotations, for example, are both massive indexes to case law. Shepard's is also an excellent case finder. Always try to use more than one finding aid to locate any particular category of primary authority you are checking. (Also try to use finding aids published by different companies, because the same publisher will often repeat the same material in different formats.) When multiple finding aids keep turning up the same cases, statutes, or other laws, it is a sign that you can stop.

3. *Comprehensive via checklists.* Work with checklists to be sure that you are covering all the bases in the law library. One indication of when it is time to stop is when you are able to check off everything on your checklists, particularly the research audit in Exhibit 14.1.

SECTION F   ANNOTATED BIBLIOGRAPHY AND RESEARCH PROBLEMS

An **annotated bibliography** is a report giving a list of library material on a particular topic, with a brief description of how the material relates to the topic. An annotated bibliography on contributory negligence, for example, would list the major cases, statutes, periodical articles, etc. and would explain in a sentence or two what each says about contributory negligence. The same would be true of an annotated bibliography on a set of facts that you are researching. If the facts present more than one research issue, you would do an annotated bibliography for each issue, or you would subdivide a single annotated bibliography into sections so that it would be clear to the reader which issue you are covering at any given place in the bibliography. The annotated bibliography is, in effect, a progress report on your research. It will show your supervisor the status of your research. (The following instructions mainly cover the preparation of an annotated bibliography for a topic that requires the application of state and local law. The same instructions, however, would be used when doing the bibliography on a federal topic. The exception would be instruction #9, which calls for local ordinances. For all other instructions below, replace the word *state* with the word *federal* when researching a federal topic.)

INSTRUCTIONS FOR PREPARING AN ANNOTATED BIBLIOGRAPHY

1. CARTWHEEL the topic of your annotated bibliography. (See Exhibit 7.1 in chapter 7.)

2. *Annotated* here simply means that you provide some description of everything you list in the bibliography—not a long analysis, just a sentence or two explaining why you included it. If you find no relevant material in any of the following sets of books, specifically say so in your report.

3. Hand in a report that will cover what you find on the topic in the sets of books mentioned in the following instructions.

4. Statutes. Go to your state code. Make a list of the statutes on the topic. For each statute, give its citation and a brief quotation from it to show that it deals with the topic.

5. Constitutions. Go to your state constitution (usually found within your state code). Make a list of the constitutional provisions on the topic. For each provision, give its citation and a brief quotation from it to show that it deals with the topic.

6. Cases. If you found statutes or constitutional provisions on the topic, check to see if there are any cases summarized in the Notes of Decisions (see Exhibit 11.1 in chapter 11) *after* these statutes or provisions. Select several cases that deal with the topic. For each case you select, give its citation and a brief quote from the case summary in the Notes of Decisions to show that it deals with the topic.

7. Digests. Go to the Descriptive Word Index of digests (page 146). Make a list of key topics that deal with

Continued on next page

INSTRUCTIONS FOR PREPARING AN ANNOTATED BIBLIOGRAPHY—continued

the topic.

8. **Rules of court.** Go to the rules of court that cover courts in your state (page 241). Make a list of the rules, if any, that deal with the topic. For each rule, give its citation and a brief quotation from it to show that it deals with the topic.

9. **Ordinances.** Go to the ordinances that cover your city or county (page 240). Make a list of the ordinances, if any, that deal with the topic. For each ordinance, give its citation and a brief quotation from it to show that it deals with the topic.

10. **Administrative regulations.** Are there any state agencies that have jurisdiction over any aspect of the topic? If so, list the agencies. If your library has the regulations of the agencies, make a list of the regulations, if any, that deal with the topic. For each major regulation, give its citation and a brief quote from it to show that it deals with the topic (page 238).

11. **A.L.R.1st, A.L.R.2d, A.L.R.3d, A.L.R.4th, A.L.R.5th, A.L.R. Fed.** Go to these six sets of books (see Exhibit 9.3). Try to find one annotation in *each* set that deals with your topic. Give the citation of the annotation in each set. Flip through the pages of each annotation and try to find the citation of one case from a state court of your state, or from a federal court with jurisdiction over your state. Give the citation of the case.

12. **Legal periodical literature.** Use the *Index to Legal Periodicals and Books* and the *Current Legal Index* to locate four legal periodical articles that deal with the topic (page 174). Try to find at least two relevant articles in each index. Give the citations of the articles. Put a checkmark next to the citation if your library has the legal periodical in which the article is located.

13. **Legal treatises.** Go to your card or computer catalog (page 141). Find any two legal treatises (page 180) that cover your topic. Give the citation of the treatises. Sometimes you may not find entire books on

the topic. The topic may be one of many subjects in a broader treatise.

14. **Looseleafs.** Are there any looseleaf services on this topic (page 172)? Check the card or computer catalog and ask the librarian. For each looseleaf, give its citation and explain how it covers the topic.

15. *Words and Phrases.* Go to this multivolume legal dictionary (page 75). In this dictionary, locate definitions, if any, of the major words and phrases involved in your topic. Limit yourself to definitions from court opinions of your state, if any.

16. **Shepardize** every case, statute, or constitutional provision you find to make sure it is still valid (page 153).

17. **Other material.** If you come across other relevant material not covered in the above instructions, include it in the bibliography as well.

18. When in doubt about whether to include something in the bibliography, include it.

19. There is no prescribed format for the bibliography. One possible outline format you can use is as follows:

Topic: _____

   A. Statutes (Instructions 4 and 16)
   B. Constitutions (Instructions 5 and 16)
   C. Cases (Instructions 6, 7, and 16)
   D. Digests (Instruction 7)
   E. Rules of court (Instruction 8)
   F. Ordinances (Instruction 9)
   G. Administrative regulations (Instruction 10)
   H. A.L.R.1st, A.L.R.2d, A.L.R.3d, A.L.R.4th, A.L.R.5th, A.L.R. Fed. (Instruction 11)
   I. Legal periodical literature (Instruction 12)
   J. Legal treatises (Instruction 13)
   K. Looseleafs (Instruction 14)
   L. *Words and Phrases* (Instruction 15)
   M. Other material (Instruction 17)

Research Problems

 Assignment 14.1

Prepare an annotated bibliography on one of the following topics:

(a) Common-law marriage
(b) Negligence liability of a driver of a car to his or her guest passenger
(c) Negligence liability of paralegals
(d) Overtime compensation for paralegals
(e) Sex discrimination
(f) The felony-murder rule
(g) Default judgment
(h) Worker's compensation for injury on the way to work
(i) Fact situation assigned by your instructor

Assignment 14.2

In the problems that follow, include citations that support every position you take in your responses. In analyzing and researching some of the problems below, you may find it difficult to proceed unless you know more facts about the problem. In such situations, clearly state the missing facts that you need to know. In order to proceed with the analysis and research, you can assume that certain facts exist as long as you state what your factual assumptions are *and* your assumptions are reasonable given the facts that you have.

(a) In your state, what entity (e.g., legislature, committee, court, agency) has the authority to prescribe rules and regulations on who can and who cannot practice law?

(b) List the kinds (or levels) of courts (local, state, or federal) that sit in your state and identify the major powers of each court; i.e., indicate what kinds of cases each court can hear.

(c) In your state, find a statute or court opinion that defines the following words or phrases:

   (i)   Summons
   (ii) In personam
   (iii) Mandamus
   (iv) Exhaustion of administrative remedies
   (v)   Judgment
   (vi) Jurisdiction
   (vii) Warrant

(d) Mary Adams works for a National Welfare Rights Organization (N.W.R.O.) chapter in your state. She is a paralegal. An N.W.R.O. member, Mrs. Peterson, has a complaint against a local welfare department branch concerning her public assistance check. Mary Adams goes to a hearing with Mrs. Peterson to represent her. The hearing officer tells Mary that she cannot represent Mrs. Peterson because Mary is not an attorney. Is the hearing officer correct?

(e) Using the statutory codes of five different states (one of which must be your own state), find out how old a male and female must be to marry without consent of parent or guardian in each of the states.

(f) Go to any statutory code that has a pocket part. Starting with the first few pages of the pocket part, identify any three statutes that have totally repealed *or* partially modified the corresponding three statutes in the body of the bound text. Describe what the repeal or modification was. (*Note:* You may have to compare the new section in the pocket part with the old section in the body of the text to describe the change.)

———————

In the following problems, use the state law *of your state* whenever you determine from your research that state law governs the problem.

(g) John Jones was sent to a state mental hospital after being declared mentally ill. He has been institutionalized for the last five years. In his own view, he is not now mentally ill. The hospital disagrees. What can John do? What steps might he take to try to get out?

(h) Peter Thomas is convicted of petty larceny. At the time of sentencing, his attorney asks the court to grant probation in lieu of a prison term. The judge replies, "Since Mr. Thomas has had three prior felony convictions (and since one of them was for attempted rape), I could not grant him probation even if I wanted to. I sentence him to a year in prison." On appeal, the attorney argues that the judge was incorrect in ruling that she had no power to grant probation to Mr. Thomas. Is the attorney correct?

(i) Mrs. Peterson invites a neighbor to her house for dinner. Mrs. Peterson's dog bites the neighbor. Is Mrs. Peterson responsible for the injury?

(j) Sam, age fifteen, goes to a used car lot. He signs a purchase agreement on a used car: $500 down and $100 a month for the next ten months. One day after the purchase, Sam allows a friend to drive the car. The friend demolishes the car in an accident. When Sam tells the used car dealer about the accident, he is told that he must still make all payments until the purchase price has been paid. Is the dealer right?

Continued on next page

(k) An elderly woman presented the following facts to you during a legal interview. She and her husband moved into their house in 1946. Next to the house is a vacant lot. She does not know who owns the lot. She planted a small vegetable and flower garden on this lot and built a small fence around the garden. She has continued to cultivate this garden for the past twenty-seven years. Neighbors regard this garden as hers. Since her husband's death last fall, men in the neighborhood have been trying to use the garden area as a place to store their old car parts. She is troubled by this. What are her rights?

(l) Dorothy Rhodes and John Samualson are the parents of Susan Samualson. (Dorothy married Robert Rhodes after divorcing John Samualson.) Dorothy died after separating from Robert Rhodes. Susan's father (John) has disappeared.

   Mr. and Mrs. Ford were neighbors of the Rhodes. Susan lived with the Fords for a long period of time while her mother was having marital difficulties. A court granted the Fords custody and guardianship in 1988. The Social Security Administration sent Susan the Social Security benefits she was entitled to on the death of her mother. In 1990, the Fords formally adopted Susan, but did not inform the Social Security office of this; they did not know that they had to. When the Social Security office learned of the adoption, they terminated the payments for Susan and informed the Fords that the money she had received since the adoption would have to be returned.

   The Fords and Susan want to know what substantive and procedural rights they have.

(m) Jane Smith owns a small shoe repair shop. The city sanitation department determines that Jane is a carrier of a typhoid germ. She herself does not have typhoid fever, but others could become infected with the fever by coming in contact with her. The city orders Jane's shop to be closed. She and her husband are not allowed to leave the shop until arrangements can be made to transfer them to a hospital.

   (i)   Can the city quarantine Jane and her husband?
   (ii) If they enter a hospital quarantine, can they be forced to pay the hospital bill?
   (iii) Can they recover loss of profits due to the closing of their business?

(n) The Henderson family owns a $140,000 home next door to a small grocery store. The store catches fire. The firefighters decide that to get at the fire from all angles, they must break through the Henderson home, which is not on fire. Damage to the Henderson home from the activity of the firefighters comes to $40,000. Who pays for this damage?

(o) Bill and Mary are married with two children. They are happily married except for one ongoing quarrel. Bill is upset with Mary because she goes bowling every Friday night. Mary is disturbed with Bill because he plays cards every Tuesday night. To resolve their difficulty, they reach the following agreement: Bill will give up his Tuesday night cards if Mary will give up her Friday bowling. On Friday, Mary stays home. On the following Tuesday, however, Bill plays cards. He declares that he wants to continue the card playing. Mary wants him to live up to his agreement and brings a suit in court against him, charging breach of contract. (Assume that neither wants a divorce.) What result?

(p) After a series of serious accidents in which numerous riders are hurt, a bill is placed before the city council that would require all motorcyclists to wear protective helmets whenever riding. Is the bill constitutional?

(q) As a measure to enforce a standard of dental care, a bill is proposed that all the drinking water in the state be fluoridated and that every citizen be required to visit a dentist at least once a year. Is this bill constitutional?

(r) Tom Jones has terminal lung cancer. Modern technology, however, can keep him alive indefinitely. Tom requests that the hospital no longer use the technology on him. He wants to die. What are his rights?

(s) Alice Brown is seventeen years old. She is a self-styled hippie who refuses to work. Alice's parents tell her that they will fully finance a college education for her. She refuses. The parents go to court and ask that their daughter be forced to go to college and avoid ruining her life. What result?

(t) In 1942 James Fitzpatrick died, leaving an estate of $50,000. The executor tried to locate the heirs. In 1943 the probate court closed the estate and distributed the money to the heirs who

Assignment 14.2—continued

were known at the time. In 1986, an individual who says he is an heir appears. He wants to go to court to reopen the estate and claim his share of the inheritance. What result?

(u) Mary is the sole beneficiary of her father's will. Another sister is intentionally left out of the will by her father. There are no other heirs. Mary murders her father. Who gets his estate?

(v) The board of education is alarmed over increasing disturbances in the public schools. The superintendent of schools proposes that the board adopt a regulation that would authorize the school nurse, under the direction of the principal, to administer an oral tranquilizer to disruptive pupils so that they could be rendered "relatively passive" and responsive to school guidance. Discuss the legality of the regulation.

(w) The state claims that public assistance costs are bringing the finances of the state to the brink of bankruptcy. It is proposed that all children of parents receiving public assistance be required to attend vocational classes as part of their regular school curriculum. Discuss the legality of the regulation.

(x) Most kosher meat stores accept the United Kosher Butchers Association (UKBA) as the authoritative certifier that "all the religious requirements have been thoroughly observed." Associated Synagogues (AS) certifies caterers as authentic carriers of kosher food. AS refuses to certify caterers who buy meat from stores certified by the UKBA because the latter refuses to submit to supervision by the rabbinical committee of AS. Many caterers then withdraw their patronage from stores supervised by UKBA. What legal action, if any, can the UKBA take?

(y) The town of Salem has a population of 2,000. A group of avowed homosexuals moves into the area. They begin to run for public offices, with some success. The old-time townspeople become very upset. A state law gives courts the power to hospitalize mentally ill individuals. The mayor of Salem files petitions in court to have the homosexuals declared mentally ill and institutionalized. Discuss any law that might apply to these facts.

(z) Mary Perry belongs to a religion that believes that medical problems can be resolved through spiritual meditation. Her son Paul is ten years old. One day at school, Paul is rushed to a hospital after collapsing. Mrs. Perry is called at home. When she arrives at the hospital, she is told that Paul will require emergency surgery. She refuses to give her consent. The doctor tells her that if the operation is not performed within the next twenty-four hours, Paul will die. Mrs. Perry responds by saying that "God will cure my son." What legal action, if any, can be taken to protect Paul's rights and to protect Mrs. Perry's rights?

CHAPTER SUMMARY

Validation research will let you know whether the primary authority you want to rely on is good law. This kind of research is particularly important because it is not uncommon to read invalid laws that appear to be valid.

It is not always easy to answer the related questions of whether you have found everything you need to find in the library, whether what you have found is currently valid, and whether it is time to stop your research project. Try to imagine yourself in the shoes of the opponent, who is inclined to tear apart and challenge everything you have found. What would this opponent say about the product of your research and about your analysis of this prod-

uct? This perspective may help you assess the status of your research to date.

Consider using a research audit as a checklist on finding primary authority, secondary authority, and nonlegal materials; using citators and other standard updating features; keeping a research log; and consulting with people to determine whether you have left out any research steps.

The ongoing guidance of your supervisor will be critical in deciding whether it is time to stop, as will repetitiveness in what you are finding, and comprehensiveness in going through the checklists presented in this book.

KEY TERMS

validation research   annotated bibliography

LEGAL WRITING

Contents

LETTER WRITING

Chapter Outline

SECTION A   INTRODUCTION

A law office prepares a number of different kinds of writing:

- Letters
- Memoranda of law
- Appellate briefs
- Instruments
- Pleadings

Letters will be covered in this chapter. Memoranda of law and appellate briefs are covered in chapters 16 and 17. Here is an overview of instruments and pleadings:

Instruments: An **instrument** is a formal document that gives expression to a legal act or agreement. Examples of instruments include contracts, deeds, wills, leases, bonds, notes, and mortgage agreements. Many formbooks and computer programs provide models for drafting such instruments. Except for simple contracts, an attorney will rarely write an instrument from scratch. The starting point is almost always a standard form or model, which is adapted to the particular facts of the client. For guidelines on using standard forms—and on avoiding their abuse—see Exhibit 15.1.

Exhibit
How to Avoid Abusing a
Standard Form

1. A **standard form** is an example of the document or instrument that you need to draft, such as a pleading, contract, or other instrument.
2. Standard forms are found in a number of places—for example, in formbooks, in manuals, in practice texts, in some statutory codes, and in some rules of court.
3. Most standard forms are written by private attorneys. Occasionally, however, a standard form will be written by the legislature or by the court as the suggested or required format to use.
4. Considerable care must be exercised in the use of a standard form. Such forms can be deceptive in that they appear to require little more than filling in the blanks. The intelligent use of these forms usually requires much more.
5. The cardinal rule is: *adapt* the form to the particulars of the client's case.
6. Do not be afraid to change the preprinted language in the form if you have a good reason. Whenever you make such a change, bring it to your supervisor for approval.
7. You should never use a standard form unless and until you have satisfied yourself that you know the meaning of *every* word and phrase on the form. This includes **boilerplate,** which is standard language often used in the same kind of document. The great temptation of most form users is to ignore what they do not understand because the form has been used so often in the past without any apparent difficulty. Do not give in to this temptation. Find out what everything means by:
   - Using a legal dictionary
   - Asking your supervisor
   - Asking other knowledgeable people
   - Doing other legal research
8. You need to know whether the entire form or any part of it has ever been litigated in court. To find this out, do some legal research in the area of the law relevant to the form.
9. Once you have found a form that appears useful, look around for another form that attempts to serve the same purpose. Analyze the different or alternative forms available. Which one is preferable? Why? The important point is: keep questioning the validity of the form. Be very skeptical about the use of any form.
10. Do not leave any blank spaces on the form. If a question does not apply, make a notation to indicate this, such as N.A. (not applicable).
11. If the form was written for another state, be sure that the form can be adapted and is adapted to the law of your state. Often, however, an out-of-state form is simply unadaptable to your state because of the differences in the laws of the two states.
12. Occasionally, you may go to an old case file to find a document that might be used as a model for a similar document that you need to draft on a current case. All the above cautions apply to the adaptation of documents from closed case files.

Pleadings: **Pleadings** are formal statements of claims and defenses that are exchanged between parties involved in litigation. The major pleadings are the complaint, answer, counterclaim, reply to counterclaim, cross-claim, and third-party complaint. Formbooks and computers are also heavily used in drafting standard form pleadings. Companies sell software that contains sample pleadings ready to be filled in and adapted to the needs of particular clients. Or, the office may simply adapt old pleadings from its computer files. Practices such as family law and bankruptcy often use repetitive pleadings. Their files, if properly organized in the computer database, can quickly generate pleadings needed for new clients. Word processing can then be used to make needed adaptations with relative ease for most cases. (See Exhibit 15.1 on standard forms.)

SECTION B   LETTER WRITING

A law office writes many garden variety letters every day, such as a letter requesting information (see Exhibit 15.2), a letter demanding payment, a letter notifying someone that the office represents a particular person or company, a cover letter that tells the recipient you are sending ("enclosing") a document or other physical object in the letter or package. For guidelines on letter writing in general, see Exhibit 15.3.

One of the major categories of letters a law office often writes is the **confirmatory letter** in which you confirm that something important has been done or said. For example:

> "This is to confirm that you have agreed to accept $5,000 in full settlement of the contract dispute between . . . ."

> "Thank you for coming in Tuesday to discuss the extension of insurance coverage for the employees in the Southeast region of your company's operations. I want to state my understanding of what took place at the meeting. Please let me know if this is consistent with your understanding. . . ."

This kind of letter is important because it provides written confirmation of matters that might be subject to misunderstanding with the passage of time. It is also a good way to provide a record for the file. In this sense, a confirmatory letter is similar to a "memo to the file" in which you communicate something about the case that has taken place, e.g., the substance of a recent telephone conversation or the result of some research in the law library. A memo of this kind might not be important enough to send to a supervisor, but should be in the file where anyone working on the case will have access to it when using the file. The confirmatory letter is different, of course, because it goes to someone outside the office in an effort to prompt him or her to voice any disagreements with the contents of the letter.

In an **opinion letter,** the office writes to its client to explain the application of the law and advise the client what to do. Such letters try to clarify technical material. Unlike a brief or memorandum, the opinion letter does not make extensive reference to court opinions or statutes. The client's need is for clear, concise, practical advice.

Assignment 15.1

Prepare a letter for each of the following situations. You will need more facts to complete the letters (e.g., the address of the recipient, your address, and more details on the purpose of the letter). You can make up any of these facts as long as they are reasonably consistent with the facts provided. In each case, your supervisor is an attorney who wants you to draft the letter for his or her signature.

(a) The office represents Richard Clemens, who is a plaintiff in an automobile accident case against George Kiley. The latter's insurance company has offered to settle for $10,000. Draft a letter to Richard Clemens in which you tell him about the offer and ask him to call you so that you can schedule an appointment with your supervisor to discuss the offer.

Continued on next page

Assignment 15.1—continued

Point out that the supervisor is not pleased with the low amount of the offer, but that the decision on whether to accept it will be entirely up to the client.

(b) Draft a letter to a client who failed to appear at two meetings last month with her attorney (your supervisor) at the office to discuss her case. The client is Diane Rolark. She is very wealthy. The office hopes to keep her as a client in the future on other cases. Hence, the office does not want to antagonize her. The letter should remind her of the next appointment with her attorney (three weeks from today).

(c) Write an opinion letter to a client, James Duband, in which you explain any legal concept that you have learned in another course. (For example, assume that you just covered limited liability in a corporations or business law class. You could write a letter to a client in which you explain what limited liability means.) Assume that this concept is relevant to the case of this client, and that the client has written the office asking your supervisor to explain the concept as it pertains to his case.

15.2

Exhibit
Sample Letter

Gordon, Davis & Kildare
8268 Prestwick Drive
Boston, MA 02127
617-268-1899
617-268-9203 (fax)

Mary Gordon, Esq.
John Davis, Esq.
Lance Kildare, Esq.

```
                                            March 13, 1997
                                   RE: Massy Ford v. Cuttler
                                                    97-3456


Brenda A. Sarbanes
Vice President
Dennison Research Institute
74 Statler Road
Belmont, MA 02177

Dear Ms. Sarbanes:

   Our office represents Charles Cuttler in a stock distribution
suit against Massy Ford, Inc. I understand that your company
provides marketing research used in litigation. I want to obtain
some information about your services.

   Do you have any literature you could send me on the kind of
research you do? How are your fees determined? Finally, do you
have any examples of reports you have prepared in the past that we
could see?

   To give you an idea of our practice, I am enclosing our firm
brochure. Thank you for your consideration.

Sincerely,



Sean Williams
Paralegal

cc: Edith Jenkins

Encl.
SW:ebw
```

15.3 ······························ Guidelines on Letter Writing

Exhibit

1. Obtain clear instructions from your supervisor on (a) the purpose of the letter, (b) who will sign it, and (c) the date you should have a draft available for that person.
2. Determine if the office has any models for your letter. In the past, has the office ever sent out this kind of letter? If so, read them. Ask your supervisors if the letters are good examples, and if you should use them as a guide. (See Exhibit 15.1 on using models and standard forms.)
3. In form, your letter must be perfect. Here are the components to include:
   - **Heading** The heading is the letterhead, often preprinted. It contains the full name, address, telephone number, and other contact numbers of your law office. It is usually centered at the top of the page.
   - **Date** Give the full date (month, day, year) that the letter will be sent out. It is often placed at the right margin under the heading.
   - **Recipient** This is the full name, title, and address of the person who will be receiving the letter. It is often placed at the left margin.
   - **RE:** This is a brief statement that indicates the case to which the letter pertains, and occasionally the major theme of the letter (e.g., "RE: Henderson v. Jones, Civ. 92.179. Request for Extension of Time to File Responsive Declaration"). It is placed at either the right margin or the left margin.
   - **Salutation** Here you address the recipient "Dear . . . :" A colon (:) follows the last name of this person. If he or she is a doctor, professor, or important public official, use his or her title. The salutation often starts at the left margin on the line under the address.
   - **Identification Line** In the first line of the letter, let the reader know who is sending the letter, unless this is already obvious to the recipient because of prior contact.
   - **Purpose Line** Shortly after the identification line, briefly tell the reader the main purpose of the letter.
   - **Body** In the main body of the letter, explain the purpose of the letter in greater detail.
   - **Request Line** If you are asking the recipient to do something, be sure there is a specific request line in the letter that makes this clear.
   - **Closing** Here you conclude the letter. This should be a separate paragraph. Say something like, "If you have any questions about this matter, please do not hesitate to contact me." or "Thank you for your consideration in this matter." On the next line write, "Sincerely" or "Very truly yours." Place the name and title of the signer of the letter below the space for his or her signature.
   - **Copies Sent** If you are sending a copy of the letter to someone, indicate this by saying "cc:" followed by the name of the person(s) receiving the copy ("cc" stands for carbon copies; this abbreviation is still used even though carbon is seldom the method used today to make copies). Suppose you send out copies of the letter, but you do not want the recipient to know this. On the recipient's letter, you say nothing about copies. On the office copy of the letter, say "bcc:" (blind carbon copy) followed by the name of the people getting the copies. In this way, only your copy of the letter indicates who received copies. The main letter is silent ("blind") on this point.
   - **Enclosures** If you are enclosing anything with the letter, say, "Encl." If enclosing more than one item, say, "Encls."
   - **Initials** If someone else typed the letter for you, place your initials in capital letters, followed by a colon (:) and the initials (in lowercase) of the person who did the typing.
4. Grammatically, your letter must be perfect. There should be no spelling errors.
5. If the letter is to be sent to a client or another individual who is not an attorney, do not use technical words unless you define them in the letter. The only exception is when prior contact with the recipient leaves no doubt that he or she understands the words.
6. Avoid long sentences. There of course is no law specifying the number of words you should use in a sentence. Keep in mind, however, that shorter sentences are easier to understand, *particularly when dealing with technical subjects*. After you write a sentence, force yourself to decide whether the sentence would be clearer if you broke it into two or more shorter sentences (see chapter 18 on writing fundamentals).

C HAPTER SUMMARY

A law office prepares different kinds of written documents. Instruments are formal documents that give expression to a legal act or agreement. Pleadings are formal statements of claims and defenses that are exchanged between parties involved in litigation. To draft instruments and pleadings, the office may rely on standard forms. Care must be used, however, to avoid abusing such forms.

For example, the form must be adapted to the specifics of the client's case.

Among the different kinds of letters an office writes are confirmatory letters (which confirm that something important has been done or said) and opinion letters (which explain the application of the law and advise the client what to do).

KEY TERMS

instrument	boilerplate	confirmatory letter
standard form	pleadings	opinion letter

MEMORANDUM OF LAW

Chapter Outline

SECTION A   **KINDS OF MEMORANDA**

A **memorandum of law** is a written analysis of a legal problem. (The plural is *memoranda*; the shorthand is *memo*.) More specifically, it is a written explanation of how the law applies to a given set of facts. There are two main kinds of memoranda: (1) an internal or interoffice memorandum, and (2) an external or advocacy memorandum. The differences are outlined in Exhibit 16.1.

16.1

Exhibit
Characteristics of
Interoffice and External
Memoranda of Law

Interoffice Memorandum of Law
- Emphasizes both the strengths and the weaknesses of the client's position on each issue (objective)
- Emphasizes both the weaknesses and the strengths of the opposing party's known or anticipated position on each issue (objective)
- Predicts the court's or the agency's probable decision on each issue
- Recommends the most favorable strategy for the client to follow

External Memorandum of Law
- Emphasizes the strengths but minimizes or ignores the weaknesses of the client's position on each issue (adversary)
- Emphasizes the weaknesses but minimizes or ignores the strengths of the opposing party's position on each issue (adversary)
- Argues for a favorable decision on each issue

Interoffice Memorandum of Law

The main audience of your **interoffice memorandum of law** is your supervisor; the memo is an internal document.[1] Your goal in the memo is to analyze the law in order to make a prediction of how a court or other tribunal will resolve the dispute in the client's case. It is extremely important that this memo present the strengths *and weaknesses* of the client's case. The supervisor must make strategy decisions based in part on what you say in the memo. Hence the supervisor must have a realistic picture of what the law is. Many students find it very difficult to present strengths and weaknesses in the same memo. They devote the vast majority of the memo to arguments that favor one side. This kind of writing is inappropriate in an interoffice memorandum of law. Force yourself to find arguments that support both sides—no matter which side is the client of your office and no matter which side you think should win. A hallmark of the professional is the ability to step back and assess a problem objectively. This means being able to analyze strengths and weaknesses of both sides.

Although most interoffice memoranda of law are objective in the sense that they present both sides of the controversy, there are exceptions. The supervisor, for example, might explicitly ask for a memo containing the arguments supporting one side only. He or she may not want to read both sides at the moment or may feel that the office already has a grasp of one side and therefore wants a memo focused on the authority supporting the other side. Such a memo, of course, is still internal; it is not meant to be read by anyone outside the office.

External or Advocacy Memorandum of Law

The main audience of your **external memorandum of law** is someone outside the office, usually a judge or official in an administrative agency. Your goal in this memo is to try to convince the reader to take a certain action in the client's case. Hence, the memo is an advocacy document. In it, you are highlighting the strengths of the client's case and the weaknesses of the opponent's case.

Different terminology is sometimes used for this kind of memo:

---

1. Sometimes it is referred to as an **intraoffice memorandum of law** because it stays within the office.

- **Points and authorities memorandum:** An external memorandum submitted to a trial judge or hearing officer.
- **Trial memorandum:** An external memorandum submitted to a trial judge (also called a *trial brief*).
- **Hearing memorandum:** An external memorandum submitted to a hearing officer or administrative law judge within an administrative agency.

When the document is submitted to an appellate court, it is called an *appellate brief*. The structure of the appellate brief is considered in chapter 17.

———————

Most of the discussion that follows is on the internal interoffice memo. The external advocacy memo is mentioned only when there are significant differences.

SECTION B   STRUCTURE OF AN INTEROFFICE MEMORANDUM OF LAW

The organization and structure of a legal memorandum will vary a great deal depending on the complexity of the client's case; there is no official structure that will be appropriate in every situation. Find out what preferences your supervisor has, if any. Check office memos in old case files and ask your supervisor whether to use their format as a guide. Often the primary factor influencing the choice of structure will be the number of issues treated in the memorandum. Exhibit 16.2 illustrates the structure of a relatively uncomplicated memorandum involving only one issue.

16.2

Exhibit
Organization of a One-Issue Interoffice Memorandum of Law

> **INTEROFFICE MEMORANDUM OF LAW**
>
> TO: [*supervisor*]   RE: [*subject of memorandum*]
> FROM: [*your name*]
> DATE: [*today's date*]
> CASE: [*names of the parties*]
> OFFICE FILE NUMBER: [   ]
> DOCKET NUMBER: [   ]
>
> **STATEMENT OF ASSIGNMENT**
>
> [*State what your supervisor asked you to do.*]
>
> **ISSUE AND CONCLUSION**
>
> [*State the issue being treated and briefly—in less than a full sentence if possible; also briefly state the conclusion or answer to this issue.*]
>
> **FACTS**
>
> [*State the facts of the client's case.*]
>
> **ANALYSIS**
>
> [*State and discuss the relevant primary and secondary authorities with counteranalysis.*]
>
> **CONCLUSION**
>
> [*State your conclusion in greater depth plus your recommendations, if any, for further action in the case.*]

More often, however, the memorandum will involve several issues. A clear presentation of your research and analysis in such a memorandum often requires a somewhat more elaborate structure. Exhibit 16.3 illustrates how a multiple-issue memorandum could be structured.

16.3

Exhibit
Organization of a
Multiple-Issue Interoffice
Memorandum of Law

INTEROFFICE MEMORANDUM OF LAW

TO: [*supervisor*]   RE: [*subject of memorandum*]
FROM: [*your name*]
DATE: [*today's date*]
CASE: [*names of the parties*]
OFFICE FILE NUMBER: [   ]
DOCKET NUMBER: [   ]

STATEMENT OF ASSIGNMENT

[*State what your supervisor asked you to do.*]

A. SUMMARY OF ISSUES AND CONCLUSIONS

ISSUE I.

[*State the first issue.*]

CONCLUSION

[*Briefly summarize your conclusion on the first issue.*]

ISSUE II.

[*State the second issue.*]

CONCLUSION

[*Briefly summarize your conclusion on the second issue.*]

ISSUE III.

[*State the third issue.*]

CONCLUSION

[*Briefly summarize your conclusion on the third issue.*]

ISSUE IV.

[*State the fourth issue.*]

CONCLUSION

[*Briefly summarize your conclusion on the fourth issue.*]

B. FACTS

[*State the facts of the client's case that are relevant to all four issues.*]

C. ANALYSIS

ISSUE I.

[*Restate the first issue. Then discuss the relevant primary and secondary authorities, present the counteranalysis, and state your conclusion on this issue.*]

ISSUE II.

[*Restate the second issue. Then discuss the relevant primary and secondary authorities, present the counteranalysis, and state your conclusion on this issue.*]

ISSUE III.

[*Restate the third issue. Then discuss the relevant primary and secondary authorities, present the counteranalysis, and state your conclusion on this issue.*]

ISSUE IV.

[*Restate the fourth issue. Then discuss the relevant primary and secondary authorities, present the counteranalysis, and state your conclusion on this issue.*]

D. CONCLUSION

[*Summarize your conclusions on all the issues.*]

E. RECOMMENDATIONS

F. APPENDIX

[*Include long items referred to in the memo, e.g., statistical tables, the full text of statutes.*]

Although not all supervisors agree on the preferred structure of an interoffice memorandum of law, here is a description of the features many supervisors would like to see in such memos:

1. Heading
2. Statement of the assignment
3. Issues
4. Facts
5. Discussion or analysis
6. Conclusion
7. Recommendations
8. Appendix

Heading

The **heading** of the memo contains basic information about you and the nature of the memo:

a. A **caption** centered at the top of the page stating the kind of document it is (Interoffice Memorandum of Law)
b. The name of the person to whom the memo is addressed (usually your supervisor)
c. Your name (the author of the memo)
d. The date the memo was completed and submitted
e. The name of the case (client's name and opponent, if any)
f. The office file number
g. The court **docket number** (if the suit has already been filed and the clerk of the court has assigned a docket number)
h. The subject matter of the memo following the notation **RE:**, meaning "in the matter of" or "concerning"

The example in Exhibit 16.4 illustrates how this information might be set forth in a memo written on behalf of client Brown, who is suing Miller.

16.4

Exhibit
Heading of Interoffice
Memorandum

INTEROFFICE MEMORANDUM OF LAW

TO: Jane Patterson, Esq.
FROM: John Jackson, Paralegal
DATE: March 13, 1994
CASE: Brown v. Miller
OFFICE FILE NUMBER: 94-1168
DOCKET NUMBER: C-34552-94

RE: Whether substituted service
is allowed under Civil
Code § 34-403(g)

Note that the subject-matter description (RE) in this example briefly indicates the nature of the question you are treating in the memorandum. This information is needed for at least two reasons. First, the average law office case file contains a large number of documents, often including several legal memoranda. A heading that at least briefly indicates the subject of the memorandum makes it easier to locate the memorandum in the client's file. Second, your memo might be examined sometime in the future, long after the case is over. Many offices keep copies of old office memoranda in files or in computer databases. They are cataloged by subject matter for reference in future cases. The subject-matter heading on the memo facilitates the cataloging, filing, and retrieving of such memos.

Including the date on which the memorandum was completed and submitted is important for similar reasons. Although your analysis and conclusions may have been accurate at the time the memorandum was written, the law may have changed by the time the memorandum is examined again. When the reader sees the date of the memorandum, he or she will know from what date subsequent legal research will be needed.

Statement of the Assignment

Soon after you are given an interoffice memorandum assignment, you should write out what you were asked to do. State the parameters of the assignment. If limitations or restrictions were imposed (e.g., not to cover a particular issue), include them in your written statement. If you have any difficulty writing the statement, consult with your supervisor immediately. The time to clarify what you are to do—and what you are not to do—is before you spend extensive amounts of time researching, analyzing, and writing. Here is an example:

> **Statement of Assignment**
> You have asked me to prepare a memorandum of law limited to the question of whether our client, Joan Davis, is required to return the overpayment she received from the Department of Revenue and Disbursements. You asked me to discuss Ohio law only.

Include this statement of the assignment after the heading. The value of clearly articulating the boundary lines of the memo cannot be overemphasized.

Issues

Before discussing **legal issues,** review the discussion in Chapter 11 on breaking rules into their **elements** (page 210). An element is a portion of a rule that is a precondition to the applicability of the entire rule. As pointed out in Figure 11.3 in chapter 11, one of the benefits of element identification is that it will assist you in identifying legal issues. Once you have laid out the elements, ask yourself which ones will be in controversy or contention because the two sides will not agree on how these elements apply to the facts. Each **element in contention** becomes the basis of a legal issue.

There are two ways to phrase legal issues. An example of a *shorthand statement of a legal issue* would be, "Does § 34 apply?" or "Can a van be burglarized?" A more *comprehensive statement of a legal issue* would consist of:

- A brief quote from the element in contention, and
- Several of the important facts relevant to that contention

For example, suppose that you are analyzing the following rule and facts:

> § 92. The operator of any vehicle riding on a sidewalk shall be fined $100.
> Facts: Fred rides his ten-speed bicycle on the sidewalk. He is charged with violating § 92.

The element breakdown and issue statement would be as follows:

Elements of § 92.

1. Operator
2. Any vehicle
3. Riding
4. On a sidewalk

Issue: Is a ten-speed bicycle a "vehicle" under § 92?

The parties will probably agree that Fred rode his bicycle on a sidewalk and that Fred was the operator of his bicycle. The first, third, and fourth elements, therefore, should not be made into legal issues. The only disagreement will be over the second element. Hence, it is the basis of an issue. Note the quotation marks around the element in contention (vehicle) and the inclusion of an important fact that is relevant to this contention (it was a ten-speed bicycle).

Assignment 16.1

Provide a comprehensive phrasing of the legal issue or issues in each of the following situations:

(a) *Facts:* Harry Franklin works for the XYZ Agency. In one of the Agency's personnel files is a notation that Paul Drake, another Agency employee, was once arrested for fraud. Harry obtains this information from this file and tells his wife about it. (She also knows Paul.) Harry is unaware that Paul has told at least three other employees about his fraud arrest. *Regulation: 20(d).* It shall be unlawful for any employee of the XYZ Agency to divulge confidential material in any file of the Agency.

(b) *Facts:* Jones has a swimming pool in his backyard. The pool is intended for use by the Jones family members and guests who are present when an adult is there to supervise. One hot summer night, a neighbor's child opens an unlocked door of a fence that surrounds the Jones's yard and goes into the pool. (There is no separate fence around the pool.) The child knows that he should not be there without an adult. No one else is at the pool. The child drowns. *Statute: § 77.* Property owners are liable for the foreseeable harm that occurs on their property.

(c) *Facts:* Dr. Carla Jones is the family physician of the Richardson family. After an appointment with Mary Richardson, age 16, Dr. Jones prescribes birth control pills. Mary tells Dr. Jones that she can't afford the pills and does not want her parents to know she is taking them. Dr. Jones says she will give Mary a supply of the pills at no cost in exchange for an afternoon of office clerical work at Dr. Jones's office. *Statute: § 25-403.* A pharmacist must not sell prescription drugs to a minor.

Often you must state and discuss certain issues *on the assumption* that the court or agency will decide against you on prior issues that you discuss early in the memorandum. Suppose that the client is a defendant in a negligence action. The first issue may concern the liability of the defendant: Was the defendant negligent or not? The memorandum will cover the liability question and will attempt to demonstrate in the discussion or analysis of this issue why the defendant is *not* liable. All the evidence and authority supporting nonliability will be examined under this issue. At the time the memorandum is written, of course, this issue will not have been resolved. Hence, you must proceed on the assumption that the client will lose the first issue and be prepared for other issues that will then arise. For example, all issues concerning damages (how much money must be paid to a plaintiff who has successfully established liability) should be anticipated and analyzed in the event that the liability issue is lost. The statement of the damage issue in the memorandum should be prefaced by language such as:

In the event that we lose the first issue, then we must discuss the issue of . . . .

or

On the assumption that the court finds for [the other party] on the liability issue, the damages question then becomes whether . . . .

No matter how firmly you believe in your prediction of what a court or agency will do on an issue, be prepared for what will happen in the event that your prediction eventually proves erroneous. This must be done in an internal memorandum, in an external memorandum (hearing or trial), and in an appellate brief.

Facts

Your statement of the facts of the client's case is one of the most important components of the memorandum. In this statement, a party tells his or her story through all the legally significant facts, i.e., those facts that help establish all the elements of the **causes of action** and defenses being asserted. (A cause of action is a set of facts that give a party a right to judicial relief; it is a legally acceptable reason for suing.) In addition, several background facts are included in the statement of the facts. You should take great pains to see that it is concise, highly accurate, and well organized.

a. *Conciseness:* An unduly long fact statement only frustrates the reader. Try to eliminate any unnecessary facts from the statement. One way of doing this is to carefully review your fact statement *after* you have completed your analysis of the issues. If your statement contains facts that are not subsequently referred to in your analysis, it may be that those facts are not particularly relevant to your memorandum and can be eliminated in your final draft. Otherwise, go back and discuss them in your analysis.

b. *Accuracy:* In many instances you will be drafting the memorandum for an attorney who is preparing to go before a court or agency for the first time; there may be no prior proceedings. Hence, there will be no record and no official findings of fact. The temptation will be to indulge in wishful thinking—to ignore adverse facts and to assume that disputed facts will be resolved in favor of the client. Do not give in to this temptation. You must assess the legal consequences of both favorable *and* unfavorable facts. If a particular fact is presently unknown, put aside your writing, if possible, and investigate whatever evidence exists to prove the fact one way or the other. If it is not practical to conduct an investigation at the present time, then you should provide an analysis of what law will apply based on your most reasonable estimate of what an investigation may uncover. (When you get to the recommendations section of the memo, be sure to include investigation that the office should undertake later.) The need for accuracy does not mean that you should fail to state the facts in the light most favorable to the client. It simply means that you must be careful to avoid making false or misleading statements of fact.

c. *Organization:* A disorganized statement of facts not only prevents the reader from understanding the events in question but also interferes with an understanding of your subsequent analysis. In general, it is best to start with a short one- or two-sentence summary of the nature of the case. If the case has already been in court, include the prior proceedings to date in this summary. Then provide a *chronological* statement of the detailed facts. Occasional variations from strict chronological order can be justified as long as they do not interfere with the flow of the story.

Discussion or Analysis

Here you present the law (primary authority) and explain its applicability to the facts. In other words, you try to answer the issues. For memos that require interpretation of statutes, the following organizational structure is suggested:

- State the entire section or subsection of the statute that you are analyzing. Include only what must be discussed in the memo. If the section or subsection is long, you may want to place it in an appendix to the memo. If you are going to discuss more than one section or subsection, treat them separately in different parts of the memo unless they are so interrelated that they must be discussed together.
- Break the statute into its elements. (An element is a portion of a rule that is a precondition of the applicability of the entire rule.) List each element separately. (See "Organizing a Memorandum of Law" in the benefits of element analysis in Exhibit 11.3 in chapter 11.)
- Briefly tell the reader which elements will be in contention and why. In effect, you are telling him or her why you have phrased the issue(s) the way you did earlier in the memo.
- Go through each element you have identified, one at a time, spending most of your time on the elements that are most in contention.
- For the elements not in contention, simply tell the reader why you think there will not be any dispute about them. For example, you anticipate that both sides probably will agree that the facts clearly support the applicability or nonapplicability of the element.

- For the elements in contention, present your interpretation of each element; discuss court opinions that have interpreted the statute, if any; discuss regulations and administrative decisions that have interpreted the statute, if any; discuss the legislative history of the statute, if available; discuss scholarly interpretation of the statute, if any, in legal periodicals or other secondary authority. (Be sure that you have laid the foundation for the use of secondary authority. See Figure 4.2 in chapter 4.)
- Give opposing viewpoints for the elements in contention. Try to anticipate how the other side will interpret these elements. For example, what counterarguments will the other side probably make through court opinions or legislative history?

Conclusion

Give your personal opinion (based on your legal analysis and legal research) as to which side has the better arguments. Do not state any new arguments in the conclusion. Simply state your own perspective—in summary fashion—on the strengths and weaknesses of your arguments.

Recommendations

State recommendations you feel are appropriate in view of the analysis and conclusion that you have provided. For example, further facts should be investigated, further research should be undertaken, a letter should be written to the agency involved, the case should be litigated or settled, etc. Make the recommendations as specific as possible.

Appendix

At the end of the memo, include special items, if any, that you referred to in the memo, such as photographs, statistical tables, or the full text of statutes or other primary authority. If the statute or other primary authority you are relying on in the memo is relatively brief, print it in the body of the memo or in a footnote where it can be easily found by the reader. Only when your quote is fairly long should you include it in full in the appendix *in addition to* your treatment of the pertinent parts (elements) in the discussion/analysis section of the memo.

SECTION C   **SAMPLE INTEROFFICE MEMORANDUM OF LAW**

What follows is an interoffice memorandum of law that conforms with this structure. Assume that the supervisor wants this memorandum within a few hours after the assignment is given to you. You are asked to provide a preliminary analysis of a statute. Hence, at this point there has been no time to do any research on the statute, although the memo should indicate what research will be needed.

```
                INTEROFFICE MEMORANDUM OF LAW
TO: Tim Farrell, Esq.                    RE: Whether Donaldson has
FROM: Mary Jones, Paralegal                  violated § 17
DATE: March 23, 1990
CASE: Department of Sanitation v. Jim Donaldson
OFFICE FILE NUMBER: 90-114
DOCKET NUMBER: (none at this time; no action has been filed)

A. ASSIGNMENT
  You have asked me to do a preliminary analysis of 23 State Code
Ann. § 17 (1980) to assess whether our client, Jim Donaldson, has
violated this statute. No research on the statute has been under-
taken thus far, but I will indicate where such research might be
helpful.
```

Continued on next page

—*continued*

B. LEGAL ISSUE
   When a government employee is asked to rent a car for his
agency, but uses the car for personal business before he signs
the lease, has this employee violated § 17, which prohibits the
use of "property leased to the government" for nonofficial purposes?

C. FACTS
   Jim Donaldson is a government employee who works for the State
Department of Sanitation. On February 12, 1990, he is asked by his
supervisor, Fred Jackson, to rent a car for the agency for a two-
year period. At the ABC Car Rental Company, Donaldson is shown
several cars available for rental. He asks the manager if he could
test drive one of the cars for about 15 minutes before making a
decision. The manager agrees. Donaldson then drives the car to his
home in the area, picks up a TV, and takes it to his sister's
home. When he returns, he tells the manager that he wants to rent
the car for his agency. He signs the lease and takes the car to
the agency. The supervisor, however, finds out about the trip that
Donaldson made to his sister with the TV. Donaldson is charged
with a violation of § 17. Because he is a new employee at the
agency, he is fearful that he might lose his job.

D. ANALYSIS Donaldson is charged with violating 23 State Code
Ann. § 17 (1980), which provides as follows:

> § 17. Use of Government Property
> An employee of any state agency shall not directly or indi-
> rectly use government property of any kind, including property
> leased to the government, for other than officially approved
> activities.

To establish a violation of this statute, the following elements
must be proven:
   (1) An employee of any state agency

   (2) (a) shall not directly use government property of any kind
           including property leased to the government, or

       (b) shall not indirectly use government property of any
           kind including property leased to the government

   (3) for other than officially approved activities

The main problem in this case will be the second element.

   (1) Employee of a state agency
      Donaldson works for the State Department of Sanitation,
   which is clearly a "state agency" under the statute.
   (2) Use of property leased to the government
      The central issue is whether Donaldson used property leased
   to the government. (The rented car was not owned by the government. Hence it was not "government property." And Donaldson
   acted "directly" rather than "indirectly," such as by causing
   someone else to drive the car.) There should be no dispute
   that when Donaldson drove the car to his sister's, he directly
   used property. But was it "property leased to the government"?
      Donaldson's best argument is a fairly strong one. His posi-
   tion will be that when he made the trip to his sister's, he
   had not yet signed the lease. He would argue that "leased"
   means contractually committed to rent. Under this definition,
   the car did not become property leased to the government until
   after he returned from his sister's house. No costs were

—*continued*

incurred by the government because of the test drive. Rental payments would not begin until the car was rented through the signing of the lease.

The supervisor, on the other hand, will argue for a broader definition of "leased"— that it means the process of obtaining a contractual commitment to rent, including the necessary steps leading up to that commitment. Under this definition, the car was leased to Donaldson when he made the unauthorized trip. The test drive was arguably a necessary step in making the decision to sign a long-term leasing contract.

The goal of the legislature in enacting § 17 should be kept in mind when trying to determine the meaning of any of the language of § 17. The legislature was trying to avoid the misuse of government resources. Public employees should not take advantage of their position for private gain. To do so would be a violation of the public trust. Yet this is what Donaldson did. While on the government payroll, he obtained access to a car and used it for a private trip. Common sense would lead to the conclusion that leasing in § 17 is not limited to the formal signing of a leasing contract. Anything that is necessarily part of the process of signing that contract should be included. The legislature wanted to prevent the misuse of government resources in all necessary aspects of the leasing of property.

It is not clear from the facts whether the manager of the ABC Rental Company knew that Donaldson was considering the rental on behalf of a government agency when he received permission to take the test drive. The likelihood is that he did know it, although this should be checked. If the manager did know, then Donaldson probably used the fact that he was a government employee to obtain the permission. He held himself out as a reliable individual because of the nature of his employment. This reinforces the misuse argument under the broader definition of "leased" presented above.

I have not yet checked whether there are any court opinions or agency regulations interpreting § 17 on this point. Nor have I researched the legislative history of the statute. All this should be done soon.

(3) Officially Approved Activities

Nothing in the facts indicates that Donaldson's supervisor, Fred Jackson, gave him any authorization to make the TV trip. Even if Jackson had authorized the trip, it would probably not be "officially" approved, since the trip was not for official (i.e., public) business.

E. CONCLUSION

Donaldson has the stronger argument based on the language of the statute. The property simply was not "leased" at the time he made the TV trip. I must admit, however, that the agency has some very good points in its favor. Unlike Donaldson's technical argument, the agency's position is grounded in common sense. Yet on balance, Donaldson's argument should prevail.

F. RECOMMENDATIONS

Some further investigation is needed. We should find out whether the ABC Rental Company manager knew that Donaldson was a government employee at the time he asked for the test drive. In addition, legal research should be undertaken to find out if any

Continued on next page

—*continued*

court opinions and agency regulations exist on the statute. A check into the legislative history of § 17 is also needed.

Finally, I recommend that we send a letter to Donaldson's supervisor, Fred Jackson, explaining our position. I have attached a draft of such a letter for your signature in the event you deem this action appropriate.

There is one matter that I have not addressed in this memo. Donaldson is concerned that he might lose his job over this incident. Assuming for the moment that he did violate § 17, it is not at all clear that termination would be an appropriate sanction. The statute is silent on this point. Let me know if you want me to research this issue.

Farrell, Grote, & Schweitzer
Attorneys at Law
724 Central Plaza Place
West Union, Ohio 45693
513-363-7159

Timothy Farrell, Esq.
Angela Grote, Esq.
Clara Schweitzer, Esq.

                                                     March 25, 1990
                                                     RE: James Donaldson
                                                         90-114

Frederick Jackson
Field Supervisor
Department of Sanitation
3416 34th St. NW
West Union, Ohio 45693

Dear Mr. Jackson:

    Our firm represents Mr. James Donaldson. As you know, some question has arisen as to Mr. Donaldson's use of a car prior to the time he was asked to rent it for your agency on February 12, 1990. Our understanding is that he was asked to go to the ABC Car Rental Company in order to rent a car that was needed by your agency, and that he did so satisfactorily.

    Your agency became responsible for the car at the moment Mr. Donaldson signed the lease for the car rental. What happened prior to the time the lease was signed is not relevant. The governing statute (§ 17) is quite explicit. It forbids nonofficial use of property "leased" to the government. Such use did not occur in this case. No one has questioned Mr. Donaldson's performance of his duty once he "leased" the car.

    If additional clarification is needed, we would be happy to discuss the matter with you further.

Sincerely,

Timothy Farrell, Esq.
TF:ps

Assignment 16.2

The Pepsi Cola Bottling Company is authorized to do business in Florida. It wishes to prevent another Florida company from calling itself the Pepsi Catsup Company because this name violates § 225.25. The Pepsi Catsup Company denies that its name is in violation of this statute. The Secretary of State has the responsibility of enforcing this statute.

48 State Code Ann. § 225.25 (1979). The name of a company or corporation shall be such as will distinguish it from any other company or corporation doing business in Florida.

Your supervisor asks you to prepare a preliminary memorandum of law on the applicability of this statute. The office represents the Pepsi Catsup Company. Do no legal research at this time, although you should point out what research might be helpful. After you complete the memo, draft a letter to the Secretary of State giving the position of your office on the applicability of the statute. (You can make up the names and addresses of the people involved as well as any dates that you need.)

CHAPTER SUMMARY

A memorandum of law is a written analysis of a legal problem that explains how the law applies to a given set of facts. The audience of an internal or interoffice memorandum of law is your supervisor. In this memo you analyze the law and predict how a court or other tribunal will resolve the dispute. The audience of an external or advocacy memorandum of law is someone outside the office, such as a hearing officer. In this memo you analyze the law to try to convince the reader to take a certain action in the client's case.

The structure or organization of a memorandum of law depends on the preferences of your supervisor and the complexity of the case being analyzed due to the number of issues involved. The major components of many interoffice memoranda of law are: heading, statement of the assignment, legal issues (which are based on the elements in contention), facts, discussion or analysis, conclusion, recommendations, and appendix.

KEY TERMS

memorandum of law
interoffice memorandum
   of law
intraoffice memorandum
   of law

external memorandum of law
points and authorities
   memorandum
trial memorandum
hearing memorandum

heading
caption
docket number
RE:
legal issues

elements
elements in contention
causes of action

APPELLATE BRIEF

► *Chapter Outline*

Section A. Introduction
Section B. Sections of an Appellate Brief

SECTION A   INTRODUCTION

An **appellate brief** is a document, submitted to an appellate court, in which a party asks the court to approve, modify, or reverse what a lower court has done. The party preparing the brief *files* it in an appellate court and *serves* it on all opposing parties in the litigation. The appellate brief is one of the most sophisticated kinds of writing in a law office.[1]

The first appellate brief that is usually submitted is the *appellant's* brief. The **appellant** is the party initiating the appeal. Then the *appellee's* brief is filed in response. The appeal is taken against the **appellee** (sometimes called the **respondent**). Finally, the appellant is often allowed to submit a **reply brief** to counter the position taken in the appellee's brief.

Occasionally, a court will permit a nonparty to the litigation to submit an appellate brief. This is referred to as an **amicus curiae** (friend of the court) brief (page 39). The amicus brief advises the court on how to resolve the controversies before it. For example, the National Conference of American Bishops might ask to submit an amicus brief in a case in which the Conference is not a party but that raises the issue of a state's right to tax church activities other than worship services.

SECTION B   SECTIONS OF AN APPELLATE BRIEF

Not all appellate briefs have the same structure. Rules of court often specify what structure or format the brief should take, the print size, number of the copies to be submitted, etc. The following are the major components of many appellate briefs:

(a) *Caption:* The **caption** states the names of the parties, the name of the court, the court file or docket number, and the kind of appellate brief it is. The caption goes on the front cover of the brief (page 40).

(b) *Statement of Jurisdiction:* In the **statement of jurisdiction,** there is a short statement explaining the subject-matter jurisdiction of the appellate court. For example:

This Court has jurisdiction under 28 U.S.C. § 1291 (1967).

The jurisdiction statement may point out some of the essential facts that relate to the jurisdiction of the appellate court, such as how the case came up on appeal. For example:

On January 2, 1978, a judgment was entered by the U.S. Court of Appeals for the Second Circuit. The U.S. Supreme Court granted certiorari on February 6, 1978. 400 U.S. 302.

Later in the brief there is a Statement of the Case that often includes more detailed jurisdictional material.

(c) *Table of Contents:* The **table of contents** is an outline of the major components of the brief, including **point headings,** and the pages in the brief on which everything begins. A point heading is the party's conclusion it wants the court to adopt for a particular issue. The function of the table of contents is to provide the reader with quick and easy access to each portion of the brief. Because the page numbers will not be known until the brief is completed, the table of contents is the last section of the brief to be written. The following excerpt from the respondent's brief illustrates the structure of a table of contents that includes the point headings as part of the "argument."

```
                          TABLE OF CONTENTS

                                                              Page
     Opinions Below ................................................. 1
     Jurisdiction ................................................... 2
```

---

1. The word *brief* has other meanings as well. See the beginning of chapter 10 (and the glossary) for definitions of *brief of a case* and *trial brief.*

TABLE OF CONTENTS—continued

(d) *Table of Authorities:* The **table of authorities** lists all the cases, statutes, regulations, administrative decisions, constitutional provisions, charter provisions, ordinances, court rules, and secondary authority relied on in the brief. All the cases are listed in alphabetical order, all the statutes are listed in alphabetical and numerical order, etc. The page numbers on which each of these authorities is discussed in the brief are presented so that the table acts as an index to these authorities.

TABLE OF AUTHORITIES

Page

CASES:

    Smith v. Jones, 24 F.2d 445 (5th Cir. 1974) ... 2, 4, 12

    Thompson v. Richardson, 34 Miss. 650, 65 So. 109 (1930) ... 3, 9

    Etc.

CONSTITUTIONAL PROVISIONS

    Art. 5, Miss. Constitution ... 12, 17

    Art. 7, Miss. Constitution ... 20

    Etc.

STATUTES

    Miss. Code Ann. § 23(b) (1978) ... 2, 8, 23

    Miss. Code Ann. § 45 (1978) ... 7

    Etc.

LAW REVIEW ARTICLES

    John Colom, *Sex Discrimination in the 1980s*, 35 Miss. Law Journal 268 (1982) ... 19

Etc.

(e) *Questions Presented:* The label used for the **questions presented** section of the brief varies. Other names for it include "Points Relied on for Reversal," "Points in Error," "Assignments of Error," "Issues Presented," etc. Regardless of the label, its substance is essentially the same: it is a statement of the legal issues that the party wishes the appellate court to consider and decide.

(f) *Statement of the Case:* In the **statement of the case,** the dispute and lower court proceedings to date are summarized, the essential facts of the case are presented, and (often) the jurisdictional data are included. (Some courts require a separate *statement of facts* in addition to a statement of the case.)

In the following excerpt from a statement of the case, note the specific references to pages in the **transcript.** The transcript is the word-for-word account of what happened in the lower court. An appellate court **reviews** what occurred below; it does not hold hearings to determine what the facts were. It examines—*reviews*—the facts found by the trial court in order to decide whether the conclusions reached by the trial court on those facts were correct.

> These are actions based upon the Federal Tort Claims Act, 28 U.S.C. § 1346(b), initiated by the appellants, Garrett Freightlines, Inc. and Charles R. Thomas in the United States District Court for the District of Idaho. The appellant alleged that appellee's employee, Randall W. Reynolds, while acting within the scope of his employment, negligently caused injury to appellants. The United States denied that the employee was acting within the scope of his employment.
>
> On March 27, 1973, appellant Garrett made a motion for limited summary judgment as to whether Reynolds was acting within the scope of his employment when the collision occurred. The actions of Garrett and Thomas were consolidated by order of the court, and appellee later moved for summary judgment (see trial transcript, page 204).
>
> The District Court held that under the authority of dicta in *Berrettoni v. United States,* 436 F.2d 1372 (9th Cir. 1970), Reynolds was not within the scope of his employment when the accident occurred and granted appellee's motion for summary judgment. It is from that order and judgment that the injured now appeals.
>
> Staff Sergeant Reynolds was a career soldier in the United States Military and, until November 9, 1970, stationed at Fort Rucker, Alabama. On or about July 30, 1970, official orders directed that Reynolds be reassigned to the Republic of Vietnam. . . .

(g) *Summary of Argument:* In the **summary of argument,** the major points to be made in the brief are summarized.

(h) *Argument:* In the **argument,** the attorney explains the legal positions of the client presented in the order of the point headings listed in the table of contents. All the primary and secondary authority relied on is analyzed.

(i) *Conclusion:* The **conclusion** states what action the attorney is asking the appellate court to take.

(j) *Appendixes:* The **appendixes** contain excerpts from statutes or other primary authority, excerpts from the trial transcript, charts, descriptions of exhibits entered into evidence at the trial, etc.

Assignment 17.1

Go to the rules of court that cover the highest state court in your state. Find the rules on the format of the first appellate brief filed by an appellant. Summarize the components that this brief must have. Compare these components with those outlined in this chapter.

CHAPTER SUMMARY

An appellate brief is a formal written argument to a state or federal court of appeals on why the lower court's decision should be affirmed, modified, or reversed.

The major components of an appellate brief are: caption, statement of jurisdiction, table of contents, table of authorities, ques-

tions presented, statement of the case, summary of the argument, argument, conclusion, and appendixes.

KEY TERMS

appellate brief
appellant
appellee
respondent
reply brief

amicus curiae
caption
statement of jurisdiction
table of contents
point headings

table of authorities
questions presented
statement of the case
transcript
reviews

summary of argument
argument
conclusion
appendixes

Writing Fundamentals

SECTION A   INTRODUCTION

Legal writing has a bad reputation. Few think that attorneys write well. Why do lawyers have this reputation? One critic says that a young attorney soon learns that the only way to avoid being wrong is never to say anything clearly![1] Some judges react negatively to writing that falls into this category. United States District Judge Lynn N. Hughes, of Houston once forced a trial attorney to rewrite a pleading by eliminating "all excessive capitalization, empty formalisms, obscure abstractions, and grammatical imbecilities." In this chapter the goal is to avoid a similar condemnation of our own writing.

SECTION B   SOME OF THE BASICS[2]

1. Comma (,)

1.1   Use a **comma** to separate two words or figures that might otherwise be misunderstood. **EX:** Instead of hundreds, thousands came.

1.2   Use a comma between an introductory phrase and a direct quotation of only a few words. **EX:** He said, "Now or never."

1.3   Use a comma to indicate the omission of a word or words. **EX:** Then we had much; now, nothing.

1.4   Use a comma between two or more *coordinate adjectives*. (A coordinate adjective modifies a noun separate from other adjectives. Adjectives are coordinate if you can scramble them without changing the meaning of the sentence.) **EX:** The school instituted relevant, lengthy classes. **COMPARE:** He was arrested with an illegal time bomb.

1.5   Use a comma before and after Jr., Sr., Esq., Ph.D., Inc. within a sentence. **EX:** Henry Smith, Jr., chairperson.

1.6   Use a comma to set off parenthetical words, phrases, or clauses. **EX:** Paul Dix, who was then Secretary of State, opposed the bill.

1.7   Use a comma between an introductory dependent clause and the subsequent independent clause. **EX:** Beset by enemies, he resigned.
But do not use a comma after a short prepositional phrase. **EX:** At night he was too tired to study.

1.8   Use a comma to set off a nonrestrictive clause. (A clause is nonrestrictive if it is not essential to the meaning of the sentence. Nonrestrictive clauses use *which*. Restrictive clauses are essential and use *that*.) **EX:** The judge dismissed the case, which surprised no one. **COMPARE:** The clerk refused to stamp the complaint that was not notarized.

1.9   Use a comma to set off words or phrases in apposition or in contrast. **EX:** Mary Smith, her attorney, filed the motion. The third case, *In re Jones,* is next.

1.10 Use a comma after each word in a series of three or more words or phrases joined at the end by *and* or by *or*. **EX:** The office employed attorneys, paralegals, and secretaries. You can go now by bus, take the van at noon, or drive with the rest of the group this evening.

1.11 Use a comma before a conjunction in a compound sentence that joins two independent clauses. **EX:** The first trial took two weeks, but the third lasted one day. **COMPARE:** I enjoyed everything but the finale.

---

1. Ann Lousin, *Firms, Not Law Schools, Create Bad Writers*, National Law Journal (June 11, 1990), at 12.
2. Based on William Statsky and Richard Gladstein, *Grammar, Composition & Style* (1981)(Richard Nakamura & Cheryl Jannarone, contributing editors); Office of the Federal Register, *Legal Drafting Style Manual* (1977); G.P.O., *Style Manual* (1973, 1984); Office of Legislative Counsel, D.C. City Council, *Legislative Drafting Manual* (1979); Department of the Treasury, *Effective Writing* (1975); and Gray, *Writing a Good Appellate Brief,* 88 Case and Comment 44 (1983).

1.12 Use a comma after a noun or phrase in direct address. **EX:** Senator, will you support the amendment?

1.13 Use a comma inside the closing quotation mark. **EX:** "Freedom is out of the question," he asserted.

1.14 Do not use a comma before a zip code. **EX:** Boston, MA 02127

1.15 Do not use a comma to set off a short prepositional phrase. **EX:** With me the money is safe. **COMPARE:** In view of all the considerations placed before me, I accept.

1.16 Do not use a comma before a parenthesis. **EX:** All paralegals (temporary and full-time) were present.

2. Semicolon (;)

2.1 Use a **semicolon** to separate items in a list when commas are already used within some of the items in the list. **EX:** He traveled to Boston, Massachusetts; Salem, Oregon; and Reno, Nevada.

2.2 Use a semicolon to separate independent clauses that are not joined by *and, but, yet, or,* or *nor.* **EX:** The plaintiff is indigent; the defendant is wealthy. **COMPARE:** He is late, but we can proceed. (See also 1.11 above.)

2.3 Use a semicolon between independent clauses joined by *however, therefore, thus, moreover, indeed,* and *then.* **EX:** Richards is a great judge; however, he is unpredictable.

2.4 Use a semicolon between independent clauses joined by phrases like *for example, for instance, in fact.* **EX:** There are advantages to settling the case; for example, the trial will be avoided.

2.5 Place semicolons outside quotation marks. **EX:** The witness said there was "no one present"; however, the jury felt otherwise.

3. Colon (:)

3.1 Use a **colon** to call attention to and to introduce a formal quotation. **EX:** The judge angrily concluded by saying: "This is the last extension I will grant!"

3.2 Use a colon between two independent clauses (or sentences) when the second explains, summarizes, or comments on the first. (Start the second with a capital letter). **EX:** The jury finally resolved the issue: It found for the defendant.

3.3 Use a colon to introduce a list, especially when the list is introduced by the words *the following* and *as follows.* **EX:** Bring the following documents: the motion, the response, and the brief.

3.4 Use a colon after a salutation in a formal letter. **EX:** Dear Mr. Henderson:

3.5 Use a colon to separate a title of a book from its subtitle. **EX:** *Introduction to Paralegalism: Perspectives, Problems, and Skills.*

3.6 Use a colon when stating clock time. **EX:** 5:12 A.M.

3.7 Do not use a colon after the verb *to be* or after a preposition. **EX:** The memo is concise and effective. (**NOT:** The memo is: concise and effective.) They picketed on sidewalks, streets, and parking lots. (**NOT:** They picketed on: sidewalks, streets, and parking lots.)

4. Dash (—)

4.1 Use a **dash** to mark a sudden break or abrupt change of thought. **EX:** He said— and no one contradicted him—that he is innocent.

4.2 Use a dash to mark or set off a brief summary. **EX:** Fortitude, energy, and luck— we will need them all to win.

4.3   Do not use a dash immediately after a comma, colon, or semicolon. **EX:** The box contains the following evidence: guns, knives, and spears. **NOT:** The box contains the following evidence:—guns, knives, and spears.

5. Parallelism

5.1   Items in a list should be of equal value. All items that are parallel in thought must be alike in construction (general rule).

5.2   If you want the list to contain nouns, do not allow a verb to replace one of the nouns.
Do not say: The attorney wanted an extension and to settle.
Say: The attorney wanted an extension and a settlement.

5.3   If the first item in your list is an *ing* word, the remaining item(s) in the list should be *ing* words.
Do not say: He enjoys debating, bargaining, and negotiation.
Say: He enjoys debat*ing*, bargain*ing*, and negotiat*ing*.

5.4   If the first item in your list is an *ed* verb, the remaining item(s) in the list should be *ed* verbs.
Do not say: He is exhausted, frightened, and in a state of shock.
Say: He is exhaust*ed*, frighten*ed*, and shock*ed*.

5.5   If the first item in your list is a prepositional phrase, the remaining item(s) in the list should be prepositional phrases.
Do not say: The agency agreed with Dan, with Mary, and me.
Say: The agency agreed *with* Dan, *with* Mary, and *with* me.

5.6   Avoid placing some items in the list in the active voice (e.g., John calls) and others in the passive voice (e.g., Jim is called.)
Do not say: As the conditions are met by Ted, Bob accepts them.
Say: As Ted meets the conditions, Bob accepts them.

5.7   If the first item in your list is a noun, don't make the remaining item in the list a clause. Or make every item in the list a clause.
Do not say: He asked for her help and that I refrain from interfering.
Say: He asked for her help and for my noninterference.
OR: He asked that she help and that I refrain from interfering.

5.8   Other parallelism rules:
(a)   If the first item in the list is an infinitive (e.g., to call), all items in the list should be infinitives.
(b)   If the first item in the list is a phrase (e.g., the date *of payment*), all items in the list should be phrases.
(c)   If the first item in the list is a clause (e.g., which is now available), all items in the list should be clauses.
(d)   If the first item in the list begins with an article (e.g., the, an, a), all items in the list should begin with an article.

6. Spelling

6.1   Although there are a few useful spelling rules (e.g., i before e except after c . . .), most spelling problems are resolved by *memorizing* the correct spelling. Don't wait for spelling rules. Start memorizing now. Here are some frequently misspelled words in law that you should memorize (after checking their meaning, if unsure):

aberration	aluminum	biased	cigarette	counseling
abridgment	analogous	calendar	cocaine	defense
abysmal	anomalous	canceled	colossal	dependent
accessory	anonymous	cancellation	commingle	descendant
accommodate	appalling	cannot	consensus	dissension
acknowledgment	assassinate	casual	consignor	divorcee
adviser	behoove	catalog	controlling	embarrass
aide	benevolence	causal	corollary	employee

enclose	heterogeneous	labeled	partisan	specious
encumber	hijack	liaison	patrolled	statute
encumbrance	idiosyncrasy	libeled	percent	subpoena
encyclopedia	illicit	license	perquisite	surreptitious
enforcement	impaneled	likable	personal	surveillance
enrollment	impasse	lineage	personnel	threshold
entrench	imperiled	liquor	practice	totaled
entrust	indict	livable	precedent	trafficking
exonerate	inequity	lodestar	prerequisite	transferable
fetal	ingenious	maneuver	pretense	transferor
fetish	innocuous	marijuana	preventive	transferred
fiche	innuendo	marshaled	promissory	traveled
foresee	inquire	meager	quarreling	traveler
germane	inquiry	mileage	questionnaire	traveling
glamour	installment	milieu	racket	vacillate
goodbye	instill	modeled	registrar	villain
grievous	judgeship	moneys	reinforce	vitamin
gruesome	judgment	movable	rescission	warranty
harass	kidnapped	offense	scurrilous	willful
heinous	kidnapper	oneself	separate	
hemorrhage	kidnapping	parallel	skillful	

6.2   Place *i* before *e* except after *c* or after an *ay* sound.

> **I before E:** believe, belief, field, relief, relieve, grief, siege, friend, yield, niece
> **Except after C:** receive, receipt, conceive, ceiling, deceive, conceit
> **Except after AY sound:** neighbor, weigh, freight, sleigh
> **Further Exceptions:** their, neither, weird, foreign, seize, society, height, ancient, conscience, efficient, sufficient

6.3   Add *es* to form the plural of words that already end in *s*, *ch*, *sh*, *x*, or *z*.

bus/busses	flush/flushes	box/boxes
glass/glasses	dish/dishes	fox/foxes
business/businesses	bush/bushes	buzz/buzzes
church/churches	tax/taxes	

6.4   To form the plural of a word ending in *y*, add *s* if the letter before the *y* is a vowel.

attorney/attorneys	boy/boys
play/plays	key/keys
survey/surveys	monkey/monkeys
day/days	Sunday/Sundays

6.5   To form the plural of a word ending in *y*, change the *y* to *i* and add *es* if the letter before the *y* is a consonant.

story/stories	baby/babies
butterfly/butterflies	bureaucracy/bureaucracies
company/companies	lady/ladies
blueberry/blueberries	sixty/sixties
candy/candies	summary/summaries

6.6   In forming the plurals of compound terms, the significant word takes the plural form:

assistant directors	heirs at law
assistant attorneys	inspectors general
attorneys at law	judge advocates
brothers-in-law	mothers-in-law
comptrollers general	notaries public
courts-martial	prisoners of war
daughters-in-law	rights-of-way
general counsels	trade unions
grants-in-aid	

7. Possessive ('s) (')

7.1 If a singular or a plural noun does not end in *s*, the *possessive* is formed by adding *'s*.
EX: man's fears; men's fears   child's money; children's money

7.2 If the noun is singular and ends in *s*, the possessive is formed by adding *'s*.
EX: Judge Jones's opinion   Lois's attorney   the boss's report

7.3 If the noun is plural and ends in *s*, the possessive is formed by adding an apostrophe (').
EX: ten actors' parts   all the hostesses' tips

7.4 For joint possession, follow the above rules for the last noun only.
EX: Bill and Ed's family   father and sons' game

7.5 Possessive pronouns do not take apostrophes.
Say: its car is broken   **Not:** it's car is broken
Say: whose car is it   **Not:** who's car is it
Say: the cars are ours   **Not:** the cars are our's
Say: the car is hers   **Not:** the car is her's
Say: the cars are theirs   **Not:** the cars are their's
Say: the cars are yours   **Not:** the cars are your's

8. Numerals

8.1 Spell out numbers of one or two words, except for dates, street numbers, and math calculations. **EX:** seven, thirty-two, two thousand, twenty million; June 2; 6 Main Street; 4 + 4

8.2 Use numerals for numbers of three or more words.
EX: 157   2,567   3,100,000

8.3 When a sentence begins with a number, always write out the number. **EX:** Five hundred paralegals attended the conference.

9. Subject-Verb Agreement

9.1 Subject and verb must agree in number regardless of whether nouns or pronouns appear between the subject and verb. **EX:** The courts on the first floor complex of the building are [not *is*] in session. (The subject of the sentence is *courts,* not *complex* or *building*.)

9.2 Subjects connected by *and* are usually plural for purposes of agreement. **EX:** Verbose writing and inconsistent reasoning irritate [not *irritates*] the senior partner.

9.3 Subjects joined by *or* or by *nor* usually require a verb that agrees with the closer subject. **EX:** Smith or Hill teaches [not *teach*] in the spring. Neither the mortgage nor the contracts are [not *is*] available. Either the administrators or the secretary uses [not *use*] that computer.

9.4 The following indefinite pronouns are usually singular: *anyone, anybody, each, either, everyone, everybody, everything, neither, none, no one, somebody, someone*. **EX:** everyone appreciates [not *appreciate*] the gesture; none of the judges is [not *are*] available.

9.5 The words *all, any, most, none,* and *some* require a singular or a plural verb depending on their meaning in the sentence. **EX:** Most of his assets are [not *is*] gone. Most of his energy is [not *are*] gone.
    In the first sentence *most* refers to *assets,* a plural word. Hence we need a plural verb, *are*. In the second sentence, *most* refers to *energy,* a singular word. Hence we need a singular verb, *is*.

9.6 Collective nouns such as *committee, crowd, class, majority,* and *family* usually require a singular verb. **EX:** The family sleeps (not *sleep*) there. The majority of the court favors (not *favor*) capital punishment.

9.7 Nouns singular in meaning but plural in form normally require singular verbs. **EX:** All politics is [not *are*] local.

9.8 The title of a book or periodical requires a singular verb even if plural in form. **EX:** The *Daily News* is (not *are*) on sale.

9.9 A relative pronoun (*who, that, which*) used as a subject requires a singular or plural verb to agree with its antecedent. **EX:** Judge Bennett is one of the local judges who has (not *have*) spoken.

10. Pronoun-Noun Agreement

10.1 Pronouns must agree with their **antecedents** in number. **EX:** Each one of these women must make her [not *their*] position known. (The antecedent of the pronoun is "each one"—singular, not "women"—plural.)

10.2 When antecedents are connected by *and*, use a plural pronoun. **EX:** Tom and Joe won their [not *his*] party's nomination.

10.3 When antecedents are connected by *or* or by *nor*, the pronoun should agree with the nearest antecedent. **EX:** Tom or Joe will show his [not *their*] plans first. The city and the towns have presented their [not, *has presented its*] budget.

10.4 Collective nouns such as *committee, crowd, class, board, audience, majority, team,* and *family* take singular or plural pronouns according to whether the collective noun functions in the singular (as a unit) or in the plural (as individuals within the unit). **EX:** Try to persuade the board of directors that it is wrong. The board of directors disagree on whether their salaries should be increased.

10.5 Indefinite pronouns are usually singular: *anyone, anybody, each, either, everyone, everybody, everything, neither, no one, nobody, somebody, someone.* **EX:** Each of the boys brought his (not *their*) car. Everyone appreciates his [not *their*] mentor. **OR:** Everyone appreciates her [not *their*] mentor.

SECTION C   IMPROVING CLARITY

11. Unnecessary Language

11.1 Do not use circumlocutions. A **circumlocution** is a pair of words that have the same effect. Here is a list of circumlocutions commonly found in the law. Avoid using them. Pick one of the words and discard the other.

Do not say:	*Say:*	*Or say:*
alter and change	alter	change
any and all	any	all
by and with	by	with
each and every	each	every
final and conclusive	final	conclusive
full and complete	full	complete
made and entered into	made	entered
null and void	null	void
order and direct	order	direct
over and above	over	above
sole and exclusive	sole	exclusive
type and kind	type	kind
unless and until	unless	until

11.2. Omit excess language. If language adds nothing to the sentence, don't use it. There is an easy test to find out if your phrase, clause, or sentence is carrying excess baggage. Remove it and ask yourself whether you have altered the meaning or emphasis desired. If not, keep it out.

Compare the sentences in these two columns:

A	B
Your maximum recovery is $100 under the provisions of the Warsaw Convention.	Your maximum recovery is $100 under the Warsaw Convention.

When we remove "the provisions of" from the first sentence, we lose neither meaning nor emphasis. Hence, we don't need it. Compare the following versions of the same sentence:[3]

He consulted *with* a doctor *in regard to* his injuries.	He consulted a doctor *about* his injuries.
He drove to the left *due to the fact* that the lane was blocked.	He drove to the left *because* the lane was blocked.
This product is used for *hair-dyeing purposes.*	This product is used to *dye hair.*
The continuance was requested *in order to obtain the presence of a witness who was not then available.*	The continuance was requested *because a witness was unavailable.*

Read these sentences, with and without the italicized words.

The court directed a verdict in favor of the defendant *and against the plaintiff.* (Verdicts for defendants usually are against the plaintiff.)

The car was green *in color.* (This distinguishes it from the car that was green in size!)

A delivery was made every Tuesday *on a regular weekly basis.* (What does *every Tuesday* mean if not weekly and regularly?)

Use the language in the second column unless you have a valid reason to use the language in the first column:

Do not say:	*Say:*
(1) all of the	(1) all the
(2) by means of	(2) by *or* with
(3) does not operate to	(3) does not
(4) during the course of	(4) during
(5) in the time of	(5) during
(6) in order to	(6) to
(7) or in the alternative	(7) or
(8) period of time	(8) period *or* time
(9) provision of law	(9) law
(10) State of New Jersey	(10) New Jersey
(11) until such time as	(11) until

11.3. Use shorter words when longer ways of expressing the same idea add nothing. Use the language in the second column unless you have a valid reason to use the language in the first column:

Do not say:	*Say:*
(1) adequate number of	(1) enough
(2) prohibited from	(2) shall not
(3) at such time as	(3) when
(4) during such time as	(4) while
(5) enter into a contract	(5) contract (verb)
(6) for the duration of	(6) during

3. Grey, *Writing a Good Appellate Brief*, 88 Case and Comment 44, 48–50 (No. 6, November/December 1983). Reprinted by special permission of the Lawyers Cooperative Publishing Co.

(7)	for the purpose of	(7)	for
(8)	for the purpose of entering	(8)	to enter
(9)	for the reason that	(9)	because
(10)	give consideration to	(10)	consider
(11)	give recognition to	(11)	recognize
(12)	have need of	(12)	need
(13)	in case	(13)	if
(14)	in a number of	(14)	in some
(15)	in cases in which	(15)	when
(16)	in connection with	(16)	in *or* on
(17)	in regard to	(17)	about
(18)	in relation to	(18)	about *or* toward
(19)	in the case of	(19)	if *or* in
(20)	in the event of	(20)	if
(21)	in the matter of	(21)	in *or* on
(22)	in the majority of instances	(22)	usually
(23)	in view of	(23)	because *or* since
(24)	is able to	(24)	can
(25)	is applicable	(25)	applies
(26)	is binding on	(26)	binds
(27)	is dependent on	(27)	depends on
(28)	is entitled to	(28)	may
(29)	is in attendance at	(29)	attends
(30)	is permitted to	(30)	may
(31)	is required to	(31)	shall
(32)	is unable to	(32)	cannot
(33)	is directed to	(33)	shall
(34)	it is your duty to	(34)	you shall *or* you must
(35)	make an appointment of	(35)	appoint
(36)	make a determination of	(36)	determine
(37)	make application	(37)	apply
(38)	make payment	(38)	pay
(39)	make provision for	(39)	provide for
(40)	on a few occasions	(40)	occasionally
(41)	on behalf of	(41)	for
(42)	on the part of	(42)	by *or* among
(43)	provided that	(43)	if
(44)	subsequent to	(44)	after
(45)	with reference to	(45)	on

11.4. Use a less complicated or less fancy way of expressing the same idea. Use the language in the second column unless you have a valid reason to use the language in the first column:

Do not say:		*Say:*	
(1)	accorded	(1)	given
(2)	afforded	(2)	given
(3)	cause it to be done	(3)	have it done *or* do it
(4)	contiguous to	(4)	touching
(5)	deem	(5)	consider
(6)	endeavor (as a verb)	(6)	try
(7)	evince	(7)	show
(8)	expiration	(8)	end
(9)	expires	(9)	ends
(10)	have knowledge of	(10)	know
(11)	forthwith	(11)	immediately
(12)	in accordance with	(12)	under

(13)	in the event of	(13)	if
(14)	in the event that	(14)	if
(15)	in the interest of	(15)	for
(16)	is applicable	(16)	applies
(17)	is authorized to	(17)	may
(18)	is directed to	(18)	shall
(19)	is empowered to	(19)	may
(20)	is entitled (for a name)	(20)	is called
(21)	is hereby authorized	(21)	may
(22)	is not prohibited	(22)	may
(23)	per annum	(23)	per year
(24)	provided that	(24)	if
(25)	render service	(25)	give service

Assignment 18.1

Rewrite any of the following sentences that contain language that can be simplified without interfering with the effectiveness of the sentence.

(a) You are required to pay the fine.

(b) The period of time you have to render assistance is three months.

(c) For the duration of construction, it shall be unlawful for a person to enter or to attempt entry.

(d) If you are unable to enter into a contract with him for the materials, the oral commitment is still binding on you.

(e) She consulted with a lawyer with respect to possible litigation.

(f) She accepted the appointment due to the fact that she was qualified.

(g) It is green in color.

(h) Ask the witness questions about the bills.

(i) Judge Jones is currently on the bench.

11.5 Use shorter sentences. There is no rule on how long a sentence must be. Yet in general we can say that the longer a sentence is, the more difficult it is to follow. Too many long sentences ask too much of the reader. This is not to say that a reader cannot understand such sentences. It simply means that you are taxing the patience of readers when you subject them to long, involved sentences.

Unfortunately, sentences are almost always too long in legal writing. Here is an example from a legal memorandum. In the rewrite, we have broken a fifty-four–word sentence into four smaller, more readable sentences:

> **Weak:** Claims for child support were not fully and finally adjudicated pursuant to a North Carolina divorce judgment where the North Carolina court did not have personal jurisdiction over the husband and could not adjudicate any child support claims without jurisdiction and therefore Florida is not precluded from collecting monies from the husband toward arrearages.

> **Better:** The North Carolina divorce judgment did not fully and finally adjudicate the claims for child support. The court in this state did not have personal jurisdiction over the husband. It could not adjudicate any child support claims without jurisdiction. Florida is therefore not precluded from collecting monies from the husband toward arrearages.

Other examples:

> **Weak:** In May of 1995, a district personnel administrator informed Mary Miller that the district had decided to transfer her to a different school which was a decision that was based on information Miller pro-

vided, however the administrator had never talked to Miller in person prior to the decision.

Better: In May of 1995, a district personnel administrator informed Mary Miller that the district had decided to transfer her to a different school. The district based its decision on information Miller provided. The administrator, however, never talked to Miller in person prior to the decision.

Weak: Her new job at the firm as the legal administrator in charge of personnel and finances was enjoyable, lucrative, educational, and challenging, but confusing and frightening at times.

Better: Her new job at the firm as legal administrator in charge of personnel and finances was enjoyable, lucrative, educational, and challenging. It was also confusing and frightening at times.

Weak: The final issue for discussion concerns the status of the national and international parties that has been the main stumbling block in the contract negotiations thus far.

Better: The final issue for discussion is the status of the national and international parties. This issue has been the main stumbling block in contract negotiations thus far.

Weak: There is no need for you to submit a revised report to the Board unless you wish to include new matter which should have been included in an earlier report provided that the new matter covers only procedural issues except for those procedural issues that have already been resolved by the commission.

Better: You do not have to submit a revised report to the Board. An exception is when you wish to include new matter on procedural issues that should have been included in an earlier report. These procedural issues must not be ones that the Commission has already resolved.

 Assignment 18.2

Rewrite any of the following sentences that are too long.

(a) The board can, within sixty days of the receipt of a certification from the secretary, take action to return ownership to persons of corporations certified as owners from whom the property was acquired by expropriation or by purchase under threat of expropriation.

(b) A short time later, as George approached the intersection of Woodruff and Fuller, someone in the middle of the street started shooting, but George kept driving when he heard about fifteen shots that sounded like different guns firing, one of which hit his Pontiac, damaging the front windshield and dashboard.

(c) By way of illustration, presidential candidate Ross Perot and basketball player Michael Jordan arguably may have achieved such pervasive fame as to have become public figures for all purposes, while Dr. Jack Kevorkian may have voluntarily placed himself into the public controversy over euthanasia and physician-assisted suicide so as to have become a public figure for a limited range of issues.

12. Action Verbs and Adjectives

A **nominalization** is a noun formed from a verb or adjective. Examples include the noun *consideration* from the word *consider,* or the noun *effectiveness* from the adjective *effective.* Nominalizations are not grammatically incorrect. In most cases, however, they weaken a sentence. Unfortunately, the legal profession seems addicted to nominalizations. Avoid this addiction yourself.

12.1   Prefer action verbs to nominalization based on these verbs. Compare the sentences in these two columns:

A	B
He realizes the effort is futile.	He came to the realization that the effort is futile.
She decided to retire.	She made the decision to retire.
The court determined who should pay.	A determination of who should pay was made by the court.

Which do you prefer: *realizes* or *came to the realization? decided* or *made the decision? determined* or *determination was made?* The nominalizations in column B are *realization, decision,* and *determination.* The sentences in column A are more forceful and direct. Those in column B are more stilted and verbose. Using nominalizations often leads to longer words and longer sentences. They also encourage the use of passive voice, as in the third example.

Do not say:	*Say:*
(1) give consideration to	(1) consider
(2) give recognition to	(2) recognize
(3) have knowledge of	(3) know
(4) have need of	(4) need
(5) in the determination of	(5) to determine
(6) is applicable	(6) applies
(7) is dependent on	(7) depends on
(8) is in attendance at	(8) attends
(9) make an appointment of	(9) appoint
(10) make application	(10) apply
(11) make payment	(11) pay
(12) make provision for	(12) provide for

12.2   Prefer adjectives to nominalizations based on these adjectives. Adjectives turned into nouns can also interfere with effective writing. Compare the sentences in these two columns:

A	B
The program is viable.	The program has viability.
I admired her persuasive argument.	I admired the persuasiveness of her argument.

The nouns *viability* and *persuasiveness* in column B are needlessly pretentious. They seem calculated to impress someone. This can be distracting because it tends to draw attention to the person writing or speaking and away from the meaning of the sentence itself.

Assignment 18.3

Rewrite the following sentences by removing all nominalizations.

(a)   They entered a moot-court competition.
(b)   The assessment of the property by County Water Board is $11,000.
(c)   He needs time for reflection, preparation, and supervision.
(d)   They agreed on the importance of the project.
(e)   The figures need more specificity and certitude.

13. Active Voice/Passive Voice

13.1 Use **active voice** rather than **passive voice** by making the doer of the action the subject and main focus of the sentence. Compare the sentences in the following two columns:

A (passive voice)	B (active voice)
The decision was announced by the judge.	The judge announced the decision.
The report will be prepared.	I will prepare the report.
The court was cleared.	The clerk cleared the court.
By Friday the bridge will have been blown up by the workers.	By Friday, the workers will have blown up the bridge.
The strike was ended by the injunction.	The injunction ended the strike.

The verbs in the sentences in the A column are in the passive voice. The verbs in the sentences in the B column are in the active voice. What are the differences between these two kinds of sentences?

Sentences with verbs in the *passive voice* have the following characteristics:

- The doer of the action is either unknown or given less emphasis than what was done.
- The doer of the action, if referred to at all, is mentioned after the action itself.
- The subject of the sentence receives the action. The subject is acted upon.

If you do not mention the doer of the action in the sentence, the verb form is a **truncated passive.** In the following sentence, for example, you don't know who fired Jim:

Jim was fired at noon.

Sentences with verbs in the active voice have the following characteristics:

- The doer of the action is the important focus.
- The doer of the action is mentioned before the action itself.
- The subject of the sentence performs the action. The subject is the doer of the action.

The passive voice is often less effective because it is less direct and often less clear. It can dilute the forcefulness of a statement.

> **Weak:** It is no longer allowed to take library books overnight.
> **Better:** The law library no longer allows you to take books overnight.
> **Or:** The law library no longer allows borrowers to take books overnight.

The action in these sentences is the prohibition on taking books overnight. In the rewrite, we know who has performed this action—the law library. In the first sentence, we are not sure. The subject (and center of attention) in the rewrite is the law library; the subject (and center of attention) in the first sentence is the prohibition—the action.

 Assignment 18.4

Rewrite any of the following sentences that use the passive voice. If you need to add any facts to the sentences to identify the doer of the action, you may make them up.

(a) As the semester came to a close, the students prepared for their exams.
(b) Examinations are not enjoyed.
(c) No drugs were prescribed after the operation.
(d) It has been determined that your license should be revoked.

Continued on next page

Assignment 18.4—continued

(e) Consideration is being given this matter by the attorney.

(f) It is believed by district officials that the expense is legal.

(g) The fracture was discovered by the plaintiffs in 1992.

14. Positive Statements

14.1 Phrase something positively rather than negatively whenever possible. There is an odd tendency in the law to phrase things negatively: "Do not execute the deed that way"; "Do not contact the defendant"; "Do not render payment", etc. Generally, it is more effective to phrase things positively.

> **Weak:** Do not exceed the limit.
>
> **Better:** Stay within the limit.
>
> **Weak:** It is not difficult to assess the damages.
>
> **Better:** It is easy to assess the damages.
>
> **Or:** We can assess the damages with ease.

Assignment 18.5

Phrase the following sentences positively.

(a) The prosecutor argued that the state should not be put through the burden of proving causation; it should be the plaintiff who has this burden.

(b) It is unlikely that the evidence will fail to reveal the presence of heroin.

(c) We must not interfere with the right of a landowner to prevent trespassers from entering the land.

(d) It is not unreasonable to expect payment on time.

15. Pronoun References

15.1 Be careful with pronoun references. Use pronouns only when the nouns to which the pronouns refer are unmistakably clear. Using pronouns with ambiguous referents can confuse the meaning of a sentence. If the pronoun could refer to more than one person or object in a sentence, repeat the name of the person or object to avoid ambiguity.

> **Do not say:** After the administrator appoints a deputy assistant, he shall supervise the team. [Who does the supervising? The administrator or the deputy? If the latter is intended, then:]
>
> **Say:** After the administrator appoints a deputy assistant, the deputy assistant shall supervise the team.

16. That/Which

16.1 If a clause is essential to the meaning of the sentence, use *that* without comma(s). Every clause gives the reader some information. The question is, how important is this information to the meaning of the sentence? If it is essential to the understanding of the sentence, you must use *that* rather than *which*. For example:

> You must return the books *that* are overdue.

The clause at the end of the sentence identifies the book you must return. You do not have to return every borrowed book, only the overdue ones. Therefore, you must use *that*. Clauses that are essential to the meaning of a sentence are **restrictive clauses**. Note that there is no comma after the word *books*. Commas interrupt the flow of a sentence. Generally, you do not want to interrupt something that is essential to the meaning of a sentence. Hence, we do not use commas with restrictive clauses.

16.2   If a clause is not essential to the meaning of the sentence, use *which* with comma(s). If the clause is not essential to the meaning of the sentence, it is a **nonrestrictive clause**. Use *which* with such clauses, and set them off with comma(s):

> The Adams County Courthouse, which is located on a one-acre lot, was the scene of a lynching in 1912.

If you removed the *which* clause, you would not affect the meaning of the sentence. The clause adds geographical information, but it is not essential to the reader's ability to know what courthouse the writer is discussing. Here is another example:

> Ted has driven all of Mary's cars, which he enjoys a great deal.

The information about enjoyment is not essential to our knowledge of the cars that Ted drove.

16.3   The correct use of *that* and *which* is your clauses helps the reader understand the meaning you intend in the sentence. Some clauses are not clearly restrictive or clearly nonrestrictive. It may depend on the meaning you intend. The proper use of *that* and *which* can help communicate your intent:

> The clerk accepted Janice Kiley's filings that she had notarized.

This sentence is correct if the writer means the clerk could accept only notarized filings and hence did not accept her unnotarized ones. We need the clause to know what filings the clerk accepted. The clause is restrictive. Therefore, we use *that* without commas. But:

> The clerk accepted Janice Kiley's filings, which she had notarized.

This sentence is correct if the writer meant that the clerk could accept either notarized or unnotarized filings. Kiley happened to notarize everything she filed, but the clerk did not require this to accept them. We don't need the clause to know what filings the clerk accepted. The clause is nonrestrictive; therefore, use *which* with commas.

 Assignment 18.6

Correct the *that/which* problems, if any, in the following sentences. Explain your responses. If your answer depends on the meaning intended in the sentence, explain the possibilities.

(a) She is the general counsel for the corporation, that I own.

(b) I own a briefcase which is handmade.

(c) My posted grade that now everyone knows about was C−.

(d) The derogatory comment which my client received at home is the basis of the litigation.

(e) Congress, which is open to the public, consists of the House and Senate.

SECTION D   GENDER-NEUTRAL LANGUAGE

17. Sexist Language

17.1   Use gender-neutral language if your intent is to refer to both sexes, and if gender-neutral language is available. Here are some examples:

Gender-Specific Language	*Gender-Neutral Language*
(1) draftsman	(1) drafter, writer
(2) fireman	(2) firefighter
(3) policeman	(3) officer, police officer
(4) workman	(4) worker, laborer, employee
(5) foreman	(5) supervisor, manager
(6) man	(6) person, human, humankind
(7) man hours	(7) worker hours
(8) manpower	(8) work force, personnel
(9) mankind	(9) humanity, humankind, human race, people
(10) mailman	(10) postal worker, postal carrier, letter carrier
(11) chairman	(11) chair, chairperson, moderator, monitor, head
(12) clergyman	(12) minister, member of the clergy, rabbi, priest
(13) congressman	(13) Member of Congress, legislator, senator, representative
(14) insurance man	(14) insurance agent
(15) stewardess	(15) flight attendant
(16) wife	(16) homemaker
(17) repairman	(17) electrician
(18) middleman	(18) agent
(19) salesman	(19) seller, sales representative
(20) businessman	(20) seller, executive, manager, supervisor, capitalist, entrepreneur, merchant

17.2   Use *he or she* or plural pronouns. Using *he or she* can sometimes be effective to eliminate sexism. This phrase, however, is awkward; you should avoid overusing it. A better technique is to write in the plural so that you do not have to use the offending singular gender-specific pronoun. Make the antecedent plural so that you can use a gender-neutral plural pronoun. (An *antecedent* is the word, phrase, or clause to which a pronoun refers.)

Weak: Every judge in the country has his own style.

Better: Every judge in the country has his or her own style.

Best: Judges in the country have their own style.

17.3   Use *you* if this does not inappropriately shift the point of view. The second-person pronoun *you* is, of course, gender-neutral. Use it whenever possible.

Weak: Every juror must take his role seriously.

Or: Every juror must take her role seriously.

Better: As a juror, you must take your role seriously.

Note, however, that this is not a solution if using the second person is an inappropriate shift in the point of view you have established in your paper. Point of view is the perspective from which you are writing. It can be first person (e.g., *we* should vote, *I* am a candidate); second person (e.g., *you* need to register); or third person (e.g., *they* used absentee ballots). If, for example, you have been consistently using the third person in your paper, you should not abruptly shift to the second person to solve the sexism problem.

17.4   Repeat the noun. Another way to avoid gender-specific language is to repeat the noun so that you do not need to use a pronoun.

> **Weak:** Before an attorney accepts a new client in the office, he must be sure there is no conflict of interest.

> **Better:** Before an attorney accepts a new client in the office, the attorney must be sure there is no conflict of interest.

> **Best:** Before attorneys accept a new client in the office, they must be sure there is no conflict of interest.

The use of the pronoun *he* in the first sentence is inappropriate for another reason. What does *he* refer to? The client? The attorney? Does the client or the attorney have to make sure there is no conflict of interest? The antecedent of this pronoun is not clear. The second sentence avoids this ambiguity by repeating the noun *attorney* so that the reader does not have to guess whether the pronoun *he* refers to the attorney or to the client. The third alternative eliminates this problem altogether by using the plural pronoun *they*. Its antecedent is clearly the plural word *attorneys,* not the singular word *client.*

17.5   Rewrite your sentence to avoid the problem. Sometimes gender-neutral language is not available, does not appear to fit what you want to say, or has already been overused. If so, rewrite the sentence to sidestep the problem entirely. This may be the only effective remedy available. For example:

> **Weak:** A member of the legislature must be diplomatic if he wants to succeed.

> **Better:** Members of the legislature must be diplomatic in order to succeed.

> **Or:** Legislators must be diplomatic to succeed.

> **Or:** To succeed, legislators must be diplomatic.

17.6   Do not use the passive voice as a solution. Writers sometimes use the passive voice as a technique for eliminating sexism in their writing.

> **Weak:** The court requires a juror to base his decision solely on the evidence presented.

> **Rewrite 1:** It is required that a juror's decision be based solely on the evidence presented.

Rewrite 1 is as ineffective as the original sentence because of the passive voice. Here is a better alternative:

> **Rewrite 2:** The court requires jurors to base their decisions solely on the evidence presented.

 Assignment 18.7

Rewrite the following paragraph by eliminating inappropriate gender-specific language.
Every paralegal in the country needs to study his textbooks carefully. If he fails to do so, he runs the risk of faulty preparation for his career.

Assignment 18.8

For each exercise, select *a* or *b* as the most acceptable alternative based on the rules and guidelines in this chapter. Explain each answer.

- **1**
  - **a.** To Holmes Marshall was a great judge.
  - **b.** To Holmes, Marshall was a great judge.
- **2**
  - **a.** The client described his old dilapidated apartment building.
  - **b.** The client described his old, dilapidated apartment building.
- **3**
  - **a.** Henry Jackson, Esq., is the attorney of record.
  - **b.** Henry Jackson, Esq. is the attorney of record.
- **4**
  - **a.** Moral turpitude he remarked is an important criterion.
  - **b.** Moral turpitude, he remarked, is an important criterion.
- **5**
  - **a.** On their way to court, they stopped for breakfast.
  - **b.** On their way to court they stopped for breakfast.
- **6**
  - **a.** Kline a recently elected judge received the assignment.
  - **b.** Kline, a recently elected judge, received the assignment.
- **7**
  - **a.** We studied torts, civil procedure, and contracts.
  - **b.** We studied torts, civil procedure and contracts.
- **8**
  - **a.** The client did not sue but he demanded an apology.
  - **b.** The client did not sue, but he demanded an apology.
- **9**
  - **a.** "I did not perjure myself", he insisted.
  - **b.** "I did not perjure myself," he insisted.
- **10**
  - **a.** Bring the notes; the law books, old and new; and the briefs.
  - **b.** Bring the notes, the law books, old and new, and the briefs.
- **11**
  - **a.** Tort law is difficult, however, it is also challenging.
  - **b.** Tort law is difficult; however, it is also challenging.
- **12**
  - **a.** Jon said, "I accept the offer;" therefore, the case ended.
  - **b.** Jon said, "I accept the offer"; therefore, the case ended.
- **13**
  - **a.** Examine the following statutes, § 23, § 57, and § 107.
  - **b.** Examine the following statutes: § 23, § 57, and § 107.
- **14**
  - **a.** Read *Evidence, A Guide for the Practitioner.*
  - **b.** Read *Evidence: A Guide for the Practitioner.*
- **15**
  - **a.** Three fears, exposure, arrest, and prison, are in his mind.
  - **b.** Three fears—exposure, arrest, and prison—are in his mind.
- **16**
  - **a.** His orders were for her to accept the offer and that she resign.
  - **b.** His orders were for her to accept the offer and to resign.
- **17**
  - **a.** The committee considered the offer and discussed alternatives.
  - **b.** The committee considered the offer and alternatives were discussed.

Assignment 18.8—continued

- **18**
  Which of the following lines has no spelling errors?
  a. abridgment, acknowledgment, accommodate, embarrass, foresee, commingle
  b. heinous, parallel, willful, maneuver, statute, precedent, liaison, harrass
- **19**
  a. The courts decree requires both hospitals compliance.
  b. The court's decree requires both hospitals' compliance.
- **20**
  a. Consideration is being given to this matter by the attorney.
  b. The attorney is considering this matter.
- **21**
  a. It is believed by district officials that the expense is legal.
  b. District officials believe that the expense is legal.
- **22**
  a. The plaintiffs discovered the fracture in 1992.
  b. The fracture was discovered by plaintiffs in 1992.
- **23**
  a. I found 174 regulations.
  b. I found one hundred seventy four regulations.
- **24**
  a. The judge, along with his colleagues, hope for a raise.
  b. The judge, along with his colleagues, hopes for a raise.
- **25**
  a. A complete set of regional reporters is expensive.
  b. A complete set of regional reporters are expensive.
- **26**
  a. Each of us deserve a raise.
  b. Each of us deserves a raise.
- **27**
  a. No one, not even my coworkers, know what I will do.
  b. No one, not even my coworkers, knows what I will do.
- **28**
  a. Neither the clerks nor the paralegal works there.
  b. Neither the clerks nor the paralegal work there.
- **29**
  a. Neither Mary nor Elaine allowed their opinions to be known.
  b. Neither Mary nor Elaine allowed her opinions to be known.
- **30**
  a. The chairman objected.
  b. The chair objected.
- **31**
  a. Helen assaulted him in the course of the discussion.
  b. Helen assaulted him during the discussion.
- **32**
  a. The court deemed the mother to be unfit.
  b. The court considered the mother to be unfit.
- **33**
  a. He resigned during the course of the trial.
  b. He resigned during the trial.
- **34**
  a. The judge acted for the purpose of encouraging a settlement.
  b. The judge acted to encourage a settlement.

Continued on next page

Assignment 18.8—continued

- **35**
  - **a.** Ted made the request in order to strike the evidence.
  - **b.** Ted made the request to strike the evidence.
- **36**
  - **a.** You must phone in the event that they cancel the meeting.
  - **b.** You must phone if they cancel the meeting.
- **37**
  - **a.** The offer is accepted provided that you lower the price.
  - **b.** The offer is accepted if you lower the price.
- **38**
  - **a.** Avoid all contact whatsoever with the defendant.
  - **b.** Avoid all contact with the defendant.
- **39**
  - **a.** We will reject all offers over and above $10,000.
  - **b.** We will reject all offers over $10,000.
- **40**
  - **a.** You shall report at noon.
  - **b.** You are directed to report at noon.
- **41**
  - **a.** The clause is binding on all parties.
  - **b.** The clause binds all parties.
- **42**
  - **a.** The law requires you to make payment at the beginning of the month.
  - **b.** The law requires you to pay at the beginning of the month.
- **43**
  - **a.** My acceptance is dependent on the amount of your offer.
  - **b.** My acceptance depends on the amount of your offer.
- **44**
  - **a.** It is not unreasonable to expect payment on time.
  - **b.** It is reasonable to expect payment on time.

CHAPTER SUMMARY

A writer must have command of certain writing basics, such as commas, semicolons, colons, dashes, parallelism, spelling, possessives, numerals, subject-verb agreement, and pronoun-noun agreement. Avoid unnecessary language by eliminating circumlocutions, taking out excess language, using shorter words, preferring less complicated language, and using shorter sentences. Prefer action verbs and adjectives to nominalizations, the active voice to the passive voice, and positive statements over negative ones. Be sure that all pronoun references are clear and that you have properly made the distinction between that clauses and which clauses. Finally, use gender-neutral language.

KEY TERMS

comma	parallelism	nominalization	restrictive clause
semicolon	possessive	active voice	nonrestrictive clause
colon	antecedents	passive voice	
dash	circumlocution	truncated passive	

BIBLIOGRAPHY OF LEGAL RESEARCH AND CITATION GUIDES ON STATE LAW

Alabama

H. Johnson & T. Coggins, *Guide to Alabama State Documents . . .* (American Ass'n of Law Libraries, 1993).

G. Schrader, *Alabama Law Bibliography* (Barrister Press, 1990).

L. Kitchens, *Alabama Practice Materials,* 82 Law Library Journal 703 (1990).

Alaska

A. Ruzicka, *Alaska Legal and Law Related Publications* (American Ass'n of Law Libraries, 1984).

Arizona

K. Shimpock-Vieweg & M. Alcorn, *Arizona Legal Research Guide* (Hein, 1992).

R. Teenstra et al., *Survey of Arizona Law-Related Documents* (American Ass'n of Law Libraries, 1984).

A. Torres, *Arizona Practice Materials,* 80 Law Library Journal 577 (1988).

K. Fitzhugh, *Arizona Practice Materials,* 81 Law Library Journal 277 (1989).

Arkansas

L. Foster, *Arkansas Legal Bibliography* (American Ass'n of Law Libraries, 1988).

California

D. Martin, *California Law Guide, 3d* (Butterworth, 1995).

D. Henke, *California Law Guide, 2d* (Parker, 1976, 1995 Supp.).

L. Dershem, *California Legal Research Handbook* (Rothman, 1996).

V. Mackay & L. Peritore, *California Government Publications and Legal Resources* (American Ass'n of Law Libraries, 1991).

K. Castetter, ed., *Locating the Law: A Handbook for Non-Librarians, 2d* (So. Calif. Ass'n of Law Libraries, 1989).

T. Dabagh, *Legal Research Guide for California Practice* (Hein, 1985).

M. Fink, *Research in California Law, 2d* (Dennis, 1964).

R. Formichi, *California Style Manual, 3d* (1986).

J. Hanft, *Legal Research in California, 2d* (Bancroft-Whitney, 1996).

B. Ochal, *California Current State Practice Materials,* 74 Law Library Journal 281 (1981).

Colorado

G. Alexander et al., *Colorado Legal Resources* (American Ass'n of Law Libraries, 1987). *See also* 16 Colorado Lawyer 1795 (1987).

S. Weinstein, *Colorado Legal Source Materials—1981,* 10 Colorado Lawyer 1816 (August 1981).

M. Fontenot, *Colorado Practice Materials,* 88 Law Library Journal 427 (1996).

Connecticut

L. Cheeseman & A. Bielefield, *Connecticut Legal Research Handbook* (Conn. Law Book Co., 1992).

S. Bysiewicz, *Sources of Connecticut Law* (Butterworth, 1987).

D. Voisinet et al., *Connecticut State Legal Documents* (American Ass'n of Law Libraries, 1985).

District of Columbia

L. Chanin et al., *Legal Research in the District of Columbia . . .* (Hein, 1995).

C. Ahearn, *Selected Information Sources for the District of Columbia, 2d* (American Ass'n of Law Libraries, 1985).

Florida

M. Kaplan et al., *Guide to Florida Legal Research, 4th* (Fla. Bar, Cont. Legal Education, 1994).

N. Martin, *Florida Legal Research and Source Book* (D&S Publishers, 1990).

E. Tribble & C. Beane, eds., *Guide to Florida Legislative Publications & Information Sources, 3d* (Capitol, 1990).

C. Roehrenbeck, *Florida Legislative Histories* (D&S Publishers, 1986).

Florida Style Manual (Fla. State Univ. Law Review, 1991).

Georgia

L. Chanin & S. Cassidy, *Guide to Georgia Legal Research and Legal History* (Harrison, 1990).

R. Stillwagon, *Georgia Legal Documents* (American Ass'n of Law Libraries, 1991).

Hawaii

R. Kahle, *How to Research Constitutional, Legislative and Statutory History in Hawaii* (Hawaii Legislative Reference Bureau, 1986).

J. Dupont & B. Keever, *The Citizens Guide: How to Use Legal Materials in Hawaii* (1983).

Idaho

P. Cervenka et al., *Idaho Law-Related State Documents* (American Ass'n of Law Libraries, 1989).

L. Seeger, *Idaho Practice Materials,* 87 Law Library Journal 534 (1995).

Illinois

L. Wendt, *Illinois Legal Research Manual* (Butterworth, 1989).

C. Nyberg et al., *Illinois State Documents* (American Ass'n of Law Libraries, 1986).

L. Wendt, *Researching Illinois Legislative Histories,* 1982 Southern Illinois University Law Journal 601.

Indiana

L. Fariss & K. Buckley, *An Introduction to Indiana State Publications for the Law Librarian* (American Ass'n of Law Libraries, 1982).

Iowa

A. Secrest, *Iowa Legal Documents Bibliography* (American Ass'n of Law Libraries, 1990).

Kansas

J. Custer, *Kansas Legal Research & Reference Guide, 2d* (Kansas Bar Ass'n, 1997).

M. Wisnecki, *Kansas State Documents for Law Libraries* (American Ass'n of Law Libraries, 1984).

Kentucky

A. Torres, *Kentucky Practice Materials,* 84 Law Library Journal 509 (1992).

W. Gilmer, *Guide to Kentucky Legal Research, 2d* (State Bar Library, 1985).

Louisiana

W. Chiang, *Louisiana Legal Research, 2d* (Butterworth, 1990).

M. Hebert, *Louisiana Legal Documents and Related Publications* (American Ass'n of Law Libraries, 1990).

M. Cunningham, *Guide to Louisiana and Selected French Materials and Citation,* 67 Tulane Law Review 1305 (1993).

Maine

W. Wells, *Maine Legal Research Guide* (Tower Publishing, 1989).

M. Seitzinger, *Uniform Maine Citations* (1983).

Maryland

M. Miller, *Ghost Hunting: Finding Legislative Intent in Maryland* (Md. State Law Library, 1984).

L. Davis, *An Introduction to Maryland State Publications* (American Ass'n of Law Libraries, 1981).

L. Chanin, *Legal Research in the District of Columbia, Maryland, and Virginia* (Hein, 1995).

Massachusetts

M. Botsford et al., *Handbook of Legal Research in Massachusetts* (Mass. Continuing Legal Education, 1988).

L. McAuliffe & S. Steinway, *Massachusetts State Documents Bibliography* (American Ass'n of Law Libraries, 1985).

Michigan

R. Beer & J. Field, *Michigan Legal Literature, 2d* (Hein, 1991).

N. Bosh, *Research Edge* (Institute of Continuing Legal Education, 1993).

J. Doyle, *Michigan Citation Manual* (Hein, 1986).

S. Yoak & M. Heinen, *Michigan Legal Documents* (American Ass'n of Law Libraries, 1982).

Legal Research Guide for Michigan Libraries (Mich. Ass'n of Law Libraries, 1982).

D. Johnson, *Michigan Practice Materials,* 73 Law Library Journal 672 (1980).

J. Doyle, *Michigan Citation Manual* (1986).

Minnesota

M. Baum & M. Nelson, *Guide to Minnesota State Documents . . .* (American Ass'n of Law Libraries, 1986).

A. Soderberg & B. Golden, *Minnesota Legal Research Guide* (Hein, 1985).

Mississippi

B. Cole, *Mississippi Legal Documents . . .* (American Ass'n of Law Libraries, 1987).

Missouri

M. Nelson, *Guide to Missouri State Documents . . .* (American Ass'n of Law Libraries, 1991).

Montana

F. Snyder, *The Citation Practices of the Montana Supreme Court,* 57 Montana Law Review 453 (1966).

S. Jordan, *Montana Practice Materials,* 84 Law Library Journal 299 (1992).

Nebraska

M. Fontenot et al., *Nebraska State Documents Bibliography* (American Ass'n of Law Libraries, 1988).

P. Hill, *Nebraska Legal Research and Reference Manual* (Butterworth, 1983).

Nevada

K. Henderson, *Nevada State Documents Bibliography . . .* (American Ass'n of Law Libraries, 1984).

New Jersey

C. Allen, *A Guide to New Jersey Legal Bibliography . . .* (Rothman, 1984).

P. Axel-Lute, *New Jersey Legal Research Handbook, 2d* (NJ Institute for Continuing Legal Education, 1996).

C. Senezak, *New Jersey State Publications* (American Ass'n of Law Libraries, 1984).

Manual on Style (NJ Administrative Office of the Courts, 1979).

New Mexico

P. Wagner & M. Woodward, *Guide to New Mexico State Publications, 2d* (American Ass'n of Law Libraries, 1991).

New York

R. Carter, *Legislative Intent in New York State* (NY State Library, 1981).

R. Carter, *New York State Constitution: Sources of Legislative Intent* (Rothman, 1988).

S. Dow & K. Spencer, *New York Legal Documents* (American Ass'n of Law Libraries, 1985).

E. Gibson, *New York Legal Research Guide* (Hein, 1988).

Brown, *An Annotated Bibliography of Current New York State Practice Materials,* 73 Law Library Journal 28 (1980).

New York Rules of Citation, 2d (St. John's Law Review, 1991).

North Carolina

J. McKnight, *North Carolina Legal Research Guide* (Rothman, 1994).

T. Steele & D. Diprisco, *Survey of North Carolina State Legal and Law-Related Documents* (American Ass'n of Law Libraries, 1987).

North Dakota

For All Intents and Purposes: Essentials in Researching Legislative Histories (ND Legislative Council, 1981).

Ohio

C. Corcas, *Ohio Legal and Law-Related Documents . . .* (American Ass'n of Law Libraries, 1986).

D. Gold, *A Guide to Legislative History in Ohio* (Ohio Legislative Service Comm'n, 1985).

Ohio Legal Resources . . . 4th (Ohio Library Council, 1996).

M. Putnam & S. Schaefgen, *Ohio Legal Research Guide* (Hein, 1996).

Manual of the Forms of Citation Used in the Ohio Official Reports (Ohio Supreme Court, 1992).

Style Manual (Ohio Northern Univ. Law Review, 1980).

Oklahoma

C. Corcas, *Oklahoma Legal and Law-Related Documents . . .* (American Ass'n of Law Libraries, 1983).

Oregon

L. Buhman et al., *Bibliography of Law-Related Oregon Documents* (American Ass'n of Law Libraries, 1986).

K. Beck, *Oregon Practice Materials,* 88 Law Library Journal 288 (1996).

Pennsylvania

J. Fishman, *Bibliography of Pennsylvania Law: Secondary Sources* (Pa. Legal Resources Institute, 1992).

J. Fishman, *An Introduction to Pennsylvania Publications . . .* (American Ass'n of Law Libraries, 1986). *See also* 78 Law Library Journal 74 (1986).

C. Moreland & E. Surrency, *Research in Pennsylvania Law, 2d* (Oceana, 1965).

Guide to Citation (Pa. Commonwealth Court, 1981).

Rhode Island

C. McConaghy, *Selective Bibliography for the State of Rhode Island* (American Ass'n of Law Libraries, 1993).

Legal Research in Rhode Island (RI Law Institute, 1989).

South Carolina

P. Benson, *A Guide to South Carolina Legal Research and Citation* (SC Bar Continuing Legal Education, 1991).

R. Mills & J. Schultz, *South Carolina Legal Research Handbook* (Hein, 1976).

South Dakota

S. Etling, *A Primer on Citation* (South Dakota Law School Foundation, 1996).

D. Jorgensen, *South Dakota Legal Documents* (American Ass'n of Law Libraries, 1988).

D. Jorgensen, *South Dakota Legal Research Guide* (Hein, 1988).

Tennessee

L. Laska, *Tennessee Legal Research Handbook* (Hein, 1977).

D. Picquet & R. Best, *Law and Government Publications of the State of Tennessee* (American Ass'n of Law Libraries, 1988).

L. Laska, *Tennessee Rules of Citation* (1982).

Texas

M. Allison & K. Schleuter, *Texas State Documents for Law Libraries* (American Ass'n of Law Libraries, 1986).

L. Brandt, *Texas Legal Research: An Essential Lawyering Skill* (Texas Lawyer Press, 1995).

K. Gruben & J. Hambleton, *A Reference Guide to Texas Law and Legal History, 2d* (Butterworth, 1987).

P. Permenter & S. Ratliff, *Guide to Texas Legislative History* (Legislative Reference Library, 1986).

K. Gruben, *An Annotated Bibliography of Texas Practice Materials,* 74 Law Library Journal 87 (1981).

Texas Law Review Manual on Style, 7th (1992).

Texas Rules of Form, 8th (1992).

Utah

K. Staheli, *Utah Practice Materials,* 87 Law Library Journal 50 (1995).

Vermont

V. Wise, *A Bibliographic Guide to the Vermont Legal System, 2d* (American Ass'n of Law Libraries, 1991).

Virginia

J. Eure, *A Guide to Legal Research in Virginia* (Va. Law Foundation, 1989).

J. Lichtman & J. Stinson, *A Law Librarian's Introduction to Virginia State Publications* (American Ass'n of Law Libraries, 1988).

L. Chanin, *Legal Research in the District of Columbia, Maryland, and Virginia* (Hein, 1995).

Washington (state)

Gallagher Law Library, *Washington Legal Researcher's Deskbook, 2d* (Gallagher Law Library, 1996).

S. Burson, *Washington State Law-Related Publications* (American Ass'n of Law Libraries, 1984).

M. Cerjan, *Washington Legal Researchers Deskbook* (Wash. Law School Foundation, 1994).

West Virginia

S. Stemple et al., *West Virginia Legal Bibliography* (American Ass'n of Law Libraries, 1990).

Wisconsin

R. Danner, *Legal Research in Wisconsin* (Univ. of Wash, Extension Law Dept, 1980).

J. Oberla, *An Introduction to Wisconsin State Documents . . .* (American Ass'n of Law Libraries, 1987).

Wyoming

N. Greene, *Wyoming State Legal Documents* (American Ass'n of Law Libraries, 1985).

CASE LAW ON THE INTERNET

For statutory law and other primary authority on the Internet, see Exhibit 11.4 in chapter 11. Some of the Internet sites presented in Exhibit 11.4 are linked to the sites below, and vice versa. Not all courts have their case law online. For additional leads to the law of your state, check the general home page for your state, where you will often find links to a variety of state laws. Here is the address of the home page of most states (insert your state's abbreviation in place of the **xx**): **http://www.state.xx.us**

I. FEDERAL CASES

All Federal Courts

http://www.ljextra.com/public/daily/coaall.html

http://www.law.cornell.edu/opinions.html

http://law.house.gov/6.htm

http://www.legalonline.com/courts.htm

http://www.virtualchase.com/govdoc/opinions.htm

United States Supreme Court

http://supct.law.cornell.edu/supct/index.html

ftp://ftp.cwru.edu/hermes

United States Court of Appeals (1st Circuit)

http://www.law.emery.edu/1circuit

United States Court of Appeals (2nd Circuit)

http://www.law.pace.edu/lawlib/legal/us-legal/judiciary/second-circuit.html

United States Court of Appeals (3rd Circuit)

http://www.law.vill.edu/Fed-Ct/ca03.html

United States Court of Appeals (4th Circuit)

http://www.law.emery.edu/4circuit

United States Court of Appeals (5th Circuit)

http://www.ca5.uscourts.gov

United States Court of Appeals (6th Circuit)

  http://www.law.emery.edu/6circuit

United States Court of Appeals (7th Circuit)

  http://www.kentlaw.edu/7circuit

United States Court of Appeals (8th Circuit)

  http://www.wulaw.wustl.edu/8th.cir

United States Court of Appeals (9th Circuit)

  http://www.law.vill.edu/Fed-Ct/ca09.html

United States Court of Appeals (10th Circuit)

  http://www.law.emory.edu/10circuit/index.html

United States Court of Appeals (11th Circuit)

  http://www.law.emory.edu/11circuit/index.html

  http://www.mindspring.com/~wmundy/opinions.html

United States Court of Appeals (Federal Circuit)

  http://www.ll.georgetown.edu/Fed-Ct/cafed.html

  http://www.fedcir.gov

United States Court of Appeals (District of Columbia Circuit)

  http://www.ll.georgetown.edu/Fed-Ct/cadc.html

II. STATE CASES

All States

  http://www.law.cornell.edu/opinions.html

  http://www.legalonline.com/courts.htm

  http://lawlib.wuacc.edu/washlaw/uslaw/statelaw.html

  http://www.piperinfo.com/state/states.html

  http://www.piperinfo.com/pl03/statedir.html

  http://www.virtualchase.com/govdoc/opinions.htm

ALABAMA

  http://www.alalinc.net

ALASKA

  http://www.alaska.net/~akctlib

ARIZONA

  http://www.state.az.us/co/cindex.htm

ARKANSAS

  http://www.state.ar.us/supremecourt

  http://courts.state.ar.us

CALIFORNIA

http://www.courtinfo.ca.gov/opinions

COLORADO

http://www.cobar.org/coappcts/scndx.htm

CONNECTICUT

http://www.pita.com

DELAWARE

http://www.widener.edu/law/lic/delaw.htm

FLORIDA

http://nersp.nerdc.ufl.edu:80/~lawinfo/flsupct/index.html

http://justice.courts.state.fl.us

GEORGIA

http://www.state.ga.us/Courts/Supreme

HAWAII

http://www.hsba.org/Hawaii/Court/Court/Curr/courin.htm

IDAHO

http://www.state.id.us/judicial/judicial.html

ILLINOIS

http://www.state.il.us/court/default.htm

INDIANA

http://www.law.indiana.edu/law/incourts/incourts.html

http://www.state.in.us/judiciary/opinions

KANSAS

http://www.law.ukans.edu/kscourts/kscourts.html

LOUISIANA

http://www.law.cornell.edu/states/louisiana.html#opinions

http://www.lasc.org

http://www.pita.com

MAINE

http://www.courts.state.me.us/mescopin.home.html

MARYLAND

http://courts.state.md.us/T40

MASSACHUSETTS

http://www.lweekly.com/sjc.htm

http://www.socialaw.com

http://199.103.225.210/masslaw

MICHIGAN

http://www.icle.org/michlaw/index.htm

MINNESOTA

http://www.courts.state.mn.us

MISSISSIPPI

http://www.mslawyer.com

MISSOURI

http://www.osca.state.mo.us/courts/Judicial2.nsf

MONTANA

http://www.lawlibrary.mt.gov/OPININS.HTM

NEBRASKA

http://www.nol.org/legal/index.html

NEW HAMPSHIRE

http://www.state.nh.us/courts/supreme.htm

NEW JERSEY

http://www.state.nj.us/judiciary/appdiv/homepage.htm

http://www.state.nj.us/judiciary/supreme.htm

http://njlawnet.com/opinions.html

NEW MEXICO

http://www.fscll.org

NEW YORK

http://www.law.cornell.edu/ny/ctap/overview.html

http://ucs.ljx.com/ctpages.html

NORTH CAROLINA

http://www.nando.net/insider

NORTH DAKOTA

http://sc3.court.state.nd.us

OHIO

http://www.sconet.ohio.gov

OKLAHOMA

http://www.ou.edu/okgov

PENNSYLVANIA

http://www.cerf.net/penna-courts

http:www.lawresearch.com/v3/cspaj.htm

RHODE ISLAND

http://www.ribar.com/Courts/courts.html

http://www.pita.com

SOUTH CAROLINA

http://www.law.sc.edu/opinions/opinions.htm

SOUTH DAKOTA

http://www.sdbar.org/opinions/index.htm

TENNESSEE

http://www.tsc.state.tn.us/opinions/opinopts.htm

TEXAS

http://www.window.state.tx.us/txgovinf/txcoca.html

UTAH

http://courtlink.utcourts.gov

http://www.versuslaw.com

VERMONT

http://dol.state.vt.us/WWW_ROOT/000000/HTML/SUPCT.HTML

http://dol.state.vt.us:70/1GOPHER_ROOT3%3a%5bSUPCT%5D

VIRGINIA

http://www.courts.state.va.us/opin.htm

WASHINGTON (STATE)

http://www.wa.gov/courts/opinpage/home.htm

http://www.cdlaw.com

WEST VIRGINIA

http://www.state.wv.us/wvsca/opinions.htm

WISCONSIN

http://www.wisbar.org/Wis/index.html

WYOMING

http://courts.state.wy.us/OPINION.HTM

COURT OPINIONS FOR ASSIGNMENTS

The following cases are to be used when completing Assignments.

United States v. Kovel

United States Court of Appeals
Second Circuit, 1961, 296 F.2d 918

FRIENDLY, Circuit Judge.

This appeal from a sentence for criminal contempt for refusing to answer a question asked in the course of an inquiry by a grand jury raises an important issue as to the application of the attorney-client privilege to a non-lawyer employed by a law firm.

Kovel is a former Internal Revenue agent having accounting skills. Since 1943 he has been employed by Kamerman & Kamerman, a law firm specializing in tax law. A grand jury in the Southern District of New York was investigating alleged Federal income tax violations by Hopps, a client of the law firm; Kovel was subpoenaed to appear on September 6, 1961. The law firm advised the Assistant United States Attorney that since Kovel was an employee under the direct supervision of the partners, Kovel could not disclose any communications by the client or the result of any work done for the client, unless the latter consented; the Assistant answered that the attorney-client privilege did not apply to one who was not an attorney.

On September 7, the grand jury appeared before Judge Cashin. The Assistant United States Attorney informed the judge that Kovel had refused to answer "several questions . . . on the grounds of attorney-client privilege"; he proffered "respectable authority . . . that an accountant, even if he is retained or employed by a firm of attorneys, cannot take the privilege." The judge answered "You don't have to give me any authority on that." A court reporter testified that Kovel, after an initial claim of privilege had admitted receiving a state-

ment of Hopps' assets and liabilities, but that, when asked "what was the purpose of your receiving that," had declined to answer on the ground of privilege "Because the communication was received with a purpose, as stated by the client"; later questions and answers indicated the communication was a letter addressed to Kovel. After verifying that Kovel was not a lawyer, the judge directed him to answer, saying "You have no privilege as such." The reporter then read another question Kovel had refused to answer, "Did you ever discuss with Mr. Hopps or give Mr. Hopps any information with regard to treatment for capital gains purposes of the Atlantic Beverage Corporation sale by him?" The judge again directed Kovel to answer reaffirming "There is no privilege—You are entitled to no privilege, as I understand the law."

Later on September 7, they and Kovel's employer, Jerome Kamerman, now acting as his counsel, appeared again before Judge Cashin. The Assistant told the judge that Kovel had "refused to answer some of the questions which you had directed him to answer." A reporter reread so much of the transcript heretofore summarized as contained the first two refusals. The judge offered Kovel another opportunity to answer, reiterating the view, "There is no privilege to this man at all." Counsel referred to New York Civil Practice Act, § 353, which we quote in the margin.*

Counsel reiterated that an employee "who sits with the client of the law firm . . . occupies the same status . . . as a clerk or stenographer or any other lawyer . . ."; the judge was equally clear that the privilege was never "extended beyond the attorney." The court held [Kovel] in contempt, sentenced him to a year's imprisonment, ordered immediate commitment and denied bail. Later in the day, the grand jury having indicted, Kovel was released until September 12,

---

*"An attorney or counselor at law shall not disclose, or be allowed to disclose, a communication, made by his client to him, or his advice given thereon, in the course of his professional employment, nor shall any clerk, stenographer or other person employed by such attorney or counselor . . . disclose, or be allowed to disclose any such communication or advice."

at which time, without opposition from the Government, I granted bail pending determination of this appeal.

Here the parties continue to take generally the same positions as below—Kovel, that his status as an employee of a law firm automatically made all communications to him from clients privileged; the Government, that under no circumstances could there be privilege with respect to communications to an accountant. The New York County Lawyers' Association as *amicus curiae* has filed a brief generally supporting [Kovel's] position.

Decision under what circumstances, if any, the attorney-client privilege may include a communication to a nonlawyer by the lawyer's client is the resultant of two conflicting forces. One is the general teaching that "The investigation of truth and the enforcement of testimonial duty demand the restriction, not the expansion, of these privileges," 8 Wigmore, *Evidence* (McNaughton Rev. 1961), § 2192, p. 73. The other is the more particular lesson "That as, by reason of the complexity and difficulty of our law, litigation can only be properly conducted by professional men, it is absolutely necessary that a man . . . should have recourse to the assistance of professional lawyers, and . . . it is equally necessary . . . that he should be able to place unrestricted and unbounded confidence in the professional agent, and that the communications he so makes to him should be kept secret . . . ," Jessel, M. R. in *Anderson v. Bank*, 2 Ch.D. 644, 649 (1876). Nothing in the policy of the privilege suggests that attorneys, simply by placing accountants, scientists or investigators on their payrolls and maintaining them in their offices, should be able to invest all communications by clients to such persons with a privilege the law has not seen fit to extend when the latter are operating under their own steam. On the other hand, in contrast to the Tudor times when the privilege was first recognized, the complexities of modern existence prevent attorneys from effectively handling clients' affairs without the help of others; few lawyers could now practice without the assistance of secretaries, file clerks, telephone operators, messengers, clerks not yet admitted to the bar, and aides of other sorts. "The assistance of these agents being indispensable to his work and the communications of the client being often necessarily committed to them by the attorney or by the client himself, the privilege must include all the persons who act as the attorney's agents." 8 Wigmore, *Evidence*, § 2301; Annot., 53 A.L.R. 369 (1928).

Indeed, the Government does not here dispute that the privilege covers communications to non-lawyer employees with "a menial or ministerial responsibility that involves relating communications *to an attorney*." We cannot regard the privilege as confined to "menial or ministerial" employees. Thus, we can see no significant difference between a case where the attorney sends a client speaking a foreign language to an interpreter to make a literal translation of the client's story; a second where the attorney, himself having some little knowledge of the foreign tongue, has a more knowledgeable non-lawyer employee in the room to help out; a third where someone to perform that same function

has been brought along by the client; and a fourth where the attorney, ignorant of the foreign language, sends the client to a non-lawyer proficient in it, with instructions to interview the client on the attorney's behalf and then render its own summary of the situation, perhaps drawing on his own knowledge in the process, so that the attorney can give the client proper legal advice. All four cases meet every element of Wigmore's famous formulation, § 2292, "(1) Where legal advice of any kind is sought (2) from a professional legal advisor in his capacity as such, (3) the communications relating to that purpose, (4) made in confidence (5) by the client, (6) are at his instance permanently protected (7) from disclosure by himself or by the legal advisor, (8) except the protection be waived," . . . § 2301 of Wigmore would clearly recognize the privilege in the first case and the Government goes along to that extent; § 2301 would also recognize the privilege in the second case and § 2301 in the third unless the circumstances negated confidentiality. We find no valid policy reason for a different result in the fourth case, and we do not read Wigmore as thinking there is. Laymen consulting lawyers should not be expected to anticipate niceties perceptible only to judges—and not even to all of them.

This analogy of the client speaking a foreign language is by no means irrelevant to the appeal at hand. Accounting concepts are a foreign language to some lawyers in almost all cases, and to almost all lawyers in some cases. Hence the presence of an accountant, whether hired by the lawyer or by the client, while the client is relating a complicated tax story to the lawyer, ought not destroy the privilege, any more than would that of the linguist in the second or third variations of the foreign language theme discussed above; the presence of the accountant is necessary, or at least highly useful, for the effective consultation between the client and the lawyer which the privilege is designed to permit. By the same token, if the lawyer has directed the client, either in the specific case or generally, to tell his story in the first instance to an accountant engaged by the lawyer, who is then to interpret it so that the lawyer may better give legal advice, communications by the client reasonably related to that purpose ought fall within the privilege; there can be no more virtue in requiring the lawyer to sit by while the client pursues these possibly tedious preliminary conversations with the accountant than in insisting on the lawyer's physical presence while the client dictates a statement to the lawyer's secretary or is interviewed by a clerk not yet admitted to practice. What is vital to the privilege is that the communication be made *in confidence* for the purpose of obtaining *legal* advice *from the lawyer*. If what is sought is not legal advice but only accounting service, or if the advice sought is the accountant's rather than the lawyer's, no privilege exists. We recognize this draws what may seem to some a rather arbitrary line between a case where the client communicates first to his own accountant (no privilege as to such communications, even though he later consults his lawyers on the same matter, *Gariepy v.*

United States, 189 F.2d 459, 463 (6th Cir. 1951)),[‡] and others, where the client in the first instance consults a lawyer who retains an accountant as a listening post, or consults the lawyer with his own accountant present. But that is the inevitable consequence of having to reconcile the absence of a privilege for accountants and the effective operation of the privilege of client and lawyer under conditions where the lawyer needs outside help. We realize also that the line we have drawn will not be so easy to apply as the simpler positions urged on us by the parties—the district judges will scarcely be able to leave the decision of such cases to computers; but the distinction has to be made if the privilege is neither to be unduly expanded nor to become a trap.

The judgment is vacated and the cause remanded for further proceedings consistent with this opinion.

[‡]We do not deal in this opinion with the question under what circumstances, if any, such communications could be deemed privileged on the basis that they were being made to the accountant as the client's agent for the purpose of subsequent communication by the accountant to the lawyer; communications by the client's agent to the attorney are privileged, 8 Wigmore, *Evidence,* § 2317-1.

Quinn v. Lum and Cronin, Fried, Sekiya & Kekina
Civ. No. 81284
Hawaii Court of Appeals

On January 25, 1984, Richard K. Quinn, Attorney at Law, a Law Corporation, filed suit against Rogerlene Lum, a member of the Hawaii Association of Legal Assistants (HALA) and formerly legal secretary with the Quinn firm, for injunctive relief based on the allegation that Mrs. Lum possesses confidential client information from her work as Quinn's legal secretary, which information would be transmitted to the co-defendant, Mrs. Lum's new employer, Cronin, Fried, Sekiya & Kekina, Attorneys at Law, if she were to begin her employment with the Cronin firm as a legal assistant.

On or about January 3, 1984 Mrs. Lum notified Quinn that she had accepted a position as a paralegal with the Cronin firm. Quinn subsequently discussed and corresponded with Mr. Cronin regarding the hiring of Mrs. Lum, who was scheduled to begin work with the Cronin firm on January 30, 1984. Mr. Cronin repeatedly refused Quinn's request that she not be hired by the Cronin firm.

On January 26, a hearing on the application for a temporary restraining order was heard by Judge Philip T. Chun of the Circuit Court of the First Circuit, State of Hawaii. The application was denied.

Quinn alleges in the pleadings filed with the Court in Civil No. 81284 that Mrs. Lum's employment with the Quinn firm from December 1, 1982 to January 17, 1984, and as Mr. Quinn's secretary from April 25, 1983 to January 17, 1984, included attendance at the firm's case review committee meetings. Confidential discussions occurred concerning case evaluation, settlement evaluation, strategy and tactics between Quinn, his associates, and their clients.

Cronin et al. are attorneys of record for the plaintiffs in *Firme v. Honolulu Medical Group and Ronald P. Peroff, M.D.* Quinn's firm represents the defendants. The case was set for trial on March 19, 1984. According to exhibits attached to the records filed in the instant case, Mr. Cronin recognized the *Firme* situation and agreed that Mrs. Lum would not be involved in the *Firme* case in her new employment, nor would his firm "[ever] seek to obtain any information from her concerning cases with which she was involved while in [Quinn's] office, nor would we have her work on any while here." Mr. Cronin goes on to say in his January 24 letter to Quinn that Quinn should consult with his clients in the *Firme* case as to whether Quinn's "attempt . . . to stop Mrs. Lum from working for [the Cronin firm] is with their approval."

Quinn also alleges that while his firm is known in the Honolulu legal community as one which represents hospitals, doctors and other health care providers, the Cronin firm is known as a plaintiff medical malpractice firm. Quinn lists in several pleadings that on more than one occasion, these firms found themselves adversaries in the same cases.

[Quinn contends] that this action was brought not to "bar Lum from working as a legal secretary or even as a paralegal, since that would be ludicrous given the size of Hawaii's legal community." In fact, Quinn states he would have "no objection to Lum's working for any other law firm in Hawaii other than one which specializes in medical malpractice plaintiffs' work, like [Cronin's]."

A subsequent hearing on the original complaint for injunctive relief was then held in Judge Ronald Moon's court on February 6. Plaintiff's motion for a preliminary injunction that would bar such employment "for at least two years" was denied, with the judge noting *Quinn v. Lum* as a case of first impression.

The Court explained its decision in light of the standards to be met before a preliminary injunction could be issued, as dealt with in depth by Mrs. Lum's attorney, David L. Fairbanks, who is also the current President of the Hawaii State Bar Association.

The standards which must be met in order to obtain a preliminary injunction, as listed by Judge Moon, follow:

1. The Court did not feel there was a substantial likelihood that plaintiff would prevail on the merits. If an injunction were to be issued, it would:
   "[E]ssentially prevent a paralegal or legal secretary, [or] attorney from joining any law firm that may have had some case in the past, . . . cases pending at the present time, or potential cases which may be worked on in the future" (Transcript of the Hearing, page 82).
2. The evidence is lacking regarding irreparable damage to Richard Quinn's clients.
3. The public interest would not be served by issuing such an injunction.

When an attorney enters practice in the State of Hawaii, he or she agrees to abide and be governed by the Hawaii Code of Professional Responsibility. This code does not attempt to govern the ethical actions of the non-attorneys. While Canon 37 of the American Bar Association's Code of Professional Responsibility, adopted pre-1971, states that a lawyer's employees have the same duty to preserve client confidences as the lawyer, this Canon is not included in the Hawaii code. Compliance, therefore, with the same rules of ethics guiding the Hawaii attorney is currently left to the discretion—and conscience—of the non-attorney.

If an attorney in Hawaii breaches the Code of Professional Responsibility, the office of Disciplinary Counsel may choose to investigate the matter and may pass the matter on to the Disciplinary Board and possibly, to the Hawaii Supreme Court for adjudication.

If an employee of a law office becomes suspect of some breach of ethics or acts of omission, the employing attorney becomes responsible for the employee's deeds. For example, if a legal secretary fails to file the complaint the day the Statute of Limitations expires thinking the next day would suffice, it is the attorney who is responsible to the client. The attorney can fire the secretary "for cause" but the attorney, nevertheless, stands responsible. It appears the only way for an attorney to further censor the employee directly is via a civil suit for tortious damages.

Whether a permanent injunction can or will be granted has yet to be seen in this case. What is clear is that neither the office of Disciplinary Counsel nor the Hawaii Supreme Court would or could become involved; they have no jurisdiction over the non-attorney working in a law office.

Brown v. Hammond
United States District Court, Eastern District, Pennsylvania, 1993, 810 F. Supp. 644

WALDMAN, District Judge.

Plaintiff is a former employee of defendant attorney and his law firm. She is suing for wrongful discharge after having "blown the whistle" on the defendants' allegedly improper billing practices. Jurisdiction is based on diversity of citizenship.* Defendants have moved to dismiss the complaint for failure to state a claim upon which relief can be granted, pursuant to Fed.R.Civ.P. [Federal Rule of Civil Procedure] 12(b)(6).

I. LEGAL STANDARD

The purpose of a Rule 12(b)(6) motion is to test the legal sufficiency of a complaint. See *Sturm v. Clark,* 835 F.2d 1009, 1111 (3d Cir. 1987). In deciding a motion to dismiss for failure to state a claim, the court must "accept as true all the allegations in the complaint and all reasonable inferences that can be drawn therefrom, and view them in the light most favorable to the non-moving party." See *Rocks v. Philadelphia,* 868 F.2d 644, 645 (3d Cir. 1989). Dismissal is not appropriate unless it clearly appears that plaintiff can prove no set of facts in support of his claim which could entitle him to relief. See *Hishon v. King & Spalding,* 467 U.S. 69, 73, 104 S. Ct. 2229, 2232, 81 L. Ed. 2d 59 (1984). . . . A complaint may be dismissed when the facts pled and the reasonable inferences drawn therefrom are legally insufficient to support the relief sought. . . .

II. FACTS

The pertinent factual allegations in the light most favorable to plaintiff are as follows. From November 4, 1990 to April 4, 1991, plaintiff was employed by defendants at-will as a paralegal and secretary. The time she spent on client matters was billed to clients as "attorney's time" without any notice to such clients that the work was done by a non-lawyer. Her supervisors directed her at times to bill her work directly as attorney's time despite her protests that the practice was improper. She then informed various authorities and affected clients of this practice. Plaintiff does not allege that she had any responsibility for overseeing the firm's billing practices.

Defendants responded by imposing new work rules with respect to hours of employment which applied only to and discriminated against plaintiff. She was subsequently terminated.

In count I, plaintiff asserts that she was terminated in violation of public policy for reporting the wrongful actions of defendants. In count II, she asserts that she was terminated in violation of public policy for refusing to perform wrongful actions. . . .

III. DISCUSSION

It is well established under Pennsylvania law that "absent a statutory or contractual provision to the contrary . . . either party [may] terminate an employment relationship for any or

no reason." *Geary v. United States Steel Corp.,* 456 Pa. 171, 175–176, 319 A.2d 174 (1974). An employer may determine, without any fair hearing to an at-will employee, that the employer simply wishes to be rid of him. *Darlington v. General Electric,* 350 Pa. Super. 183, 210, 504 A.2d 306 (1986). An employer's right to terminate an at-will employee has been characterized as "virtually absolute." *O'Neill v. ARA Services, Inc.,* 457 F. Supp. 182, 186 (E.D. Pa. 1978).

Pennsylvania law does recognize, however, a nonstatutory cause of action for wrongful discharge from employment-at-will, but only in the quite narrow and limited circumstance where the discharge violates a significant and recognized public policy. *Borse v. Piece Goods Shop,* 963 F.2d 611, 617 (3d Cir. 1992); *Geary,* supra; *Darlington,* supra. Such a public policy must be "clearly mandated" and of a type that "strikes at the heart of a citizen's social right, duties and responsibilities." *Novosel v. Nationwide Insurance Co.,* 721 F.2d 894, 899 (3d Cir. 1983). *Geary* signals a "narrow rather than expansive interpretation of the public policy exception." *Bruffett v. Warner Communications, Inc.,* 692 F.2d 910, 918 (3d Cir. 1982). Public policy exceptions "have been recognized in only the most limited of circumstances." *Clay v. Advanced Computer Applications, Inc.,* 522 Pa. 86, 89, 559 A.2d 917 (1989).

While courts generally look to constitutional or legislative pronouncements, some courts have found an expression of significant public policy in professional codes of ethics. See *Paralegal v. Lawyer,* 783 F. Supp. 230, 232 (E.D. Pa. 1992); *Cisco v. United Parcel Services,* 328 Pa. Super. 300, 476 A.2d 1340 (1984). . . .

The court in [the] *Paralegal* [v. *Lawyer* case] found that the Pennsylvania Rules of Professional Conduct as adopted by the Pennsylvania Supreme Court pursuant to state constitutional powers, Pa. Const. art. 5, § 10(c), could provide the basis for a public policy exception to the at-will employment rule. See *Paralegal* [v. *Lawyer*], 783 F. Supp. at 232 (finding public policy against falsifying material facts and evidence from rules 3.3(a)(1), 3.4(a), and 3.4(b)). In that case, a paralegal whose employer was being investigated by the state bar was terminated after she learned that the attorney-employer had created a false record to exculpate himself and so informed the lawyer who was representing the employer in disciplinary proceedings.

Taking plaintiff's allegations as true, defendants would appear to have violated the Pennsylvania Rules of Professional Conduct by misrepresenting to clients who had performed work for which they were paying or by effectively permitting the unauthorized practice of law by a non-lawyer. See Rule 1.5 (regulating fees); Rule 5.5(a) (prohibiting aiding non-lawyers in unauthorized practice of law); Rule 7.1 (prohibiting false or misleading communications about lawyer's services); 8.4(c) (defining "professional misconduct" to include dishonesty, fraud, deceit or misrepresentation).

Based upon pertinent precedent and persuasive authority, the court must distinguish between gratuitous disclosure of improper employer conduct and disclosures by persons responsible for reporting such conduct or for protecting the

---

*Plaintiff is a citizen of Texas, and defendants are citizens of Pennsylvania. The amount in controversy exceeds $50,000.

public interest in the pertinent area. See *Smith v. Calgon Carbon Corp.*, 917 F.2d 1338, 1345 (3d Cir. 1990), cert. denied, 111 S. Ct. 1597, 113 L. Ed. 2d 660 (1991) (discharged chemical company employee not responsible for reporting improper emissions or spills); *Field v. Philadelphia Electric Co.*, 388 Pa. Super. 400, 565 A.2d 1170 (1989) (nuclear safety expert discharged for making statutorily required report to federal agency). See also *Hays v. Beverly Enters.*, 766 F. Supp. 350 (W.D. Pa.), aff'd, 952 F.2d 1392 (3d Cir. 1991) (physician's duty does not extend to plaintiff nurse); *Gaiardo v. Ethyl Corp.*, 697 F. Supp. 1377 (M.D. Pa. 1986), aff'd, 835 F.2d 479 (3d Cir. 1987) (plaintiff not supervisor or responsible for quality control).

The court concludes that plaintiff's termination for gratuitously alerting others about defendants' improper billing practice does not violate the type of significant, clearly mandated public policy required to satisfy the new narrow exception to Pennsylvania's rigid at-will employment doctrine.

By her own characterization what plaintiff did was to "blow the whistle" on wrongful conduct by her employer. The Pennsylvania Whistleblower Law, 43 Pa. C.S.A. [Consolidated Statutes Annotated] § 1421 et seq., protects from retaliatory adverse employment action employees of public bodies or entities receiving public appropriations who report wrongdoing.** That Law, which excludes from its protection wholly private employment, has been found not to codify any previously existing legal right or privilege and held not to constitute an expression of clearly mandated public policy in the context of private at-will employment.† See *Smith*, 917 F.2d at 1346;

Cohen v. Salick Health Care, Inc., 772 F. Supp. 1521, 1531 (E.D. Pa. 1991) (employee discharged for alerting employer's prospective contractee of inflated financial projections); *Wagner v. General Electric Co.*, 760 F. Supp. 1146, 1155 (E.D. Pa. 1991) (employee discharged after expressing criticism of employer's product to customers).

On the other hand, courts are less reluctant to discern important public policy considerations where persons are discharged for refusing to violate the law themselves. See *Smith*, 917 F.2d at 1344; *Woodson v. AMF Leisureland Centers, Inc.*, 842 F.2d 699 (3d Cir. 1988) (refusal to sell liquor to intoxicated patron); *Shaw v. Russell Trucking Line, Inc.*, 542 F. Supp. 776, 779 (W.D. Pa. 1982) (refusal to haul loads over legal weight); *McNulty v. Borden, Inc.*, 474 F. Supp. 1111 (E.D. Pa. 1979) (refusal to engage in anti-trust violations). No employee should be forced to choose between his or her livelihood and engaging in fraud or other criminal conduct. To the extent that plaintiff appears to allege that she was also terminated for refusing herself to engage directly in fradulent billing, her action may proceed. . . .

An appropriate order will be entered.

ORDER

AND NOW, this 12th day of January, 1992, upon consideration of defendants' Motion to Dismiss Plaintiff's Complaint, consistent with the accompanying memorandum, IT IS HEREBY ORDERED that said Motion is GRANTED in part and DENIED in part in that [count I] of plaintiff's complaint [is] DISMISSED.

**While the Whistleblower Law protects covered employees who report impropriety to outside authorities, it does not authorize such employees to voice complaints directly to clients of a public or publicly funded entity.

†Because of the special nature of the attorney-client relationship, an attorney's misrepresentation about the source, quality, nature or cost of work performed is arguably more reprehensible than such misrepresentation to clients and customers by other suppliers of goods and services. It is not, however, sufficiently different in kind therefrom to satisfy the narrow public policy exception to Pennsylvania's stringent at-will employment doctrine.

SOME USAGE GUIDELINES FOR FORMAL WRITING

ability, capacity

Ability is the mental, physical, financial, or legal power to do something. Capacity is the ability to absorb, contain, or hold something.

EX: <u>ability</u> to communicate effectively; <u>ability</u> to pay; a courtroom filled to <u>capacity</u>

abjure, adjure

Abjure means to repudiate or renounce. Adjure means to command something, often under oath.

EX: <u>abjure</u> the belief; <u>adjure</u> them to stop the picketing

above

"Above" is frequently used in the law to refer to material previously discussed.

EX: the doctrine discussed <u>above</u>; the <u>above</u> material
Make sure that the reference is clear. Will the reader know what you are referring to "above"? If not, avoid using the word. Use a less vague reference.

EX: the doctrine discussed on page 24; the material in section C

accept, except

Accept means to receive with approval or to agree with. As a verb, except means to leave out; as a preposition, it means other than.

EX: <u>accept</u> the offer; <u>excepted</u> from the requirements; all the cases <u>except</u> the ones that were overruled

accident, mishap

An accident is an unexpected occurrence, which may or may not be bad. A mishap is an unfortunate, usually minor, accident.

EX: money found by <u>accident</u>; suffer a <u>mishap</u>

accordance, in accordance with

Avoid using such overly formal language.
SAY: as you requested
RATHER THAN: <u>in accordance with</u> your request

acknowledge, admit, concede

These words mean to accept the existence or truth of something, often with some hesitation. When something is admitted, is is usually done much more reluctantly than when it is acknowledged. Concede means to yield.

EX: <u>acknowledge</u> the mistake; <u>admit</u> guilt; <u>concede</u> the argument

actual, real

Both words mean existing in fact. Real suggests something demonstrative or objectively present.

EX: <u>actual</u> intent; <u>real</u> evidence

adjacent, contiguous

Adjacent means lying near or close by; contiguous means touching or in actual contact.

EX: Maine and Rhode Island are <u>adjacent</u> states; Maine and New Hampshire are <u>contiguous</u> states

adjudge, judge

Adjudge means to adjudicate, to make a formal decision. Judge also means to consider and to rule, but it can be used in less formal settings.

EX: <u>adjudged</u> to be in contempt; <u>judge</u> of character

adoptive, adopted

Adoptive means related by adoption. Adopted refers to the person accepted by others through the legal process of adoption.

EX: <u>adoptive</u> father; <u>adopted</u> child (don't say <u>adopted</u> father)

adverse, averse

Adverse means opposed or against one's interest. Averse means a feeling of distaste, a disinclination.

EX: <u>adverse</u> claim, <u>adverse</u> circumstances; <u>averse</u> to the settlement offer

advice, advise

Advice is a noun meaning opinion, counsel, recommendation, or suggestion. Advise is a verb meaning to counsel or give advice to.

EX: the lawyer <u>advised</u> the client to accept the <u>advice</u> of the doctor

advise, notify, inform (see also *advice*)

Advise is an overly formal way to say notify or inform.
SAY: <u>notify</u> us of the verdict
RATHER THAN: <u>advise</u> us of the verdict

affect, effect (see also *effect; impact*)

Affect is a verb meaning to have an influence on. As a verb, effect means to bring something about or to cause. As a noun, effect means the result.
EX: the ruling <u>affects</u> all contractors; the supervisor <u>effected</u> changes; the <u>effect</u> of the verdict

aforementioned, aforesaid

These words are verbose ways of saying "mentioned earlier."
SAY: the theory discussed on page 5
RATHER THAN: the <u>aforementioned</u> theory or the <u>aforesaid</u> theory

aggravate, irritate, annoy

Aggravate means to make something worse, to add to the problem. Avoid using it to mean to annoy or to provoke. Irritate means to vex, harass, or disturb. "Annoy" is a less severe form of "irritate."
EX: <u>aggravate</u> an injury; <u>irritate</u> the judge

aid, aide

Aid means help or support. Aide is a person who provides help or support, an assistant.
EX: <u>aid</u> provided by the <u>aide</u>

alibi

Do not use this word to mean excuse or apology in general. Use it as the legal defense of being somewhere else at the time of the crime.

allege, contend

Allege means to state that something is true without proving it. Contend means to maintain or assert a position. Do not use contend unless disagreement exists. When it does not exist, "say" or "said" are preferable.
EX: the report <u>alleged</u> fraud; to respond to the report, she <u>contended</u> that there was no fraud

allow, permit

Allow means to let happen, suggesting the absence of an affirmative prohibition. Permit is more forceful, suggesting an affirmative authorization.
EX: the animals were <u>allowed</u> to wander; the judge did <u>permit</u> the extension

all ready, already

All ready means fully prepared, or completely ready. Already means earlier, previously, or before.
EX: they were <u>all ready</u>; <u>already</u> gone

all right, alright

All right is often misspelled as alright. Never use the latter word.

all together, altogether

All together means in agreement or present in one place. Altogether means completely or entirely.
EX: the lawyers were <u>all</u> <u>together</u> for a bench conference; the statement was not <u>altogether</u> true

allude, refer

Use allude for an indirect reference, and refer for a direct or specific reference.
EX: the witness <u>alluded</u> to the problem; the lawyer <u>referred</u> to exhibit Z

allusion, illusion

Allusion is an indirect reference. Illusion is a false image or hallucination.
EX: an <u>allusion</u> that she was involved in organized crime; the <u>illusion</u> of grandeur

alternative, alternate

Alternative means one of two possibilities. An alternate is a substitute.
EX: the <u>alternative</u> of prison or probation; an <u>alternate</u> on the jury
Use alternative only when there is a choice between two options. If there are more than two, say "choice," "preference," "selection," "pick," etc.
SAY: three <u>choices</u>
RATHER THAN: three <u>alternatives</u>

ameliorate, mitigate

Ameliorate means to improve or make better. Mitigate means to make less severe.
EX: <u>ameliorate</u> his living conditions; <u>mitigate</u> the damages

amiable, amicable

Both words mean friendly. Amiable suggests a sweetness, while amicable emphasizes the lack of bitterness or hostility.
EX: <u>amiable</u> personality; <u>amicable</u> settlement

among, between

Generally, use "among" when comparing more than two items, and "between" when comparing two items. Between can be used when more than two items are involved if each item is being considered individually or in relation to each other.
EX: listed <u>among</u> the wounded; divided <u>between</u> employee and employer; understanding <u>between</u> nations; <u>between</u> the lines

amoral, immoral, unmoral

Amoral means neither moral nor immoral; not to be judged by moral standards. Immoral means contrary to moral standards. Unmoral means unable to distinguish right from wrong. It has close to the same meaning as amoral. The same is true of nonmoral, meaning not connected with morality.
EX: animals are <u>amoral</u>; an <u>immoral</u> gambling contract; <u>unmoral</u> behavior of the mentally incompetent adult

amount, in the amount of

"In the amount of" is verbose. Use "for" whenever possible.
SAY: a check <u>for</u> $100
RATHER THAN: a check <u>in the amount of</u> $100

amount, number

Amount refers to things in the aggregate or in bulk. Number refers to things that can be counted one by one.
EX: <u>amount</u> of tension; <u>amount</u> of nitrogen; <u>number</u> of volumes

ampersand (&)

An ampersand (&) is the symbol for the word "and." Use it only if it is part of the official name of a company or firm.

Do not use an ampersand or the plus sign (+) as shorthand.
SAY: reversed and remanded
RATHER THAN: reversed & remanded

and/or

Avoid using this phrase in formal writing; it can be ambiguous. When you mean "one or the other or both," say so explicitly.
SAY: the affidavit must be signed by the plaintiff, or her attorney, or both
RATHER THAN: the affidavit must be signed by the plaintiff and/or her attorney

and which

Use this phrase in a clause only if "which" appears in a preceding clause. If possible, rewrite to avoid using "which."
SAY: the first course which I took and which I passed
RATHER THAN: the first course I took and which I passed
EVEN BETTER: the first course I took and passed

angle

In formal writing, do not use this word to mean point of view.
SAY: her perspective on the case
RATHER THAN: her angle on the case

announce, annunciate

Both words mean to proclaim or declare. Announce is preferred.

ante, anti

Ante is a prefix that means before, prior, or in front of. Anti is a prefix that means opposed to or against. A hyphen is not needed unless anti precedes a proper name or the letter "i."
EX: antenuptial agreement; anteroom; antidiscrimination ordinance; anti-American demonstration

anticipate, expect

Anticipate is an overly formal (and sometimes ambiguous) substitute for the word expect.
SAY: expect opposition; we expect the letter to go out today
RATHER THAN: anticipate opposition; we anticipate that the letter will go out today
Anticipate is proper when you mean to look forward to something occurring.
EX: anticipate the visit

any (see also *either*)

Do not use this word if it adds nothing to the sentence.
SAY: it does not help; are we nearer?
RATHER THAN: it does not help any; are we any nearer?

anybody, any body

Say "anybody" (one word) when you mean any person. Say "any body" (two words) when you are referring to corpses or focusing on specific items.
EX: anybody can answer; the police did not find any body
Anybody takes a singular verb.
EX: anybody is eligible

anymore, any more

Anymore means "from now on," or "at the moment." Any more means "something additional."

EX: the court does not sit anymore; are there any more forms?

any one, anyone (see also *anybody*)

Say "any one" (two words) only when you are referring to any single person or thing. Say "anyone" when you are referring to persons or things in general.
EX: any one of the proposals is acceptable; anyone can come

anyplace

Avoid using this colloquial substitute for anywhere.
SAY: sit anywhere
RATHER THAN: sit anyplace

apparent, evident

Both words mean obvious and clear, but with different shades of meaning. Apparent suggests the use of reasoning, while evident suggests the presence of objective or external indications.
EX: it is apparent the theory will not succeed; evident defects

appraise, apprise

Appraise means to evaluate or to judge. Apprise means to give notice or to inform. Do not spell apprise with a "z" (apprize).
EX: appraise the furniture; apprise the suspect of her rights

apt, prone, likely, liable

All of these words can mean probably, having a tendency, or inclined. Use apt or prone when referring to a natural tendency or habit that is unpleasant or undesirable.
EX: apt to fall; prone to error; likely to succeed
The primary meaning of liable is legally responsible. Avoid using it to mean probability, even in an unpleasant or undesirable context.
SAY: apt to overdrink and have an accident
RATHER THAN: liable to overdrink and have an accident

arbitrate, mediate

To arbitrate is to render a decision at the invitation of both parties. To mediate is to act as go-between to encourage the parties to come to a mutually satisfactory resolution on their own.

as, because, since (see also *because*)

Do not use "as" as a substitute for the other words listed.
SAY: he filed the claim because (or since) he qualified for it
RATHER THAN: he filed the claim as he qualified for it

as . . . as

When "as" is used in a comparison, complete the sentence in order to determine whether the pronoun that follows should be nominative or objective.
EX: she is as wise as I (the nominative "I" is used because if you completed the sentence, it would read: "she is as wise as I am.")
EX: the verdict shocked him as much as me (the objective "me" is used because if you completed the sentence, it would read: "the verdict shocked him as much as it shocked me.")

as if, as though

"As though" is preferable to "as if" in formal writing. Use a subjunctive verb after this phrase.

SAY: the witness acts as though he were knowledgeable
RATHER THAN: the witness acts as if he is knowledgeable

ask a question
The phrase is redundant: Either of the two words alone is sufficient.
SAY: ask her; question her
RATHER THAN: ask her a question

as per, as regards, with regard to
Avoid using these clumsy expressions.
SAY: as you instructed; concerning your letter; about your application
RATHER THAN: as per your instructions; as regards your letter; with regard to your application

as such
Avoid using this awkward phrase.
SAY: the coins are rare and valuable
RATHER THAN: The coins are rare; as such, they are valuable

assume, presume
While these words are often used interchangeably, assume suggests a reasoning process, whereas presume means to take for granted without proof.
EX: from reading the transcript, I assumed that he was present; presumed to be innocent

assure, insure, ensure
Assure means to give confidence and to set one's mind at ease. Ensure and insure are often interchangeable. When you mean to guarantee against the risk of loss, insure is most commonly used.
EX: assure the defendant that we will do our best; insure the spouse, with the child as beneficiary; insure the car against theft

as to
Generally, this phrase should not be used as a substitute for "about."
SAY: we are unsure about the trial date
RATHER THAN: we are unsure as to the trial date

as to whether
Avoid using this awkward and wordy phrase.
SAY: unsure whether to come
RATHER THAN: unsure as to whether to come

as well as, both
"As well as" and "both" do not need to be used together.
SAY: both John and Jim
RATHER THAN: both John as well as Jim

at about
Avoid using this phrase.
SAY: arrived at noon; arrived about noon
RATHER THAN: arrived at about noon

at present
Omit this phrase if it adds nothing to the sentence.
SAY: we are preparing a handbook
RATHER THAN: we are preparing a handbook at present

attached hereto
The phrase is almost always redundant.

SAY: the document is attached
RATHER THAN: the document is attached hereto

at this point in time
A wordy way to say "now."

author
Avoid using this word as a verb. As a noun, use it for men and women; do not use the word authoress.
SAY: write the memo; she is an author
RATHER THAN: author the memo; she is an authoress

awhile, a while
"Awhile" is an adverb that means "for a short time." (Hence, do not use the word "for" before awhile since it is already included in its meaning.) The word "while" is a noun meaning a period of time. "A while" therefore, means "a period of time." "For" can be used with this phrase.
EX: wait awhile until I return, wait for a while before you decide to litigate

back down, back up, back out
Generally, these words are colloquial and should not be used in formal writing.

backward, backwards
Both words are proper as adverbs. Only "backward" is proper as an adjective.
EX: move backward, move backwards; a backward move (not a backwards move)

bad, badly
"Bad" and "badly" are often misused with verbs such as look and feel.
SAY: I feel bad
RATHER THAN: I feel badly (unless you mean that your sense of touch is weak or impaired)
Use badly as an adverb.
EX: sung badly
Also, "badly" should not be used to mean "very much."

be advised that
Avoid using this overly formal phrase.
SAY: you must appear
RATHER THAN: be advised that you must appear

because, reason is because
"Because" means "for the reason that" or "since." Hence it is redundant to say, "reason is because."
SAY: he was fined because of the report
RATHER THAN: he was fined; the reason is because of the report.
If you need to say the "reason is," say the "reason is that" rather than the "reason is because."
EX: the reason he succeeded is that he worked harder than the others

beside, besides
Do not say "besides" when you mean "next to."
SAY: beside the lake
RATHER THAN: besides the lake
"Besides" is an adverb meaning "moreover." It can also mean "in addition to" and "except for."

between you and I

The correct phrase is "between you and me." The preposition "between" takes the objective case.

biannual, semiannual, biennial

Biannual and semiannual mean occurring twice a year. Biennial means occurring once every two years or lasting two years.

EX: <u>biannual</u> conferences in March and November; <u>semiannual</u> conferences in March and November, <u>biennial</u> congress in 1990 and 1992

bimonthly, semimonthly

Bimonthly means occuring every other month. Semimonthly means occurring twice a month.

EX: <u>bimonthly</u> meetings in January, March, and May; <u>semimonthly</u> reports on the first and last week of each month

biweekly, semiweekly

Biweekly means occurring every two weeks. Semiweekly means occurring twice a week.

EX: <u>biweekly</u> meetings are on the 1st and 15th of the month; <u>semiweekly</u> report every Monday and Friday

The word "regular" is redundant with biweekly, semiweekly, weekly, monthly, daily, yearly, etc.

SAY: a biweekly meeting; a monthly meeting

RATHER THAN: a <u>regular</u> biweekly meeting; a <u>regular</u> monthly meeting

black, blacks, white, whites

Do not capitalize these words when referring to race.

blame on

Rewrite to avoid using this phrase.

SAY: he <u>blamed</u> Joe

RATHER THAN: he placed the <u>blame</u> <u>on</u> Joe

brake, break

Brake is a device for stopping something. Break means to split or crack something.

EX: excessive pressure will <u>break</u> the truck's <u>brake</u>

breadth, breath, breathe

Breadth is a side-to-side measurement. Breath is air taken in and out in respiration. Breathe is the verb meaning to inhale and exhale air.

EX: three inches in <u>breadth</u>; her first <u>breath</u> after awaking; <u>breathe</u> slowly

bring, take

Use "bring" when moving toward something and "take" when moving away from something.

EX: <u>bring</u> the treatise to the library; <u>take</u> the treatise out of the library

EX: <u>bring</u> the exhibits with you (they are somewhere else at present); <u>take</u> the exhibits with you (they are now here and can be removed)

but what, but that

Avoid using these colloquial phrases.

SAY: I have no doubt <u>that</u> he is competent

RATHER THAN: I have no doubt <u>but</u> <u>that</u> (or <u>but</u> <u>what</u>) he is competent

but yet

This phrase is redundant.

SAY: we thought we understood torts, <u>but</u> we failed the exam

RATHER THAN: we thought we understood torts, <u>but</u> <u>yet</u> we failed the exam

can, may

"Can" indicates the ability or freedom to do something. "May" indicates permission.

EX: she <u>can</u> do legal research; she <u>may</u> use the law library

cancel out

The "out" in this phrase is redundant.

cannot

Do not spell this as two words (can not) unless you are placing great emphasis on the word "not."

cannot but, can't but, cannot help but

Avoid using these awkward phrases.

SAY: <u>cannot</u> help admiring

RATHER THAN: <u>cannot</u> <u>but</u> admire; <u>can't</u> <u>help</u> <u>but</u> admire

can't

Spell this word out in formal writing: cannot.

canvas, canvass

Canvas is the noun meaning a heavy piece of fabric. Canvass is the verb meaning to solicit or request.

EX: stand on the <u>canvas</u>; he <u>canvassed</u> the block for votes

capitol, capital

Capitol is a building, an edifice. The main meanings of capital are a city, a form of wealth, and chief.

EX: visiting the Senator at the <u>capitol</u> in Albany, the <u>capital</u> of New York

case of

This phrase is usually redundant.

SAY: in *Johnson v. Smith*

RATHER THAN: in the <u>case</u> <u>of</u> *Johnson v. Smith*

center around, center on

Avoid using the phrase "center around." Instead, say "center on" or "center in."

SAY: the brief <u>centered</u> <u>on</u> the estoppel theory

RATHER THAN: the brief <u>centered</u> <u>around</u> the estoppel theory

character, nature

Avoid using these words unnecessarily.

SAY: the argument is specious

RATHER THAN: the argument is of a specious <u>character</u>

cite, site, sight

Cite means to make reference to written material. A site is a place or location. Sight is the ability to see.

EX: <u>cite</u> the opinion; <u>site</u> of the accident; impaired <u>sight</u>

claim, assert, maintain

Use claim to imply doubt or a legal right. Use assert or maintain to emphasize truth.

EX: a fraud <u>claim</u>; he <u>asserted</u> that he was not there; he <u>maintained</u> that he was not there

close proximity

This phrase is redundant since proximity means close in place or time.

SAY: the car is <u>close</u> to the edge

RATHER THAN: the car is in <u>close</u> <u>proximity</u> to the edge

closure, cloture

Closure is the act of closing something; a conclusion. Cloture is a legislative procedure that terminates debate so that a vote can be taken.

EX: bring the matter to <u>closure</u>; <u>cloture</u> was invoked to end the filibuster

collusion, connivance

Collusion is an agreement to defraud, using the forms of the law. Connivance is an indirect consent or permission to allow another to commit an unlawful act.

EX: <u>collusion</u> by the husband and wife in pretending that grounds for divorce existed; <u>connivance</u> of the mayor in not notifying the police when she heard that the money was going to be embezzled

commence, begin, initiate

For everyday events, use begin. For normal legal matters and other relatively important events, use commence. For very serious events, use initiate.

EX: <u>begin</u> work; <u>commence</u> litigation; <u>initiate</u> the investigation

common, ordinary

Common suggests what is shared by many. Ordinary suggests a lack of distinction.

EX: <u>common</u> knowledge; <u>ordinary</u> soldier

compare, contrast

When you compare, you emphasize similarities *and* differences. When you contrast, you emphasize differences.

EX: <u>compare</u> the two offers; <u>contrast</u> the civil law with the common law

compare and contrast

This phrase is redundant since "compare" means to point out similarities and differences.

compare to, compare with

"Compare to" suggests an existing similarity. "Compare with" suggests calling attention to differences and similarities.

EX: he was flattered when Jones <u>compared</u> him <u>to</u> the partner; <u>compare</u> the testimony <u>with</u> the prior statements

complement, compliment

Complement means to supplement, complete, or bring to a whole. Compliment means a flattering remark.

EX: the colors <u>complement</u> the design; an unexpected <u>compliment</u>

compose, comprise, include

Compose means to constitute or make up. Comprise means to consist of or to include. The parts compose the whole; the whole comprises the parts.

EX: the twelve counties <u>compose</u> the state; the state <u>comprises</u> twelve counties

When you say include, you are usually referring to less than all of the parts. When you say comprise, you are usually referring to all of the parts.

EX: the play <u>comprises</u> three acts; the play <u>includes</u> songs and dances

concept, conception

Concept is a thought or general idea. Conception is one's understanding of something.

EX: the <u>concept</u> of equity; they had no <u>conception</u> of the magnitude of the loss

concur with, concur in

Say "concur with" when the agreement is with a person. Say "concur in" when the agreement is with anything else.

EX: Judge Smith <u>concurred</u> <u>with</u> Judge Jones; I <u>concur</u> <u>in</u> the result

connotation, denotation

Connotation is the suggestive or secondary meaning of the word or phrase. Denotation is the literal meaning of the word or phrase.

EX: the <u>connotation</u> of widow is loneliness and grief; its <u>denotation</u> is a woman whose husband has died

consecutive, successive

Consecutive means following without interruption. Successive means following in logical order, which may or may not involve interruption.

EX: a <u>consecutive</u> sentence is served immediately after the prior sentence; <u>successive</u> defeats in 1982, 1985, and 1990

consensus of opinion

This phrase is redundant.

SAY: the <u>consensus</u> was to adjourn

RATHER THAN: the <u>consensus</u> <u>of</u> <u>opinion</u> was to adjourn

consistently, constantly

Consistently means uniformly. Constantly means persistently, continually recurring.

EX: <u>consistently</u> wrong; <u>constantly</u> interrupting

contact

Do not use this word to mean to get in touch with.

SAY: telephone him, write to him, communicate with him.

RATHER THAN: <u>contact</u> him

contagious, infectious

Contagious means transmitted by physical contact. Infectious means transmitted without actual contact (e.g., through disease-carrying organisms in water, air, etc.).

contemptible, contemptuous

Contemptible means deserving contempt. Contemptuous means showing contempt.

EX: <u>contemptible</u> lie; he was <u>contemptuous</u> of the police officer

continual, continuous

Continual means happening over and over, but with interruptions. Continuous means happening without interruption.

EX: <u>continual</u> harassment; <u>continuous</u> weekend snow

convince, persuade

Convince means to cause someone to believe something. Persuade means to induce someone to act.

EX: she <u>convinced</u> me that I had a cause of action; she <u>persuaded</u> me to litigate

cooperate together

A redundant phrase.

SAY: they <u>cooperated</u> on the project

RATHER THAN: they <u>cooperated</u> <u>together</u> on the project

controversial issue, noncontroversial issue

An issue is a question about which there is disagreement. Therefore, to call an issue "controversial" is redundant, and to call it "noncontroversial" is a non sequitur. By definition, an issue must be controversial.

co-respondent, correspondent

A co-respondent is someone with whom your spouse allegedly committed adultery. A correspondent is someone with whom you communicate in writing.

EX: she was named as the <u>co-respondent</u> in the wife's divorce action against her husband; a <u>correspondent</u> in China

could of, should of, would of

The "of" in these phrases should be "have."

SAY: <u>could</u> <u>have</u> succeeded; <u>should</u> <u>have</u> succeeded; <u>would</u> <u>have</u> succeeded

RATHER THAN: <u>could</u> <u>of</u> succeeded; <u>should</u> <u>of</u> succeeded; <u>would</u> <u>of</u> succeeded

Also avoid using the contractions "could've," "should've," and "would've."

counsel, council, consul

Counsel is a lawyer or a group of lawyers. Counsel also means the advice by a respected or knowledgeable person. Council is an organized body set up to govern or to give advice. A consul is a government official who lives in another country in order to represent his or her country's commercial interests.

EX: <u>counsel</u> for the corporation, wise <u>counsel</u> received from the accountant; rural county <u>council</u>, <u>council</u> of elders; trade problems handled by the <u>consul</u>

counselor, councilor

A counselor is someone who gives advice. A councilor is a member of a council. The preferred spelling is with one "l" as indicated here.

EX: <u>counselor</u> at law; an elected <u>councilor</u>

country, nation

A country is a physical or geographic territory. A nation is a group of people with common customs, history, etc.

EX: France is a <u>country</u> at war; America is a <u>nation</u> of immigrants

couple

When referring to a man and a woman, couple can take a plural or a singular verb as long as you are consistent. The plural is preferred.

SAY: the <u>couple</u> <u>are</u> donating <u>their</u> time

RATHER THAN: the <u>couple</u> <u>are</u> donating <u>its</u> time

course, in the course of

"In the course of" is redundant.

SAY: <u>during</u> the trial

RATHER THAN: <u>in</u> the <u>course</u> of the trial

credible, creditable, credulous

Credible means plausible, worthy of belief. Creditable means worthy of praise. Credulous means gullible, overly inclined to believe.

EX: a <u>credible</u> witness; he did a <u>creditable</u> job digesting the transcripts; he is unusually <u>credulous</u> for a person with so much education

criterion, criteria

Criterion is the singular of criteria. The preferred plural of criterion is criteria rather than criterions.

EX: the <u>criterion</u> used by the commission <u>is</u> efficiency; the <u>criteria</u> used by the commission <u>are</u> efficiency and experience

criticize, critique

Avoid using critique as a verb.

SAY: <u>criticize</u> the presentation; <u>give</u> <u>a</u> <u>critique</u> of the presentation

RATHER THAN: <u>critique</u> the presentation

currently

Omit this word if it adds nothing to the sentence.

SAY: we are preparing a handbook

RATHER THAN: we are <u>currently</u> preparing a handbook

customary, usual, habitual

Customary means commonly practiced. Usual means that which is normal and frequent. Habitual means acting by habit or constantly repeating a certain behavior.

EX: it was <u>customary</u> for the court to adjourn at noon; his <u>usual</u> hostility; <u>habitual</u> liar

data, datum

Datum means information. Data is the plural of datum and should, therefore, take a plural verb. Although some grammarians feel that data can also take a singular verb, in formal writing, use a plural verb.

SAY: the <u>data</u> <u>are</u> available

RATHER THAN: the <u>data</u> <u>is</u> available

dead end, dead-end

Dead end is a noun meaning the end of something, like a road. It also means a stalemate or impasse. The adjective form is dead-end.

EX: the negotiations reached a <u>dead</u> <u>end</u>; a <u>dead-end</u> job

deadly, deathly

Deadly means tending to cause, or causing death. Deathly means resembling death.

EX: <u>deadly</u> use of force; <u>deathly</u> apparition

decided, decisive, incisive

Decided means definite, without doubt. Decisive means resolute or conclusive. Incisive means perceptive, sharp.

EX: a <u>decided</u> advantage; a <u>decisive</u> victory; an <u>incisive</u> remark

decimate

Literally, this word means to kill every tenth person (a Roman form of punishment). It also means to destroy a large part of something. If, however, you are referring to destruction in a proportion other than ten percent, do not use decimate.

SAY: <u>destroyed</u> half the population

RATHER THAN: <u>decimated</u> half the population

decline, refuse

Decline means to say no politely. Refuse means to say no with a note of insistence or irritation.

EX: <u>decline</u> the invitation; <u>refuse</u> to answer

deduce, induce

Deduce is to reason from the general facts to a specific conclusion (from cause to effect). This is known as "a priori" reasoning. Induce is to reason from specific facts to a general conclusion (from effect to cause). This is known as "a posteriori" reasoning.

EX: since all employees we talked to had received the notice, we <u>deduced</u> that this employee received it; from the fact that workers had accidents at the machine on March 13th, March 26th, and July 31st, we <u>induced</u> that the machine was dangerous.

deem, consider, think

Deem is an overly formal way to say consider or think.

SAY: we <u>think</u> the matter is closed; we <u>consider</u> the matter closed

RATHER THAN: we <u>deem</u> the matter closed

defective, deficient

Defective means having a flaw. Deficient means insufficient, lacking in amount or degree.

EX: <u>defective</u> computer; <u>deficient</u> in research skills

definite, definitive

Definite means clearly defined. Definitive means decisive and authoritative.

EX: <u>definite</u> plans; <u>definitive</u> ruling

definitely, absolutely, positively

Avoid using these words when you mean clearly or certainly.

SAY: without doubt, I am going

RATHER THAN: I am <u>definitely</u> going; I am <u>absolutely</u> going; I am <u>positively</u> going

EVEN BETTER: I am going

delusion, illusion

Both words mean a false image. A delusion is more permanent or fixed than an illusion.

EX: he acted under the <u>delusion</u> that he was George Washington; his <u>illusion</u> of grandeur vanished when he lost the election

demise, death

Demise is an overly formal word for death.

SAY: an untimely <u>death</u>

RATHER THAN: and untimely <u>demise</u>

democracy, republic

When you use the word democracy, you are emphasizing the power of the people. When you use the word republic, you are emphasizing the power of the people through their elected representatives.

depository, depositary

Depository is a place where something is kept or stored. Depositary is a person who has been entrusted with something. Occasionally, however, depositary is also used to refer to a place.

EX: he placed the money in the <u>depository</u>; he gave the money to the <u>depositary</u>

device, devise

A device is an invention or a product of some kind. A devise is a gift of real property (and sometimes personal property) by a will.

EX: gambling <u>device</u>; a <u>devise</u> to his daughter

diagnosis, prognosis

Diagnosis is a process of studying something. It is also the opinion based on such a study. Prognosis is a prediction.

EX: a <u>diagnosis</u> of the illness; the <u>prognosis</u> for recovery

different

Avoid the redundant use of this word.

SAY: he will visit three cities

RATHER THAN: he will visit three <u>different</u> cities

different from, different than

Generally, "different from" is preferable to "different than."

EX: intent is <u>different</u> <u>from</u> apprehension

differ from, differ with

Use "differ from" when emphasizing dissimilarity between things. Use "differ with" when emphasizing differences between persons.

EX: civil law <u>differs</u> <u>from</u> common law; he <u>differed</u> <u>with</u> the judge

dilemma, predicament

Dilemma involves a choice between two possibilities that are relatively equal in their undesirability. A predicament is a problem or an embarrassing situation.

EX: he faced the <u>dilemma</u> of accepting the forfeiture or the fine; the <u>predicament</u> of being without funds in a strange town

diminish, minimize

Diminish means to make something smaller. Minimize means to make something as small as possible.

EX: <u>diminish</u> the available assets; he tried to <u>minimize</u> his responsibility

disburse, disperse

Disburse means to pay out. Disperse means to scatter or disseminate.

EX: <u>disburse</u> the funds; <u>disperse</u> the crowd

disclose, divulge, said (see also *indicate*)

Do not use "disclose" or "divulge" for "said" unless you mean that something is being revealed or uncovered rather than merely communicated.

SAY: he <u>said</u> that he was tired

RATHER THAN: he <u>disclosed</u> that he was late; he <u>divulged</u> that he was late (unless you mean that this information had some significance)

discover, invent

Discover means to obtain knowledge of something that has existed but has been unknown. Invent means to produce or create something that has never existed.

EX: <u>discover</u> gold, <u>discover</u> rampant cheating; <u>invent</u> a more powerful computer

discreet, discrete

Discreet means being prudent, cautious. Discrete means separate, distinct.

EX: <u>discreet</u> about revealing the news; <u>discrete</u> sections of the brief

disinterested, uninterested

Disinterested means impartial, having no bias. Uninterested means indifferent.

EX: a <u>disinterested</u> witness; he was so <u>uninterested</u> that he fell asleep during the performance

disorganized, unorganized

Disorganized means disorder, usually in reference to that which was once organized. Unorganized means never having been organized.

EX: <u>disorganized</u> file after considerable use; <u>unorganized</u> notes at the beginning of her research

disposition, temperament

Disposition means one's usual frame of mind. Temperament is a more narrow word that refers to one's emotional outlook or traits.

EX: a <u>disposition</u> to accept things at face value; a volatile <u>temperament</u>

divert, avert

Divert means to distract or turn something off course. Avert means to turn away or prevent.

EX: <u>divert</u> their attention from the speaker, <u>avert</u> disaster

divide, separate

Divide means to partition or split something into parts according to a prior arrangement or plan. It is also used in the sense of splitting into opposing groups or camps. Separate means to partition or disconnect something by removing a component part or by keeping the parts away from each other.

EX: the judge must <u>divide</u> the assets; the issue will <u>divide</u> the community; the judge ordered the bailiff to <u>separate</u> the witnesses

divided into, composed of

"Divided into" means to partition or split something into its parts. "Composed of" means to constitute the parts of something.

EX: the profits were <u>divided</u> <u>into</u> four shares; the jury is <u>composed</u> <u>of</u> teachers, tellers, insurance agents, and housewives

dollars

Do not use this word if you also use the dollar sign.
SAY: he paid $200
RATHER THAN: he paid $200 <u>dollars</u>

dominant, predominant

Both words mean controlling or exercising the most control. "Predominant," however, suggests being overriding or uppermost at a particular time.

EX: the <u>dominant</u> forces seeking change; during the meeting, the shareholders were the <u>predominant</u> force

don't, doesn't

Avoid frequent use of contractions in formal writing.
SAY: <u>do</u> <u>not</u> go; <u>does</u> <u>not</u> speak the language
RATHER THAN: <u>don't</u> go; <u>doesn't</u> speak the language

doubt that, doubt whether, doubt if

Use "doubt that" in a negative statement, in a question, and in a statement of unbelief. Use "doubt whether" to express uncertainty. Avoid "doubt if" since it is generally considered too informal.

EX: there is no <u>doubt</u> <u>that</u> the jury will convict; do you <u>doubt</u> <u>that</u> the jury will convict?; there is little <u>doubt</u> <u>that</u> the jury is biased; we <u>doubt</u> <u>whether</u> any hope of recovery exists

drunk, drunken

Use "drunk" as a predicate. Use "drunken" as an adjective.

EX: he is <u>drunk</u>; a <u>drunken</u> customer

due to the fact that, because

The "due to" phrase is a wordy way to say because.
SAY: he lost <u>because</u> he did not file
RATHER THAN: he lost <u>due</u> <u>to</u> <u>the</u> <u>fact</u> <u>that</u> he did not file

during the time that, during the course of

These are redundant phrases.
SAY: arrested <u>while</u> soliciting votes; arrested <u>during</u> the conference
RATHER THAN: arrested <u>during</u> <u>the</u> <u>time</u> <u>that</u> he was soliciting votes; arrested <u>during</u> <u>the</u> <u>course</u> <u>of</u> the conference

dying, dyeing

Dying means losing one's life. Dyeing is the coloring of material.

each other, one another

The traditional view is that "each other" should be used only when referring to two people, and "one another" to more than two.

EX: the plaintiff and defendant would not look at <u>each</u> <u>other</u>; the five attorneys sent memos to <u>one</u> <u>another</u>
The possessive is 's rather than s'.

EX: Bob and Bill used each other's books; the three students used one another's books.

eager, anxious

Eager means impatient and desirous. Anxious means worried or distressed.

EX: <u>eager</u> to leave the hospital; <u>anxious</u> about the doctor's report

eatable, edible

These words, meaning fit to be eaten, are interchangeable.

ecology, environment

Ecology is a narrower word meaning the relationships between organisms and their surroundings. Environment means the total circumstances in a certain setting.

economic, economical

Economic refers to the production and management of wealth. Economical means prudent, not wasteful.

EX: <u>economic</u> forecast; an <u>economical</u> use of limited resources

effect (see also *affect*)

Effect can be a noun (meaning the result), or a verb (meaning to bring something about or to cause). As a verb is is overly formal.

SAY: the administrator <u>made</u> changes
RATHER THAN: the administrator <u>effected</u> changes

effective, efficient
Effective means producing the desired result. Efficient means producing the desired result without wasting effort or time.
EX: an <u>effective</u> remedy; an <u>efficient</u> management team

e.g., i.e.
E.g. (exempli gratia) means for example; i.e. (id est) means in other words, or, that is.
EX: the terms of the will, <u>i.e.</u>, what she wanted to do with her property; the terms of the will, <u>e.g.</u>, her husband receives the car, her son receives the stock, her daughter receives the business.

either, any
Use "either" when you are referring to two. Use "any" when referring to more than two.
EX: they will hire <u>either</u> John or Mary; I will read <u>any</u> of the three books.

either, neither
Either takes a singular verb, even if followed by "of" and a plural. The same is true of neither.
EX: <u>either</u> theory <u>is</u> acceptable; <u>either</u> of the theories <u>is</u> acceptable
EX: <u>neither</u> theory <u>is</u> acceptable; <u>neither</u> of the theories <u>is</u> acceptable

either . . . or, neither . . . nor
"Or" goes with "either." "Nor" goes with "neither."
SAY: <u>neither</u> the judge <u>nor</u> the jury
RATHER THAN: <u>neither</u> the judge <u>or</u> the jury
Use a singular verb unless one of the joined nouns is plural. If so, the verb should agree with the noun closest to the verb.
EX: <u>neither</u> the judge <u>nor</u> the jury <u>is</u> in the courtroom
EX: <u>neither</u> the jurors <u>nor</u> the judge <u>is</u> in the courtroom
EX: <u>neither</u> the judge <u>nor</u> the jurors <u>are</u> in the courtroom

elicit, illicit
Elicit means to bring out or to call forth. Illicit means illegal.
EX: <u>elicit</u> a response; <u>illicit</u> transaction

else but, else besides, else except
The word "else" can be redundant when used with "but," "besides," or "except."
SAY: no one <u>but</u> John came; no one <u>besides</u> John came; no one <u>except</u> John came.
RATHER THAN: no one <u>else</u> <u>but</u> John came; no one <u>else</u> <u>besides</u> John came; no one <u>else</u> <u>except</u> John came.

emigrate, immigrate
Emigrate means to leave a country and settle elsewhere. The person who emigrates is an emigrant. Immigrate means to come into a country to settle. The person who immigrates is an immigrant.
EX: John <u>emigrated</u> from Poland. He is an <u>emigrant.</u> Mary <u>immigrated</u> to America. She is an <u>immigrant.</u>

eminent, imminent, immanent
Eminent means prominent or distinguished. Imminent means near at hand. Immanent means inherent, remaining within.

EX: an <u>eminent</u> authority on torts; <u>imminent</u> threat; <u>immanent</u> in human nature

empathy, sympathy
Empathy means identifying with the emotions of another. It is a stronger word than sympathy, which means understanding and compassion.
EX: <u>empathy</u> between the brothers; <u>sympathy</u> for the victim

employ, use
Do not use employ when you mean use.
SAY: they <u>used</u> ingenuity
RATHER THAN: they <u>employed</u> ingenuity

enclose, inclose
The preferred spelling is enclose.

enclosed herein, enclosed please find, please find enclosed
These phrases are redundant.
SAY: a copy is <u>enclosed</u>
RATHER THAN: <u>enclosed</u> <u>herein</u> is a copy; <u>enclosed</u> <u>please</u> <u>find</u> a copy

endorse, indorse
These words mean to place one's signature on something as part of a legal transfer. They also mean to approve of something. The preferred spelling is endorse.

enormous, immense
Enormous means extraordinarily large. Immense means so large that the regular means of measurement are not adequate.
EX: an <u>enormous</u> box, the <u>immense</u> ocean floor

envious, jealous
Envious means feeling upset and resentful about what another has. Jealous means feeling fear or apprehension about being replaced.
EX: <u>envious</u> of her success; <u>jealous</u> of the time he spent with her

episode, incident, event
All three words mean an occurrence. Episode suggests that the occurrence is part of a sequence or series of occurrences. An incident is a minor occurrence. An event is an important occurrence.
EX: another <u>episode</u> of violence in their feud; he thought nothing of the <u>incident</u>; all were present for the <u>event</u>

equal, perfect, unique
These are absolute words. Avoid using comparative language with them.
SAY: <u>equal</u> to; is <u>perfect</u>; is <u>unique</u>
RATHER THAN: <u>more</u> <u>equal</u> than; <u>most</u> <u>perfect</u> of; <u>less</u> <u>unique</u> than

equivocal, ambiguous, obscure
Equivocal means intentionally unclear. Ambiguous means unclear because more than one meaning is possible. Obscure means not easily understood, often because it is almost hidden.
EX: an <u>equivocal</u> response; an <u>ambiguous</u> clause; an <u>obscure</u> reference

ergo
This word means therefore or consequently. Avoid using it in formal writing.

Esq.

If "Esq." is used after an attorney's name, do not use Mr., Ms., etc., and, do not use the word attorney.

SAY: Mary Smith, <u>Esq.</u>

RATHER THAN: Ms. Mary Smith, <u>Esq.</u>, Attorney at Law

essay, assay (as verbs)

Essay means to make an attempt. Assay means to subject to analysis.

EX: <u>essay</u> the project; <u>assay</u> the liquid

essential, necessary

Essential is stronger than necessary. When something is necessary, it is required and very important, but not always indispensable. When something is essential, it is vital in the sense of continued existence or validity.

EX: an <u>essential</u> element of the tort; a <u>necessary</u> meeting

estimate, estimation

Estimate means a preliminary calculation or opinion. Estimation means the process of reaching an estimate.

EX: only an <u>estimate</u> could be provided; the <u>estimation</u> would take several weeks

et al.

Et al. means "and other persons" (et alii). Avoid using it even in case citations.

etc., for example; etc., such as

Do not use "etc." when you introduce a list by "for example" or "such as." Etc. would be redundant.

SAY: for example, lawyers, paralegals, secretaries

RATHER THAN: for example, lawyers, paralegals, secretaries, etc.

every one, everyone

"Every one" means each individual person or thing. "Everyone" means every person.

EX: <u>every one</u> of the containers has been inspected; <u>everyone</u> must attend

everyplace, everywhere

Everywhere is more standard than everyplace.

everywhere that

"That" is superfluous in this expression.

SAY: <u>everywhere</u> I went

RATHER THAN: <u>everywhere that</u> I went

evidence, show

Do not use evidence to mean show.

SAY: their condition <u>showed</u> no weakness

RATHER THAN: their condition <u>evidenced</u> no weakness

exact replica

The word "exact" is redundant.

except for the fact that

This can be shortened to "except that."

excess verbiage

The word "excess" is redundant, since verbiage means excess words.

exhaustive, exhausting

Exhaustive means comprehensive. Exhausting means tiring, wearing oneself out.

EX: <u>exhaustive</u> study of the opinions; an <u>exhausting</u> performance

expect, suppose, believe, guess

Do not use "expect" when you mean suppose, believe, or guess.

SAY: I <u>believe</u> the jury will reach a verdict today.

RATHER THAN: I <u>expect</u> the jury will reach a verdict today

explicit, express

Both words mean clearly expressed. Explicit means defined, spelled out. Express is often used in reference to intention or a state of mind.

EX: <u>explicit</u> erotica; <u>express</u> offer

explicit, implicit

Explicit means clearly expressed. Implicit means implied, understood but not directly expressed.

EX: an <u>explicit</u> rejection by letter; an <u>implicit</u> rejection by silence

expound, explain

Expound is an overly technical, and often pompous, way to say explain.

extant, extent

Extant means still in existence. Extent means the range or distance of something.

EX: <u>extant</u> language; the <u>extent</u> of the damage

facilitate, help

Help or make easier is preferable to facilitate.

SAY: <u>help</u> the project

RATHER THAN: <u>facilitate</u> the project

fact, opinion

Do not say fact when you mean opinion. If the statement is a matter of judgment, it is an opinion no matter how strongly one feels it to be true. Facts must be capable of objective verification.

EX: <u>Fact</u>: insurance rates have increased. <u>Opinion</u>: insurance rates are burdensome

factor

A factor is that which contributes to a result. Hence the phrase "contributing factor" is redundant. Factor is a vague word. Avoid using it when possible.

SAY: we must consider cost

RATHER THAN: cost is a <u>factor</u> we must consider

fact that

This phrase is often superfluous.

SAY: he admits he was there

RATHER THAN: he admits the <u>fact that</u> he was there

farther, further

Farther means more distance physically. Further means more distant in degree, quantity, or time.

EX: they drove <u>farther</u> than expected; the judge would not tolerate <u>further</u> disruption

faze, phase

Faze means to disturb or bother. Phase means an aspect or a stage of something.

EX: the jury was not <u>fazed</u> by the revelation; the next <u>phase</u> of the project

feasible, possible

Feasible means capable of being done, often to a fair probability. Possible means capable of happening, however slight the odds may be.

EX: a feasible plan; a possible rejection

female, woman, girl, lady, feminine

Some consider "female" to be objectionable except in scientific or research contexts. The preferable words are woman, girl, lady, and feminine.

SAY: the suspect is a woman; her feminine appeal

RATHER THAN: the suspect is a female; her female appeal

fewer, less, smaller

Use "fewer" when referring to numbers, or items that can be counted. Use "less" with mass or collective nouns, and when the emphasis is on degree. Use smaller when referring to size.

EX: fewer applications; less hostility; smaller room

field

This word is overused and rarely adds anything to a sentence.

SAY: she studied law

RATHER THAN: she studied the field of law

fight with, fight along with, fight against

Avoid using the phrase "fight with" when it is not clear whether the fight is "along with" or "against."

SAY: he fought along with the British; or, he fought against the British

RATHER THAN: he fought with the British

figuratively, literally

Figuratively means symbolically, or, "in a manner of speaking." Literally means actually or really.

EX: he was figuratively on fire with rage; the bailiff literally lifted him out of the seat

final culmination

The word "final" is redundant.

finalize, complete, conclude

Avoid using the word finalize, meaning to put into final form. Acceptable substitutes are complete, conclude, etc.

finding, holding

A finding is a formal determination of what the facts are. The verb is find. A holding is a formal determination of how the law applies to the facts. The verb is hold.

EX: the court found that the defendant did not file the report, and held him in contempt

fire, dismiss, discharge

Do not use "fire" to mean dismiss or discharge someone from employment. It is too informal.

firstly, secondly, etc.

When presenting a list, it is preferable to say first, second, third, etc., rather than firstly, secondly, thirdly, etc.

first of all

"Of all" is unnecessary.

fit, fitted

The past tense of fit is fit *or* fitted.

EX: the shoes fit; the shoes fitted

Use fitted, however, when you mean "to cause to fit" or "to make the right size."

EX: the seamstress fitted the dress

fix

Use this word to mean to fasten securely or attach. Avoid the colloquial use of fix to mean arrange, repair, prepare, etc.

flammable, inflammable, nonflammable

Flammable and inflammable have the same meaning. They both mean easily ignited or likely to burn. Nonflammable means the opposite.

EX: gasoline is flammable (or inflammable); specially treated mattresses are nonflammable

flaunt, flout

Flaunt means to brag or show off. Flout means to show contempt for or to defy openly.

EX: flaunt his wealth; flout the regulations

flier, flyer

Both words mean one who flies, and a handbill or circular. Flier is the preferred spelling.

forbear, forebear

As nouns, both words mean an ancestor, but forebear is the preferred spelling. As a verb, forbear (not forebear) means to resist or restrain.

EX: created by her forebears; forbear responding

forbid . . . from

Do not use this construction.

SAY: forbid you to enter

RATHER THAN: forbid you from entering

forced, forceful, forcible

Forced means involuntary or unnatural. Forceful means having strength or effectiveness. Forcible means brought about by physical force.

EX: forced landing; forceful argument; forcible entry

formally, formerly

Formally means formal or in accordance with custom. Formerly means at an earlier time.

EX: dressed formally; formerly in charge of operations

former, latter

Use "former" when referring to the first to two items mentioned. Do not use it to refer to the first of three or more items. Use "latter" when referring to the last of two items mentioned. Do not use it to refer to the last of three or more items.

SAY: When Smith, Jones, and Davis objected, Smith spoke for the group. When Smith, Jones, and Davis objected, Davis resigned. When Davis resigned, he was replaced by the treasurer.

RATHER THAN: When Smith, Jones, and Davis objected, the former spoke for the group. When Smith, Jones, and Davis objected, the latter resigned. When Davis resigned, the latter was replaced by the treasurer.

formulate, form

Formulate is a wordy substitute for form or devise. Limit formulate to scientific settings.

SAY: form an opinion

RATHER THAN: formulate an opinion

for the purpose of
This phrase should be replaced by "to" whenever possible.
SAY: came <u>to</u> negotiate
RATHER THAN: came <u>for</u> <u>the</u> <u>purpose</u> of negotiation

for the reason that
This phrase should be replaced by "because" whenever possible.
SAY: rejected <u>because</u> the report contained errors
RATHER THAN: rejected <u>for</u> <u>the</u> <u>reason</u> <u>that</u> the report contained errors

for your information
This phrase adds nothing. Do not use it.

freak, freakish
These words refer to what is highly unusual or abnormal. Freak is a noun, freakish is an adjective. Do not use freak as an adjective.
EX: a <u>freak</u> of nature; a <u>freakish</u> occurrence (not a <u>freak</u> occurrence)

free gift, free pass, for free
By definition, gifts and passes are free. Free is redundant in such phrases. The word "for" is also unnecessary in the phrase "for free."
SAY: a <u>gift</u> of wine; a <u>pass</u> to the game; given to him <u>free</u>
RATHER THAN: a <u>free</u> <u>gift</u> of wine; a <u>free</u> <u>pass</u> to the game; given to him <u>for</u> <u>free</u>

from . . . to
The following statement is ambiguous: "from March to April." Do you mean from the beginning of March to the beginning of April? From the end of March to the end of April? Be more precise.
EX: during March through April

future plans
The word "future" usually adds nothing since most plans are for a later period. The same is true of the word "ahead" in the phrase "plan ahead," and the word "advance" in the phrase "advance plans."

garnish, garnishee
Both words are verbs meaning to attach a debtor's property in the possession of another. Garnishee is also a noun meaning the debtor against whom garnishment has been sought. Another meaning of garnish is to embellish, to add something for flavor or color.
EX: <u>garnish</u> his wages; <u>garnishee</u> his wages; the <u>garnishee</u> lost his job; <u>garnish</u> the salad

gauge, gage
Both words mean a standard or an instrument of measurement, but the preferred spelling is gauge. A less common meaning of gage is a challenge or pledge.
EX: pressure <u>gauge</u>

general consensus, general public
These are redundant phrases since "consensus" and "public" already incorporate the concept of "general."

get, got, gotten
Get means to acquire, to reach, to become, etc. Although this verb can be acceptable in formal writing, you should consider using alternative language for simplicity and precision.
SAY: was arrested; must go; dressed for the trip; I have a headache; seek revenge; I must finish; we obtained the funds
RATHER THAN: <u>got</u> arrested; <u>got</u> to go; <u>get</u> dressed for the trip; I've <u>got</u> a headache; <u>get</u> back at him; I <u>have</u> <u>got</u> to finish; we <u>have</u> <u>gotten</u> the funds
There are times, however, when get seems more natural than substitutes.
COMPARE: <u>get</u> up in the morning; <u>get</u> a book
WITH: <u>arise</u> in the morning; <u>obtain</u> a book

glance, glimpse
A glance is a brief look. A glimpse is a brief, incomplete, or partial look
EX: a <u>glance</u> at her watch; a <u>glimpse</u> of the president in the car

good, well
Good is an adjective. Use it before nouns and with linking verbs such as be, seem, taste, appear, look.
EX: a <u>good</u> response; the chances look <u>good</u>.
Well is an adverb and an adjective. As an adjective, it refers to a person's health.
EX: spoke <u>well</u> (adverb); feel <u>well</u> (adjective)
In the last example (feel well), if you were referring to the sense of touch rather than to health, "well" would be an adverb.

graduated from, was graduated from
The institution does the graduating, not the student. Hence the traditional view is that the passive form (was graduated from) is needed. Today, however, both forms are acceptable. Be sure to include the preposition "from."
EX: she <u>graduated</u> <u>from</u> Duke; she <u>was</u> <u>graduated</u> <u>from</u> Duke

grievous, grievious
There is no such word as grievious. It is a common misspelling of grievous.
EX: <u>grievous</u> crime

grisly, grizzly
Grisly means gruesome. Grizzly means gray.
EX: a <u>grisly</u> crime; a <u>grizzly</u> bear

half, a half a
Avoid using the phrase "a half a" or "a half an."
SAY: a <u>half</u> hour
RATHER THAN: a <u>half</u> <u>an</u> hour

happen, transpire, occur, take place
For an accidental or chance event, use occur or happen; for a planned event, use take place.
EX: the accident <u>happened</u> at noon; the hearing will <u>take</u> <u>place</u> at noon
Transpire means to become known or to leak out. Do not use it to mean to happen or to take place.
SAY: they were surprised by what <u>occurred</u> at the scene
RATHER THAN: they were surprised by what <u>transpired</u> at the scene

healthful, healthy

Healthful means conducive to health. Healthy means possessing good health.

EX: exercise is <u>healthful</u>; John is <u>healthy</u>

herein, hereto, herewith

Avoid using these words. They are too formal and often redundant.

SAY: discussed in this letter

RATHER THAN: discussed <u>herein</u>

here is, here are

Here takes a singular or plural verb depending on the noun that follows the verb.

EX: here <u>is</u> the law library; here <u>are</u> the law libraries; here <u>are</u> Harvard and Yale

hitherto

Use a less cumbersome substitute whenever possible.

SAY: <u>previously</u> unknown

RATHER THAN: <u>hitherto</u> unknown

hoard, horde

Hoard means a hidden supply of something. Horde means a large number of something.

EX: a <u>hoard</u> of food; a <u>horde</u> of shoppers

hopefully

Strict grammarians object to the use of this word to mean "it is hoped" or "if all goes well." Use it only when you mean "in a hopeful manner."

SAY: I hope the court's decision will resolve the matter

RATHER THAN: <u>hopefully</u>, the court's decision will resolve the matter

however

Avoid using "however" to start a sentence when you mean "nevertheless" or "yet." The phrase "but however" is redundant. Use one of these words, not both. Use a semicolon before however when it begins the second independent clause in a sentence.

EX: The lawyers are ready; <u>however</u>, the court is not.

identical with, identical to

"Identical with" is preferred.

EX: your signature is <u>identical</u> <u>with</u> the one on the document

identify with

Use the reflexive pronoun with this phrase.

SAY: she <u>identified</u> <u>herself</u> <u>with</u> the character

RATHER THAN: she <u>identified</u> <u>with</u> the character

if, whether

"Whether" is preferable to "if" when introducing a clause that refers to alternatives.

SAY: let me know <u>whether</u> you can attend

RATHER THAN: let me know <u>if</u> you can attend

Note the ambiguity of the "if" clause. If the person *cannot* attend, there is no need to let you know. The "whether" clause makes it clear that you want to know either way.

if not

Avoid this phrase when it is not clear what you mean. The danger is that what follows "if not" may be incorrectly interpreted negatively.

SAY: the busiest <u>and</u> (or <u>and</u> <u>probably</u>) the most honest judge

RATHER THAN: the busiest, <u>if</u> <u>not</u> the most honest, judge (this sentence suggests that the judge is not honest

if . . . then

Omit "then" when it adds nothing.

SAY: <u>if</u> he loses, he will resign

RATHER THAN: <u>if</u> he loses, <u>then</u> he will resign

illegible, unreadable, legible, readable

Illegible and unreadable both mean difficult to read. Unreadable has the additional meaning of dull.

Similarly, legible and readable mean capable of being read. Readable has the additional meaning of interesting.

impact, affect

As a verb, affect is preferable to impact.

SAY: the rule <u>affects</u> everyone

RATHER THAN: the rule <u>impacts</u> everyone

impeach, remove

Someone who is impeached is *not* removed or dismissed. Impeach simply means accuse, attack, or discredit.

EX: a president is <u>impeached</u> when accused of high crimes and misdemeanors by the House; a president is <u>removed</u> from office when tried and convicted by the Senate

impervious, oblivious, forgetful

Impervious means incapable of being affected; impenetrable. Oblivious means lacking memory, and being unaware. Forgetful means not remembering due to a problem or defect of memory .

EX: <u>impervious</u> to criticism; <u>oblivious</u> of the passage of time; <u>forgetful</u> as ever, he missed the appointment

imply, infer

Imply means to signal or to hint at a meaning. Infer means to deduce something from the signal or the hint. It is the writer or speaker who implies. It is the reader or listener who infers.

EX: the director <u>implied</u> she was dissatisfied with the report; the staff <u>inferred</u> that the director wanted the report changed

impractical, practical, impracticable, practicable

Impractical means not prudent or sensible. Practical means wise or realistic. Impracticable means not capable of being carried out. Practicable means feasible, capable of being done.

EX: to read a book in a day may be <u>practicable</u> because you have done it before, but <u>impractical</u> because of other things you must do today

impudent, impertinent, imprudent

Impudent means brash and disrespectful. Impertinent is less strong. It means impolite, in bad taste. Imprudent means unwise.

EX: they were shocked by her <u>impudent</u> criticism; an <u>impertinent</u> question; an <u>imprudent</u> purchase

in, at

Both words refer to a location. Use "at" when the focus is on a specific location. Use "in" when the focus is on more general boundaries.

EX: I live <u>in</u> the Northeast; I work <u>at</u> Smith, Jones & Jackson

in, into

"In" means inside of, within an area or space. "Into" has the same meaning, but is used with motion or action verbs.

EX: the file is <u>in</u> her briefcase; she went <u>into</u> the court

in advance of, prior to, before

Before is preferable to "in advance of" and "prior to."

SAY: compliance <u>before</u> the hearing

RATHER THAN: compliance <u>in advance</u> of the hearing

in a position to

Avoid using this wordy phrase.

SAY: we cannot accept the offer

RATHER THAN: we are <u>not in a position</u> to accept the offer

in connection with

When you mean "about" or "on," do not use this awkward phrase

SAY: the Center prepared a report <u>on</u> the accident

RATHER THAN: the Center prepared a report <u>in connection with</u> the accident

incredible, incredulous

Incredible means implausible, not to be believed. Incredulous means skeptical, showing disbelief.

EX: he told an <u>incredible</u> story; we were <u>incredulous</u> of his story

indefinitely, forever

Indefinitely means "having no precise limits or boundaries." This is not the same as "a very long time." When you mean the latter, use a word such as forever.

EX: a job that could end tomorrow or in twenty years is a job that will last <u>indefinitely</u>; housework is a job that lasts <u>forever</u>

indicate, say, said, remark; state; insist (see also *allege*)

Say and said are preferred over more formal substitutes (e.g., indicate, remark) that do little more than provide variation for the sake of variation.

SAY: he <u>said</u> that he wanted the position; she would not <u>say</u> if the product was available

RATHER THAN: he <u>remarked</u> that he wanted the position; she would not <u>indicate</u> if the product was available

"State" is properly used when making a formal, full, or detailed declaration.

EX: for the record, he <u>stated</u> that he wanted to withdraw

"Insist" is properly used when someone is being very firm in a position.

EX: she <u>insisted</u> that she did not receive the funds

individual, person

Do not indiscriminately substitute individual (as a noun) for person. Say individual when you are emphasizing one from the group.

EX: an unknown <u>person</u> came forward; no one doubted the right of an <u>individual</u> to dissent from the party position

inflict, afflict

Inflict means to cause something burdensome to be endured. Afflict means to cause distress and suffering, to make miserable.

EX: <u>inflict</u> extra work on them; <u>afflicted</u> with the disease

informant, informer

These words are interchangeable.

in length, in size, in number

Omit these phrases if they are redundant.

SAY: from top to bottom, the wall is eleven feet; the handle is small; he bought ten

RATHER THAN: from top to bottom, the wall is eleven feet <u>in length</u>; the handle is small <u>in size</u>; he bought ten <u>in number</u>

in order to, in order that

These phrases often add nothing to a sentence.

SAY: file the pleading <u>to</u> state the case; delivered early <u>so that</u> they could prepare

RATHER THAN: file the pleading <u>in order to</u> start the case; delivered early <u>in order that</u> they could prepare

input

Avoid using this word except when discussing science or computers.

SAY: your valuable <u>participation</u> in preparing the speech

RATHER THAN: your valuable <u>input</u> in preparing the speech

in receipt of, received

Received is preferable to the awkward, "in receipt of"

SAY: we have <u>received</u> your application

RATHER THAN: we are <u>in receipt of</u> your application

inside of, inside, outside of, outside

Omit "of."

SAY: fell <u>inside</u> the elevator; the property <u>outside</u> city limits

RATHER THAN: fell <u>inside of</u> the elevator; the property <u>outside of</u> city limits

insoluble, insolvable, unsolvable

Insoluble means incapable of being dissolved. Insolvable and unsolvable mean incapable of being solved.

EX: <u>insoluble</u> substance; <u>insolvable</u> crime

in spite of the fact that, although

Although is preferable to the wordy, "in spite . . . ."

SAY: he went <u>although</u> he protested

RATHER THAN: he went in <u>spite of the fact that</u> he protested

instantaneously, instantly

Instantaneously means without perceptible delay. Instantly means at once.

EX: he responded <u>instantaneously</u>; he died <u>instantly</u>

instinct, intuition

Instinct means unlearned behavior. Intuition means knowledge gained outside the normal process.

EX: an <u>instinct</u> for survival; an <u>intuition</u> that she was not being told everything

intentional, voluntary, unintentional, involuntary

An intentional act is one done with a particular intention, or one done deliberately. An unintentional act is one done without a certain intention, or one done deliberately. Conduct is voluntary or involuntary depending on whether it is the product of a free will.

EX: his contact with her body was <u>intentional</u>; his driving into the wall was <u>unintentional</u>; his denunciation of his country was <u>voluntary</u>; his sneeze was <u>involuntary</u>

interment, internment

Interment means burial. Internment means imprisonment or confinement.

EX: <u>interment</u> will be on Monday morning; <u>internment</u> of those captured

in terms of

Avoid using this phrase when it adds nothing.

SAY: there was confusion <u>about</u> the amount

RATHER THAN: there was confusion <u>in</u> <u>terms</u> <u>of</u> the amount

interpersonal, personal

Avoid using interpersonal if you mean nothing more than personal.

SAY: <u>personal</u> relationships

RATHER THAN: <u>interpersonal</u> relationships

interrelationship

Avoid interrelationship if you mean nothing more than relationship.

SAY: <u>relationship</u> between the two countries

RATHER THAN: <u>interrelationship</u> between the two countries

in that, since

"Since" is preferable to "in that."

SAY: they accepted the offer <u>since</u> the terms were sufficient

RATHER THAN: they accepted the offer <u>in</u> <u>that</u> the terms were sufficient

in the event that, if

Avoid using the first phrase when "if" is adequate.

SAY: <u>if</u> you succeed

RATHER THAN: <u>in</u> <u>the</u> <u>event</u> <u>that</u> you succeed

in the immediate vicinity of

Avoid using this phrase when all you mean is "near."

SAY: the accident occurred <u>near</u> the school

RATHER THAN: the accident occurred <u>in</u> <u>the</u> <u>immediate</u> <u>vicinity</u> <u>of</u> the school

in the light of

Avoid this cliché. If you use it, do not say "in light of." The "the" must be included.

into, in to (see also *in, into*)

"Into" and "in to" are distinct. Compare the following:

EX: she went <u>into</u> the court; she went <u>in</u> <u>to</u> obtain the file

invariably, frequently

Invariably means not changing, constant. It does not mean often or frequently.

EX: he is <u>invariably</u> late (if you mean there has never been a time when he was not late); he is <u>frequently</u> late (if you mean he is often late)

invited guest

The word "invited" is redundant, since guest means one who is invited.

in which

Omit this phrase if it adds nothing.

SAY: the courteous way she was treated

RATHER THAN: the courteous way <u>in</u> <u>which</u> she was treated

its, it's

"It's" is a contraction for "it is." For the possessive, say "its," never "it's." If you cannot substitute "it is" for "it's,' do not use the latter.

SAY: <u>it's</u> contagious; <u>its</u> product

RATHER THAN: <u>its</u> contagious; <u>it's</u> product

Even when correctly used, contractions should be limited to speaking. In formal writing, say "it is."

EX: <u>it</u> <u>is</u> contagious

I wish to state that

Avoid using the verbose phrase.

SAY: the report is inadequate

RATHER THAN: <u>I</u> <u>wish</u> <u>to</u> <u>state</u> <u>that</u> the report is inadequate

join together

The phrase is redundant. Drop the "together" (even though the Bible cautions us not to put asunder what has been divinely "joined together.")

SAY: <u>join</u> the two factions

RATHER THAN: <u>join</u> the two factions <u>together</u>

judicial, judicious

Judicial mean pertaining to the courts. Judicious means demonstrating wise judgment.

EX: the volume contains <u>judicial</u> opinions; a <u>judicious</u> choice

jurist, judge, justice

Jurist does not mean judge. A jurist is someone skilled or versed in the law. This can include more than judges. The distinction between judge and justice depends on local custom. Members of the highest court in a judicial system are often called justices; others in that system, judges.

knot

Knot is a nautical unit of speed. Do not add "per hour."

SAY: traveled twenty <u>knots</u>

RATHER THAN: traveled twenty <u>knots</u> <u>per</u> <u>hour</u>

know-how

Avoid using this word in formal writing.

SAY: reputation for competence in management

RATHER THAN: reputation for management <u>know-how</u>

laceration, cut

Laceration is a pompous way of referring to a cut.

last

Avoid ambiguity in the word "last" (e.g., the <u>last</u> case he tried). Do you mean the last case of his career (there were no more)? If so, say "final" or add language to make this clear.

EX: the <u>final</u> case he tried, or the <u>last</u> case he tried <u>before</u> <u>he</u> <u>resigned</u>

Or do you mean the most recent case that he tried (more are expected)?

EX: the <u>latest</u> case he tried, or the <u>most</u> <u>recent</u> case he tried

lay, lie

Lay means to place; it must have an object. Lie means to rest or recline; it does not take an object.

EX: <u>lay</u> the pen on the desk; <u>lie</u> on the couch.

Do not confuse the principal parts of these two verbs. <u>Lay</u>: laid, laid, laying. <u>Lie</u>: lay, lain, lying.

EX: <u>laid</u> a pen on the desk; caught <u>laying</u> the pen in his pocket; I <u>lay</u> there for two hours; I <u>have lain</u> there for hours; <u>lying</u> in bed

Lie also means to communicate a falsehood intentionally. The principal parts of this verb are lie, lied, lied.

lead, led

Lead means to show the way, to head. Led is the past tense and past participle of lead. Avoid the error of thinking that the past tense and past participle of lead is lead.

SAY: the evidence <u>led</u> him to the conclusion

RATHER THAN: the evidence <u>lead</u> him to the conclusion

A similar confusion can exist with the verb forms mislead, misled.

let's, let us

Avoid the contraction "let's" in formal writing.

SAY: <u>let us</u> continue

RATHER THAN: <u>let's</u> continue

lighted, lit

Both of these words are acceptable as the past tense and past participle of light.

EX: <u>lighted</u> the cigarette; <u>lit</u> the cigarette

lightening, lightning

Lightening means making something lighter or less heavy. Lightning means a flash in the sky.

EX: <u>lightening</u> of the load; fear of <u>lightning</u>

likely

When used as an adverb to mean probably, "likely" should be preceded by "very," "quite," and similar words.

SAY: the jury will <u>very</u> <u>likely</u> find for the plaintiff

RATHER THAN: the jury will <u>likely</u> find for the plaintiff

loath, loathe

Loath means reluctant or unwilling. Loathe means to detest.

EX: she is <u>loath</u> to accept the position; she <u>loathes</u> the very idea of taking the position

loose, lose

Loose (as an adjective) means not fastened. Lose means to be unable to find, to be deprived of.

EX: a <u>loose</u> fitting; <u>lose</u> the case

loud, loudly

Use loud as an adjective (a <u>loud</u> noise) rather than as an adverb. The adverb is loudly.

SAY: speak <u>loudly</u>

RATHER THAN: speak <u>loud</u>

major

Use this word to mean important or significant only when it is clear that you are making a comparative state-ment or are viewing an event, object, or concept in relation to something else.

EX: a <u>major</u> announcement (as opposed to all other announcements)

Even when correctly used, major is overused. Consider alternatives such as principal, chief, etc.

majority, most of

Use majority when you are specifically comparing the majority with the minority. If you are simply referring to the larger number, "most" is preferable.

SAY: <u>most</u> of the agents approved

RATHER THAN: the <u>majority</u> of the agents approved (unless you specifically mean over 50%)

majority, plurality

Majority means more than half. Plurality means the largest number, but still less than half.

Assume there are seven justices on the bench. In a case, three justices write an opinion together, two others write a separate opinion, one justice writes an opinion by herself, and the seventh justice does not participate. There is no <u>majority</u> opinion, since more than half of the justices (i.e., four or more) did not join together. The opinion in which the three justices joined is the <u>plurality</u> opinion.

In an election, plurality also means the number by which the winner exceeds the votes for his or her nearest rival.

male, man, boy, masculine

Use "male" only in scientific or research contexts. Otherwise, use man, boy, or masculine.

manner

Replace this word with an adverb when possible.

SAY: written <u>clearly</u>; spoken <u>forcefully</u>

RATHER THAN: written <u>in a clear manner</u>; spoken <u>in a forceful manner</u>

marital, martial

Marital means pertaining to marriage. Martial means pertaining to the armed forces or war.

EX: <u>marital</u> discord; <u>martial</u> law

materialize, happen, appear, take place

Materialize means to take a real form, to cause to become actual. Do not use it to mean happen, appear, or take place.

SAY: goals that did not <u>materialize</u>

RATHER THAN: the event <u>materialized</u> at noon

maybe, may be

"Maybe" is an adverb; "may be" is a verb phrase.

EX: <u>maybe</u> the verdict will be favorable; it <u>may be</u> that the verdict is favorable

media, medium

Media is the preferred plural of medium. While mediums is also acceptable, medias never is. Media takes a plural verb.

SAY: all the <u>media are</u> waiting for the interview; TV is a mass <u>medium</u>

RATHER THAN: all the <u>media</u> is waiting for the interview; TV is a mass <u>media</u>

meretricious, meritorious

Meretricious means involving vulgarity, insincerity, or unlawful sexual relations. Meritorious means having merit, deserving serious judicial inquiry, or going to the heart or essence of the case.

EX: a <u>meretricious</u> relationship; a <u>meritorious</u> defense

moot

In the law, moot means no real controversy.

EX: the question is <u>moot</u> because the company has already received what it wanted

The word also means subject to debate or pertaining to debate.

EX: <u>moot</u> court

more importantly

The "ly" is unnecessary. Say "more important."

more preferable

This phrase is redundant. Say "preferable."

more than one

This phrase is singular and takes a singular verb.

EX: <u>more than one</u> lawyer <u>is</u> present

mutual, common

The focus of mutual is the relationship with or between things. The focus of common is the relationship shared with a group.

EX: <u>mutual</u> respect between the rivals; the <u>common</u> concerns of the delegates

mutual cooperation

This phrase is redundant. Drop "mutual."

nature

Avoid "nature" when you mean kind, type, or sort. In its place be specific about what you mean.

SAY: the settlement is troublesome because of its failure to resolve every issue

RATHER THAN: the <u>nature</u> of the settlement is troublesome

necessaries, necessities

Both words mean that which is necessary. Use necessaries when referring to what is needed to sustain human life at a certain standard of living.

needless to say

Avoid using this phrase. If what follows this phrase was really "needless to say," you would not have said it.

none

None takes a singular verb if it goes with a singular noun. None takes a plural verb if it goes with a plural noun, unless you want to emphasize "not one."

EX: <u>none</u> of the prior hostility <u>was</u> evident; <u>none</u> of the applicants <u>were</u> present; <u>none</u> of the applicants <u>was</u> present (if you wanted to stress that "not one" of the applicants was present)

no question but that

Omit the "but" in this phrase.

not

Avoid the ambiguous use of this word.

EX: all lawyers are <u>not</u> competent

Do you mean that all lawyers are incompetent? Or do you mean that not all lawyers are competent? Change the sentence to say what you mean.

not only . . . but also

Follow the rules of parallelism when you use this construction. Be sure that what follows "not only" is of the same grammatical construction as what follows "but also."

SAY: the judge <u>not only</u> revoked the sale <u>but also</u> suspended the license

RATHER THAN: the judge <u>not only</u> revoked the sale <u>but also</u> the license was subjected to suspension

EVEN BETTER: the judge revoked the sale and suspended the license

noxious, obnoxious

Noxious means harmful to your health or morals. Use obnoxious when you mean disagreeable or offensive.

EX: <u>noxious</u> gas; <u>obnoxious</u> conduct

number

The word "number" takes a plural verb when preceded by "a" and a singular verb when preceded by "the."

EX: a number of lawyers <u>are</u> available; <u>the</u> number of Ohio lawyers <u>is</u> decreasing

official, officious

Official means authoritative, pertaining to an office. Officious means meddlesome, volunteering when not asked.

EX: an <u>official</u> answer; an <u>officious</u> clerk

on, upon

Whenever possible, say "on" rather than "upon."

SAY: there are few things <u>on</u> which they agreed

RATHER THAN: there are few things <u>upon</u> which they agreed

one, one's

Avoid the stilted use of "one" as a substitute for a personal pronoun.

SAY: The property must be maintained; you should take care of your property; I must take care of my property; we must take care of our property.

RATHER THAN: <u>one</u> must take care of <u>one's</u> property

one of those . . . who

This construction takes a plural verb when "who" refers to a plural.

EX: he is <u>one of those</u> judges <u>who are</u> upset (plural verb because "who" refers to a plural noun, judges)

When, however, you add "the only," "who" clearly refers to the singular "one" and takes a singular verb.

EX: he is <u>the only one of those</u> judges <u>who is</u> upset (singular verb because "who" refers to the singular "one")

onetime, one-time

Onetime means former. One-time means only once.

EX: a <u>onetime</u> judge; a <u>one-time</u> chance to win

only

To avoid confusion, place "only" as close as possible to the word it modifies.

EX: the confusion can <u>only</u> be alleviated by a change in policy (if you mean that the confusion cannot be corrected entirely)

EX: the confusion can be alleviated <u>only</u> by a change in policy (if you mean that the confusion can be alleviated but there is just one way to do it—by a change in policy)

on the basis of

Rewrite to avoid using this vague phrase.

SAY: the person who earned the most points won

RATHER THAN: the decision was made <u>on</u> <u>the</u> <u>basis</u> <u>of</u> points earned

on the part of

Avoid using this wordy phrase.

SAY: discontent <u>among</u> the workers

RATHER THAN: discontent <u>on</u> <u>the</u> <u>part</u> <u>of</u> the workers

opaque, transparent

Something is opaque if you cannot see through it, transparent if you can.

ophthalmologist, optician, optometrist

An ophthalmologist is a doctor who specializes in eye diseases. An optician is one who makes and sells eyeglasses, usually not a doctor. An optometrist is a nondoctor who can test for some eye defects and prescribe lenses. Another word for ophthalmologist is oculist.

optimistic, pessimistic

Avoid using optimistic to refer to specific events. Use it to convey a general sense of looking at things in their best light.

SAY: an <u>optimistic</u> attitude

RATHER THAN: an <u>optimistic</u> sign

Say "hopeful" when referring to specifics.

The same is true of pessimistic; apply it to a general outlook that the worst will probably happen. When referring to specifics, say ominous, discouraging, etc.

ordinance, ordnance

Ordinance means a law passed by a city or county government, usually the local legislature. Ordnance means military weapons or the weapons division of the military.

orient, orientate

These words have the same meaning. Orient is preferred.

other than

Avoid using this phrase when "except" is adequate.

SAY: all counts were dismissed <u>except</u> the third

RATHER THAN: all counts were dismissed <u>other</u> <u>than</u> the third

overall

Avoid using this vague, overused word whenever possible. Consider alternatives such as total, general, aggregate, average, comprehensive, whole, complete.

SAY: the <u>complete</u> plan; the <u>comprehensive</u> plan

RATHER THAN: the <u>overall</u> plan

over with

The "with" is redundant.

SAY: the case is <u>over</u>

RATHER THAN: the case is <u>over</u> <u>with</u>

EVEN BETTER: the case is <u>finished</u>; the case is <u>completed</u>

paid, payed

The past tense and past participle of pay is paid. Payed is mainly a nautical term.

panacea

A panacea is a remedy of all diseases or difficulties. Do not use it to refer to one disease or difficulty.

parameter, perimeter

Parameter is a scientific word meaning an arbitrary constant or variable. Do not use it to mean boundary, limit, range, or scope.

SAY: stay within the <u>limits</u> of the budget

RATHER THAN: stay within the <u>parameters</u> of the budget

Perimeter means boundary, or the outer limits of an area.

EX: the <u>perimeter</u> of the field

partially, partly

When the emphasis is on a part of an object, use partly. When you mean "to a certain degree," use partially.

EX: she is <u>partially</u> dependent on her uncle for support; the memo is <u>partly</u> done

particular

This word often adds nothing to the sentence.

SAY: he was unable to attend at this time

RATHER THAN: he was unable to attend at this <u>particular</u> time

party, person

Other than in a legal context, do not refer to a person as a party.

SAY: they took the wounded <u>person</u> to the hospital

RATHER THAN: they took the wounded <u>party</u> to the hospital

past history, past experience

The word "past" is redundant in these phrases.

peaceful, peaceable

Peaceful means undisturbed. Peaceable means inclined toward or promoting peace.

EX: a <u>peaceful</u> setting; a <u>peaceable</u> way to resolve the dispute

pendant, pendent

Pendant, a noun, means something that hangs. Pendent, an adjective, means hanging or suspended.

EX: a <u>pendant</u> around her neck; <u>pendent</u> jurisdiction

people, persons

Use people when referring to a large number. Use persons when referring to relatively few, or when referring to them as individuals.

EX: the <u>people</u> in the stadium; the <u>persons</u> arrested

per cent, percent

The preferred spelling is "per cent." It takes a singular verb if the number is singular and a plural verb if the number is plural.

EX: ten per cent of the brief <u>is</u> done; ten per cent of the cases <u>are</u> frivolous

period of

Omit this phrase if it adds nothing to the sentence.
SAY: he kept a record for two months
RATHER THAN: he kept a record for a <u>period</u> <u>of</u> two months

per se

This phrase means in itself, by itself, intrinsically. Unless you are referring to a specific legal doctrine (e.g., libelous per se), do not use this phrase in your writing. It usually adds little more than pomposity.

personal, personally

Avoid using these words if they add nothing to the meaning of the sentence.
EX: a <u>personal</u> friend (as opposed to what other kind of friend?)
EX: she attended <u>personally</u> (how else could she attend?)
EX: <u>personally</u>, I disagree (how else could you disagree?)

phenomenon, phenomena

Unless you are referring to a perceptible event that is remarkable or impressive in some way, avoid calling it a phenomenon.
The preferred plural of phenomenon is phenomena, not phenomenons.

plane, plain

Plane means a level of development or achievement. Plain means clear, simple, undecorated.
EX: research on a sophisticated <u>plane</u>; the <u>plain</u> meaning rule

plans and specifications

Unless you are making a clear distinction between that which is a "plan" and that which is a "specification," this phrase is redundant. Say "plans."

plus

Do not use "plus" to connect main clauses.
SAY: he failed the course <u>and</u> he left the city
RATHER THAN: he failed the course <u>plus</u> he left the city
Plus takes a singular verb unless the subject is plural. Plus is a preposition, not a conjunction. It does not affect the number of the verb.
EX: ten <u>plus</u> ten <u>is</u> twenty; their objections <u>plus</u> the error <u>are</u> recorded

point of view, viewpoint, standpoint

Whenever possible, try to find substitutes for these words.

SAY:	RATHER THAN:
legally	from a legal <u>point</u> <u>of</u> <u>view</u>
his opinion	his <u>point</u> <u>of</u> <u>view</u>
her judgment	her <u>viewpoint</u>
economically	from an economic <u>standpoint</u>

population, populace

Population means the people, the number of persons in a certain group or territory. Populace means the common people.
EX: the male <u>population</u> of the town; a land reform program acceptable to the <u>populace</u>

possess

Unless you are referring to a legal doctrine, use simpler words such as have, has, and own.

SAY: he <u>has</u> a sense of humor
RATHER THAN: he <u>possesses</u> a sense of humor

practically, virtually

Practically means in a practical manner, and in all important respects. Do not use it to mean "almost." Virtually means in fact, although not formally.
EX: <u>practically</u> exonerated; <u>virtually</u> extinct

precedence, precedent

Precedence means going before, having priority. Precedent means something that happened in the past that can be helpful in similar situations in the future.
EX: whoever files first has <u>precedence</u>; the 1943 case is a clear <u>precedent</u>

precipitate, precipitous

Precipitate means happening suddenly and often carelessly. Precipitous means very steep.
EX: he cautioned against <u>precipitate</u> action; a <u>precipitous</u> climb

premises

This word has two meanings: (a) propositions supporting a conclusion, and (b) land and the buildings on it. In both senses, premises takes a plural verb.
EX: she claims that faulty <u>premises</u> <u>are</u> in the analysis; the <u>premises</u> <u>are</u> vacant

prepared

Prepared is not a substitute for "willing" or "ready."
SAY: he is not <u>ready</u> to acknowledge defeat
RATHER THAN: he is not <u>prepared</u> to acknowledge defeat

prescribe, proscribe

Prescribe means to provide rules or guidelines, and to recommend. Proscribe means to prohibit.
EX: she <u>prescribed</u> medication; the court <u>proscribed</u> picketing

presentiment, presentment

Presentiment means a premonition. A presentment is an accusation of crime initiated by a grand jury based on its own knowledge. It also means giving or producing a negotiable instrument to the drawee for its acceptance, or to the drawer or acceptor for payment.

present incumbent

The word present is redundant.

previous to, prior to

"Before" is preferable to either phrase.
SAY: she held the position before 1989
RATHER THAN: she held the position <u>previous</u> <u>to</u> 1989, or she held the position <u>prior</u> <u>to</u> 1989

principal, principle

Principal means the most important (adjective), the head of a school (noun), and money on which interest is earned (noun). Principle means a basic truth (noun).
EX: her <u>principal</u> argument in the brief; the <u>principle</u> of cause and effect

private industry

The word private is redundant.

pseudo, quasi

Pseudo means false. Quasi means resembling, to some degree.

EX: <u>pseudo</u> doctor; <u>quasi</u>-legislation

qualified expert

At a trial we speak of an expert who has been qualified, meaning that he or she has gone through a prescribed process in order to be allowed to testify. In any other context it is redundant to refer to a qualified expert. By definition, experts are qualified.

question of whether, question as to whether, question arises as to whether, question is whether

Pare down these phrases whenever possible.

SAY: The <u>question</u> <u>is</u> <u>whether</u> the contract is void

RATHER THAN: The <u>question</u> <u>arises</u> <u>as</u> <u>to</u> <u>whether</u> the contract is void

EVEN BETTER: Is the contract void?

quote

Use quote as a verb when repeating someone else's words exactly as written or spoken. Do not use quote as a noun. Say quotation instead.

raise, rise

Raise takes an object; rise does not.

EX: <u>raise</u> the price; production costs <u>rise</u>

rarely ever, seldom ever

The word "ever" in these phrases is redundant.

SAY: she <u>rarely</u> attends; he <u>seldom</u> participates

RATHER THAN: she <u>rarely</u> <u>ever</u> attends; he <u>seldom</u> <u>ever</u> participates

The following constructions, however, are proper: "rarely if ever" and "seldom if ever."

rational, rationale

Rational (an adjective) means reasonable or logical. Rationale (a noun) means the reason or explanation for something.

EX: a <u>rational</u> plan to solve the problem; the <u>rationale</u> of the court's decision

reason why

In place of this phrase, say "reason that," "reason," "because," etc.

SAY: laziness is the <u>reason</u> he failed

RATHER THAN: laziness is the <u>reason</u> <u>why</u> he failed

EVEN BETTER: he failed <u>because</u> of his laziness

rebellion, revolt, revolution, riot

Rebellion: an organized uprising designed to overthrow the government (it usually fails; if it succeeds, it is a revolution).

Revolt: extensive opposition to a custom, law, authority, or government.

Revolution: the overthrow of a government and the substitution of a new government.

Riot: sudden violent disruption of public order.

rebut, refute, deny

To rebut a charge is to counter it by offering opposing evidence or arguments. To refute a charge is to counter it by offering other evidence that proves it is wrong. To deny a charge is simply to say that it is wrong.

EX: she <u>rebutted</u> Bill's claim that she was lazy by staying late that night to finish the report; she <u>refuted</u> the claim that she did not pay for the item by producing the sales receipt for it; she <u>denied</u> that she was late

recipient

Received is preferable to recipient.

SAY: she <u>received</u> a raise

RATHER THAN: she was the <u>recipient</u> of a raise

refer back

The word "back" is usually redundant, even when you are discussing something that is earlier or comes before.

SAY: <u>refer</u> to chapter one

RATHER THAN: <u>refer</u> <u>back</u> to chapter one

relate

Do not use this word to mean to have rapport with.

SAY: John and Fred work well together

RATHER THAN: John and Fred <u>relate</u> well together

relevant, irrelevant

These words mean pertinent or not pertinent to something specific. Adding the word "to" often makes this relationship clear. When you call something relevant or irrelevant, your reader should not have to ask, "to what?"

SAY: the training is <u>irrelevant</u> <u>to</u> my current job

RATHER THAN: the training is <u>irrelevant</u>

remediable, remedial

Remediable means that which can be corrected. Remedial means providing a remedy.

EX: the mistake is <u>remediable</u>; a <u>remedial</u> statute

replica

Replica is a copy or reproduction of the original made by the original artist. Do not use replica to mean model or miniature.

SAY: he built a <u>model</u> of the White House to scale

RATHER THAN: he built a <u>replica</u> of the White House to scale

represent

Represent means "stands for." Do not use it as a substitute for "is."

SAY: this paycheck <u>is</u> the amount he received

RATHER THAN: this paycheck <u>represents</u> the amount he received

resume, résumé

Resume means to begin again. Résumé (note the accents) means a summary of past employment, education, etc.

rightly, rightfully

Rightly means correctly or accurately. Rightfully means morally, properly, or fairly.

EX: he <u>rightly</u> concluded that the document is missing; he <u>rightfully</u> claimed that he owned the document

rob

Persons and places are robbed; things are not.

EX: <u>rob</u> a stranger; <u>rob</u> a bank; <u>steal</u> the money

rules and regulations

Do not use this phrase unless you are sure that there is a clear distinction between a rule and a regulation. Often there is no such distinction.

Sabbath

Sabbath is not a synonym for Sunday. For Jews, the Sabbath is Saturday.

said

Do not use said as an adjective to mean aforementioned.
SAY: this buyer; the XYZ Company
RATHER THAN: the said buyer; the said company

sanction

Depending on context, this word can mean permission or penalty.
EX: they went on the trip after it received the sanction of the board; there are sanctions for the offense in the statute

savings

With the article "a," do not use the plural, "savings."
SAY: a saving of hundreds of dollars
RATHER THAN: a savings of hundreds of dollars

scan

Avoid using this word, since it may not be clear which of the following two equally acceptable meanings you intend: to read very carefully, or to look over quickly.

seasonable, seasonal

Seasonable means within the agreed time, or appropriate to the season. Seasonal means that which depends on or is controlled by the seasons.
EX: seasonable acceptance of the offer; seasonable rain; seasonal employment

secular, sectarian

Secular means nonspiritual, worldly. Sectarian means pertaining to a particular religion or sect.
EX: secular music; sectarian education

sensual, sensuous

Both words mean pertaining to the senses. Sensual is often used in a physical or sexual context. Sensuous is often used in an aesthetic context.
EX: a sensual dress; a sensuous painting

sentiment, sentimentality

Both words refer to emotions or feelings. A sentiment is often sincere, while sentimentality is often affected or excessive.

serve, service

As a verb, the primary meaning of service is to maintain and keep repaired.
EX: service the computer
Do not use service to mean give services to, or to provide a general benefit. Instead, use serve.
SAY: the company serves the county
RATHER THAN: the company services the county
Two exceptions are debts (debts can be serviced) and breeding animals (animals can be serviced).

sic [sic]

Use sic in brackets [sic] to indicate that any errors in a quotation are in the original and hence are not copying mistakes of yours.
EX: "the wound did not heel [sic] in time"

simplistic

Simplistic means oversimplified. It does not mean simple. It also is not the same as simplified, which means made less complex.
EX: a simplistic plan is naive; a simple plan can be very profound and effective; a simplified version of a plan may be so general that it is now simplistic

slow

Slow is primarily an adjective, but it can function as an adverb. Nevertheless, when you need an adverb, slowly is preferred.
SAY: drive slowly
RATHER THAN: drive slow

specie, species

Specie means coined money. Species means a category or classification. The spelling is the same for the singular and the plural—species.
EX: payment in specie; this species is prevalent in Peru

stationary, stationery

Stationary means standing still. Stationery means writing paper.
EX: a stationary object; a stationery store

stimulant, stimulus

A stimulant is a temporary arousal or acceleration of activity. (The plural is stimulants.) A stimulus is anything that causes a response. (The plural is stimuli.)
EX: the drug acted as a stimulant so that she could stay awake; the stimulus of the rivalry

straight, strait

Straight means not curved. Strait means a water passage.
EX: a straight line; travel through the strait

strategy, tactics

Strategy is the overall plan to achieve a particular goal. Tactics are the means to implement the strategy. A strategy is a plan. A tactic is a technique.
EX: a conference to prepare strategy for the case; military tactics

structure

As a verb, this word is often used pretentiously.
SAY: create a place to work
RATHER THAN: structure an environment for work

subsequent, subsequently

"Later" is preferable to either one of these words.
SAY: a later development; later, she resigned
RATHER THAN: a subsequent development; subsequently, she resigned

subsequent to

"After" is preferable.
SAY: he resigned after the release of the report
RATHER THAN: he resigned subsequent to the release of the report

suffer from

When you have a sickness or illness, you suffer <u>from</u> it, not <u>with</u> it.

SAY: suffer <u>from</u> tuberculosis

RATHER THAN: suffer <u>with</u> tuberculosis

supra

Avoid "supra" to refer the reader to previously cited material. It is often cumbersome for the reader to go back to find the previous cite. Either repeat the full cite or give the cite in abbreviated form.

take delivery

A needlessly technical way to say receive.

SAY: expected to <u>receive</u> the goods on Tuesday

RATHER THAN: expected to <u>take delivery</u> of the goods on Tuesday

target

Target means something you aim or fire at.

EX: an easy <u>target</u>; the <u>target</u> of criticism

It is overused in the sense of goal, purpose, or objective.

SAY: the <u>goal</u> of the program is to eliminate illiteracy

RATHER THAN: the <u>target</u> of the program is to eliminate illiteracy

than

When "than" is used in a comparison, complete the sentence in order to determine whether the following pronoun should be nominative or objective.

EX: she is wiser <u>than</u> I (the nominative "I" is used because if you completed the sentence, it would read: "she is wiser <u>than</u> I am")

Complete the sentence and rewrite it, if necessary, to avoid ambiguity.

EX: she likes Paul better <u>than</u> <u>me</u> (the objective "me" is used if you mean: "she likes Paul better <u>than</u> she likes <u>me</u>." The latter phrasing is clearer.)

EX: she likes Paul better <u>than</u> I (the nominative "I" is used if you mean: "she likes Paul better <u>than</u> <u>I</u> like him." The latter phrasing is clearer.)

thankfully

This word means "in a thankful way." Do not use it to mean "I am grateful that."

SAY: we prayed together <u>thankfully</u>

RATHER THAN: <u>thankfully</u>, we no longer pray together

that

When "that" is a conjunction, it can be omitted if it is not needed for clarity.

SAY: the court said he could have an extension

RATHER THAN: the court said <u>that</u> he could have an extension

But,

SAY: the court said <u>that</u> in 1989 we would have to file again

RATHER THAN: the court said in 1989 we could have to file again

The "that" is necessary to make clear that the court did not make the statement in 1989.

Also do not repeat "that" needlessly.

SAY: the manager feels <u>that</u> when the case is over, there is no need to remain

RATHER THAN: the manager feels <u>that</u> when the case is over, <u>that</u> there is no need to remain

that, which

Use "that" to begin a restrictive clause. A restrictive clause is also called a limiting or defining clause. It modifies and defines. The meaning of a restrictive clause is essential to the sentence. Do not use commas to set off a restrictive clause.

EX: the opinion does not apply to sales <u>that</u> are paid by check (the clause is restrictive; it defines a certain category of sales)

Use "which" to begin a nonrestrictive clause. A nonrestrictive clause is also called a nonlimiting or nondefining clause. It modifies but does not define. It gives additional, nonessential information. The meaning of a restrictive clause is not essential to the sentence. If a clause can be dropped without changing the basic meaning of the sentence, it is a nonrestrictive clause. Commas are used to set off nonrestrictive clauses.

EX: the legal profession, <u>which</u> began centuries ago, has many different kinds of lawyers within it (the clause is nonrestrictive; it modifies the profession, but does not define or restrict it)

there

The verb following "there" should be singlular or plural depending on whether the true subject of that verb is singular or plural.

EX: there <u>are</u> many mansions (plural verb "are" because the subject, mansions, is plural)

EX: there <u>is</u> an error in the memo (singular verb "is" because the subject, error, is singular)

EX: there <u>appears</u> to be a flaw (singular verb "<u>appears</u>" because the subject, flaw, is singular)

there, their, they're

"There" is primarily an adverb. "Their" is the possessive of they. "They're" is a contraction of "they are."

EX: the library is <u>there</u>; <u>their</u> responsibility; <u>they're</u> finished

In formal writing use "they are" rather than the contraction "they're."

thereafter, therein, therefrom, wherein

Use less pompous substitutes for these words whenever possible (e.g., after that, then, from then on, in that place, in that way).

thing

Avoid using this word.

SAY: the part of the proposal that he objected to

RATHER THAN: the <u>thing</u> about the proposal that he objected to

this

Be sure the reader knows what "this" refers to. Avoid using "this" as a general reference to what precedes it.

SAY: I want to enter the health field and to pursue my music education. <u>Both</u> <u>of</u> <u>these</u> <u>goals</u> will take considerable effort.

RATHER THAN: I want to enter the health field and to pursue my music education. This will take considerable effort.

this is to inform you that
Avoid using this phrase.
SAY: you are terminated
RATHER THAN: this is to inform you that you are terminated

though, although
As conjunctions, these words are interchangeable.
EX: although closed to the general public, the theater was opened on holidays; though closed to the general public, the theater was opened on holidays

thrust
Avoid using this word when you mean general direction.
SAY: the main theme of the plan
RATHER THAN: the thrust of the plan

to, too, two
"To" is a preposition. "Too" is an adverb. "Two" is a number.
EX: go to the library; too difficult; two briefs

tortuous, torturous, tortious
Tortuous, means twisting or winding. Torturous means painful. Tortious means pertaining to a tort.
EX: a tortuous street; a torturous experience; a tortious interference

total
Eliminate this word when it adds nothing.
SAY: he purchased 233 volumes
RATHER THAN: he purchased a total of 233 volumes

toward, towards
Both spellings are correct, but toward is preferred.

track, tract
A track is a mark, route, or course of action. A tract is land, a pamphlet, or a verse.
EX: track and field; the distribution of the tract

transitory, transient
Both words mean for a limited time. Use transitory when the emphasis is short-lived. Use transient when the emphasis is remaining a short time.
EX: transitory pain; transient guest

treachery, treason
Treachery means any betrayal. Treason means a betrayal of one's country.

treble, triple
Both words can mean three times or threefold. Unless you are referring to a rule that uses treble (e.g., treble damages), you should use triple.

troubled
People or their faculties are troubled, not things or events.
SAY: troubled conscience
RATHER THAN: troubled company

type
When you mean kind or sort, you must say "type of."
SAY: that type of lawyer
RATHER THAN: that type lawyer

unaware, unawares
Unaware is the adjective. Unawares is the adverb.
EX: unaware of the error; caught unawares

undersigned
Do not use this word to refer to the signer(s) of a document.

unexceptional, unexceptionable
Unexceptional means usual or normal. Unexceptionable means not subject to objections.
EX: the unexceptional behavior of the animals observed; unexceptionable title

unilateral, bilateral
Unilateral means involving one side only. Bilateral means involving both sides.
EX: a unilateral concession by Italy; a bilateral commitment of France and Italy

unsanitary, insanitary
These words are interchangeable. Unsanitary is more common.

unsatisfied, dissatisfied
Unsatisfied means unpaid, and failure to meet standards or expectations. Dissatisfied means disappointed or upset.
EX: unsatisfied judgment; dissatisfied by your rudeness

use, usage
Use means in operation or service. Usage means customary practice.
EX: the use of the computer; a former usage among Christians

utilize, use
Use is preferable to the more pompous utilize.
SAY: use the library
RATHER THAN: utilize the library

valuable, valued
Valuable means worth money or of considerable importance. Valued means highly esteemed, whether or not a monetary value is attached.
EX: a valuable ring; a valued experience

very
This word is frequently overused. Either omit it or find a substitute.
SAY: the assignment is difficult; the assignment is unusually difficult
RATHER THAN: the assignment is very difficult

viable
This word means able to survive, and also practical. Avoid using the word unless it is very clear to the reader why you are saying something is survivable or practical.

SAY: the proposal is <u>viable</u> because it provides for adequate funding and competent staff
RATHER THAN: the proposal is <u>viable</u>

virus
A virus is not a disease. It is an agent that causes a disease.
SAY: sick with the measles caused by a <u>virus</u>
RATHER THAN: sick with a <u>virus</u>

visit, visit with
Say "visit" rather than "visit with" in formal writing.
SAY: <u>visit</u> her neighbor
RATHER THAN: <u>visit</u> <u>with</u> her neighbor

voiced
This word is often part of wordy phrases that should be avoided.
SAY: he <u>objected</u> <u>to</u> the resolution; she is <u>dissatisfied</u> <u>with</u> the plan
RATHER THAN: he <u>voiced</u> <u>objections</u> <u>to</u> the resolution; she <u>voiced</u> <u>dissatisfaction</u> <u>with</u> the plan

was, were
To express conditions contrary to fact, use "were."
EX: if I <u>were</u> a judge; if she <u>were</u> elected
"Was" can be used when referring to the simple past that is not necessarily contrary to fact.
EX: if she <u>was</u> a member of the bar at the time, she was not in active practice

well-
Note the hyphen in the spelling of the following words when they precede the noun they modify:

well-being	well-known
well-defined	well-meaning
well-done	well-rounded
well-founded	well-thought-of

West, East, South, North
Capitalize these words when referring to a region of the country.

what
Generally, you should avoid beginning a sentence with "what."
SAY: The weather bothered him.
RATHER THAN: <u>What</u> bothered him was the weather.

whereas
An overused word in the law. Use a substitute when you can.
SAY: the plaintiff withdrew, while the defendant proceeded
RATHER THAN: the plaintiff withdrew, <u>whereas</u> the defendant proceeded

wherewithal
"Means" is preferable.
SAY: the <u>means</u> to survive
RATHER THAN: the <u>wherewithal</u> to survive

whether or not
"Or not" is often redundant when a choice of alternatives is stated or implied. If you remove "or not" and the sentence still conveys the meaning, keep it out.

SAY: we did not know <u>whether</u> to go
RATHER THAN: we did not know <u>whether</u> <u>or</u> <u>not</u> to go
"Or not" is sometimes needed.
EX: you must leave school <u>whether</u> <u>or</u> <u>not</u> you can afford the tuition

while
While means "during the time that."
EX: he read <u>while</u> he waited
Do not use while to mean but, and, although, or whereas.
SAY: Mary is the attorney in charge <u>and</u> Paul is her assistant
RATHER THAN: Mary is the attorney in charge <u>while</u> Paul is her assistant

who, whom (see also *that, which*)
Although there are general rules on when to use who and whom, the rules are often broken because the word "whom" has come into general disfavor.
Use "who" when it stands for the subject.
EX: the lawyer <u>who</u> argued the case (who is the subject of argued)
EX: the lawyer <u>who</u> I think argued the case (who is still the subject of argued)
EX: <u>who</u> do you think will win? (who is the subject of will win)
Use "whom" when it stands for the object of a verb or preposition.
EX: the judge <u>whom</u> the lawyers hated has resigned (whom is the object of the verb hated)
EX: to <u>whom</u> will the honor go? (whom is the object of the preposition to)
Widespread usage has produced some exceptions. The following examples are considered correct in spite of the above rules.
EX: <u>who</u> did you talk to? <u>who</u> did you see?
Except when used directly in front of a preposition (e.g., "to whom," "for whom") whom is generally disfavored.

who's, whose
"Who's" is the contraction for "who is." Avoid using contractions in formal writing.
EX: <u>Who</u> <u>is</u> the officer in charge?
RATHER THAN: <u>Who's</u> the officer in charge?
Never use who's as the possessive. The possessive for who and which is whose.
SAY: <u>Whose</u> book is this?
RATHER THAN: <u>who's</u> book is this?
Whose can refer to people or to things.
EX: the man <u>whose</u> car I borrowed; the flower <u>whose</u> fragrance I love

within, in
"In" is often a good substitute for "within."
SAY: he will stay <u>in</u> the building
RATHER THAN: he will stay <u>within</u> the building

with respect to
Avoid using this wordy phrase.
SAY: we deny all of your allegations of negligence
RATHER THAN: <u>with</u> <u>respect</u> <u>to</u> your claim of negligence, we deny all of your allegations

with the purpose of

This phrase is often redundant unless you want to emphasize the state of mind.

SAY: he entered the library to study

RATHER THAN: he entered the library <u>with</u> <u>the</u> <u>purpose</u> <u>of</u> studying

witness

Do not use this word as a verb unless you are talking about evidence in a legal case.

SAY: we saw a play at the theater

RATHER THAN: we <u>witnessed</u> a play at the theater

won't, wont

"Won't" is a contraction that means "will not." Avoid using contractions in formal writing. "Wont" means used to or accustomed.

EX: he is <u>wont</u> to complain

would seem, would appear

Avoid using such vague expressions.

SAY: I think the building is vacant

RATHER THAN: it <u>would</u> <u>appear</u> that the building is vacant

writer, the writer

Do not refer to yourself as "the writer" in your writing. Use a personal pronoun ("I") or find some other way to draw attention to yourself.

wrong, wrongly

Wrong is an adjective and an adverb.

EX: the <u>wrong</u> spelling; you spelled it <u>wrong</u>

Wrongly is also an adverb. Place it in front of the word it modifies.

EX: <u>wrongly</u> identified

xerox

Say "Xerox" when you are referring to a copy made by a Xerox machine. If not, say photocopy.

x-ray, X-ray, x ray, X ray

The preferred spelling is x-ray.

Glossary

A

abstract A summary of the important point of a text; an overview. *See also* digests.

act *See* statute.

active voice The grammatical verb form in which the doer of the action is the main focus. *See also* passive voice.

acts and resolves A set of books containing the session laws of a state legislature, printed chronologically rather than by subject matter. *See also* session laws.

administrative agency A unit of government whose primary mission is to carry out or administer the statutes of the legislature and the executive orders of the chief of the executive branch.

administrative code A collection of administrative regulations organized by subject matter rather than by date.

administrative decision A resolution of a controversy between a party and an administrative agency involving the application of the regulations, statutes, or executive orders that govern the agency. Sometimes called a *ruling*.

administrative law judge (ALJ) A hearing officer who presides over a hearing at an administrative agency. Also called *hearing examiner* and *trial examiner*.

Administrative Procedure Act (APA) The statute that governs procedures before federal administrative agencies. Many states have their own APA for state agencies.

administrative regulation A law of an administrative agency designed to explain or carry out the statutes and executive orders that govern the agency. Also called a *rule*.

administrative rule *See* administrative regulation.

administrative ruling *See* administrative decision.

advance session law service *See* legislative service.

advance sheet A pamphlet that comes out before (in advance of) a later pamphlet or hardcover volume.

adversarial memorandum *See* external memorandum of law; memorandum of law.

agency reports A study or analysis prepared by an administrative agency. Often useful for background research.

ALJ *See* administrative law judge.

A.L.R., A.L.R.2d, etc. *American Law Reports*. A set of annotated reporters published by Lawyers Co-op (of the West Group) that contain the full text of selected opinions plus extensive research papers on issues raised in these opinions. The research papers are called annotations.

A.L.R. Blue Book of Supplemental Decisions The set of books that enables you to update annotations in A.L.R.1st.

A.L.R. Digest to 3d, 4th, 5th, Federal The digest that summarizes and acts as an index to the annotations in A.L.R.3d, A.L.R.4th, A.L.R.5th, and A.L.R. Fed.

ALR Federal Quick Index A single-volume index to the annotations in A.L.R. Fed.

ALR Federal Tables A volume that tells you what annotations have mentioned a particular federal opinion, statute, or regulation.

A.L.R. First Series Quick Index A single-volume index to the annotations in A.L.R.1st.

ALR Index A multivolume index to annotations in A.L.R.2d, A.L.R.3d, A.L.R.4th, A.L.R.5th, and A.L.R. Fed.

ALR Quick Index 3d, 4th, 5th A single-volume index to the annotations in A.L.R.3d, A.L.R.4th, A.L.R.5th.

A.L.R.2d Digest A digest that summarizes and acts as an index to the annotations in A.L.R.2d.

A.L.R.2d Later Case Service The set of books that enables you to update annotations in A.L.R.2d.

American Digest System Three sets of digests that provide small-paragraph summaries of court opinions written by every federal and every state court that publishes its opinions. The three digests are the *General Digest,* the *Decennial Digests,* and *Century Digest.*

American Jurisprudence 2d (Am. Jur. 2d) A national legal encyclopedia published by Lawyers Co-operative Publishing (of the West Group).

American Law Institute A group of private scholars that publishes the Restatements.

American Law Reports An annotated reporter that prints selected opinions plus annotations on issues in these opinions. *See also* A.L.R., A.L.R.2d, etc.

amicus curiae Friend of the court.

amicus curiae brief A friend-of-the-court brief. An appellate brief submitted by someone who is not a party to the litigation.

Am. Jur. 2d *See American Jurisprudence 2d.*

analogous Relevant because it covers the facts of the research problem. Something is *on point* when it is similar although there might be some differences.

Ann. Abbreviation for annotated.

annotated (ann.) With notes or commentaries added to something.

annotated bibliography A bibliography that briefly states why each entry was included.

annotated reporter A set of books that contain the full text of court opinions plus commentary (annotations) on them.

annotated statutory code A collection of statutes organized by subject matter rather than by date, along with notes and commentary.

annotation An explanatory note or commentary. Extensive notes based on issues within opinions within the six sets of *American Law Reports. See also* A.L.R., A.L.R.2d, etc.; *American Law Reports.*

Annotation History Table A table at the end of the *ALR Index* that tells you which annotations have been supplemented or superseded.

antecedents Words, phrases, or clauses to which pronouns refer.

APA *See* Administrative Procedure Act.

appellant The party bringing an appeal because of dissatisfaction with something the lower tribunal did.

appellate brief A document submitted to an appellate court in which a party seeks approval, modification, or reversal of what a lower court has done. The brief is filed in an appeals court and served on opposing parties.

appellee The party against whom an appeal is brought. Also called the *respondent*.

appendixes Additions to a volume or document printed after the body of the text.

argument That portion of an appellate brief in which a party's legal positions are presented in the order of the point headings in the table of contents.

at common law (1) All the case law and statutory law in England and in the American colonies before the American Revolution. (2) Judge-made law that exists until changed by statute. *See also* common law.

Atlantic Digest A regional digest of the West Group that gives summaries of state opinions of Conn., Del., D.C., Me., Md., N.H., N.J., Pa., R.I., and Vt.

Atlantic 2d (**A.2d**) A regional reporter of the West Group that prints the state court opinions of Conn., Del., D.C., Me., Md., N.H., N.J., Pa., R.I., and Vt.

attorney general The chief attorney for the government. *See also* opinion of the attorney general.

authority Whatever a court could rely on in reaching its decision. *See also* mandatory authority; primary authority; secondary authority.

Authority Reference [in C.F.R.] The reference to the enabling statute that is the authority for an administrative regulation in the *Code of Federal Regulations*.

Auto-Cite An online program of LEXIS that tells you whether an opinion you are checking is good law. For example, you will be told whether the opinion has been overruled or criticized by another opinion. You will also be given the opinion's parallel cites. Auto-Cite is an online citator. *See also* citator.

B

background research Checking secondary sources to give you a general understanding of an area of law that is new to you.

Ballentine's Law Dictionary A single-volume legal dictionary.

Bankruptcy Reporter (**B.R.**) A reporter of the West Group that contains federal court opinions on bankruptcy law.

below (1) The lower tribunal that heard the case before it was appealed. (2) Later in the document.

bibliography A list of citations to materials that is organized for a specific purpose. *See also* annotated bibliography.

bicameral [legislature] A legislature with two chambers. A *unicameral* legislature has one chamber.

bill A proposed statute.

black letter law A statement of a fundamental or basic principle of law.

Black's Law Dictionary A single-volume legal dictionary.

Blue and White Book The set of books that enables you to find parallel cites to cases for one state.

Bluebook (also called blue book) (1) *A Uniform System of Citation,* the bible of citation form. (2) The *National Reporter Blue Book,* a source for parallel cites. (3) The *A.L.R. Blue Book of Supplemental Decisions,* a set of books that allows you to update the annotations in A.L.R.1st.

BNA *See* Bureau of National Affairs.

boilerplate Standard language that is commonly used in a certain kind of document. Standard verbiage.

Boolean A search that allows words to be specifically included or excluded through operatives such as AND, OR, and NOT.

brief (1) Shorthand for appellate brief. A document submitted to an appellate court in which a party seeks approval, modification, or reversal of what a lower court has done. The brief is filed in an appeals court and served on opposing parties. (2) A document submitted to any court in support of a particular position. (3) A summary of the main or essential parts of a court opinion. (4) Shorthand for a trial brief, which is an attorney's personal notes on how to conduct a trial.

bulletin A publication issued on an ongoing or periodic basis.

bulletin board systems Inexpensive, relatively small, user-run versions of a commercial information service.

Bureau of National Affairs (BNA) A law publisher, particularly of looseleaf services.

C

California Reporter (**Cal. Rptr.**) A reporter of the West Group that contains opinions of California state courts.

call number The identification number that enables you to find a publication on the shelves of a library.

CALR Computer-assisted legal research.

caption The title and other identifying information of something such as an opinion, complaint, or appellate brief.

caption (of opinion) The title of an opinion (usually consisting of the names of the parties), the name of the court that wrote it, the docket number, the date of decision—all printed just before the opinion begins.

CARTWHEEL A technique designed to help you think of a large variety of words and phrases to check in the index and table of contents of a law book.

case (1) A court opinion, which is a written explanation of how the court applied the law to the facts before it to resolve a legal dispute. Opinions are printed in volumes called *reporters* or *reports*. The words *case* and *opinion* are often used interchangeably. (2) A pending matter on a court's docket. (3) A client matter being handled by a law office, whether or not litigation is involved.

casebook A law-school textbook containing numerous edited court opinions.

case name citator *See Shepard's Case Names Citator.*

case notes Summaries of and commentary upon a court opinion; published in a law review.

cause of action Facts that give a party the right to judicial relief. A legally acceptable reason for suing.

CCH *See* Commerce Clearing House.

CD-ROM Compact disk–read-only memory. An information storage system that uses optical technology or laser beams to store and allow you to read large quantities of information.

Century Digest One of the three digests within the American Digest System; covers opinions written between 1658 and 1896.

certiorari *See* writ of certiorari.

C.F.R. *See Code of Federal Regulations.*

CFR Index and Finding Aids The pamphlet that acts as the index to the *Code of Federal Regulations.*

CFR Parts Affected A table in the *Federal Register* that tells you which pages in the *Federal Register* contain material that has affected (e.g., changed, renumbered) regulations in the *Code of Federal Regulations* since the last edition of the C.F.R. was published.

charter The fundamental law of a municipality or other local unit of government authorizing it to perform designated governmental functions.

circuit A territory over which a particular court has jurisdiction. The federal court system is divided into United States Circuits.

circumlocution A pair of words that have the same effect; unnecessarily wordy language.

CIS *See* Congressional Information Service.

citation A reference to any material printed on paper or stored in a computer database. It is the "address" where you can locate and read the material. *See also* parallel cite; pinpoint cite; public domain citation; short form citation.

citator A book (or CD-ROM or online service) containing lists of citations that can help you assess the current validity of an item and can give you leads to other relevant materials.

cite (1) [noun] A citation. (2) [verb] To give the volume number, page number, or other information that will enable you to locate material in a library.

cite checking Reading every cite in a document to determine whether the format of the cite conforms to the citation rules being used (e.g., the Bluebook rules), whether the quotations in the cite are accurate, etc.

cited material The case, statute, regulation, or other document that you are shepardizing.

citing material The case, article, or annotation that mentions whatever you are shepardizing, i.e., that mentions the cited material.

civil law system The legal system of many Western European countries other than England. (England and the United States have a common law system.) A civil law system places a greater emphasis on statutory or code law than the common law system.

C.J.S. *See Corpus Juris Secundum.*

CLE Continuing legal education. Undertaken after an individual has received his or her primary education or training in a law-related occupation.

CLE materials Continuing-legal-education materials prepared for attorneys after they have completed law school.

code A set of rules, organized by subject matter.

Code of Federal Regulations (C.F.R.) A publication of the federal government that prints many of the regulations adopted by federal administrative agencies.

Code of Federal Regulations Index A multivolume index to the *Code of Federal Regulations*, published by R. R. Bowker.

codified To arrange laws by subject matter regardless of when they were enacted.

codified cite The citation to a statute that has been printed in a code, and therefore has been organized by subject matter. *See also* session law cite.

codify To arrange material by subject matter.

colon A punctuation mark (:) used to introduce a list or quotation, follow a salutation in a formal letter, etc.

comma A punctuation mark (,) used to separate elements of a sentence, e.g., coordinate adjectives, nonrestrictive clause, three or more items in a list.

command An instruction typed into a computer.

comment A study of a legal issue published in a legal periodical, often written by a law student.

Commerce Clearing House (CCH) A law publisher, particularly of looseleaf services.

committee print A compilation of information prepared by committee staff members on a bill, consisting of comparative analysis of related bills, statistics, studies, reports, etc.

committee report A summary of a bill and a statement of reasons for and against its enactment.

common law (1) Judge-made law created by the courts to resolve a dispute within a particular litigation in the absence of controlling enacted law, such as a statute or constitutional provision, that governs the dispute. (2) Case law; all court opinions. (3) The legal system that the United States inherited from England. (4) All the case law and statutory law in England and in the American colonies before the American Revolution. *See also* at common law; enacted law.

comprehensive brief A summary of a court opinion consisting of the following ten parts: citation, parties, objectives of parties, theories of the litigation, history of the litigation, facts, issue, holding, reasoning, and disposition.

conclusion The answer of the writer to a legal question or issue posed in a memorandum or appellate brief.

concurring opinion An opinion written by less than a majority of the judges on the court that agrees with the *result* reached by the majority but not with all of its reasoning.

confirmatory letter A letter restating or confirming that something important has been done or said.

conflicts of law An area of the law that determines what law applies when a choice must be made between the laws of different, coequal legal systems (e.g., those of two states).

Cong. Rec. *See Congressional Record.*

Congressional Information Service (CIS) Publisher of legislative history materials for federal statutes.

Congressional Record (Cong. Rec.) The official collection of the day-to-day happenings of Congress.

connectors Characters, words, or symbols used to show the relationship between the words and phrases in a query.

consolidated litigation More than one lawsuit being resolved in the same opinion.

constitution The fundamental law that creates the branches of government and that identifies basic rights and obligations.

construction Interpretation.

construe To interpret.

continuing legal education (CLE) Legal training a person receives after completing his or her primary or formal education. *See* CLE materials.

copyright page The page in a law book that provides the copyright year of the book.

Corpus Juris Secundum (C.J.S.) A national legal encyclopedia published by West.

court rules *See* rules of court.

cumulated Consolidated older and newer material. *See also* cumulative.

cumulative The most recent volume or issue contains all the material in the prior volumes or issues and consolidates this older material with new material; that which repeats earlier material and consolidates it with new material in one place.

Current Law Index A multivolume index to literature in legal periodicals; published by Information Access Corporation.

D

dash A punctuation mark (—) used to mark a sudden break or change of thought, to set off a brief summary, etc.

Decennial Digest One of the three digests within the American Digest System; they cover opinions written in ten-year periods.

decision *See* administrative decision; opinion.

Defendant-Plaintiff Table A table of cases in West digests that lists the defendant's name first.

defense A response to a claim of the other party, setting forth reason(s) the claim should be denied. The response may be an allegation of facts, a presentation of a legal theory, etc..

delta symbol (Δ) The symbol used by Shepard's to indicate that the year is the year of the citing material, not of the cited material.

depository library A private or public library that receives free federal government publications to which it must allow the general public access.

Descriptive Word Index (DWI) An index to the digests of West.

descriptive words Language to check in an index consisting of parties, places, or things, basis of action or issue, defenses, and relief sought.

deskbook A single-volume collection of the rules of court for one or more courts, usually in the same judicial system.

Dewey Decimal System A system of cataloging library books and materials in a library that does not use the Library of Congress Classification System.

dictum A statement made by a court that was not necessary to resolve the specific legal issues before the court. The plural of dictum is *dicta*.

digests (1) Volumes that contain summaries of court opinions. These summaries are sometimes called *abstracts* or *squibs*. (2) Volumes that contain summaries of annotations in A.L.R., A.L.R.2d, A.L.R.3d, etc. (3) The digest volumes of *Martindale-Hubbell Law Directory*, consisting of summaries of the law of the fifty states and of foreign countries.

discretionary statute A statute that allows something to be done, but does not require or mandate it. *See also* mandatory statute.

disposition The order of a court reached as a result of its holdings.

dissenting opinion An opinion that disagrees with the result and the reasoning used by the majority.

district court *See* United States District Court.

docket A list of cases on a court's calendar.

docket number A consecutive number assigned to a case by the court when the case is filed by the party bringing the litigation.

documentation The manual on operating a computer; the accompanying documents.

DWI *See* Descriptive Word Index.

E

edition A version of a text that is usually a revision of an earlier version.

ejusdem generis A rule of construction that a general word or phrase should be interpreted as being of the same kind as the specific words or phrases that the general one follows.

electronic citation *See* public domain citation.

element A portion of a rule that is a precondition of the applicability of the entire rule.

element in contention An element of the rule about which the parties do not agree. The disagreement may be over the meaning of the element or how it applies to the facts.

enabling statute A statute that authorizes an agency to write regulations or to perform other specific tasks.

enacted law Any law that is not created within litigation. Examples include constitutions, statutes, administrative regulations, ordinances, and rules of court.

en banc The entire membership of a court; by the entire court.

encyclopedia *See* legal encyclopedia.

Encyclopedia of Associations An extensive list of associations and their functions.

et al. And others.

et seq. And following.

executive agreement An agreement between the United States and a foreign country that does not have to be approved by the Senate.

executive branch The branch of government that carries out, executes, or administers the law.

executive department agencies Administrative agencies that exist within the executive branch of government, often at the cabinet level.

executive order A law issued by the chief executive pursuant to specific statutory authority or to the executive's inherent authority to direct the operation of governmental agencies.

exhausted administrative remedies Has gone through all methods available in an administrative agency to resolve a dispute before asking a court to review what the agency did.

external memorandum of law A memorandum written primarily for individuals outside the office to convince them to take a certain course of action. *See also* memorandum of law.

F

F.3d *See Federal Reporter 3d*.

fact comparison Identifying fact similarities, differences, and gaps between the facts in an opinion and the facts of a client's case in order to determine whether the opinion applies. *See also* rule comparison.

federalism The division of powers between the federal government and the state governments.

Federal Cases A reporter that contains opinions of federal courts up to 1880.

Federal Claims Reporter A West reporter containing opinions of the United States Court of Federal Claims.

Federal Digest A West digest that summarizes federal cases decided through 1939.

Federal Practice Digest, 2d A West digest that summarizes federal cases decided from 1961 to 1975.

Federal Practice Digest, 3d A West digest that summarizes federal cases decided from 1975.

Federal Practice Digest, 4th A West digest that summarizes federal cases decided since publication of *Federal Practice Digest, 3d*.

Federal Register (Fed. Reg.) A daily publication of the federal government that prints proposed regulations of federal agencies, executive orders, etc.

Federal Reporter 3d (F.3d) A West reporter that currently contains the opinions of the United States Courts of Appeals.

Federal Rules Decisions A West reporter that contains opinions of the United States District Courts on issues of civil and criminal procedure, plus articles and speeches on procedural issues.

Federal Supplement (F. Supp.) A West reporter that currently contains the opinions of the United States District Courts.

Fed. Reg. *See Federal Register.*

field A subdivision of information in WESTLAW cases and other documents that is separately searchable. *See also* segments.

  field search In WESTLAW, a search that is limited to a certain part of cases in its databases.

file A group of related data records, e.g., employee records.

first impression New; that which is coming before the court for the first time.

foreword A beginning section of a book in which the publisher explains some of the features of the book. Sometimes called a *preface*.

formbook A manual that contains forms, checklists, practice techniques, etc. Sometimes called a *practice manual* or *handbook*.

FRCP Federal Rules of Civil Procedure.

F.R.D. *See Federal Rules Decisions.*

Freestyle The natural language system for phrasing queries in LEXIS. In WESTLAW it is called WIN.

F. Supp. *See Federal Supplement.*

full faith and credit The doctrine stating that one state must recognize and enforce valid public acts of other states, e.g., a valid court judgment.

full-text search A search through all of the information (usually every word) in a database.

G

General Digest One of the three digests within the American Digest System; they cover opinions written since the last *Decennial Digest* was published.

general index An index that often covers multivolume publications such as *Corpus Juris Secundum*.

generic citation *See* public domain citation.

glossary A dictionary, often at the end of a book, that defines many of the words and phrases used in the book.

Government Printing Office (GPO) The federal government agency that prints many government documents.

grammatical connectors (/p, /s) Ways to phrase a computer research query so that the search is limited to documents with words that fall within the same paragraph (/p) or within the same sentence (/s).

H

handbook *See* formbook.

heading The beginning of a memorandum that lists who the memo is for, who wrote it, what it is about, etc.

headnote A small-paragraph summary of a portion of a court opinion, written by a private publisher.

hearing examiner *See* administrative law judge.

hearing memorandum A memorandum of law submitted to a hearing officer.

HELP key A key on a computer keyboard that will lead you to online assistance in using specific computer software or hardware.

Historical Note Information on the legislative history of a statute printed after the text of the statute.

history of a case In *Shepard's Citations*, a list that gives you the citation of every decision that was part of the same litigation as the case you are shepardizing (e.g., affirmed it). Also called *subsequent history*. *See also* treatment of a case.

holding A court's specific answer to a specific question or issue that arises out of specific facts before the court. Whatever a court says beyond those facts is dictum. Also called a *ruling*. *See also* dictum.

home page The page on the Internet (usually the opening page) that introduces a computer user to the site of an organization or individual.

hornbook A treatise that summarizes an area of the law.

hypertext A method of displaying and linking information located in different places in the same document or in different documents.

I

id. [Abbreviation for Latin *ibidum*] The same as something previously mentioned; the same as the immediately preceding authority cited.

Illinois Decisions (Ill. Dec.) A West reporter containing Illinois cases.

ILP *See Index to Legal Periodicals and Books.*

independent regulatory agency An administrative agency (often existing outside the executive department) created to regulate an aspect of society.

index An alphabetical list that tells you where important words and concepts are covered in a book.

Index and Finding Aids to Code of Federal Regulations A Lawyer's Co-op publication that, among other things, tells you what statutes are the basis of particular regulations in C.F.R.

Index Medicus An index to literature in medical periodicals.

Index to Annotations Now called *ALR Index*. The set of books that is the main index to annotations in A.L.R.2d, A.L.R.3d, A.L.R.4th, A.L.R.5th, and A.L.R. Fed.

Index to Legal Periodicals and Books (ILP) A multivolume index to legal periodical literature published by H.W. Wilson. The ILP is also available on CD-ROM and online.

Index to the Code of Federal Regulations A multivolume index to the *Code of Federal Regulations* published by Congressional Information Service.

infra Below; mentioned or referred to later in the document.

in personam jurisdiction *See* personal jurisdiction.

In re In the matter of.

Insta-Cite An online program of LEXIS that tells you whether an opinion you are checking is good law. For example, you will be told whether the opinion has been overruled or criticized by another opinion. Insta-Cite is an online citator. *See* citator.

instrument A formal document that gives expression to a legal act or agreement (e.g., a mortgage).

interfiled *See* interfiling.

interfiling Inserting pages anywhere within an existing text; for example, in a looseleaf volume.

interim edition An early edition of the *Supreme Court Reporter.*

interlibrary loan Borrowing something from a library that obtained it from another library on your behalf.

Internet A self-governing network of networks to which millions of computer users all over the world have access.

interoffice memorandum of law An internal memorandum of law whose audience is your supervisor. Also called an *intraoffice memorandum of law.*

Interpretative Notes and Decisions The summaries of cases interpreting federal statutes in *United States Code Service. See also* Notes of Decisions.

interstate compact An agreement between two or more states governing a problem of mutual concern.

intraoffice memorandum of law *See* interoffice memorandum of law.

issue (1) an installment of a series (e.g., an issue of the *Harvard Law Review*). (2) *See* legal issue.

J

jargon Technical language; language that does not have an everyday meaning.

judicial branch The branch of government with primary responsibility for interpreting laws and resolving disputes that arise under them.

jump cite *See* pinpoint cite.

Jurisdictional Table of Cited Statutes and Cases A table at the beginning of annotations in A.L.R.5th that gives you a state-by-state breakdown of which sections of the annotation cover specific statutes and cases.

K

k (1) A measure of capacity in a computer system. (2) A WESTLAW equivalent of a digest key number.

Kardex A file in which the library records the volume numbers and dates of incoming publications that are part of subscriptions.

KeyCite An online case citator available on WESTLAW.

key facts A critical fact; a fact that was essential or very important to the holding of the court.

key number A general topic and a number of a subtopic. It is the heart of the system used by West to organize the millions of small-paragraph summaries of court opinions in digests.

key number system The organization of digests through key numbers. *See* digests; key number.

key-word search A search through a list of specified words that function like an index to a database.

KF call number The category used for identifying many law books in the Library of Congress (LC) Classification System.

L

Later Case Service See A.L.R.2d Later Case Service.

Latest Case Service Hotline An 800 number that helps you update an annotation.

law directory A list of attorneys.

law journal *See* law review; legal periodical.

law review A legal periodical published by a law school. Sometimes called a *law journal.*

laws *See* session laws.

Lawyer's Co-operative Publishing Company (Lawyer's Co-op) A major publisher of law books, e.g., *American Jurisprudence 2d,* American Law Reports. (Now part of the West Group.)

Lawyer's Edition (L. Ed.) *See United States Supreme Court Reports, Lawyers' Edition.*

L. Ed. *See United States Supreme Court Reports, Lawyers' Edition.*

legal analysis The application of rules of law to facts in order to answer a legal question or issue. The goal is to solve a legal dispute, to prevent such a dispute from arising, or to prevent the dispute from getting worse.

legal counsel The chief attorney, usually of a government. Also called *attorney general.*

legal dictionary A collection of definitions of legal terms. May be in a volume, on a CD-ROM, or online.

legal encyclopedia A multivolume set of books that alphabetically summarizes almost every major legal topic.

legal issue A question of law; a question of what the law is, or what the law means, or how the law applies to a set of facts. If the dispute is over the truth or falsity of the facts, it is referred to as a *question of fact* or a *factual dispute.*

legal newsletter A special-interest report (published daily, weekly, etc.) covering practical suggestions and current developments in a particular area of the law.

legal newspaper A newspaper (published daily, weekly, etc.) devoted to legal news.

legal periodical In the broadest sense, a publication on legal topics that is usually sold by subscription and issued at regular intervals—other than a publication that simply updates or supplements another publication. Legal newspapers and legal newsletters fit within this definition of *legal periodical.* More commonly, the phrase refers to subscriptions published by academic institutions, commercial companies, or bar associations.

Legal Resource Index An index to literature in legal periodicals; published by Information Access Corporation. It is available on microfilm, on LegalTrac, on WESTLAW, and on LEXIS.

legal thesaurus A volume that provides word alternatives for words used in legal writing and in the formulation of research queries in computer-assisted legal research.

LegalTrac A CD-ROM index to legal periodical literature.

legal treatise A book written by a private individual (or by a public individual writing as a private citizen) that provides an overview, summary, or commentary on a legal topic.

legislation (1) The process of making statutory law. (2) A statute.

legislative branch The branch of government with primary responsibility for making or enacting the law.

legislative history All of the events that occur in the legislature before a bill is enacted and becomes a statute.

legislative intent The purpose of the legislature in enacting a particular statute.

legislative service A publication that prints recently enacted session laws. Also called *session law service,* or *advance session law service.* In addition, it may print bills, which are proposed statutes.

LEXIS The legal research computer service of Reed Elsevier Co.

lexsee A command in LEXIS that tells the service to retrieve a specific document, other than a statute, when you already know the citation.

lexstat A command in LEXIS used to retrieve a specific statute when you already know its citation. The comparable command in WESTLAW is *fi.*

Library of Congress (LC) Classification System A system of cataloging library books and materials. Many law books under this system are catalogued under KF call numbers.

List of Sections Affected (LSA) A pamphlet that tells you what pages in the *Federal Register* have material that has affected (e.g., changed, renumbered) regulations in the *Code of Federal Regulations* since the last edition of the C.F.R. was prepared.

listserv A program that manages computer mailing lists automatically. This includes receiving and distributing messages from and to the members of the list.

litigation status The procedural category of a party during any stage of litigation, e.g., plaintiff, defendant, appellant.

load To move a program or information from a disk drive into the computer.

lobbyists Individuals whose sole function is to monitor and try to influence the content of proposed legislation.

looseleaf A hardcover book with easily removable pages, usually through a three-ring binder structure.

looseleaf filing Inserting current pages and removing outdated pages in looseleafs. *See also* interfiling.

looseleaf service A multipurpose collection of materials on a particular area of law. It might contain recent court opinions, relevant legislation, administrative regulations, etc.

LSA *See List of Sections Affected.*

M

majority opinion The opinion whose result and reasoning are supported by at least half plus one of the judges on the court.

mandatory authority Whatever a court must rely on in reaching its decision.

mandatory primary authority Any law that a court must follow to help it resolve a legal dispute.

mandatory statute A statute that requires something to be done.

Maroon Book The shorthand name of the citation guide formally entitled *The University of Chicago Manual of Legal Citation.* It is the major competitor of the more widely used citation guide, *The Bluebook: A Uniform System of Citation. See also* Bluebook.

Martindale-Hubbell Law Digest The volumes of the *Martindale-Hubbell Law Directory* that summarize the law of every state and most countries of the world.

Martindale-Hubbell Law Directory A national directory of attorneys. It also has digest volumes that summarize the law of every state and most countries of the world.

Matthew Bender A law publisher, particularly of looseleaf services.

Medline A computer research system for medical periodicals.

memorandum of law A *memorandum* is simply a note, a comment, or a report. A legal memorandum is a written explanation of what the law is and how it might apply to a fact situation.

memorandum opinion *See* per curiam opinion.

microfiche *See* microform.

microform Images or photographs that have been reduced in size. Microforms can be *microfilms,* which store material on reels or cassettes, or *microfiche* or *ultrafiche,* which store material that has been reduced by a factor of 100 or more on a single sheet of film.

Military Justice Reporter A West reporter containing the full text of opinions of the United States Court of Military Appeals and the Courts of Military Review.

Modern Federal Practice Digest A West digest that summarizes federal cases decided between 1939 and 1961.

monitor a bill Finding current information on the status of a proposed statute in the legislature.

N

National Reporter Blue Book A set of books that enables you to find parallel cites to cases of many state courts.

National Reporter System A set of reporters of the West Group that consists of the seven regional reporters (e.g., A.2d, N.E.2d, etc.) as well as reporters covering federal courts (e.g., F.3d).

network Several computers connected together to share printers or hard disk drives.

New York Supplement (N.Y.S.) A West reporter containing opinions of New York state courts.

NEXIS An online service providing access to a great deal of news, financial and medical data, etc. Affiliated with LEXIS.

nominalization A noun formed from a verb or adjective.

nominative reporter A reporter volume that is identified by the name of the person responsible for compiling and printing the opinions in the volume.

nonauthority (1) Any primary or secondary authority that is not on point. (2) Any invalid primary authority. (3) Any book that is solely a finding aid.

nonrestrictive clause A clause (part of a sentence) that is not essential to the meaning of a sentence.

North Eastern 2d (**N.E.2d**) A regional reporter of the West Group that prints state court opinions of Ill., Ind., Mass., N.Y., and Ohio.

North Western Digest A regional digest of the West Group that summarizes state opinions of Mich., Minn., Neb., N.D., S.D., and Wis.

North Western 2d (**N.W.2d**) A regional reporter of the West Group that prints state court opinions of Mich., Minn., Neb., N.D., S.D., and Wis.

Notes of Decisions Summaries of court opinions that have interpreted a statute. The notes are printed after the statute in annotated codes.

nutshell A legal treatise (written in pamphlet form) that summarizes a topic that is covered in a law school course.

O

official reporter A reporter that is published under the authority of the government, often printed by the government itself. *See also* unofficial reporter.

official statutory code A statutory code published by the government or by a private company with special permission of or authority from the government.

offprint reporter *See* special edition state reporter.

on all fours The facts are exactly the same, or almost the same.

online Being connected to a host computer system or information service—usually through telephone lines.

online tutorial A program available on a computer that explains the basics of specific software or hardware.

on point Similar, although there might be some differences. Something is *analogous* if it covers the facts of the research problem.

open stacks Collections of books and other materials in a library that users can browse on their own.

opinion A court's written explanation of how it applied the law to the facts before it to resolve a legal dispute. Also called a *case*. Opinions are printed in volumes called *reporters*.

opinion letter A letter to a client explaining the application of the law and advising the client what to do.

opinion of the attorney general Formal legal advice given by the chief law officer of the government to another government official or agency.

ordinance A law passed by the local legislative branch or government (e.g., city council) that declares, commands, or prohibits something.

outline A pamphlet that summarizes and outlines a legal subject.

override To supersede; to change the result of another body or person. For example, Congress can override a presidential veto by a two-thirds vote.

overrule To change the holding of an opinion in a different litigation. An *overruled* opinion no longer has value as precedent. *See also* reverse.

P

/p *See* grammatical connectors (/p, /s).

Pacific Digest A regional digest of the West Group that summarizes state opinions of Alaska, Ariz., Cal., Colo., Haw., Idaho, Kan., Mont., Nev., N.M., Okla., Or., Utah, Wash., and Wyo.

Pacific 2d (**P.2d**) A regional reporter of the West Group that prints state court opinions of Alaska, Ariz., Cal., Colo., Haw., Idaho, Kan., Mont., Nev., N.M., Okla., Or., Utah, Wash., and Wyo.

parallel cite An additional reference to printed or online sources where you will be able to read the same material, word-for-word.

parallelism Using a consistent (i.e., parallel) grammatical structure when phrasing logically related ideas in a list.

Parallel Table of Authorities and Rules A table that tells you what statutes are the basis of particular regulations in the C.F.R. The table is published in *Index and Finding Aids to Code of Federal Regulations,* published by Lawyer's Co-op.

paraphrase To phrase something partly or entirely in your own words.

passive voice The grammatical verb form in which the object of the action (rather than the doer) is main focus. *See also* active voice.

Pattern Jury Instructions Suggested instructions to a jury that can be adapted to the specifics of a particular trial.

per curiam opinion A court opinion that does not name the individual judge who wrote the opinion for the court; usually a short opinion that raises issues the court has decided frequently. Also called a *memorandum opinion.*

Permanent A.L.R. Digest A digest that summarizes and acts as an index to the annotations in A.L.R.1st.

personal jurisdiction The court's power over a particular person. Also called *in personam jurisdiction.*

persuasive authority Whatever a court relies on in reaching its decision that it is not required to rely on.

pinpoint cite A reference to a specific page number in a document (e.g., a case) in addition to the page number where the document begins. In some documents, the pinpoint reference is to a specific paragraph number in the document. Also called a *jump cite.*

plagiarism Use of someone else's writing without appropriate citation.

Plaintiff-Defendant Table A table of cases in West digests that list the plaintiff's name first.

pleading A formal document that contains allegations or other responses of the parties in a trial. The major pleadings are the complaint and answer.

PL number *See* Public Law number.

pocket part An insert that fits into a small pocket built into the inside back (and occasionally front) cover of a hardcover volume.

pocket veto A rejection of a bill passed by the legislature without an explicit veto from the chief executive. He or she does nothing with the bill, and the legislature adjourns within ten weekdays after he or she receives it.

point heading A party's conclusion to one of its major arguments it is making in an appellate brief.

points and authorities memorandum A memorandum of law submitted to a judge or hearing officer. Sometimes called a *trial memorandum.*

popular name A phrase or short title that is used to identify a statute.

Popular Name Table An alphabetical list of statutes by their popular names, cross-referencing to where they can be found in the statutory code.

possessive Pertaining to a noun or pronoun that shows

ownership or possession.

practical manual *See* formbook.

precedent A prior decision that can be used as a standard in a later similar case.

preface *See* foreword.

preliminary prints The advance sheets for *United States Reports*.

Prentice Hall A law publisher, particularly of looseleaf services.

primary authority Any *law* that a court could rely on in reaching its decision.

private law *See* statute.

private statute *See* statute.

prospective Applying to facts arising only after a certain date (e.g., the date of enactment of a statute). *See also* retroactive.

protocols Sets of standards that allow computer users to communicate with each other online.

public domain Free; accessible to anyone at no cost.

public domain citation A citation that is medium-neutral. To find the material in the citation, you do not have to use the traditional volume and page numbers of a commercial publisher such as West. Also called a *generic citation*. If the reference is to documents online, the public domain citation is called an *electronic citation*.

public law *See* statute.

Public Law number (Pub. L.) A consecutive number assigned to a statute that is of general public interest and that will eventually be printed in a code. *See also* statute.

public statute *See* statute.

publisher's page The first few pages in a book that give information about the publisher, such as other materials it publishes.

Q

quasi-adjudication An administrative decision of an administrative agency that has characteristics of a court opinion.

quasi-independent regulatory agency An administrative agency that has characteristics of both an executive department agency and of an independent regulatory agency.

quasi-judicial power Like or similar to a court.

quasi-legislation A regulation of an administrative agency that has characteristics of the legislation (statutes) of a legislature.

query A question that asks a computer to find something in its database.

question of law/question of fact *See* legal issue.

questions presented A statement of the legal issues in an appellate brief that the party wants the appellate court to consider and decide.

Quick Index *See A.L.R. First Series Quick Index, ALR Federal Quick Index,* and *ALR Quick Index 3d, 4th, 5th.*

R

RE: Concerning.

reasoning An explanation of why the court answered the legal issues the way it did—why it reached particular holdings.

record (1) The official collection of all the trial pleadings, exhibits, orders, and word-for-word testimony given during the trial. (2) A collection of data fields that constitute a single unit (e.g., employee record).

regional digest A digest that summarizes court opinions that are printed in full in its corresponding regional reporter.

regional reporter A reporter that contains state court opinions of states within a region of the country.

register A set of books that contain administrative regulations (e.g., the *Federal Register*).

regulation Any governmental or nongovernmental method of controlling conduct. *See also* administrative regulation.

remand Send a case back to a lower tribunal with instructions from the appellate court.

reply brief An appellate brief of the appellant that responds to the appellate brief of the appellee.

reported Printed in a traditional reporter.

reporter (1) A set of volumes containing the complete text of court opinions. *See also* annotated reporter; official reporter. (2) A set of volumes containing the complete text of administrative decisions. (3) Some looseleaf services use the word *Reporter* in their titles even though they often contain more than reports of opinions and decisions.

reports The name often given to an official reporter (e.g., *United States Reports*). *See also* committee report.

respondent *See* appellee.

Restatements Scholarly publications of the American Law Institute (ALI) that attempt to formulate (restate) the existing law of a given area.

restrictive clause A clause (part of a sentence) that is essential to the meaning of the sentence.

retroactive Applying to facts arising before as well as after a certain date (e.g., the date of enactment of a statute).

reverse To change the result of an opinion on appeal in the same litigation. *See also* overrule.

reviews Examines in order to determine whether any errors of law were made.

root expander (!) The exclamation mark that stands for one or more characters or letters added to the root of a word.

rule *See* administrative regulation.

rule comparison Comparing the rule interpreted in an opinion with the rule involved in a client's case in order to help determine whether the opinion applies. *See also* fact comparison.

rules of court The procedural laws that govern the mechanics of litigation before a particular court. Also called *court rules*.

ruling *See* administrative decision; holding.

S

/s *See* grammatical connectors (/p, /s).

same case on appeal Every decision that is part of the same litigation as the case you are shepardizing; the history of the case.

scope note The summary of coverage of a topic within a West digest.

search engine An Internet site that uses hypertext to function as a massive index to the data available on the Internet.

search query A computer research question; what you ask the computer in order to find out something in a database.

search resources Tools to find primary authority. The tools include catalogs, digests, annotations, Shepard's, and looseleaf services. Also called *research resources*.

secondary authority Any *nonlaw* that a court could rely on in reaching its decision.

section (§) A portion of a statute, regulation, or book.

segments Subdivisions of information in LEXIS cases and other documents that are separately searchable. *See also* field.

segment search In LEXIS, a search that is limited to a certain part of cases in its databases.

self-editing Subjecting what you have written to your own criticism and review.

semicolon A punctuation mark (;) separating items in lists that already contain a comma, some independent clauses, etc.

serial publication An ongoing publication to which one purchases a subscription.

series A set of books with its own internal volume-numbering system. When a new series in the set begins, the volume number starts again with 1.

session law cite The citation to a statute that has not yet been printed in a code and therefore is organized chronologically. *See also* codified.

session laws The uncodified statutes (public and private) of the legislature. The statutes are printed chronologically rather than by subject matter. Public session laws are later codified in statutory codes. Session laws are also called *acts and resolves, laws,* and *statutes at large. See also* statute; *United States Statutes at Large.*

session law service *See* legislative service.

shepardize To use the volumes (CD-ROM or online versions) of *Shepard's Citations* to obtain validation and other data on the primary or secondary authority that you are researching. Among the data provided when *shepardizing* are whether a statute has been repealed, whether an opinion has been appealed, and the parallel cites for the opinion.

Shepard's Case Names Citator A citator that allows you to find parallel cites to cases.

Shepard's Code of Federal Regulations Citations A citator that allows you to shepardize the regulations in the *Code of Federal Regulations. See also* shepardize.

Shepard's Federal Citations A citator that allows you to shepardize opinions in F.3d and F. Supp. *See also* shepardize.

Shepard's Federal Statute Citations A citator that allows you to shepardize the statutes in Congress found in the *United States Code* and in *United States Statutes at Large. See also* shepardize.

Shepard's United States Citations A citator that allows you to shepardize opinions of the United States Supreme Court. *See also* shepardize.

short form citation An abbreviated citation of an authority that you provide after you have already given a full citation of that authority.

slip law The first printing of an act; a single statute (public or private) that is printed separately, often in a small pamphlet. The act is next printed as a *session law. See* session laws. Finally, some statutes are printed in a *statutory code. See* statutory code.

slip opinion A single court opinion, which for many courts is the first printing of the case.

South Eastern Digest A regional digest of the West Group that summarizes state court opinions of Ga., N.C., S.C., Va., and W. Va.

South Eastern 2d **(S.E.2d)** A regional reporter of the West Group that prints state court opinions of Ga., N.C., S.C., Va., and W. Va.

Southern 2d **(So. 2d)** A regional reporter of the West Group that prints state court opinions of Ala., Fla., La., and Miss.

South Western 2d **(S.W.2d)** A regional reporter of the West Group that prints state court opinions of Ark., Ky., Mo., Tenn., and Tex.

special edition state reporter A reporter that prints the court opinions of one state, which are also printed within the regional reporter covering that state. Also called an *off-print reporter.*

special interest groups Organizations that serve particular groups of people (e.g., unions).

specific fact research Finding the primary and secondary authority that covers the specific facts of your research problem.

squibs *See* digests.

standard form A preprinted form used frequently for various kinds of transactions or proceedings.

stare decisis Doctrine stating that courts should decide similar cases in the same way unless there is good reason for the court to do otherwise. A reluctance to reject precedent—prior opinions.

star paging A notation (e.g., an asterisk or star) next to text within a page of an unofficial reporter, indicating where the same text is found in an official reporter. *See also* official reporter.

Stat. *See United States Statutes at Large.*

statement of jurisdiction That portion of an appellate brief that explains the subject-matter jurisdiction of the appellate court.

statement of the case That portion of an appellate brief that summarizes the dispute and lower court proceedings to date, presents the essential facts, and often includes the jurisdictional data.

statute A law passed by the legislature declaring, commanding, or prohibiting something. The statute is contained in a document called an *act.* If the statute applies to the general public or to a segment of the public, it is called a *public law* or *public statute.* If the statute applies to specifically named individuals or to groups—and has little or no permanence or general interest—it is called a *private law* or *private statute. See also* discretionary statute; mandatory statute; official statutory code; unofficial statutory code.

statute in derogation of the common law A statute that changes the common law. *See* common law.

statutes at large A set of books containing session laws of a legislature, printed chronologically rather than by subject matter.

statutory code A collection of statutes organized by subject matter rather than by date.

statutory history table A table that gives you information on the prior versions of a statute, e.g., its former number or citation.

subject-matter jurisdiction The power of the court to resolve a particular category of dispute.

subscript In word processing (and other computer programs) and printing, a character that prints below the usual text baseline.

subsequent history *See* history of a case.

summary of argument The portion of an appellate brief that summarizes the major points made in the brief.

superscript In word processing (and other computer programs) and printing, a character that prints above the usual text baseline.

superseded annotation An annotation that has been completely rewritten by another annotation.

supplemented annotation An annotation that has been added to or expanded on (supplemented) by another annotation.

supra Above; mentioned or referred to earlier in the document.

Supremacy Clause The clause in the United States Constitution that says federal law controls over state or local law whenever a federal question is raised.

supreme court The highest court in a judicial system. (In New York, however, the supreme court is a trial court.)

Supreme Court Reporter A West unofficial reporter containing cases of the United States Supreme Court.

syllabus (1) A one-paragraph summary of an entire court opinion, usually written by a private publisher rather than by the court. (2) In *Shepard's Citations*, the headnotes of an opinion that summarize a portion of the opinion.

T

table of authorities A list of the primary and secondary authority the writer is using in an appellate brief, memorandum, or other document. The table usually indicates on what page(s) in the document each authority is discussed or mentioned.

table of cases A list of all the cases printed or referred to in the volume, and where they are found in the volume.

Table of Cases and Circuits A table at the beginning of annotations in A.L.R. Fed. that tells you what sections of the annotation cover specific federal courts.

table of contents A sequential outline of the major components of a book, brief, or other document and where they begin in it.

Table of Jurisdictions Represented A table at the beginning of annotations in A.L.R.1st, 2d, 3d, and 4th that tells you what sections of the annotation cover specific states.

Table of Key Numbers A table that tells you which General Digest volumes, if any, have cases digested under the key numbers you are searching.

Table of Laws, Rules, and Regulations A table that tells you which annotations discuss specific federal statutes or federal regulations. This table is in the last volume of the *Index to Annotations*.

table of statutes A list of all the statutes printed or referred to in the volume, and where they are found in the volume.

Tables of Statutes, Rules, and Regulations Cited A table in *American Jurisprudence 2d* that tells you where certain statutes, rules of court, and regulations are discussed in

the volumes of this legal encyclopedia.

Tables volume Volumes within the *United States Code,* the *United States Code Annotated,* and the *United States Code Service* that provide information such as how to translate a Statute at Large (session law) cite into a U.S.C./U.S.C.A./U.S.C.S. cite.

TAPP (Things, Act, Persons, Places) A system for organizing a research problem into categories and concepts that can be checked in indexes and tables of contents of legal materials. *See also* CARTWHEEL.

Tentative Draft A preliminary report of the American Law Institute containing the proposed version of a Restatement.

term of art A word or phrase that has a special or technical meaning.

Thomas The Internet site for information on Congress; <http://thomas.loc.gov>

thumbnail brief A summary of a court opinion consisting of the following six parts: citation, facts, issue, holding, reasoning, and disposition.

title page A page at the beginning of a book that lists the name of the book, the author(s), the publisher, etc. On this page, or on the next page, the latest copyright date of the book is printed.

topic and key number *See* key number.

Total Client-Service Library Charts published by Lawyers Co-operative Publishing Company (LCP) that lead you to LCP publications and other research services on specific topics.

trace a key number To find out what case law is digested under the same key number in different digests of the West Group.

transcribed Copied or written out, word for word.

transcript A word-for-word account.

treatise *See* legal treatise.

treatment of a case In *Shepard's Citations*, a list that gives you the citation of other decisions in unrelated litigation that have discussed (treated) the case you are shepardizing (e.g., criticized or followed it). *See also* history of a case.

treaty An international agreement between two or more foreign governments.

trial brief An attorney's set of notes on how to conduct a trial, often placed in a *trial notebook.* Sometimes called a *trial manual* or *trial book.*

trial examiner *See* administrative law judge.

trial manual *See* trial brief.

trial memorandum *See* points and authorities memorandum.

trial notebook A collection of documents, arguments, and strategies that an attorney plans to use during a trial. Sometimes referred to as the *trial brief.* (It can also mean the notebook in which the trial brief is placed.)

truncated passive A form of passive voice in which the doer of the action is not mentioned. *See also* passive voice.

U

ultrafiche *See* microform.

unicameral [legislature] A legislature with one chamber. A *bicameral* legislature has two chambers.

Uniform System of Citation Also called "the Bluebook." A publication that provides guidelines on citation form.

uniform state laws Proposed statutes presented to all the state legislatures by the National Conference of Commissioners on Uniform State Laws.

Union List of Legislative Histories A publication that lists which law libraries have collected the legislative histories of particular federal statutes.

United States Circuit Court See circuit.

United States Code (U.S.C.) The official collection of the statutes of Congress, published by the federal government.

United States Code Annotated (U.S.C.A.) An unofficial collection of the statutes of Congress, published by the West Group.

United States Code Congressional and Administrative News (U.S.C.C.A.N.) A set of books published by the West Group that acts as an advance session law service for the statutes of Congress. U.S.C.C.A.N. prints every public law, many committee reports, and other data needed to trace the legislative history of a federal statute. See legislative service.

United States Code Service (U.S.C.S.) An unofficial collection of the statutes of Congress, published by LEXIS.

United States Code Service Advance The advance session law service containing recently enacted federal statutes that will be printed in *United States Code Service*.

United States Court of Appeals The main federal appellate court just below the United States Supreme Court.

United States District Court The main federal trial court.

United States Law Week (U.S.L.W.) A looseleaf service, published by Bureau of National Affairs (BNA), that prints every opinion of the United States Supreme Court.

United States Reports (U.S.) An official reporter containing opinions of the United States Supreme Court.

United States Statutes at Large (Stat.) A set of books containing session laws of Congress, printed chronologically rather than by subject matter.

United States Supreme Court The highest court in the federal judicial system.

United States Supreme Court Bulletin (S. Ct. Bull.) An unofficial reporter containing opinions of the United States Supreme Court; published by Commerce Clearing House.

United States Supreme Court Digest (Lawyer's Edition) A digest summarizing opinions of the United States Supreme Court; published by LEXIS.

United States Supreme Court Digest (West) A digest summarizing opinions of the United States Supreme Court; published by West.

United States Supreme Court Reporter See *Supreme Court Reporter*.

United States Supreme Court Reports, Lawyer's Edition (L. Ed.) An unofficial reporter containing opinions of the United States Supreme Court.

universal character (*) The asterisk, which stands for any character or letter in a computer search query.

University of Chicago Manual of Legal Citation The competitor to *The Bluebook: A Uniform System of Citation.*

unofficial reporter A reporter printed by a private or commercial printer/publisher without specific authority from the government.

unofficial statutory code A statutory code published by a private company without special permission from or authority of the government.

unpublished case An opinion that the court decides is not important enough for general publication. Also called an *unpublished opinion.* Such a case is not printed in traditional reporters. Therefore it is called an *unreported case* or *unreported opinion.* Although you still may be able to read them online through LEXIS and WESTLAW, such cases cannot be relied on in the same manner as traditionally reported opinions.

unpublished opinion See unpublished case.

unreported case See unpublished case.

unreported opinion See unpublished case.

U.S.C. See *United States Code.*

U.S.C.A. See *United States Code Annotated.*

U.S.C.C.A.N. See *United States Code Congressional and Administrative News.*

U.S.C.S. See *United States Code Service.*

USCS Advance See *United States Code Service Advance.*

users group Individuals using the same computer product who meet to discuss their experiences with it.

U.S.L.W. See *United States Law Week.*

V

validation research Using citators and other sources to check the current validity of every authority you intend to rely on in your document.

Veterans Appeals Reporter A reporter that prints opinions of the United States Court of Veterans Appeals and of other courts hearing appeals from this court.

veto Rejection by the chief executive of a bill passed by the legislature. *See also* pocket veto.

virtual law library A library that exists in a computer-generated environment.

W

WESTLAW The legal research computer service of the West Group.

West Publishing Company A major publisher of law books (e.g., the National Reporter System). West also produces WESTLAW, a computer-assisted legal research system.

West's Legal Directory An online list (available on WESTLAW) of attorneys around the country.

White Book See Blue and White Book.

WILSONLINE A computer-assisted legal research system that provides online access to the *Index of Legal Periodicals and Books.*

WIN The natural-language system for phrasing queries in WESTLAW. In LEXIS it is called Freestyle.

World Wide Web (WWW) A tool that allows you to navigate locations on the Internet that are often linked by *hypertext.*

Words and Phrases A multivolume legal dictionary. Most of its definitions come from court opinions. It is published by West.

writ of certiorari An order by an appellate court requiring a lower court to certify the record of a lower court proceeding and to send it up to the appellate court, which has decided to accept an appeal of the proceeding. The writ is used in a case in which the appellate court has discretion to accept or reject the appeal.

Index